Negotiations of Gender and Property through Legal Regimes (14th–19th Century)

Legal History Library

VOLUME 48

The titles published in this series are listed at *brill.com/lhl*

Negotiations of Gender and Property through Legal Regimes (14th–19th Century)

Stipulating, Litigating, Mediating

Edited by

Margareth Lanzinger, Janine Maegraith, Siglinde Clementi, Ellinor Forster and Christian Hagen

BRILL
NIJHOFF

LEIDEN | BOSTON

Cover Illustration: "WELCHER MAN(N) AI(N) POSS WEIB HAT […]" – "The man who has a wicked wife", Bayerische Bild-Enzyklopädie: das Weltbild eines wissenschaftlich-magischen Hausbuches aus dem frühen 16. Jahrhundert, Biblioteka Jagiellońska, BJ Rkp. Przyb. 35/64, fol 95v. Jagiellonian Digital Library https://jbc.bj.uj.edu.pl/dlibra/publication/283753/edition/271106.

This book has been funded by the Südtiroler Wissenschaftsfonds (2014–2016), FWF Austrian Science Fund (2016–2020, P 29394), and the Competence Centre for Regional History, Free University of Bozen-Bolzano.

Library of Congress Cataloging-in-Publication Data

Names: Stipulating, Litigating, Mediating: Negotiation Processes within the Competing Fields of Gender and Property (Conference) (2015 : Libera università di Bolzano) | Lanzinger, Margareth, editor. | Maegraith, Janine Christina, editor. | Clementi, Siglinde, editor. | Forster, Ellinor, editor. | Hagen, Christian, editor. | Libera università di Bolzano, host institution.
Title: Negotiations of gender and property through legal regimes (14th-19th century) : stipulating, litigating, mediating / edited by Margareth Lanzinger, Janine Maegraith, Siglinde Clementi, Ellinor Forster and Christian Hagen.
Description: Leiden, The Netherlands : Koninklijke Brill NV, [2021] | Series: Legal history library, 1874-1793 ; volume 48 | Includes index.
Identifiers: LCCN 2021003390 (print) | LCCN 2021003391 (ebook) | ISBN 9789004454187 (cloth) | ISBN 9789004456204 (ebook)
Subjects: LCSH: Marital property–Europe–History–Congresses. | Inheritance and succession–Europe–History–Congresses. | Women's rights–Europe–History–Congresses. | LCGFT: Conference papers and proceedings.
Classification: LCC KJC1162.A6 S75 2015 (print) | LCC KJC1162.A6 (ebook) | DDC 346.404/2–dc23
LC record available at https://lccn.loc.gov/2021003390
LC ebook record available at https://lccn.loc.gov/2021003391

Typeface for the Latin, Greek, and Cyrillic scripts: "Brill". See and download: brill.com/brill-typeface.

ISSN 1874-1793
ISBN 978-90-04-45418-7 (hardback)
ISBN 978-90-04-45620-4 (e-book)

This book is printed on acid-free paper and produced in a sustainable manner.

Contents

Acknowledgments

This book is the result of an international conference entitled "Stipulating – Litigating – Mediating. Negotiation Processes within the Competing Fields of Gender and Property" which took place from 22 to 24 October 2015 at the University of Bozen/Bolzano. The conference was part of the research project "Legal Spaces and Gender Order as Social Processes in a Trans-regional Perspective: Negotiating and Stipulating in Urban and Rural Contexts of South Tirol from the Fifteenth to the Early Nineteenth Century", funded by the Südtiroler Wissenschaftsfonds (2014–2016). The project was based at the Institute for History and European Ethnology, University of Innsbruck (https://www.uibk.ac.at/geschichte-ethnologie/forschung/projekt_rechtsraeume.html) and at Geschichte und Region / Storia e regione, Bolzano in cooperation with the South Tyrolean Provincial Archive and the Centre – now Competence Centre – for Regional History, Free University Bozen/Bolzano https://storiaeregione.eu/en/projects/details/rechtsraeume-geschlechterordnungen-als-soziale-prozesse-transregional. The research team consisted of Ellinor Forster, Margareth Lanzinger, Siglinde Clementi, Janine Maegraith, and Christian Hagen.

The project team undertook the editing of the present volume and was supported in their work by the subsequent research project entitled "The Role of Wealth in Defining and Constituting Kinship Spaces / Vermögen als Medium der Herstellung von Verwandtschaftsräumen vom 16. bis zum 18. Jahrhundert" (P 29394). This project was funded by the FWF Austrian Science Fund (2016–2020) and based at the University of Vienna (http://kinshipspaces.univie.ac.at/en/). We would like to thank our two funding bodies for making this publication possible as well as the University of Bolzano and the Kompetenzzentrum für Regionalgeschichte / Centro di competenza Storia regionale / Competence Centre for Regional History and especially Siglinde Clementi for organising and supporting the conference.

The editorial team would also like to thank Catherine Brooke Penaloza Patzak and Christine Brocks for their invaluable contributions in editing the English articles, which come from many different countries. Their final edits have helped make this volume more coherent.

Tables and Graphs

Tables

Graphs

Notes on Contributors

Marie-Pierre Arrizabalaga
holds a full professorship in American Studies at CY Cergy Paris Université, France. Her research considers family, inheritance, and emigration in the nineteenth and twentieth centuries. She is interested in family strategies and mechanisms to maintain family patrimony intact and secure decent emigration to excluded sons and daughters. Her approach involves the gender, micro-longitudinal, historical demographic analysis of family behaviours to explain inheritance practices and emigration to the United States. She has published 17 articles in journals, 21 chapters in books, and edited or co-edited five books. See: https://www.cyu.fr/marie-pierre-arrizabalaga

Laura Casella
is Professor of Early Modern and Gender History at the University of Udine. She was Visiting Professor (2011) at the École des Hautes Études en Sciences Sociales, Paris and Marseille, and has given lectures and seminars at several French Universities. Her research focuses on the political and cultural role of élites, the history of border areas, family and gender history. Presently, she is working on everyday women's writing in North Eastern Italy from the sixteenth to the nineteenth centuries. Her recent publications include *Construire les liens de famille dans l'Europe moderne,* edited with Anna Bellavitis and Dorit Raines (2013) and *La famiglia aristocratica: una storia del potere, una storia domestica* (2019).

Isabelle Chabot
is Associate Professor in Medieval History at the University of Padua and a specialist in social history and medieval family history. She focuses on the gender relations within kinship. She has also investigated the elaboration of family memory in late medieval Florence, dowry and inheritance rules, and practices of circulation and devolution of property between women and men from a comparative perspective, as well as the development of dotal charity between the Middle Ages and the early modern time. In addition, she looks at female poverty, women's work, and the multiple activities of family survival, as well as the relationship between women and justice. Her publications include *La dette des familles. Femmes, lignage et patrimoine à Florence aux XIVe et XVe siècles* (2011), *Ricostruzione di una famiglia. I Ciurianni di Firenze tra XII e XV secolo, con edizione critica del "Libro propio" di Lapo di Valore Ciurianni e successori*

(*1326–1429*) (2012), and *L'economia della carità. Le doti del Monte di Pietà di Bologna* (*secoli XVI–XX*) (1997).

Siglinde Clementi
is Vice Director of the Competence Centre for Regional History at the Free University of Bozen-Bolzano, where she leads the research area gender and women's history. Her research interests are gender and women's history, micro-history, history of the body and of medicine in the early modern period, cultural history of birth and of nobility, regional history of Tyrol. She leads numerous research projects, such as "Wealth arrangements, gender relations and kinship in Tyrolean nobility in the early modern period" and the interdisciplinary project "'Naturally' relating to land. Mountain farming in the Alps – an ethnographic study". Her publications include *Körper, Selbst und Melancholie. Die Selbstzeugnisse des Landadeligen Osvaldo Ercole Trapp* (*1634–1710*) (2017).

Simona Feci
is Associate Professor of Medieval and Modern Legal History at the University of Palermo's Law Department. She was member of the Executive Board of the Società italiana delle storiche (Association of Italian Women Historians) (2014–2018) and was active as its President (2016–2020). She has published on the topics of women's legal history, family history, history of justice and judicial systems in early modern Italy, and violence against women in the past. Her publications include *Pesci fuor d'acqua. Donne a Roma in età moderna: diritti e patrimoni* (2004), as editor with Laura Schettini, *La violenza contro le donne nella storia. Contesti, linguaggi, politiche del diritto* (*secc. XV-XXI*) (2017), and articles on marital lawsuits before the seventeenth-century S. Romana Rota (2010).

Ellinor Forster
is Assistant Professor at the Institute for History and European Ethnology at the University of Innsbruck. In 2015 she was Visiting Fellow for Humanities at the Silesian University in Opava (Czech Republic), in 2016/2017 Scholar at the Austrian Historical Institute in Rome, and in 2017/18 Senior Lecturer at the Department of Modern and Contemporary History at the Johannes Kepler University in Linz. She has published on spatial concepts, cultural history of politics and administration, legal and gender history in the eighteenth and nineteenth century.

Andrea Griesebner
is History Professor at the University of Vienna. From 2014 to 2017 she acted as vice chair, and from 2017 to 2020 as chair, of the History Department. Between

2011 und 2020 she directed three research projects on Catholic marriage jurisdiction from the sixteenth to the mid-nineteenth century, which were financed by the Austrian Science Fund (FWF) and by the Anniversary Fund of the National Bank of Austria. During the academic year 2002 she was Visiting Professor at the History Department at Georgetown University, Washington DC, USA. Her research covers early modern cultural, criminal, law, and gender history, theory and methodology of history, and feminist theory.

Christian Hagen
is Research Associate at the University of Kiel. He studied Medieval and Modern History, Sociology and Political Sciences at the Universities of Kiel and Bologna. In 2013 he received his PhD in History on the medieval urbanisation of Tyrol and published it in 2015 with the title *Fürstliche Herrschaft und kommunale Teilhabe. Die Städte der Grafschaft Tirol im Spätmittelalter*. In 2014 and 2015 he was Research Associate of the project "Legal spaces and gender order as social processes in a trans-regional perspective" (Bolzano). This was followed by post-doc research for the project "Creditors and debtors: Christian and Jewish loan markets in late medieval German cities" at the University of Kiel. His further interests are Medieval economic, social, and cultural history, history of towns and urbanisation, European and regional history.

Margareth Lanzinger
is Professor of Economic and Social History at the University of Vienna. Her work focuses on kinship, family and marriage, property and wealth, inheritance practices and marital property regimes, cultural history of administration, including a major comparative study of marriages between relatives. She has been Visiting Professor and guest lecturer at the Free University of Berlin, at the University of Hanover, and at the University of Siegen. She is a member of numerous international research networks, editorial teams, and working groups, including the international research network "Gender Differences in the History of European Legal Cultures". Her publications include *The Routledge History of the Domestic Sphere (16th to 19th Century)* (2020), co-edited with Joachim Eibach.

Janine Maegraith
is a social historian of early modern central Europe. 2014–2015 she was part of the research project "Legal spaces and gender order as social processes in a trans-regional perspective. Negotiating and stipulating property in urban and rural contexts of Southern Tyrol from the 15th to the early 19th century" (Südtiroler Wissenschaftsfonds) at the University of Innsbruck. Since 2016 she

is research associate at the University of Vienna and is working on the project "The Role of Wealth in Defining and Constituting Kinship Spaces from the Sixteenth to the Eighteenth Century" (FWF Austrian Research Fund, Project number P 29394 and P 33348). She is currently writing her book titled *Lives in a Negotiated Community: Courts, Neighbours, and the Market in Early Modern Tyrol.*

Silvia Mattivi
graduated with a degree in Historical Studies from the University of Trento. Her thesis, supervised by Professor Giovanni Ciappelli, focused on a family book written between 1710 and 1821 and was awarded by the Autonomous Province of Trento as a "degree thesis recognised of great interest for the history of Trentino". After that, she received her master's degree in History of European Civilisation with a thesis focusing on the register compiled by the notary Antonio da Pomarolo between 1351 and 1357, supervised by Professor Emanuele Curzel. This thesis was chosen by the University of Trento as the "best degree thesis of the Faculty of Humanities for the academic year 2009–2010" and was also awarded by the Province of Trento. Results of the research concerning the register of Antonio da Pomarolo were reported in an article written by Silvia Mattivi and published in *Studi Trentini* 2012.

Beatrice Moring
joined the Cambridge Group for the History of Population in 1996. In 2007, after spending some years at the University of Essex, she became Associate Professor in Social and Economic History at the University of Helsinki. Her research interests are women and work, household and economy, inheritance, and social stratification. She has recently published a monograph *Widows in European Economy and Society 1600–1920* (Boydell and Brewer, 2017); in 2012 she edited the volume *Female Economic Strategies in the Modern World* and, in 2019, the special issue *Making the Invisible Visible* of *Historicka Demografie*. Her current projects are a comparative publication on women and family property and a monograph on women in factory work and the first female industrial inspectors.

Craig Muldrew
is Professor of Early Modern Economic and Social History at the University of Cambridge. His research focuses on two areas. The first is the investigation of the economic and social role of trust in the development of the market economy in England between 1500 and 1700. The second is the living standards and work of agricultural labourers in the early modern English economy. He

is the author of *The Economy of Obligation: The Culture of Credit and Social Relations in Early Modern England* (1998) and *Food, Energy and the Industrious Revolution: Work and Material Culture in Agrarian England, 1550–1780* (2011).

Regina Schäfer
studied History, Literature, Sociology, and Journalism at the Universities of Mainz (Germany) and Dijon (France). She is Research Associate at the Department of Late Medieval History and Comparative Regional Studies at the Johannes Gutenberg University in Mainz. Her research interests primarily focus on social history in the fifteenth century (social mobility, nobility and rural life, legal practice). She was part of a team to edit and translate the court records of the village Ingelheim and is currently working on the project "Finance, Law, Administration and Government in late medieval towns: Aberdeen and Augsburg in comparison" (FLAG).

Georg Tschannett
studied History at the University of Vienna. In July 2015 he passed the viva for his PhD-thesis on *Separations from Bed and Board in Vienna* (1783–1850). His research foci are gender history and the history of law. From 2011 to 2015 he was a researcher for the project "Matrimony before the Court" at the University of Vienna. From 2015 to 2016 he worked at the follow up research project "Marriage Litigations from the 16th to the 19th Century. Regional and Social Differentiation," both financed by the Austrian Research Fund (FWF). He works at the Federal Administrative Court of Austria since 2017.

CHAPTER 1

Families and Property: Stipulating, Litigating, Mediating

Margareth Lanzinger, Janine Maegraith, Siglinde Clementi, Ellinor Forster, and Christian Hagen

1 Introduction

Family property as capital in the form of houses, land, movables, financial assets, and rights were of great importance in the past. Together with the use of commons, it was, aside from the property of corporations and religious institutions, the main form of capital. Houses and land as part of family property, for example, could be transferred, sold, exchanged, leased, or bequeathed. But this always involved legal customs and rights, consequently entailing competition between the entitled parties that produced high conflict potential. The means by which individuals prevented or solved such conflicts and safeguarded the property, agency, and social background of those concerned had significant impact on the social and economic development of societies. In order to address these themes, the authors of this volume have made use of multiple types of documents: from court records, marriage contracts, divorce proceedings, wills, old age provision contracts, probate inventories, and inheritance proceedings to diaries of patricians, notary books, law codes, and retirement contracts. The chapters are thematically interrelated and address marital property regimes in relation to the practices and legal regulations of inheritance patterns and with consideration to inter-familial negotiation, conflict, and resolution. Inheritance patterns inevitably bred conflict and safeguarding strategies such as contracts or wills, which initially appear to evidence similar modes of action. Upon closer examination, however, these strategies reveal differences that correspond to specific property laws and regulations, such as dowry systems in the Italian states, separate and common marital property systems in other areas, or coverture in England – in other words, Europe's basic property transmission systems.

This international or inter-regional approach challenges our understanding and definition of legal expressions and their meanings in different languages and legal cultures. Within the essays, specific expressions have been preserved and explained rather than just translated in order to avoid obscuring their

 | DOI:10.1163/9789004456204_002

significance, and with it the inherent differences of legal cultures and property regimes. "Dowry", for instance, or "marriage portion" are distinct terms that refer to different legal contexts, while the distinction between a "gender guardian" and "*Momper*", or advocate, is explained in turn. It is also important to keep in mind that the understanding of particular legal expressions might vary according to context, where it was used and by whom, and this could in turn affect the social position of those involved.[1] The concluding commentary by Margareth Lanzinger, entitled "Wealth in its Diverse Meanings and Contexts", discusses and synthesises the themes and results of the chapters, and highlights the volume's most central considerations.

This volume builds on the work and debates of social history, in which inheritance law and practice, real estate, and generational issues have been important themes.[2] It also draws on a breadth of work in social anthropology on inheritance and reproduction, the work of Jack Goody, for example, who has stressed the need for comparative historical research on every level. With regard to property transfer, Goody points out in his book *Production and Reproduction. A Comparative Study of the Domestic Domain* that "strategies of inheritance" and arrays of potential alternatives vary not only between societies but also between social groups.[3] His detailed assessments of different dowry systems (dowry and bride price) in Africa and Eurasia and diverse means of wealth and property devolution have also been pioneering.[4] Such extensive comparison can help illuminate structural distinctions. In order to understand practice and its implications, however, a more up-close perspective might be helpful. A micro-historical

1 Ida Fazio discusses this problem by considering the different meanings and social compositions of "dote", see Ida Fazio, "Le ricchezze delle donne: verso una riproblematizzazione," *Quaderni storici* 101 (1999), pp. 539–50, here p. 546.

2 Cf., for example, Gérard Béaur, Christian Dessureault, and Joseph Goy, eds., *Familles, terre, marchés. Logiques économiques et stratégies dans les milieux ruraux (XVIIe–XIXe siècles)* (Rennes: Presses universitaires de Rennes, 2004); Antoinette Fauve-Chamoux, "The Stem Family, Demography and Inheritance: the Social Frontiers of Auto-Regulation," in *The European Peasant Family and Society. Historical Studies*, ed. Richard L. Rudolph (Liverpool: Liverpool University Press, 1995), pp. 86–113; Andreas Gestrich, "Neuzeit," in Andreas Gestrich, Jens-Uwe Krause, and Michael Mitterauer, *Geschichte der Familie* (Stuttgart: Kröner, 2003), pp. 364–652, here 364–99; Hannes Grandits and Patrick Heady, eds., *Distinct Inheritance: Property, Family and Community in a Changing Europe* (Münster: LIT, 2003); Giovanni Levi, *Das immaterielle Erbe. Eine bäuerliche Welt an der Schwelle zur Moderne* (Berlin: Wagenbach, 1986).

3 Jack Goody, *Production and Reproduction. A Comparative Study of the Domestic Domain* (Cambridge: Cambridge University Press, 1976).

4 Jack Goody and Stanley Jeyaraja Tambiah, *Bridewealth and Dowry* (Cambridge: Cambridge University Press, 1973).

perspective facilitates the observation of processes involved in various forms of property transfer and administration, and analysis of the roles of women and men enrich the debate by challenging macro-level findings.[5]

Many of these ideas have been taken up in the historiography, but a number of others remain understudied. A key theme is the relationship between kinship and marital property, and the desire of testators and successors to retain their socio-economic status. This volume therefore addresses a significant gap in the literature: a cross-period European comparison of different property regimes brought into conversation with inheritance patterns and resulting gender-specific negotiations and conflicts. Earlier work has laid a sturdy foundation for this subject, looking, for example, at diverse inheritance regulations and practices, and at marriage in the context of household formation.[6] This body of work has also considered the gendered character of legal thought and practice in different European regions with regard to inheritance practices, property rights, dowry systems, and marital property regimes. Additional themes include women's access to property; the regulation of familial ownership and marital property arrangements; the manner in which marital property was separated in instances of legal separation of marriage; and the ways in which specific norms were applied in practice.[7] The Rural History in Europe series published by Brepols greatly advances research on comparative European issues, including, for example, questions of property rights or full ownership rights, and the effect of land markets and long-term economic change in Europe on the development of agriculture and the emergence of capitalism in the countryside.[8] These are only a few of the recent directions in

5 See also Fazio, "Le ricchezze," p. 545.

6 For example, the volume Anne-Lise Head-König, ed., *Inheritance Practices, Marriage Strategies and Household Formation in European Rural Societies* (Thurnout: Brepols, 2012), offers a comparison of different inheritance regulations and practices and marriage in the context of household formation in rural societies. It focuses on diverse inheritance models and analyses demographic consequences – but not in the context of marital property regimes. In her introduction Anne-Lise Head-König underlines "that marriage and household patterns in rural societies cannot be explained by inheritance customs alone". Anne-Lise Head-König, "Inheritance Regulations and Inheritance Practices, Marriage and Household in Rural Societies. Comparative Perspectives in a Changing Europe," in ibid., pp. 17–48, here p. 17.

7 Jutta Gisela Sperling and Shona Kelly Wray, eds., *Across the Religious Divide. Women, Property, and Law in the Wider Mediterranean (ca. 1300–1800)* (New York and London: Routledge, 2010).

8 Gérard Béaur, Phillipp R. Schofield, Jean-Michel Chevet, and María Teresa Pérez Pícazo, eds., *Property Rights, Land Markets and Economic Growth in the European Countryside (13th–20th Centuries)* (Turnhout: Brepols, 2013). This volume concentrates more on the debate surrounding economic progress and less on the interrelationship of social, economic, legal, and gender aspects.

a growing body of literature that address the importance of property structure, negotiation, and gender relations.[9]

From this research, two other significant topics that remain understudied have emerged: the diversity of means for anticipating, preventing, and managing conflict and the importance of pre- and extra-judicial arbitration with a variety of existing authorities. The diversity of means is in part based on the many diverse legal cultures. It is our hypothesis, however, that this diversity is also a reflection of structurally inherent axes of competition that affect varying configurations of men and women and correspond to the interplay between marital property regimes and inheritance structures or configurations of the dotal property system. Thus, depending on their respective positions, men and women had the potential to become either opponents or allies. This applies to widows and widowers, the guardians of children as well as the kin of the deceased; there was competition between successors to an estate and his or her non-inheriting siblings, as well as between stepmothers or fathers and their stepchildren and guardians. Case analyses can on the one hand shed light on the power of law and structurally inherent competition, and on the other locate options within structural frameworks. They can also provide a means of identifying and illustrating the many possible outcomes. It is in consideration of such conflicts and their anticipation, prevention, and management that contractual agreements and contracts as such can be understood as documents that were central in marital, familial, and kinship contexts, and where wealth was negotiated and, therefore, economic decisions were made.[10] This shows the need to expand European-wide research. Moreover, existing lively international academic exchanges demonstrate that a long-term and comparative approach is required. This volume links this research to wider historiographic debates and findings about living conditions across social strata, economic development, and social roles.

9 Special issue of Geschichte und Region / Storia e regione 27–2 (2018), "Vermögen und Verwandtschaft / Patrimonio e parentela", ed. by Siglinde Clementi and Janine Maegraith; Annette Caroline Cremer, ed., *Gender, Law and Material Culture. Immobile Property and Mobile Goods in Early Modern Europe* (London and New York: Routledge 2021).

10 See Craig Muldrew, "The Culture of Reconciliation: Community and the Settlement of Economic Disputes in Early Modern England," *The Historical Journal* 39–4 (1996), pp. 915–42; Christian Hagen, Margareth Lanzinger, and Janine Maegraith, "Verträge als Instrumente der Vermögensabsicherung im südlichen Tirol vom 14. bis zum 18. Jahrhundert," *Historische Anthropologie* 25–2 (2017), pp. 188–212.

2 Stipulating – Litigating – Mediating

Until today, family property retains importance as capital and marital, familial, and kinship relations continue to be largely shaped by transfers of resources and claims on property.[11] These transfers can relate to real estate, movables, and money as well as to rights and provisions.[12] Both historical and contemporary transfers and entitlements generate potential conflicts of interest between spouses, siblings, and half- or stepsiblings, between different generations, between widows and children's guardians, to name only a few familial constellations. This is evidenced in numerous medieval, early modern, and nineteenth-century court proceedings, agreements, and contracts. While these conflicts transcend individual cases, they are inevitably channelled by prevalent legal regimes as well as the respective conceptions of marriage and kinship and the power attributed to these. Wealth and inheritance conflicts

---

11 See, for example, Maria Ågren and Amy Louise Erickson, eds., *The Marital Economy in Scandinavia and Britain 1400–1900* (Aldershot: Ashgate, 2005); Anna Bellavitis, *Famille, genre, transmission à Venise au XVIe siècle* (Rome: École Française de Rome, 2008); Simonetta Cavaciocchi, ed., *La famiglia nell'economia europea, secc. XIII–XVIII. The Economic Role of the Family in the European Economy from the 13th to the 19th Centuries. Atti della "Quarantesima Settimana di Studi", 6–10 aprile 2008* (Florence: Firenze University Press, 2009); Antoinette Fauve-Chamoux, "Widows and their Living Arrangements in Preindustrial France," *The History of the Family* 7–1 (2002), pp. 101–16; Beatrice Moring, ed., *Female Economic Strategies in the Modern World* (London: Pickering & Chatto, 2012); Beatrice Moring and Richard Wall, *Widows in European Economy and Society, 1600–1920* (Woodbridge: Boydell Press, 2017); Maria Ågren, *Domestic Secrets. Women & Property in Sweden 1600–1850* (Chapel Hill, NC: University of North Carolina Press, 2009); Margarida Durães, Antoinette Fauve-Chamoux, Llorenç Ferrer i Alòs, and Jan Kok, eds., *The Transmission of Well-Being: Gendered Marriage Strategies and Inheritance Systems in Europe (17th–20th Centuries)* (Bern and New York: Peter Lang, 2009); David Warren Sabean, Simon Teuscher, and Jon Mathieu, eds., *Kinship in Europe. Approaches to Long-Term Development (1300–1900)* (New York and Oxford: Berghahn, 2007).

12 This approach, which involves a broad definition of wealth, was developed within the context of an on-going research project entitled "The Role of Wealth in Defining and Constituting Kinship Spaces / Vermögen als Medium der Herstellung von Verwandtschaftsräumen vom 16. bis zum 18. Jahrhundert" (P 29394). This project is funded by the FWF Austrian Science Fund (2016–2020) and based at the University of Vienna, see http://kinshipspaces.univie.ac.at/en/. See Christian Hagen, Margareth Lanzinger, and Janine Maegraith, "Competing Interests in Death-related Stipulations in South Tirol c. 1350–1600," in *Planning for Death: Wills, Inheritance and Property Strategies in Medieval and Reformation Europe*, ed. Mia Korpiola and Anu Lahtinen (Leiden: Brill, 2018), pp. 88–118; Margareth Lanzinger and Janine Maegreaith, "Houses and the Range of Wealth in Early Modern Gender- and Intergenerational Relationships," *Jahrbuch für Europäische Geschichte / European History Yearbook* 18 (2017), pp. 14–34, open access https://doi.org/10.1515/9783110532241-002.

were ubiquitous within the patriciate and the nobility.[13] However, a number of familial disputes among the lower social strata have likewise been recorded and researched, particularly marital conflicts in which property and wealth constituted a significant factor.[14]

In the past, intergenerational and marital property transfer comprised a large proportion of a generation's assets in comparison to market purchases. It is therefore important to not only analyse the market ratio of property in comparison with market transactions but also to study negotiations of property, resulting conflicts, resolutions between kin, and marital relations. In many cases, it was the interplay between inheritance practice and marital property law that shaped and defined the nature of and the potential for conflict, leading to property disputes. The question of whether succession was based on impartible or partible inheritance was a matter of some significance. So too was the question of which of the children – all of the sons, only the eldest or another sibling – were preferred as successors. But family property was interwoven with the question of marital property. It mattered whether marital property was combined or remained separate, and in the case of the latter whether the origin of that wealth was considered relevant, and if property brought into and generated during marriage was differentiated. Preferences

13 See, for example, Siglinde Clementi, "Undivided Brothers – Renouncing Sisters. Family Strategies of Low Nobility in Sixteenth- and Seventeenth-Century Tyrol," in *Gender, Law and Economic Well-Being in Europe from the Fifteenth to the Nineteenth Century. North versus South?*, ed. Anna Bellavitis and Beatrice Zucca Micheletto (London: Routledge, 2019), pp. 149–63; Simone Derix, *Die Thyssens. Familie und Vermögen* (Paderborn: Ferdinand Schöningh, 2016); Sophie Ruppel, *Verbündete Rivalen: Geschwisterbeziehungen im Hochadel des 17. Jahrhunderts* (Cologne, Weimar, and Vienna: Böhlau, 2006); Britta Schneider, *Fugger contra Fugger. Die Augsburger Handelsgesellschaft zwischen Kontinuität und Konflikt (1560–1597/98)* (Augsburg: Wißner, 2016); Siegrid Westphal, "Dynastische Konflikte der Ernestiner im Spiegel von Reichshofrats- und Reichskammergerichtsprozessen," in *Das Reichskammergericht im Spiegel seiner Prozessakten. Bilanz und Perspektiven der Forschung*, ed. Friedrich Battenberg and Bernd Schildt (Cologne, Weimar, and Vienna: Böhlau, 2010), pp. 225–50; Antonio Terrasa-Lozano, "Legal Enemies, Beloved Brothers: High Nobility, Family Conflict and the Aristocrats' two Bodies in Early-Modern Castile," *European Review of History: Revue européenne d'histoire* 17–5 (2010), pp. 719–34; Lyndan Warner, ed., *Stepfamilies in Europe, 1400–1800* (London: Routledge, 2018).

14 See, for example, Julie Hardwick, *Family Business. Litigation and the Political Economies of Everyday Life in Early Modern France* (Oxford: Oxford University Press, 2009); Alexandra Lutz, *Ehepaare vor Gericht. Konflikte und Lebenswelten in der Frühen Neuzeit* (Frankfurt a. M. and New York: Campus, 2006); Sylvia Möhle, *Ehekonflikte und sozialer Wandel. Göttingen 1740–1840* (Frankfurt a. M. and New York: Campus, 1997); Nicole Grochowina, *Das Eigentum der Frauen. Konflikte vor dem Jenaer Schöppenstuhl im ausgehenden 18. Jahrhundert* (Cologne, Weimar, and Vienna: Böhlau, 2009); Warner, *Stepfamilies*.

and disadvantages could also be guided by social, economic, cultural, and political principles, which shaped the transmission of assets and negotiated or stipulated intergenerational and marital arrangements such as property transfers, contracts, wills, marriage, or dowry contracts.[15]

Conflict shaped familial interaction, involved arbiters, occupied courts of law and, according to our thesis, promoted a culture of contract drafting that anticipated the potential for conflict.[16] Contracts also constituted the conclusion of situations that were regarded to be in need of negotiation. They could also be a source of dispute, necessitating additional negotiation that led to settlement or compromise, such legal acts being assigned a contractual quality. Contracts could be amended, changed, or entirely rescinded. Families, kinship and social groups, local and regional societies, and legal institutions assigned varying significance to conflict prevention and peace maintenance over time and space. The French *lettres de cachet*,[17] for example, resulted in imprisonment and an astonishingly high number of these entailed familial conflicts between spouses or parents and children.[18] In contrast to this severe form of "conflict resolution", contracts in southern Tyrol proved an often used and flexible instrument to guard against and mediate wealth-related conflicts.[19]

15 See, for example, Giulia Calvi and Isabelle Chabot, eds., *Le ricchezze delle donne. Diritti patrimoniali e poteri familiari in Italia (XIII–XIX)* (Turin: Rosenberg & Sellier, 1998); Siglinde Clementi, "Deren von Wolkenstein. Familienstrategien, Heirat und Geschlechterbeziehungen bei den Wolkenstein-Trostburg (um 1500 bis 1650)," in *Die Wolkensteiner. Facetten des Tiroler Adels in Spätmittelalter und Neuzeit*, ed. Gustav Pfeifer and Kurt Andermann (Innsbruck: Wagner, 2009), pp. 111–47; Barbara B. Diefendorf, "Women and Property in *Ancien Régime* France. Theory and Practice in Dauphiné and Paris," in *Early Modern Conceptions of Property*, ed. John Brewer and Susan Staves (London and New York: Routledge, 1995), pp. 170–93; Martha C. Howell, *The Marriage Exchange. Property, Social Place, and Gender in Cities of the Low Countries, 1300–1550* (Chicago and London: The University of Chicago Press, 1998); Mia Korpiola and Anu Lahtinen, eds., *Planning for Death: Wills, Inheritance and Property Strategies in Medieval and Reformation Europe* (Leiden: Brill, 2018); Margareth Lanzinger, Gunda Barth-Scalmani, Ellinor Forster, and Gertrude Langer-Ostrawsky, *Aushandeln von Ehe. Heiratsverträge der Neuzeit im europäischen Vergleich* (Cologne, Weimar, and Vienna: Böhlau, 2010, 2nd edition 2015).

16 See Hardwick, *Family Business*, p. 6; Derix, *Die Thyssens*, esp. chapter 3.

17 They were petitions made by small merchants or craftsmen to greengrocers, second-hand dealers, servants or carriers addressed to the police lieutenant of Paris or the royal chancellery to obtain an "order" to restrict the freedom of another person. These petitions became increasingly common over time.

18 Arlette Farge and Michel Foucault, *Le désordre des familles. Lettres de cachet des Archives de la Bastille au XVIIIe siècle* (Paris: Gallimand, 1989), Engl. trans.: *Disorderly Families. Infamous Letters from the Bastille Archives* (Minneapolis: University of Minnesota Press, 2016).

19 Hagen, Lanzinger, and Maegraith, "Verträge als Instrumente".

Conflicts are ubiquitous. With or without contracts, they emerged and escalated in different ways and could not always be resolved through settlement or arbitration.[20] Prolonged familial disputes and spousal separation or divorce were conflicts that could have economic consequences.[21] Litigating, negotiating, and mediating were not only means of resolving disputes; they might also accompany them and prove necessary beyond the formal confines of a given conflict.[22] In addition to written law, these central elements of conflict proceedings constituted an important reference point, even in circumstances where there was room for interpretation and in which circumvention strategies were utilised. Julie Hardwick has emphasised this entanglement, describing it as a "combination of neighbourhood opinion and judges' preferences, as well as jurisdictional rules [that] created powerful local legal cultures".[23] This also suggests that conflict shaped social affairs in various ways. Analysis of wealth-related disagreements arising from the specific inheritance practice and marital property law of southern Tyrol, for example, has shown that relationships between husband and wife and their kin were structured by wealth in a complex way. This implies that gender inequality had a powerful influence on claims as well as on the potential for conflict.[24] In this respect, we consider conflict to be not only a break but also an opportunity for the renewal of and struggle for relationships with regard to wealth and all social interactions. Thus, conflicts "provide useful windows into the familial relations" of the persons involved, as Llyod Bonfield concludes from his study of "testamentary disputes".[25] The question remains whether conflict was the engine or product of social change, or both.[26]

20 See the recently completed PhD thesis by Detlef Berghorn, "Eine (Fall-)Geschichte in Beziehungen: Verwandtschaft als Streitzusammenhang im hohen Adel des Alten Reiches (16. bis 19. Jahrhundert)" (PhD diss. University of Hanover, 2018) where he analyses a 250-year dispute between nobles.

21 See, for example, Siegrid Westphal, Inken Schmidt-Voges, and Anette Baumann, *Venus und Vulcanus. Ehen und ihre Konflikte in der Frühen Neuzeit* (Munich: Oldenbourg, 2011).

22 Justyna Wubs-Mrozewicz, for example, suggests the term "conflict management" to refer to the fact that many conflicts were never "resolved", Justyna Wubs-Mrozewicz, "Conflict Management and Interdisciplinary History. Presentation of a New Project and an Analytical Model," *tseg* 15–1(2018), pp. 89–107.

23 Hardwick, *Family Business*, p. 6.

24 Margareth Lanzinger and Janine Maegraith, "Konkurrenz um Vermögen im südlichen Tirol des 16. Jahrhunderts," *L'Homme*. Z.F.G. 27–1 (2016), pp. 15–31.

25 Lloyd Bonfield, *Devising, Dying and Dispute. Probate Litigation in Early Modern England* (Farnham: Ashgate, 2012), p. 11.

26 See Caroline Arni and Mischa Suter, "Editorial," *Historische Anthropologie* 24–3 (2016), pp. 309–12, here p. 310 (special issue on "Konflikt").

If practiced carefully, national, and regional comparisons can highlight specific characteristics that have been previously overlooked. This method can also help us identify factors and historical contexts, options, and limitations that shaped each specific legal framework and constituted the foundation for distinctive differences between European legal spaces. Jack Goody, for example, quotes a Dutch factor, or merchant, William Bosman, who in 1705 published his observations on the Gold Coast: "here are no tedious Disputes on account of Marriage Settlements [...]. The Bride brings no other Fortune than her Body, nor does the Man want much."[27] Bosman observed the absence of a dowry or marriage portion in this area. But, in emphasising that there were no "tedious Disputes", he also inadvertently pointed to the Western European link between property transfer and dispute. While outside perspectives can lead to problematic interpretations of observed areas, they can also help identify differences and specificities. The "Stipulating – Litigating – Mediating" conference held in Bozen/Bolzano in October 2015 on which this volume is based pushed the cross-regional approach further into a European-wide debate. This debate benefited from a strong foundation in international panels such as the research network "Gender Differences in the History of European Legal Cultures", which established a broad network of scholars and considered farther-flung legal spaces such as Northern Europe and the Ottoman Empire.[28] The conference showed the great potential of a debate that had the capacity to reach beyond specific European legal spaces and contexts, and evaluate implications and differences between, for example, a stringent dotal system and a more open marital property regime, or transitional spaces, variations, and their relation to different inheritance practices.

27 Quoted in Goody, *Production and Reproduction*, p. 6; William Bosman, *A New and Accurate Description of the Coast of Guinea, Divided into the Gold, the Slave, and the Ivory Coasts* (London: Printed for Sir Alfred Jones by Ballantyne, 1705).

28 Grethe Jacobsen, Helle Vogt, Inger Dübeck, and Heide Wunder, eds., *Less Favored – More Favored. Proceedings from a Conference on Gender in European Legal History, 12th–19th Centuries, September 2004* (Copenhagen: The Royal Library, 2005), http://www5.kb.dk/da/nb/publikationer/fundogforskning-online/less_more/, accessed 5 October 2018; Karin Gottschalk, ed., *Gender Difference in European Legal Cultures. Historical Perspectives* (Stuttgart: Steiner, 2013); Grethe Jacobsen and Heide Wunder, eds., *East Meets West. A Gendered View of Legal Traditions* (Kiel: Solivagus, 2015). Regarding the conferences and workshops see https://www.uni-giessen.de/fbz/fb04/institute/geschichte/fruehe_neuzeit/personen/cremer-annette/gender%20differences, accessed 5 October 2018.

3 Family Property, Law, and Legal Custom in Southern Tyrol

Evidently, the historiography on these themes is comprehensive, however, an interrelation of the themes and more inter-regional comparison of different legal spaces remains to be done. For late medieval and early modern southern Tyrol, for example, the question of differing transactions of property, their ratios, and the various conflict-prone constellations concerning property proved to be a pivotal factor within the issues of property transfer and negotiations of property.[29] This approach is based on comparative long-term empirical research. We began to develop this theme with a volume entitled *Aushandeln von Ehe*, "negotiating marriage", which analysed three marital property regimes based on a regional approach and a shared set of questions. This work established two key findings: first, that inheritance practices need to be contextualised alongside marital property regimes in order to understand the logics and implications of property transfers, and second, access to and the disposal of immobile property or financial assets could have the effect of turning gender roles upside down.[30] The next step was a research project addressing the negotiation and stipulation of property in the urban and rural contexts of southern Tyrol from the fifteenth to the early nineteenth century.[31] Our primary interest was the influence of the law on the organisation of society, with a special focus on marital property and inheritance practices. During the transition from the late medieval to the early modern period, political authorities increasingly

---

29 This analysis is the focus of the aforementioned project entitled "The Role of Wealth in Defining and Constituting Kinship Spaces". The project investigates the impact that kinship entitlements had on the land market in early modern southern Tyrol and the ways in which wealth defined kinship spaces.

30 Lanzinger, Barth-Scalmani, Forster, and Langer-Ostrawsky, *Aushandeln von Ehe*; Margareth Lanzinger, "Paternal Authority and Patrilineal Power: Stem Family Arrangements in Peasant Communities and Eighteenth-Century Tyrolean Marriage Contracts," in *The Power of the Fathers. Historical Perspectives from Ancient Rome to the Nineteenth Century*, ed. Margareth Lanzinger (London: Routledge, 2015), pp. 65–89; Margareth Lanzinger, "Marriage Contracts in Various Contexts: Marital Property Rights, Sociocultural Aspects and Gender-specific Implications. Late-Eighteenth-Century Evidence from two Tirolean Court Districts," *Annales de démographie historique* 121–1 (2011), pp. 69–97. For a medieval perspective see Gabriela Signori, *Von der Paradiesehe zur Gütergemeinschaft. Die Ehe in der mittelalterlichen Lebens- und Vorstellungswelt* (Frankfurt a. M. and New York: Campus, 2011).

31 The full project title is "Legal Spaces and Gender Order as Social Processes in a Transregional Perspective: Negotiating and Stipulating in Urban and Rural Contexts of South Tirol from the Fifteenth to the Early Nineteenth Century", the project was funded by the Südtiroler Wissenschaftsfonds (2014–2016).

attempted to unify law, and in some cases even to create new laws.[32] As a result, 'old' common practice – which only in part and in some areas aligned with property law – was confronted with 'new' legislation. Interestingly, for instance in Tyrol, 'new' legislation often upheld common practice.

There are two reasons why southern Tyrol was particularly well-suited to an analysis of the relationship between law and legal practice: first, this was a region in which two legal cultures met – we have evidence from as early as the fifteenth century of the use of both Italian and German legal institutions and instruments in this area. Second, with regard to the written law codes in the county of Tyrol and the prince-bishopric of Trento, the analysed documents show that a variety of practical interpretations of that law survived into the nineteenth century and with this various means for individuals to negotiate those laws.[33] This flexibility may well reflect the ways in which historical actors upheld local customs by interpreting the laws accordingly or using existing legal gaps, for example, in inheritance law.[34] Differences in the use of legal institutions can also be seen in the continued use of the notarial system in German-speaking areas such as Neumarkt or Kaltern into the seventeenth century. Such early modern legal pluralism can be identified in the contexts of differing municipal or ecclesiastical law, different legal practices in town and countryside, and in the adaptation of the Italian dowry system in areas such as Neumarkt and Kaltern, which excluded non-noble marrying daughters from their inheritance.[35]

The research project traced these differences and adaptations from the fifteenth to the early nineteenth century, with a combined focus on gender relations and how varieties in legal authority allocated to women and men structured their relationships. The extent to which women and men were given independence in negotiation or stipulation could expand or limit their agency and their sphere of influence within society, a scope that was subject to change

32 Korpiola and Lahtinen, *Planning for Death*.

33 See Peter Oestmann, *Rechtsvielfalt vor Gericht. Rechtsanwendung und Partikularrecht im Alten Reich* (Frankfurt a. M.: Klostermann, 2002).

34 See also Fazio, "Le ricchezze," p. 542. Fazio stresses the necessity of analysing the interpretation of laws for gaps and plurality, rather than just the juxtaposition of law and practice.

35 The exclusion of non-noble daughters provided with a dowry from paternal inheritance is considered as an essential feature of the Mediterranean dowry system and stands in contrast to marital property regimes in the German-speaking and other northern areas. For a comparison see the special issue and the introduction of *Geschichte und Region / Storia e Regione* 19–1 (2010), "Heiratsgüter / Doti", ed. Siglinde Clementi and Marina Garbellotti; Margareth Lanzinger, "Variationen des Themas: Mitgiftsysteme," in Lanzinger, Barth-Scalmani, Forster, and Langer-Ostrawsky, *Aushandeln von Ehe*, pp. 469–92.

over time. Consequently, negotiating and stipulating are two central concepts in the transitional space of law and practice, especially when considering marriage property and inheritance law. The court was not, however, the only venue for negotiating such cases; there were also infrajudicial means for resolving conflict, stipulating, and mediating.[36]

4 Family Property at Stake: Approaches and Results

In order to contextualise our results and bring them into conversation with other legal cultures, property laws and practices, we organised the international conference entitled "Stipulating – Litigating – Mediating. Negotiation Processes within the Competing Fields of Gender and Property" in 2015. The conference aimed at identifying how property was negotiated between kin and marital relations, between men and women, and especially how different positions were interrelated. It raised issues concerning how specific constellations of inheritance structures and marital property regime conflicts arose, how they were prevented, or resolved. Such analyses must account for different socio-economic positions such as property status and power relations, marital status, family status including the presence of underage children, stepfamilies, migration status, life course stages, and chronologies of change.

The meeting brought together historians from Austria, France, Finland, Germany, Great Britain, and Italy who study property issues, configurations, circumstances, and patterns of conflict in very different legal and social contexts – including urban, rural, and aristocratic milieus – from the late Middle Ages to the nineteenth century. The conference was marked by an exceptionally lively and fruitful discussion regarding differences between basic European models of property arrangement with respect to inheritance patterns, dowry systems, and marital property regimes, and the implications of these considerations for the agency and social standing of women and men. The result is a constructive exchange between scholars specialising in different legal cultures – which still tend to be discussed in separate forums – with the intention to stimulate additional research.

36 For the concept of infrajudicial see Benoît Garnot, ed., *L'infrajudiciaire du Moyen Age à l'époche contemporaine. Actes du colloque de Dijon 5–6 octobre 1995* (Dijon: Editions universitaires de Dijon, 1996); Franziska Loetz, "L'infrajudiciaire. Facetten und Bedeutung eines Konzepts," in *Kriminalitätsgeschichte. Beiträge zur Sozial- und Kulturgeschichte der Vormoderne*, ed. Andreas Blauert and Gerd Schwerhoff (Konstanz: UVK, 2000), pp. 545–62.

This volume presents contributions that originated from the conference in Bolzano. They address unresolved questions regarding property transfer, gender relations, and household economy: how might some legal cultures have engendered conflict or influenced the negotiation practices and agency of participants? Were some inheritance and marital property structures particularly conflict-prone? How was conflict handled, or what precautions were implemented to avoid conflict? What impact did conflict have on gender balance, power distribution, and property structures? By focusing on the familial level and kinship structures, the chapters shed light on various European practices and the implications of different inheritance and marital property regimes on property and gender relations. The widely discussed English perspective on coverture, women's ownership, and landholding, and the significance of inheritance and marital property, which is based on the groundbreaking research of the Cambridge Group and elaborated in the work of Amy Erickson and Jane Whittle,[37] is complemented by a range of European case studies that demonstrate the diversity of practices, their underlying logic, and the effects that those practices had on the social and economic structures of society.

The aim of this volume is to identify crucial fields, such as the differing extents of testamentary freedom, inheritance practices, and marital property regimes, that more often than not, continue to be analysed separately. Scope is essential with regard to testamentary freedom and could differ by area; from wholly free in England, for example, to partially restricted as in the county of Tyrol, to no freedom to bequeath by last will, as was the case in the duchy of Schleswig.[38] But all these were affected by issues such as whether or not inheritance practices followed partible or impartible principles, favoured the eldest, youngest, or several sons over daughters, and whether marital property regimes were common or separate. These issues mattered, and they had an effect on social organisation as well as interpersonal relations. Differences in marital property regimes determined whether it was the widowed spouse, the descendants, or next of kin that had precedence over the property rights of

37 See Amy Louise Erickson, *Women and Property in Early Modern England* (London: Routledge, 1993); Amy Louise Erickson, "Coverture and Capitalism," *History Workshop Journal* 59–1 (2005), pp. 1–16; in the context of the family-land bond debate cf. Jane Whittle, "Inheritance, Marriage, Widowhood and Remarriage: a Comparative Perspective on Women and Landholding in North-East Norfolk, 1440–1580," *Continuity and Change* 13–1 (1998), pp. 33–72.

38 Peter Landau, "Die Testierfreiheit des Deutschen Rechts im späten Mittelalter und in der frühen Neuzeit," *Zeitschrift der Savigny-Stiftung für Rechtsgeschichte. Germanistische Abteilung* 114–1 (1997), pp. 56–72.

the deceased. Aside from these differing systems, which had significant ramifications for the positions of spouses and siblings, there was also a huge variety of practices within property regimes.

The contours of the debates and comparisons presented here are shaped by a careful attention to these variants, identification of their underlying parameters, and an understanding of their differences and impact. Methodologically speaking, this is a synergy of social and legal history, historical kinship studies, historical and social anthropology, history of the family, gender history, and economic history. This multi-stranded approach brings together perspectives from different European regions and aims to compare methods of negotiation, power of disposition, structurally inherent conflict, disputes, and modes of resolution. Such an approach deepens analysis by identifying stages in the life course, contexts that were particularly conflict-prone, and by suggesting potential tendencies and chronologies of change. Each of the analyses also explores the significance of gender.

5 The Contributions

The book is divided into four sections. The first section, "Differentiated Patterns", discusses the diverse legal cultures of Italy, a German territory in the Rhine Valley, Nordic countries, and the Western Pyrenees. It introduces an inter-regional comparison and opens up a wide range of different approaches and changes over time: from the much debated Italian exclusion of women from inheritance, the juridical flexibility that increased legal options for late-medieval German women and men, and Nordic women's agency and focus on old age security, to gendered negotiations in the Western Pyrenees in the wake of the Civil Code. We also find variety in the realm of conflict, be it with regard to gender, birth order, age, or marital property, conflict was taken to local courts (which often acted as arbitrators), resolved outside of court, and negotiated by neighbours or family members.

In this section, Simona Feci stresses the importance of equal access to family assets and the negative consequences of the exclusion of women from intestate inheritance in Italy. With a focus on the Italian peninsula, she analyses the discussion of partial or whole exclusion of women from inheritance in customary and statutory law from the Middle Ages to the nineteenth century. She shifts the debate away from a focus on the dowry to a more comprehensive view that equally considers the legal and customary decisions that largely excluded women from inheritance and the relation of this to the dowry. Thus, she opens the field to more probing questions regarding the introduction of exclusion, changes in legal practice over time, and debates that arose in the nineteenth century.

Regina Schäfer examines inheritance disputes from the late medieval German Ingelheim court records with the aim of filling the gap in our understanding of the legal, social, and economic situation of women in late medieval urban and rural areas during this transitional time. Inheritance disputes appear only rarely in those court records, being the most complex legal matters with which the court was faced. Schäfer's detailed case studies reveal that numerous conflicts arose from the regulation of inheritance and partition of marital property following the death of one spouse. The fact that descendants were favoured over surviving spouses also posed a threat, particularly to widowed spouses and especially widows. Schäfer shows how women attempted to protect themselves from this through remarriage, negotiating legal safeguards at court, and appointing a legal representative (*Momper*). Women were present at court and negotiated their cases both in and outside court. Courts preferred consensus and attempted to delay or defer decisions to arbitration courts. In the sixteenth century, written law and the implementation of Roman law brought about a decrease in the late medieval potential for women to represent their own interests in court.

Beatrice Moring analyses the ways in which women secured their livelihoods for widowhood and old age. Looking at property transfer contracts with retirement clauses in the Nordic countries from the seventeenth to nineteenth centuries, she demonstrates how women negotiated their active and on-going roles on the family farm and secured provision in old age and illness. These contracts reflect the agency of women with access to landed property and evidence their intention to maintain a certain standard of living. The contracts can also be understood as a counterbalance to increasing commercialisation and tension between the rural and urban spheres in the nineteenth century: a retirement contract formed a mortgage for family land, thus rendering its sale or auction less profitable. This being the case, retirement contracts can be seen as an attempt to protect the loss of family land to non-kin and to maintain a widow's livelihood and inclusion in its ownership.

Marie-Pierre Arrizabalaga contrasts inheritance negotiations in the Western Pyrenees before the French Revolution with the changes following the introduction of the Civil Code in 1804. Before the French Revolution, there was a practice known as "primogeniture regardless of gender". According to this Basque custom, succession to land was regulated by birth order, with family land being inherited by the first-born child regardless of gender. The second-born would be entitled to a dowry and the third-born remained at home. This was thus an area in which daughters could become heiresses. The Civil Code of 1804 replaced this custom and mandated equal inheritance, which heightened the consequence of gender in succession strategies instead of removing its dominant role in the Western Pyrenees. Arrizabalaga shows how families circumvented the new law and perpetuated customary inheritance practices, a process realised through negotiation with and agreement of extended family members. Nonetheless, new gendered inequalities led to new conflicts between siblings.

"Spaces of Transition", the second section, deepens the analysis of rural and urban differences and change over time, highlighting opportunities forged by customary law and the remarkable autonomy of fourteenth-century propertied women in the wake of the plague. With a focus on the role of women in patrimonial issues, Silvia Mattivi analyses notarial registers of mid-fourteenth-century Trento. She finds that women gained economic independence and trustworthiness by administering their own economic affairs. Considering familial connections as linked with social and economic relations, she examines the couple as an economic and social unit in the community, agency in the choice of marriage partners, dowry negotiation, inheritance practices, and the economic independence of women as demonstrated in their wills. Her most striking finding is the active involvement of middle-class women in their husbands' professional activity. The social and economic changes that occurred in this period and potential demographic changes stemming from the 1348 plague resulted in women's increased economic agency.

Christian Hagen examines legal inheritance practices and matrimonial property regime in late medieval Tyrol. He traces several early modern features back to late medieval developments and discovers legal continuities leading up to sixteenth-century law codes in Tyrol. As there are no written normative sources from that time, this continuity has primarily been established via his analysis of legal practice. By referring to several case studies based on marriage contracts, wills, and widows' claims for reimbursement in which there was either an aim to avoid conflict or in which conflict arose, Hagen demonstrates a remarkable continuity in the separation of marital property and inheritance practices that lasted well into the sixteenth century. He also shows the importance of the involvement of not only next of kin, but friends, neighbours, and the community in legal cases. This involvement was likely crucial during a period in which oral agreements were still common and may have contributed to rendering arbitration more common than litigation.

The importance of arbitration is also asserted in Janine Maegraith's chapter. She analyses the transitional spaces between rural and urban areas in sixteenth-century southern Tyrol. Basing her research on local court books, she examines the conflicts stemming from the separation of marital property and an emphasis on consanguinity in Tyrol, and how these were resolved. She investigates gender-specific practices of property distribution, in particular landownership as evidenced in marital property arrangements and property agreements for widowhood. Although women were less frequently in possession of land, they had control over some assets, participated in the credit market, and, in some cases, enjoyed usufruct. Occasionally, marriage portions proved a powerful tool for negotiation because pay-outs to widows had the potential to overburden an estate. Nonetheless, during marriage women saw their property increase only marginally, and the separation of marital property and a tendency to favour sons perpetuated a gender imbalance in landownership. This imbalance is mirrored by the fact that the situation of men that married into property was very similar to that of unpropertied widows, and implies that in addition to gender and kinship, property itself was also a crucial factor in shaping the social position of men and women. Transitional spaces had the potential to pave the way for better terms of negotiation for women as well as men, but each of Maegraith's case studies shows that access to property and the legal regulation for property transfer were decisive in securing a more advantageous position.

The third section, "Social Spaces – Legal Cultures: Patricians and Nobles" addresses wealth transmission and women's property among the upper social strata. Late medieval Florentine patrimonial disputes involving women are used as sources to analyse the interplay between family justice and public justice, with one study investigating women's agency in conflict and mediation in the Friulian borderlands, and another a guardianship dispute between a widowed mother and her brother-in-law in southern Tyrol. Isabelle Chabot makes use of extensive archival material, including court records and personal documents, to reconstruct several case studies involving patrician patrimonial and inheritance conflicts in late medieval Florence. Such conflicts were a structural phenomenon, and dense archival documentation as well as a close study of statutory law allows her to examine both the origin of conflicts and their resolutions. Her focus is on the restitution of dowries, but she also discusses cases in which daughters claimed more than the dowry they had received from their paternal inheritance, thus challenging the *exclusio propter dotem*. Chabot finds that extrajudicial arbitration interacted with public justice in the course of litigation, and that widows were able to act more autonomously in the context of informal private negotiations. The *lex de testamentis* of 1477 introduced a formidable change to this flexibility, in that it prevented daughters from challenging the paternal will and the *donationes cause mortis*, thus leaving Florentine women with no opportunity to make a claim on portions of paternal inheritance.

Laura Casella's chapter offers a new perspective on the history of border territories. She examines the nobility in Friuli, a border territory situated between

Venice and the county of Gorizia, and decisions regarding the transfer of familial property. Significant in her analysis is the incorporation of a broad range of ego documents, from the writings of noblewomen to legal materials. These rarely studied documents provide new insight into women's agency as well as economic and managerial involvement in property transfer and management. Her incorporation of this material allows for the alignment of the political and conflictual history of border areas with that of their social history. Casella's close reading of women's ego-documents has led her to conclude that early modern Friulan aristocratic women had a large sphere of influence in economic and legal decisions, and that this condition was not confined to widowhood. Women made decisions regarding the transfer of property, defended their interests in the public and private spheres and, thus, were active in the realms of conflict as well as mediation.

Based on the seventeenth-century case study of the Trentino-Tyrolean noble Family Trapp, Siglinde Clementi demonstrates that the potential for conflict in the realm of familial property arose between parties representing different legal positions. The dispute between widow Maria Anna Trapp née Thun, who had accepted guardianship over her son and regency over her deceased husband Osvaldo Trapp's estate, and her brother-in-law Ernesto reveals several axes of conflict resulting from two different legal perspectives: one protecting the interests of the son and thus favouring the widow as his guardian, and the other respecting the institution of undivided fraternal property and thus the interests of the Trapp brothers. In addition, the interplay of power relations and gender stereotypes had a significant influence on the proceedings and administration of family property. Clementi finds that although, as a result of undivided fraternal property, women of the lower nobility faced considerable legal restrictions in property matters, the separation of marital property and the custom of dowry with renunciation of inheritance, these women nonetheless had potential to gain power and agency. Initially the court decided in Maria Anna Trapp's favour, but in the end her son was persuaded by the social influence of his uncle, who maintained the mother's weaker position as a woman. This case reveals contrasts between legal institutions and family interests, the decisive nature of power relations, and the multi-layered nature of early modern legal interests.

In the fourth and final section, "Urban and Rural Spaces: Ascribing and Defending Property, Bequests and Occupation", Craig Muldrew's chapter complements his study *Food, Energy and the Industrious Revolution.*[39] Here, he

39 Craig Muldrew, *Food, Energy and the Industrious Revolution: Work and Material Culture in Agrarian England, 1550–1780* (Cambridge: Cambridge University Press, 2011).

focuses on wills made by early modern English agricultural labourers who had very little to leave. Few among the poorer inhabitants left wills or made inventories, and Muldrew estimates that only about seven percent of labourers were probated. He investigates why some poor people in early modern England made wills or had inventories drawn up despite facing registration costs and analyses the wills of 120 agricultural labourers in Cambridgeshire that could be linked with a probate inventory. Muldrew's interpretation combines several current research strands: his own work on living standards among agricultural labourers, Alexandra Shepard's work on the self-worth of witnesses in trials that came before the English Church Courts, and Sebastian Keibek's approach that corrects wealth bias in inventory studies.[40] As it appears that many who claimed to have been without assets were either young, paupers, or very old, Muldrew's results point to age and life course as significant factors in the analysis of assets. He also suggests the gaps in our understanding of this phenomena, resulting from missing data, could provide insight to age distribution and the number of paupers and people on the road. The identification of these gaps renders it all the more important to correct the available data for wealth bias. His analysis of household possessions shows that ownership of some land or animals did not necessarily indicate ownership of more household goods. Muldrew asserts that according to Shepard's work, wills could express testators' worth, and although labourers had comparably little disposable wealth, in relative terms even small assets were important. But there were other reasons for making a will that went beyond an assertion of worth, such as avoiding potential family conflict and providing for family members.

With a focus on the negotiation of wealth in urban divorce settlements, Andrea Griesebner investigates a Catholic "merchantess" in the Archduchy of Austria below the Enns, who was sued by her second husband for "unauthorised separation" at the end of the eighteenth century. Based on various sources, Griesebner reconstructs the case study of the merchantess Eva Maria Neudorferin, her first marriage, and the dispute that arose out of Neudorferin's second marriage in order to shed light on the ingrained nature of the relationship between property, power, and gender. The author draws on a rich fund of civil and criminal justice material to portray the conflicts between the merchantess and her second husband, who had married into her property. Griesebner concludes that in the Archduchy landed property, businesses, and

40 Alexandra Shepard, *Accounting for Oneself: Worth, Status, and the Social Order in Early Modern England* (Oxford: Oxford University Press, 2015); Sebastian Keibek, "Correcting the Probate Record for Wealth Bias," Cambridge Working Papers in Economic and Social History No. 28, March 2017.

trade licenses were not passed along a patrilineal line but rather bequeathed to the surviving spouse and children, which enabled widows to continue the trade. This practice had the potential to result in a situation where a newly propertied widow married an unpropertied husband, who then found himself in an economically inferior status to his wife. This specific constellation led to conflict more often than cases of wives who married into a household. One reason for this might have been the presence of two incompatible legal concepts: a non-gendered matrimonial property model and a gender model that asserted the superiority of men and gave husbands power over their wives. This ambivalence is strikingly revealed by Griesebner's case study, and so too is the fact that, preceding the Josephine Civil Code of 1786, married women enjoyed a strong position in the Archduchy of Lower Austria. The civil code strengthened the position of husbands and mandated the separation of marital property. Similarly to Gertrude Langer-Ostrawsky,[41] Griesebner finds that couples continued to use marriage contracts to come to an agreement regarding community of marital property following the introduction of that legal code with separation of marital property.

Georg Tschannett takes a new perspective on studying divorce and separation, looking beyond divorce itself to focus on property disputes: he investigates the causes of disputes that led to divorce from bed and board, examines who brought what property into these unions and establishes the parameters of couples' wealth. With a focus on eighteenth to nineteenth-century divorce case-files from the magistrate of the city of Vienna, Tschannett establishes the ways in which property was divided, and considers the consequences of divorce and the effects these consequences had on the living conditions of husbands and wives. He finds that disputes often had a long history and that, in many cases, couples had reached extra-judicial agreements before coming to court. He establishes that while partners often agreed on the need for a divorce, the consequences of divorce and property-related issues regularly gave rise to additional dispute. Spouses' reactions within these disputes indicate that apart from legal norms other factors such as gender, age, life course, social position, and the distribution of property between spouses were decisive. Tschannett demonstrates that daughters who inherited businesses and widows who brought businesses into a second marriage were in a strong position to negotiate their futures. Couples with small businesses relied on continued cooperation and strived

41 Gertrude Langer-Ostrawsky, "Vom Verheiraten der Güter. Bäuerliche und kleinbäuerliche Heiratsverträge im Erzherzogtum Österreich unter der Enns," in Lanzinger, Barth-Scalmani, Forster, and Langer-Ostrawsky, *Aushandeln von Ehe*, pp. 27–76.

to remain business partners. In contrast, alimony-related issues were central factors in deciding the living conditions of couples coming from middle-class and civil-service backgrounds. Tschannett shows the importance of the role of the court as arbitrator, and that property related disputes were just as central as post-mortem disputes.

Regardless of whether disputes were prevented or not, the factors of negotiation, arbitration, and stipulation – in and outside of court – always took centre stage when the time came for people to settle economic decisions and social relations. The outcomes of mediation processes were pivotal in deciding social and economic standing and in gender and power relations, and the case studies published here highlight the importance of legal regulations and practices – and the legal loopholes therein – in safeguarding actors that were less privileged by virtue of economy, gender, or marital status.

References

Ågren, Maria. *Domestic Secrets. Women & Property in Sweden 1600–1850*. Chapel Hill, NC: University of North Carolina Press, 2009.

Ågren, Maria, and Amy Louise Erickson, eds. *The Marital Economy in Scandinavia and Britain 1400–1900*. Aldershot: Ashgate, 2005.

Arni, Caroline, and Mischa Suter. "Editorial." *Historische Anthropologie* 24–3 (2016): pp. 309–12.

Béaur, Gérard, Christian Dessureault, and Joseph Goy, eds. *Familles, terre, marchés. Logiques économiques et stratégies dans les milieux ruraux (XVIIe–XIXe siècles)*. Rennes: Presses universitaires de Rennes, 2004.

Béaur, Gérard, Phillipp R. Schofield, Jean-Michel Chevet, and María Teresa Pérez Pícazo, eds. *Property Rights, Land Markets and Economic Growth in the European Countryside (13th–20th Centuries)*. Turnhout: Brepols, 2013.

Bellavitis, Anna. *Famille, genre, transmission à Venise au XVIe siècle*. Rome: École Française de Rome, 2008.

Berghorn, Detlef. "Eine (Fall-)Geschichte in Beziehungen: Verwandtschaft als Streitzusammenhang im hohen Adel des Alten Reiches (16. bis 19. Jahrhundert)." PhD diss., University of Hanover, 2018.

Bonfield, Lloyd. *Devising, Dying and Dispute. Probate Litigation in Early Modern England*. Farnham: Ashgate, 2012.

Calvi, Giulia, and Isabelle Chabot, eds. *Le ricchezze delle donne. Diritti patrimoniali e poteri familiari in Italia (XIII–XIX)*. Turin: Rosenberg & Sellier, 1998.

Cavaciocchi, Simonetta, ed. *La famiglia nell'economia europea, secc. XIII–XVIII. The Economic Role of the Family in the European Economy from the 13th to the*

19th Centuries. Atti della "Quarantesima Settimana di Studi", 6–10 aprile 2008. Florence: Firenze University Press, 2009.

Clementi, Siglinde. "Deren von Wolkenstein. Familienstrategien, Heirat und Geschlechterbeziehungen bei den Wolkenstein-Trostburg (um 1500 bis 1650)." In *Die Wolkensteiner. Facetten des Tiroler Adels in Spätmittelalter und Neuzeit*, edited by Gustav Pfeifer and Kurt Andermann, pp. 111–47. Innsbruck: Wagner, 2009.

Clementi, Siglinde. "Undivided Brothers – Renouncing Sisters. Family Strategies of Low Nobility in Sixteenth- and Seventeenth-Century Tyrol." In *Gender, Law and Economic Well-Being in Europe from the Fifteenth to the Nineteenth Century. North versus South?*, edited by Anna Bellavitis and Beatrice Zucca Micheletto, pp. 149–63. London: Routledge, 2019.

Clementi, Siglinde, and Janine Maegraith, eds. "Vermögen und Verwandtschaft/ Patrimonio e parentela. " Special issue of *Geschichte und Region / Storia e regione* 27–2 (2018).

Cremer, Annette Caroline, ed. *Gender, Law and Material Culture. Immobile Property and Mobile Goods in Early Modern Europe*. London and New York: Routledge, 2021.

Derix, Simone. *Die Thyssens. Familie und Vermögen*. Paderborn: Ferdinand Schöningh, 2016.

Diefendorf, Barbara B. "Women and Property in *Ancien Régime* France. Theory and Practice in Dauphiné and Paris." In *Early Modern Conceptions of Property*, edited by John Brewer and Susan Staves, pp. 170–93. London and New York: Routledge, 1995.

Durães, Margarida, Antoinette Fauve-Chamoux, Llorenç Ferrer i Alòs, and Jan Kok, eds. *The Transmission of Well-Being: Gendered Marriage Strategies and Inheritance Systems in Europe (17th–20th Centuries)*. Bern and New York: Peter Lang, 2009.

Erickson, Amy Louise. "Coverture and Capitalism." *History Workshop Journal* 59–1 (2005): pp. 1–16.

Erickson, Amy Louise. *Women and Property in Early Modern England*. London: Routledge, 1993.

Farge, Arlette, and Michel Foucault. *Le désordre des familles. Lettres de cachet des Archives de la Bastille au XVIIIe siècle*. Paris: Gallimand, 1989, English translation: *Disorderly Families. Infamous Letters from the Bastille Archives*. Minneapolis: University of Minnesota Press, 2016.

Fauve-Chamoux, Antoinette. "The Stem Family, Demography and Inheritance: the Social Frontiers of Auto-Regulation." In *The European Peasant Family and Society. Historical Studies*, edited by Richard L. Rudolph, pp. 86–113. Liverpool: Liverpool University Press, 1995.

Fauve-Chamoux, Antoinette. "Widows and their Living Arrangements in Preindustrial France." *The History of the Family* 7–1 (2002): pp. 101–16.

Fazio, Ida. "Le ricchezze delle donne: verso una riproblematizzazione." *Quaderni storici* 101 (1999): pp. 539–50.

Garnot, Benoît, ed. *L'infrajudiciaire du Moyen Age à l'époche contemporaine. Actes du colloque de Dijon 5–6 octobre 1995*. Dijon: Editions universitaires de Dijon, 1996.

Gestrich, Andreas. "Neuzeit." In Andreas Gestrich, Jens-Uwe Krause, and Michael Mitterauer, *Geschichte der Familie*, pp. 364–652. Stuttgart: Kröner, 2003.

Goody, Jack. *Production and Reproduction. A Comparative Study of the Domestic Domain*. Cambridge: Cambridge University Press, 1976.

Goody, Jack, and Stanley Jeyaraja Tambiah. *Bridewealth and Dowry*. Cambridge: Cambridge University Press, 1973.

Gottschalk, Karin, ed. *Gender Difference in European Legal Cultures. Historical Perspectives*. Stuttgart: Steiner, 2013.

Grandits, Hannes, and Patrick Heady, eds. *Distinct Inheritance: Property, Family and Community in a Changing Europe*. Münster: LIT, 2003.

Grochowina, Nicole. *Das Eigentum der Frauen. Konflikte vor dem Jenaer Schöppenstuhl im ausgehenden 18. Jahrhundert*. Cologne, Weimar, and Vienna: Böhlau, 2009.

Hagen, Christian, Margareth Lanzinger, and Janine Maegraith. "Competing Interests in Death-related Stipulations in South Tirol c. 1350–1600." In *Planning for Death: Wills, Inheritance and Property Strategies in Medieval and Reformation Europe*, edited by Mia Korpiola and Anu Lahtinen, pp. 88–118. Leiden: Brill, 2018.

Hagen, Christian, Margareth Lanzinger, and Janine Maegraith. "Verträge als Instrumente der Vermögensabsicherung im südlichen Tirol vom 14. bis zum 18. Jahrhundert." *Historische Anthropologie* 25–2 (2017): pp. 188–212.

Hardwick, Julie. *Family Business. Litigation and the Political Economies of Everyday Life in Early Modern France*. Oxford: Oxford University Press, 2009.

Head-König, Anne-Lise, ed. *Inheritance Practices, Marriage Strategies and Household Formation in European Rural Societies*. Thurnout: Brepols, 2012.

Head-König, Anne-Lise. "Inheritance Regulations and Inheritance Practices, Marriage and Household in Rural Societies. Comparative Perspectives in a Changing Europe." In *Inheritance Practices, Marriage Strategies and Household Formation in European Rural Societies*, edited by Anne-Lise Head-König, pp. 17–48. Thurnout: Brepols, 2012.

Howell, Martha C. *The Marriage Exchange. Property, Social Place, and Gender in Cities of the Low Countries, 1300–1550*. Chicago and London: The University of Chicago Press, 1998.

Jacobsen, Grethe, Helle Vogt, Inger Dübeck, and Heide Wunder, eds. *Less Favored – More Favored. Proceedings from a Conference on Gender in European Legal History, 12th–19th Centuries, September 2004*. Copenhagen: The Royal Library, 2005. http://www5.kb.dk/da/nb/publikationer/fundogforskning-online/less_more/.

Jacobsen, Grethe, and Heide Wunder, eds. *East Meets West. A Gendered View of Legal Traditions*. Kiel: Solivagus, 2015.

Keibek, Sebastian. "Correcting the Probate Record for Wealth Bias." Cambridge Working Papers in Economic and Social History No. 28, March 2017.

Korpiola, Mia, and Anu Lahtinen, eds. *Planning for Death: Wills, Inheritance and Property Strategies in Medieval and Reformation Europe*. Leiden: Brill, 2018.

Landau, Peter. "Die Testierfreiheit des Deutschen Rechts im späten Mittelalter und in der frühen Neuzeit." *Zeitschrift der Savigny-Stiftung für Rechtsgeschichte. Germanistische Abteilung* 114–1 (1997): pp. 56–72.

Langer-Ostrawsky, Gertrude. "Vom Verheiraten der Güter. Bäuerliche und kleinbäuerliche Heiratsverträge im Erzherzogtum Österreich unter der Enns." In Margareth Lanzinger, Gunda Barth-Scalmani, Ellinor Forster, and Gertrude Langer-Ostrawsky. *Aushandeln von Ehe. Heiratsverträge der Neuzeit im europäischen Vergleich*, pp. 27–76. Cologne, Weimar, and Vienna: Böhlau, 2010, 2nd edition 2015.

Lanzinger, Margareth. "Marriage Contracts in Various Contexts: Marital Property Rights, Sociocultural Aspects and Gender-specific Implications. Late-Eighteenth-Century Evidence from two Tirolean Court Districts." *Annales de démographie historique* 121–1 (2011): pp. 69–97.

Lanzinger, Margareth. "Paternal Authority and Patrilineal Power: Stem Family Arrangements in Peasant Communities and Eighteenth-Century Tyrolean Marriage Contracts." In *The Power of the Fathers. Historical Perspectives from Ancient Rome to the Nineteenth Century*, edited by Margareth Lanzinger, pp. 65–89. London: Routledge, 2015.

Lanzinger, Margareth. "Variationen des Themas: Mitgiftsysteme." In Margareth Lanzinger, Gunda Barth-Scalmani, Ellinor Forster, and Gertrude Langer-Ostrawsky. *Aushandeln von Ehe. Heiratsverträge der Neuzeit im europäischen Vergleich*, pp. 469–92. Cologne, Weimar, and Vienna: Böhlau, 2010, 2nd edition 2015.

Lanzinger, Margareth, Gunda Barth-Scalmani, Ellinor Forster, and Gertrude Langer-Ostrawsky. *Aushandeln von Ehe. Heiratsverträge der Neuzeit im europäischen Vergleich*. Cologne, Weimar, and Vienna: Böhlau, 2010, 2nd edition 2015.

Lanzinger, Margareth, and Janine Maegraith. "Houses and the Range of Wealth in Early Modern Gender- and Intergenerational Relationships." *Jahrbuch für Europäische Geschichte / European History Yearbook* 18 (2017): pp. 14–34, open access https://doi.org/10.1515/9783110532241-002.

Lanzinger, Margareth, and Janine Maegraith. "Konkurrenz um Vermögen im südlichen Tirol des 16. Jahrhunderts." *L'Homme*. Z.F.G. 27–1 (2016): pp. 15–31.

Levi, Giovanni. *Das immaterielle Erbe. Eine bäuerliche Welt an der Schwelle zur Moderne*. Berlin: Wagenbach, 1986.

Loetz, Franziska. "L`infrajudiciaire. Facetten und Bedeutung eines Konzepts." In *Kriminalitätsgeschichte. Beiträge zur Sozial- und Kulturgeschichte der Vormoderne*, edited by Andreas Blauert and Gerd Schwerhoff, pp. 545–62. Konstanz: UVK, 2000.

Lutz, Alexandra. *Ehepaare vor Gericht. Konflikte und Lebenswelten in der Frühen Neuzeit*. Frankfurt a. M. and New York: Campus, 2006.

Möhle, Sylvia. *Ehekonflikte und sozialer Wandel. Göttingen 1740–1840*. Frankfurt a. M. and New York: Campus, 1997.

Moring, Beatrice, ed. *Female Economic Strategies in the Modern World*. London: Pickering & Chatto, 2012.

Moring, Beatrice, and Richard Wall. *Widows in European Economy and Society, 1600–1920*. Woodbridge: Boydell Press, 2017.

Muldrew, Craig. *Food, Energy and the Industrious Revolution: Work and Material Culture in Agrarian England, 1550–1780*. Cambridge: Cambridge University Press, 2011.

Muldrew, Craig. "The Culture of Reconciliation: Community and the Settlement of Economic Disputes in Early Modern England." *The Historical Journal* 39–4 (1996): pp. 915–42.

Oestmann, Peter. *Rechtsvielfalt vor Gericht. Rechtsanwendung und Partikularrecht im Alten Reich*. Frankfurt a. M.: Klostermann, 2002.

Ruppel, Sophie. *Verbündete Rivalen: Geschwisterbeziehungen im Hochadel des 17. Jahrhunderts*. Cologne, Weimar, and Vienna: Böhlau, 2006.

Sabean, David Warren, Simon Teuscher, and Jon Mathieu, eds. *Kinship in Europe. Approaches to Long-Term Development (1300–1900)*. New York and Oxford: Berghahn, 2007.

Schneider, Britta. *Fugger contra Fugger. Die Augsburger Handelsgesellschaft zwischen Kontinuität und Konflikt (1560–1597/98)*. Augsburg: Wißner, 2016.

Shepard, Alexandra. *Accounting for Oneself: Worth, Status, and the Social Order in Early Modern England*. Oxford: Oxford University Press, 2015.

Signori, Gabriela. *Von der Paradiesehe zur Gütergemeinschaft. Die Ehe in der mittelalterlichen Lebens- und Vorstellungswelt*. Frankfurt a. M. and New York: Campus, 2011.

Sperling, Jutta Gisela, and Shona Kelly Wray, eds. *Across the Religious Divide. Women, Property, and Law in the Wider Mediterranean (ca. 1300–1800)*. New York and London: Routledge, 2010.

Terrasa-Lozano, Antonio. "Legal Enemies, Beloved Brothers: High Nobility, Family Conflict and the Aristocrats' two Bodies in Early-Modern Castile." *European Review of History: Revue européenne d'histoire* 17–5 (2010): pp. 719–34.

Warner, Lyndan, ed. *Stepfamilies in Europe, 1400–1800*. London: Routledge, 2018.

Westphal, Siegrid. "Dynastische Konflikte der Ernestiner im Spiegel von Reichshofrats- und Reichskammergerichtsprozessen." In *Das Reichskammergericht im Spiegel seiner Prozessakten. Bilanz und Perspektiven der Forschung*, edited by Friedrich Battenberg and Bernd Schildt, pp. 225–50. Cologne, Weimar, and Vienna: Böhlau, 2010.

Westphal, Siegrid, Inken Schmidt-Voges, and Anette Baumann. *Venus und Vulcanus. Ehen und ihre Konflikte in der Frühen Neuzeit*. Munich: Oldenbourg, 2011.

Whittle, Jane. "Inheritance, Marriage, Widowhood and Remarriage: a Comparative Perspective on Women and Landholding in North-East Norfolk, 1440–1580." *Continuity and Change* 13–1 (1998): pp. 33–72.

Wubs-Mrozewicz, Justyna. "Conflict Management and Interdisciplinary History. Presentation of a New Project and an Analytical Model." *tseg* 15–1(2018): pp. 89–107.

PART 1

Differentiated Patterns

CHAPTER 2

The Exclusion of Women from Inheritance Rights: An Unresolved Issue?

Simona Feci

On 28 February 2005, during the 49th session of the *Commission on the Status of Women* (CSW), the then secretary of the United Nations Kofi Annan outlined seven strategic priorities for guaranteeing gender parity, among which was number 4: "Guarantee women's and girls' property and inheritance rights.[1] How can women climb out of poverty without access to land and housing? And without that security, how can they protect themselves against the impact of HIV/AIDS?" he asked.[2] Ten years later, on 25 September 2015, the UN unveiled *Transforming Our World: The 2030 Agenda for Sustainable Development*. The 17 goals identified by the working group include as the fifth: "Achieve gender equality and empower all women and girls". A number of the 169 objectives associated with the 17 goals explicitly address the need to bring about equality between women's and men's access to economic resources and landownership.[3]

These two examples show that the exclusion of women from inheritance and unequal access to family assets and specific resources are issues of pressing current concern at the level of both strategies for international development and research associated therewith.[4] Women's exclusion from inheritance is also an open question in the field of historical research, especially research into practices of inter- and intra-generational asset transmission in past centuries in Europe.

1 Translated by John Francis Phillimore. I am extremely grateful to Laurie Nussdorfer for her attentive reading of the original text and its translation.

2 http://www.un.org/press/en/2005/sgsm9738.doc.htm, accessed 12 February 2017.

3 See, for instance, "5.a Undertake reforms to give women equal rights to economic resources, as well as access to ownership and control over land and other forms of property, financial services, inheritance and natural resources, in accordance with national laws", in *Report of the Open Working Group of the General Assembly on Sustainable Development Goals* (1 August 2014) available at http://undocs.org/A/68/970; http://www.undp.org/content/undp/en/home/mdgoverview/post-2015-development-agenda.html, accessed 12 February 2017.

4 Cf. Elizabeth Cooper and Kate Bird, "Inheritance: a Gendered and Intergenerational Dimension of Poverty," *Development Policy Review* 30 (2012), pp. 527–41.

 | DOI:10.1163/9789004456204_003

On closer inspection, inheritance disparity proves to be an underlying principle of the whole of the medieval and early modern patrimonial system and, at least in Italy, continued to have decisive consequences for social organisation and public administration up until the nineteenth century. None the less, and for all its centrality, the exclusion of women from intestate succession in the Italian peninsula has been the victim of a skewed perspective that has tended to privilege, in Italian historiography at any rate, analyses focused on the dowry system (*sistema della dote*). The reasons for this invisibility derive in part from the inadequate dialogue between women's history and legal history. It is also a result of the attention that historical research has devoted to the *agency* of women – the autonomy, initiative, and entrepreneurship of women, and their negotiation of extant norms to their own best advantage – at the expense of gender asymmetries.[5] Notwithstanding the wealth of existing research into modes of asset transference, wider European scholarship has failed to engage fruitfully with the issue.[6]

In this contribution, I will first show how deeply the exclusion of women was embedded in Italian legislation of the medieval and early modern periods, and then discuss some aspects that sparked debate among jurists and disputes between private citizens. These two lines of enquiry, regulation and practical problems, are the necessary starting point for further research into and reflection on the succession and social reproduction strategies actually pursued by families.

1 Italian Statutes

According to the Roman law of Justinian, all legitimate descendants have an equal claim to inheritance, regardless of sex. In the Italian peninsula in the

5 Cf. Paola Lanaro and Gian Maria Varanini, "Funzioni economiche della dote nell'Italia centro-settentrionale (tardo medioevo/ inizi età moderna)," in *La famiglia nell'economia europea. Secc. XIII–XVIII / The Economic Role of the Family in the European Economy from the 13th to the 18th Centuries. Atti della "XL Settimana di Studi dell'Istituto Internazionale di Storia Economica F. Datini" (Prato, 6–10 aprile 2008)*, ed. Simonetta Cavaciocchi (Florence: Firenze University Press, 2009), pp. 81–102.

6 See as exceptions Laurent Mayali, *Droit savant et coutumes. L'exclusion des filles dotées, XII*[e]*–XV*[e] *siècles* (Frankfurt a. M.: Klostermann, 1987); Maria Teresa Guerra Medici, "City Air: Women in the Medieval City," in *Donne tra Medioevo ed Età Moderna in Italia: ricerche*, ed. Giovanna Casagrande (Perugia: Morlacchi, 2005), pp. 23–51; Jutta Sperling, "Dowry or Inheritance? Kinship, Property, and Women's Agency in Lisbon, Venice, Florence (1572)," *Journal of Early Modern History* 11 (2007), pp. 197–238.

medieval and early modern period, however, the property rights of women were governed by the principle of exclusion from inheritance *ab intestato* which is the right in the case of intestate deaths. The exact nature and scope of such exclusion could vary according to local context and over the course of time, generally in the direction of greater rigour. Nonetheless, the principle is incorporated in custom and statutory legislation with a substantial degree of consistency from the middle of the twelfth century on.[7] It is useful to recognise at the outset that the statutes thus violated, either explicitly or indirectly, a crucial principle of Roman law.

In the late seventeenth century, the eminent jurist and future cardinal Giovan Battista De Luca instigated Pope Innocent XI's *Constitutio super statutariis successionibus* (1680). With this measure, the pontiff officially confirmed all local arrangements regarding *ab intestato* inheritance in the Papal States that favoured males to the detriment of women.[8] In his posthumously published *Commentaria* (1684) on this legislation, De Luca included relevant clauses from almost 200 Italian communal statutes – largely but not wholly from the papal domains – which endorsed the *exclusio* principle.[9] The result is a precise geography of the diffusion of this system of passing on family assets from one generation to the next, which rewards men at the expense of their female relatives and runs counter to Roman law as compiled in the *Corpus iuris civilis* (Novel 118, in particular).[10] Present in all the major cities of the Papal States, the exclusion also affected women the length and breadth of Italy, from Genoa to the cities of the Grand Duchy of Tuscany (Arezzo, Florence, Pisa, Lucca, and Siena), from Milan, Mantua, and Pavia to Naples, Bari, and the Kingdom of the Two Sicilies, as well as in centres overlooked by De Luca but whose laws are known to us, such as the Venetian Republic, the Patriarchate of Friuli, and the territories of the Savoy.[11]

---

7 Cf. Manlio Bellomo, *Ricerche sui rapporti patrimoniali tra i coniugi: contributo alla storia della famiglia medievale* (Milan: Guffré, 1961), p. 176; Thomas Kuehn, *Law, Family and Women. Toward a Legal Anthropology of Renaissance Italy* (Chicago and London: The University of Chicago Press, 1991), chapter 10: *Some Ambiguities of Female Inheritance Ideology in the Renaissance.*

8 Read the papal *Constitutio* in Giovan Battista De Luca, *Commentaria ad constitutionem Innocentii XI PM de Statutariis successionibus* (Lugduni: J.A. Cranmer and P. Perachon, 1697); Maria Teresa Guerra Medici, "L'esclusione delle donne dalla successione legittima e la Constitutio super statutariis successionibus di Innocenzo XI," *Rivista di storia del diritto italiano* 56 (1983), pp. 261–94.

9 De Luca, *Commentaria*, pp. 75–165.

10 http://droitromain.upmf-grenoble.fr/Corpus/Nov118.htm, accessed 12 February 2017.

11 Franco Niccolai, *La formazione del diritto successorio negli statuti comunali del territorio lombardo-tosco* (Milan: Giuffrè, 1940), pp. 65–108; Felice Amato Duboin,

With a few irregularities, these local laws constitute a coherent regulatory framework that encompasses three main issues: first, the nature of the exclusion, or from what kind of inheritance (paternal, maternal, etc.) women were excluded, to what extent, and whether all or only some types of assets were involved; second, the extent of agnatic kinship to which women were subordinated in the order of succession before they could receive legacies; and third, the relationship between exclusion and the bestowal of dowries, specifically the possibility of looking at the dowry as a substitute for the *legittima* – that is the portion of the inheritance that the testator must legally give to legitimate offspring and other specific categories of successors.

The compendia of customs and statutes that have come down to us from the second half of the twelfth century and more robustly in the course of the thirteenth, register the statement and spread of the principle of unequal succession rights between offspring according to gender, and at the same time establish a linkage between the exclusion of women and the right to receive a dowry. The jurist Alberto da Gandino (d. 1310) defined *exclusio propter masculos* – exclusion because of male descendants – as a *consuetudo Lombardiae* or a Lombard custom, but Alberico da Rosate (d. 1360) noted in his *Quaestiones statutorum* that, according to Lombard law and generally according to urban statutes, the brother excludes the sister from succession because he provides her with a dowry – "*de iure lombardo et communiter ex statutis civitatum frater excludit sororem a successione eam dotando*".[12] There is no doubt that the bestowal of a dowry automatically barred the dowried woman from inheriting from the man who had awarded her the same, and it is in fact precisely in the

Raccolta per ordine di materie delle leggi, provvidenze, editti, manifesti, ecc., vol. VII (Turin: Mancio, Speirani e Co., 1831), pp. 232–67; Giulia Calvi and Isabelle Chabot, eds., *Le ricchezze delle donne. Diritti patrimoniali e poteri familiari in Italia (XIII–XIX sec.)* (Torino: Rosenberg & Sellier, 1998); Isabelle Chabot, *La dette des familles. Femmes, lignage et patrimoine à Florence aux XIVe et XVe siècles* (Rome: École française de Rome, 2011); Elisa Mongiano, *Patrimonio e affetti: la successione legittima nell'età dei codici* (Turin: G. Giappichelli, 1999); Andrea Romano, "Successioni e difesa del patrimonio familiare nel Regno di Sicilia," in *Marriage, Property and Succession*, ed. Lloyd Bonfield (Berlin: Duncker and Humblot, 1992), pp. 71–154. Sardinia is an exception: see Monica Miscali, "Famiglia, patrimonio e strategie di trasmissione della proprietà in Sardegna nell'Ottocento," *Nuevo Mundo Mundos Nuevos*, Colloques (2008), available online, http://nuevomundo.revues.org/26123; DOI: 10.4000/nuevomundo.26123, accessed 13 September 2015.

12 Andrea Romano, *Famiglia, successioni e patrimonio familiare nell'Italia medievale e moderna* (Torino: G. Giappichelli, 1994), p. 47.

context of succession norms that we encounter the recognition of women's rights to receive a dowry.[13]

But the recorded customs and statutory provisions go further, as the jurist Alberto Bruno (d. 1541) makes clear in his treatise *De statutis a successionibus foeminas excludentibus*, the bestowal of a dowry is not the only reason for the exclusion, it simply constitutes one particular item within the general ambit of *exclusio propter masculos*.[14] In fact, as Thomas Kuehn has observed in relation to early thirteenth-century Milanese practices, while dowries justified the exclusion of daughters and sisters from the *de cuius* – the deceased – and given that in general terms men are privileged over women (*favor agnationis*), "it would seem that women's exclusion had as much to do with men as with dowry". He rightly makes the point that at the time when the Milanese customs were codified (1216), "dowry was perhaps not yet the norm for marital property consignments": in fact, the dowry coexisted with the *quarta* (that is, a formal donation of Lombard/Frankish origin made by the husband to the wife), although the latter was by this point reduced to somewhat of a relic.[15]

The relationship between inheritance and dowry has been the subject of analysis for a good while now, and this has established that the dowry cannot be viewed as an anticipated settlement of inheritance claims. We can now add

---

13 See *Statuti pistoiesi del secolo XIII: studi e testi*, ed. Renzo Nelli and Giuliano Pinto, vol. 3 (Pistoia: Società pistoiese di storia patria, 2002); *Statutum potestatis comunis Pistorii (1296)*, ed. Ludovico Zdekauer (Pistoia: Società pistoiese di storia patria, 2002), pp. 55–56 (l. II, VII); *Lo statuto del comune di Bologna dell'anno 1335*, ed. Anna Laura Trombetti Budriesi (Rome: nella sede dell'Istituto Palazzo Borromini, 2008), p. CLXXII. In the German speaking area, in contrast, this was not automatically the case. See the contribution by Siglinde Clementi in this volume.

14 Alberto Bruno et al., *Tractatus facilis, ac perutilis, atque quotidano usu approbatus: de statutis à successionibus foeminas, necnon cognatorum lineam excludentibus* [...] (Venice: [Andrea Zenaro, al segno della Fontana], 1549).

15 Cf. Thomas Kuehn, "Gender and Law in Milan," in *A Companion to Late Medieval and Early Modern Milan. The Distinctive Features of an Italian State*, ed. Andrea Gamberini (Leiden and Boston: Brill, 2014), pp. 406–31, here p. 410; Thomas Kuehn, " '*Dos non teneat locum legittime*': Dowry as a Woman's Inheritance in Early Quattrocento Florence," in *Law and Marriage in Medieval and Early Modern Times: Proceedings of the Eighth Carlsberg Academy Conference on Medieval Legal History 2011*, ed. Per Andersen et al. (Copenhagen: DJØF Publishing, 2012), pp. 231–48. *"En quelque sorte, le raisonnement qui fera la fortune de l'exclusion se trouve inversé. La dot est moins la cause de l'exclusion que une conséquence, sort de contropartie équitable, un artifice permettant, conformément aux idéaux romains, d'atténuer la rigueur d'une règle qui privilégie les héritiers de sexe masculin."* Mayali, *L'exclusion*, pp. 23–24.

a few more arguments to those adduced by Diane Owen Hughes forty years ago and prompted by the same legislation.[16]

In the first place, all the statutes emphasise the quantitative dimensions of the dowry, insisting that it be "appropriate" (*congrua*), and in a few rare cases actually state that it should be of equal value to the *legittima*. None the less, it is usually envisaged or allowed, that dowries be lower than the sum women might expect as equal heirs. In the case of the Veronese statutes, a 1277 supplement specifies that a paternal estate should be divided between a brother (as heir) and sister (for her dowry) in the proportion of three quarters to one-quarter. Should there be two sisters, the proportions were fixed at two-thirds to one-third, and with three or more sisters at half to the male and half divided among the females. If there was more than one brother, each would receive double the legacy of each of the girls, regardless of the number of sisters.[17] Provisions or specific sub-paragraphs almost always enjoin the women to be content with what they receive as dowries, and forbid them or their descendants from initiating action against the heirs of the deceased to obtain a supplementary sum to bring the dowry up to the level of the *legittima*.[18]

It should also be said that – local usages aside – by the late Middle Ages it had become customary to have dowried girls pledge an oath not to make claims on the *legittima*, or to specifically renounce it. Piacenza's statute (1346, III, 36) does not prescribe an explicit exclusion of girls from legitimate inheritance, but it does acknowledge the validity of the renunciation of all inheritance claims on the paternal estate that girls commit themselves to upon receiving a dowry from their father.[19] In the first half of the fourteenth century, Bartolo da Sassoferrato recorded: "*hodie est consuetudo quod filiae feminae faciant pactum de non succedendo et iurant et valet istud pactum*" – today it is common that daughters enter a valid agreement to renounce (their) succession by oath.[20] By the sixteenth century such sworn waivers were regular practice in various areas of the peninsula, from the Kingdom of Naples to the Duchy of Savoy.[21]

16 Diane Owen Hughes, "From Brideprice To Dowry in Mediterranean Europe," *Journal of Family History* 3 (1978), pp. 262–96.

17 Cf. Gino Sandri, *Gli statuti veronesi del 1276 colle correzioni e le aggiunte fino al 1323* (Venice: Deputazione di storia patria per le Venezie, 1940), chapter 100.

18 Cf. Bellomo, *Ricerche*, pp. 176–79.

19 Cf. Francesco Ercole, "Il diritto delle persone e il diritto di famiglia nel codice civile parmense studiato nei lavori preparatorii," *Rivista di diritto civile*, 5–6 (1912), pp. 561–642 and 721–807, here p. 774.

20 Romano, *Famiglia*, p. 45.

21 Cf. Mongiano, *Patrimonio*, p. 46, note 24; Romano, *Famiglia*, p. 45, note 108.

The dowry was then at best a conspicuous and inescapable curtailment of female prerogative over family assets. Studies furthermore present no indication that there is anything in the idea that an unequal siphoning of wealth according to the sex of the heirs might have been disavowed in practice, all extant research underlines the important role of the dowry in the economy of the family.[22] It was, if anything, family demography that carried the most weight in the destination of assets.[23] What's more, specific categories of assets, houses, or fortresses, for example, or real estate more generally, could not be handed down to a female descendant of the lineage.[24] None the less, we should emphasise that feudal law did not inhibit women from succeeding to a fief, particularly in the southern areas of the peninsula.[25]

Secondly, although the exclusion of a dowried girl in some cases involved only inheritance of the bestower's assets, it was more often extended to any other legacy that might come down to her as well. The statute of Casale (in Monferrato), for example, stipulates that a girl provided with a dowry by one of her relations (father, mother, brother, etc.) is barred from inheriting from any of them if there are extant male relations up to the fourth degree. Thus, even if this statute holds that a dowry should be considered *pro competenti legitima* – as appropriate *legitima*, the generalised exclusion demonstrates that such an equivalence is only interpretive and in no way substantive. And in fact, the motivation adduced refers specifically to the ruling principle of asset transmission by which "*per masculos conservantur familiae et agnationes*" – the families and kinship lines are preserved by male descendants.[26] In their wills, fathers or other men in the family apportioned dowries to the females as legacies, while male descendants are named as "heirs".

Moreover, exclusion from inheritance also applied to daughters and descendants who were nubile and had not been provided with dowries at the

22 Cf. Beatrice Zucca Micheletto, "À quoi sert la dot? Aliénations dotales, économie familiale et stratégies des couples à Turin au XVIIIe siècle," *Annales de démographie historique* 121 (2011), pp. 161–86.

23 Cf. Lanaro and Varanini, "Funzioni," p. 92.

24 Cf. Niccolai, *La formazione*, p. 71.

25 Cf. Guerra Medici, "City Air;" Cristina Danusso, "La donna e i feudi: uno sguardo alla prassi successoria dell'Italia centro-settentrionale fra Tre e Quattrocento," *Rivista di storia del diritto italiano* 65 (1992), pp. 181–239.

26 Chapter *De mulieribus dotatis non succedentibus patri nec matri nec fratribus aut patruis, aliis agnatis existentibus*, Duboin, *Raccolta*; see also the statutory law of Cuneo: "*mulier dotata sit exclusa non solum a bonis dotantis sed etiam a bonis quorumcumque ascendentium vel descendentium, trasversalium et collateralium, stantibus fratribus ex parte patris sive filiis fratrum masculis*", chapter 153.

time of their kinsman's death. Statutes were established in Padua in 1222 for the exclusion of women from inheriting from not only their fathers, but their mothers as well, provided their brothers found them husbands and supplied them with dowries commensurate with their estate, their honour, and the conventions of the city.[27]

Customs and statutes are aimed at guaranteeing women's property rights and to establish suitable systems for securing these through forms of social pressure and legal mechanisms. Nevertheless, these rights – in almost all cases – are made to coincide with dowries (and with the provision of sustenance until these are delivered), rather than with inheritance. A further example: in Arezzo (1337), the exclusion from paternal (and maternal) inheritance gave rise to girls' right to a dowry, which, if not respected, was transmuted into a credit against the paternal estate. This credit related exclusively to the dowry, however, and not to the possibility of advancing a claim on an equal footing with male heirs.[28]

Such an eventuality is, however, present in a few statutes. According to Roman law in Genoa (as clarified by a statute from 1375), if an individual died *ab intestato*, an undowried daughter could compete with her male kin for the inheritance. Be that as it may, the same chapter recognises her only the right to a dowry.[29] In Cherasco (near Cuneo, in Piedmont), too, a statute ordains that if a brother or an uncle of a young woman whose father has not, before dying, provided her with a dowry, refuses to do so himself, she should be given access to the inheritance "*secundum legem romanam*" – according to Roman law. We may nonetheless assume that this measure was chiefly intended to prompt the men of the family to look after the claims of their kinswomen on the paternal estate and provide them with maintenance. In practice, a generic commitment to provide a dowry was enough to ensure a woman's exclusion.

In confirmation of the conceptual incompatibility of women and inheritance, we need only look at the terminology employed when a voluntary or legal measure threatened to put brothers and sisters on the same level. In the Kingdom of Naples, the word used for the customary provision "that became

---

27 The "*medesima norma si osservi anche riguardo alle non maritate dal padre o dalla madre, morto o morta senza lasciare testamento, purché il fratello o i fratelli siano tenuti a maritarle e a fornire loro la dote secondo le loro disponibilità, l'onore e le consuetudini della città.* [...]", *Statuti del comune di Padova*, translated by Guido Beltrame, Guerrino Citton and Daniela Mazzon (Cittadella: Biblos, 2000), p. 234 (XVI, 582).

28 Cf. *Statuto del comune*, p. 223; Bellomo, *Ricerche*, p. 177.

29 Cf. Vito Piergiovanni, *Gli statuti civili e criminali di Genova nel Medioevo. La tradizione manoscritta e gli statuti* (Genova: ECIG, 1980), p. 215, note 25.

effective when a father named a nubile co-heir with her male siblings, when brothers consented to a sister inheriting an equal portion, or when brothers refused to consent to a sister's marriage so as not to provide a dowry", once she had passed her sixteenth birthday and made a request to marry, was *masculatio*.[30]

A final element making it impossible to consider a dowry a sort of advance on inheritance concerns the actual legal nature of dowries themselves, that is, the fact that the assets handed over as dowry were subject to specific rules regarding use, administration, and transmission, that were much more restrictive than those governing inherited property.

The geography of Italian statutes thus comprises at least two types of text: one entailing the *exclusion* of women from legitimate inheritance, after which (but not because of which) a dowry would be apportioned them; the other entailing an *endowment* which, in as much as it was conferred in place of the *legittima*, excluded the dowried girl (and her descendants) from the line of inheritance of the bestower (and in some cases others as well). The first, then, excludes women from inheritance, while the second removes them from it, although in practice there was a tendency for the two forms to overlap.[31]

It is important to note that the arguments used in the statutes to justify this inequality of transmission insist on the agnatic principle rather than on the provision of a dowry. Women's inability to perpetuate a lineage is one well-known assumption, whose roots lie in Ulpian's celebrated dictum: "*Mulier autem familiae suae et caput et finis est*" (D. 50.16.195, par. 5) – a woman is the beginning and the end of her own family. The equivalence between lineage and property was asserted by jurists such as Bartolo da Sassoferrato (d. 1357) and Alberico da Rosate from at least the fourteenth century onwards and is the source of the reasoning behind limiting transmission to males.[32] A number of statutes echo, and to some degree flesh out, these values and assumptions. For example, Cesena's fifteenth century statutes open with the following statement: "*Cum per filios et liberos masculini sexus magis quam per foeminas defunctorum domus et memoria conservetur et diu quadam successione ad longissimos*

30 Guerra Medici, "L'esclusione," p. 270 (translated from the original Italian text).

31 Cf. Mongiano, *Patrimonio*, p. 45.

32 Giovanni Rossi, "I fedecommessi nella dottrina e nella prassi giuridica di ius commune tra XVI e XVII secolo," in *La famiglia nell'economia europea. Secc. XIII–XVIII / The Economic Role of the Family in the European Economy from the 13th to the 18th Centuries. Atti della "XL Settimana di Studi dell'Istituto Internazionale di Storia Economica F. Datini" (Prato, 6–10 aprile 2008)*, ed. Simonetta Cavaciocchi (Florence: Firenze University Press, 2009), pp. 175–202, here p. 176.

annos duratura trahat, conservationi eorum salubriter attendentes necessario statuendo duximus providere." Because house and memory of the deceased is better preserved by sons and male children than by women, and so that the succession continues for many years, we consider it necessary to ensure that the preservation of this is properly observed by stipulating this.[33] Fabriano's statutes from the same century also refer to the public interest behind such provisions: "*Cum iuris ratio multis casibus masculinum sexum praeferat foeminino et eum digniorem reputet, pro bono et utilitate Communis provida deliberatione duximus statuendum* [...]." Because regarding the law, in many cases the male gender is preferred to the female gender, and the former is regarded to be worthier in order to provide for the common good and the common benefit we considered to stipulate [...].[34]

The *favor agnationis*, the greater public importance of the male lineage, the desire to forestall disputes and ensure harmony, and plain misogyny come together to justify the principle of exclusion and the development of legal expedients *contra ius* – against the law – that is, inconsistent with or in direct contradiction to Justinian's corpus of Roman law.[35] The text of a fifteenth century statute from the small town of Ceva (Piedmont) does not hesitate to admit as much: "*ita quod fratres masculi extantes semper succedant, foeminis exclusis ex toto, canonici seu civili juris dispositione non obstante, cui intelligatur expresse derogatum.*" Since in case there are brothers, they always take succession and women are excluded from everything, and any canonical or civil order to the contrary shall be deemed null and void.[36]

In the fifteenth-century version of the Constitutions of Friuli it is stated that women, as women, are not expected to inherit under the terms envisaged by Roman law.[37] This assertion echoes the same *contra ius* decision imposed by force and upheld by parliament in 1371 against the then Patriarch of Aquileia,

33 De Luca, *Commentaria*, p. 100.

34 De Luca, *Commentaria*, p. 106.

35 Romano, *Famiglia*, p. 48: "*mulieres aliquando earum bona dilapidant*" (Gaeta); *Gli statuti del comune di Treviso, sec. 13.–14*, ed. Bianca Betto (Rome: nella sede dell'Istituto, 1986), 2, pp. 283–84: "[...] *maxime cum actus et consilia mulierum reperiantur interdum adversus bonos mores et propria commoda laborare*" (Treviso).

36 Duboin, *Raccolta*, VII.

37 Cf. *Costituzioni della Patria del Friuli nel volgarizzamento di Pietro Capretto del 1484 e nell'edizione latina del 1565*, ed. Anna Gobessi and Ermanno Orlando (Rome: Viella, 1998), chapter 136: "*le donne, per respetto de la conditione feminile non son accetade a succeder in la hereditate segondo rason commune*"; and chapter 180 "*salve niente de mancho le constitutioni che dispone circa le donne exchiuse de la ereditate contra la disposizione de rason communa, a le quali non volemo che sia pregiudicado*".

Marquard of Randeck. The prelate had moved to eliminate the clauses regarding the exclusion of dowried daughters from paternal inheritance in favour of male kin from the text of the revised Constitutions of 1366, for being "*notorie et manifeste contra ius divinum, canonicum et civile ac naturale et etiam contra omnem iuridicam consuetudinem*" – generally and obviously against divine, canonical, and civic and natural law as well as against any legal custom.[38]

2 Rivalry and Conflict

In light of the dominant tendency of the legislation to privilege males over females, the problem of conflict engendered by this skewed inheritance of assets and the exclusion of women appears of considerable interest. It is an issue that intersects with the theme of conflict between brothers and sisters, which has itself become the subject of important studies.[39]

The first point worth noting is the substantial acquiescence of women to this disparity of treatment of which they were the victims. Neither my own research nor previous studies into testamentary behaviour have revealed any departure from the regulatory position. Parents generally accept the principle of exclusion, even if they at times make efforts to balance out the effects or attenuate the economic consequences: fathers in particular when they have only female descendants or their progeny are infants,[40] mothers in more complex and flexible ways, and involving all their children, both males and females.[41]

Nevertheless, it is useful to set up a comparison using one or two exceptional texts that comment critically on the issue. In the first half of the seventeenth century, the famous Venetian nun Arcangela Tarabotti addressed herself to

38 *Costituzioni della Patria del Friuli*, chapter 75.

39 Giulia Calvi and Caroline Blutrach-Jelin eds., "Sibling Relations in Family History: Conflicts, Cooperation and Gender Roles (Sixteenth to Nineteenth Centuries)," *European Review of History: Revue européenne d'histoire* 17 (2010), pp. 695–704, here 699; Agnès Fine, Christiane Klapisch-Zuber, and Didier Lett eds., "Liens et affects familiaux," *Clio. Femmes, Genre, Histoire* 34 (2011), pp. 7–16; Fabrice Boudjaaba, Christine Dousset, and Sylvie Mouysset eds., *Frères et sœurs du Moyen Âge à nos jours / Brothers and Sisters from the Middle Ages to the Present* (Bern: Peter Lang, 2016).

40 See Simona Feci, "Guardare al futuro. Il destino dei figli minori nei testamenti paterni (Roma, sec. XVII)," in *Famiglie. Circolazione di beni, circuiti di affetti in età moderna*, ed. Renata Ago and Benedetta Borello (Rome: Viella, 2008), pp. 83–116; Lanaro and Varanini, "Funzioni," p. 92.

41 Cf. *Storia della maternità*, ed. Marina d'Amelia (Rome and Bari: Laterza, 1997).

fathers of families: "If you would not accompany your daughters to wealthy and noble wedding rites with high-ranking and wealthy spouses, as your vainglory requires, then join them at least in more modest marriages. Divide up your estates and wealth among them without preference, for that is the will of God. Do not aim at raising one of them to the summit of worldly pomp by casting the others down into a chaos of wretchedness and damnation's abyss. Temper the wealth of your sons, and remember that your daughters are also your flesh and blood; do not wish to constrain the feelings that God has left free to all His creatures."[42]

Even the shrewd Arcangela Tarabotti (1604–1652), then, in her campaign against an inheritance system that sustained patrilineage and encouraged the practice of the forced consignment of supernumerary girls to convents, pressed for the equal treatment of girls, without going so far as to specifically advocate parity of inheritance between all heirs, regardless of sex.

Earlier in the century another Venetian, Moderata Fonte (1555–1592), raised the issue in her dialogue *The Worth of Women* (*I meriti delle donne*), denouncing the injustice of the treatment meted out to women. Some fathers failed to provide for their daughters while they were alive, and then when they die they "leave everything, or the lion's share of their riches, to males and deny them [the girls] their due inheritance"; others would do better to at least make provision in their last wishes. "Then there are others [women] who are lucky enough to be left a dowry by their father, or to receive a share in his estate along with their brothers if he dies intestate, but who then find themselves imprisoned in the home like slaves by their brothers, who deprive them of their rights and seize their portion for themselves, in defiance of all justice, without ever attempting to find them a match. And so the poor things have no choice but to grow old at home under their brothers' rule, waiting on their nephews and nieces, and they spend the rest of their lives buried alive."[43] Notwithstanding

42 Arcangela Tarabotti, *Paternal Tyranny*, Edited and Translated by Letizia Panizza (Chicago and London: The University of Chicago Press, 2004), p. 54. "*Se non potete accompagnar le* [...] *vostre figliole ad Imenei dovitiosi e nobili, conforme rieccherebbe la vostra vanagloria, congiungetele in matrimonii alti meno e più modesti. Dividete frà di loro senza partialità i poderi, e le ricchezze vostre, che così vuole Iddio; né vogliate sollevarne una alla sommità delle grandezze mondane, precipitando l'altre in un chaos di miserie et in un'abisso di dannatione. Moderate il lusso de' maschi e riccordatevi che le femine ancora son vostra carne*": Arcangela Tarabotti, *La semplicità ingannata. Edizione critica e commentata*, ed. Simona Bortot (Padova: Il Poligrafo, 2007), pp. 200–01.

43 Moderata Fonte (Modesta dal Pozzo), *The Worth of Women, Wherein Is Clearly Revealed Their Nobility and Their Superiority to Men*, edited and translated by Virginia Cox (Chicago and London: The University of Chicago Press, 1997), p. 63. "[Women] *cui pure i lor padri, o per buona sorte lasciano loro la dote, o morendo ab intestato di ragione succedono in parte*

their denunciation of the wrongs suffered by women, the protagonists of the dialogue continued to view marriage, with a generous dowry provided by loving fathers or brothers, as the best prospect for which women could hope. Even this text, then, finds it difficult to openly claim an equal inheritance, although Cornelia, one of the two speakers in the dialogue, imagines an ideal state where a woman might receive a "dowry" without marrying, or in other words achieve complete economic independence.[44]

Other male and female testimonies corroborate this point of view: justice consists in an equal, proportionate provision of dowries to the whole cohort of daughters, without privileging one at the expense of the legitimate rights of the others. And, more generally, it consists in a guarantee of those rights like dowry, sustenance, or spending money, that the female members of the family can legitimately expect from the estate at regularly intervals and in reasonable amounts.[45]

Therefore, as far as I can see, we do not find voices raised against the exclusion of women from inheritance until the late eighteenth century, at which point criticism is levelled at the whole *ancien régime* including the asymmetry in the status of men and women. I offer just two examples, again from Italy. In 1797 in Mantua, Carolina Arienti Lattanzi declared in a public lecture entitled *The Enslavement of Women* (*La schiavitù delle donne*) that the dowry system was harmful to women because it prevented them from sharing paternal inheritance on equal terms with their brothers.[46] In an even more pointed manner, the Ligurian Jacobin newspaper *Il Difensore della Libertà* published a brief statement in its 43rd issue on 21 October 1797 from self-styled *cittadine* (*citoyennes*, as it were) – and supported by more than 2,500 signatures – that criticised the claims of the men in the government of the Ligurian Republic to being "defenders of liberty" and denounced "the egotism of their sex" as demonstrated by their removal of the article of the draft constitution that

nelle facoltà co' fratelli, sono da quelli tenute in casa per ischiave ed usurpato la lor ragione, e goduto il loro, contra ogni giustizia, senza mai trattar di locarle; e così convengono sotto il loro imperio invecchiarsi in casa, servendo ai nepoti e finiscono la lor vita sepolte innanzi che morte". Moderata Fonte (Modesta dal Pozzo), *Il merito delle donne* (Venice: Domenico Imberti, 1600), p. 23.

44 Fonte, *Il merito*, p. 59.

45 See, for instance, Simona Feci, "I Mattei 'di Paganica': una famiglia romana tra XV e XVII secolo," *Dimensioni e problemi della ricerca storica* 1 (2011), pp. 81–113, here p. 97.

46 "*La stessa istituzione delle doti ci divenne pregiudicievole* [*dal momento che*] *fossimo escluse dall'avere un'euguale diritto coi maschi alla distribuzione della paterna eredità.*" Laura Pisano and Christiane Veauvy, *Parole inascoltate: le donne e la costruzione dello Stato-nazione in Italia e in Francia* (*1789–1860*) (Rome: Editori Riuniti, 1994), p. 194.

treated men and women equally with regard to inheritance rights from the definitive version just then being approved.[47] In short, in the midst of the revolutionary climate the more alert female minds identified in equal inheritance, as in, for example, the notion of complete liberty to dispose of their own assets, areas of the law that revealed the limits of the supposed universality of the "rights of man," and exposed the hollowness of its claims.

Even in the centuries preceding the revolutionary age of codification, the persistence of the *favor agnationis*, the ubiquity of women's exclusion, and the difficulty of imagining equality on the part of those directly concerned, did not entirely avoid controversy in regard to medieval and early modern inheritance law, both on technical-juridical grounds and on that of general feeling (and – we might add – practice). These conflicts produced uncertainty in the interpretations of jurists and fuelled family quarrels.

We must bear in mind that women were not excluded *tout court* from inheritance, but were lower, and behind male members of the line, on the ladder of potential inheritors. Thus, a first issue concerned the substance of this subordination and, in particular, the rivalry sparked between the daughter and other more distant male kin when the deceased had only female descendants. If the exclusion of sisters in favour of their brothers and male *ex fratre* nephews was undisputed, over time local customs came to differ in the extent to which male kin were to be preferred to daughters or other female descendants of the deceased, generally widening its scope. In Siena between the mid-thirteenth and the mid-fourteenth centuries, the norm progressed from only excluding the daughter of the dead person in favour of the son to promoting all male descendants.[48] In Padua in 1222, daughters were excluded from the paternal and maternal inheritance only in favour of their brothers, while two centuries later they were demoted, along with their descendants of both sexes, beneath male ascendants and collateral kin up to the third canonical degree.[49]

---

47 *"Conosciamo però che sbalzare dalla nullità assoluta in cui siamo state per tanti secoli immerse, a quel grado di esistenza politica che, malgrado l'uguaglianza, godete voi esseri privilegiatissimi, sarebbe urtare troppo direttamente contro i pregiudizi* [...] *Ne abbiamo una trista ma evidente prova, nell'esito infelice del progetto di Costituzione, che ci parificava ai nostri fratelli nelle successioni legittime. L'egoismo mascolino si è rivoltato, ed il Governo provvisorio* [...] *ha barbaramente troncato un articolo che faceva onore alla giustizia e ai lumi della commissione". Il Difensore della Libertà* (Genova: nella stamperia del cittadino Andrea Frugoni e C., 1797–1798), 43, 21 October 1797, p. 169, http://www.internetculturale.it/jmms/iccuviewer/iccu.jsp?id=oai%3Awww.internetculturale.sbn.it%2FTeca%3A20%3ANT0000%3AIEI0105960_40922&mode=all&teca=MagTeca+-+ICCU, accessed 27 October 2016.

48 Cf. Chabot, *La dette*, pp. 30–31.

49 *Gli statuti de Padova tradotti de latino in vulgare* [...] (Padova: G. Fabriano, 1551), chapter 17.

Nonetheless, this extension of the degrees of male kin to be interposed between women and their access to the estates of fathers or grandfathers did become a matter for argument, in so far as the feelings of family-minded fathers, and of legislators, were exercised over it.

One legal case, studied a few years back by Claudio Povolo, illustrates the ramifications of such a situation, and highlights both the differences between experts and public perception.[50] We are in Carnia in the 1530s and a case comes before the patriarchal court of Udine between a young woman, one Caterina Corradazzo, and her uncles concerning the estate of her father. The girl, the only child of the deceased, appeals to the established custom of the small town where she lives. Her fellow townspeople testify that if a man dies intestate and without male descendants, the daughter inherits his goods, excluding male ascendants, in this case her father's brothers. The uncles had brought the case before the tribunal at Udine, invoking the fifteenth-century Constitutions of the Patriarchate of Friuli. Even so, this legislative body too declared in favour of Caterina, since, even if demoted behind her uncles, she would still have had the right to a dowry equal to the *legittima*, which in this case would have been reckoned at half the assets of the deceased.[51] The Constitutions laid down, in fact, a sliding scale of inheritance rights: exclusion from paternal inheritance in the face of male descendants of the deceased where a dowry had been given (even if less than the *legittima*); the assignment of a dowry equal to a full share where there are surviving male ascendants or lateral kin (that is, the father of the deceased, the brothers and *ex fratre* nephews); full inheritance if the father had designated as heir someone unrelated to the family.

Exclusion therefore is structured as a demotion in the order of possible inheritors that is absolute when the deceased has brothers or male nephews, but relative and variable when the daughter is in competition with other agnatic relatives of the deceased. And to judge from *consilia* or legal proceedings, the contention between daughters and relatives was an open question. It should further be noted that, as in the case just examined, confrontation

50 Claudio Povolo, "Eredità anticipata o esclusione per causa di dote? Un caso di pluralismo giuridico nel Friuli del Cinquecento," in *Padre e figlia*, ed. Luisa Accati (Torino: Rosenberg et Sellier, 1994), pp. 41–73.

51 "*Secondo l'antica consuetudine e intenzione de' nostri maggiori di conservare le facoltà ne' maschi, basti alla figlia la dote, ancorché minore della legittima. Se però il padre non avrà lasciato discendenti maschi eredi, ma agnati ascendenti o trasversali, le femmine abbiano la dote non minore della legittima. Se gli eredi istituiti sono estranei la figliola lesa nella legittima potrà rompere il testamento e succedere ab intestato, fermi però i legati. Fino al matrimonio abbia comunque congrui alimenti*". Niccolai, *La formazione*, p. 87.

was often initiated not by the woman directly concerned, but by the woman's heirs: men, therefore, vying with other men.

The legislation itself is at odds on the point, and we have to make sense of it by re-examining and clarifying the wording of the texts. An example is provided by Turin's statute, which ruled that, in the absence of males, the daughters of a deceased father or mother should inherit *ab intestato,* but should be relegated behind male kin in the case of landed property. With time, however, this proviso became a bone of contention and amendment was urged. In 1489, "*pro evitandis rixis litibus ac quaestionibus quae saepius oriuntur propter diversas opiniones interpretationis verborum ipsius statute*" – to avoid bitter quarrel and court proceedings, which often originated from different opinions on the interpretation of the wording in the statutes themselves, the Senate (*Consiglio maggiore di credenza*) drew up a new version favourable to women that obtained a decree of ratification from the *vicario cittadino*, but was never approved by the Duke or entered in the book of statutes.[52] The Citizens' Council was accordingly able to make good the omission at the beginning of the seventeenth century and took the opportunity to extend the prerogative conceded to daughters to the sisters of the deceased.[53]

Another example of this increased sensitivity towards daughters of a deceased in comparison to more remote kin can be discerned – in a contrary sense – in the motives behind Innocent XI's 1680 promulgation of the *Constitutio super statutariis successionibus*, to which I referred at the beginning of this contribution. The tendency of magistrates and jurists to interpret the texts of statutes in such a way as to nullify the intention of the provisions, which was to perpetuate lineages through male inheritance, had become so conspicuous that it provoked protests and litigation.[54]

Another controversial legal aspect concerns the relationship between dowry and *legittima*. Although, as we have seen, medieval and early modern jurists were well aware that the exclusion of women derived from the principle of *favor agnationis*, its important practical implications rendered clarification of whether the single rule governing legitimate inheritance envisaged the

52 Dubois, *Raccolta*, VII: p. 22, note A: "*Si quis vel aliqua ab intestato decesserit de dicta civitate Taurini aut de loco Grugliasci, nullo facto ordinamento rerum suarum et nullis relictis filiis masculis legitimis ex eo vel ea legitime procreatis, relictis tamen filia vel filiabus suis legittimis, quod ipsa filia vel ipsae filiae ipsius sic decedentis succedant et succedere debeant tam in domibus quam in aliis bonis ipsius sic decedentis*" (1489).

53 Dubois, *Raccolta*, VII, p. 22, note A.

54 De Luca, *Commentaria*.

exclusion of women *propter masculos*, or rather *propter dotem* was a question well worth their attention.[55]

In fact, the possibility of women being included among the heirs of a deceased had a bearing on the amount of the *legittima* due to the sons: with four or more children, the portion rose from a third to a half of the deceased's estate, so that counting the females among the numbered children, and awarding them a dowry *loco legitimae* which was lower than the legitimate portion, increased the proportion of the estate available to the males. If, on the other hand, the exclusion was clear-cut (or they had already been provided with dowries, and married off during the father's lifetime) they could not be numbered among those having a right to a share in the inheritance.

Bologna's fourteenth-century statute specifies that, consistent with exclusion *propter dotem*, women are not to be considered or numbered as heirs.[56] In Milan, on the other hand, the prevailing interpretation of the statute counted the excluded women together with their brothers in determining the *legittima*, "even if the dowry does not take the place of the *legittima*", because they were initially excluded and then, subsequently, dowried.[57] Following the authoritative judgement delivered by Bartolo di Sassoferrato, however, learned opinion in the early modern period counted the women in a purely instrumental spirit (*ad utilitatem masculorum* – to the advantage of the male descendants), that is, in order to enable their male relations to aspire to at least half the paternal estate (and not merely a third) and to curtail the proportion of disposable assets that the deceased could direct elsewhere in his will. For the whole of the seventeenth century the highest court in the State of Milan interpreted the statute in the sense that the excluded, dowried daughters could not be included in the total of inheriting children, thereby precluding any analogy between dowry and *legittima*. In assessing the statutes of Pavia, however, the same tribunal took the opposite line. In the belief that this was *ad favorem filiorum masculorum* – to the advantage of the sons – other high courts of the early modern era, such as the Roman Rota and the Neapolitan Royal Council, found it opportune to include girls, although excluded from inheriting, in the

55 Anna Maria Monti, *Iudicare tamquam Deus. I modi della giustizia senatoria nel Ducato di Milano tra Cinque e Settecento* (Milan: Giuffrè, 2003), pp. 305–20.

56 *Lo statuto del comune di Bologna*, 566.

57 *Statuti di Milano volgarizzati con note e spiegazioni* [...] (Milan: G. Galeazzi, 1773), p. 123: "*Resta dunque stabilito che le femmine escluse dalla successione a favore de' maschi fanno numero e parte nella legittima e l'accrescono a comodo de' maschi escludenti, quantunque la dote non succeda in luogo della legittima.*"

roster of children determining the proportion of the paternal estate reserved for the *legittima*.

3 Conclusions

In conclusion, I would like to touch on the early nineteenth century circumstances and legal reasoning that led to a change in inheritance paradigms in Italy sufficient to favour the introduction of legislation intended to level the playing-field between males and females.

We have seen how the impact of Jacobinism in Italy, as indeed elsewhere, brought about a reversal of the old inheritance system, such as imposing equality with male siblings, thus, making female siblings equal with male siblings and at least consider the possibility of women sharing in the paternal estate. But the changes thus introduced needed to find solid legal underpinnings to justify their inclusion in, or exclusion from, post Restoration legislative codes.

The legal reasoning adduced for and against the introduction of a new inheritance regime poses an interesting study and embraces the relationship between Roman law and local custom, between Roman and Justinian law, and between history and human nature – or better, between custom and natural law.

A starting point for examining the trajectory of change is provided by the seventeenth-century writings of G.B. De Luca, cited above, in the form of his *Commentaria* and *Dottor volgare* (1673).[58] In justifying the imposition of an inheritance system that was not only inequitable but, above all, contrary to *ius comune*, the cardinal deployed not arguments of principle, but rather embarked on a long excursus through legal history to demonstrate that – contrary to the opinion of the jurists – medieval and early modern statutes had not modified Roman law. In fact, he argued that Justinian's *Corpus iuris civilis* had never been applied in Italy, and that the Longobards, in this field, had developed codes analogous to "the ancient customs of the people". With the medieval rediscovery of Justinian law, however, a divergence arose between "the common people" and the experts, whose literal interpretations went against the "understanding and usage" of communities. The statutes, by contrast, in opting for unequal inheritance, had aligned themselves with "the ancient laws of the Romans and the Longobards, which is to say, the age-old and unbroken

58 Giovanni Battista De Luca, *Il dottor volgare, ovvero Il compendio di tutta la legge civile, canonica, feudale e municipale* […] (Florence: V. Batelli e compagni, 1839–1843), I–IV.

customs of the country". For this reason, according to De Luca, such legislation cannot be considered a departure from the Corpus, but rather an unwillingness to adopt its dispensations: it was "a statement of their intention not to embrace this part at least of these civil laws newly disinterred and introduced, as being contrary to their customs and inclinations, which still persist and hold sway, being entirely natural to the area". It further follows from this reconstruction of history that the statutes cannot be read and applied to the letter, because they are decadent legislative measures "made in barbarous times, and in out-of-the-way places, by people more foolish than learned" and often confused and obscure. One should rather attend to the spirit of the provisions, that is, to the legislators' intentions, and uphold these.[59]

A contrary alliance opposing De Luca's "ancient customs of the people" and pre-Justinian Roman law arose in the Curia at the beginning of the nineteenth century between natural and Justinian law, viewed as the expression par excellence of Roman law, which in its systematic and dogmatic abstraction would become the vector through which the assumed principles of natural law would shape modern codifications.

What then are the considerations that the cautious cardinals and papal prelates gave voice to, in 1818, with a view to mitigating a draft civil law that would too drastically curtail the traditional regulatory role of the church in the field of inheritance? In agreeing that the daughters and sisters of the deceased should be excluded in favour of male relations of the same kinship status, but preferred to male kin of more distant degree, the ecclesiastics declared: "In this fashion all anomalies and bitterness are averted. A modest agnatic bias is combined with the wishes of nature, the interests of families and the rights of blood, [...]. Just as it was harsh to exclude a full-sister in favour of a remote male cousin, so it seems reasonable to exclude a woman from transverse inheritance up to the fourth degree in favour of equidistant males, e.g. her own brothers. Thus, without offending charitable feelings we can check the pernicious accumulation of wealth in the hands of the weaker sex, and the impoverishment of the sex whose sweat has created estates, which alone can further the name and political status of the family, and whom it is well to encourage with the hope of recompense, just as it is dangerous to embolden the other sex."[60]

---

59 De Luca, *Il dottor volgare*, III, pp. 183–84.

60 Mirella Mombelli Castracane, *La codificazione civile nello Stato pontificio*, vol. 1: *Il progetto Bartolucci del 1818* (Naples: Edizioni scientifiche italiane, 1987), p. 452: "*In tal modo si evita ogni amarezza, ed ogni anomalia. Si combina il favore discreto dell'agnazione col voto di natura, l'interesse delle famiglie coi diritti del sangue,* [...]. *Quanto forse era crudo l'escludere una germana in grazia d'un trasversale remoto, altrettanto sembra ragionevole l'esclusione*

Against the background of these preliminary explorations, I would point to many questions that need further investigation: the introduction of exclusion, connections to feudal law, mutations over time, treatment at the hands of learned law, the systematic study of *consilia* and jurisprudence, economic and social research into actual practice, and finally the debates accompanying eventual abolition of the exclusion of women in inheritance in the course of the nineteenth century.

References

Bellomo, Manlio. *Ricerche sui rapporti patrimoniali tra i coniugi: contributo alla storia della famiglia medievale.* Milan: Guffré, 1961.

Boudjaaba, Fabrice, Christine Dousset, and Sylvie Mouysset, eds. *Frères et sœurs du Moyen Âge à nos jours / Brothers and Sisters from the Middle Ages to the Present.* Bern: Peter Lang, 2016.

Bruno, Alberto, et al. *Tractatus facilis, ac perutilis, atque quotidano usu approbatus: de statutis à successionibus foeminas, necnon cognatorum lineam excludentibus* [...]. Venice: [Andrea Zenaro, al segno della Fontana], 1549.

Calvi, Giulia, and Caroline Blutrach-Jelin, eds. "Sibling Relations in Family History: Conflicts, Cooperation and Gender Roles (Sixteenth to Nineteenth Centuries)." *European Review of History: Revue européenne d'histoire* 17 (2010): pp. 695–704.

Calvi, Giulia, and Isabelle Chabot, eds. *Le ricchezze delle donne. Diritti patrimoniali e poteri familiari in Italia (XIII–XIX sec.)*. Torino: Rosenberg & Sellier, 1998.

Chabot, Isabelle. *La dette des familles. Femmes, lignage et patrimoine à Florence aux XIV*[e] *et XV*[e] *siècles*. Rome: École française de Rome, 2011.

Cooper, Elizabeth, and Kate Bird. "Inheritance: A Gendered and Intergenerational Dimension of Poverty." *Development Policy Review* 30 (2012): pp. 527–41.

Costituzioni della Patria del Friuli nel volgarizzamento di Pietro Capretto del 1484 e nell'edizione latina del 1565, edited by Anna Gobessi and Ermanno Orlando. Rome: Viella, 1998.

D'Amelia, Marina, ed. *Storia della maternità*, Rome and Bari: Laterza, 1997.

della femmina dall'eredità di un trasversale fino al quarto grado in grazia di altri agnati equidistanti, e.g. dei fratelli della stessa esclusa. Così, senza tradire i sentimenti della carità s'impedisce il pernicioso accumulamento delle ricchezze nel sesso debole, e l'impoverimento nel sesso, i sudori del quale formano i patrimonj, che solo propaga il nome e l'esistenza politica della famiglia, e che tanto meglio è incoraggiare colla speranza degli emolumenti, quanto è pericoloso chiamarvi l'altro sesso."

Danusso, Cristina. "La donna e i feudi: uno sguardo alla prassi successoria dell'Italia centro-settentrionale fra Tre e Quattrocento." *Rivista di storia del diritto italiano* 65 (1992): pp. 181–239.

De Luca, Giovan Battista. *Commentaria ad constitutionem Innocentii XI PM de Statutariis successionibus*. Lugduni: J.A. Cranmer and P. Perachon, 1697.

De Luca, Giovanni Battista. *Il dottor volgare, ovvero Il compendio di tutta la legge civile, canonica, feudale e municipale* [...]. Florence: V. Batelli e compagni, 1839–1843.

Il Difensore della Libertà (Genova: nella stamperia del cittadino Andrea Frugoni e C., 1797–1798).

Duboin, Felice Amato. *Raccolta per ordine di materie delle leggi, provvidenze, editti, manifesti, ecc.*, vol. VII. Torino: Mancio, Speirani e Co., 1831.

Ercole, Francesco. "Il diritto delle persone e il diritto di famiglia nel codice civile parmense studiato nei lavori preparatorii." *Rivista di diritto civile*, 5–6 (1912): pp. 561–642 and 721–807.

Feci, Simona. "Guardare al futuro. Il destino dei figli minori nei testamenti paterni (Roma, sec. XVII)." In *Famiglie. Circolazione di beni, circuiti di affetti in età moderna*, edited by Renata Ago and Benedetta Borello, pp. 83–116. Rome: Viella, 2008.

Feci, Simona. "I Mattei 'di Paganica': una famiglia romana tra XV e XVII secolo." *Dimensioni e problemi della ricerca storica* 1 (2011): pp. 81–113.

Fine, Agnès, Christiane Klapisch-Zuber, and Didier Lett, eds. "Liens et affects familiaux." *Clio. Femmes, Genre, Histoire* 34 (2011): pp. 7–16.

Fonte, Moderata (Modesta dal Pozzo). *Il merito delle donne*. Venice: Domenico Imberti, 1600.

Fonte, Moderata (Modesta dal Pozzo). *The Worth of Women, Wherein Is Clearly Revealed Their Nobility and Their Superiority to Men*, edited and translated by Virginia Cox. Chicago and London: The University of Chicago Press, 1997.

Guerra Medici, Maria Teresa. "City Air: Women in the Medieval City." In *Donne tra Medioevo ed Età Moderna in Italia: ricerche*, edited by Giovanna Casagrande, pp. 23–51. Perugia: Morlacchi, 2005.

Guerra Medici, Maria Teresa. "L'esclusione delle donne dalla successione legittima e la Constitutio super statutariis successionibus di Innocenzo XI." *Rivista di storia del diritto italiano* 56 (1983): pp. 261–94.

Kuehn, Thomas. "'*Dos non teneat locum legittime*': Dowry as a Woman's Inheritance in Early Quattrocento Florence." In *Law and Marriage in Medieval and Early Modern Times: Proceedings of the Eighth Carlsberg Academy Conference on Medieval Legal History 2011*, edited by Per Andersen et al., pp. 231–48. Copenhagen: DJØF Publishing, 2012.

Kuehn, Thomas. "Gender and Law in Milan." In *A Companion to Late Medieval and Early Modern Milan. The Distinctive Features of an Italian State*, edited by Andrea Gamberini, pp. 406–31. Leiden and Boston: Brill, 2014.

Kuehn, Thomas. *Law, Family and Women. Toward a Legal Anthropology of Renaissance Italy*. Chicago and London: The University of Chicago Press, 1991.

Lanaro, Paola, and Gian Maria Varanini. "Funzioni economiche della dote nell'Italia centro-settentrionale (tardo medioevo/ inizi età moderna)." In *La famiglia nell'economia europea. Secc. XIII–XVIII / The Economic Role of the Family in the European Economy from the 13th to the 18th Centuries. Atti della "XL Settimana di Studi dell'Istituto Internazionale di Storia Economica F. Datini" (Prato, 6–10 aprile 2008)*, edited by Simonetta Cavaciocchi, pp. 81–102. Florence: Firenze University Press, 2009.

Mayali, Laurent. *Droit savant et coutumes. L'exclusion des filles dotées, XIIe–XVe siècles*. Frankfurt a. M.: Klostermann, 1987.

Miscali, Monica. "Famiglia, patrimonio e strategie di trasmissione della proprietà in Sardegna nell'Ottocento." *Nuevo Mundo Mundos Nuevos*, Colloques (2008), http://nuevomundo.revues.org/26123; DOI: 10.4000/nuevomundo.26123, accessed 13 September 2015.

Mombelli Castracane, Mirella. *La codificazione civile nello Stato pontificio, vol. 1: Il progetto Bartolucci del 1818*. Naples: Edizioni scientifiche italiane, 1987.

Mongiano, Elisa. *Patrimonio e affetti: la successione legittima nell'età dei codici*. Torino: G. Giappichelli, 1999.

Monti, Anna Maria. *Iudicare tamquam Deus. I modi della giustizia senatoria nel Ducato di Milano tra Cinque e Settecento*. Milan: Giuffrè, 2003.

Niccolai, Franco. *La formazione del diritto successorio negli statuti comunali del territorio lombardo-tosco*. Milan: Giuffrè, 1940.

Owen Hughes, Diane. "From Brideprice To Dowry in Mediterranean Europe." *Journal of Family History* 3 (1978): pp. 262–96.

Piergiovanni, Vito. *Gli statuti civili e criminali di Genova nel Medioevo. La tradizione manoscritta e gli statuti*. Genova: ECIG, 1980.

Pisano, Laura, and Christiane Veauvy. *Parole inascoltate: le donne e la costruzione dello Stato-nazione in Italia e in Francia (1789–1860)*. Rome: Editori Riuniti, 1994.

Povolo, Claudio. "Eredità anticipata o esclusione per causa di dote? Un caso di pluralismo giuridico nel Friuli del Cinquecento." In *Padre e figlia*, edited by Luisa Accati, pp. 41–73. Torino: Rosenberg et Sellier, 1994.

Report of the Open Working Group of the General Assembly on Sustainable Development Goals (1 August 2014), http://undocs.org/A/68/970; http://www.undp.org/content/undp/en/home/mdgoverview/post-2015-development-agenda.html, accessed 12 February 2017.

Romano, Andrea. *Famiglia, successioni e patrimonio familiare nell'Italia medievale e moderna*. Torino: G. Giappichelli, 1994.

Romano, Andrea. "Successioni e difesa del patrimonio familiare nel Regno di Sicilia." In *Marriage, Property and Succession*, edited by Lloyd Bonfield, pp. 71–154. Berlin: Duncker and Humblot, 1992.

Rossi, Giovanni. "I fedecommessi nella dottrina e nella prassi giuridica di ius commune tra XVI e XVII secolo." In *La famiglia nell'economia europea. Secc. XIII–XVIII / The Economic Role of the Family in the European Economy from the 13th to the 18th Centuries. Atti della "XL Settimana di Studi dell'Istituto Internazionale di Storia Economica F. Datini" (Prato, 6–10 aprile 2008)*, edited by Simonetta Cavaciocchi, pp. 175–202. Florence: Firenze University Press, 2009.

Sandri, Gino. *Gli statuti veronesi del 1276 colle correzioni e le aggiunte fino al 1323*. Venice: Deputazione di storia patria per le Venezie, 1940.

Sperling, Jutta. "Dowry or Inheritance? Kinship, Property, and Women's Agency in Lisbon, Venice, Florence (1572)." *Journal of Early Modern History* 11 (2007): pp. 197–238.

Gli statuti de Padova tradotti de latino in vulgare [...]. Padova: G. Fabriano, 1551.

Statuti del comune di Padova, translated by Guido Beltrame, Guerrino Citton, and Daniela Mazzon. Cittadella: Biblos, 2000.

Gli statuti del comune di Treviso, sec. 13.–14, edited by Bianca Betto. Rome: nella sede dell'Istituto, 1986.

Statuti di Milano volgarizzati con note e spiegazioni [...]. Milan: G. Galeazzi, 1773.

Statuti pistoiesi del secolo XIII: studi e testi, edited by Renzo Nelli and Giuliano Pinto, vol. 3. Pistoia: Società pistoiese di storia patria, 2002.

Statutum potestatis comunis Pistorii (1296), edited by Ludovico Zdekauer. Pistoia: Società pistoiese di storia patria, 2002.

Lo statuto del comune di Bologna dell'anno 1335, edited by Anna Laura Trombetti Budriesi. Rome: nella sede dell'Istituto Palazzo Borromini, 2008.

Tarabotti, Arcangela. *La semplicità ingannata. Edizione critica e commentata*, edited by Simona Bortot. Padova: Il Poligrafo, 2007.

Tarabotti, Arcangela. *Paternal Tyranny*, edited and translated by Letizia Panizza. Chicago and London: The University of Chicago Press, 2004.

Zucca Micheletto, Beatrice. "À quoi sert la dot? Aliénations dotales, économie familiale et stratégies des couples à Turin au XVIIIe siècle." *Annales de démographie historique* 121 (2011): pp. 161–86.

CHAPTER 3

Inheritance Disputes from Ingelheim Court Records on the Threshold of the Early Modern Period (Fourteenth to Fifteenth Centuries)

Regina Schäfer

"Marriage meant setting up a new household to become an independent unit"[1] – and the death of one of those spouses destabilised that economic unit. The remaining relatives of the deceased had to rearrange themselves and establish new economic units. Contemporary legal norms, economic theory, and juridical conflicts tell us about the efforts and issues in these processes. Widows and widowers generally either remarried or retired. There is some remarkable research on the situation of widows in rural areas of Germany during early modern times, especially on women fighting for their inheritance.[2] There is also research on noblewomen and widows in the Middle Ages.[3] But

1 Hilde Sandvik, "Decision-making on Marital Property in Norway, 1500–1800," in *The Marital Economy in Scandinavia and Britain 1400–1900*, ed. Maria Ågren and Amy Louis Erickson (Aldershot: Ashgate, 2004), pp. 111–26, here p. 111.

2 Stefan Brakensiek, Michael Stolleis, and Heide Wunder, eds., *Generationengerechtigkeit? Normen und Praxis im Erb- und Ehegüterrecht 1500–1850* (Berlin: Duncker & Humblot, 2006); Hendrikje Carius, *Recht durch Eigentum: Frauen vor dem Jenaer Hofgericht (1648–1806)* (Munich: Oldenbourg, 2012); Karin Gottschalk, "Erbe und Recht. Die Übertragung von Eigen in der frühen Neuzeit," in *Erbe. Übertragungskonzepte zwischen Natur und Kultur*, ed. Stefan Willer, Sigrid Weigel, and Bernhard Jussen (Berlin: Suhrkamp, 2013), pp. 85–125; Michaela Hohkamp, "Wer will erben? Überlegungen zur Erbpraxis in geschlechtsspezifischer Perspektive in der Herrschaft Triberg von 1654–1806," in *Gutsherrschaft als soziales Modell*, ed. Jan Peters (Munich: Oldenbourg, 1995), pp. 327–41; Margareth Lanzinger, *Das gesicherte Erbe. Heirat in lokalen und familialen Kontexten. Innichen 1700–1900* (Vienna, Cologne, and Weimar: Böhlau, 2003); Susanne Rouette, "Erbrecht und Besitzweitergabe. Praktiken in der ländlichen Gesellschaft Deutschlands, Diskurse in Politik und Wissenschaft," in *Ländliche Gesellschaften in Deutschland und Frankreich, 18.–19. Jahrhundert*, ed. Rainer Prass, Jürgen Schlumbohm, Gérard Béaur, and Christophe Duhamelle (Göttingen: Vandenhoeck & Ruprecht, 2003), pp. 145–66; Nicole Grochowina, *Das Eigentum der Frauen. Konflikte vor dem Jenaer Schöppenstuhl im ausgehenden 18. Jahrhundert* (Cologne, Weimar, and Vienna: Böhlau, 2009); Nicole Grochowina, *Eigentumskulturen und Geschlecht in der Frühen Neuzeit* (Leipzig: Leipziger Universitäts-Verlag, 2005); *Female Economic Strategies in the Modern World*, ed. Beatrice Moring (London: Pickering & Chatto, 2012).

3 Karl-Heinz Spieß, "Lordship, Kinship, and Inheritance among the German High Nobility in the Middle Ages and Early Modern Period," in *Kinship in Europe. Approaches to*

 | DOI:10.1163/9789004456204_004

we still know little about the situation of women in cities,[4] and even less about their living conditions in rural areas in the late Middle Ages.[5] Scholars tend to assume the early modern situation was similar to the Middle Ages. This idea of the *longue durée* came along with a supposed persistence of social situations in rural areas from the fourteenth to the eighteenth century. However, Steven Ozment, Lyndal Roper, and others have demonstrated the effects of the reformation on family life. Protestantism tended to view women almost exclusively as wives subordinate to their husband or as daughters who should be trained for their roles as wives. The legacy of Protestantism led to a renewal of patriarchalism.[6] Hence, the situation of women might have been different in

---

Long-term Development (1300–1900), ed. David Warren Sabean, Simon Teuscher, and Jon Mathieu (New York and Oxford: Berghahn, 2007), pp. 57–75; Claudia Zey, ed., *Mächtige Frauen? Königinnen und Fürstinnen im europäischen Mittelalter (11.–14. Jahrhundert)* (Ostfildern: Thorbecke, 2015); Wolfgang Haubrichs and Patricia Oster, eds., *Zwischen Herrschaft und Kunst: fürstliche und adlige Frauen im Zeitalter Elisabeths von Nassau-Saarbrücken (14.–16. Jh.)* (Saarbrücken: Kommission für saarländische Landesgeschichte, 2013); Jörg Rogge, ed., *Fürstin und Fürst. Familienbeziehungen und Handlungsmöglichkeiten* (Stuttgart: Thorbecke, 2004); Bettina Elpers, *Regieren, Erziehen, Bewahren. Mütterliche Regentschaften im Hochmittelalter* (Frankfurt a. M.: Klostermann, 2003).

4 Kathrin Pajcic, *Frauenstimmen in der spätmittelalterlichen Stadt? Testamente von Frauen aus Lüneburg, Hamburg und Wien als soziale Kommunikation* (Würzburg: Königshausen & Neumann, 2013); Gabriela Signori, *Versorgen – Vererben – Erinnern. Kinder- und familienlose Erblasser in der städtischen Gesellschaft des Spätmittelalters* (Göttingen: Vandenhoeck & Ruprecht, 2001); Rudolf Hagemann and Heide Wunder, "Heiraten und Erben. Das Baseler Ehegüterrecht und Ehegattenerbrecht," in *Eine Stadt der Frauen. Studien und Quellen zur Geschichte der Baslerinnen im späten Mittelalter und zu Beginn der Neuzeit (13.–17. Jahrhundert)*, ed. Heide Wunder (Basel: Schwabe, 1995), pp. 150–66; Heinrich Rüthing, *Höxter um 1500. Analyse einer Stadtgesellschaft* (Paderborn: Bonifatius-Druckerei, 1986); Thomas Weibel, *Erbrecht und Familie. Fortbildung und Aufzeichnung des Erbrechts in der Stadt Zürich – vom Richtebrief zum Stadterbrecht von 1716* (Zürich: Chronos, 1988); Sandra Cavallo and Lyndan Warner, eds., *Widowhood in Medieval and Early Modern Europe* (London: Longman, 1999).

5 Katharina Simon-Muscheid, "Der weite Weg zur Erbschaft: Weibliche Rechtswege und Strategien im späten Mittelalter," in *Lesarten der Geschichte: Ländliche Ordnungen und Geschlechterverhältnisse. Festschrift für Heide Wunder zum 65. Geburtstag*, ed. Jens Flemming, Pauline Puppel, Werner Troßbach, Christina Vanja, and Ortrud Wörner-Heil (Kassel: kassel university press, 2004), pp. 402–17; Wilhelm Brauneder, *Die Entwicklung des Ehegüterrechts in Österreich. Ein Beitrag zur Dogmengeschichte und Rechtstatsachenforschung des Spätmittelalters und der Neuzeit* (Salzburg: Wilhelm Fink, 1973).

6 Lyndal Roper, *The Holy Household. Women and Morals in Reformation Augsburg* (Oxford: Clarendon Press, 1989); Steven Ozment, *When Fathers Ruled. Family Life in Reformation Europe* (Cambridge, Mass.: Harvard University Press, 1983); Steven Ozment, *The Bürgermeister's Daughter. Scandal in a Sixteenth-Century German Town* (New York: St. Martin's Press, 1998); Heinrich Richard Schmidt, "Nothurft vnd Hußbruch. Haus, Gemeinde und Sittenzucht im Reformiertentum," in *Ehe – Familie – Verwandtschaft. Vergesellschaftung in*

the late Middle Ages. Relations changed within not only the family but society as well. As Heide Wunder concisely put it, post 1500, rule with peasants became rule over peasants.[7] The fifteenth and early sixteenth centuries were a period of political and social change and transition. Villages and towns were increasingly integrated into extensive complexes of territorial power. Lordship became more and more territorial, with marked borders. The lords made increased attempts to bring the inhabitants of villages and towns under their dominion and to integrate foreigners. Adapting the idea of the good father who ruled the country, the prince or the city council tried to regulate the lives of their subordinates.[8]

The legal and social situation of communities and of women within those communities thus varied in essence from town to town, but the sixteenth century was a turning point. In addition, the political landscape of the Rhine Valley was marked by close proximity of different seignories. Some villages were partitioned or had more than one lord; Ingelheim was part of the Emperor's properties but impawned to the Count Palatine. The structure of territorial and small-town societies in the Late Middle Ages is thus far more heterogeneous and intriguing than the situation in the middle of the sixteenth century.[9]

1 Ingelheim and the Ingelheim Court Records

In the fifteenth century Ingelheim, situated in the south-west of Germany near the city of Mainz, an important central location in the middle of Germany, was a village of roughly 800 inhabitants. A unique and extraordinary set of records from the medieval Ingelheim court have fortunately been preserved – at least

Religion und sozialer Lebenswelt, ed. Andreas Holzem and Ines Weber (Paderborn: Ferdinand Schöningh, 2008), pp. 301–23.

7 Heide Wunder, *Die bäuerliche Gemeinde in Deutschland: Von der Herrschaft mit Bauern zur Herrschaft über Bauern* (Göttingen: Vandenhoeck & Ruprecht, 1986).

8 Ernst Schubert, *Fürstliche Herrschaft und Territorium im späten Mittelalter* (München: Oldenburg, 1996, 2nd edition 2006); Gerd Schwerhoff, "Frühneuzeitliche Stadtgeschichte im Cultural Turn – eine Standortbestimmung," in *Neue Stadtgeschichte(n): die Reichsstadt Frankfurt im Vergleich*, ed. Julia Schmidt-Funke and Matthias Schnettger (Bielefeld: transcript Verlag, 2018), pp. 11–41.

9 Raoul Hippchen, Heidrun Ochs, and Regina Schäfer, "Der Mittelrhein. Konkurrenz der Herrschaften und Motor des Handels," in *Schrei nach Gerechtigkeit. Leben am Mittelrhein am Vorabend der Reformation*, ed. Winfried Wilhelmy (Regensburg: Schnell und Steiner, 2015), pp. 17–25.

in parts.[10] These provide a comprehensive view of routines and procedures of a local court that handled all kinds of civil and penal proceedings that were of relevance to the community, from unpaid wages to insult, from property transfer to unnatural death.[11]

Simon Teuscher has shown how oral tradition was transformed by seigneurial and written orders in the fifteenth century; over the course of the Late Middle Ages forms of communication changed fundamentally.[12] Many aspects of life in a village community were yet to be subject to regulation by governing parties. During this period rules and methods of supervising and controlling aspects of daily life, such as police ordinances, were put into place.[13] The introduction of Roman law was in its earliest stages. Different and overlapping legal systems coexisted, and had yet to be replaced by a single hierarchical legal system. While earlier research has emphasised the divide between oral and written culture, recent research is looking at the process of mediating law and rights, and the tension caused by diverging concepts of legality.[14] The Ingelheim court served as a local court as well as a consultation court (*Oberhof*) for villages and individuals within a 50-kilometre radius. This is fortunate for our task, because we have two kinds of court records: the high court records (*Oberhofprotokolle*), consisting of decisions made by the court as advising court (*Oberhof*), and the *Haderbücher*, the local court records that document discussions in front of the local court. We find that the court acted quite differently depending on whether they were faced with solving a local issue or an outsider asking for a judgment on a difficult case. Legal history is concentrating on the high court

10 Rainer Opitz, "Kodikologie und Quellenwert der frühen Haderbücher," in *Die Ingelheimer Haderbücher – Mittelalterliches Prozessschriftgut und seine Auswertungsmöglichkeiten*, ed. Franz J. Felten and Harald Müller (Ingelheim: Vandenhoeck & Ruprecht, 2010), pp. 29–41.

11 Regina Schäfer, "Friede durch Recht. Zur Funktion des Dorfgerichts in der Gemeinde," in *Dorf und Gemeinde. Grundstrukturen der ländlichen Gesellschaft in Spätmittelalter und Frühneuzeit*, ed. Kurt Andermann and Oliver Auge (Epfendorf: bibliotheca academica, 2012), pp. 65–85.

12 Simon Teuscher, *Lords' Rights and Peasant Stories: Writing and the Formation of Tradition in the Later Middle Ages* (Philadelphia: University of Pennsylvania Press, 2012).

13 Karl Härter, "Gute Ordnung und Policey des Alten Reiches in der Region: Zum Einfluß der Reichspoliceygesetzgebung auf die Ordnungsgesetzgebung süddeutscher Reichstände," in *Das Reich in der Region während des Mittelalters und der Frühen Neuzeit*, ed. Rolf Kießling and Sabine Ullmann (Konstanz: UVK, 2005), pp. 187–223.

14 Christine Reinle, "Umkämpfter Friede. Politischer Gestaltungswille und geistlicher Normenhorizont bei der Fehdebekämpfung im deutschen Spätmittelalter," in *Rechtsveränderung im politischen und sozialen Kontext mittelalterlicher Rechtsvielfalt*, ed. Stefan Esders and Christine Reinle (Münster: Lit, 2005), pp. 143–70.

records focussing on legal norms and practice.[15] For social historians the local court records are more fruitful since they provide an insight into the discussion within the local community of Ingelheim.

The local court records (*Haderbücher*), which are preserved for the period between 1387 and 1534, mention cases of severe punishment, even death penalties. But these are rare. About ninety percent of the records deal with unpaid debts, which reflects the dependency of the wine growing economy on advance financing and credit.[16] Many legal proceedings resemble dunning procedures. Only a minor portion of the records are connected to inheritance disputes. Verdicts are moreover rare in the local court records; this differs from the high court records, where the same court, albeit in another function, issued sentences to requesting courts in all cases.[17] The scarcity of decisions in the local court records needs an explanation. I presume that the primary aim of the Ingelheim court was to restore peace in the community. Finding a consensus between the parties was preferred over passing out judgements that would most likely deepen the conflict. The court therefore tried to delay decisions, deferring these to arbitration courts and forcing the opposing parties to swear peace until the next session. In some cases, the court explicitly declared that the dispute should not be brought to court again but rather be settled outside of court.[18] The primary aim of the court was not the enforcement of law, but keeping peace and securing the independence of Ingelheim and its special status within the Rhine Palatinate (*Pfalzgrafschaft*).[19]

15 Alexander Krey, *Die Praxis der spätmittelalterlichen Laiengerichtsbarkeit. Gerichts- und Rechtslandschaften des Rhein-Main-Gebietes im 15. Jahrhundert im Vergleich* (Cologne, Weimar, and Vienna: Böhlau, 2015).

16 Gerhard Fouquet, "Kredit in der ländlichen Gesellschaft und Wirtschaft im späten Mittelalter. Das Beispiel Ober-Ingelheim," in *Zins und Gült. Strukturen des ländlichen Kreditwesens in Spätmittelalter und Frühneuzeit*, ed. Kurt Andermann and Gerhard Fouquet (Epfendorf: bibliotheca academica, 2016), pp. 17–40.

17 *Die älteren Urteile des Ingelheimer Oberhofes*, vol. 1–4, ed. Adalbert Erler (Frankfurt a. M.: Klostermann, 1952–1963).

18 *Das Oberingelheimer Haderbuch 1476–1485*, ed. Werner Marzi (Alzey: Rheinhessische Druckwerkstätte, 2011), fol. 4r, 4v, 36v, 61r–v, 172r, 182r = Ober-Ingelheimer Haderbuch 1476–1484, Bl. 004, 004v, 036v, 061–061v, 172v, 182, accessed 28 July 2020, https://www.haderbuecher.de/baende/1476-1485-ober-ingelheim/blatt/band-1-oi-1476-1484-bl-004/. So far, five Haderbücher are online – including translations into modern German, the transliterated medieval text, and a facsimile of each page: Nieder-Ingelheim 1468–1485, Ober-Ingelheim 1476–1485, Groß-Winternheim 1490–1502, Ober-Ingelheim 1518–1529, Nieder-Ingelheim 1521–1530. In the following, I use the citation *Ober-Ingelheimer Haderbuch 1476–1484*.

19 Schäfer, "Friede," pp. 65–85.

These particular court records are the result of disputes. They obviously reveal little about families who lived in harmony. Still, problems with families, and mostly problems of inheritance, were by far the most difficult matters with which the court had to deal. The Ingelheim court records are exceptionally extensive and detailed. The records reveal a wealthy community of significant size with an excellent infrastructure: a market, fortifications, a hospital, and a school. Ingelheim society was stratified: nobleman and day labourer, mayor and maid all appeared before the court. Such a community had ceased to be plain rural, but could not yet be considered fully urban.[20] The region was also marked by high mobility; serfdom was not common, and people could easily leave the village and move abroad, or settle down and continue their life in Ingelheim.

Before diving deeper into the matter of negotiation processes within the converging fields of gender and property, one sample from the court records will prove a useful point of departure. A synopsis and interpretation of the discussion in front of the court shall follow:

> Jtem Rudiger hait sich verdingt Peter Snaden sin wort zu thune und hait das buch geigen Karlen und Jeckeln von Siemern laißen offen und das alleß verbot. Und begert Adam den bottel zuverhoren. Dar off sagt Adam wie daß Hans Klee off eyn zijt yn Peders husche krancke gelegen und des selben legers auch gestorben. Do sihe Peder kommen und yme in sin husche geruffen. Also habe Hans Klee sinen bruder und eynen swager bij yme gehabt. Und Hans Klee sagt wie daß Peder Snade eynen kauffe ummb yne gethan hette und die selbe scholt habe er Pedern mit wißen und willen sins bruder und swagers die zijt geben vor sin eigen gut. Doch also daß er yne den leger halten und yme das beste thun soll. Do habe er wider Hansen bruder und swager gesagt: kommet Hans nu off sall dann auch die scholt Peders sin ader nit. Haben sie yme geantwort das laißen sie gescheen. Komme er off er mags Pedern wider geben ader nit das krudde sie nit dann. Sie verwilligen diese gift do bij sij er gewest. Und

20 Michael Matheus, "Winzerdörfer: Wirtschafts- und Lebensformen zwischen Stadt und Land. Überlegungen zu einem Siedlungstyp in vergleichender europäischer Perspektive," in *Landwirtschaft und Dorfgesellschaft im ausgehenden Mittelalter*, ed. Enno Bünz (Ostfildern: Thorbecke, 2020); Regina Schäfer, "Ingelheim im Spätmittelalter – eine Gemeinde zwischen Dorf und Stadt," in *Alltag, Herrschaft, Gesellschaft und Gericht im Spiegel der spätmittelalterlichen Ingelheimer Haderbücher. Ein Begleitband zum Editionsprojekt "Ingelheimer Haderbücher,"* ed. Werner Marzi and Regina Schäfer (Alzey: Rheinhessische Druckwerkstätte, 2012), pp. 47–63.

> was das ymm rechten byndt laiße er gescheen. Rudiger als von Peders wegen hait die sage verbot und sagt haben die czwene eynene genugen dar an das laiße er gescheen. Ist des nit so stehe er do und sihe sins rechten bodijg.
>
> Dar off hait sich Ancze Duppengießer verdingt Karlen und Jeckeln yre worte zu thune und hait sin undertinge verbot als recht ist. Und hait auch verbot daß der bottel erkent daß Hans Klee krancke gelegen der selben kranckheit auch gestorben. Dwile dann der bottel von Peders wegen/ und nit von bescheit des scholteißen ader gerichts do gewesten so hoffen Karlen und Jeckel daß sie die sage nit yren solle als er sagen wollen. Dann Hans Klee sij ir gemachter vatter gewesten und da ummb soll er yne das ire nit enweg geben dwile die handt gebrochen ist. Und hett erßs macht gehabt so solt erßs gethain hain vor scholteßen und scheffen alsdann gewonheit ist. Und sunderlich dwile er yn syme doit bette gelegen hait so soll erßs nit macht hain. Und stilt das zu recht.
>
> Rudiger als von Peders wegen sagt de jnsage Ancze als von der czweier wegen gethain hoffe Peder daß yne die nit yrren solle dann eß finde sich in dem buch genuge yne mit des bottels sage nit. So hoffe Peder bij syme rechten jn maißen er dann vor geretten zu bliben. Und hait eß auch zu recht gestalt.
>
> Das ist gelengt ad socios. Das hain sie verbot.[21]

In 1480 Karl and Jeckel of Simmern, the two stepsons of the deceased Hans Klee, were seeking recompense from Peter Snade from Ingelheim, who had been nursing Hans Klee, and in whose house their stepfather had breathed out his life. Peter Snade had managed to bring Hans Klee to make a gift by will to his advantage on his deathbed in the presence of Klee's brother, brother-in-law, and the bailiff. The court session took place on the occasion of the bailiff's statement, who had been called upon as a witness by Peter Snade. Snade also declared himself willing to state under oath that the gift by will had been made as described. The stepsons countered his arguments by denying their stepfather's right to disinherit them and by putting casting doubt on the legality of the gift, as the will had been declared on the deathbed and not before the complete court board. Neither of the parties presented their case directly, this was done by two of the four supporters (*Fürsprecher*) installed at the court, who argued on their behalves. The court decided in favour of the stepsons. Peter Snade was to be reimbursed for his expenses while caring for Hans Klee on his

21 *Ober-Ingelheimer Haderbuch 1476–1485*, fol. 146r–146v.

deathbed. Everything else was to be returned to the heirs. But this verdict did not close the case, they argued for some time about the amount and conditions of the payment. In the end, an agreement was reached outside of court.[22]

In the period from 1387 to 1534, covered by the records, cases like this one range into the hundreds.[23] While many of the court cases cannot be properly defined and were probably settled outside of court, inheritance disputes constituted the majority of the cases that were brought back to court again and again, consuming much of the court's time. The collection of court records comprises nineteen volumes, varying in size between 100 and 300 pages and each containing several thousand entries. Most entries are very short, making bare mention without further detail that the case of person A complaining about person B had been brought before court. Only ten to twenty percent of those complaints developed into full legal cases. The Ingelheim court records provide detailed insight into the process of negotiating conflict and the legal practices exercised therein. At the time, Ingelheim was a community of three villages (Ober-Ingelheim, Nieder-Ingelheim, Großwinternheim) under immediate authority of the emperor but, as mentioned, impawned to the Count Palatine. The court consisted of fourteen lay judges, most of whom were members of the nobility, and presided over by the sheriff or mayor, who also acted as judge. There was also a clerk who kept the records, two bailiffs, and four so-called *Fürsprecher* who acted as semi-professional advocates. The noble lay judges were fiefs of the Count Palatine or the archbishop of Mainz, their families owned fortresses and small villages nearby; some of them lived in Ingelheim, others in the Rheingau on the other side of the river Rhine. They had some basic education; a few, but not all, knew how to read Latin and most were trained in the practices of administration, none had studied law. It was customary law they dealt with in an oral tradition, the court did not use written textbooks.[24] Their decisions, however, were based on legal custom and local or territorial law, which can no longer be described as merely traditional law. There were fixed lawsuit procedures that forced all parties involved to submit to the decisions of the court. The court avoided being bound to written law and

22 *Ober-Ingelheimer Haderbuch 1476–1485*, fol. 155r, 157r–157v.

23 Opitz, "Kodikologie," pp. 29–41; Marita Blattmann, "Beobachtungen zum Schrifteinsatz an einem deutschen Niedergericht um 1400: die Ingelheimer Haderbücher," in *Als die Welt in die Akten kam. Prozeßschriftgut im europäischen Mittelalter*, ed. Susanne Lepsius and Thomas Wetzstein (Frankfurt a. M.: Klostermann, 2008), pp. 51–84, here pp. 55–57.

24 Hugo Loersch, *Der Ingelheimer Oberhof* (Bonn: Adolph Marcus, 1885); Regina Schäfer, "Rechtsprechung ohne Gesetz? Die Rechtsentscheidungen der Schöffen von Niedergerichten," in *Das Gesetz – The Law – La Loi*, ed. Andreas Speer and Guy Guldentops (Berlin: de Gruyter, 2014), pp. 152–78.

was thus capable of finding more flexible and suitable solutions. Unfortunately, complementary documents such as (last) wills and marriage agreements are no longer available, as they were mostly oral.[25] This means we need to resort to the court's verdicts and the statements documented in its records as our principle sources. Analysis will show that a number of basic legal concepts and regulations were in use.

2 Rules Regulating Inheritance

The medieval system of property consisted of separate and joint estates. Separation of property was most common. The notion of a separate estate comprised gifts and inheritance. Gifts from the bride's family (*Wittum* and *dos*) and the gifts made by her bridegroom (*Morgengabe*) became the wife's separate estate, but under the husband's administration. The marital estate compromised three parts: the husband's inherited property, the wife's inherited property and the common property they acquired during their marriage. If the marriage remained without children, ownership of the goods in possession of the spouses at the time of the wedding was returned to the respective parent families.[26] The assets acquired after the wedding were considered joint property (*Zuerwerb*).[27] If the couple died without children the joint property was likewise returned to the parent families, although not in equal shares. Two thirds went to the husband's family, the so-called share of the sword (*Schwertteil*), and one third went to the wife's family, the so-called share of the skirt (*Rockteil*).

In case of offspring, property had to be divided among the children, regardless of whether it had been acquired by their parents through inheritance or labour. Female and male children inherited equal shares as soon as one of their parents died. The allocation of the inheritance shares was negotiated by the relatives (*frunde*). Upon the death of one partner, the transmission of property to the surviving partner and to the next generation had to be negotiated. If all children died before one or both of their parents, grandchildren inherited in their place and in the same manner. If a child's death preceded the death of a parent (but not the deaths of the siblings), his or her descendants were

25 Signori, *Versorgen*, p. 67.

26 Gunter Gudian, *Ingelheimer Recht im 15. Jahrhundert* (Aalen: Scientia, 1968), p. 163; Erler, *Die älteren Urteile*, no. 245.

27 Gudian, *Ingelheimer Recht*, pp. 174–75; Brauneder, *Entwicklung*, pp. 235–51; Weibel, *Erbrecht*, pp. 47–49.

ruled out as heirs. Unlike in early modern Germany, where genealogical lines were of greater relevance, grandchildren of deceased children were not entitled to inherit from their grandparents.[28] This was particularly important with regard to real estate, which was passed on irrespective of how, and as a result of whom, it had become a part of the marital property. Descendants were thus clearly favoured over the surviving spouse, who was left empty-handed. Upon enquiry by another court, the Ingelheim court explicitly stated that according to prevailing legal norms, the widow was not entitled to an inheritance.[29]

This situation constituted a threat to the welfare of the surviving spouse, be there children or not. Inheriting children, grandchildren, and spouses' respective families were likely to take measures to oust her or him from the estate in order to get their hands on the assets. In the following, this will be shown to be the case primarily for widows; widowers faced a similar, though slightly different fate.[30]

In many cases, the inheritance rules described above were only applied to real estate assets, and not to mobile assets, which to some degree attenuated the potentially disastrous economic effect on the survivor. In Ingelheim it was common that a couple shared the use of the land, even if it was not possessed by both partners equally.[31] Widows would regularly use the land until their own deaths, and were thus protected against being ousted from their homes at the time of their husbands' deaths. Widows, in fact, were only granted usufruct, and remained under obligation to maintain the estate, to pay any interest, and so forth. If they failed to meet these obligations, potential assets would return to the spouses' parent families.[32] The widow had the right to only lifelong usufruct of the land, not ownership. She could use the property, but was not allowed to sell it. These rights and obligations remained unchanged if the widow married again, excluding her new husband from any right linked to her former marriage. The land was still treated as separate property, belonging to the lineage of each spouse. If the new marriage remained childless, and both widow and her new husband died, all assets were returned to the respective parent families, namely the widow's family and those of her first and her

28 Gudian, *Ingelheimer Recht*, pp. 183 and 191; Weibel, *Erbrecht*, p. 171.

29 Gudian, *Ingelheimer Recht*, p. 165.

30 Ibid., pp. 188–89; Sandra Cavallo and Lyndan Warner, "Introduction," in *Widowhood*, pp. 3–23, here p. 3.

31 *Ober-Ingelheimer Haderbuch 1518–1529*, fol. 208r–v.

32 Gudian, *Ingelheimer Recht*, pp. 184–88. Cf. Signori, *Versorgen*, pp. 86–91; Weibel, *Erbrecht*, pp. 174–76.

second husband.[33] Children and grandchildren descending from the second marriage only inherited from their parents or grandparents, respectively.

These regulations could be circumvented by concluding an inheritance contract before the court. Spouses could agree to turn their separate estates into a joint estate. In Ingelheim, testators were considered to have the right to dispose freely of their possessions. This total discretion over the distribution of their property contradicts the legal norms of inheritance. Men and women could circumvent the legal norms before the court and with the consent of their relatives. In most cases, spouses would mutually declare the survivor to be their testamentary heir.[34] In this period, the degree of testator's freedom had yet to be regulated and the court therefore left considerable room for maneuver. Inheritance agreements could not be cancelled unilaterally. Inheritance contracts could be restricted to specific assets or declare the surviving spouse the sole heir to the complete fortune, in which case none of the assets would be returned to the respective family of birth. In this case, the widow would receive the complete estate following the death of her husband.

The birth of a child rendered all inheritance contracts invalid. Children stemming from the current marriage were favoured over stepchildren and inherited equal shares regardless of their gender. Stepchildren were treated in the same way as children from the current marriage if both spouses had agreed before court that all children should be treated alike, inheriting equal shares (*Einkindschaft*).[35] The consent of the children of the first marriage was necessary for the stepchildren to be considered equal heirs.[36] In our sample inheritance dispute, the new and childless husband Hans Klee had apparently adopted his wife's children from her first marriage, Jeckel and Karl von Simmern, who then became the sole heirs of their estate.

Inheritance disputes were fought between all manner of family members and relatives, be they parents, children, grandparents, grandchildren, blood and step-relatives, or others. Such disputes could be rooted in conflicting legal

---

33 Gudian, *Ingelheimer Recht*, pp. 176–78.

34 Ibid., pp. 161–65. This was common in the city of Frankfurt as well. Cf. Walther Karl Zülch, *Frankfurter Künstler 1223–1700* (Frankfurt a. M.: Diesterweg, 1935), p. 51. In the villages that are now in Switzerland the declarations were called "Mächtnisse"; Weibel, *Erbrecht*, pp. 64–121 (Zurich); Signori, *Versorgen* (Basel).

35 Gudian, *Ingelheimer Recht*, pp. 208–10. Gabriela Signori, "Pflegekinder, Stiefkinder, Morgengabskinder: Formen sozialer Eltern- bzw. sozialer Kindschaft in der Gesellschaft des Spätmittelalters," in *Freundschaft und Verwandtschaft. Zur Unterscheidung und Verflechtung zweier Beziehungssysteme*, ed. Johannes F. K. Schmidt, Martine Guichard, Peter Schuster, and Fritz Trillmich (Konstanz: UVK, 2007), pp. 165–80.

36 Zülch, *Frankfurter Künstler*, p. 171 with an example of a goldsmith from Frankfurt.

regulations or principles, or in attempts to exploit certain weaknesses or disadvantages of heirs apparent, such as ill health, absence from or unfamiliarity with the place, minority, and even grief. Our sample case demonstrates a conflict between the will of the deceased and what the heirs believed to be their right. The conflict goes even deeper, Peter Snade, who benefitted from the testator's will, used blood relatives of Hans Klee, who acted as if they could freely dispose of their share of the sword. The law turned out to be in favour of the stepsons, but the fact that Peter Snade was in possession of the estate using it as if he were the proprietor put them at a disadvantage. They moreover lacked assistance from the family of their stepfather. In the end, a settlement outside the court was likely the most satisfactory, if not the only, way forward for both sides.

As remarriage was common for widows and widowers, inheritance lines became quite complex. This can be illustrated by the attempts of a wife's relatives to deprive a widower of his possessions:

> Jtem Ioest Scherer von wegen Birckerns Margrethen spricht zu Hen Gicken vnd sagt: Er, Gick, hab gehabt eyn hußfrawe genent Margreth Birckern fuent eyn wytwen Adam Peffers. Vnd nach seyn, Adams, dot, hab er, Hen Gick, Margrethen zu der eh genommen mit etlichen beweglichen vnd vnbeweglichen guttern vnd sonder leybs erben doids vorscheyden vnd abgangen. Dar vmb dan dye ytzige Margreth klegerin als die nechst gesypte freundin vnd vorwente der verstorben Margrethen, Hen Gicken hußfrawen nemlich geswister kynder myt eynander. Begert Margreth den gepurlichen teyl der zubrachten Irer wasen narung wie obsteth, Hen Gick dar von hant ab; mit recht erkannt vnd behalten. Disse clage meren myndern vt iuris.[37]

The widower was the second husband of Margreth Becker, who had previously been married to the prosperous Adam Peffer. Neither couple had own children. The second husband, Hen Gick, was now arraigned by a cousin of his late wife, who tried to get a part of the share of the skirt.

There were all kinds of gender-related inheritance problems. I would like to focus on widows first, who were largely expected to be in a better legal and social situation than wives or unmarried women. As widows often remarried,

37 *Ober-Ingelheimer Haderbuch 1518–1529*, fol. 5 (not in the partial edition Werner Marzi and Kai-Michael Sprenger, eds., *Hader und Streit in Ingelheim. Edition ausgewählter Gerichtsfälle aus dem Ober-Ingelheimer Haderbuch 1518–1529* (Ingelheim: E. Humbert Verlag, 2016)).

each widow had the potential to become a wife again. Remarried or not, both groups had to fight hard for their interests from the first marriage in order to actually get their hands on their assets.

3 The Legal and Economic Position of Widows

The death of a person, specifically of a childless one, regularly constituted a situation of crisis. Although most heirs were aware of their rights, it was often difficult to assess the inheritance and to calculate the shares to be allocated to the heirs. It was not uncommon to mutually share financial obligations between spouses at the time of the wedding, and debts and obligations were inherited along with the assets.[38] Loans and credits were common in Ingelheim, this lead to over-indebtedness on the one side and to the accumulation of wealth on the other. Vintners would borrow money in spring in hopes of equivalent returns from the sale of the new vintage in autumn.[39] The death of an individual burdened with financial obligations created uncertainties for creditors, who often reacted by filing lawsuits, especially when the debtors were childless, or by having themselves entitled to seize property at the first failure of the heirs to honour payment instalments.[40]

The legal position of a woman changed the moment her husband died, she had to pay creditors, lost property, and moreover she lost her husband's labour. A lot of widows were at a great risk for poverty. In order to avoid a precarious

38 *Ober-Ingelheimer Haderbuch 1476–1485*, fol. 15v, 30v–31r.

39 Kurt Andermann and Gerhard Fouquet, eds., *Zins und Gült: Strukturen des ländlichen Kreditwesens in Spätmittelalter und Frühneuzeit* (Epfendorf: bibliotheca academica, 2016); Gabriela Signori, *Schuldenwirtschaft. Konsumenten- und Hypothekarkredite im spätmittelalterlichen Basel* (Konstanz: UVK, 2015); Gabriela Signori, ed., *Prekäre Ökonomien. Schulden in Spätmittelalter und Früher Neuzeit* (Konstanz: UVK, 2014); Hans-Jörg Gilomen, "Der Kleinkredit in spätmittelalterlichen Städten. Basel und Zürich im Vergleich," in *Städtische Wirtschaft im Mittelalter: Festschrift für Franz Irsigler zum 70. Geburtstag*, ed. Rudolf Holbach (Cologne, Weimar, and Vienna: Böhlau, 2011), pp. 109–48; Ulrich Pfister, "Le petit crédit rural en Suisse aux XVIe–XVIIe siècles," *Annales, Histoires, Sciences Sociales* 49 (1994), pp. 1339–57; Laurence Fontaine, "Die Bauern und die Mechanismen der Kreditvergabe," in *Schuldenlast und Schuldenwerk. Kreditnetzwerke in der europäischen Geschichte 1300–1900*, ed. Gabriele Clemens (Trier: Kliomedia, 2008), pp. 109–30; Rodrigue Lavoie, "Endettement et pauvreté en Provence d'après les listes de la justice comtale XIV–XVe siècle," *Provence historique* 23 (1973), pp. 201–16; Maryse Guenette, "Au Carrefour de la misère: les poursuites pour dettes à Brignoles et à Saint-Maximin au milieu du XIVe siècle," *Canadian Journal of History* 26 (1991), pp. 225–40.

40 *Ober-Ingelheimer Haderbuch 1476–1485*, fol. 3r, 13r, 51v. *Ober-Ingelheimer Haderbuch 1518–1529*, fol. 2v (not in the partial edition Marzi and Sprenger, *Hader und Streit in Ingelheim*).

situation a widow's relatives and or husband could arrange for protective measures – delaying the moment of bequest by declaring a community of accrued gain during the lifetime of husband and wife was one means of doing this. Alternatively, the terms of a dower could be arranged at the time of engagement. The widow might be promised 20 to 60 Gulden after her husbands' death as a tenancy for life.[41] In other German regions we see widows having the right of abode in the conjugal home – this was not common in Ingelheim. Children could renounce a part of their inheritance in favour of their mother or father. In one case, the inheritance was divided into three parts: two for the children and the third for their father. This need not necessarily be seen as an indicator of selfless love and understanding between generations. Such solutions could be beneficial for all parties. The heirs abstained from a third, but they received land and money immediately. It was advantageous for widowers (or widows) as well. Rather than being granted the use of land that was legally their children's, they now owned it.

Many heirs, especially widows, were ill-prepared for the transition of possessions and properties. On their deathbeds, men usually declared the debts they had incurred and had yet to repay to a close relative.[42] Upon the deaths of their husbands widows were often thrust into an existential crisis, and some relinquished their inheritance.[43] This was done by laying her coat on his grave in a symbolic gesture of withdrawing the marital community, as the following example shows:[44]

> Jtem Drubein hait Elsen, Philips Hennen seligen witwen zu gesprochen wie daß Heppgin von Bubenheim yre hußwert selige eyn phert gekaufften habe ummb den schriber zu Odernheim vor XVI gulden. Aso habe yre bruder Kloppel und sie yne off die zijt gebetten burge zu werden. Sie wollen yne losen sonder allen schaden. Daß sie yne nu nit von schaden doint das schade yme XX gulden und heist yne des eyn ja ader neyn obe sie solichs geretten habe ader nit. Dar off sagt Else: des offgemeßen schadens sij sie zuvor abe unschuldig, sie worde sin dann erzugt als recht were. Furter so sij yre hußwert selige XX jare doit gewesten. Also habe sie off die zijt den mantel off dem grabe laißen liegen. Auch habe sie Drubein nuste

41 Gudian, *Ingelheimer Recht*, pp. 185–88.

42 *Ober-Ingelheimer Haderbuch 1476–1485*, fol. 12v, 17v; cf. Gudian, *Ingelheimer Recht*, pp. 170 and 223.

43 Cf. the situation of the artist in Frankfurt; Zülch, *Frankfurter Künstler*, pp. 34, 47, and 178.

44 *Ober-Ingelheimer Haderbuch 1476–1485*, fol. 17v. In Zurich widows had to pay one third of the debts; Weibel, *Erbrecht*, pp. 54–55.

gerett und wes er sie wider anlange des sij sie unschuldijg. Die unscholt ist gestalten noch hude zu XIIII tagen. Das haint sie beide verbot.

Drubein accuses Else, the widow of Henne Philipp, that her first husband Heppgin of Bubenheim once bought a horse from the cleric of Odernheim for 16 Gulden. Else and her brother Kloppel had asked him, Drubein, to act as guarantor for them. They had promised to timely pay their debts and hold him harmless but they failed to do so, and he lost 20 Gulden. He asks her to admit or reject the suit. Else answers: Her first husband died more than twenty years ago. She laid her coat on his grave and left it. She promised Drubein nothing. She declares herself innocent. The court prolongs her innocence for fourteen days. Both parties accept the adjudgment. Children, however, had no way of relinquishing an inheritance and assumed all obligations of their parents.

There is no such thing as a typical widow, but widows faced a very distinct set of situations. Women in general, and widows in particular, should not, as was common in the older historiography, be reduced to mere victims; they had means to shape their fates. We find widows who enjoyed comfortable lives and others who had to fight very hard for their rights. It becomes apparent that some widows chose to carry on their business even when they had adult sons. There are widows who were designated heir by their own son,[45] and others who left Ingelheim to settle down with relatives living abroad. In the following, I will present four cases to illustrate the spectrum of situations facing widows from the middling social strata in Ingelheim: two examples of widows arguing with their relatives – one fighting her stepmother and another filing a lawsuit against her son-in-law; these will be followed by two rather sad cases of widows who suffered from illnesses. As there already is some research into noblewomen and their conflicts, I will avoid that topic. We cannot tell much about lower class women, they were rarely present before court, but the final examples show us how in cases of illness women could lose everything.[46]

The first case gives us an impression of the ways in which inheritance was negotiated, when relatives did not agree on the terms. Let's hear a witness:

Dicta testis Smußers Ketten contra Heijdesheim Otilianj:

Jtem Niclaus Bender, burger zu Obern Jngelnheijm als getzuge Ketten Peter Schmußer seligen nachgelaijßen witwen zu Heijseßheijm

45 In Frankfurt 1410 Gipel Schnitzler named his mother as his heir; Zülch, *Frankfurter Künstler*, p. 28.

46 Valentin Groebner, *Ökonomie ohne Haus. Zum Wirtschaften armer Leute in Nürnberg am Ende des 15. Jahrhunderts* (Göttingen: Vandenhoeck & Ruprecht, 1993).

furgestelt. Nach dem er deß mit recht erlangt waß kuntschafft der warheijt zu sagenŋ vff schuldigung dinstags nach Oculi mej nehst hije vor vff jnen bescheen. Also hait der Schultheiß als richter jnen angenomen mit gelobden vnd eijden wije recht beladen dije warheijt zu sagen niemants zu liebe oder zü leijde weder vmb mijdde gabe fruntschafft fijhenschafft etc., sunder luterlichen durch deß rechten willen. Dar nach vor der pene vnd schult deß meijneijdts vnd falschlicher kunde getrulich gewarnet vnd vermant etc vnd vff gemeijn fragstucke befragt, sagt der kunde:

Er sij alt vmb XL jare, eijn wingarter vnd bender, nit jm ban oder keijserlicher acht, von niemant kunde zu sagen vnderricht, gebeten oder besuldet, keijnem teijll verwendt etc. vnd verslug sich [...] vnd haijtt vff alle ander gemeijnŋ[li]ch vnd woijll geantwort vnd fur [u]ff den zuspruche antwort der zuge vnd sagt:

[Vm]b xxiiii jar vff eijn Heijseßheijmer kijrb tag, sij er [je]rlich zu Heijseßheym zur kirbe gewest. Also sij zu jme komen Peter Swalbecher vnd Dijell Strohecker, die [i]en den kunde erbetten, daß er vff Bernharts sijten were, Bernharten vermoegt, daß er sich vmb daß erbteijll mit [Smu]ßern vertrueg. Vnd die benannten zwene haben jme [g]ut zü sin vor den costen; vnd Bernhart soll jme IIIi albus eijn tag zu lone geben. Also sij er [mit] Bernharten von bescheidt benanter zweijer [...]t thun wollten, dwijll sie nachbuer weren geijn [Wa]ckernheijm. Vnd er, Niclaus wart gut Smüßern vor den costen dar vff gehen moecht vnd darnach sinth sie gangen vff den mitwochen jnne der Creutze wochen geijn Niderjngelnheijm jnne Zorneß husch, alda geseßen vnd gedruncken. Also sijhen jre der vertragsman vieer vnd Anthes Wolff selig jre obman gewest. Vnd haben deßmals also vertragen die benanten Peter Smußern eijnß- vnd Bernharten Otilien man andernteijls der maijß, das Peter Smußer solt geben Bernharten vnd Otilien eeluden vor alle ansprach vnd erbfall achtzehen gulden gemeijner slechter werung. Der selbigen sijhen Bernharten worden XVII gulden vnd der ander gulden sij jnne die orten vnd daß gelache geben worden, Vnd sinth Emmel Ercken vnd er Niclaus gewest vff Bernharts sijthen vnd dan vff Smußers sijten sij zu eijnem teijll gewest Moller Henne aber der ander sij jme dem kunde jtzo nit wißentlich wer der selbig gewest. Vnd der kunde haijtt hije mit sin sage besloßen vnd geredt, er hab die warheit gesagt vnd wijß nit mehe von den sachen. Jst hije mit verlaijßen vnd jme vffgesagt wie recht.[47]

47 *Ober-Ingelheimer Haderbuch 1518–1529*, fol. 26r–v (not in the partial edition Marzi and Sprenger, *Hader und Streit in Ingelheim*).

Bernhard and Peter Smußer were arguing about an inheritance. Each party had asked two men to be mediators, usually these were relatives called *frunde*, but in this case at least one neighbour served as mediator. The parties had to agree on a fifth person to serve as an arbitrator (*Obmann*), in this case the nobleman Anthis Wolff, one of the judges. They met at a tavern excluding those directly involved in the case. If the five found a solution, both parties had to accept the terms of this arbitration. Our witness was asked to remember the results of this arbitration: Bernhard was the son of Kett and married to Ottilie. After Bernhard's death, Ottilie moved from Heidesheim near Ingelheim to Bacharach. Ottilie filed a lawsuit to claim a share of her husband's share of the sword, whereas her stepmother-in-law Kett tried to show that Bernhard and Ottilie had relinquished his share of his family's possessions in exchange for 18 Gulden. Kett relied on the testimony of the witness Niclaus Bender. Ottilie ignored a call to appear before the court in Ingelheim to listen to the witness, declaring she did not know of anything that anyone might have to say against her. Instead, she sent a bailiff with a message claiming that if she was not granted her right, she would find other means to reach her ends.[48] We do not know if this threat was put into action.

The situation between Otilie and Kett provides an example of the often problematic relationships between mothers and their stepdaughters or daughters-in-law. The second case study I would like to present shows a widow in a conflict with her son-in-law. Following the death of her daughter, Magdalena Stern sued her son-in-law Gangolf. She argued that while she was sick, she had transferred property including house, farm, and goods – which had been her husband's – to Gangolf, but only under the condition that he looked after her and secured her a suitably comfortable life until her demise, and Gangolf failed to keep his promise. Magdalena had the mayor remind Gangolf of his duties, but in vain. Then she cancelled her agreement with Gangolf, requesting him to reinstate her rights to the property, and asked the court for support. Gangolf defended himself:

> Jtem Gangolff meder gibt antwurtt vff clag so Magdalenn wittwe Stern Conratts seyn swegerfraw gegenn jme in recht furbracht. Sagt: Er hab seyn narung jme vber der hoe vff die drey vnd drey ßigk fl wertt wurdenn an Sternn Conratenn seynn swehr seligenn vnd an die vermeinte clagerinn sein swiger gelegt. Darzu alles so er vnnd seynn husfrau selig Magdalena

48 *Ober-Ingelheimer Haderbuch 1518–1529*, fol. 84r–84v (not in the partial edition Marzi and Sprenger, *Hader und Streit in Ingelheim*).

gnannt VI jar mit jrer hertenn vnd suern arbeit vberkomenn, auch die vermeinte clagerin drey jar langk ij shwerennn costenn crang gezogenn. Vnd als gedachte seynn husfrau selig gestorbenn vnd vier cleyner vnerzogen kinder verlaßenn, hab er mit rat jrerr als seyner sweger frawenn, Magdalenn der clagerin vnd beyderseits fruntschafft zur anndern ehee mit Kathereynenn Heltzen, Laurentzen dochter, ize seynn hußfrawe, gegrieffenŋ. Hab sie, Magdalena seynn swegerfrauwe, clagerin, mit jme, Gangolffenn, vnd rat der fruntschafft der zeytt vor den junghern Diether vonn Buches, schultheiß, eyn vertrag vffgericht dermas, das er der vermeinte clagerin, seyner swigerin, alle jar biß zu ende jrs lebenns gebenn vnd reychenn solt eynn fl vnd zwo ome weynns. Soliches dann er, Gangolff, auch jr guttlichenŋ biß her geben vnd entricht, des er sich auch hiemit nochmals vorheym wie gemelt zu geben erbutt, etc. Jst dernhalbenn an euch seyn bit, ine ingebrachter clagerin mit erstatung costenn vnnd schadenn ledig zuerkennen.

Daruff hot die clagerin schup ad proximum.[49]

Gangolf described the situation from his point of view. He and his late wife Magdalena, daughter of his mother-in-law of the same name, had taken care of Magdalena the elder for more than three years while Magdalena the elder was sick. Then Magdalena the younger died and Gangolf was left with four young children. His relatives and mother-in-law agreed that it was best for him and his children if he remarried, and he complied. The mayor drafted the contracts and determined that payments to Magdalena be made in the form of wine and grain, thereafter Gangolf – so he claimed – never failed to fulfil his obligations.

His former mother-in-law Magdalena obviously had felt that she had given away her property without proper compensation. She continued living on her own dowry, and did not share a home with Gangolf, his new wife, or her grandchildren, who actually used the land and house in question. The lawsuit was finally settled by arbitration. We do not know its outcome, but I think we can presume that Magdalena received higher and more regular payments and that Gangolf and his family enjoyed a quiet life in their house.

This case is interesting in several ways. Gangolf was a mower, so Magdalena and Conrad Stern, who were well established in Ingelheim and earned a comfortable living, entrusted their daughter to a man of a much lower social status. Gangolf was married to Magdalena the younger for six years, and they had four

49 *Ober-Ingelheimer Haderbuch 1518–1529*, fol. 186v–187r (not in the partial edition Marzi and Sprenger, *Hader und Streit in Ingelheim*).

living children. Gangolf also explained his desperate situation following the death of his first wife. He had to remarry to raise his children, and did so with the consent of his mother-in-law. The statement's line of argument is also interesting. Of course, we have to bear in mind that it is the court clerk reporting what the defendant said, but we still find hints about the relationship between the relatives. Gangolf referred to his wife as very hard working. He mentioned that the couple had cared for the sick Magdalena for three years. He did not ask for gratitude, but he mentioned the costs connected with this treatment. He thus hinted they had earned the house through their work. We can assume that the sick Magdalena the elder lived in the same house while she was ill, but we do not know for sure. We have examples of wives or widows living alone or in the houses of maidens who looked after them. At the time of the court proceedings Magdalena was no longer living in the shared house. This means that conflicts between mothers-in-law and sons-in-law did not always take place in the same house.

The cases also illustrate that in Ingelheim the nuclear family configuration was typical, at least for the social strata that appeared at court – we have many other examples of this.[50] The high mobility of men and women augmented the scattering of family members across the wider region. Extended family rarely lived under one roof, and if so, only temporarily in times of crisis. Once children came of age they usually left the houses of their parents. Ottilie, Kett, and Magdalena represent widows who were actively fighting for their rights, and were furthermore well situated. But there are others. When they become seriously ill widows quickly fell into a precarious economic state.

Else Back, neé Smith, came from the small village of Ober-Hilbersheim to marry Clese Back, a man from Ingelheim. Clese had previously been married to Katherin Stortzkop. Clese had been Katherin's second husband, and she brought a small fortune – both her first husband and parents had been wealthy – and two underaged children into the marriage. Following the death of Katherin, Clese married Else. They had no children of their own, but fostered Katherin's children so that they would have the right to live on the property, which belonged to the children. Clese died after the children had come of age. Else, who was much younger than her husband, and not much older than

50 Peter Laslett and the Cambridge Group for the History of Population and Social Structure proved this for households in seventeenth-century England. Peter Laslett and Richard Wall, eds., *Household and Family in Past Time: Comparative Studies in the Size and Structure of the Domestic Group over the Last Three Centuries in England, France, Serbia, Japan and Colonial North America, with Further Materials from Western Europe* (Cambridge: Cambridge University Press, 1972).

her stepchildren, lost her eyesight. Her stepchildren did not take care of her – but they were never asked to do so, and this was never discussed. Else Back continued to live as a blind widow for nearly ten years, and hired caretakers, neighbours, to whom she paid 20 Gulden a year. She eventually decided that, unless she was able to find a more long-term-solution, her land and income would not suffice to provide for her expenses. So she made a contract arranged by the mayor with Hans von Floßstadt. This agreement resembles a retirement contract. Hans von Floßstadt promised her tenancy for life and to care for her until she died (*helfen und versehen*) – if she surrendered all she possessed to him. And this is what she did, and – of course – following her death her relatives went to court complaining that Hans von Floßstadt had taken possession of land that belonged to the children. After years of the case pending in court, it was decided that Hans was to be reimbursed for his expenses and everything else was to be returned to the heirs.[51]

We find several instances of elderly people living alone in their houses. Old, sick, and disabled people – both women and men – were often expected to look after themselves. Only the destitute received poor relief. Disease and maturity were treated with pragmatism, and usually without special interest. The Ingelheim court records and other sources show that elderly people had to move several times before they found a place to settle for the rest of their lives.[52] But we also have examples of old or ill individuals who were looked after by someone.[53] If the old were bedfast, they needed caretakers. They could be cared for in their own homes, the home of a family member, or in that of a neighbour. Sometimes it was not their closest kin but strangers who took care of them – a neighbour rather than the husband, a brother instead of a daughter, and co-workers instead of the sons. The old and infirm had to pay their caretakers, and sometimes these people tried to take advantage of the situation – as was the case of the dying Hans Klee mentioned above.[54] Support from relatives had to be asked for, sometimes even officially. We also have examples of widows and widowers who felt neglected and disinherited their children,[55]

---

51 *Ober-Ingelheimer Haderbuch 1518–1529*, fol. 107r–108v; cf. Marzi and Sprenger, *Hader und Streit in Ingelheim*, pp. 106–26.

52 Cordula Nolte, ed., *Phänomene der "Behinderung"* im *Alltag: Bausteine zu einer Disability History der Vormoderne* (Affalterbach: Didymos Verlag, 2014).

53 Signori, *Versorgen*, pp. 80 and 167–68.

54 *Ober-Ingelheimer Haderbuch 1518–1529*, fol. 138r. Cf. Signori, *Versorgen*, pp. 233–37.

55 *Ober-Ingelheimer Haderbuch 1518–1529*, fol. 138r; (not in the partial edition Marzi and Sprenger, *Hader und Streit in Ingelheim*). Cf. Signori, *Versorgen*, pp. 80–81, 150–51, and 153–54.

or (step)parents who tried to take possession of their children's assets.[56] A final case might serve to illustrate the complexity of women's situations.

In 1521 a man named Theis Hadamar filed a lawsuit against Merge the younger, minor daughter of the deceased Hans von Isenach. An excerpt from the testimony of one of Merge the youngers' guardians will illustrate this highly complicated case:

> Merge, Hanß Jsennachs dochter als eijn vnertzogenŋ [kin]dt, nach dem sin mutter Merge vßsatzes halber diß fleckens verwijset. Jrer anfrauwen Jsennachs Kettern heijm getzogen, hat die selbig Jsennachs Ketter auch diß jars denn wingarten schniden laijßen. Hat Merge Jsennachs nachgelaißen witwen jnne eijnem vermeijnten nichtigen kauffe Henne Knoden vnderstanden zu zustellen. Daß aber solicher kauffe nichtig sij, hait Merge one verwilligung der oberigheijt vnd der anfrauwen nit zu thun gehat. Deß zum rechten getzogen. Nach maijls hait Philips furgewendt, eijn losüng wije jn clage furgetragen. Jst jn jme selbst nichts. Vnd furter Thijs Hadamarn zu stellen, daß nit sin gewest. Hat die genannte Jsennachs Kette als die anfrauwe angesucht Diethart Bueches, schulteißen, solich jre enckeln zu schutzen vnd schirmen vnd zu handthaben.[57]

Merge the older, mother of the accused Merge the younger (Mergelin) and wife of the deceased Hans von Isenach, had sold a vineyard to Hans Knode and Theis Hadamar. And Theis Hadamar had been forced to give it back, as the sale was deemed unlawful. He was offered the money he had paid, but refused to take it. Now he tried to prove that the dispossession was illegal.

Kett, the grandmother of Merge the younger, was born in the town of Eisenach, about 200 kilometres away from Ingelheim. She settled down in Ingelheim and gave birth to Hans von Isenach (= Eisenach). Hans married a girl named Merge and they had a daughter, who was called Merge after her mother. When Hans von Isenach died, Hans' mother Kett left Ingelheim and went back to Eisenach, where her relatives lived. Her daughter-in-law, Merge the elder, became leprous and had to leave Ingelheim and her underaged daughter Mergelin. Before doing so, Merge – the mother – wrote to her mother-in-law Kett and asked for support. As can be gleaned from the statement of the complainant, Theis Hadamar, the case was even more complicated:

56 *Ober-Ingelheimer Haderbuch 1518–1529*, fol. 28r–28v (not in the partial edition Marzi and Sprenger, *Hader und Streit in Ingelheim*). Cf. Zülch, *Frankfurter Künstler*, pp. 120 and 167.

57 *Ober-Ingelheimer Haderbuch 1518–1529*, fol. 24v (not in the partial edition Marzi and Sprenger, *Hader und Streit in Ingelheim*).

> jtem ist ware zuvor [...] Philips Trubeyn von syner schw[ester] zu jrer Mergen schwiegerfrau [gebeten] zu gehen. Sie bytten, jre, Mergen krancken frawen mit gelt jre [...] zu hylff vnd stuer kommen.
>
> Jtem Philipsen von Jsenachs Ketten geantwort, syn schwester zu sagen, sie moge jre keyn gelt schicken, sie soll das haußs vff dem Marck gelegen oder wyngarten verkauffen, jre lybs narong do von zuhaben. Vnd das jst ware.
>
> Jtem das Merg der beclagtin mutter awß verhenckniß des allmechtigen gottes mit dem außsatz beladen; vnd also jrer lypzucht halben etliche jrer habe als wyngarten zuverkauffen genoittiengt worden jst. [...]
>
> Sonder vnd one das die beclagte Merg anfrawe Jsenachs Ket etc als legittima tuturia solichen vfflichen kauff der zu Jngelnheym wußlich vnd onverborgenlich geschen zu hyndern oder den kaufer abzutryben vnderstanden haben. [...][58]

We learn that the ill Merge the elder asked her brother, Philipp Drubein, to help her. He contacted her mother-in-law, Kett. Kett Isenach acted as *legittima tuturia* for her granddaughter. She told her daughter-in-law, who begged for help, that she would not send her any money, but that Merge could sell a house in Ingelheim and vineyards. We can thus conclude that the death of her husband had left Merge the elder with a right to servitude but nothing else, and as a result of her medical condition she was not able to draw any benefit from her rights. The family property was owned by her underaged daughter; and the grandmother Kett was the daughter's legitimate guardian, even after she had left Ingelheim. In order to raise money, Merge the elder sold some vineyards to her brother. He sold them to another man, who finally sold them to Theis Hadamar, mentioned at the outset. According to the new owner, Merge had sold the vineyards with the consent of her mother-in-law, Kett. Kett thought otherwise. After gaining the support of her relatives in Eisenach, she activated the mayor, had two legal guardians appointed to her grandchild, and successfully rescinded the sale. The guardian argued that Merge had no right to sell property without the consent of the authority – council and court – and the grandmother of her daughter. The new owner was quite unwilling to return the land, and refused to take the money. The men had obviously benefitted from Merge's emergency and paid a small price for very good vineyards. Moreover, Theis was insulted by the brisk way in which the legal guardians had

58 *Ober-Ingelheimer Haderbuch 1518–1529*, fol. 29/b–30; another testimony fol. 44v–45r.

acted – even picking grapes from the vineyard. In the end, the case was settled outside of court.[59]

We thus have three women and three generations with different fates: Merge the elder who had to leave family, house, and village as a result of her contagious illness. She must have been desperate, and was trying hard to raise money to improve her living conditions outside the shelter of society – we know nothing of her fate. Merge the younger was an orphan, but she seems to have been well situated. Kett, her grandmother and mother-in-law of Merge the elder, had left Ingelheim to return to the town from which she came, Eisenach. She left her minor grandchild in Ingelheim, but remained her guardian and cared for her. Kett tried to secure Merge's inheritance and asked the mayor to give her grandchild two guardians, who Kett paid. The cousins of Hans von Eisenach who were still living in Eisenach also tried to help her grandniece, Merge the younger, by writing letters to the court to support her and secure payment for the guardians.[60] Potential emotional aspects do not receive mention. Even if discussions in front of the court were often emotional – each party believed itself to be in the right – this was rarely reported. There is little 'romantic' element in this intergenerational relationship.

4 Wives and Their Legal and Economic Standings

In many cases, remarrying was the best women could do to avoid poverty. Some women married men above their own status,[61] others married their farm hand,[62] and there are other cases of business-minded women who remained single. Some had to leave their underaged children, but children of the first marriage usually lived with their mother and stepfather. Heirs could force their mother into a marriage or use remarriage as a threat; they tried to guard themselves against potential problems by means of inheritance contracts, agreements on the dower, and renunciations of inheritance. Children often received partial payments in advance of the inheritance upon the wedding of

59 *Ober-Ingelheimer Haderbuch 1518–1529*, fol. 21v–25r, 28r–28v.

60 *Ober-Ingelheimer Haderbuch 1518–1529*, fol. 162r–162v.

61 There are similar cases in Frankfurt. After his second wife died the painter Johannes Becht married his maidservant; Zülch, *Frankfurter Künstler*, pp. 179 and 232.

62 *Ober-Ingelheimer Haderbuch 1518–1529*, fol. 28r–28v (not in the partial edition Marzi and Sprenger, *Hader und Streit in Ingelheim*).

their mother to another man.[63] As our examples show, however, such measures were not always successful.

There is a great deal of variance in how wives could acquire, possess, and dispose of mobile and immobile property, and in how they presented their cases before court. Although faced with several restrictions, being under the guardianship of their husbands did not entirely prevent wives from taking part in legal conflicts or from appearing before court. Rather, the records show that wives bought goods, both for household use and for trade. Access to money also varied. As mentioned, the wife's separate estate was under her husband's administration. A husband could not sell his wife's land without her approval; a sale without the wife's approval was invalid.[64] But husbands could secure access to their wives' real estate by making them appoint a legal representative, called a *Momper*, for themselves. A *Momper* was not a gender guardian but a trustee entitled to act in the name of the woman or man he represented. Clerics, noblemen, and men and women living far away but owning property in Ingelheim also used *Mompers* as trustees. One was free to choose anyone as a *Momper*, and men and women often appointed relatives, judges, or advocates. And some wives appointed their husbands as *Mompers*. The appointment of a *Momper* could be repealed before court, but I do not have a single example of a wife revoking her husband's capacity as a *Momper*. The access of wives to their own estates was restricted while their husbands were alive.

Men and women were responsible for keeping inherited land, and we must assume that they tried to do so. At the same time, there was an active land market. Land was swapped, shared, given to subtenants or even fragmented into tiny portions; for the most part land was not allodial but leased and/or burdened with charges. Families were often under great pressure and loaded with debt, and one of the only ways to access money was to mortgage land. Women responded in various ways to this situation. Their scope of action was limited by their husbands and or male relatives as well as dependent on their economic wealth and ability to obtain money in critical situations. Families usually kept at least one gold or silver piece in reserve to use it as a pawn in case of emergency.[65] And nearly everyone in Ingelheim owned (or rented) at least a small piece of land or a garden. But the activity of women was not yet

63 Loersch, *Der Ingelheimer Oberhof*, no. 50, 51, 193, and 217; *Ober-Ingelheimer Haderbuch 1518–1529*, fol. 42v (not in the partial edition Marzi and Sprenger, *Hader und Streit in Ingelheim*).

64 Gudian, *Ingelheimer Recht*, pp. 216–18.

65 *Ober-Ingelheimer Haderbuch 1518–1529*, fol. 1a–1v/a (not in the partial edition Marzi and Sprenger, *Hader und Streit in Ingelheim*).

limited by their family status; that is, they were yet not obliged to have a gender guardian. We find very active women in business and in front of the court – married women, widows, and unmarried women.

5 Litigate – Argue – Mediate

Many of the conflicts documented in the court records are inter-family ones, and are often, though not always, connected to inheritance disputes. Such was the case of a widow who sued her brother-in-law for stealing a cask of wine, a deed that turned out to be an attempt at getting a part of the share of the sword.[66]

As a rule, relatives tried to get a family off to a good start by arranging for the eventuality. An oral marriage contract pronounced in the presence of witnesses, which fixed the dowry, the bequest and so on, was nearly always part of the engagement procedure. But widows' situations were dependent on more than their marriage settlements and financial circumstances. I would suggest that there are six main factors which influenced the chances of a woman to ensure her livelihood: first legal norms, second specific provisions made in the marriage contract or a special designation as heir, third, her relationship to her relatives (*frunde*) and husband, fourth, her financial situation, fifth, her local presence, in this case in Ingelheim, and the ability to act directly on-site and finally, sixth the woman's personality. Thus, we have widows who enjoyed comfortable lives, and widows who were abandoned or pushed around.

Settlement of an inheritance was often a long on-going process in which the rights of the testator had to be reconciled with those of the heirs, who were often split into groups with conflicting interests, that might require accounting for the existence of competing legal systems. A clear and hierarchical legal system emerged only slowly. The court's verdicts and customary law clearly favoured the rights of children over those of the testator and the widow. Sometimes inheritance conflicts became existential: the rights of children stood in conflict with those of the testator regarding the use of his possessions to provide for sickness and old age. The right of a creditor stood against that of a widow to get rid of her first husband's debts. Given that upon remarriage a widow's debts would become her new husband's debts, withdrawing from the first marriage was a social privilege which improved a widow's chances for a new marriage. But it could leave the creditor empty-handed.

66 *Ober-Ingelheimer Haderbuch 1476–1485*, fol. 70r–70v.

There was a difference between legal norms and legal practice. The fifteenth century saw the ongoing co-existence of legal systems and statutes. There was customary law, verdicts, the influence of natural law, unwritten established rights, and acts before court and sealed documents. Transfers of ownership had to take place in court. But the court made frequent and consequent use of adjournment, postponement, and delegation – giving the parties a chance to find a solution outside of court. While the court usually did not hesitate to make a decision when asked for a verdict in conflicts that were external to Ingelheim, local conflicts were regularly settled through arbitration – and this means by the *frunde*, the relatives of both parties. We also have hints about non-legal but local norms that were of relevance within the community. Deviant behaviour was discussed in public and sanctioned by the community. The way in which a husband was expected to manage a joint estate was also a matter of local norm, as was children's treatment of their parents, and vice versa. People gossiped about husbands who purloined their wives' or families' property. As personal reputation was essential in receiving credit, and credit was a necessary aspect of everyone's welfare, these norms could not be neglected.[67] We can also assume that in most cases the wife's relatives were able to secure her (and their own) financial interests. That said, we only have opportunity to get to know cases in which this system of social governance failed.

Women are present in the court records: widows, as well as wives, and unmarried women. It did not seem to matter that buyers or lenders were married and female.[68] This can be found before and after 1500, but there are indications that the legal position of women suffered a decline. While it was possible for a woman to represent her husband before court when he was unavailable, and even to act in her own name until around 1480, this was disputed in the 1520s. Ewald Sumer argued that he was not compelled to answer the complaint of Else Schnade because she was married. Being female, she was not meant to act without a *Momper* or male relative. So her case was not justified, and he was to be cleared.[69] A defendant argued that women should not give testimony in

---

67 Regina Schäfer, "Talking about Deviance? Insult and Humiliation in the Ingelheim Court Records," in *Recounting Deviance: Forms and Practices of Presenting Divergent Behaviour in the Late Middle Ages and Early Modern Period*, ed. Jörg Rogge (Bielefeld: transcript, 2016), pp. 25–56.

68 Hans-Jörg Gilomen, "Frauen als Schuldnerinnen und Gläubigerinnen in der Stadt Basel in den 1420er Jahren," in Signori, *Prekäre Ökonomien*, pp. 103–37.

69 *Ober-Ingelheimer Haderbuch 1518–1529*, fol. 268: "*Denn sie habe einen Ehemann, der wie ein Mann vor Gericht mit ihm zu handeln fähig sei, zudem Verwandte. Daraus folgt, dass sie als eine Weibsperson ohne Momper vor Gericht nicht förmlich oder fruchtbringend handeln kann oder vermag. Er bittet zu erkennen, dass er wegen dieser Ungeschicklichkeit und*

criminal cases.[70] Modern society and the reformation encouraged this development strengthening the role of the *paterfamilias*. Roman law favoured men. Written law diminished the opportunity to negotiate in front of the court. Law became more predictable, but stricter. The court was now looking for a just solution instead of an appropriate solution. In the Middle Ages the court was a place to negotiate rights, but not the only place. Its primary objective was to preserve public order, peace, and Ingelheim's status as a quasi-autonomous community.[71] Finding a consensus was preferential to giving judgements that would deepen the conflict. Thus, the court tried to delay decisions or defer them to arbitration courts.

This changed at the beginning of the sixteenth century. The role of the court changed along with society. In early modern times we find only noblemen as judges in Ingelheim, and the court acted as town lord. Ingelheim became proper part of the Rhine Palatinate. The court was no longer the high court (*Oberhof*) of other local courts, its jurisdictional area became fixed, and the high court system ceased to exist. We do not have any written court records from Ingelheim after 1540, but there are court records from the village of Nierstein nearby that date to the 1660s. The court was fairly similar in function, but the cases dealt with are quite different in the seventeenth century, often concerning witchcraft and moral aberration.[72] The judges acted as superiors who controlled the subordinate village. These developments influenced the opportunities available for women to act. The early modern period saw a push towards strengthening patriarchal structures that diminished the presence and standing of women in court, and left them with one fewer place to negotiate their rights.

References

Andermann, Kurt, and Gerhard Fouquet, eds. *Zins und Gült: Strukturen des ländlichen Kreditwesens in Spätmittelalter und Frühneuzeit*. Epfendorf: bibliotheca academica, 2016.

---

sonst von der vermeintlichen Klägerin frei gesprochen werde mit Erstattung von Kosten und Schaden."

70 *Ober-Ingelheimer Haderbuch 1518–1529*, fol. 130v.

71 Regina Schäfer, "Frieden und Ruhe im Ort – Zur Funktion des Gerichts in der Gemeinde," in Marzi and Schäfer, *Alltag, Herrschaft, Gesellschaft*, pp. 81–96.

72 *Das Protokollbuch des Niersteiner Rittergerichts (1654–1661)*, ed. Kerstin Riedel and Sigrid Schmitt (Darmstadt and Marburg: Historische Kommission für Hessen, 1999).

Blattmann, Marita. "Beobachtungen zum Schrifteinsatz an einem deutschen Niedergericht um 1400: die Ingelheimer Haderbücher." In *Als die Welt in die Akten kam. Prozeßschriftgut im europäischen Mittelalter*, edited by Susanne Lepsius and Thomas Wetzstein, pp. 55–84. Frankfurt a. M.: Klostermann, 2008.

Brakensiek, Stefan, Michael Stolleis, and Heide Wunder, eds. *Generationengerechtigkeit? Normen und Praxis im Erb- und Ehegüterrecht 1500–1850*. Berlin: Duncker & Humblot, 2006.

Brauneder, Wilhelm. *Die Entwicklung des Ehegüterrechts in Österreich. Ein Beitrag zur Dogmengeschichte und Rechtstatsachenforschung des Spätmittelalters und der Neuzeit*. Salzburg: Wilhelm Fink, 1973.

Carius, Hendrikje. *Recht durch Eigentum: Frauen vor dem Jenaer Hofgericht (1648–1806)*. Munich: Oldenbourg, 2012.

Cavallo, Sandra, and Lyndan Warner. "Introduction." In *Widowhood in Medieval and Early Modern Europe*, edited by Sandra Cavallo and Lyndan Warner, pp. 3–23. London: Longman, 1999.

Cavallo, Sandra, and Lyndan Warner, eds. *Widowhood in Medieval and Early Modern Europe*. London: Longman, 1999.

Ehlers, Bettina. *Regieren, Erziehen, Bewahren. Mütterliche Regentschaften im Hochmittelalter*. Frankfurt a. M.: Klostermann, 2003.

Erler, Adalbert, ed. *Die älteren Urteile des Ingelheimer Oberhofes*, vol. 1–4. Frankfurt a. M.: Klostermann, 1952–1963.

Fontaine, Laurence. "Die Bauern und die Mechanismen der Kreditvergabe." In *Schuldenlast und Schuldenwerk. Kreditnetzwerke in der europäischen Geschichte 1300–1900*, edited by Gabriele Clemens, pp. 109–30. Trier: Kliomedia, 2008.

Fouquet, Gerhard. "Kredit in der ländlichen Gesellschaft und Wirtschaft im späten Mittelalter. Das Beispiel Ober-Ingelheim." In *Zins und Gült. Strukturen des ländlichen Kreditwesens in Spätmittelalter und Frühneuzeit*, edited by Kurt Andermann and Gerhard Fouquet, pp. 17–40. Epfendorf: bibliotheca academica, 2016.

Gilomen, Hans-Jörg. "Der Kleinkredit in spätmittelalterlichen Städten. Basel und Zürich im Vergleich." In *Städtische Wirtschaft im Mittelalter: Festschrift für Franz Irsigler zum 70. Geburtstag*, edited by Rudolf Holbach, pp. 109–48. Cologne, Weimar, and Vienna: Böhlau, 2011.

Gilomen, Hans-Jörg. "Frauen als Schuldnerinnen und Gläubigerinnen in der Stadt Basel in den 1420er Jahren." In *Prekäre Ökonomien. Schulden in Spätmittelalter und Früher Neuzeit*, edited by Gabriela Signori, pp. 103–37. Konstanz: UVK, 2014.

Gottschalk, Karin. "Erbe und Recht. Die Übertragung von Eigen in der frühen Neuzeit." In *Erbe. Übertragungskonzepte zwischen Natur und Kultur*, edited by Stefan Willer, Sigrid Weigel, and Bernhard Jussen, pp. 85–125. Berlin: Suhrkamp, 2013.

Grochowina, Nicole. *Das Eigentum der Frauen. Konflikte vor dem Jenaer Schöppenstuhl im ausgehenden 18. Jahrhundert*. Cologne, Weimar, and Vienna: Böhlau, 2009.

Grochowina, Nicole. *Eigentumskulturen und Geschlecht in der Frühen Neuzeit.* Leipzig: Leipziger Universitäts-Verlag, 2005.

Groebner, Valentin. *Ökonomie ohne Haus. Zum Wirtschaften armer Leute in Nürnberg am Ende des 15. Jahrhunderts.* Göttingen: Vandenhoeck & Ruprecht, 1993.

Gudian, Gunter. *Ingelheimer Recht im 15. Jahrhundert.* Aalen: Scientia, 1968.

Guenette, Maryse. "Au Carrefour de la misère: les poursuites pour dettes à Brignoles et à Saint-Maximin au milieu du XIVe siècle." *Canadian Journal of History* 26 (1991): pp. 225–40.

Hagemann, Rudolf, and Heide Wunder. "Heiraten und Erben. Das Baseler Ehegüterrecht und Ehegattenerbrecht." In *Eine Stadt der Frauen. Studien und Quellen zur Geschichte der Baslerinnen im späten Mittelalter und zu Beginn der Neuzeit (13.–17. Jahrhundert)*, edited by Heide Wunder, pp. 150–66. Basel: Schwabe, 1995.

Härter, Karl. "Gute Ordnung und Policey des Alten Reiches in der Region: Zum Einfluß der Reichspoliceygesetzgebung auf die Ordnungsgesetzgebung süddeutscher Reichstände." In *Das Reich in der Region während des Mittelalters und der Frühen Neuzeit*, edited by Rolf Kießling and Sabine Ullmann, pp. 187–223. Konstanz: UVK, 2005.

Haubrichs, Wolfgang, and Patricia Oster, eds. *Zwischen Herrschaft und Kunst: fürstliche und adlige Frauen im Zeitalter Elisabeths von Nassau-Saarbrücken (14.–16. Jh.).* Saarbrücken: Kommission für saarländische Landesgeschichte, 2013.

Hippchen, Raoul, Heidrun Ochs, and Regina Schäfer. "Der Mittelrhein. Konkurrenz der Herrschaften und Motor des Handels." In *Schrei nach Gerechtigkeit. Leben am Mittelrhein am Vorabend der Reformation*, edited by Winfried Wilhelmy, pp. 17–25. Regensburg: Schnell und Steiner, 2015.

Hohkamp, Michaela. "Wer will erben? Überlegungen zur Erbpraxis in geschlechtsspezifischer Perspektive in der Herrschaft Triberg von 1654–1806." In *Gutsherrschaft als soziales Modell*, edited by Jan Peters, pp. 327–41. Munich: Oldenbourg, 1995.

Krey, Alexander. *Die Praxis der spätmittelalterlichen Laiengerichtsbarkeit. Gerichts- und Rechtslandschaften des Rhein-Main-Gebietes im 15. Jahrhundert im Vergleich.* Cologne, Weimar, and Vienna: Böhlau, 2015.

Lanzinger, Margareth. *Das gesicherte Erbe. Heirat in lokalen und familialen Kontexten. Innichen 1700–1900.* Vienna, Cologne, and Weimar: Böhlau, 2003.

Laslett, Peter, and Richard Wall, eds. *Household and Family in Past Time: Comparative Studies in the Size and Structure of the Domestic Group over the Last Three Centuries in England, France, Serbia, Japan and Colonial North America, with Further Materials from Western Europe.* Cambridge: Cambridge University Press, 1972.

Lavoie, Rodrigue. "Endettement et pauvreté en Provence d'après les listes de la justice comtale XIV–XVe siècle." *Provence historique* 23 (1973): pp. 201–16.

Loersch, Hugo. *Der Ingelheimer Oberhof.* Bonn: Adolph Marcus, 1885.

Marzi, Werner, ed. *Das Oberingelheimer Haderbuch 1476–1485.* Alzey: Rheinhessische Druckwerkstätte, 2011.

Marzi, Werner, and Kai-Michael Sprenger, eds. *Hader und Streit in Ingelheim. Edition ausgewählter Gerichtsfälle aus dem Ober-Ingelheimer Haderbuch 1518–1529*. Ingelheim: E. Humbert Verlag, 2016.

Matheus, Michael. "Winzerdörfer: Wirtschafts- und Lebensformen zwischen Stadt und Land. Überlegungen zu einem Siedlungstyp in vergleichender europäischer Perspektive." In *Landwirtschaft und Dorfgesellschaft im ausgehenden Mittelalter*, edited by Enno Bünz. Ostfildern: Thorbecke, 2020.

Moring, Beatrice, ed. *Female Economic Strategies in the Modern World*. London: Pickering & Chatto, 2012.

Nolte, Cordula, ed. *Phänomene der "Behinderung" im Alltag: Bausteine zu einer Disability History der Vormoderne*. Affalterbach: Didymos Verlag, 2014.

Opitz, Rainer. "Kodikologie und Quellenwert der frühen Haderbücher." In *Die Ingelheimer Haderbücher – Mittelalterliches Prozessschriftgut und seine Auswertungsmöglichkeiten*, edited by Franz J. Felten and Harald Müller, pp. 29–41. Ingelheim: Vandenhoeck & Ruprecht, 2010.

Ozment, Steven. *The Bürgermeister's Daughter. Scandal in a Sixteenth-Century German Town*. New York: St. Martin's Press, 1998.

Ozment, Steven. *When Fathers Ruled. Family Life in Reformation Europe*. Cambridge, Mass.: Harvard University Press, 1983.

Pajcic, Kathrin. *Frauenstimmen in der spätmittelalterlichen Stadt? Testamente von Frauen aus Lüneburg, Hamburg und Wien als soziale Kommunikation*. Würzburg: Königshausen & Neumann, 2013.

Pfister, Ulrich. "Le petit crédit rural en Suisse aux XVIe–XVIIe siècles." *Annales, Histoires, Sciences Sociales* 49 (1994): pp. 1339–57.

Reinle, Christine. "Umkämpfter Friede. Politischer Gestaltungswille und geistlicher Normenhorizont bei der Fehdebekämpfung im deutschen Spätmittelalter." In *Rechtsveränderung im politischen und sozialen Kontext mittelalterlicher Rechtsvielfalt*, edited by Stefan Esders and Christine Reinle, pp. 143–70. Münster: Lit, 2005.

Riedel, Kerstin, and Sigrid Schmitt, eds. *Das Protokollbuch des Niersteiner Rittergerichts (1654–1661)*. Darmstadt and Marburg: Historische Kommission für Hessen, 1999.

Rogge, Jörg, ed. *Fürstin und Fürst. Familienbeziehungen und Handlungsmöglichkeiten*. Stuttgart: Thorbecke, 2004.

Roper, Lyndal. *The Holy Household. Women and Morals in Reformation Augsburg*. Oxford: Clarendon Press, 1989.

Rouette, Susanne. "Erbrecht und Besitzweitergabe. Praktiken in der ländlichen Gesellschaft Deutschlands, Diskurse in Politik und Wissenschaft." In *Ländliche Gesellschaften in Deutschland und Frankreich, 18.–19. Jahrhundert*, edited by Rainer Prass, Jürgen Schlumbohm, Gérard Béaur, and Christophe Duhamelle, pp. 145–66. Göttingen: Vandenhoeck & Ruprecht, 2003.

Rüthing, Heinrich. *Höxter um 1500. Analyse einer Stadtgesellschaft*. Paderborn: Bonifatius-Druckerei, 1986.

Sandvik, Hilde. "Decision-making on Marital Property in Norway, 1500–1800." In *The Marital Economy in Scandinavia and Britain 1400–1900*, edited by Maria Ågren and Amy Louis Erickson, pp. 111–26. Aldershot: Ashgate, 2004.

Schäfer, Regina. "Friede durch Recht. Zur Funktion des Dorfgerichts in der Gemeinde." In *Dorf und Gemeinde. Grundstrukturen der ländlichen Gesellschaft in Spätmittelalter und Frühneuzeit*, edited by Kurt Andermann and Oliver Auge, pp. 65–85. Epfendorf: bibliotheca academica, 2012.

Schäfer, Regina. "Frieden und Ruhe im Ort – Zur Funktion des Gerichts in der Gemeinde." In *Alltag, Herrschaft, Gesellschaft und Gericht im Spiegel der spätmittelalterlichen Ingelheimer Haderbücher. Ein Begleitband zum Editionsprojekt "Ingelheimer Haderbücher,"* edited by Werner Marzi and Regina Schäfer, pp. 81–96. Alzey: Rheinhessische Druckwerkstätte, 2012.

Schäfer, Regina. "Ingelheim im Spätmittelalter – eine Gemeinde zwischen Dorf und Stadt." In *Alltag, Herrschaft, Gesellschaft und Gericht im Spiegel der spätmittelalterlichen Ingelheimer Haderbücher. Ein Begleitband zum Editionsprojekt "Ingelheimer Haderbücher,"* edited by Werner Marzi and Regina Schäfer, pp. 47–63. Alzey: Rheinhessische Druckwerkstätte, 2012.

Schäfer, Regina. "Rechtsprechung ohne Gesetz? Die Rechtsentscheidungen der Schöffen von Niedergerichten." In *Das Gesetz – The Law – La Loi*, edited by Andreas Speer and Guy Guldentops, pp. 152–78. Berlin: de Gruyter, 2014.

Schäfer, Regina. "Talking about Deviance? Insult and Humiliation in the Ingelheim Court Records." In *Recounting Deviance: Forms and Practices of Presenting Divergent Behaviour in the Late Middle Ages and Early Modern Period*, edited by Jörg Rogge, pp. 25–56. Bielefeld: transcript, 2016.

Schmidt, Heinrich Richard. "Nothurft vnd Hußbruch. Haus, Gemeinde und Sittenzucht im Reformiertentum." In *Ehe – Familie – Verwandtschaft. Vergesellschaftung in Religion und sozialer Lebenswelt*, edited by Andreas Holzem and Ines Weber, pp. 301–23. Paderborn: Ferdinand Schöningh, 2008.

Schubert, Ernst. *Fürstliche Herrschaft und Territorium im späten Mittelalter*. München: Oldenburg, 1996, 2nd edition 2006.

Schwerhoff, Gerd. "Frühneuzeitliche Stadtgeschichte im Cultural Turn – eine Standortbestimmung." In *Neue Stadtgeschichte(n): die Reichsstadt Frankfurt im Vergleich*, edited by Julia Schmidt-Funke and Matthias Schnettger, pp. 11–41. Bielefeld: transcript Verlag, 2018.

Signori, Gabriela. "Pflegekinder, Stiefkinder, Morgengabskinder: Formen sozialer Eltern- bzw. sozialer Kindschaft in der Gesellschaft des Spätmittelalters." In *Freundschaft und Verwandtschaft. Zur Unterscheidung und Verflechtung zweier*

Beziehungssysteme, edited by Johannes F. K. Schmidt, Martine Guichard, Peter Schuster, and Fritz Trillmich, pp. 165–80. Konstanz: UVK, 2007.

Signori, Gabriela, ed. *Prekäre Ökonomien. Schulden in Spätmittelalter und Früher Neuzeit*. Konstanz: UVK, 2014.

Signori, Gabriela. *Schuldenwirtschaft. Konsumenten- und Hypothekarkredite im spätmittelalterlichen Basel*. Konstanz: UVK, 2015.

Signori, Gabriela. *Versorgen – Vererben – Erinnern. Kinder- und familienlose Erblasser in der städtischen Gesellschaft des Spätmittelalters*. Göttingen: Vandenhoeck & Ruprecht, 2001.

Simon-Muscheid, Katharina. "Der weite Weg zur Erbschaft: Weibliche Rechtswege und Strategien im späten Mittelalter." In *Lesarten der Geschichte: Ländliche Ordnungen und Geschlechterverhältnisse. Festschrift für Heide Wunder zum 65. Geburtstag*, edited by Jens Flemming, Pauline Puppel, Werner Troßbach, Christina Vanja, and Ortrud Wörner-Heil, pp. 402–17. Kassel: kassel university press, 2004.

Spieß, Karl-Heinz. "Lordship, Kinship, and Inheritance among the German High Nobility in the Middle Ages and Early Modern Period." In *Kinship in Europe. Approaches to Long-term Development (1300–1900)*, edited by David Warren Sabean, Simon Teuscher, and Jon Mathieu, pp. 57–75. New York and Oxford: Berghahn, 2007.

Teuscher, Simon. *Lords' Rights and Peasant Stories: Writing and the Formation of Tradition in the Later Middle Ages*. Philadelphia: University of Pennsylvania Press, 2012.

Weibel, Thomas. *Erbrecht und Familie. Fortbildung und Aufzeichnung des Erbrechts in der Stadt Zürich – vom Richtebrief zum Stadterbrecht von 1716*. Zürich: Chronos, 1988.

Wunder, Heide. *Die bäuerliche Gemeinde in Deutschland: Von der Herrschaft mit Bauern zur Herrschaft über Bauern*. Göttingen: Vandenhoeck & Ruprecht, 1986.

Zey, Claudia, ed. *Mächtige Frauen? Königinnen und Fürstinnen im europäischen Mittelalter (11.–14. Jahrhundert)*. Ostfildern: Thorbecke, 2015.

Zülch, Walther Karl. *Frankfurter Künstler 1223–1700*. Frankfurt a. M.: Diesterweg, 1935.

CHAPTER 4

Landed Property, Power, and Female Old Age Security in the Nordic Countries

Beatrice Moring

Widows have often been seen as the victims of male structures – poor, deprived, and sidelined. It has been assumed that when a woman was freed from the control of her husband, she lost vital economic protection. In her book about gender and poverty, Rachel Fuchs puts forward the very general view that for nineteenth-century European women widowhood and old age were riddled with poverty, neglect by family and kin, and a great deal of dependence on assistance from welfare institutions.[1] One of the issues that has been raised in connection with studies of women and economy in the past, is the claim that women lacked agency, that all of the power remained in the hands of men.[2] In their summary of the contributions to the volume *Widowhood in Medieval and Early Modern Europe*, Sandra Cavallo and Lyndon Warner underline the different positions of widowed women and men. While men continued their lives as before, women in some parts of Europe had considerable difficulties in accessing and utilising the property to which they were legally entitled. In their efforts to generalise, the experiences of noble widows from southern Europe are amalgamated with and believed to illustrate those of women from other social groups and geographic areas.[3] Lynn Abrams has raised the question of whether despite of decades of research into the history of women we are still trapped in an historical narrative that remains predominantly male. The image of women as the victims of male society can easily be added as an extra chapter, while the actors in politics, economy, social development, organisations

1 Rachel Fuchs, *Gender and Poverty in Nineteenth-Century Europe* (Cambridge: Cambridge University Press, 2005), pp. 235–36.

2 Isabelle Chabot, "Lineage Strategies and the Control of Widows in Renaissance Florence," in *Widowhood in Medieval and Early Modern Europe*, ed. Sandra Cavallo and Lyndan Warner (London: Longman, 1999), pp. 127–44.

3 Sandra Cavallo and Lyndan Warner, Introduction to *Widowhood in Medieval and Early Modern Europe*, ed. Sandra Cavallo and Lyndan Warner (London: Longman, 1999), pp. 3–23, here pp. 14–15 and 22–23.

 | DOI:10.1163/9789004456204_005

etc. are men.[4] Although the accounts of struggles by noble women to control their property are undoubtedly correct, they are likely to provide a poor guide to the experiences of women of less lofty status. Many widows with access to property would have been the former wives of farmers and craftsmen, rather than part of the nobility.

Marie Pierre Arrizabalaga and Margareth Lanzinger have, based on studies of France and Austria, queried the notion of the absence of female agency. They have demonstrated that women could inherit landholdings and other property and participate in the process of transfer. They also revealed that women made choices, assessed their options, and secured their property.[5] Hilde Sandvik and Beatrice Moring have also presented evidence of female agency within and after marriage in rural communities of Norway and Finland.[6]

Property transfer contracts with retirement clauses have sometimes been interpreted as if extracting assets and setting up a new household would have been the only true measure of economic authority for a widow. However, studies of living arrangements and contracts themselves often indicate family interaction.[7] The aim of this study is to demonstrate how women in the Nordic past exercised their will and desire to maintain an active role on the family farm even in old age, and at the same time created safeguards in collaboration with family members for a decent existence even in the eventuality of illness and incapacity. The aim is also to analyse the retirement contract as a means of retaining a modicum of power in a situation of societal change and increasing

4 Lynn Abrams, "Introduction: Gendering the Agenda," in *Gender in Scottish History since 1700*, ed. Lynn Abrams, Eleanor Gordon, Deborah Simonton, and Eileen J. Yeo (Edinburgh: Edinburgh University Press, 2006), pp. 1–16, here pp. 3–4.

5 Marie Pierre Arrizabalaga, "Gender and Migration in the Pyrenees in the Nineteenth Century: Gender-Differentiated Patterns and Destinies," in *Female Economic Strategies in the Modern World*, ed. Beatrice Moring (London: Pickering & Chatto, 2012), pp. 127–44; Margareth Lanzinger, "Women and Property in Eighteenth-Century Austria: Separate Property, Usufruct and Ownership in Different Family Configurations," in Ibid., pp. 145–59.

6 Hilde Sandvik, "Decision-Making on Marital Property in Norway, 1500–1800," in *The Marital Economy in Scandinavia and Britain 1400–1900*, ed. Maria Ågren and Amy Louise Erickson (Aldershot: Ashgate, 2005), pp. 111–26; Beatrice Moring, "Property and Power: Women and the Holding and Transmission of Assets," in *The Logic of Female Succession: Rethinking Patriarchy and Patrilineality in Global and Historical Perspectives*, ed. Emiko Ochiai (Kyoto: International Research Center for Japanese Studies, 2002), pp. 75–100.

7 Anu Pylkkänen, "Forming the Marital Economy in the Early Modern Finnish Countryside," in *The Marital Economy in Scandinavia and Britain 1400–1900*, ed. Maria Ågren and Amy Louise Erickson (Aldershot: Ashgate, 2005), pp. 75–88, here pp. 75–79; Beatrice Moring, "Retirement Contracts and the Economics of Widowhood in the Nordic Countries," *Continuity and Change* 21–3 (2006), pp. 383–418; Beatrice Moring, "Rural Widows, Economy and Co-Residence in the 18th and 19th Centuries," *The History of the Family* 15–3 (2010), pp. 239–54, here p. 242.

tensions between urban and rural interest groups. A concept that crystalises in the struggle to hold on to land and traditional values in the face of increasing commercialisation of society.

1 The Data

For Scandinavia the retirement contract is of some importance, as in the late eighteenth century twenty percent of all Finnish widows lived in retirement and in rural Sweden thirty percent of the widows were in this position.[8] In order to illuminate the issue of standard of living in rural retirement, this research has explored 182 original Finnish retirement contracts from the 1830s to the 1880s. The court records where these contracts originate also include information about the sale, contract or ownership transfer relating to specific properties (or portions thereof) over a period of several decades recording intra familial or extra familial transfers or mortgages with the land as security. In addition, the transcripts of 281 land transfers that have a retirement contract for the time period from 1850 to 1920, and extracts from parish registers relating to the individuals involved, have been examined. For comparative purposes, 188 retirement contracts from Finnish court records from 1620 to 1700 have been analysed using the court record register Tuokko at the National Archives Helsinki.[9]

Retirement contracts and court records relating to nineteenth-century land transfers in central Sweden have also been included using the document collection of Fredriksson, *Sandhems gårdskrönikor*. Comparative seventeenth-century retirement agreements have been extracted from the printed collections of court records from northern Sweden.[10] Utilising the study of Olov Åberg and Johan Öster, the contents of 175 retirement contracts from Northern Sweden have been analysed,[11] as well as seven original contracts from the

8 Gunnar Fougstedt and Antti Raivio, *Suomen väestön sääty ja ammattiryhmiys v. 1751–1805* (Helsinki: Tilastokeskus, 1953), pp. 44–48.

9 The National Archives, Helsinki, Finland, Court records for the judiciary district of Aland, KO b 12 1855; Court records of the judiciary district of Ostrobothnia KO b 12 1830–31, KO b 18 1881, KO b 2 1864, 1865.

10 Algot Hellbom, *Tingsprotokoll for Njurunda* (Sundsvall: Medelpads hembygdsforening, 1983); Kjell Hoffman, *Jämtlands domböcker och landstingsprotokoll 1647–1648* (Östersund: Landsarkivet i Östersund, 1989).

11 Olov Åberg and Johan Öster, "Efter avslutad färd en hederlig begravning, Undantagsinstitutionen i Neder Luleå och Raneå socken 1790–1895," *Uppsala Papers in Economic History* 37 (University of Uppsala, 1995).

parish of Ljustorp that have been made available by the local history society. The information on Norwegian retirement contracts has been gathered from Beate Homlong's thesis which is based on analysis of 615 contracts from western Norway.[12] Nineteenth-century contracts from three earlier studies by Hugo Högnäs, Kaaperi Kivialho and Onni Koskikallio have likewise been included in the analysis.[13]

Although it has been demonstrated that many contracts were often not implemented during the lifetime of the old farmer,[14] they could play a role in the economic security of his widow. As there are clear indications that the presence of a woman affected the contents of an agreement, the contracts have been examined for information about issues with a bearing on the female sphere. Special attention has therefore been given to stipulations regarding living quarters, the use of resources and space, the allocation of grain and other foodstuffs, and the right to keep or make use of animals.

2 The Legal and Economic Position of Married and Widowed Women in Nordic Society

The issues of vital importance for an assessment of the position of widows in past societies are the right of widows to property and economic activity and the right of widows to make independent decisions about themselves and their children. The pre-Christian and later medieval laws of Sweden included the following formula to be uttered by the father of the bride for the establishing of a legal marriage: "I give you my daughter, to honour and to be your wife, to half the bed, to locks and keys and to one-third of all you have or will have of movable property as has been set down by the law."[15]

---

12 Beate Homlong, " 'I vores eiende lemstue', Kårskipnaden i Etne 1716–1901" (MA thesis., University of Bergen, 1995).

13 Hugo Högnäs, *Sytning och arvslösen i den folkliga sedvänjan i Pedersöre och Nykarlebybygden 1810–1914* (Åbo: Åbo akademi, 1938); Kaaperi Kivialho, *Maatalouskiinteistöjen omistajavaihdokset ja hinnanmuodostus Halikon tuomiokunnassa 1851–1910* (Helsinki: Kansantaloudellinen yhdistys, 1927), and Onni Koskikallio, *Maatalouskiinteistöjen eläkerasituksesta Pirkkalan ja Ruoveden tuomiokunnissa vuosina 1800–1913* (Helsinki: Helsingin yliopisto, 1927).

14 Moring, "Retirement Contracts," pp. 389–91 and 411–12.

15 Olof Hultman, *Upplandslagen* (Helsingfors: Svenska litteratursallskapet i Finland, 1916); Birgit Sawyer, *Kvinnor och familj id et forn- och medeltida Skandinavien* (Skara: Viktoria bokförlag, 1992), pp. 16–17; Jyrki Knuuttila, *Avioliitto oikeudellisena ja kirkollisena instituutiona Suomessa vuoteen 1629* (Helsinki: Suomen Kirkkohistoriallinen Seura, 1990), pp. 31–34; Ruth Donner, ed., *King Magnus Eriksson's Law of the Realm* (Helsinki: Ius Gentium

When embarking upon marriage, a woman often joined the family of her husband, bringing with her a dowry of cattle, textiles, and money. When her parents died, she inherited a share of the parental property, or all of it if there were no siblings. The husband and his family endowed the wife with one-third of the marital property to be used by her in widowhood.[16] While the marriage lasted, the husband had control over the family economy with certain restrictions. Until the end of the seventeenth century a husband could not sell land that his wife had inherited except with the permission of her family. When couples lived on the wives' land the husband became the head of the farm, not the owner. Family land ran strictly through the bloodline and could not be inherited by a spouse. If the couple had children, the property of the wife was ultimately to be divided between them. If the couple remained childless the dowry had to be re-paid to her family once she died. Widows also had the right to reclaim their property in the eventuality that they decided to leave the house of their late husbands and never enjoyed upkeep in old age. All money earned during the marriage was joint property, of which the wife owned one-third, but any money that a woman had earned before marriage was her own. Women were not obliged to cover their husbands' old debts.[17]

While the law[18] saw men as the representative of the house in society, this was not always the case in practice. In the absence of the husband, the wife acted as his deputy. She appeared in court on behalf of her husband and

---

Association, 2000), pp. 17–18; Karl Robert Villehad Wikman, *Om de fornnordiska formerna for aktenskapets ingaende* (Helsingfors: Societas Scientiarum Fennica, 1959), pp. 9–13.

16 Fr. Hallager and Fr. Brandt, *Kong Christian den fjerdes Norske Lov af 1604* (Kristiania: Fellberg & Landmark, 1855), p. 68; Rudolf Huebner, *A History of Germanic Private Law* (London: John Murray, 1918), pp. 599 and 625–26; Anu Pylkkänen, "Avioliiton historiaa," in *Suomen oikeushistorian pääpiirteet*, ed. Pia Letto-Vanamo (Helsinki: Gaudeamus, 1991), pp. 80–97, here p. 83; Heikki Ylikangas, "Huomenlahja Ruotsin keskiaikaisten lakien valossa," *Historiallinen Aikakauskirja* (1967), pp. 14–25, here pp. 15–18; *Kulturhistoriskt Leksicon for Nordisk Middelalder* (*KLNM*), vol. 3 (Malmo: Allhem, 1958), p. 682; E. A. Virtanen, "Historiska uppgifter om morgongåvan bland allmogen i västra Finland," *Budkavlen* (1964–65), pp. 82–87.

17 Huebner *A History*, pp. 629–30 and 648; Pylkkänen, "Avioliiton," pp. 84–85.

18 The regional legislation in Sweden-Finland was compiled between 1347–1352 in the Magnus Eriksson's Law of the Realm, the first national law code. It was re-issued in 1442 with few modifications as the law of the realm of King Kristoffer. It experienced little change until the Law Code of 1734, which introduced some innovations, but retained most of the old regulations regarding landownership and transfer, with the exception of redefining retirement as property transfer rather than headship transfer. In the mid 1850s and 1860s, female inheritance rights were extended for rural areas and the rights of the extended family to intervene in property deals curtailed; see Donner, *King Magnus Eriksson's*, pp x–xii; see also note 19.

handled disputes, taxation, debts, fines, taking up of farmland, inheritance issues and took the responsibility for problems caused by children and servants of the house. Even though the law did not require the permission of the wife to sell land acquired during the marriage or land inherited by men, the sixteenth- and seventeenth-century sales documents usually carry the names of both husband and wife, or state that the wife has given her permission to the transaction. The Law for Norway of Christian V in 1687 increased the economic power of husbands and restricted wives' rights to permitting or objecting to land sales and conducting economic transactions in the husbands' absence. In practice, however, these clauses were disregarded both by women and local communities, including the representatives of the local legal system, in instances in which adhering to the law was inconvenient.[19] The fact that women did not continuously remain in the background in relation to economic matters has also been observed for other parts of Northern Europe.[20]

In eighteenth-century Sweden and Finland, the new administrative class promoted changes in the economic legislation and focused on the individual rather than the family. The farming class fought all changes to property and inheritance legislation, but over time the power of the family and kin was curtailed. The right of the wider kinship group to revoke a land sale was abolished in 1734. The right of married women to engage in independent economic activity was circumscribed, however, though their signature was still necessary for any sale of land. From the nineteenth century on the power of the husband could be restricted through tying up assets in prenuptial contracts, and a so called "good man", or trustee who retained control of the capital, could be used for the preservation of property for the duration of the marriage. In the late nineteenth century, the property of husband and wife was separated, and each gained control over their own earnings.[21]

19 John E. Roos, *Suomen vanhimmat tuomiokirjat*, vol. 2: *Ala Satakunnan tuomiokirja 1550–1552* (Helsinki: Valtionarkisto, 1964); Anu Pylkkänen, *Puoli vuodetta, lukot ja avaimet* (Helsinki: Lakimiesliiton kustannus, 1990), pp. 278–82 and 351–52; Hilde Sandvik, "Kjönnsperspektiv pa tidlig moderne tids ökonomi," in *Fra kvinnehistorie til kjönnshistorie*, ed. Kare Tönneson (Oslo: Oslo University, 1994), pp. 93–106, here pp. 97 and 101–02.

20 Ellen E. Kittell, "Guardianship over Women in Medieval Flanders: a Reappraisal," *Journal of Social History* 31–4 (1980), pp. 897–930.

21 Pylkkänen, "Avioliiton," pp. 93–94; Knut Fredriksson, *Sandhems gårdskrönikor*, vol. 5 (Falköping: Sandhems hembygdsforening, 1988), p. 653. Despite the annexation of Finland by Russia in 1809, property legislation remained unaltered, with the old Swedish laws remaining in place and being gradually augmented or altered in the later part of the century by local (Finnish) parliament.

When husbands died their property was inventoried for division between widows and any children. In addition to a third of all the marital property (excluding inherited land), rural widows were provided with a bed complete with bedding and a set of clothes (the morning gift). In some cases, they retained their engagement gifts as personal property. In urban areas such as in Denmark widows received one half of the property, and by the early twentieth century the widow's share was fifty percent in most Nordic countries. Even though widows had no rights to their husbands' family land, they could retain the headship if their children were young. Widows could even remarry and remain at the helm of the holding, although the new husband could never become the owner of the landed property of his stepchildren. At retirement, the widow had the right to expect care from whichever child had been granted the headship.[22]

3 Generational Transfer, the Single Heir System, and the Retirement Contract

Inheritance legislation in the Nordic countries made a distinction between land and other property. It granted all children inheritance rights, although boys inherited a larger share than girls, and both boys and girls could inherit land. Already even medieval legislation supported the principle of transmitting landholdings undivided to a single heir and dividing only the movable portion of the property. Land division was only deemed acceptable in instances where the farmland could be extended through taking up new fields or through land purchase. The necessity of guarding holdings against fragmentation makes an explicit appearance in Norwegian medieval legislation, dividing the children into the categories of a main heir with right to the parental holding and other siblings to be compensated with money and movables. While the laws granted parents the right to expect care in old age irrespective of their economic situation, they also stated that parents with land or assets were to compensate their

22 Hultman, *Upplandslagen*, pp. 48–51; *KLNM* 3, pp. 682–685; Huebner, *A History*, pp. 644–45 and 651; Hallager and Brandt, *Kong Christian*, pp. 73 and 77; Pylkkänen, "Avioliiton," pp. 94–96; Åke Holmbäck and Elias Wessen, *Svenska landskapslagar*, vol. 3: *Hälsingelagen* (Stockholm: Geber, 1940), p. 361. Urban areas were subject to different rules, codified in the fourteenth century in Magnus Erikssons Stadslag (The law for towns of Magnus Eriksson). As urban property did not include family land, widows inherited half the property in addition to their morning gift providing there were children; see Beatrice Moring, "The Standard of Living of Widows: Inventories as an Indicator of the Economic Situation of Widows," *The History of the Family* 12–4 (2007), pp. 233–49, here p. 242.

children for that care. This particular piece of legislation created the opportunity to transfer landholdings en bloc to a single heir who, in receiving the land, was obliged to shoulder the care for the parents and the family economy. Land fragmentation was thereby avoided, and opportunities were created to facilitate a gradual shift of tasks from one generation to another and to provide departing children with a dowry over the family life course.[23]

Although the expression "retirement contract" has been used to describe the public declaration, and later document, whereby parents promised to transfer their land to a particular child in exchange for care, the declaration was not immediately followed by a withdrawal from active work. The main purpose of the "contract" was to name the parties involved and render the transfer legal. As land was often transmitted along the male line, the eldest son was usually, although not always the chosen heir. In cases of early death of a male head, the widow acted as head for shorter or longer periods. As the legal owner of one-third of all movable property, cattle, money, tools etc., such property was included in the transfer when she ultimately decided to retire.[24]

In the sixteenth century, a more or less standard formula was used in the retirement declarations documented in court records:

> Poval Kivenranta declared in front of the court that he will take Staffan Hakulin to be his son as he has none of his own. He is to serve, feed clothe and care for him and his wife until they die and then he is to become their rightful heir, and if Poval Kivenranta dies before his wife she promises her land to him as it is her father's land.[25]
>
> Came in front of the court Valborg Larsdotter and declared, that she was giving her beloved son Lasse Olsson her share of the movables of the farm, as much as it might be, in gratitude for the care he has given her and intends to give, to clothe, feed and care for until she dies, as is witnessed by 12 men.[26]
>
> Stepped in front of the court Karin Siffredsdotter of Leistla, and made known that she gave her 2 daughters called Biritt and Valbor all her movable goods, and particularly she gave Valbor 1 oxen more than to Biritt, for

23 Hultman, *Upplandslagen*; *KLNM* 20, pp. 464–65; Åke Holmbäck, *Svenska landskapslagar, Äldre Svearätt* (Stockholm: Geber, 1919), pp. 112–13; Holmbäck and Wessen, *Svenska landskapslagar*; Kjeld Helland Hansen, "Föllog, föderad, kår," *Heimen* 11 (1958–1960), pp. 173–77; Kjeld Helland Hansen, "Kårskipnaden," *Heimen* 13 (1966), pp. 182–95.

24 Moring, "Property and Power," pp. 82–83 and 96.

25 National Archives, Helsinki, Finland, Joroinen, court records 11 September 1561.

26 National Archives, Helsinki, Finland, Eurajoki court records 23 July 1550.

> their true service to her that they have given her, and will give hereafter until the day she dies, as will be examined by 12 men.[27]

In the second instance we find that the daughters were running the farm jointly, and that the maternal property was specifically cattle-based.

Co-residence continued as the most common form of retirement in rural seventeenth-century Sweden and Finland. The sharing of bread and a home makes it difficult to assess the changes a person who retired from the headship encountered. Retirement could be a legal formality rather than an actual intention of withdrawing from the headship, particularly in the case of males.[28] A transfer to a daughter or a younger son, bypassing the eldest, generally involved declarations in court including an explanation of why a younger child or son-in-law was to receive the farm. In order to ensure that the compensation to the person providing the care was legally valid, it was even possible in some parts of Finland to publicly adopt that person. A declaration in court could also be sufficient. For example: "Jöran Sigfridson in Bodwijk stood up in front of the court and gave his farm to his son-in-law Hans Michilson, who is to take care of him in his old age, like a rightful son does for his parents, and run the farm, which has been offered to his other children, but they have found livelihoods on other farms through marriage."[29]

As the first example shows, a transfer of land via the female line was perfectly acceptable. The fact that males with inheritance claims had declined to take on the obligations, however, was established in court to avoid future complications. In addition, a fictional male to male link could be created through the act of adoption. In the majority of cases the issue was settled while both parties of the couple were alive. After the death of the husband the obligations of care extended to his widow. If the heir did not fulfil his promises the agreement could be changed or revoked in the local court. In actual fact a considerable proportion of property issues in Finnish and Swedish court records consist of the registration of retirement, adoption, property division, wills, or the forming of a house corporation, in connection with an ownership transfer, in return for care.[30]

---

27 National Archives, Helsinki, Finland, Ulvila court 2 April 1552.

28 Hoffman, *Jämtlands domböcker*, pp. 47–48, 60, and 68.

29 Hammarland, 20 November 1643, quoted from Johan Stiernhook, *Alandska Domböcker 1641–1643*, ed. John E. Roos (Helsingfors: Alands landskapsstyrelse, 1946), p. 107.

30 National Archives, Helsinki, Finland, seventeenth-century Court records; Marja Taussi Sjöberg, *Rätten och kvinnorna, fran släktmakt till statsmakt i Sverige* (Stockholm: Atlantis, 1996), pp. 190–91.

4 Landownership and the Transfer from Oral to Written Agreements

In the seventeenth century, the ownership of a farm had been understood as resting with the old head until his death, even if the headship and the actual running of the farm had been transferred to the younger generation. This legal stance made it possible to revoke or change retirement agreements in case of disagreements or practical problems like the death of the chosen successor. After the introduction of the legal code of 1734 in Sweden and Finland, the change in headship became understood as a change in ownership. The implications of this were that a flexible system changed into one of definite ownership transfer. In Norway, retirement contracts had been constructed as sales contracts for centuries sometimes stipulating a sale of, for example, half of the farm to the heir.[31]

During the eighteenth century, a large proportion of farms in Sweden and Finland were on crown land. In some cases, the old head made a will in favour of the heir, but often an application was only submitted to the court for the verification of a headship transfer. The new head then became liable for paying all taxes. In practice, however, a number of the old farmers never retired from headship. The old and young couples continued sharing living space, meals, and work.[32] When a farmer died young his widow often took over. Studies of local communities in eighteenth-century Sweden and Finland have indicated that ten to sixteen percent of farms were run by a widow.[33] In such cases, the widow herself had to see to the timing and nature of her retirement. Farmers themselves did not always distinguish between their own land and that of the crown, and the generational transfer on the one was not much different from that on the other. Legally of course the farmer did not actually own the land, and while kinship succession had been practiced for centuries, in theory the authorities were entitled to name the successor. The issue of the position of a childless widow of a crown farmer was therefore legally speaking not

31 Axel Charpentier, *Om sytning* (Helsingfors: J. Simelii arvingar, 1896), pp. 106–07; Helland Hansen, "Kårskipnaden," pp. 187–190.

32 Eli Hecksher, *Svensk arbete och liv* (Stockholm: Bonniers, 1980), pp. 144 and 188–89; Eino Jutikkala, *Suomen talonpojan historia* (Helsinki: Suomen kirjallisuuden seura, 1958), pp. 300–05; Ragna Ahlback, *Kokar* (Helsingfors: Svenska litteratursallskapet i Finland, 1955), pp. 36–37 and 305; Moring, "Retirement Contracts," p. 392.

33 Martin Dribe and Christer Lundh, "Gender Aspects on Inheritance Strategies and Land Transmission in Rural Scania, Sweden," in *The Logic of Female Succession: Rethinking Patriarchy and Patrilineality in Global and Historical Perspectives*, ed. Emiko Ochiai (Kyoto: International Research Center for Japanese Studies, 2002), pp. 53–74, here p. 63; Moring, "Property and Power," pp. 75–100, here p. 82.

unambiguous. In 1811, a regulation was passed in Finland granting the widow of a crown farmer not only the right to stay on the farm as long as she lived, but also the right to set up a retirement contract when she became too old and ill to care for the farm or be cared for by the next landholder. An Imperial decree of 1852 further underlined the legality of a crown farmer's right to retire and be taken care of on his farm in old age.[34]

Despite the legal alteration linking change of headship to change of ownership, itemised retirement contracts remained rare throughout the eighteenth century. Some transfers and retirement agreements can be found in wills and inventories.[35] The care of the widow and the provision of a separate room could be noted in other documents that might be drawn up. In one example from 1731, the old mother was provided with a room, but was guaranteed the right to join the rest of the family by the fire in the main room when she so wished.[36]

5 Securing the Land and Life in Old Age, the Purpose of the Nineteenth Century Contract

While during the sixteenth century contracts could be drafted with the assumption that the heir was going to prosper and therefore be capable of clothing and caring for the old parent, the situation became different in the nineteenth century. Crown land was brought into private hands in Finland and Sweden as well as in Norway, and what was owned outright could also be lost. Land was increasingly bought and sold, and it was also used as security for loans. Legal changes strengthened the inheritance claims of younger children, and the single heir system rested on less secure foundations than before.[37] As retirement contracts were legally a mortgage on the land, they affected the value of a farm in cases of sale or transfer. On the other hand, retirement contracts granted

34 Högnäs, *Sytning*, 3; *Samling af Placater, Forordningar, Manifester och Pabud samt andre Allmanna Handlingar hwilka i Stor-Furstendomet Finland sedan 1808 ars borjan ifran trycket utkommit*, 1831 (Helsingfors: Senaten, 1831), pp. 146–48; Kivialho, "Maatalouskiinteistöjen," p. 73.

35 National Archives, Helsinki, Finland, Inventories, Brando parish, 23 September 1708, Brando parish, 8 September 1706, mf ES 3501.

36 Saini Laurikkala, *Varsinais-Suomen talonpoikain asumukset ja kotitalousvälineet 1700-luvulla* (Turku: Turun Yliopisto, 1947), pp. 52, 56, and 84.

37 Borje Sidbäck, *Fran forntid till nutid* (Vasa: Sidbäck hembygdsforening, 1992), pp. 18–19; Högnäs, *Sytning*, pp. 42–44 and 224; Gabriel Nikander, "Sytningsfolk i Sibbo," *Kalender utgiven av Svenska Folkskolans Vanner* (1917), pp. 71–74.

the right of residence for life, and whatever was stipulated in a legal retirement contract could not be revoked by creditors or new owners. The transfer of land from tenant farms to freehold in Norway commenced in the 1660s when only twenty percent of the farmland was owned by the farmers themselves, with the rest owned by the church, the crown, or the nobility. By the early decades of the nineteenth century, farmers had acquired more than fifty percent of the land, and considerable regional differences can be detected in landownership and the number of detailed retirement contracts. Ståle Dyrvik tentatively posed the question of whether there was a correlation between retirement contracts and a high proportion of freeholds. Regional variation in co-residence levels were indeed a feature of the Norwegian countryside.[38] The regional variation in landownership in Finland is also reflected in the prevalence of retirement contracts. In regions where the farms retained their crown nature, or where land sale was of marginal importance, there are few or no detailed nineteenth century retirement contracts to be found.[39]

In 1852, a law was introduced at the instigation of the Finnish urban bourgeoisie, that the existence and nature of retirement contracts must be disclosed to creditors when using land as security for loans. In 1864, restrictions were introduced regarding the creation of a second retirement contract, and thereafter a share of retirement payments – in cash or kind – could be frozen for retirees' outstanding personal debts. In 1878, the right of family members to buy back land going out of the family was restricted to the children and parents of the previous owner.[40] This change brought about the potential for an intensification in buying and selling of land. It also made it more difficult for families to hold on to land or buy it back if an auction had taken place at the initiative of creditors. The regions in Finland with active land markets, borrowing for agricultural investments and a high proportion of private land

38 Ståle Dyrvik, "Overgangen til sjolveige i Norge," *Historisk tidsskrift* 56–1 (1977), pp. 1–17.

39 Beatrice Moring, *Skärgårdsbor. Hushåll, familj och demografi i finländsk kustbygd på 1600–1700- och 1800-talen* (Helsingfors: Societas Scientiarum Fennica, 1994), pp. 56–63; Beatrice Moring, "Family Strategies, Inheritance Systems and the Care of the Elderly in Historical Perspective: Eastern and Western Finland," *Historical Social Research* 23–1/2 (1998), pp. 67–82, here p. 70; Pylkkänen, *Puoli vuodetta*, pp. 180 and 362; Jutikkala, *Suomen talonpojan*, pp. 320–323; National Archives, Helsinki, Finland, Probate inventories Korpo; Orvar, Löfgren, "Family and Household among Scandinavian Peasants," *Ethnologia Scandinavica* (1974), pp. 17–52, here pp. 41–42; Ahlback, *Kokar*, p. 36.

40 Högnäs, *Sytning*, pp. 2–4; Kaisa Korpijaakko, "Maanomistusoikeuden kehityksesta ruotsalais-suomalaisen oikeusjarjestyksen mukaan," in *Oikeudellisen sääntelyn kehityslinjoja*, ed. Jukka Kekkonen, Kaisa Korpijaakko, and Heikki Ylikangas (Helsinki: Gaudeamus, 1986), pp. 66–70; Kivialho, "Maatalouskiinteistöjen," p. 66.

were Ostrobothnia in the northwest and Finland Proper in the south west. During the nineteenth century these regions also show an increased intensity, unparalleled in other parts of the country, of drawing up detailed retirement contracts.

An analysis of contracts from nineteenth-century northwest Finland shows that a large proportion of farms with detailed retirement contracts were burdened with debts. The majority of the transfers were between parents and children, and more than ninety percent of these transfers were conducted as giving and receiving a conditional gift. The heir promised care for the parents and took responsibility for debts and the inheritance shares of younger siblings (cattle, money, a wedding party). Some of the contracts included clauses that increased the retirement payments if the land went out of the family. Practically all of the contracts included a long list of items in the case that joint housekeeping could not be maintained and each contract carefully stipulated that the person responsible was not specifically the son or daughter but "whoever holds the farm". If the heir lost the farm to the creditors, the old couple was secured by the contract and the payments to the other children could also be sought in court, particularly if they had been set out as the price for the farm. When the heir ran the farm successfully, contracts were seldom implemented, apart from the sections about having a heated retirement room, sharing meals, and receiving one pair of shoes per year.[41]

6 The Structure of the Contract, Time and Place, and the Parties: the Female Voice

Nineteenth century contracts retain a remarkably uniform structure. They start with the property, name, administrative number, village, judicial district, the name and kinship status of the new owners, they state whether the transaction is a sale or gift, and in case of sale the sum that is being paid, has been paid, or will be paid. Sometimes the actual money is to be paid to siblings at the time of their marriage, or combined with gifts in kind, such as animals. In cases of generational transfer, the majority of contracts state that the old and new owners will continue with co-residence and common economy and only certain items or animals will be set aside as private property of the retirees. Another section usually followed this, making arrangements for a long list of

41 Kivialho, "Maatalouskiinteistöjen," p. 97; *Vallgrund Min Hembygd*, vol. 2: *Skrifter utgivna av Vallgrunds hembygdsforening* (Vasa: Vallgrunds hembygdsforening, 1982), p. 83.

goods and payments and the right of use of specific parts of the farm, for the eventuality that the couples might not get along or that the farm left family hands. At the end of the document there were declarations by both parties that they were satisfied with the contract, the date and place, and the signatures of two witnesses. It would seem that the text was often dictated to a scribe, minor court official or somebody else in the parish with the ability to draw up legal documents, as this person also stated his identity. The timing of contract presentation for verification at the local court varied. Courts held autumn and spring sessions and were not always open for business. Court sessions were not held continuously in every parish and generally people waited for a convenient time to approach them for verification. Sometimes contracts were only presented at court once one of the parties had died or some other economic transaction was due.[42]

While the majority of retirement contracts were negotiated during the lifetime of both parents and subsequently held by the survivor (often the widow), a certain percentage were drawn up by widows after the death of their husbands. These contracts show that in many cases in which the land was transferred to a child the retiree had no intention of actually retiring, particularly not from headship. The contract was made for future use, when the farmer and his wife became older and infirm, or if the farm were to go out of the family. The words used were: "For the rest of our lives we expect to retain undiminished headship on the farm or if we decide to retire from it we require the following retirement payments [...]". "If a situation arises that will make it necessary for us to retire from the headship we expect following retirement payments". "As long as I want I will retain the privilege of mother and head of the housekeeping, but when I no longer maintain this activity my son is to provide me with the following retirement payments [...]".[43]

If the new head was a kinsman, the expectation was generally that co-residence would remain the model even after retirement. Some contracts between parents and children only stated that the child was to feed, clothe and care for the parents. Others reflect concerns for the future. When the farm was sold outside the family a retirement settlement was included in the

42 Högnäs, *Sytning*, pp. 231–32; Hugo Högnäs, "Arvejord och sytningsfolk," *Kalender utgiven av Svenska Folkskolans Vänner* (1941), pp. 78–88, here pp. 78–79; Åberg and Öster, "Efter avslutad". A calculation from nineteenth-century southwestern Finland revealed that the value of the retirement contract represented less in sales between relatives and a higher price was charged from strangers. The difference in price could be as much as twenty-five percent (Kivialho, "Maatalouskiinteistöjen," p. 132).

43 Hognas, *Sytning*, pp. 49 and 189.

transaction. On rare occasions a remote relation or non-relation was taken in as an heir and carer in old age as had been the fashion in previous centuries.[44] On one hand the increased survival rate of children made it more likely for parents to be able to name a son or daughter as heir, but on the other hand the survival of siblings in greater numbers created pressures on existing assets.

7 The Necessary Items – Grain, Milk, Potatoes

The lists of items found in the contracts reveal views regarding necessities held by the rural population in nineteenth-century Scandinavia. If creditors took over and the farm was auctioned, it would be foolish to expect a positive attitude from the new owner who necessarily saw the old couple or widow as a nuisance. Housing was almost universally listed as the first and foremost issue in nineteenth-century Finnish contracts (see Table 4.1): 99.5 percent had stipulations concerning residence, 80.9 percent a room for personal use at the farm, 18.3 percent a separate building on the farm, and 0.3 percent made no changes to the current residence pattern. Close on the heels of these were stipulations that the room or residence was to be heated at the expense of the farm or that a specific amount of firewood was to be provided (536 detailed contracts Ostrobothnia).[45]

Of food items, grain appears in all the contracts, generally two barrels of rye and one or two barrels of barley per person; the presence of potatoes mirrors the rising importance of this plant for the everyday diet. The importance of dairy production for the rural economy is revealed through the inclusion of milk deliveries, or the right to milk a specific cow. Sometimes butter or cheese is also listed. Salted fish, a staple, is frequently included, as is dried or salted beef and pork and salt, some contracts, however, request a lamb for slaughter rather than the processed product. A common specification is the free use of a horse for trips to church and market, and contracts often end with requests of care in illness and a respectable funeral. Shoes and boots are present in many contracts, luxury items like coffee, sugar, tobacco, and alcohol become ever more present over the nineteenth century while cotton, hemp, and candles are only occasionally listed. A study from late eighteenth- and nineteenth-century western Norway reveals similar lists of provisions: free housing on the farm, in a specific room or a separate building, free heating or firewood, cows, sheep,

44 Moring, "Retirement Contracts," pp. 393–95.
45 Moring, "Retirement Contracts," pp. 412–13.

TABLE 4.1 Details of provisions in nineteenth-century Finnish retirement contracts

Item	Percent of contracts
Free housing	80–100
Heating or firewood	60–98
Grain	100
Milk or milk a cow/day	28–67
Keep cow	28–33
Wool or keep sheep	29–94
Meat	48–60
Fish	42–87
Potatoes	23–60
Potato patch	4–35
Use of horse	48–85
Care and funeral	40–50

Sources: National Archives, Helsinki,Contracts, collections: KO b 12 1830–31, KO b 18 1881, KO b 2 1864, 1865, KO b 12 1855; The Regional Archive of Turku, Retirement contracts in the collection of Kaaperi Kivialho; Hugo Högnäs, *Sytning och arvslösen i den folkliga sedvänjan i Pedersöre och Nykarlebybygden 1810–1914* (Åbo, 1938); Kaaperi Kivialho, *Maatalouskiinteistöjen omistajavaihdokset ja hinnanmuodostus Halikon tuomiokunnassa 1851–1910* (Helsinki, 1927); Onni Koskikallio, *Maatalouskiinteistöjen eläkerasituksesta Pirkkalan ja Ruoveden tuomiokunnissa vuosina 1800–1913* (Helsinki, 1927) altogether 973 contracts between 1810–1920

and their upkeep, grain deliveries, potatoes and salt, the right to milk cows on the farm or deliveries of milk, baking rights and milling rights.[46]

The contract below is a good example of both the structure and content of a retirement agreement for husband and wife with a transfer to a family member:

> I Johan Erik Carlsson in agreement with my wife Christina Catharina Matsdotter give and donate to my son Carl Johan Johanson 2/3 of our freehold farm nr 3 in Golby and Jomala parish Aland, consisting of 7/16 mantal and valued at 200 silver roubles. However my brother in law

46 Högnäs, *Sytning*, pp. 95–96, 103, 128, 134, 139, 155, 160–65, 176, 285, and 480; Helland Hansen, "Kårskipnaden," p. 188; Homlong, "I vores eiende lemstue," pp. 144, 148–151, and 155; Åberg and Öster, "Efter avslutad".

> Johan Fagerholm is to keep the croft on our land, that was awarded him with a contract of the 14 November 1820. When we have retired from the 2/3 of the farm we are to be provided with houseroom in the main building of the farm and also hold the chamber by the porch and a storage shed for our own use. *Food together with the farmer of whatever kind is provided for him.* Two sheep, 1 barrel of rye, a well tilled and fertilised field for the cultivation of 2 boxes of flaxen, and 2 strips for cultivation on the eastern side. 2 pairs of shoes, horse and equipment on holidays to and from church and other necessary trips, and love, respect and care until we die.
>
> If for some reason I and my wife would not be satisfied to *eat at the table of the farm* we can request the following items; 1 barrel of rye and the share in the field shall not be requested but in addition to the right to use the mill we are to have every October 3 barrels of rye, ½ barrel of barley, 8 box peas, 2 kap wheat, 2 barrels potatoes, 1 ½ lispund[47] dry meat, 1 lisp smoked pork, 2 lispund butter, ¼ barrel salted Baltic herring, 1 pint sweet and 1 jug of sour milk per day. If one of us dies then the deliveries are cut by half.
>
> The head of the farm is also to give us 2 silver roubles and 4 kappa salt. Our grain is to be milled at the windmill of the farm. Baking, brewing and washing is to take place in the spaces that the farmer uses for such activities. In addition, we are to have delivered to the room in which we reside dry and chopped firewood. In return we renounce the ownership and right to 2/3 of the freehold farm nr 3 in Golby in all its parts and whatever can be acquired in the future, for ourselves and our descendants in favour of our son Carl Johan Johanson and his wife Gustava Wilhemina Malmqvist for them to keep and cultivate. 30 November 1853
>
> Johan Erik Carlson, farmer on nr 3 in Golby, Christina Catharina Matsdotter, wife
>
> We declare ourselves satisfied with the document above in all parts and promise to fulfil it or it is to be fulfilled by whoever owns this farm Carl Johan Johanson, farmers' son, Wihelmina Malmqvist, wife.[48]

This contract clearly indicates the intention by the two generations to have common economy and living space. The "chamber by the porch" made it possible for the old couple to put a bed in a separate room, with the "houseroom

47 Lispund = 8.5 kilograms.

48 The National Archives, Helsinki, Finland, Aland, Court records 1851–1855, 596–97; emphasis by the author.

in the main building" being the shared living space of the entire household. "Food together" is an unambiguous statement, the parties were going to share their meals. The stipulations of a flaxen plot are only a confirmation of the female custom of having individual flaxen plots where the plants could be tended to produce what would ultimately become high quality linen. Most nineteenth-century retirement contracts list shoes, as these were not manufactured in-house but bought from shoemakers. Listing a number of deliveries as a plan b is the common structure of the contracts. While disagreements between family members that resulted in separation of the economy was not a common occurrence, a long list of requests could render the land unattractive to outsiders.

8 Quantities and Standard of Living

The needs of an old person were understood as a warm room, sufficient food and clothes, access to activity within the farm if desired, transport, care in illness and old age, and a decent funeral. The structure of the needs remains surprisingly constant over the centuries. Calculations for the late nineteenth century and the early decades of the twentieth, transforming the various items in the contracts into money, indicate that a retirement contract for one person in western Finland was roughly the equivalent of two rural male servants' annual wages or the wages of three female servants. A similar calculation for nineteenth-century western Norway indicates an average retirement contract value of about two female servants' wages or one and a half male servants' wages.[49]

An analysis of stipulations in contracts for two persons versus those for one indicate that a surviving spouse was expected to need slightly less than a single person. A widow who participated in a contract with her husband, with a fifty percent reduction at demise of one of the parties, was slightly less well off than a widow who set up her own contract. The provisions of grain in nineteenth-century Finland show remarkable uniformity; two and a half or three barrels of grain per person seems to have been the standard. Data from northern Sweden are almost identical. The provisions of potatoes varied more, from as little as one to as much as four barrels per person and year.[50] The generosity of

49 Kivialho, "Maatalouskiinteistöjen," pp. 109 and 240; Homlong, "I vores eiende lemstue," p. 164; Fritz Hodne, *Norges okonomiske historie 1815–1970* (Oslo: Cappelen, 1981), p. 181.

50 Högnäs, *Sytning*, pp. 95–99; Kivialho, "Maatalouskiinteistöjen," p. 105; Koskikallio, *Maatalouskiinteistöjen*, pp. 64–67; Theodor Forssell, *Tutkimuksia talodellisista oloista Suomen maaseudulla*, vol. 2:1 (Helsinki, 1887), pp. 12–13; J. H. Ilvonen, *Tutkimuksia*

the contracts in nineteenth-century Finland, at the expense of potential non-related new owners, shows the construction of new security mechanisms. The size of the payments often reflected the proximity of the relationship.[51] The quantities in the contracts were generally sufficient or exceeded the needs of retirees even after a reduction taking place upon the death of one of the partners. The combination of grain, potatoes, milk, fish etc. as outlined in these contracts provided more sustenance for one person than was consumed by a poor family of four in the 1880s.[52]

One of the reasons for such arrangements was the inclusion of provisions for younger children. The parents wanted to make sure that whatever happened, the livelihood of minors remained secure until they could earn their keep and were married in style. This was the custom in all regions where retirement contracts have been located.[53] A small farm with limited output could be, relatively speaking, heavily burdened by these provisions, if the contract would have been interpreted literally in practice, while a large one could easily manage. Representatives of the middle classes that were attacking the retirement system in nineteenth-century parliamentary discourse would naturally see the payments as a burden, because when they got their hands on a farm as a result of unpaid debts, the contracts were implemented in full. If the farm stayed in the family, the items were not supplied or demanded but the two generations retained a joint economy. Since the middle ages farmers and their widows had traded their farms against security in old age. The restructuring of the retirement contract enabled them to retain a familiar life pattern despite threats to their lifestyle posed by a rising market economy and altered legislation.

As stated above, widows with young children tended to run the farm until one of the sons or daughters had married and acquired the skills necessary to head a farming enterprise. Ulrika Karlsdotter was widowed in 1862, when her eldest son was only nine years old. The household was fairly wealthy, and the assets considerable. She headed the farm for eighteen years; at the time of

---

taloudellisista oloista Suomen maaseudulla, 4: 16 (Helsinki: SKS, 1888), pp. 12–13; Åberg and Öster, "Efter avslutad".

51 Högnäs, *Sytning*, p. 93; Kivialho, "Maatalouskiinteistöjen," p. 132.

52 Isacson Mats, *Ekonomisk tillväxt och social differentiering. Bondeklassen i By socken 1680–1860* (Uppsala: Uppsala University, 1979), p. 120; David Hannerberg, *Svenskt agrarsamhälle under 1200 år* (Stockholm: Laromedelsforlagen, 1971), pp. 93–96; Heikkinen Sakari, Riitta Hjerppe, Yrjö Kaukiainen, Erkki Markkanen, and Ilkka Nummela, "Förändringar i levnadsstandarden i Finland 1750–1913," in *Levestandarden i Norden 1750–1914*, ed. Gunnar Karlsson (Reykjavik: University of Iceland, 1987), pp. 67–94, here pp. 69 and 92.

53 Högnäs, *Sytning*, p. 183; Koskikallio, *Maatalouskiinteistöjen*, p. 232; Archive for Popular Culture (FKA, SLS), Helsinki, Finland, Retirement Contract, Collection 1028.

her retirement her eldest son Karl was twenty-seven years old and his younger brothers twenty-four and twenty-one respectively. Their sister Karolina had married a farmer who was present at the drawing up of the contract. It is not unlikely that one or possibly both of the younger brothers were still at home, hence a specific clause regarding residence. Even though the farm was in a strong economic situation, the son Karl borrowed money several times in the 1890s, using the land as security. As the retirement contract formed a portion of the deeds, it was tied to the holding and a mortgage with priority. The family managed to retain the holding until the death of the widow in 1894.

The retirement contract for Ulrika Karlsdotter, the mother at Westergard freehold farm in Pargas parish, was drawn up in 1880 when the eldest brother bought the land shares of his siblings and became the sole owner of the farm. Among other elements the contract stated that:

> [...] the building behind the farmhouse will be used for living quarters, apart from one room for the owner. A shed for the animals and a barn are to be erected using timber from the woodland area of the farm ... One of the storage buildings will be kept for her own use, as will the woodshed next to that of the farm. She will have space in the cellar for her potatoes and space in the boat house for one boat. Three sheep and their lambs are to be fed together with the animals of the farm and allowed joint grazing. She will have a vegetable garden on the south side and four barrels of potatoes will be planted for her. All her buildings will be maintained by the farmer as well as the fencing of her vegetable garden. Horse to church and other necessary trips will be provided ... grain (rye, oats, barley), pork, fish, hay for the animals, firewood, ready to use.
>
> If our mother should die within 9 years and one of the brothers or sisters is without lodging, that sibling has the right to use the accommodation and chop firewood, until the end of the said 9 years [...].[54]

9 Men, Women, and Priorities

The views of men regarding the needs of their wives, once widowed, is reflected in stipulations that the retirement payments could be cut down by twenty-five to fifty percent upon the husband's death, however, similar reductions did not always take place following the deaths of wives. In instances in which

54 FKA, SLS, Collection 1028.

the contract had been made for a farmer and his second wife, retirement payments might be radically reduced if the widowed wife decided to remarry, and in some cases, payments would be terminated altogether. In some cases, even first wives suffered reduced benefits upon remarriage; retaining family ties was rewarded, while linking your lot with outsiders discouraged. If the widow remained single the contract secured her housing, firewood, grain, milk, meat, wool etc. "[…] when one of us dies half of these payments will be cut, except in the right to horse, housing, light and firewood" (1909). "After the death of husband or wife, half of the animal fodder will disappear but on the other hand, at the time of the year when the cow is dry, a pint of milk shall be provided per day" (1879).[55]

Analysis of the contracts reveals certain differences between those set up by men for themselves alone, with their wives, and by widows for themselves (see Table 4.2). While men alone were likely to take part in family meals with their successor and require clothes ready-made, couples were more likely to retain headship or form an economic unit with their children, while the women intended to stay active in the female domain as long as possible. Many contracts made by men alone indicate an intention to retire, retaining the right of using a horse to travel to market, mill and around the village, to be allocated tobacco and alcohol, clothes, and food. "When one of us dies the amounts are halved, if, however, I survive my wife I want the full amount of the grain, the tobacco and the alcohol" (farmer Sandbacka and his wife, 1829).[56]

The desire to keep a cow or at least have the right to milk a cow figures prominently in contracts made by couples and those of widows. The need for women to maintain activity even when restricted by old age is evidenced by the custom in northern, eastern, and central Finland that a cow was kept as long as possible and two particular sheep were sheared for old couples when such work was beyond them. Norwegian oral history collections also evidence the desire of old widows to keep their cow and their independence.[57]

In 1863, for example, the widow Borghilde in Etne parish, western Norway, wanted winter fodder for two cows and grazing land in the summer for the cows and five sheep, free right to use all premises on the farm for baking, milking, and animal care. She intended to live in the farmhouse with the family. If a problem were to arise, she had secured the right to build a house of her own on the farm grounds. She also wanted it documented that firewood was to be

55 Högnäs, *Sytning*, pp. 183–185; Homlong, "I vores eiende lemstue," pp. 121 and 175–176.

56 Helland Hansen, "Kårskipnaden," p. 193; Hognas, *Sytning*, pp. 113, 119, 130–132, and 183.

57 Högnäs, *Sytning*, p. 124; Homlong, "I vores eiende lemstue," p. 172.

TABLE 4.2 Mean quantities of food supplied in nineteenth-century Finnish retirement contracts

Item	Contract for 1 person	Contract for a couple
Grain	3 1/2 barrels	5 barrels
Potatoes	2 1/2 barrels	3 barrels
Potato patch seed potato	1 barrel	1 barrel
Fish salt and fresh	17 kg	28 kg
Milk	2,6 litres	2,7 litres
Milk 1 cow/day	2,5 litres	2,5 litres
Meat	23,7 kg	23 kg
Keep animals, 1 cow, 2 sheep	Most contracts	Most contracts

SOURCES: SEE TABLE 4.1

chopped and brought to her in the house.[58] In 1837 the farmer's widow Bond in northwest Finland similarly stipulated that: "I will milk a cow daily, all year round, using all cows equally whether they give abundant or poor milk. In addition, every year I want to milk one cow after she has had a calf, for a week [...]".[59]

In 1893 the widow Kojonen stated her desire "to keep back a cow before the property division [...]". In addition she wanted fodder "4 wagonloads of hay (225 kg per load), 1/2 a load of open field hay and 1/2 wagonload of free growing hay".[60] The widow Klockars (1844) wanted to keep "1 cow and some sheep" and fodder for them[61] as did the widow Nybonde.[62] The widow Lojlax stated her intention to "milk one cow every day of the cows of the farm".[63] The widow Kock wanted "grazing of one cow together with those of the farm every summer" (1895),[64] and in 1890 the farmer's widow Sik decided that "At the time when my cow does not milk I am to have half a pint of milk per day for two months".[65]

58 Homlong, "I vores eiende lemstue," p. 180.

59 The National Archives, Helsinki, Finland, Ostrobothnia, Court records 1842, autumn assizes, Pedersore, case 62.

60 Ostrobothnia, Court records 1893, autumn assizes, Jeppo, case 42.

61 Ostrobothnia, Court records 1845, spring assizes, Nykarleby, case 8.

62 Ostrobothnia, Court records 1851, spring assizes, Nykarleby, case 22.

63 Ostrobothnia, Court records 1894, autumn assizes, Munsala, case 49.

64 Ostrobothnia, Court records 1898, autumn assizes, Nykarleby, case 41.

65 Ostrobothnia, Court records 1887, spring assizes, Munsala, case 28.

Keeping sheep, shearing sheep, or be provided with wool for spinning and weaving were a regular feature of widows' contracts and contracts drawn up by couples. Looms and spinning wheels were sometimes mentioned as items that the women intended to keep. Women usually wanted to keep two sheep, a cow and to have fodder and shelter for these animals.[66] Some, such as the widow Levala, were specific: "I want two sheep to slaughter every year and one to shear."[67] While others like the widow Sik wanted "The right to keep a sheep together with those of the farm."[68] Some wanted to engage in the provision of fodder, the widow Hannula, for instance, stipulated that she was to have "The right to collect leaves from the wood of the farm for one sheep."[69]

The contracts of women and couples often also included stipulations regarding the right to use various buildings for brewing beer, making butter, baking bread, washing, cooking etc. In one contract the widow says outright that she is going to maintain the role of mistress of the house in the kitchen and other indoor work.[70] In cases when land went outside the family, widows' contracts might state quite bluntly, as the widow Nygard put it, "I require the room opposite the door as living quarters, where heating facilities and a baking oven are to be provided. 1/4 of the cowshed and the old stables for a barn, right to use half the hayloft and half the storage shed,"[71] or as another widow put it, "The buyer is to erect a cottage with an oven for baking [...] to provide a cattle shed for a cow and two sheep".[72] Yet another widow stipulated that "The items in the contract are to be paid to me even if I decide to move, however in this case I will be responsible for their transport. Should I move, my right to house, firewood, transport, and care will not be demanded."[73] The widow Damsten declared that she needed "Necessary space for me and my animals as long as I continue living in the farmhouse, should I decide to move I arrange for my own accommodation but the rest of the items in the contract are to be brought to me wherever I live."[74]

Such stipulations were not exclusive to the northwest. The widow Eva Johansdotter in Box village, southern Finland requested "a small potato patch

66 Högnäs, *Sytning*, pp. 119–120, 123, 129, 133, 139, and 146.
67 Ostrobothnia, Court records 1896, autumn assizes, Nykarleby, case 44.
68 Ostrobothnia, Court records 1887, spring assizes, Munsala, case 28.
69 Ostrobothnia, Court records 1887, spring assizes, Nykarleby, case 19.
70 Högnäs, *Sytning*, pp. 124–125, 144–146, 163–164, and 189; Homlong, "I vores eiende lemstue," pp. 153, 155–157, and 172.
71 Ostrobothnia, Court records 1887, spring assizes, Munsala, case 28.
72 Högnäs, *Sytning*, pp. 128–129, and 146.
73 Ostrobothnia, Court records 1878, spring assizes, Pedersore, case 18.
74 Ostrobothnia, Court records 1847, spring assizes, Munsala, case 466.

fertilised and kept in good order by the farm […] grazing for one cow and 2 sheep, and their offspring, in summer, with the animals of the farm. Chopped firewood brought into the yard and stacked in the woodshed. The right to use the farm kitchen for baking, brewing and washing without interference or comments from the family of the farmer in residence."[75]

The contracts in northern Sweden were similar in both structure and content. They also echo the female desire for space and activity. In addition to grain, potatoes, turnips, salt, and herring the widow Ingrid Sofia Bergman wanted: "2 jugs of flaxen seed and suitable field to grow it […] fodder for 1 cow, 1 sheep and 1 lamb […] As living quarters, the front chamber in the main building, necessary space in cellar and other outbuildings, necessary firewood, chopped and carted to the house […] Transport to church, mill and other necessary errands."[76]

The following document from southwest Finland is fairly typical of a widow in good health who wanted to remain active and is here cited *in extenso* :

> Today I have sold and transferred my 1/3 share of the freehold farm number 2 in Strömma village to my son Johan Erik Mattson and his wife Maria Sofia Eriksdotter, for this I require from these or *whoever holds the farm*, food, clothes, care of the kind that is due from children to their parents; however, should I not be satisfied to be at a communal table with them I request the following payments:
>
> 1. 2 barrels of rye, ½ barrel of barley, ¼ barrel of peas, 3 barrels potatoes, ½ barrel of salted Baltic herring, 2 lispund[77] dry beef, 1 fish ready for the pot per day, when such things can be obtained, ½ jug of sweet ½ jug of sour milk per day and when the cows are not milking 2 jugs of small beer, 1 pair of shoes and every other year one pair of boots, also money 5 silver roubles.
> 2. I want the chamber by the porch as living quarters and for the fire dry chopped wood as much as I might need, should the chamber need repairs they are to be sorted by *the person who heads the farm.*
> 3. I retain for myself a good and fertilised field enough to grow 1 box of *flaxen* that is to be provided by the person who holds the farm.

75 Nikander, "Sytningsfolk," p. 72.

76 Harnosand Archive, courtesy of The Local History Society of Ljustorp, Retirement contract, 21 October 1836, Asang, Ljustorp.

77 Lispund = 8.5 kilograms.

4. In addition I am to have the right to use the windmill to *grind my grain and space to bake the bread I might need.*
5. Should I be struck down by illness or for some other reason would be unable to grow and tend to my *flaxen*, or not well enough to *spin and weave* and make my clothes, then the head of the farm is to see to this and that I have what I need.
6. *Feed for two sheep* and space together with the animals of the farm.
7. Horse and necessary carriage to and from church and other necessary journeys.
   Strömma the 5th of January 1853 Albertina Olsdotter.[78]

One of the reasons for the confidence with which these women spoke is to be found in their legal right to the property and to retirement, but also in the collaborative economic system of Nordic farms. Complimentary activity during the marriage and the system of temporary authority transfer to wives gave couples good insight in the capability of each partner. It is far from unusual to find evidence of trust between husbands and wives of the farming class. Many farmers, such as the late husband quoted in the following document, were confident in the competence of their wives in taking care of the farm and the children. The position of authority with which the wife had been entrusted was one she held until she felt the time had come to retire. The family life cycle had reached a period of transition, but even at the brink of retirement she could not avoid pointing out that the decision was hers and hers alone: "In my husband Carl Petter Olson's will I was given control of the farm Stafre no. 2, in Ljustorp parish, receiving all the rights and duties of running the farm and bringing up the children. I have done so until the present day, and now I consider myself having finished the task. Therefore, I desire to hand the farm over to my children, so that *they might negotiate about the ownership*." The widow does not intend to be involved in who will run the farm or how, however, she does want a certain amount of security. "Hereby I set aside for myself the following retirement privileges payable to me every year out of the farm; 1/3 barrel of rye, 2 barrels of barley grown in old field, 2 1/4 barrel intermediate quality barley, 2 barrels of potatoes, 2 jugs of peas, [...] hops, pork and half of a 1/4 barrel of headless Baltic herring." It should, however, be noted that she is not withdrawing from active life. "In addition 1/4 barrel of potatoes and 2 pints of flaxen seed is to be planted for me in good soil, prepared and fertilised by the farmer.

78 National Archives, Helsinki, Finland, Aland, Court records 1851–1855, 384v–385r; emphasis by the author.

1/4 barrel of turnips or the equivalent is to be planted, I want the use of half of the garden and the fruit trees there [...] For my animals hay, straw from the barns [...] The right to graze a cow and a calf in the horse field [...] transport to and from church and to town when necessary." In addition, she envisages that she will not always be active. "If because of illness or old age I become incapable of caring for myself *the farmer* is to take care of me giving the respect and love a mother can expect of a child." The possibility of the farm being lost or sold is also taken into account. "Finally, if for some reason none of *the children can or will retain the farm* and it will be *sold out of the family to strangers* I will retain the following privilege; If I decide to *take out these payments* and *move to another place* to consume the same in peace and quiet. I can, if the owner insists, not take out the fertiliser or its value from the farm. As a security for these my claims I will approach the court to have these claims verified as a mortgage on the property. 25th of April 1878 Katharina Olofsdotter."[79]

Entrusting a wife with the authority to handle the economy of the family can also be seen in the will by Johan Mattson from Frotuna farm, Northern Sweden:

> I Johan Mattson, being of sound mind, hereby make known, while God makes it possible for me to state my last will.
>
> It is my sincere desire that my dear wife will have and control the farm as long as she wants, and my children should not have any say about this. She is also to control all the movables as long as she heads the farm. After the movables are inventoried she is to care for them and increase rather than decrease them, unless it is necessary for the need of the farm. However, when my dear wife hands over the movables, they are to be divided between sisters and brothers and when my dear wife hands over the control of the farm to our children she is to be given the following retirement payments:
>
> [...] 4 barrels of clean barley [...] fodder for a cow and 1 sheep and lamb, to be taken care of in the cowshed of the farmer ... flaxen seed grown together with that of the house ... potatoes planted wherever she considers suitable, the right to plant turnips in one quarter of the old cabbage patch [...] 1/2 barrel of fresh herring and 1/4 barrel of salted herring, everything brought home to the house ... As living quarters she is to have the chamber in the house and the farmer is to make sure that she is

79 Harnosand Archive, courtesy of The Local History Society of Ljustorp, Retirement contracts from Northern Sweden (acquired with the kind assistance of Arnold Thunstrom), Retirement contract of Katharina Olofsdotter, 25 April 1878; emphasis by the author.

> comfortable with as much firewood as she needs, chopped and put into her woodshed. She is to have transport to the church and back and other trips when necessary [...] All this she is to have delivered every year and at suitable times without argument.
>
> 8th of January 1818 Johan Mattsson, Frotuna.[80]

To a modern observer, the harping on cows, sheep, and flaxen seed might seem strange in a situation when a woman could decide to rest and have items delivered. Cows, as the source of milk for making butter have historically had considerable economic importance. Cows and sheep along with sickles, scythes, axes, and a wedding feast formed the inheritance of younger sisters living on farms with few assets. Engaging in the process of making clothes, from flaxen seed to Sunday shirt, from sheep to socks, was an essential part of female life, and the products often a source of pride and even boasting. Once retired and no longer in charge of the keys to the stores, a woman could remain productive and proud of her achievements. Certain skills were also identified with experience and could therefore enhance the status of an elderly person.[81]

10 Conclusions

While some retirement contracts were set up in connection with a land sale outside the family, the vast proportion of nineteenth-century Scandinavian contracts were between family members. In the 1880s, some extraordinary claims were made that the detailed retirement contracts were set up to protect the elder generation from neglect and abuse, and that the retirement provisions undermined the economic viability of farms in northern Europe.[82] When Aberg and Oster scrutinised the empirical basis for these claims they

80 Harnosand Archive, courtesy of The Local History Society of Ljustorp, Arnold Thunstrom, Will of Johan Mattsson, Frotuna, 8 January 1818.

81 Beatrice Moring, " 'Only Girls Would Participate, and They Had a Lovely Time'. Female Networks and Cooperation in the Nordic Past," *Annales de Démographie Historique* 112–2 (2006), pp. 57–75; Holger Wichman, *Norrlandskt arbetsliv under 1700-talet, lansmannens berattelser 1764 om allmogens arbeten i Medelpad, Angermanland och Jamtland* (Stockholm: Nordiska Museet, 1968), pp. 36–39, 44–47, 50, and 52–53; Birger Tornroos, *Stenbadan – ett alandskt fiskelage Bottenhavet* (Mariehamn: Alands landskapsstyrelse, 1980).

82 David Gaunt, "The Property and Kin Relationships of Retired Farmers in Northern and Central Europe," in *Family Forms in Historic Europe*, ed. Richard Wall, Jean Robin, and Peter Laslett (Cambridge: Cambridge University Press, 1983), pp. 249–80, here pp. 253–62.

discovered an astounding lack of evidence. In a far too little publicised work, they disproved the claim of conflicts between generations, and the negative economic effects of the contracts. It has also been pointed out that the arguments regarding conflict and economic instability were lifted from a nineteenth-century political debate between rural and urban interest groups, where the middle classes aimed to destabilise the farming class in the name of modernisation. Land that had sustained a family for generations could be lost in an instant, auctioned, and resold at considerable profit. The retirement contract as a mortgage on the land intruded on the profit-making process and was attacked by those representing a rising moneyed elite. The long and convoluted contracts of this period are evidence of farmers' strategies to secure the economic future of their wives and families.[83]

Studies of households in the nineteenth-century Nordic countryside support the view of the retirement contract as an insurance document against outsiders. Old women and widows generally continued as part of the household collective, even in retirement. Activity linked to childcare and textile work was part of the domain of the older generation in particular and was only affected by retirement in the sense that these tasks might have become even more predominant.[84]

The threat of loosing the land to outsiders that had no obligation towards the family can be seen in the structure of certain clauses relating to either the nature of living arrangements or to the size of payments in such an eventuality. It is not possible to establish with certainty how often the contracts were actually implemented, but they did provide a guarantee of a reasonable standard of living, and in some cases the margins were even generous enough to provide for other family members in need. However, it cannot be emphasised

83 Åberg and Öster, "Efter avslutad," pp. 25–28 and 188–90; Beatrice Moring, "Conflict or Cooperation? Old Age and Retirement in the Nordic Past," *Journal of family History* 28–2 (2003), pp. 231–57; Beatrice Moring, "Nordic Family Patterns and the North West European Household System," *Continuity and Change* 10–1 (2003), pp. 77–110; Christer Lundh and Mats Olsson, "The Institution of Retirement on Scanian Estates in the 19th Century," *Continuity and Change* 17–3 (2002), pp. 373–404; Martin Dribe and Christer Lundh, "Retirement as a Strategy for Land Transmission in Pre-Industrial Sweden," *Continuity and Change* 20–2 (2005), pp. 165–92; Sandvik, "Kjönnsperspektiv pa tidlig", pp. 101–02; Homlong, "I vores eiende lemstue"; Sandvik, "moderne tids ökonomi".

84 Moring, "Retirement contracts," pp. 404–10; Homlong, "I vores eiende lemstue"; Åberg and Öster, "Efter avslutad"; Orvar Löfgren, "Social Organisation," in *Land och stad. Svenska samhdllstyper och livsformer fran medeltid till nutid*, ed., Mats Hellspong and Orvar Löfgren (Lund: Liber, 1988), pp. 241–43 and 248–50; Orvar Löfgren, "Family and Household among Scandinavian Peasants," *Ethnologia Scandinavica* (1974), pp. 17–52, here pp. 40–43; Ole Hojrup, *Landbokvinden* (Kobenhavn: Nationalmuseet, 1966), pp. 177, 195, and 201.

often enough, that in a large proportion of these cases there was no intention of separating the households as long as the farm remained in the family. While the majority of retirement contracts were drafted during the lifetime of both parents, the parties were aware that, as when a will was drawn up, the woman was more likely to be the surviving party than the man. Contracts generally contained more than adequate provisions. The women were allocated a properly heated room of their own, food and clothing were to be provided along with the right to participate in production within the female sphere; milking a cow, access to the kitchen and garden as long as health and energy so allowed. While many husbands were eager to secure the right of their wives to function unhindered in widowhood, some also specifically included the option to set up a separate household, particularly in cases in which there was a risk that the property might be lost to outsiders. As we have seen from the previously cited instance in which the husband handed everything over to his wife to organise as best as she could, the authority of the mother was likewise recognised within the family.

It has been the aim of this chapter to highlight the prospects for potential well-being among ordinary women with access to land or property. The retirement contracts of the Nordic countries bear evidence that farmers' widows were not at the mercy of their families, who suffered them as burdens, but rather widows were active in organizing their old age, whether with their husbands or on their own following his death.

References

Åberg, Olov, and Johan Öster. "Efter avslutad färd en hederlig begravning, Undantagsinstitutionen i Neder Luleå och Raneå socken 1790–1895." *Uppsala Papers in Economic History 37*. University of Uppsala, 1995.

Abrams, Lynn. "Introduction: Gendering the Agenda." In *Gender in Scottish History since 1700*, edited by Lynn Abrams, Eleanor Gordon, Deborah Simonton, and Eileen J. Yeo, pp. 1–16. Edinburgh: Edinburgh University Press, 2006.

Ahlback, Ragna. *Kokar*. Helsingfors: Svenska litteratursallskapet I Finland, 1955.

Arrizabalaga, Marie Pierre. "Gender and Migration in the Pyrenees in the Nineteenth Century: Gender-Differentiated Patterns and Destinies." In *Female Economic Strategies in the Modern World*, edited by Beatrice Moring, pp. 127–44. London: Pickering & Chatto, 2012.

Cavallo, Sandra, and Lyndan Warner. Introduction to *Widowhood in Medieval and Early Modern Europe*, edited by Sandra Cavallo and Lyndan Warner, pp. 3–23. London: Longman, 1999.

Chabot, Isabelle. "Lineage Strategies and the Control of Widows in Renaissance Florence." In *Widowhood in Medieval and Early Modern Europe*, edited by Sandra Cavallo and Lyndan Warner, pp. 127–44. London: Longman, 1999.

Charpentier, Axel. *Om sytning*. Helsingfors: J. Simelii arvingar, 1896.

Donner, Ruth, ed. *King Magnus Eriksson's Law of the Realm*. Helsinki: Ius Gentium Association, 2000.

Dribe, Martin, and Christer Lundh. "Gender Aspects on Inheritance Strategies and Land Transmission in Rural Scania, Sweden." In *The Logic of Female Succession: Rethinking Patriarchy and Patrilineality in Global and Historical Perspectives*, edited by Emiko Ochiai. pp. 53–74. Kyoto: International Research Center for Japanese Studies, 2002.

Dribe, Martin, and Christer Lundh. "Retirement as a Strategy for Land Transmission in Pre-Industrial Sweden." *Continuity and Change* 20–2 (2005): pp. 165–92.

Dyrvik, Ståle. "Overgangen til sjolveige i Norge." *Historisk tidsskrift* 56–1 (1977): pp. 1–17.

Forssell, Theodor. *Tutkimuksia talodellisista oloista Suomen maaseudulla,* vol. 2:1. Helsinki, 1887.

Fougstedt, Gunnar, and Antti Raivio. *Suomen väestön sääty ja ammattiryhmiys v. 1751–1805*. Helsinki: Tilastokeskus, 1953.

Fredriksson, Knut. *Sandhems gårdskrönikor*, vol. 5. Falköping: Sandhems hembygdsforening, 1988.

Fuchs, Rachel. *Gender and Poverty in Nineteenth-Century Europe.* Cambridge: Cambridge University Press, 2005.

Gaunt, David. "The Property and Kin Relationships of Retired Farmers in Northern and Central Europe." In *Family Forms in Historic Europe*, edited by Richard Wall, Jean Robin, and Peter Laslett, pp. 249–80. Cambridge: Cambridge University Press, 1983.

Hallager, Fr., and Fr. Brandt. *Kong Christian den fjerdes Norske Lov af 1604*. Kristiania: Fellberg & Landmark, 1855.

Hannerberg, David. *Svenskt agrarsamhälle under 1200 år.* Stockholm: Laromedelsforlagen, 1971.

Hecksher, Eli. *Svensk arbete och liv*. Stockholm: Bonniers, 1980.

Heikkinen, Sakari, Riitta Hjerppe, Yrjö Kaukiainen, Erkki Markkanen, and Ilkka Nummela. "Förändringar i levnadsstandarden i Finland 1750–1913." In *Levestandarden i Norden 1750–1914*, edited by Gunnar Karlsson, pp. 67–94. Reykjavik: University of Iceland, 1987.

Helland Hansen, Kjeld. "Föllog, föderad, kår." *Heimen* 11 (1958–1960): pp. 173–77.

Helland Hansen, Kjeld. "Kårskipnaden." *Heimen* 13 (1966): pp. 182–95.

Hellbom, Algot. *Tingsprotokoll for Njurunda*. Sundsvall: Medelpads hembygdsforening, 1983.

Hodne, Fritz. *Norges okonomiske historie 1815–1970*. Oslo: Cappelen, 1981.

Hoffman, Kjell. *Jämtlands domböcker och landstingsprotokoll 1647–1648*. Östersund: Landsarkivet i Östersund, 1989.

Högnäs, Hugo. "Arvejord och sytningsfolk." *Kalender utgiven av Svenska Folkskolans Vänner* (1941): pp. 78–88.

Högnäs, Hugo. *Sytning och arvslösen i den folkliga sedvänjan i Pedersöre och Nykarlebybygden 1810–1914*. Åbo: Åbo akademi, 1938.

Hojrup, Ole. *Landbokvinden*. Kobenhavn: Nationalmuseet, 1966.

Holmbäck, Åke. *Svenska landskapslagar, Äldre Svearätt*. Stockholm: Geber, 1919.

Holmbäck, Åke, and Elias Wessen. *Svenska landskapslagar*, vol. 3: *Hälsingelagen*. Stockholm: Geber, 1940.

Homlong, Beate. " 'I vores eiende lemstue', Kårskipnaden i Etne 1716–1901." MA thesis, University of Bergen, 1995.

Huebner, Rudolf. *A History of Germanic Private Law*. London: John Murray, 1918.

Hultman, Olof. *Upplandslagen*. Helsingfors: Svenska litteratursallskapet i Finland, 1916.

Ilvonen, J.H. *Tutkimuksia taloudellisista oloista Suomen maaseudulla*, 4: 16. Helsinki: SKS, 1888.

Isacson, Mats. *Ekonomisk tillväxt och social differentiering. Bondeklassen i By socken 1680–1860*. Uppsala: Uppsala University, 1979.

Jutikkala, Eino. *Suomen talonpojan historia*. Helsinki: Suomen kirjallisuuden seura, 1958.

Kittell, Ellen E. "Guardianship over Women in Medieval Flanders: a Reappraisal." *Journal of Social History* 31–4 (1980): pp. 897–930.

Kivialho, Kaaperi. *Maatalouskiinteistöjen omistajavaihdokset ja hinnanmuodostus Halikon tuomiokunnassa 1851–1910*. Helsinki: Kansantaloudellinen yhdistys, 1927.

Knuuttila, Jyrki. *Avioliitto oikeudellisena ja kirkollisena instituutiona Suomessa vuoteen 1629*. Helsinki: Suomen Kirkkohistoriallinen Seura, 1990.

Korpijaakko, Kaisa. "Maanomistusoikeuden kehityksesta ruotsalais-suomalaisen oikeusjarjestyksen mukaan." In *Oikeudellisen sääntlelyn kehityslinjoja*, edited by Jukka Kekkonen, Kaisa Korpijaakko, and Heikki Ylikangas, pp. 66–70. Helsinki: Gaudeamus, 1986.

Koskikallio, Onni. *Maatalouskiinteistöjen eläkerasituksesta Pirkkalan ja Ruoveden tuomiokunnissa vuosina 1800–1913*. Helsinki: Helsingin yliopisto, 1927.

Kulturhistoriskt Leksicon for Nordisk Middelalder (KLNM), vol. 3. Malmo: Allhem, 1958.

Lanzinger, Margareth. "Women and Property in Eighteenth-Century Austria: Separate Property, Usufruct and Ownership in Different Family Configurations." In *Female Economic Strategies in the Modern World*, edited by Beatrice Moring, pp. 145–59. London: Pickering & Chatto, 2012.

Laurikkala, Saini. *Varsinais-Suomen talonpoikain asumukset ja kotitalousvälineet 1700–luvulla*. Turku: Turun Yliopisto, 1947.

Löfgren, Orvar. "Family and Household among Scandinavian Peasants." *Ethnologia Scandinavica* (1974): pp. 17–52.

Löfgren, Orvar. "Social Organisation." In *Land och stad. Svenska samhdllstyper och livsformer fran medeltid till nutid*, edited by Mats Hellspong and Orvar Löfgren. Lund: Liber, 1988.

Lundh, Christer, and Mats Olsson. "The Institution of Retirement on Scanian Estates in the 19th Century." *Continuity and Change* 17–3 (2002): pp. 373–404.

Moring, Beatrice. "Conflict or Cooperation? Old Age and Retirement in the Nordic Past." *Journal of family History* 28–2 (2003): pp. 231–57.

Moring, Beatrice. "Family Strategies, Inheritance Systems and the Care of the Elderly in Historical Perspective: Eastern and Western Finland." *Historical Social Research* 23–1/2 (1998): pp. 67–82.

Moring, Beatrice. "Nordic Family Patterns and the North West European Household System." *Continuity and Change* 10–1 (2003): pp. 77–110.

Moring, Beatrice. "'Only Girls Would Participate, and They Had a Lovely Time'. Female Networks and Cooperation in the Nordic Past." *Annales de Démographie Historique* 112–2 (2006): pp. 57–75.

Moring, Beatrice. "Property and Power: Women and the Holding and Transmission of Assets." In *The Logic of Female Succession: Rethinking Patriarchy and Patrilineality in Global and Historical Perspectives*, edited by Emiko Ochiai, pp. 75–100. Kyoto: International Research Center for Japanese Studies, 2002.

Moring, Beatrice. "Retirement Contracts and the Economics of Widowhood in the Nordic Countries." *Continuity and Change* 21–3 (2006): pp. 383–418.

Moring, Beatrice. "Rural Widows, Economy and Co-Residence in the 18th and 19th Centuries." *The History of the Family* 15–3 (2010): pp. 239–54.

Moring, Beatrice. *Skärgårdsbor. Hushåll, familj och demografi i finländsk kustbygd på 1600–1700- och 1800-talen*. Helsingfors: Societas Scientiarum Fennica, 1994.

Moring, Beatrice. "The Standard of Living of Widows: Inventories as an Indicator of the Economic Situation of Widows." *The History of the Family* 12–4 (2007): pp. 233–49.

Nikander, Gabriel. "Sytningsfolk i Sibbo." *Kalender utgiven av Svenska Folkskolans Vanner* (1917): pp. 71–74.

Pylkkänen, Anu. "Avioliiton historiaa." In *Suomen oikeushistorian pääpiirteet*, edited by Pia Letto-Vanamo, pp. 80–97. Helsinki: Gaudeamus, 1991.

Pylkkänen, Anu. "Forming the Marital Economy in the Early Modern Finnish Countryside." In *The Marital Economy in Scandinavia and Britain 1400–1900*, edited by Maria Ågren and Amy Louise Erickson, pp. 75–88. Aldershot: Ashgate, 2005.

Pylkkänen, Anu. *Puoli vuodetta, lukot ja avaimet*. Helsinki: Lakimiesliiton kustannus, 1990.

Roos, John E. *Suomen vanhimmat tuomiokirjat*, vol. 2: *Ala Satakunnan tuomiokirja 1550–1552*. Helsinki: Valtionarkisto,1964.

Samling af Placater, Forordningar, Manifester och Pabud samt andre Allmanna Handlingar hwilka i Stor-Furstendomet Finland sedan 1808 ars borjan ifran trycket utkommit, 1831. Helsingfors: Senaten, 1831.

Sandvik, Hilde. "Decision-Making on Marital Property in Norway, 1500–1800." In *The Marital Economy in Scandinavia and Britain 1400–1900*, edited by Maria Ågren and Amy Louise Erickson, pp. 111–26. Aldershot: Ashgate, 2005.

Sandvik, Hilde. "Kjönnsperspektiv pa tidlig moderne tids ökonomi." In *Fra kvinnehistorie til kjönnshistorie*, edited by Kare Tönneson, pp. 93–106. Oslo: Oslo University, 1994.

Sawyer, Birgit. *Kvinnor och familj id et forn- och medeltida Skandinavien*. Skara: Viktoria bokförlag, 1992.

Sidbäck, Borje. *Fran forntid till nutid*. Vasa: Sidbäck hembygdsforening, 1992.

Stiernhook, Johan. *Alandska Domböcker 1641–1643*, edited by John E. Roos. Helsingfors: Alands landskapsstyrelse, 1946.

Taussi Sjöberg, Marja. *Rätten och kvinnorna, fran släktmakt till statsmakt i Sverige*. Stockholm: Atlantis, 1996.

Tornroos, Birger. *Stenbadan – ett alandskt fiskelage Bottenhavet*. Mariehamn: Alands landskapsstyrelse, 1980.

Vallgrund Min Hembygd, vol. 2: *Skrifter utgivna av Vallgrunds hembygdsforening*. Vasa: Vallgrunds hembygdsforening, 1982.

Virtanen, E. A. "Historiska uppgifter om morgongåvan bland allmogen i västra Finland." *Budkavlen* (1964–65): pp. 82–87.

Wichman, Holger. *Norrlandskt arbetsliv under 1700-talet, lansmannens berattelser 1764 om allmogens arbeten i Medelpad, Angermanland och Jamtland*. Stockholm: Nordiska Museet, 1968.

Wikman, Karl Robert Villehad. *Om de fornnordiska formerna for aktenskapets ingaende*. Helsingfors: Societas Scientiarum Fennica, 1959.

Ylikangas, Heikki. "Huomenlahja Ruotsin keskiaikaisten lakien valossa." *Historiallinen Aikakauskirja* (1967): pp. 14–25.

CHAPTER 5

Negotiating Inheritance in the Western Pyrenees in the Nineteenth Century – Gender Differentiated Treatment and Destinies

Marie-Pierre Arrizabalaga

Pre-French Revolution inheritance laws in the Western Pyrenees referred little to gender, because single inheritance was a question of birth rank rather than gender. According to the ancient Basque customs, the first-born child, be it male or female, inherited all family assets, a system known as "primogeniture regardless of gender". In this context, men and women of the same birth rank were treated the same way, while those of different birth ranks (regardless of gender) were treated differently and unequally. In Basque families with three surviving children (the average family size in the eighteenth century), the first-born male or female child inherited all patrimony, while the second-born son or daughter received a dowry to marry away. As for the third-born son or daughter, he or she received nothing, because most parents could not afford another dowry. Instead, he or she enjoyed lifelong full room, board and care, celibate at home.[1] Basque practices were quite unique for the time, because a first-born daughter could become an heiress, even when she had younger brothers, and in such circumstances she inherited the family house and land to the detriment of younger siblings, male or female.[2] In the rest of the Pyrenees and of Southern France male primogeniture prevailed, and women only inherited the

1 These practices were common across the Western Pyrenees and particularly in the three provinces of the Basque Country: Labourd, Basse Navarre, and Soule. Each of these provinces had customs, as did Bearn, the province east of the Basque Country. These customs were published, translated into French, and at times analysed by authors. See *Coutumes générales, gardées et observées au Païs et baillage de Labourt, et reffort d'icelui* (Bordeaux: J.-B. Lacornée, 1760); Jean Goyhenetche, *For et coutumes de Basse-Navarre* (Bayonne: Elkar, 1985); Michel Grosclaude, *La Coutume de la Soule. Traduction, notes et commentaires* (Saint-Étienne-de-Baïgorry: Izpegi, 1993); as for the Bearn customs, see: Christian Desplat, trans., *For de Béarn d'Henri II d'Albret* (Pau: Marrimpouer, 1986).

2 For details on these issues, see Eugène Cordier, *Droit de famille aux Pyrénées. Barège, Lavedan, Béarn et Pays Basque* (Paris: Auguste Durand, 1859) and Alain Fougères, *Les Droits de famille et les successions au Pays Basque et en Béarn d'après les anciens textes* (Bergerac: H. Trillaud, 1938).

 | DOI:10.1163/9789004456204_006

family house and land in the absence of male heirs. In these areas, all women were treated unequally and unfavourably.[3]

The events of 4 August 1789 in the early months of the French Revolution abolished these ancient customs because they caused inequality and were considered "privileges". The Civil Code of 1804 replaced the custom laws in order to guarantee liberty and equality uniformly across France and to every man and woman.[4] It then became mandatory by law for families to partition assets equally between all the children, sons and daughters.[5] From then on, gender in inheritance law was to be less of an issue in France than before, because all children, male or female, became entitled to equal treatment regarding

3 For comparative analysis of inheritance practices over time, see articles and books by Bernard Derouet, "Pratiques successorales et rapport à la terre: les sociétés paysannes d'Ancien Régime," *Annales ESC* 1 (1989), pp. 173–206; Bernard Derouet, "Le partage des frères. Héritage masculin et reproduction sociale en Franche-Comté aux XVIIIe et XIXe siècles," *Annales ESC* 2 (1993), pp. 453–74; Bernard Derouet, "Transmettre la terre. Origines et inflexions récentes d'une problématique de différence," *Histoire et sociétés rurales* 2 (1994), pp. 33–67; Gérard Béaur, "Le marché foncier éclaté. Les modes de transmission du patrimoine sous l'Ancien Régime," *Annales ESC* 1 (1991), pp. 189–203; Gérard Béaur, "La transmission des exploitations: logiques et stratégies. Quelques réflexions sur un processus obscur," in *Problèmes de la transmission des exploitations agricoles (XVIIIe–XXe siècles)*, ed. Gérard Bouchard, Joseph Goy, and Anne-Lise Head-König (Rome: Ecole française de Rome, 1998), pp. 109–16; Gérard Béaur, "Land Transmission and Inheritance Practices in France during the *Ancien Régime*: Differences of Degree or Kind?," in *Family Welfare. Gender, Property, and Inheritance since the Seventeenth Century*, ed. David R. Green and Alastair Owens (Westport, Conn.: Praeger, 2004), pp. 31–46; Anne-Lise Head-König, Luigi Lorenzetti, and Béatrice Veyrassat, eds., *Famille, parenté et réseaux en Occident (XVIIe–XXe siècles)* (Genève: Société d'Histoire et d'Archéologie de Genève, 2001); Isaac Chiva and Joseph Goy, eds., *Les Baronnies des Pyrénées. Maisons, mode de vie, société*, vol. 1 (Paris: Éditions de l'EHESS, 1981); Isaac Chiva and Joseph Goy, eds., *Les Baronnies des Pyrénées. Maisons, espace, famille*, vol. 2 (Paris: Éditions de l'EHESS, 1986); Anne Zink, *L'Héritier de la maison. Géographie coutumière du Sud-Ouest de la France sous l'Ancien Régime* (Paris: Éditions EHESS, 1993); Pierre Lamaison, "La diversité des modes de transmission: une géographie tenace," *Etudes rurales* 110–111–112 (1988), pp. 119–75; Emmanuel Le Roy Ladurie, "Système de la coutume. Structures familiales et coutumes d'héritage en France au XVIe siècle," *Annales ESC* 4–5 (1972), pp. 825–46.

4 Between 1789 and 1804, the situation in France was chaotic. As a result, families continued to perpetuate ancient practices. With the implementation of the code in 1804, the egalitarian inheritance laws were forcefully imposed upon families. Yet, its implementation took time to come into full effect.

5 For analysis of the legal changes that emerged during the French Revolution from a historical perspective, see articles by Joseph Goy, "Transmission successorale et paysannerie pendant la Révolution française: un grand malentendu," *Etudes rurales* 110–111–112 (1988), pp. 45–56; Joseph Goy, "Les exclus de la transmission et la loi, 1789–1980," in *Les Exclus de la terre en France et au Quebec (XVIIe–XXe siècles). La reproduction familiale dans la différence*, ed. Gérard Bouchard, John Dickinson, and Joseph Goy (Sillery: Septentrion, 1998), pp. 21–34.

inheritance. In reality and despite the Civil Code, succession practices in the aforementioned region of the Western Pyrenees became gendered, more so than ever before. This contribution will show that Basque families circumvented the new egalitarian law in order to perpetuate some ancient unequal inheritance practices. They negotiated headship and heirship with all the children in order to reach inheritance agreements approved by all. And yet, during these negotiations and agreements, there emerged new gendered inequalities, some of which were more unfavourable to women than to men and might have generated new conflicts between siblings.

1 Sources and Methods

This analysis of gendered inequalities and conflicts in Basque inheritance practices is based upon the data derived from the reconstitution of 120 genealogies and their succession practices over three generations during the period that spanned from the early nineteenth century through the first decades of the twentieth century. In order to constitute the cohort, I selected the first twenty couples who married between 1800 and 1820 that had surviving descendants: twenty couples in each of six villages spread across the region (the four highland villages of Sare, Les Aldudes, Mendive, and Alçay, and the two lowland villages of Mendive and Amendeuix) were selected as case studies. Cross-section analysis of the data from the civil registers (births, marriages, and deaths), inheritance registrations (*Enregistrement*), land records (*Cadastre*), and marriage contracts throughout the period and across the Basque Country led to the complete reconstitution of these 120 genealogies over three generations and dating back to 1800. In the process, the lives of not only these one hundred and twenty couples could be reconstructed but also those of their children (the second generation 567 individuals) and their grandchildren (the third generation 1,039 individuals) who settled in their village, surrounding villages (over a twenty-mile radius), regional towns and cities, or overseas.[6]

The micro-longitudinal analysis of these genealogies will clearly highlight the persistence of some ancient practices regarding single inheritance,

6 The civil registers comprise birth, marriage, and death registers and together contribute to the reconstitution of individuals' life course events and their linkage with other individuals. The *Enregistrement* summarises all legal documents written by the notary: marriage contracts, inheritance arrangements, testaments, and donations. Finally, the *Cadastre* identifies the location, nature, size, and evolution of individual properties.

marriage, and migration in the nineteenth century. Indeed, these families elaborated strategies to avoid the partition of family assets and to secure the full transmission of the family house and land to one child from one generation to the next, as had been the case before the French Revolution and despite the egalitarian laws of the Civil Code of 1804. This chapter will also demonstrate that, because parents could not afford to financially compensate all children equally, compromises were reached in order to solve family conflicts and avoid forced partition. In the process, however, these compromises favoured men more than women, sons often making the best of single inheritance and/or compensations to the detriment of daughters. With time, however, some of the daughters managed to circumvent major inequalities. Still, younger female siblings often suffered greater unequal gendered treatment. As a result of their discontent, parents sometimes granted them greater freedom of movement and choices, allowing them to find new resourceful solutions to make a decent life for themselves outside the village, in cities, or overseas.

I chose to use a gendered approach to analyse Basques' new succession practices from 1800 onward because this perspective makes it possible to draw more in-depth and specific conclusions on inequalities between men and women, between male and female siblings, between siblings of the same birth order, and between siblings of different birth order. The goal of this micro-longitudinal analysis from a gender perspective applied to the study of past populations is thus to construct more thorough observations and conclusions that highlight significant gender and birth rank inequalities between male and female siblings despite the law. In the process, I will observe that over time women resisted inequalities to a greater and greater extent. In order to avoid conflicts, women were given the chance to use their personal resources (*baggages*) and capacities (*capabilities*) to circumvent these inequalities and have access to new opportunities for a decent, perhaps better life (*empowerment*).[7]

7 A number of authors have offered extensive analysis of the benefits of the use of a gender approach in the study of past populations, most notably Joan W. Scott, *De l'utilité du genre* (Paris: Fayard, 2012); Joan W. Scott, "Genre: une catégorie utile d'analyse historique," *Les cahiers du GRIF* "Le Genre de l'Histoire", 37–38 (1988), pp. 125–53; Nancy L. Green, "L'histoire comparative et le champ des études migratoires," *Annales ESC* 6 (1990), pp. 1335–50, and Françoise Thébaud, *Écrire l'histoire des femmes et du genre* (Lyon: ENS Éditions, 2007); Françoise Thébaud, "Une démographie au féminin," in *Une démographie au féminin – A Female Demography. Risques et opportunités dans le parcours de vie – Risks and Changes in the Life Course*, ed. Michel Oris, Guy Brunet, Virginie De Luca Barrusse, and Danielle Gauvreau (Bern: Peter Lang, 2009), pp. 5–23, among many others.

2 Inheritance According to Customs in the Old Regime

In order to evaluate new gender inequalities and potential conflict solutions in new inheritance strategies since 1800, it is important to explain how the old system worked before the French Revolution. The ancient Pyrenean customs or *Fors* were, depending on provinces, written in either the fifteenth or the sixteenth century.[8] They outlined ancient succession practices implemented in order to protect landownership, especially small and medium-sized properties. In the interest of the family house (the farm and land) and the family lineage within the community, the customs imposed single impartible inheritance, and therewith, the full transmission of family assets to one child in each generation.[9] These practices in the Pyrenees led to the emergence of the "house system",[10] a system which forbade property partition between children

8 In 1454, King Charles VII of France ordered the codification of the local oral regulations related to family, property, and inheritance in each of the provinces of France. He demanded that local *parlements* transcribe all these regulations and these new codes or *Fors* be approved by local *parlements*. The local customs, specific to each province, became written laws protected by the king and implemented locally up until the French Revolution.

9 While Basque customs, as well as those of the Lavedan and the Barège valleys, imposed primogeniture regardless of gender or *aînesse intégrale* (Cordier, *Droit de famille*), Bearn customs imposed male primogeniture, see Jacques Poumarède, *Les Successions dans le Sud-Ouest de la France au Moyen Age* (Paris: Presses Universitaires de France, 1972); Jacques Poumarède, "Famille et ténure dans les Pyrénées du Moyen Age au XIXe siècle," *Annales de démographie historique* (1979), pp. 347–60. Families in the Baronnies sometimes had more flexible inheritance traditions than male primogeniture, see Antoinette Fauve-Chamoux, "Le fonctionnement de la famille-souche dans les Baronnies des Pyrénées avant 1914," *Annales de démographie historique* (1987), pp. 241–62; Antoinette Fauve-Chamoux, "Household Forms and Living Standards in Preindustrial France: from Models to Realities," *Journal of Family History* 18–2 (1993), pp. 135–56; Antoinette Fauve-Chamoux, "The Stem Family, Demography and Inheritance," in *The European Peasant Family and Economy*, ed. David J. Siddle (Liverpool: Liverpool University Press, 1995), pp. 86–113. Finally, French Catalunian customs imposed male inheritance regardless of birth order, see Louis Assier-Andrieu, *Coutume et rapports sociaux. Etude anthropologique des communautés paysannes du Capcir* (Paris: Éditions du CNRS, 1981); Louis Assier-Andrieu, ed., *Une France coutumière. Enquête sur les "usages locaux" et leur codification (XIXe–XXe siècles)* (Paris: Éditions du CNRS, 1990). For additional comparative details on these practices, see Anne Zink's reference book on these issues *L'Héritier de la maison.*

10 The first reformer to propose a discussion of what characterised the "house system" and how it worked in the Pyrenees was Frédéric Le Play: Frédéric Le Play, *L'Organisation de la famille selon le vrai modèle signalé par l'histoire de toutes les races et de tous les temps* (Paris: Tequi, 1871); Frédéric Le Play, *La Réforme sociale en France déduite de l'observation comparée des peuples européens*, 3 vols. (Paris: Dentu, 1878); a discussion taken up by a number of authors who specialise on the Pyrenees such as, among others, Chiva and Goy, *Les Baronnies des Pyrénées*, vols. 1 and 2; and André Etchelecou, *Transition démographique*

and imposed cohabitation between generations for the sake of the economic viability of the farm, of the family unit, and of the lineage within the community.[11] Most importantly, this system guaranteed the economic and demographic equilibrium of communities, allowing only a stable population to establish and reproduce, and maintaining a stable number of farms to exploit the agricultural resources of the community.[12]

Thus, the Pyrenean customs determined families' specific succession regulations and in so doing, each individual's roles, rights, and obligations to the house. Single heirs (male in most of the regions) were sole owners of the farm. They were in charge of its full transmission to the next generation but were not allowed to dispose of it (even partially) without their siblings' approval. In exchange for inheritance, residency, and authority within the house, single heirs and their spouses signed marriage contracts that required cohabitation with surviving parents and their unmarried children. Those who permanently departed from the house were provided for and settled comfortably. Thus, single inheritance in the Pyrenees in the old regime was a strategy to guarantee

---

et système coutumier dans les Pyrénées occidentales (Paris: Presses Universitaires de France, 1991), and Fauve-Chamoux, "Household Forms and Living Standards".

11 On inheritance practices in other parts of France, see publications by Louis Assier-Andrieu, *Une France coutumière*; George Augustins, *Comment se perpétuer? Devenir des lignées et destins des patrimoines dans les paysanneries européennes* (Nanterre: Société d'ethnologie française, 1989); Béaur, "Land Transmission"; Rolande Bonnain, Gérard Bouchard, and Joseph Goy, eds., *Transmettre, hériter, succéder. La reproduction familiale en milieu rural: France – Québec, XVIIIe–XXe siècles* (Lyon: Presses Universitaires de Lyon, 1992); Gérard Bouchard, Joseph Goy, and Anne-Lise Head-König, eds., *Problèmes de la transmission des exploitations agricoles (XVIIIe–XXe siècles)* (Rome: Editions de l'Ecole française de Rome, 1998); Lamaison, "La diversité des modes", and Le Roy Ladurie, "Système de la coutume".

12 Previous to the French Revolution, property owners controlled land use within the community, including public land. In order to maintain their economic stability, they decided not to allow new farmers to become established in the community. They only authorised the sale of land of those who went bankrupt or were without descendants. Small plots of land were put up for sale, but these were usually bought by other owners established in the community. Margareth Lanzinger found similar practices in Innichen in the nineteenth century, in *Das gesicherte Erbe. Heirat in familialen und lokalen Kontexten, Innichen 1700–1900* (Vienna, Cologne, and Weimar: Böhlau, 2003). With the French Revolution, however, new farms were formed in France, allowing excluded children to establish themselves in the communities; Nadine Vivier shows this in *Propriété collective et identité communale. Les biens communaux en France, 1750–1914* (Paris: Publications de la Sorbonne, 1998). For a recent discussion of the relations between demography, economic resources, family behaviour, and population adaptation strategies to economic resources, see also the article by Thierry Eggerickk, "Régimes et transitions démographiques en Europe de l'Ouest. Un essai de synthèse," *Annales de Démographie Historique* 1 (2015), pp. 113–48.

continuity and perpetuity to families, lineages, and communities. While it secured a durable, honourable position for the single heirs and their spouses, it also burdened them with responsibilities for and obligations to the other household members. One of these obligations was cohabitation, several generations living together as stem families.[13] These households usually comprised

13 The stem family was indeed a traditional household form in the Basque Country: a three-generation household comprising two couples, one from each generation, living together under the same roof with their respective unmarried children. This argument was discussed by Maïte Lafourcade in *Mariages en Labourd sous l'Ancien Régime. Les contrats de mariage du pays de Labourd sous le règne de Louis XVI* (Bilbao: Universitad del País Vasco, 1989); Cordier, *Droit de famille*; and Fougères, *Les Droits de famille*. This was also a traditional household form elsewhere in the Pyrenees, see: Antoinette Fauve-Chamoux, "Les structures familiales au Royaume des familles-souches: Esparros," *Annales ESC* 3 (1984), pp. 514–28; Fauve-Chamoux, "Le fonctionnement"; Fauve-Chamoux, "The Stem Family"; Antoinette Fauve-Chamoux, "Strategies of Household Continuity in a Stem-Family Society: from Heirship to Headship," in *When Dad Died. Individuals and Families Coping with Distress in Past Societies*, ed. Renzo Derosas and Michel Oris (Bern: Peter Lang, 2002), pp. 121–39; Agnès Fine-Souriac, "La famille-souche pyrénéenne au XIXe siècle. Quelques réflexions de méthode," *Annales ESC* 3 (1987), pp. 478–87; Michel Verdon, "The Stem Family: Toward a General Theory," *Journal of Interdisciplinary History* 10–1 (1979), pp. 87–105; Michel Verdon, "Rethinking Complex Households: the Case of the Western Pyrenean 'Houses'," *Continuity and Change* 11–2 (1996), pp. 191–215; in France: Alain Collomp, *La maison du père. Famille et village en Haute-Provence aux XVIIe et XVIIIe siècles* (Paris: Presses Universitaires de France, 1983); Gérard Béaur, "Land Transmission and Inheritance Practices"; Jean Yver, *Égalité entre héritiers et exclusion des enfants dotés: essai de géographie coutumière* (Paris: Éditions Sirey, 1966); in Europe: Augustins, *Comment se perpétuer*; Bouchard, Goy, and Head-König, *Problèmes de transmission*; Bouchard, Dickinson, and Goy, *Les Exclus de la terre*; David R. Green and Alastair Owens, eds., *Family Welfare. Gender, Property, and Inheritance since the Seventeenth Century* (Westport, Conn.: Praeger, 2004); Anne-Lise Head-König, in collaboration with Péter Pozsgai, eds., *Inheritance Practices, Marriage Strategies and Household Formation* (Turnhout: Brepols, 2012); in America: a comparison between Canada and Europe with Gérard Béaur, Christian Dessureault, and Joseph Goy, eds., *Familles, terre, marchés. Logiques économiques et stratégies dans les milieux ruraux (XVIIe–XXe siècles)* (Rennes: Presses Universitaires de Rennes, 2004); Bonnain, Bouchard, and Goy, *Transmettre, hériter, succéder*; Christian Dessureault, John Dickinson, and Joseph Goy, eds., *Famille et marché (XVIe–XXe siècles)* (Sillery: Septentrion, 2003); Luigi Lorenzetti, Anne-Lise Head-König, and Joseph Goy, eds., *Marchés, migrations et logiques familiales dans les espaces français, canadien et Suisse, 18e–20e siècles* (Genève: Peter Lang, 2005); and in Asia: a comparison between Europe and Asia from Antoinette Fauve-Chamoux, "La reproduction familiale en milieu paysan: le destin des exclus," in *Les Exclus de la terre en France et au Quebec (XVIIe–XXe siècles). La reproduction familiale dans la différence*, ed. Gérard Bouchard, John Dickinson, and Joseph Goy (Sillery: Septentrion, 1998), pp. 73–91; Antoinette Fauve-Chamoux and Emiko Ochiai, eds., *The Stem Family in Eurasian Perspective. Revisiting House Societies, 17th–20th Centuries* (Bern: Peter Lang, 2009).

the aging parents, the single heir and spouse in charge of the inheritance and their children, and finally the heir's unmarried adult siblings still living in the house.[14] At this point, responsibilities and authority were legally and officially shared between parents and heirs (young and old masters). When both parents grew too old or died, all powers were transferred to the young heir.

The three Basque *Fors* were among the Pyrenean customs.[15] As opposed to other Pyrenean *Fors*, Basque customs required that the single heir was the first-born child, male or female, unless that child was unfit for headship and heirship (poor health, mental incapacity, or incompatibility of character).[16] This practice, known as *aînesse intégrale* (primogeniture regardless of gender) was rigorously implemented in the old regime in the Basque Country, and marriage contracts determined the rights and obligations of the young heirs or heiresses and their spouses to their parents, to the unmarried siblings and to the house. Though discontent and disagreements might have emerged, the younger children had no legal right to oppose the implementation of single inheritance at the time.

While the first-born, male or female child inherited the entirety of the house and land, his or her younger siblings (male or female) were only entitled to the *légitime*, that part of the family assets which parents acquired over the course of their marriage and which they later used to compensate younger sons and daughters when they married or emigrated. As marriage contracts from that

14 Le Play, *L'Organisation de la famille*, and Le Play, *La Réforme sociale*; Frédéric Le Play, Emile Cheysson, Bayard, and Fernand Butel, *Les Mélouga. Une famille pyrénéenne au XIXe siècle. Textes réunis par Alain Chenu* (Paris: Nathan, 1994). Frédéric Le Play was the first to describe the Pyrenean house system and stem family form and how vital these were for the economic survival of Pyrenean families and communities in the nineteenth century. Using censuses, Peter Laslett argued the contrary. He believed that the most prevalent household system in Western Europe was the simple family household (composed of a couple and their children) and that the stem family household was marginal. Peter Laslett and Richard Wall, eds., *Household and Family in Past Time. Comparative Studies in the Size and Structure of the Domestic Group over the Last Three Centuries* (Cambridge: Cambridge University Press, 1972). Lutz Beckner responded to Peter Laslett arguing that the best way to analyse household forms was not through the study of census lists but through the analysis of the life-cycle evolution of the household. This micro-longitudinal method clearly shows that households were often formed as stem families at the beginning and the end of the life-cycle evolution of the household. Lutz K. Berkner, "The Stem-Family and the Developmental Cycle of the Peasant Household: An Eighteenth-Century Austrian Example," *American Historical Review* 77–2 (1972), pp. 398–418. This debate later led Peter Laslett to reconsider his views on the matter. Peter Laslett, Richard Wall, and Jean Robin, eds., *Family Forms in Historical Europe* (Cambridge: Cambridge University Press, 1983).

15 For details on the three Basque provinces and *Fors*, see notes 2 and 3 above.

16 Lafourcade, *Mariages en Labourd*, pp. 47–53.

time stipulated, single heirs or heiresses need not wait until their parents died to become masters of the farm. Upon marriage, they were secured full inheritance and were known as the young masters of the house (*maîtres jeunes*). With their spouses, they assumed shared authority with their parents as co-seigneurs or co-managers of the house and land.[17] In return for these privileges, the customs or *Fors* imposed cohabitation as stem families: the young couple having to feed and care for aging parents and unmarried siblings residing with them. These stipulations thus guaranteed a decent life and retirement to all those living under the same roof.[18]

For the sake of the house and the family, and dependent on their parents' approval, heirs or heiresses were to marry persons of similar socio-economic background who originated from the same or a nearby village, and whose parents were farmers of equal status.[19] Social endogamy and homogamy (marriage within the same social and professional environment) were thus prerequisites for heirs' or heiresses' marriages. Another precondition to marriage was the obligation for spouses to bring a dowry into the marriage in order to "pay" for their place in the house.[20] In this manner, spouses were secured lifetime residence, care, and retirement in the house. Regardless of gender, the dowry was worth a portion of the value of the inherited assets. It was a cash sum of money to be available immediately upon marriage. Despite their investment in the house, these spouses (male or female) had no ownership rights over the assets inherited by heirs or heiresses. They were entitled only to participate in the management of the house and to lifelong residence and care. They only became full managers of the house with usufruct rights when the heir or the heiress died young and with underage children, and even then only until one of the children – the new heir or heiress – married into the house.[21] In the end, heirs or heiresses and their spouses had similar obligations as co-seigneurs, co-managers, and co-transmitters of the family house and land. The male or female spouses, however, never enjoyed property rights; these remained the sole prerogative of heirs or heiresses.[22]

The dowry of the heirs' or heiresses' spouses played an essential role in the property transmission strategies of the old regime, because it was used to pay debts or compensate one or even two siblings upon their permanent departure

---

17 Lafourcade, *Mariages en Labourd*, pp. 164–67.
18 Lafourcade, *Mariages en Labourd*, pp. 54–57 and 140–44.
19 Lafourcade, *Mariages en Labourd*, pp. 108–10.
20 Lafourcade, *Mariages en Labourd*, pp. 67–70.
21 Lafourcade, *Mariages en Labourd*, pp. 206–11.
22 Lafourcade, *Mariages en Labourd*, pp. 57–60; Zink, *L'Héritier de la maison*, pp. 180–87.

from the house. The dowry was used to allow a sibling to marry into a propertied family in the village or nearby, to enter religious orders, or to emigrate. When families could not collect more than one dowry, younger male or female siblings lived celibate in the family house with the heir or heiress, participating in activities around the farm and enjoying room, board, and care throughout life under the authority of the heir or heiress. This right, known as *droit de chaise*, secured a livelihood for siblings excluded from succession, allowed them to participate in decision-making, and guaranteed them social status in the community (a lower one than heirs', though).[23]

On 4 August 1789, the representatives of the French *Parlement* in Paris decided to abolish all privileges, of which local customs or *Fors* were a part, and to elaborate the Civil Code into a newly unified, centralised legal system that secured equality between siblings, male or female, across France. This decision had a great impact in the Western Pyrenees because it endangered the ancient "house system".[24] It made single inheritance illegal. In the process, it threatened the economic and demographic equilibrium of communities, in particular small and medium-sized properties, which faced impoverishment and sometimes bankruptcy as a result of equal partition. Resistance arose when the Civil Code of 1804 was enforced. As a result, propertied Basque families turned to notary officials in order to find the legal tools necessary to circumvent the law and perpetuate some aspects of their customs. They subsequently elaborated new strategies by adapting old practices to the new law, using the new prerogatives of the Civil Code to transmit a majority of assets to one child, as had been the case in the old regime, and to gain the support of the excluded children. All siblings were engaged in negotiations to perpetuate single inheritance. They ultimately, willingly or unwillingly, signed agreements that revealed new inequalities, and these were particularly detrimental to women.

3 New Inheritance Practices with the Civil Code of 1804

In the new law, propertied Basque families saw the potential for partition to cause succession conflicts and even bankruptcy. With the help of notary

23 For a comparative study of the customs in the Western Pyrenees in the old regime, see Zink, *L'Héritier de la maison*, pp. 160–75.

24 Frédérick Le Play offered a long discussion on the negative impact of the implementation of the egalitarian law of the Civil Code on successions in the Pyrenees in the nineteenth century. See Le Play, *L'Organisation de la famille*, and *La Réforme sociale*.

officials, they endeavoured to limit the risk of equal partition and found solutions to perpetuate single inheritance. According to the new law, families could not transfer the entire estate to one child, as they had done previously. In addition, single heirs or heiresses were no longer guaranteed full ownership of family assets, and certainly not upon marriage. Instead, they had to wait until both parents died to own some of the shares of inheritance previously conveyed upon marriage. It took even longer to legally collect siblings' shares. As the discussion below will show, this process lasted a lifetime, and necessitated agreements that took place when marriage contracts, testaments, and donations were signed.[25] What were the new strategies Basque families elaborated in the nineteenth century in an attempt to perpetuate single inheritance? What agreements were reached? How was conflict avoided?

Considering property size (mostly small or medium) and the limited economic opportunities for land acquisition in the Basque Country during the nineteenth century, families believed that single inheritance must prevail if they were to maintain family possession and the viability of their farms.[26] Farms were too small to survive multiple partitions. It was therefore crucial that only one child inherited the assets and that the other siblings departed from the house, with an exception being if one or two accepted celibacy and subordination in the home. This analysis of the reconstitution of 120 families shows that nineteenth century Basque families were successful in perpetuating single inheritance, selecting one child to live and work on the farm, and thus securing stability for the house and continuity for the lineage. Rare were

25 Few studies on traditional succession strategies in the Basque Country were published in the nineteenth century (Cordier, *Droit de famille*). Most appeared in the twentieth century, and underscored families' efforts to perpetuate traditional single inheritance practices over time despite the Civil Code. See Andrew Abelson, "Inheritance and Population Control in a Basque Valley before 1900," *Peasant Studies* 7–1 (1978), pp. 11–27; Ramón Barcelo, "Transmission héréditaire et systèmes de production: le cas de la Soule (Pyrénées-Atlantiques)," *Sociologie du travail* 3 (1988), pp. 443–60; Dolores Comas d'Argemir and Jean-François Soulet, eds., *La familía als Pirineus* (Andorre: Impremta Solber, 1993); William A. Douglass, *Etchalar and Murelaga. Opportunity and Rural Exodus in Two Spanish Basque Villages* (New York: St Martin's Press, 1975); William A. Douglass, "The Basque Stem-Family Household: Myth or Reality?," *Journal of Family History* 73–1 (1988), pp. 75–89; Etchelecou, *Transition démographique*; Fougères, *Les Droits de famille*; Verdon, "The Stem Family"; Verdon, "Rethinking Complex Households".

26 In the early nineteenth century, some common land was sold to landless younger sons or *cadets* in order to allow them to settle as sheepherders in *borda* shacks (sheepherders' summer housing in the mountains). Yet, this was not enough to allow the growing landless population to make a living in the local rural communities, hence massive emigration from the Pyrenees to cities and overseas, especially after 1840. See Nadine Vivier, *Propriété collective et identité communale*, esp. the third part.

the families that had no child to inherit the estate. When this happened, the assets were either sold or, as in most cases, transferred to a more distant relative (usually a niece or a nephew). In addition, as in the old regime, property owners and their single heir or heiress cohabitated as stem families – two couples, one from each generation, and their respective unmarried children living together and sharing the output of the farm.[27] Through such cohabitation, old and young couples shared decisions. Subsequently, as parents aged, young heirs assumed more authority and responsibility. This cohabitation was, however, not always peaceful. Sometimes parents retained full authority over decisions, forcing the heir, but more often heiress, to obey – hence the departure of many first-born sons eager for greater freedom. It was only when both parents died that the young couple assumed sole headship and full authority over the house and land.

Indeed, family reconstitutions highlight that nineteenth century Basque families perpetuated single inheritance, but the data also indicate that these practices evolved over time (see Table 5.1). Parents showed greater flexibility in their choice of heirs. As the data in Table 5.1 below clearly show, during the first half of the nineteenth century the majority of Basque families (52.2 percent) reproduced the *aînesse intégrale* of the old regime by transmitting assets to the first-born child, male or female. By the second half of the century, with massive post-1840 transcontinental emigration, they still transferred the house and land to only one child, but now to any one of the children, be it first-born (38.7 percent) or younger (61.3 percent), male or female. In addition, the data indicate that inheritance practices favoured women over men, as was the case at the time in other parts of the Pyrenees and Cantal (Central France), and as a

27 Marie-Pierre Arrizabalaga, "The Stem Family in the French Basque Country: Sare in the Nineteenth Century," *Journal of Family History* 1 (1997), pp. 50–69, and Marie-Pierre Arrizabalaga, "Structures familiales et destins migratoires à Sare au XIXe siècle," *Lapurdum* 2 (1997), pp. 237–55. As Frédéric Le Play showed for Pyrenean families, but contrary to Peter Laslett's arguments regarding simple family households being the most prevalent in Western Europe, this research proved that nineteenth-century Basque households continued, as had been the case in the old regime, to take on the form of stem families. As Berkner has convincingly demonstrated, this family form was more common than Peter Laslett argued. Indeed, it did not last the entire life-cycle evolution of the household and could therefore not be observed in every census. This was because this household form prevailed at the beginning and/or the end of the life cycle: when the heir or heiress married into the house and cohabitated with his or her parents. Thus, when looking into the entire life-cycle evolution of the nineteenth century households in the Basque Country, I observed that Basque households did, as in the old regime, take on the form of stem families at one point in the cycle.

result of massive emigration.[28] Indeed, among second-generation heirs around the mid-nineteenth century, 55.6 percent of the 52.2 percent first-born heirs were heiresses. Subsequently, among third-generation heirs in the late nineteenth century, only 38.7 percent were first-born heirs, 65.1 percent of whom were women. All in all, during the period women inherited more often than men (53.6 percent among the second generation and 55.9 percent among the third generation), and these women were either first-born or younger daughters.[29] The data seemed to suggest that, indeed, some daughters were treated more favourably than sons. And yet, further analysis will prove otherwise in regard to these heiresses and their sisters.

There are several reasons why fewer first-born or younger sons accepted heirship and headship in the family house. In the nineteenth century, some first-born sons and their younger male siblings became more and more resentful of the expectation that they obey their parents, and took advantage of the new economic opportunities other than inheritance to build a new life and perhaps to do better. It was clear that propertied parents had increased difficulty imposing old inheritance rules upon these young men. As a result, parents chose their first-born or younger daughters. In other cases, parents encouraged the departure of older sons in order to reduce the cost of living

---

28 Similar conclusions were reached regarding other Pyrenean families who transmitted family assets to daughters (first-born or younger) in Bearn: Christine Lacanette-Pommel, *La famille dans les Pyrénées. De la coutume au code Napoléon* (Estadens: PyréGraph, 2003); in the Baronnies: Rolande Bonnain, "Migration, exclusion et solidarité," in *Les Exclus de la terre en France et au Quebec (XVIIe–XXe siècles). La reproduction familiale dans la différence*, ed. Gérard Bouchard, John Dickinson, and Joseph Goy (Sillery: Septentrion, 1998), pp. 271–90; in Esparros: Fauve-Chamoux, "Le fonctionnement"; Fauve-Chamoux, "The Stem Family", and in Cantal in Central France (where according to Rose Duroux 60 percent of heirs were women): Rose Duroux, "Temporary Male Migration and Female Power in a Stem-Family Society: the Case of 19th Century Auvergne," in *Family Welfare. Gender, Property, and Inheritance since the Seventeenth Century*, ed. David R. Green and Alastair Owens (Westport, Conn.: Praeger, 2004), pp. 47–71. This practice had a tremendous effect on inheritance strategies and household structures, see Chiva and Goy, *Les Baronnies des Pyrénées*, vols. 1 and 2; Fauve-Chamoux, "La reproduction familiale"; Fauve-Chamoux, "Strategies of Household Continuity"; Antoinette Fauve-Chamoux, "Le rôle des femmes dans la transmission des biens en France," in *Famille et marché (XVIe–XXe siècles)*, ed. Christian Dessureault, John Dickinson, and Joseph Goy (Sillery: Septentrion, 2003), pp. 245–60.

29 See Marie-Pierre Arrizabalaga, "Les héritières de la maison au Pays Basque au XIXe siècle," *Lapurdum* 7 (2002), pp. 35–55; Marie-Pierre Arrizabalaga, "Female Primogeniture in the French Basque Country," in *The Logic of Female Succession: Rethinking Patriarchy and Patrilineality in Global and Historical Perspective*, ed. Emiko Ochiai (Kyoto: International Research Centre of Japanese Studies, 2002), pp. 31–52.

TABLE 5.1 Single inheritance in the nineteenth-century Basque Country according to sex and birth order among the second- and third-generation cohorts (percentage)*

Generation	Second generation			Third generation		
Birth rank / Status	Heiress	Heir	Total	Heiress	Heir	Total
First-born Child	55.6	44.4	52.2	65.1	34.9	38.7
Younger Child	51.5	48.5	47.8	50	50	61.3
Total	53.6	46.4	100 (N=69)	55.9	44.1	100 (N=111)

* The data (derived from the 120 genealogies above presented) concern the children (second-generation) and the grandchildren (third-generation) of the 120 couples who married in the early nineteenth century

on the farm resulting from greater demographic pressure. These sons took advantage of the new opportunities to depart to cities (with industrialization) or overseas (with emigration to the Americas) to make a decent living. There were yet other first-born sons who refused heirship and headship because it required that they married late, at 30 or later, and wait until some of their siblings had departed from the house before having families of their own. Rather than wait, these men chose to get married younger (before 30) to, for example, a local heiress. A few chose to remain celibate at home (being taken care of by the heir or heiress) or entered priesthood. Most, however, emigrated to the Americas, where they sometimes fared so well that they never envisioned returning home. Others did return, with sizable savings that they used to marry into wealthier families, and in the process experienced upward social mobility.

In order to illustrate the configuration mentioned above we will analyse the family of E. Marie and Jean-Baptiste, a couple who married in 1841. She was the heiress of a house and five hectares of land, while he brought a dowry of 2,000 francs into the marriage. Together, they had three children: Martin, Jeanne-Marie, and Pierre, first, second, and third-born respectively. Martin and Pierre emigrated to the Americas, leaving Jeanne-Marie to take over the family farm. It is difficult to tell whether this situation resulted from conflicts over authority in the house, but neither of the two sons returned from the Americas in order to assume heirship. They transferred their rights to the house to their sister, Jeanne-Marie, who married Pierre, a hotel owner, in 1876 at the age of 30. What is striking about this family story is that Jeanne-Marie waited until both parents died (her mother in 1857 and her father in 1876) before getting married and settling into the family house with her husband. She thus avoided facing parental approval for marriage and enjoyed full authority in the house. It is possible that none of the three children wanted to share decisions with their father (who had taken over his wife's family house after her death in 1857), which could have been why the two sons emigrated and the daughter married only after her father's death.[30]

As a result of sons' departures, daughters were sometimes the only option available for passing on an inheritance, and many were willing to assume the responsibilities of headship and heirship.[31] It was an honourable life choice that secured them status. Their parents, moreover, might have perceived them as being more docile and reliable. Perhaps these daughters were more willing to accept subordination to parents than their brothers. In any case, what was most important for propertied parents was that the most hard-working, compatible, and amenable child took over the family business and looked after them in old age, and many women (first-born or younger ones) were among those chosen.[32] Another constraint was that single heirs or heiresses had to accept a "proper" marriage and subordination. As in the past, their marital practices were generally endogamous and homogamous, involving men and women of similar professional and social background, whose parents were propertied farmers of equal status in the community or nearby. These families welcomed spouses with a sizable dowry to pay their place into the family house and compensate excluded children. Only daughters who had given

---

30 This case study is one of the family reconstitutions, derived from the data drawn from the civil registers and the inheritance registers presented in the early part of the chapter. The collected data indicated who the children were, what happened to them over time, and how property was distributed after both parents' death.

31 Marie-Pierre Arrizabalaga, "Migrations féminines – migrations masculines: des comportements différenciés au sein des familles basques au XIXe siècle," in *Marchés, migrations et logiques familiales dans les espaces français, canadien et suisse, 18e–20e siècles*, ed. Luigi Lorenzetti, Anne-Lise Head-König, and Joseph Goy (Bern: Peter Lang, 2005), pp. 183–195; Marie-Pierre Arrizabalaga, "Destins de femmes dans les Pyrénées au XIXe siècle: le cas basque," *Annales de Démographie Historique* 2 (2006), pp. 135–70.

32 In other parts of France, inheritance systems were less favourable to women, see: Augustins, *Comment se perpétuer*; Béaur, "Le marché foncier"; Béaur, "La transmission des exploitations"; Béaur, "Land Transmission and Inheritance Practices"; Bonnain, Bouchard, and Goy, *Transmettre, hériter, succéder*; Collomp, *La maison du père*; Derouet, "Pratiques successorales"; Derouet, "Le partage des frères"; Derouet, "Transmettre la terre"; Lamaison, "La diversité des modes"; Martine Segalen, *Quinze générations de Bas-Bretons. Parenté et Société dans le Pays Bigouden Sud, 1720–1980* (Paris: Presses Universitaires de France, 1985); and Yver, *Égalité entre héritiers*.

birth to illegitimate children were systematically excluded from heirship and headship.

Propertied families thus sacrificed the traditional rule of primogeniture regardless of gender (*aînesse intégrale*) in order to adopt a more flexible system of single inheritance regardless of gender and birth order, and one that apparently benefited women. These sacrifices had specific rationales. They served the interests of the house as well as the parents' personal concern for peaceful retirement, full succession, and uninterrupted lineage.[33] They also served the interests of some of the children, both men and women, to a certain extent but – as the demonstration below will show – differently.

4 New Family Strategies for Single Inheritance

The selection of the single heir was the first step in the new prevailing single inheritance practices, but the transmission of all assets to the selected child remained as yet a complex issue. It was vital for parents transferring the inheritance to preserve the house intact, but in a manner rendering it viable for its residents from one generation to the next. In this context, the new inheritance strategies needed to satisfy other specific requirements. They had to fit within the prerogatives of the egalitarian law, and at the same time be approved by all family members. This process led to long, complex negotiations toward a final agreement following the deaths of both parents. These agreements evidenced unequal treatment on the basis of the birth rank and sex of the children. Sons and daughters were expected to manifest generosity, self-sacrifice, and abnegation for the sake of the house and parents' peaceful retirements. And, as analysis of the data revealed, they – especially daughters – willingly or unwillingly, did.

The first legal step in the enforcement of single inheritance occurred at the time of signing the marriage contract between the single heir or heiress and his or her spouse, and therefore just before the marriage. Contrary to customs established in the old regime, parents could no longer transfer all family assets to the selected child upon marriage, but rather partially and gradually. This process toward the complete transmission of the settlement continued until the parents died. As it had become illegal for parents to transfer all assets to one child and disown the other children, new strategies needed to be established.

33 Lineage was not a question of gender in Basque tradition. It did not matter whether succession went down to daughters, because what mattered was the transmission of the house and its name, rather than the family name.

The data indicate that all marriage contracts secured the separation of marital property, protecting each person's inherited assets. The selected child was granted the extra share of assets upon marriage, a transfer of one-quarter to one-half of the assets, depending on the number of siblings. According to article 913 of the Civil Code, a property owner could bequeath an extra share of the inheritance to one child during his or her lifetime, and this share was not to be counted as part of the inheritance to be divided equally among the children.[34] Since most nineteenth-century Basque families had three or four children, the extra share usually amounted to one-quarter of the assets, which the preferred child received upon marriage. The rest (seventy-five percent of the assets) were to be distributed equally among all the children upon the parents' death. The succession records and marriage contracts of the Basque family sample reveal the systematic use of article 913. In addition to his or her extra share (worth, as mentioned above, one quarter of the assets), the heir or heiress could anticipate receiving his or her legal share (out of the remaining seventy-five percent share): each receiving twenty-five percent of the assets with three children in the family, nineteen percent with four children, or fifteen percent with five children. At this stage, it is clear that these strategies were not sufficient to prevent partition.

The second stage in single inheritance also took place upon the marriage of the heir or heiress and involved the spouse's dowry. The value of the dowry had to equal the extra share that the heir or heiress received upon marriage, usually twenty-five percent of the assets. In addition, it had to be available immediately. The dowry was used to buy the inheritance shares of the heir's or heiress' siblings. Depending on the number of siblings, the young couple as a unit became the sole owner of sixty-five percent to seventy-five percent of the assets upon the death of the parents: the heir's or heiress' extra share worth twenty-five percent of the assets; the twenty-five percent of siblings' assets bought with the spouse's dowry; and the heir's or heiress' legal share, worth fifteen to twenty-five percent of the assets. In any case, the young couple was certain to possess more than half of the assets. As a consequence, they were legally entitled to block a partition and prevent the sale of the house and land.[35] At this

34 Legally, this extra share could only amount to one-half with one child, one-third with two children, and one-quarter of the value of the assets with three or more children. In the nineteenth century this article was systematically used by propertied Basque families to legally transmit a larger portion of the assets to one child and with an average of three children per family, this portion was usually worth twenty-five percent of the assets.

35 For more details see Marie-Pierre Arrizabalaga, "Stratégies de l'indivision et rapport à la terre après le Code civil: le cas basque au XIXe siècle," in *Familles, terre, marchés. Logiques économiques et stratégies dans les milieux ruraux (XVIIe–XXe siècles)*, ed. Gérard Béaur,

stage, however, the full transmission remained incomplete. Solutions had to be found to avoid conflict and partition. It was in the implementation of this third stage that substantial inequalities emerged, some that discriminated against women, regardless of status and birth ranks, more so than men.

5 Gender Inequality with New Inheritance Practices, despite the Civil Code

5.1 *Heirs, Heiresses, and Their Spouses*

As a result of the extra share (worth twenty-five percent of the assets) and the dowry (worth twenty-five percent of the assets) being invested into the house upon marriage and used to compensate siblings, the young couple (the heir or heiress and their spouse) should have shared equal status within and power over the house and land. Indeed, upon marriage, they had control over fifty percent of the assets, half of which came from the extra share, and the other half from the dowry. Thereafter the young heir or heiress and his or her spouse had until both of the parents died to acquire the other siblings' legal shares. It was in the course of the acquisition of siblings' shares that new gender inequalities emerged between the heir or heiress and his or her spouse, and between siblings, male and female. These inequalities became visible in analysis of succession records. The documents identify the agreements stipulated in the marriage contracts and testaments. Upon a person's death, the French authorities required notary officials to declare the content of the deceased person's marriage contract (the value of the extra share, the dowry, the mutual donation agreements), as well as other family contracts, testaments, and inheritance registrations (agreements and bequests) when siblings or children had died before the deceased person.[36]

These succession documents show how the new law was enforced. The heirs' or heiresses' spouses only agreed to transfer their dowries to their in-laws if they received some compensation or recognition in return. And they did, thanks to the Civil Code marital property clause[37] that Basque families used

Christian Dessureault, and Joseph Goy (Rennes: Presses Universitaires de Rennes, 2004), pp. 171–83.

36 For details on this issue, see Marie-Pierre Arrizabalaga, "Gender and Migration in the Pyrenees in the Nineteenth Century: Gender-Differentiated Patterns and Destinies," in *Female Economic Strategies in the Modern World*, ed. Beatrice Moring (London: Pickring & Chatto, 2012), pp. 127–44.

37 The marital property clause of the Civil Code is known as *donation mutuelle entre époux*.

to guarantee rights to these spouses. The clause not only secured spouses' lifelong residence in the house, but also provided for a mutual donation of half of the other spouse's assets when deceased, all in usufruct or half in usufruct and half in property. This mutual donation was, however, reduced by half when the heir or heiress of the next generation was selected and received the extra share from the house owner as part of his or her marriage contract (that is, twenty-five percent of the assets in property).[38]

New gender inequalities emerged during these negotiations. As mentioned earlier, the dowry (equal to the extra share) was systematically absorbed into the house. As a result, the heir or heiress and spouse should have had equal rights over the assets, and therefore equal power of decision within the house. This, however, was not the case, because by the time the spouse died, the mutual bequest had usually been reduced to a quarter of the assets in usufruct, the other quarter having been transferred to the heir or heiress of the next generation. This was illegal according to the Civil Code because the dowry had been absorbed into the house through the purchase of the siblings' shares. As a consequence, the spouse was entitled to property rights over the assets that had been acquired (twenty-five percent) from the siblings using his or her dowry. In the first half of the nineteenth century, however, the only compensation the spouse obtained following the death of the heir or heiress was – as in the old regime – management of the house, residence and retirement in the house, and no more. He or she was thus protected from eviction from the house but had no property rights. And yet spouses, be they male or female, never claimed their legal rights. Management, residence, and retirement seemed their primary concern. At this stage, both male and female spouses were treated unfavourably in the same manner. Despite this unfavourable treatment and for fear of losing these residential privileges, these men and women hardly ever chose remarriage.

The situation had changed even more during the second half of the nineteenth century, with spouses receiving unequal gendered treatment. Unlike female spouses, men signed marriage contracts showing that they, as provided for by Civil Code, received half of the mutual bequest in property and the other half in usufruct, and also signed legal acts that indicated they had acquired ownership of shares bought with their dowry (twenty-five percent of the assets). Heiresses and their husbands thus became legal and official co-owners, co-managers, and co-transmitters of the house and land with equal

38 More specific explanations can be found in: Marie-Pierre Arrizabalaga, "Succession Strategies in the Pyrenees in the 19th Century. The Basque Case," *The History of the Family* 10–3 (2005), pp. 271–92.

status. Though legally possible, the wives of heirs did not enjoy this comfortable status, which they could never force into the marriage contract. By the time heirs died, their wives enjoyed only usufruct of twenty-five percent of the husbands' inherited assets, this as provided for in the marriage contract and in exchange for their dowries having been invested in the home. These widows enjoyed no benefit from the use of their dowry in the acquisition of their husbands' siblings' shares of the assets. Women had no way to circumvent such unequal treatment. Contrary to heirs' wives in Bearn, who did not hesitate to take their cases to court,[39] heirs' wives in the Basque Country never seemed to manage to enforce the Civil Code in an effort to gain property rights over the shares of assets acquired with the dowry. This explains why succession documents show that heirs owned all inherited assets while heiresses had to share ownership with their husbands. Heiresses' husbands were thus more successful in getting their in-laws to enforce the new law. Indeed, in-laws accepted this clause because they needed the full cooperation and participation of their sons-in-law in the activities of the farm in order to make the house and farm viable. Heirs' wives by contrast lived a life of service with the right to live, work, and die in the house under the authority of the heirs and thereafter the heirs of the next generation, as in the old regime, a life of subordination from the perspective of property rights.[40]

Some heiresses, however, elaborated new strategies in order to circumvent unequal treatment by maintaining full power over the house, as did heirs. Some did so by marrying late to avoid parental authority over and consent to their marital decisions (as the first example above seems to indicate). Marrying after one parent (or both) had died provided these heiresses with greater control over whom they chose to marry and the house. A very small number of other heiresses married men of lower status, men from more modest propertied families, or from sharecropping families, who had saved enough before marriage to collect a decent dowry to pay their place into a larger propertied family. Such marriages were indeed homogamous (within the same professional background) but not endogamous (within the same social background).

39 For details, see Lacanette-Pommel, *La famille dans les Pyrénées.*

40 For more details and examples, see Marie-Pierre Arrizabalaga, "Droits, pouvoirs et devoirs dans la maison basque: la place des hommes et des femmes au sein des familles basques depuis le XIXe siècle," *Vasconia. Cuadernos de Historia-Geografía* 35 (2006), pp. 155–83. See also Marie-Pierre Arrizabalaga, "Rôles et statuts des femmes dans les sociétés pyrénéennes: le Pays Basque aux XIXe–XXe siècles," in *Donne e Lavoro. Prospettive per una storia delle montagne europee, XVIII–XX secc.*, ed. Nelly Valsangiacomo and Luigi Lorenzetti (Milan: Franco Angeli, 2010), pp. 296–318.

In fact, marital alliances wherein the heiress had a higher social status than her husband were considered "unnatural", because these men became "servants" in the house.[41] In exchange for their dowry, they had the honour of marrying into a well-to-do propertied family and experience upward social mobility. For these reasons they agreed to bring a sizable dowry into the house without property right. In such cases, the heiress' husband was secured residence and retirement in the house, but he had limited, if any, power over decision-making. Upon her parents' deaths, the heiress was sole proprietor of the house. She was wholly in charge of and had full control over the estate. As a "servant", her husband helped on the farm and secured descendants. Though these strategies secured heirs and heiresses full power within the house, they were still not sufficient to secure the full transmission of the family house and land to one child. Additional strategies needed to be elaborated in order to compensate siblings, and here too new unequal and gendered treatment emerged over the course of the nineteenth century.

5.2 *Gendered Unequal Treatment between Excluded Siblings*

Though surviving parent(s) and the young heir or heiress and spouse controlled the majority of the assets and therefore blocked partition, they did not own all of the assets. The future of the house was still at stake, especially following the parents' death. As a result, families needed to elaborate additional strategies in order to gradually collect all siblings' inheritance shares through compensations and donations. As long as parents were alive, siblings could not legally demand their inheritance shares, thus giving the young couple the necessary time to save for siblings' compensation through years of hard work. And time indeed played in favour of the heir or heiress and spouse. The longer parents lived (and many lived into their 80s and 90s), the more the young inheriting couple could save before the final succession settlement. Meanwhile, the spouse's dowry contributed greatly to the successful reconstruction of assets. And in the nineteenth century, the dowry played a more vital role than ever before.

As part of the marriage contract, the heir's or heiress' spouse generally brought a cash dowry into the marriage, as mentioned previously. This provided siblings with a cash payment in compensation for their shares of the succession. This transaction was carried out in advance of the inheritance, when excluded siblings were young adults and upon their permanent departure

41 As illustrated in Pierre Bourdieu's discussion in *Le bal des célibataires. Crise de la société paysanne en Béarn* (Paris: Seuil, 2002), these men often lived a life of servitude and subordination.

from the house. Because these payments were made in advance of succession, before parents died and when the excluded siblings needed it the most (in their 20s), some children accepted smaller settlements for their legal shares of the inheritance.[42] Indeed, they usually received these upon marriage to an heir or heiress or just before departing for the Americas – sometimes long before both parents died. To ensure that these compensated siblings would not later demand additional retribution for their legal share of the inheritance, they were asked to sign legal documents accepting that early compensation as the full and final disbursement of their inheritance shares.[43] This process allowed the heir or heiress and spouse to strike a bargain, because some siblings, powerlessly and probably unhappily, accepted their inheritance shares at a lower price during a time when it was perhaps desperately needed. The young heirs and their spouses thus managed to compensate two siblings, men, or women, and enjoyed ownership of much more than half of the assets.

There were, however, gendered disparities in how early compensation was attributed. While men made good, advantageous use of said compensation, women had greater difficulty in benefiting from succession agreements. Even though excluded siblings received smaller compensation for their inheritance share than the single heir or heiress, excluded sons managed better than their excluded sisters. Prior to migration, excluded sons had worked as sheepherders or artisans and saved enough to marry heiresses of the same or higher status or to emigrate to the Americas. Most of them married women of the same socioeconomic and professional backgrounds: heiresses for sure, but excluded daughters as well, whom they married before departing from the community to cities or the Americas.[44] If the excluded sons could not marry within their

42 Though excluded siblings might not have been happy about the amount of the compensation, they accepted it because it came earlier than the law required, when they needed it the most, and enabled them to start a new life, especially in post-1840 America. For more details, see Arrizabalaga, "Stratégies de l'indivision".

43 For more details, see Marie-Pierre Arrizabalaga, "The House System in the Pyrenees: Traditions and Practices since the Modern Era," in *Finding 'Ie' in Western Society: Historical Empirical Study for the Paralleling and Contrasting Between Japan and Europe*, ed. Moto Takahashi (Matsuyama: Ehime University Economics Study Series, 2013), pp. 95–132.

44 Newly married couples settling in cities usually migrated as couples. When they chose to migrate to the Americas, however, the men usually departed alone to organise settlement, later to be joined by their wives and perhaps young children. Occasionally, single men settled in the Americas and returned to their village to get married and return to the Americas with their spouses. Most, however, married Basque friends' sisters who had emigrated after their brothers had settled comfortably.

social and professional environment (at home, in the cities, or in the Americas), many remained celibate (as the case study below will illustrate).[45]

Excluded women, for their part, received different, poorer treatment and were therefore bound to have worse destinies than excluded men. They usually married down, lower heirs or sharecroppers, men who sometimes emigrated alone to the Americas and later fetched their families to fare better in the new world. Other women settled in towns and cities in France. While some married artisans or civil servants there and maintained or improved their status through exogamous marriages, others remained single with a lower status as servants. Nonetheless, these single women refused exogamy through marriage outside their cultural and geographic environment and/or marrying down. Neither did they accept the option of remaining single in the family house under the authority of the heir or heiress. In comparison with their brothers, these women received less – if any – compensation (in the form of money or otherwise) for their shares of inheritance. Around the turn of the twentieth century, however, some of these women used "emancipating" strategies. They emigrated to the Americas to join relatives already established there. Once there, they married men of the same social and professional background (endogamy) and fared well. Excluded women, more often than their male counterparts, married in French cities or the Americas outside their background (exogamy) in an attempt to improve their conditions and enjoy greater power at home, or else they remained celibate in an attempt to maintain their freedom of movement and gain autonomy at the expense of status.[46]

Heirs and heiresses could not always compensate all the excluded siblings, and often asked siblings for benevolence and self-sacrifice in renouncing their shares of the inheritance. If the younger female siblings demanded their legal share of the inheritance in cash and in full upon both parents' death, they could put a great financial burden on the heir or heiress, force partition, and bring on the ruin of the family estate. For many of these women the value of their portion of the estate was meagre in consideration of the small size of the property and the number of siblings with whom to share the estate. Inheritance also was settled late in their life. Willingly or unwillingly, they agreed to sign

45 A detailed explanation of this issue can be found in Marie-Pierre Arrizabalaga, "Basque Migration and Inheritance in the Nineteenth Century," in *European Mobility Internal, International, and Transatlantic Moves in the 19th and early 20th Centuries*, ed. Annemarie Steidl, Josef Ehmer, Stan Nadel, and Hermann Zeitlhofer (Göttingen: V&R unipress, 2009), pp. 135–50.

46 Marie-Pierre Arrizabalaga, "Basque Women and Urban Migration in the Nineteenth Century," *The History of the Family* 10–2 (2005), pp. 99–117.

testaments donating their portions to the heir or heiress. Unable to bring dowries into their marriages, some of these women remained celibate in the family house throughout their lives, as women had in the past.[47] As the case study below illustrates, the traditional custom known as "*droit de chaise*" was thus perpetuated into the nineteenth century.

Yet, with time, fewer unmarried siblings wished to reside in the family house under the authority of the heir or heiress. Many men and women went to towns, cities, or overseas, where they sometimes lived a celibate life, unable to find an individual of the same background to marry. Some never demanded their shares of inheritance (or were forced into forsaking it) for the sake of the family line and the survival of the house. If they contested the succession, the law protected the interests of those who owned the larger shares of the estate, namely the heirs or the heiresses and their spouses (who blocked the succession and partition). In any case, by the time the final implementation of the succession took place (when both parents died), these siblings were older, had already built lives for themselves, and were no longer dependent on making a living from the money they might receive from an inheritance. It seems that by that time they had given up on their inheritances, either willingly or not.[48] Finally, in rare cases, after a life of experience in a town, city, or in the Americas, some unmarried siblings, who had never been compensated, returned to the family house for retirement and/or to die. They then signed testaments donating their shares of the inheritance to the heir or heiress, thus keeping family assets together. In this process, they enjoyed the status and privileges of family membership although they had not officially inherited their shares. Nonetheless, they enjoyed the privilege of spending the final days of their lives in the family house, where they received free care, food, and lodging until death in exchange for their inheritance shares.[49]

---

47 On issues related to excluded children and their destinies in other parts of Europe, see Bouchard, Dickinson, and Goy, *Les Exclus de la terre*; Martine Segalen and Georges Ravis-Giordani, eds., *Les cadets* (Paris: Éditions du CNRS, 1994), and Frans Van Poppel, Michel Oris, and James Lee, eds., *The Road to Independence. Leaving Home in Western and Eastern Societies, 16th–20th centuries* (Bern: Peter Lang, 2004).

48 Marie-Pierre Arrizabalaga, "Celibacy and Gender Inequalities in the Pyrenees in the Nineteenth and Twentieth Centuries," in *Gender Inequalities, Households and the Production of Well-Being in Modern Europe*, ed. Tindara Addabo, Marie-Pierre Arrizabalaga, Cristina Borderias, and Alastair Owens (London: Ashgate, 2010), pp. 219–34.

49 For a more detailed discussion of this issue, see Marie-Pierre Arrizabalaga, "Gender and Well-being in the Pyrenean Stem-family System," in *Gender and Well-being in Europe. Historical and Contemporary Perspectives*, ed. Bernard Harris, Lina Gálvez, and Helena Machado (London: Ashgate, 2009), pp. 85–102.

In an effort to illustrate many of the above arguments, we will analyse the H. genealogy.[50] Pierre H. (heir) and Marie E. (his spouse) married in Sare in 1809. While Pierre's succession declaration of 1827 showed that he owned all of his parents' assets (a house and thirty-two hectares of land), Marie E.'s succession declaration of 1852 only declared the value of her dowry: 600 francs. As indicated by a donation act, Pierre actually inherited all the assets upon his parents' death in 1815. This was illegal, because Pierre had a younger brother, Placide, and two sisters, and each was entitled to a share. The two sisters were likely compensated, while Placide chose celibacy in the family house with Pierre. When he died, Placide made the legal donation of his share to Pierre's heiress. The data thus show that Pierre became the single heir of the family, and owned all assets, while Marie owned only her dowry. The dowry, however, was probably used as an investment in the family farm or to compensate Pierre's sisters. And yet, Marie received no financial gain from her dowry. She enjoyed only the privilege of living, working, and retiring in the house. Thus, during the early nineteenth century single inheritance strategies resembled ancient customary practices in a manner that was not reproduced later in the century. This case study also illustrates how unfavourably heirs' spouses could be treated.

Pierre H. and Marie E. had six children. According to the family's notary, inheritance, and land tax records, their first-born son, Pierre, preferred emigration to heirship (perhaps refusing a late marriage). He received an early compensation to finance his emigration to Cuba, where he died celibate. Heirship was granted to Marianne, the second-born child, who received the extra share (a quarter of the assets) in 1850 when she married Pierre B., the non-inheriting son of a propertied family in the region. Pierre B. brought a dowry of 2,850 francs into the marriage, which was used to pay debts (from early compensations) and to compensate Marianne's other siblings. The young couple signed a marital property agreement that comprised the shared ownership of the property acquired during the marriage and the mutual donation of half of the assets (all in property, or half in property and half in usufruct). Both were thus guaranteed co-ownership and co-management, as well as abode, care, and retirement in the house as part of their contract. In addition, two of the six children – Jean-Placide, the third-born, and Marie-Baptiste, the sixth-born – remained celibate, entitled to lifelong work, care and retirement in the

50 This case study derives from the reconstitution data of one of the 120 couples' families over three generations presented above and which were reconstructed using the civil registers, the notary records, and the *Enregistrement* records (tax records upon inheritance). For details on the methodology, see discussion above.

family house (the customary *droit de chaise*). For many years this cohabitation showed that the household was structured as a stem-family, a practice customary in the old regime and prevailing in the nineteenth century. Finally, in exchange for room, board, and care, the unmarried siblings donated their shares of the inheritance to the heiress of the house. While Marie-Baptiste, who died in 1865, donated her share to her sister Marianne, the heiress of the house at the time, Jean-Placide, who died in 1889, donated his to Marie, his niece and the heiress of the next generation. Among Marianne's siblings, Marie (the fourth-born), also unmarried, entered a convent in the nearby town of Ustaritz and Jean-Martin (the fifth-born) received a dowry to marry Marie G., the heiress of a house and twenty-three hectares of land, in 1856.

It appears that through marriage, and more especially celibacy, the H. family was able to transfer their family assets intact from one generation to the next. Yet most unmarried siblings, and women in particular, experienced downward social mobility (as either a non-inheriting landless farmer or a nun). Family cohesion must have been strong, and they must have avoided conflict through some form of compensation. Indeed, each member signed documents (marriage contracts, purchase, or donation acts) that contributed to keeping the family assets together. Marianne H. was thus legally entitled to twenty-five percent of the family assets (the extra share) and to her equal share of the remaining seventy-five percent to be apportioned between all six children (one-sixth each) following the deaths of their parents. In addition, Pierre B. brought a dowry equal to twenty-five percent of the H. family assets, which the couple used to compensate Jean-Martin, who married an heiress, and perhaps to repay debts from earlier compensations (such as to Pierre, the first-born, residing in Cuba). Thus, Marianne H. and Pierre B. controlled at least 62.5 percent of the family assets (including twenty-five percent of the assets acquired collectively with the dowry). Throughout their lives (Marianne's in particular, because Pierre died within two years of marriage), the couple had to find modes of compensating the three other siblings, all of whom conveniently remained single, residing in either the family house (as was the case with Jean-Placide and Marie-Baptiste) or a convent (as in the case of Marie). The two who remained at home helped Marianne to maintain the farm after she became a widow (at the age of forty-one – never to remarry). Thereafter, the two siblings that remained at home signed donation acts in favour of their sister or niece in exchange for the right to live, work, and retire in the house (*droit de chaise*). The assets were then transmitted to Marie, the only child of the next generation.

Families were thus able to use the legal Civil Code prerogatives and elaborate new strategies to avoid partition. In the process they preserved some old customary practices, including single inheritance and celibacy, which contributed to the collection of inheritance shares without necessitating sibling compensation. Couples also provided unmarried siblings with a safe emigration to the Americas or a decent life and retirement at home. Because Marianne H. and Pierre B. had only one child, a daughter who naturally and legally inherited all assets upon her mother's death, inheritance was simple for the next generation.

6 Conclusions

Because the Civil Code didn't determine final succession settlements until the deaths of the two parents, heirs and heiresses and their spouses had plenty of time to reach agreements with excluded siblings and gradually collect all of the inheritance shares, thus perpetuating single inheritance. And the notary, inheritance, and land tax records indicate that they were successful in their efforts to gain ownership of all assets and prevent partition. Local notary officials contributed greatly to the realization of full succession settlements. Indeed, they used legal clauses to help propertied families perpetuate elements of ancient single inheritance practices, to arbitrate disagreements and conflicts, and to elaborate new strategies and find solutions that avoided partition. This contributed to the economic stability of communities and families throughout the nineteenth and early twentieth centuries. The land registers or *Cadastres* consulted for this research indicate that only a few houses were sold during this period (fewer than in, for example, Bearn).[51] Yet, it remains unclear whether individuals were willing participants in the family bargaining and voluntarily agreed to the collective agreements or if they were coerced into renouncing their rights to their legal shares.

This contribution shows how families in the nineteenth century used both old and new inheritance strategies, some of which generated greater gender differentiated treatment than before the Revolution. Heirs and heiresses' husbands were better treated and had more power and rights in the house than heiresses and heirs' wives. This was likely because men's work on the farm was valued more than that of women. Heiresses for their parts elaborated other strategies to circumvent unequal treatment. They married late to men of lower status, men who were happy to marry up. These men brought a dowry into the house in exchange for status but enjoyed no property rights.

51 Lacanette-Pommel, *La famille dans les Pyrénées.*

Similarly, excluded sons were better compensated and better treated than excluded daughters. Through work, they could save more money while residing at home. And they invested these savings in marriage or emigration. They thus acquired more wealth than women, received better compensation for their shares of inheritance than their sisters, and were therefore capable of using it toward settling into better life circumstances. There can be no question that excluded women were at more of a disadvantage than excluded men. They made up for these disadvantages and unfair treatment by marrying outside of their environments (exogamy) or by marrying excluded men who settled in cities or in the Americas, where they fared well. These couples, made up of excluded men and women made the best of it, gaining in decision-making power, equality, and liberty. Finally, celibacy affected both men and women equally, men because they refused to marry outside of their environments or communities – notably in the Americas[52] – and women because it allowed them to enjoy greater autonomy and freedom of movement in French cities.

In all cases, and in spite of reduced early compensation, excluded men and women enjoyed greater freedom of movement (in villages, cities, or the Americas), of choice (for endogamous or exogamous marriages), and of destiny – even though some may have experienced downward social mobility. It is clear that equal partition was never fully implemented, and this remained the case even after World War Two, resulting in prevailing gender inequalities. In more recent decades, however, with men and women having greater access to better education and employment opportunities in cities and in the Americas, inheritance has been increasingly assumed by men, who have had difficulty finding a spouse who agrees to marry into the house, even without a dowry. Women have actually acquired greater liberty and emancipation, refusing a life of hard work with little recognition on the farm. Today this issue remains crucial for rural farmers and families in the Basque Country and other regions, because men assume heirship and women choose to settle in urban settings, threatening the future of rural communities and of farming in many parts of contemporary France.

52 I am currently working on a research project on French immigration to California between 1880 and 1940, from a gender perspective. I am also working on the study of French immigrants' naturalization applications in the same period, a comparative gendered analysis of French immigrant men's and women's integration process into Southern California, with a special consideration being given to their regional French origins, the type of settlement they envisioned in California, and their integration processes.

References

Abelson, Andrew. "Inheritance and Population Control in a Basque Valley before 1900." *Peasant Studies* 7–1 (1978): pp. 11–27.

Arrizabalaga, Marie-Pierre. "Basque Migration and Inheritance in the Nineteenth Century." In *European Mobility Internal, International, and Transatlantic Moves in the 19th and early 20th Centuries*, edited by Annemarie Steidl, Josef Ehmer, Stan Nadel, and Hermann Zeitlhofer, pp. 135–50. Göttingen: V&R unipress, 2009.

Arrizabalaga, Marie-Pierre. "Basque Women and Urban Migration in the Nineteenth Century." *The History of the Family* 10–2 (2005): pp. 99–117.

Arrizabalaga, Marie-Pierre. "Celibacy and Gender Inequalities in the Pyrenees in the Nineteenth and Twentieth Centuries." In *Gender Inequalities, Households and the Production of Well-Being in Modern Europe*, edited by Tindara Addabo, Marie-Pierre Arrizabalaga, Cristina Borderias, and Alastair Owens, pp. 219–34. London: Ashgate, 2010.

Arrizabalaga, Marie-Pierre. "Destins de femmes dans les Pyrénées au XIXe siècle: le cas basque." *Annales de Démographie Historique* 2 (2006): pp. 135–70.

Arrizabalaga, Marie-Pierre. "Droits, pouvoirs et devoirs dans la maison basque: la place des hommes et des femmes au sein des familles basques depuis le XIXe siècle." *Vasconia. Cuadernos de Historia-Geografía* 35 (2006): pp. 155–83.

Arrizabalaga, Marie-Pierre. "Female Primogeniture in the French Basque Country." In *The Logic of Female Succession: Rethinking Patriarchy and Patrilineality in Global and Historical Perspective*, edited by Emiko Ochiai, pp. 31–52. Kyoto: International Research Center of Japanese Studies, 2002.

Arrizabalaga, Marie-Pierre. "Gender and Migration in the Pyrenees in the Nineteenth Century: Gender-Differentiated Patterns and Destinies." In *Female Economic Strategies in the Modern World*, edited by Beatrice Moring, pp. 127–44. London: Pickring & Chatto, 2012.

Arrizabalaga, Marie-Pierre. "Gender and Well-being in the Pyrenean Stem-family System." In *Gender and Well-being in Europe. Historical and Contemporary Perspectives*, edited by Bernard Harris, Lina Gálvez, and Helena Machado, pp. 85–102. London: Ashgate, 2009.

Arrizabalaga, Marie-Pierre. "Les héritières de la maison au Pays Basque au XIXe siècle." *Lapurdum* 7 (2002): pp. 35–55.

Arrizabalaga, Marie-Pierre. "Migrations féminines – migrations masculines: des comportements différenciés au sein des familles basques au XIXe siècle." In *Marchés, migrations et logiques familiales dans les espaces français, canadien et suisse, 18e–20e siècles*, edited by Luigi Lorenzetti, Anne-Lise Head-König, and Joseph Goy, pp. 183–95. Bern: Peter Lang, 2005.

Arrizabalaga, Marie-Pierre. "Rôles et statuts des femmes dans les sociétés pyrénéennes: le Pays Basque aux XIXe–XXe siècles." In *Donne e Lavoro. Prospettive per una storia delle montagne europee, XVIII–XX secc.*, edited by Nelly Valsangiacomo and Luigi Lorenzetti, pp. 296–318. Milan: Franco Angeli, 2010.

Arrizabalaga, Marie-Pierre. "Stratégies de l'indivision et rapport à la terre après le Code civil: le cas basque au XIXe siècle." In *Familles, terre, marchés. Logiques économiques et stratégies dans les milieux ruraux (XVIIe–XXe siècles)*, edited by Gérard Béaur, Christian Dessureault, and Joseph Goy, pp. 171–83. Rennes: Presses Universitaires de Rennes, 2004.

Arrizabalaga, Marie-Pierre. "Structures familiales et destins migratoires à Sare au XIXe siècle." *Lapurdum* 2 (1997): pp. 237–55.

Arrizabalaga, Marie-Pierre. "Succession Strategies in the Pyrenees in the 19th Century. The Basque Case." *The History of the Family* 10–3 (2005): pp. 271–92.

Arrizabalaga, Marie-Pierre. "The House System in the Pyrenees: Traditions and Practices since the Modern Era." In *Finding 'Ie' in Western Society: Historical Empirical Study for the Paralleling and Contrasting Between Japan and Europe*, edited by Moto Takahashi, pp. 95–132. Matsuyama: Ehime University Economics Study Series, 2013.

Arrizabalaga, Marie-Pierre. "The Stem Family in the French Basque Country: Sare in the Nineteenth Century." *Journal of Family History* 1 (1997): pp. 50–69.

Assier-Andrieu, Louis. *Coutume et rapports sociaux. Etude anthropologique des communautés paysannes du Capcir*. Paris: Éditions du CNRS, 1981.

Assier-Andrieu, Louis, ed. *Une France coutumière. Enquête sur les "usages locaux" et leur codification (XIXe–XXe siècles)*. Paris: Éditions du CNRS, 1990.

Augustins, George. *Comment se perpétuer? Devenir des lignées et destins des patrimoines dans les paysanneries européennes*. Nanterre: Société d'ethnologie française, 1989.

Barcelo, Ramón. "Transmission héréditaire et systèmes de production: le cas de la Soule (Pyrénées-Atlantiques)." *Sociologie du travail* 3 (1988): pp. 443–60.

Béaur, Gérard. "La transmission des exploitations: logiques et stratégies. Quelques réflexions sur un processus obscur." In *Problèmes de la transmission des exploitations agricoles (XVIIIe–XXe siècles)*, edited by Gérard Bouchard, Joseph Goy, and Anne-Lise Head-König, pp. 109–16. Rome: Ecole française de Rome, 1998.

Béaur, Gérard. "Land Transmission and Inheritance Practices in France during the *Ancien Régime*: Differences of Degree or Kind?" In *Family Welfare. Gender, Property, and Inheritance since the Seventeenth Century*, edited by David R. Green and Alastair Owens, pp. 31–46. Westport, Conn.: Praeger, 2004.

Béaur, Gérard. "Le marché foncier éclaté. Les modes de transmission du patrimoine sous l'Ancien Régime." *Annales ESC* 1 (1991): pp. 189–203.

Béaur, Gérard, Christian Dessureault, and Joseph Goy, eds. *Familles, terre, marchés. Logiques économiques et stratégies dans les milieux ruraux (XVIIe–XXe siècles)*. Rennes: Presses Universitaires de Rennes, 2004.

Berkner, Lutz K. "The Stem-Family and the Developmental Cycle of the Peasant Household: An Eighteenth-Century Austrian Example." *American Historical Review* 77–2 (1972): pp. 398–418.

Bonnain, Rolande. "Migration, exclusion et solidarité." In *Les Exclus de la terre en France et au Quebec (XVIIe–XXe siècles). La reproduction familiale dans la différence*, edited by Gérard Bouchard, John Dickinson, and Joseph Goy, pp. 271–90. Sillery: Septentrion, 1998.

Bonnain, Rolande, Gérard Bouchard, and Joseph Goy, eds. *Transmettre, hériter, succéder. La reproduction familiale en milieu rural: France – Québec, XVIIIe–XXe siècles.* Lyon: Presses Universitaires de Lyon, 1992.

Bouchard, Gérard, Joseph Goy, and Anne-Lise Head-König, eds. *Problèmes de la transmission des exploitations agricoles (XVIIIe–XXe siècles)*. Rome: Éditions de l'Ecole française de Rome, 1998.

Chiva, Isaac, and Joseph Goy, eds. *Les Baronnies des Pyrénées. Maisons, mode de vie, société*, vol. 1. Paris: Éditions de l'EHESS, 1981.

Chiva, Isaac, and Joseph Goy, eds. *Les Baronnies des Pyrénées. Maisons, espace, famille*, vol. 2. Paris: Éditions de l'EHESS, 1986.

Collomp, Alain. *La maison du père. Famille et village en Haute-Provence aux XVIIe et XVIIIe siècles*. Paris: Presses Universitaires de France, 1983.

Comas d'Argemir, Dolores, and Jean-François Soulet, eds. *La familía als Pirineus*, Andorre: Impremta Solber, 1993.

Cordier, Eugène. *Droit de famille aux Pyrénées. Barège, Lavedan, Béarn et Pays Basque.* Paris: Auguste Durand, 1859.

Coutumes générales, gardées et observées au Païs et baillage de Labourt, et reffort d'icelui. Bordeaux: J.-B. Lacornée, 1760.

Derouet, Bernard. "Le partage des frères. Héritage masculin et reproduction sociale en Franche-Comté aux XVIIIe et XIXe siècles." *Annales ESC* 2 (1993): pp. 453–74.

Derouet, Bernard. "Pratiques successorales et rapport à la terre: les sociétés paysannes d'Ancien Régime." *Annales ESC* 1 (1989): pp. 173–206.

Derouet, Bernard. "Transmettre la terre. Origines et inflexions récentes d'une problématique de différence." *Histoire et sociétés rurales* 2 (1994): pp. 33–67.

Desplat, Christian, trans. *For de Béarn d'Henri II d'Albret*. Pau: Marrimpouer, 1986.

Dessureault, Christian, John Dickinson, and Joseph Goy, eds. *Famille et marché (XVIe–XXe siècles)*. Sillery: Septentrion, 2003.

Douglass, William A. *Etchalar and Murelaga. Opportunity and Rural Exodus in Two Spanish Basque Villages*. New York: St Martin's Press, 1975.

Douglass, William A. "The Basque Stem-Family Household: Myth or Reality?." *Journal of Family History* 73–1 (1988) pp. 75–89.

Duroux, Rose. "Temporary Male Migration and Female Power in a Stem-Family Society: the Case of 19th Century Auvergne." In *Family Welfare. Gender, Property, and Inheritance since the Seventeenth Century*, edited by David R. Green and Alastair Owens, pp. 47–71. Westport, Conn.: Praeger, 2004.

Eggerickk, Thierry. "Régimes et transitions démographiques en Europe de l'Ouest. Un essai de synthèse." *Annales de Démographie Historique* 1 (2015): pp. 113–48.

Etchelecou, André. *Transition démographique et système coutumier dans les Pyrénées occidentales*. Paris: Presses Universitaires de France, 1991.

Fauve-Chamoux, Antoinette. "Household Forms and Living Standards in Preindustrial France: from Models to Realities." *Journal of Family History* 18–2 (1993): pp. 135–56.

Fauve-Chamoux, Antoinette." La reproduction familiale en milieu paysan: le destin des exclus." In *Les Exclus de la terre en France et au Quebec (XVII*^e^*–XX*^e^ *siècles). La reproduction familiale dans la différence*, edited by Gérard Bouchard, John Dickinson, and Joseph Goy, pp. 73–91. Sillery: Septentrion, 1998.

Fauve-Chamoux, Antoinette. "Le fonctionnement de la famille-souche dans les Baronnies des Pyrénées avant 1914." *Annales de démographie historique* (1987): pp. 241–62.

Fauve-Chamoux, Antoinette. "Le rôle des femmes dans la transmission des biens en France." In *Famille et marché (XVI*^e^*–XX*^e^ *siècles)*, edited by Christian Dessureault, John Dickinson, and Joseph Goy, pp. 245–60. Sillery: Septentrion, 2003.

Fauve-Chamoux, Antoinette. "Les structures familiales au Royaume des familles-souches: Esparros." *Annales ESC* 3 (1984): pp. 514–28.

Fauve-Chamoux, Antoinette. "Strategies of Household Continuity in a Stem-Family Society: from Heirship to Headship." In *When Dad Died. Individuals and Families Coping with Distress in Past Societies*, edited by Renzo Derosas and Michel Oris, pp. 121–39. Bern: Peter Lang, 2002.

Fauve-Chamoux, Antoinette. "The Stem Family, Demography and Inheritance." In *The European Peasant Family and Economy*, edited by David J. Siddle, pp. 86–113. Liverpool: Liverpool University Press, 1995.

Fauve-Chamoux, Antoinette, and Emiko Ochiai, eds. *The Stem Family in Eurasian Perspective. Revisiting House Societies, 17th–20th Centuries*. Bern: Peter Lang, 2009.

Fine-Souriac, Agnès. "La famille-souche pyrénéenne au XIXe siècle. Quelques réflexions de méthode." *Annales ESC* 3 (1987): pp. 478–87.

Fougères, Alain. *Les Droits de famille et les successions au Pays Basque et en Béarn d'après les anciens textes*. Bergerac: H. Trillaud, 1938.

Goy, Joseph. "Les exclus de la transmission et la loi, 1789–1980." In *Les Exclus de la terre en France et au Quebec (XVII*^e^*–XX*^e^ *siècles). La reproduction familiale dans la différence*, edited by Gérard Bouchard, John Dickinson, and Joseph Goy, pp. 21–34. Sillery: Septentrion, 1998.

Goy, Joseph. "Transmission successorale et paysannerie pendant la Révolution française: un grand malentendu." *Etudes rurales* 110–111–112 (1988): pp. 45–56.

Goyhenetche, Jean. *For et coutumes de Basse-Navarre*. Bayonne: Elkar, 1985.

Green, David R., and Alastair Owens, eds. *Family Welfare. Gender, Property, and Inheritance since the Seventeenth Century*. Westport, Conn.: Praeger, 2004.

Green, Nancy L. "L'histoire comparative et le champ des études migratoires." *Annales ESC* 6 (1990): pp. 1335–50.

Grosclaude, Michel. *La Coutume de la Soule. Traduction, notes et commentaires*. Saint-Étienne-de-Baïgorry: Izpegi, 1993.

Head-König, Anne-Lise, in collaboration with Péter Pozsgai, eds. *Inheritance Practices, Marriage Strategies and Household Formation*. Turnhout: Brepols, 2012.

Head-König, Anne-Lise, Luigi Lorenzetti, and Béatrice Veyrassat, eds. *Famille, parenté et réseaux en Occident (XVIIe–XXe siècles)*. Genève: Société d'Histoire et d'Archéologie de Genève, 2001.

Lacanette-Pommel, Christine. *La famille dans les Pyrénées. De la coutume au code Napoléon*. Estadens: PyréGraph, 2003.

Lafourcade, Maïte. *Mariages en Labourd sous l'Ancien Régime. Les contrats de mariage du pays de Labourd sous le règne de Louis XVI*. Bilbao: Universitad del País Vasco, 1989.

Lamaison, Pierre. "La diversité des modes de transmission: une géographie tenace." *Etudes rurales* 110–111–112 (1988): pp. 119–75.

Lanzinger, Margareth. *Das gesicherte Erbe. Heirat in familialen und lokalen Kontexten, Innichen 1700–1900*. Vienna, Cologne, and Weimar: Böhlau, 2003.

Laslett, Peter, and Richard Wall, eds. *Household and Family in Past Time. Comparative Studies in the Size and Structure of the Domestic Group over the Last Three Centuries*. Cambridge: Cambridge University Press, 1972.

Laslett, Peter, Richard Wall, and Jean Robin, eds. *Family Forms in Historical Europe*. Cambridge: Cambridge University Press, 1983.

Le Play, Frédéric, *La Réforme sociale en France déduite de l'observation comparée des peuples européens*, 3 vols. Paris: Dentu, 1878.

Le Play, Frédéric. *L'Organisation de la famille selon le vrai modèle signalé par l'histoire de toutes les races et de tous les temps*. Paris: Tequi, 1871.

Le Play, Frédéric, Emile Cheysson, Bayard, and Fernand Butel. *Les Mélouga. Une famille pyrénéenne au XIXe siècle. Textes réunis par Alain Chenu*. Paris: Nathan, 1994.

Le Roy Ladurie, Emmanuel. "Système de la coutume. Structures familiales et coutumes d'héritage en France au XVIe siècle." *Annales ESC* 4–5 (1972): pp. 825–46.

Lorenzetti, Luigi, Anne-Lise Head-König, and Joseph Goy, eds. *Marchés, migrations et logiques familiales dans les espaces français, canadien et Suisse, 18e–20e siècles*. Genève: Peter Lang, 2005.

Poumarède, Jacques. "Famille et ténure dans les Pyrénées du Moyen Age au XIXe siècle." *Annales de démographie historique* (1979): pp. 347–60.

Poumarède, Jacques. *Les Successions dans le Sud-Ouest de la France au Moyen Age*. Paris: Presses Universitaires de France, 1972.

Scott, Joan W. *De l'utilité du genre*. Paris: Fayard, 2012.

Scott, Joan W. "Genre: une catégorie utile d'analyse historique." *Les cahiers du GRIF* "Le Genre de l'Histoire", 37–38 (1988): pp. 125–53.

Segalen, Martine. *Quinze générations de Bas-Bretons. Parenté et Société dans le Pays Bigouden Sud, 1720–1980*. Paris: Presses Universitaires de France, 1985.

Segalen, Martine, and Georges Ravis-Giordani, eds. *Les cadets*. Paris: Éditions du CNRS, 1994.

Thébaud, Françoise. *Écrire l'histoire des femmes et du genre*. Lyon: ENS Éditions, 2007.

Thébaud, Françoise. "Une démographie au féminin." In *Une démographie au féminin – A Female Demography. Risques et opportunités dans le parcours de vie – Risks and Changes in the Life Course*, edited by Michel Oris, Guy Brunet, Virginie De Luca Barrusse, and Danielle Gauvreau, pp. 5–23. Bern: Peter Lang, 2009.

Van Poppel, Frans, Michel Oris, and James Lee, eds. *The Road to Independence. Leaving Home in Western and Eastern Societies, 16th–20th centuries*. Bern: Peter Lang, 2004.

Verdon, Michel. "Rethinking Complex Households: the Case of the Western Pyrenean 'Houses'." *Continuity and Change* 11–2 (1996): pp. 191–215.

Verdon, Michel. "The Stem Family: Toward a General Theory." *Journal of Interdisciplinary History* 10–1 (1979): pp. 87–105.

Vivier, Nadine. *Propriété collective et identité communale. Les biens communaux en France, 1750–1914*. Paris: Publications de la Sorbonne, 1998.

Yver, Jean. *Égalité entre héritiers et exclusion des enfants dotés: essai de géographie coutumière*. Paris: Éditions Sirey, 1966.

Zink, Anne. *L'Héritier de la maison. Géographie coutumière du Sud-Ouest de la France sous l'Ancien Régime*. Paris: Éditions EHESS, 1993.

PART 2

Spaces of Transition

CHAPTER 6

After the Plague: Women, Marriage, and Property in Trento during the Second Half of the Fourteenth Century

Silvia Mattivi

This chapter presents a reflection on the juridical, economic, and social relationships that could be found in the city of Trento in the middle of the fourteenth century. The main focus will be on the role of women regarding patrimonial issues. In particular, I hypothesise that women seemed to have gained more economic independence after the plague, and that, according to what we can find in the documents, more of them administered their properties and their inheritances autonomously. We can see in many notarial acts that, starting in the twelfth century, women belonging to different social classes turned into active subjects in economic and legal issues, achieving not only patrimonial independence, but also trustworthiness.[1] We should consider that in the thirteenth century there were many economic and social changes, and it is possible that the plague – and the demographic reduction that followed it – contributed considerably to these changes. Therefore, while we are reading some documents, we cannot avoid speculating there are some relevant connections between the plague and the increased autonomy of women.

The majority of the data and information analysed comes from the notarial register *Instrumenta capitularia 4,* compiled by the notary Antonio da Pomarolo between the years 1351 and 1357.[2] This register contains many documents of various types, among which there are *cartae dotis* and/or *matrimonii*, wills, partitions related to inheritance proceedings, donations, and documents referring to property rights. On the one hand these documents describe conflicting situations within the family groups. On the other hand, they demonstrate the remarkable autonomy of women in possession of the ability to manage their property and draw-up contracts.

1 Giovanna Petti Balbi, "Forme di credito femminile: osservazioni introduttive", in Giovanna Petti Balbi and Paola Gugliemotti, eds., *Dare credito alle donne. Presenze femminili nell'economia tra medioevo ed età moderna (Convegno internazionale di studi, Asti, 8–9 ottobre 2010)* (Asti: Centro Studi "Renato Bordone", 2012), pp. 9–24, here p. 12.

2 Trento, Archivio Capitolare (ACapTn), *Instrumenta capitularia* (IC) 4.

 | DOI:10.1163/9789004456204_007

1 The Register Written by Antonio Da Pomarolo

As is known, notary documents have been given great attention in recent decades. These sources provide relevant information about many features of the society in which the notary lived, even at times in an unintentional way. Notaries usually, in fact, compiled registers and wrote documents in order to perform their jobs rather than in an effort to record historical facts. In the Archivio capitolare in Trento, which is nowadays located in the Archivio diocesano, there is a series named *Instrumenta Capitularia*, that consists of about one hundred volumes drafted between the thirteenth and the eighteenth centuries.[3] The register *Instrumenta capitularia 4* (IC4) was compiled by notary Antonio da Pomarolo between the years 1351 and 1357.[4] It is a nearly intact *liber extensorum* that contains 372 documents. The fact that this register is kept in the Archivio capitolare does not imply that the clients of Antonio da Pomarolo were exclusively canons of the cathedral of Trento. On the contrary, reading through the documents we can see that both private citizens and public institutions turned to this notary. It is therefore difficult for us to understand the role Antonio actually played: was he an ordinary notary to whom the canons turned? Or was he in ongoing cooperation with the chapter of the cathedral? We must also take into account that we have little information not only on the occupational activity of Antonio, but also on his life: in addition to the register mentioned, only 18 *instrumenta* written by Antonio da Pomarolo are conserved, thanks to these we know that he worked as notary in Trento from about 1349 to 1369.

If we pay attention to the clients of Antonio da Pomarolo, we can easily notice that he mentioned about 1,000 people in his register. We do not have conclusive information about the number of inhabitants in Trento during this period but, if we consider that during the sixteenth century around 5,000 people lived in the city,[5] and that the register was drafted shortly after the plague,

3 For information about this series see: Emanuele Curzel, "Per la storia del Capitolo della Cattedrale di Trento nel Trecento e nel Quattrocento: la serie degli Instrumenta Capitularia," *Studi Trentini di Scienze Storiche* 71 (1992), pp. 223–60; and Emanuele Curzel, *I canonici e il Capitolo della cattedrale di Trento dal XII al XV secolo* (Bologna: EDB, 2001), pp. 34–38.

4 See Silvia Mattivi, "Il registro del notaio Antonio da Pomarolo (1351–1357)," *Studi Trentini. Storia* 91 (2012), pp. 295–321; and Silvia Mattivi, "Il registro del notaio Antonio da Pomarolo (1351–1357). Economia e società a Trento alla metà del Trecento" (PhD diss., Università degli Studi di Trento, 2009/2010).

5 Gian Maria Varanini, "Città alpine del tardo medioevo," in *Il Gotico nelle Alpi 1350–1450*, ed. Enrico Castelnuovo and Francesca de Gramatica (Trento: Provincia Autonoma di Trento – Castello del Buonconsiglio, 2002), pp. 35–52, here p. 39.

we can presume that a remarkable part of the population turned to Antonio. The social origins of these citizens differed greatly: Antonio worked for the canons and for other religious institutions such as the Benedictine monastery of San Lorenzo and that of Santa Chiara, the hospitals situated in the city, and the convent of San Francesco. The noble Rampreto da Scena, other notaries, peasants, artisans, and business owners turned to Antonio too. Not all of them were regular clients. Some of them went to Antonio only once or are just named in the witness list. But other names appear frequently in the documents, which allows us to hypothesise something more about their families, their properties, and their occupational status. This is the case with, for example, Bartolomeo *sartor*, Giovanni *merzader* and Martino *ciroicus*. These three men owned houses and fields and were among those present as participants or witnesses at many legal acts.

2 Marriage and Relationships in Trento after the Plague

It is important to highlight that, judging from these sources, familial and emotional relations were often connected with economic and social relations. As a result, it is necessary that this research considers all the documents in the register, because each document, although perhaps not focused on a marriage or an engagement, could contain information about relationships between families and between citizens. Economic relations in each of the social community groups mentioned in the register were often strengthened through a marriage, creating in this way complex relationships that often generated disagreements and hostility among community members. Consequently, these members often turned to a notary to demand that a dowry was delivered, or to reach an agreement about the division of an inheritance. A marriage was often a way of strengthening social connections. In fact, the couple as a unit was considered the economic and social basis of the community.[6]

If we pay specific attention to the 26 *cartae dotis* and/or *matrimonii* of the register, we can see that in every document the celebration was *per verba de presenti* and not *per verba de futuro*.[7] This can be illustrated with the

6 See, for example, Gabriela Signori, *Von der Paradiesehe zur Gütergemeinschaft. Die Ehe in der mittelalterlichen Lebens- und Vorstellungswelt* (Frankfurt a. M. and New York: Campus, 2011), p. 123.

7 Before the Council of Trento set definite rules for marriage, there was no unique form to celebrate this event. The only really important thing was that both the bride and

following content from a document that reports a contract of a dowry and marriage.

> 1353 January 26 (Saturday). Trento, in the house of *magister* Giovanni *merzader*, son of the deceased *ser* Nicolò da Ton. Present: the above-named *magister* Giovanni, Lorenzo son of the deceased *ser* Biondo from Vigolo, Benasunto called *Covalerius osterius*, Paolo called *Pevrada stazonerius* and Bettino son of the deceased *dominus Savoldus* from Bergamo, all of whom are residents in Trento.
>
> *Magister Çesius cimator*, son of the deceased Odorico from Terlago, receives as dowry from *domina* Salafia, daughter of the deceased Michele from Venosta resident in Trento, his legitimate bride and wife, 100 *lire* of *denarii trentini* both in money and in movable goods.
>
> *Domina* Salafia is asked *per verba de presenti*, at the presence of the witnesses and the notary Antonio, if she desires to marry *magister Zesius* as her legitimate bridegroom and husband, and answers: *"sic vollo libenter"*. *Magister Zesius* is asked if he desires *domina* Salafia as his legitimate bride and wife, and answers: *"sic vollo libenter"* and gives her a golden ring as sign of the wedding.[8]

---

the groom expressed clearly their intention to marry. The two expressions *per verba de presenti* and *per verba de futuro* indicated, respectively, the intention to marry in that moment (*verba de presenti*) and the promise to marry in the future (*verba de futuro*). That was essential to distinguish between marriage and engagement. On marriage before the Council of Trento see, for example, Jean Gaudemet, *Il matrimonio in Occidente* (Torino: SEI, 1996); Daniela Lombardi, *Matrimoni di antico regime* (Bologna: Il Mulino, 2001); Silvana Seidel Menchi and Diego Quaglioni eds., *Matrimoni in dubbio. Unioni controverse e nozze clandestine in Italia dal XIV al XVIII secolo* (Bologna: Il Mulino, 2001); Trevor Dean and Kate J. P. Lowe eds., *Marriage in Italy, 1300–1650* (Cambridge: Cambridge University Press, 1998).

8 ACapTn, IC4, n. 84, c. 46v: "*1353 gennaio 26 (sabato). Trento, nella casa di abitazione di magister Giovanni merzader del fu ser Nicolò da Ton. Presenti detto magister Giovanni, Lorenzo del fu ser Biondo da Vigolo, Benasuto detto Covalerius osterius, Paolo detto Pevrada stazonerius e Bettino del fu dominus Savoldus da Bergamo, tutti abitanti a Trento. Magister Çesius cimatore del fu Odorico da Terlago riceve come dote da parte della domina Salafia del fu Michele da Venosta abitante a Trento, sua sposa e moglie legittima, 100 lire di denari trentini in denari e beni mobili. La domina Salafia, interrogata per verba de presenti di fronte ai testimoni soprascritti e ad Antonio notaio se vuole il detto magister Zesius come suo legittimo sposo e marito, risponde: 'sic vollo libenter'. Magister Zesius, interrogato se vuole la detta domina Salafia come sua legittima sposa e moglie, risponde: 'sic vollo libenter' e le dona un anello d'oro in segno dell'avvenuto matrimonio.*"

All these documents were written following the same pattern, to which few changes were made. As was common in Northern Italy, the ceremony was celebrated in the house of either the father, a relative, or friends of the bride. It was often officiated by the notary.[9] In the presence of the witnesses and the notary, the bride was asked if she desired to marry the man who had been promised her; the same question was then asked to the man. After both answered *"sic vollo libenter"*, the husband gave his wife a golden ring. All the weddings described in the register were celebrated using these sentences. The practice of asking the bride before the bridegroom is likewise attested in Trento during the thirteenth century,[10] and was likely the most common custom. These sentences were often symmetrical, to show the commitment of both bride and groom.[11]

These formulaic expressions established that the two people married freely and, these alongside the public exchange of the ring, both of which were made in the presence of witnesses, were central components of the celebration that helped avoid confusion between engagement and marriage and, consequently, doubts about the legitimacy of the union. Up until the Council of Trent, in fact, Italian wedding rituals were highly diversified.[12] It was of great relevance in all cases to make sure that neither the bride nor the groom had been forced to marry against their will. For this reason, and given that until the sixteenth century the church did not organise the wedding,[13] and the presence of a priest was not required (the blessing could be given at a moment that did not correspond with the ceremony), the notary[14] or one of the witnesses were commissioned to ask the bridal couple the ritual questions. Antonio da Pomarolo did not mention other customs such as, for example, touching the hands, a gesture that marked and was associated with the engagement in surrounding areas such as Emilia Romagna, Veneto, Friuli, and Tuscany.[15] Like in Tuscany, Emilia Romagna, Southern Italy and other European regions, the most important symbolic act was probably the gift of the ring.

---

9 Daniela Lombardi, *Storia del matrimonio: dal Medioevo ad oggi* (Bologna: Il Mulino, 2011), p. 35.

10 Ginevra Zanetti, "La stipulazione del matrimonio a Trento nel secolo XIII (estratto)," *Rivista di Storia del diritto italiano* 16–1 (1943), pp. 7–77, here p. 11.

11 Gaudemet, *Il matrimonio in Occidente*, p. 133.

12 Ottavia Niccoli, "Baci rubati. Gesti e riti nuziali in Italia prima e dopo il Concilio di Trento," in *Il gesto nel rito e nel cerimoniale dal mondo antico ad oggi*, ed. Sergio Bettelli and Monica Centanni (Florence: Ponte alle Grazie, 1995), pp. 224–47, here pp. 225–26.

13 Christiane Klapisch-Zuber, *La famiglia e le donne nel Rinascimento a Firenze* (Rome and Bari: Laterza, 1995), p. 128.

14 Zanetti, "La stipulazione," p. 11.

15 For weddings before the Council of Trento see, for example, Lombardi, *Storia del matrimonio*, esp. pp. 29–30, 45, and 61.

3 Influence on the Dowry

As regards the dowry, it was usually comprised of money and/or movable goods, real estate, or a combination of these. It is important to note that the notary often drafted only one document that contained all the information about both the engagement and the wedding. That in no way means, however, that there were no previous agreements. Neither is there any mention in the register of the transfer of bride into their new homes, which in other places took place after the ceremony and was of interest to the whole community. This omission does not help us understand where the newlyweds went to live, if they lived with relatives, or on their own. It is highly likely, that the rituals celebrated by people of lower social levels were less solemn and shorter than those celebrated by nobles and aristocrats.[16]

As mentioned above, we have no information on previous agreements; the notarial acts drafted by Antonio da Pomarolo do not mention preceding negotiations. As it was usual in most European areas, a marriage in Trentino likely implied various earlier stages managed not by the bride and groom, but by their families. We can only speculate about the agreements arranged by people of the lower-middle class. A hypothesis can be based on the occupations of citizens involved and the relations between each, at least in consideration of the fathers and uncles of the bride and groom. In some cases, we know that they were business partners, but in the majority of the cases analysed it is not possible to establish the kinds of relations that linked the families. Beyond this, it is clear that people tended to marry someone belonging to their same social level: the daughter of a shoemaker usually married the son of another shoemaker, or of a farmer, or of an artisan, but never the son of a rich draper. Although the church was trying to control the celebrations, the wedding continued to be essentially a means of allegiance between families,[17] the purposes of which were to strengthen their social position and to create new relationships.

Antonio da Pomarolo's register enables us to learn about family relationships in more detail, for example, in the case of Dorotea, daughter of Giacomo *apotecarius* from Verona. The dowry of Dorotea, who married Francesco, son of the deceased Nicolò *merzader*, on 20 July 1355, was rather high in comparison to those of other women mentioned in the register: 1,200 *lire* of *denarii trentini*. Francesco was Giovanni *merzader*'s brother. Giovanni, whose

16 Klapisch-Zuber, *La famiglia*, p. 130.

17 Lombardi, *Matrimoni di antico regime*, p. 27.

marriage contract was mentioned above, was a very active client of Antonio. The family of the bridegroom owned many buildings and fields, probably inherited from the father Nicolò. We also know from the register that Giovanni had been guardian of his brother until at least a few months before the wedding. The *carta matrimonii* is similar to others conserved in the register: after both the bride and groom were asked the questions and the gift of the ring was exchanged, Francesco was given the dowry. In a *carta debiti* drafted the same day, however, it is claimed that he had not actually received the dowry from his father-in-law. The *instrumentum* is now crossed out: Antonio did this every time an issue was considered closed or a controversy settled. To put the amount of Dorotea's dowry into perspective, we should consider that in the same period the maintenance of the chaplain of the monastery of San Lorenzo came to 20 *ducati* a year (100 *lire*).[18] That dowry is comparable or even higher than those of some noble women of the period. In 1348 Caterina Thun's dowry, for example, amounted to 1,000 *lire*, in 1362 Ganga Gandi's one to 2,000; lower were the dowries of Polla, who in 1317 married Egnone Gandi (100 *lire*), and that of Serauda of Castel Belvesino Thun in 1302.[19]

On 23 July 1355, in the house of Giacomo *apotecarius* from Verona, Francesco gave Dorotea 200 *lire* of *denarii trentini* as morning gift (*morgengab*). On the same day, Dorotea gave up all claims on the inheritance of her father, her mother, and her brother; the only exception was constituted by the 1,200 *lire* of her dowry. These two events, the morning gift and the exclusion from a share in the paternal, maternal, and fraternal inheritance, are attested in other documents within and outside the register. It is important to consider that Roman and German law coexisted in the area of Trentino: according to Roman law the nuptial union is based on the agreement of bride and groom, and German law implies that a marriage is fundamentally based on the transfer of the authority over the woman (*mundium*) from the father to the husband.[20] The morning gift, or *pretium verginitatis*, also referred to as *donatio antelecti* by Antonio da Pomarolo, was a German tradition that consisted of a marriage gift, usually constituted of money, given by the husband to his wife after the first night of marriage. It symbolised the consummation of marriage and, therefore, the validity of it.[21]

---

18 Emanuele Curzel, *Documenti papali per la storia trentina* (*fino al 1341*) (Bologna: Il Mulino, 2004), p. 611.

19 Marco Bettotti, *La nobiltà trentina nel medioevo* (*metà XII–metà XV secolo*) (Bologna: Il Mulino, 2002), pp. 177–78.

20 Gaudemet, *Il matrimonio in Occidente*, p. 19.

21 There are not enough documents in Antonio da Pomarolo's register containing information about the morning gift to establish whether it corresponded to the *controdote* or if it

This custom was not followed by all the couples mentioned in the register, but only – as it seems – by Dorotea and by Binia, daughter of the deceased *Hendrigus.* The morning gift was in fact disappearing during that period.[22] The amount of the dowry was in some way proportional to that of the present given by the husband. These had nothing to do with the presents mentioned among the Langobards, which were so high that king Liutprando had to issue a law in order to prevent the morning gift from exceeding a quarter of the property of the husband.[23]

Similar to Dorotea's renunciation of her inheritance, this can be explained by the custom, testified in Trentino and in other areas for this period, according to which the dowry was considered part of the inheritance that would otherwise have gone to a woman. As a result of this custom brides were not allowed to claim anything else, and could not inherit their fathers' estates, which usually went to their male siblings. We have verification of the existence of the *exclusio propter dotem* among noble families of Trentino during this period.[24] Dotal and hereditary property were considered different and were not interchangeable. In many areas, however, local customs may have had more influence than the law.[25] The exclusion from the inheritance of the father corresponded to the need for the family estate to remain undivided. To avoid division, sons were favoured in the succession. That does not necessarily imply a married woman had to be completely excluded in the testamentary

was only a word that substitutes for the expression "*controdote*". It is highly likely that in these cases this gift, given by the husband to his wife, has something to do both with the original morning gift and the *controdote*, mixing the two traditions, however the scarcity of acts written by Antonio da Pomarolo regarding this usage makes it impossible for us to reach a definite conclusion on this matter. For additional information see, for example, Serena Luzzi, *Stranieri in città: presenza tedesca e società urbana a Trento (secoli XV–XVIII)* (Bologna: Il Mulino, 2003).

22 Diane Owen Hughes, "Il matrimonio nell'Italia medievale," in *Storia del matrimonio*, ed. Michela de Giorgio and Christiane Klapisch-Zuber (Rome and Bari: Laterza, 1996), pp. 5–61, here pp. 36–37; Manlio Bellomo, *Ricerche sui rapporti patrimoniali tra coniugi. Contributo alla storia della famiglia medievale* (Varese: Giuffrè, 1961), pp. 12.

23 Owen Hughes, "Il matrimonio", p. 35. The morning gift was originally a gift composed of some objects for the woman (everyday objects and decorations). Over time it began to include money and immovable properties, becoming so considerable that King Liutprando decided to regulate it. The medieval morning gift had already become something different from this old tradition and was not so consistent as to necessitate a law to regulate the sum given by the husband. In Italy during the Middle and Modern Ages, the morning gift was often called *antelectum*. Antonio da Pomarolo has made use of both expressions.

24 Bettotti, *La nobiltà trentina*, p. 180.

25 Signori, *Von der Paradiesehe*, pp. 60–61.

succession,[26] because fathers could leave something more to their daughters in their will.

Returning to the marriage habits described in the register, we cannot avoid recognizing that there are many similarities with practices in other cities. In Renaissance Florence, for example, after the agreements between two families, the fiancé went to the bride's house where a notary asked the ritual questions and registered the consents. Other rituals then followed: the ring given by the groom to the bride, the donation of some presents from the bridegroom to the family of the bride, and a banquet given by the family of the bride.[27] The two last practices were not mentioned in Pomarolo's register. Very relevant was, both in Trento and in Florence, that the dowry was handed over in part or *in toto* before the bride moved to her new house.[28]

From register IC4 it is clear that, if he was living, the father of the bride handed over the dowry during the ceremony. In one case, that of Binia, daughter of *Hendrigus*, the notary wrote that the dowry – two fields and 100 *lire* of *denarii trentini* – was handed over by the father and his daughter together. Sometimes the father of the bridegroom played a role as well: in the

26 Bellomo, *Ricerche*, p. 164. This is unfortunately not the appropriate venue for an in-depth examination of the ancient laws of Trento. For the statutes see, among others, Marco Bellabarba, "Gli statuti del principato vescovile di Trento. Tradizioni, simboli e pluralità di un diritto urbano," in *Legislazione e prassi istituzionale nell'Europa medievale. Tradizioni normative, ordinamenti, circolazione mercantile (secoli XI–XV)*, ed. Gabriella Rossetti (Naples: Liguori, 2001), pp. 329–52; Franco Cagol, "Il comune di Trento in antico regime," in *"Volendo questo illustrissimo magistrato Consolare". Trecento anni di editoria pubblica a Trento*, ed. Mauro Hausbergher (Trento: Provincia Autonoma di Trento, Soprintendenza per i Beni librari e archivistici, 2005), pp. XI–XLVII; Emanuele Curzel, *Trento* (Spoleto: Centro italiano di studi sull'alto Medioevo, 2013); Tomaso Gar, "Statuti della città di Trento colla designazione dei beni del comune nella prima metà del secolo XIV" (Trento: Monauni, 1858); Desiderio Reich, "Del più antico statuto della città di Trento" (estratto dal "Programma dell'i.r. Ginnasio Superiore di Trento") (Trento: Seiser, Giovanni 1889); Hans von Voltelini, *Gli antichi statuti di Trento* (Rovereto: Accademia roveretana degli Agiati, 1989, orig. Germ. 1903); Mariano Welber and Marco Stenico, *Gli statuti dei sindici nella tradizione trentina* (Trento: UCT, 1997); Laura Giuliani, "Per la riedizione delle 'Designationes communium civitatis Tridenti' del 1339: prime ipotesi di ricerca" (PhD diss., Università degli studi di Trento, 2007–2008); Carlo Bortoli, "Per un'edizione dei testi statutari del Comune di Trento dei secoli XIV–XV" (PhD diss., Università degli studi di Trento, 2009/2010); Christian Zendri, "Hans von Voltelini e gli antichi statuti di Trento. Spunti di ricerca," *Studi Trentini. Storia* 91 (2012), pp. 469–81; and Christian Zendri "I primi statuti di Trento fra tradizione manoscritta e problemi di datazione," *Studi Trentini. Storia* 95 (2016), pp. 315–24.

27 Klapisch-Zuber, *La famiglia*, pp. 117–18.

28 Ibid., p. 160.

case of Binia, the dowry was given to the father-in-law and not only to the bridegroom.

The situation was more complex when the father of the bride was deceased. In eighteen cases out of twenty-six – and this is the particularity of this group of documents – the bride gave her dowry to her husband. In two additional cases an uncle is mentioned in association with the dowry. In all but one case where the notary failed to register an entry, the fathers of each of the eighteen women that handed over their dowries were deceased. It is known that fathers played a vital role in negotiations about the marriage and the dowry among the noble or in rich families, and this usually occurred among the lower social levels as well; it was therefore not common for a woman, even if she was an orphan, to autonomously managed her dowry without the support of a male relative.[29] If we analyse these documents more carefully, we can easily notice that the two groups – the eighteen women who handed over their dowry themselves on the one hand, and on the other the two women supported by their uncles – are different not only because the eighteen women were orphans, but also because of variance in the amounts of their dowries and their social status. The eighteen brides of the first group belonged to a medium or low class, and their dowries were not very high. Many of them brought with them a sum lower than 100 *lire* of *denarii trentini*. The highest among these was the dowry of *Savorita,* daughter of the deceased Negro, with 200 *lire* of *denarii trentini*. These dowries could not be compared to that of Caterina daughter of the deceased Gislemberto, who brought 1,550 *lire* into the marriage and was supported by her uncle Bartolomeo *sartor*, a very rich and active client of the notary Antonio. We must also consider that, after all, some relatives of the bride were very often among the witnesses, perhaps to show their support; nevertheless, the independence of those eighteen women gives the impression as having been considerable, and we will reflect on this later. In one instance, the mother of the bride was also involved: she entered into a contractual agreement to pay a portion of her daughter's dowry in instalments, during the wedding celebration, however the bridegroom had declared that he had already received the dowry. We cannot avoid thinking that this sort of contract might have been linked to the payment of some debts. That would further describe a different, and more complex, kind of relationship.

29 Lombardi, *Storia del matrimonio*, pp. 23, 27 and 65–66.

4 Economic Independence of Women in Wills

Wills are another form of document that provide us with information about the role of women in the Tridentine society during the fourteenth century. As mentioned above, a woman could inherit a portion of her father's, mother's, or relatives' estate, even after she had been given a dowry, if her father decided to leave her something in his last will and testament. Research done by Luciano Maino regarding fifty wills written in Trento between the twelfth and the fifteenth century found that the most common custom was to leave more to male descendants. In instances where the husband established that the whole of his estate was to be inherited by his wife, he usually included a series of conditions referring to the exclusion from one portion or from the whole inheritance should the widow remarry.[30]

In the register IC4 there are three wills, two of which refer to the last wishes of women. One of these contains interesting details. This is the will of Eleonora, drafted on 2 October 1354. Therein, the notary wrote that her two nieces, Lucia, and Caterina, were to receive sums of 50 and 100 *lire* of *denarii trentini* respectively. The portion for Lucia would have been given to Eleonora's nephew Giovanni if the same Lucia had not married him. Caterina, on the other hand, would have been excluded from the inheritance if she committed adultery or failed to keep herself pure and chaste. These kinds of conditions would generally not have come under consideration had the heirs been men.

Another notarial act contains the last wishes of Marco, son of the deceased *Hendricus*, and was compiled by Antonio da Pomarolo on 15 March 1354. After leaving a sum to the poor and for his spiritual salvation, the testator listed a series of debts that his sons had to repay. He then established that 50 *lire* of *denarii trentini* was to be given to his servant Antonia, and 60 to her son. He finally chose his two sons as his sole heirs. It is rather rare that something was left to a servant, but this is not the only known case. In another will, compiled on 4 September 1390, Lola from Trento, a widow, decided her sole heir was to be her servant Gilda, on the condition that the same would not sell any real estate without the permission of her legal representative, the notary Francesco, until the age of twenty.[31] The most common practice was for women to choose their husbands as sole heirs or, in instances where the husband was deceased, sons, brothers, or nephews. Although we do find wills in which mothers or daughters are mentioned as sole heirs, it seems that women tended to leave their

30 Luciano Maino, *50 testamenti medioevali nell'Archivio capitolare di Trento (secoli XII–XV)* (Ferrara: Liberty House, 1999), p. 41.

31 Ibid., pp. 135–37.

property to male relatives. Be that as it may, these wills provide us with some important information: each of these women owned amounts of money, and moveable and immovable property that they decided to leave to one relative or another.

5 Cooperation in the Professional Activities of the Family

Other documents clearly evidence that women participated in economic matters of the family, as is the case, for example, in matters relating to rents, buying, and selling. In some instances, we see that a good was sold or rented by both the wife and husband, rather than by the husband alone. It is not possible for us to understand if these women participated in the economic situation of the family more than they had before the plague, or if they were simply managing their dowries. In my opinion, it is highly likely that they had reached a greater economic autonomy; otherwise, the notary would have noted – as he did in some documents – that the goods had belonged to the dowry. I would also add to this consideration the fact that the names of these women can be found in other notarial acts regarding the occupation of their husbands. It is reasonable to hypothesise that they cooperated in the professional activity of their husbands and, consequently, could have obtained more power in family economic matters. A *carta solutionis* kept in the register describes a highly relevant case in this respect, wherein Caterina, wife of Negro, returned 10,200 *lire* to her father, who had lent her that rather high sum two years previously. It seems that Caterina managed this money without the supervision of her husband. We do not know what Caterina used this money for, nor if Negro was the *cimator pannorum* mentioned elsewhere in the register as client of Antonio da Pomarolo. Regardless, that sum was likely connected with the activity of her husband.

Different was the situation of widows, who were protagonists of buying and selling, and had no need of help from male relatives. Some researchers have found that since as early as the thirteenth century widows became increasingly less subject to the legal protection of both their families of birth and that of their husbands.[32] Nevertheless, we cannot avoid speculating about whether or not the increased economic autonomy of women in the Middle Ages that

32 Claudia Opitz, "La vita quotidiana delle donne nel tardo Medioevo (1250–1500)," in *Storia delle donne in Occidente*, vol. 2: *Il Medioevo*, ed. George Duby and Michelle Perrot (Rome and Bari: Laterza, 1990), pp. 330–402, here p. 382.

has been evidenced by many of the examined documents is likewise related to the plague, as a result of which a considerable number of individuals perished and many families were drastically reduced. Many girls and women became orphans as a result of the plague and were therefore obliged to themselves manage issues that had previously been administered by the *pater familias* or other male relatives.

6 Conclusions

Apart from the *Cronica* of Giovanni from Parma, a canon often mentioned in the register analysed here, we have little information about the plague in Trento during the fourteenth century.[33] Giovanni from Parma narrates that there was an outbreak in Trento on 2 June 1348 that lasted six months and killed five sixths of the inhabitants. As this is the only narration of the facts, we are not able to establish how many people really perished, but it is certain that the plague claimed many victims. Register IC4 provides some clues on the effects of this situation on the population of the town. Nearly all of the people mentioned had lost a mother or father or were managing the inheritance of another relative. The most emblematic case is perhaps that of two brothers, Giovanni and Giuliano, who in a *carta divisionis* agreed upon the division of the properties not only of their parents, but of their brothers as well. The notary Antonio wrote of fifty-four inheritance proceedings, which means that at least fifty-four people had recently died – "at least" because in some cases the inheritance involved more than one individual. Documents describing the situation in previous decades are missing, and as a result it is clear that it will be impossible for us to come to any understanding about why these people died. But we can speculate that women reached a new level of economic independence due to the fact that many of their male relatives had died. In addition, we can also presume that the choice of the spouse, at least in the lower-class families, was perhaps only partially imposed.

It may seem unusual that in the absence of a male relative many women in the second half of the fourteenth century could decide for themselves who to marry and how to manage their dowries, however female participation in the management of family property was nothing new in Trento, and was

33 See Emanuele Curzel, Lorenza Pamato, and Gian Maria Varanini, "Giovanni da Parma, canonico della cattedrale di Trento, e la sua cronaca (1348–1377)," *Studi Trentini di Scienze Storiche* 80 (2001), pp. 211–39.

the case in other areas as well.[34] Documents kept in the archival fond of the *Congregazione della Carità* drafted between the years 1300 and 1380 show us that some women, widows and otherwise, autonomously stipulated location and sales contracts.[35] This appears to have been the case for transactions of goods of low value made by lower-middle class individuals. In cases of disagreement, male relatives were sometimes named in the notarial act alongside the woman when she went to the notary. Again, granting the proper precautions, it could be possible to presume that women of middle or low social levels had more economic independence and were less controlled by their families. In his research on the nobility, Bettotti has found that there was probably more cooperation between husband and wife in Trentino regarding the family estate than in other areas.[36]

In conclusion, it is important to take into account that the period considered here saw many economic and social changes. The development of a monetary and commercial economy changed the lives of women: their participation in social, economic, religious, and political situations increased throughout Europe. Women had always been present in familial activities, in production and buying and selling, but now the participation of lower to middle-class women in the professional activities of their husbands likely provided them with more independence than that enjoyed by noblewomen.[37] As few artisans employed shop boys, the help of family members was necessary. As has been shown elsewhere, women's work was an important contribution to the development of a town's economy.[38] We can hypothesise that, precisely because of this economic importance women of the lower-middle social levels in Trento, as in other areas, experienced more independence and freedom in the management of goods belonging to their properties. Furthermore, it is reasonable to assume that the plague that occurred in the town in 1348 increased the economic independence of many women.

---

34 See, for example, Petti Balbi and Guglielmotti, *Dare credito.*

35 See Silvia Roatti, "Istituzioni ecclesiastiche e società a Trento nel Trecento. Dalle pergamene della Congregazione di Carità (con un'appendice di 234 regesti di documenti inediti (1300–1380)" (PhD diss., Università degli studi di Trento, 1991/1992).

36 Bettotti, *La nobiltà trentina*, p. 185.

37 Carla Casagrande, "La donna custodita," in *Storia delle donne in Occidente*, vol. 2: *Il Medioevo,* ed. George Duby and Michelle Perrot (Rome and Bari: Laterza, 1990), pp. 88–128, here pp. 88–89.

38 Opitz, "La vita quotidiana," pp. 338 and 362.

References

Bellabarba, Marco. "Gli statuti del principato vescovile di Trento. Tradizioni, simboli e pluralità di un diritto urbano." In *Legislazione e prassi istituzionale nell'Europa medievale. Tradizioni normative, ordinamenti, circolazione mercantile (secoli XI–XV)*, edited by Gabriella Rossetti, pp. 329–52. Naples: Liguori, 2001.

Bellomo, Manlio. *Ricerche sui rapporti patrimoniali tra coniugi. Contributo alla storia della famiglia medievale.* Varese: Giuffrè, 1961.

Bettotti, Marco. *La nobiltà trentina nel medioevo (metà XII–metà XV secolo).* Bologna: Il Mulino, 2002.

Bortoli, Carlo. "Per un'edizione dei testi statutari del Comune di Trento dei secoli XIV–XV". PhD diss., Università degli Studi di Trento, 2009/2010.

Cagol, Franco. "Il comune di Trento in antico regime." In *"Volendo questo illustrissimo magistrato Consolare". Trecento anni di editoria pubblica a Trento,* edited by Mauro Hausbergher, pp. XI–XLVII. Trento: Provincia Autonoma di Trento, Soprintendenza per i Beni librari e archivistici, 2005.

Casagrande, Carla. "La donna custodita." In *Storia delle donne in Occidente,* vol. 2: *Il Medioevo,* edited by George Duby and Michelle Perrot, pp. 88–128. Rome and Bari: Laterza, 1990.

Curzel, Emanuele. *Documenti papali per la storia trentina (fino al 1341).* Bologna: Il Mulino, 2004.

Curzel, Emanuele. *I canonici e il Capitolo della cattedrale di Trento dal XII al XV secolo.* Bologna: EDB, 2001.

Curzel, Emanuele. "Per la storia del Capitolo della Cattedrale di Trento nel Trecento e nel Quattrocento: la serie degli Instrumenta Capitularia." *Studi Trentini di Scienze Storiche* 71 (1992): pp. 223–60.

Curzel, Emanuele. *Trento.* Spoleto: Centro italiano di studi sull'alto Medioevo, 2013.

Curzel, Emanuele, Lorenza Pamato, and Gian Maria Varanini. "Giovanni da Parma, canonico della cattedrale di Trento, e la sua cronaca (1348–1377)," *Studi Trentini di Scienze Storiche* 80 (2001): pp. 211–39.

Dean, Trevor, and Kate J. P. Lowe, eds. *Marriage in Italy, 1300–1650.* Cambridge: Cambridge University Press, 1998.

Gar, Tomaso. "Statuti della città di Trento colla designazione dei beni del comune nella prima metà del secolo XIV." Trento: Monauni, 1858.

Gaudemet, Jean. *Il matrimonio in Occidente.* Torino: SEI, 1996.

Giuliani, Laura. "Per la riedizione delle 'Designationes communium civitatis Tridenti' del 1339: prime ipotesi di ricerca". PhD diss., Università degli studi di Trento, 2007–2008.

Klapisch-Zuber, Christiane. *La famiglia e le donne nel Rinascimento a Firenze.* Rome and Bari: Laterza, 1995.

Lombardi, Daniela. *Matrimoni di antico regime*. Bologna: Il Mulino, 2001.

Lombardi, Daniela. *Storia del matrimonio: dal Medioevo ad oggi*. Bologna: Il Mulino, 2011.

Luzzi, Serena. *Stranieri in città: presenza tedesca e società urbana a Trento (secoli XV–XVIII)*. Bologna: Il Mulino, 2003.

Maino, Luciano. *50 testamenti medioevali nell'Archivio capitolare di Trento (secoli XII–XV)*. Ferrara: Liberty House, 1999.

Mattivi, Silvia. "Il registro del notaio Antonio da Pomarolo (1351–1357). Economia e società a Trento alla metà del Trecento." PhD diss., Università degli Studi di Trento, 2009/2010.

Mattivi, Silvia. "Il registro del notaio Antonio da Pomarolo (1351–1357)." *Studi Trentini. Storia* 91 (2012): pp. 295–321.

Niccoli, Ottavia. "Baci rubati. Gesti e riti nuziali in Italia prima e dopo il Concilio di Trento." In *Il gesto nel rito e nel cerimoniale dal mondo antico ad oggi*, edited by Sergio Bettelli and Monica Centanni, pp. 224–47. Florence: Ponte alle Grazie, 1995.

Opitz, Claudia. "La vita quotidiana delle donne nel tardo Medioevo (1250–1500)." In *Storia delle donne in Occidente*, vol. 2: *Il Medioevo*, edited by George Duby and Michelle Perrot, pp. 330–402. Rome and Bari: Laterza, 1990.

Owen Hughes, Diane. "Il matrimonio nell'Italia medievale." In *Storia del matrimonio*, edited by Michela de Giorgio and Christiane Klapisch-Zuber, pp. 5–61. Rome and Bari: Laterza, 1996.

Petti Balbi, Giovanna. "Forme di credito femminile: osservazioni introduttive." In *Dare credito alle donne. Presenze femminili nell'economia tra medioevo ed età moderna*, edited by Giovanna Petti Balbi and Paola Gugliemotti (Convegno internazionale di studi, Asti, 8–9 ottobre 2010), pp. 9–24. Asti: Centro Studi "Renato Bordone", 2012.

Reich, Desiderio. "Del più antico statuto della città di Trento" (estratto dal "Programma dell'i.r. Ginnasio Superiore di Trento"). Trento: Seiser, Giovanni, 1889.

Roatti, Silvia. "Istituzioni ecclesiastiche e società a Trento nel Trecento. Dalle pergamene della Congregazione di Carità (con un'appendice di 234 regesti di documenti inediti (1300–1380)." PhD diss., Università degli studi di Trento, 1991/1992.

Seidel Menchi, Silvana, and Diego Quaglioni, eds. *Matrimoni in dubbio. Unioni controverse e nozze clandestine in Italia dal XIV al XVIII secolo*. Bologna: Il Mulino, 2001.

Signori, Gabriela. *Von der Paradiesehe zur Gütergemeinschaft. Die Ehe in der mittelalterlichen Lebens- und Vorstellungswelt*. Frankfurt a. M. and New York: Campus, 2011.

Varanini, Gian Maria. "Città alpine del tardo medioevo." In *Il Gotico nelle Alpi 1350–1450*, edited by Enrico Castelnuovo and Francesca de Gramatica, pp. 35–52. Trento: Provincia Autonoma di Trento – Castello del Buonconsiglio, 2002.

von Voltelini, Hans. *Gli antichi statuti di Trento*. Rovereto: Accademia roveretana degli Agiati, 1989, orig. Germ. 1903.

Welber, Mariano, and Marco Stenico, *Gli statuti dei sindici nella tradizione trentina*. Trento: UCT, 1997.

Zanetti, Ginevra. "La stipulazione del matrimonio a Trento nel secolo XIII (estratto)." *Rivista di Storia del diritto italiano* 16–1 (1943): pp. 7–77.

Zendri, Christian. "I primi statuti di Trento fra tradizione manoscritta e problemi di datazione." *Studi Trentini. Storia* 95 (2016): pp. 315–24.

Zendri, Christian. "Hans von Voltelini e gli antichi statuti di Trento. Spunti di ricerca." *Studi Trentini. Storia* 91 (2012): pp. 469–81.

CHAPTER 7

Along Family Line and Next of Kin: Negotiating and Safeguarding Dowries and Inheritance in Late Medieval Tyrol

Christian Hagen

By the Middle Ages, the idea that inheritance could lead to a multitude of conflicts had already been well-established. Contemporary literature repeatedly alludes to this topic, particularly with regard to nobility and succession to rulership.[1] While the struggle for political control following the death of a family member always represented a specific circumstance, such struggles often entailed disputes concerning succession and property. This potential for conflict over property between families, spouses, siblings, or different generations, seems to have been acknowledged as a common problem.

This potential is reiterated in phrases that reoccur throughout the related sources. Fear of dispute is explicitly named as the reason that individuals chose to put last wills and testamentary contracts down in writing. A noble widow strove to discourage discord between her heirs (*in vera dileccione ad restinguendas futuras discordias et brigas confessa et manifesta fuit* […]) by dividing an interest that she had previously received from her husband.[2] In addition to a concern for salvation, many late medieval last wills refer to a wish to prevent dispute as a primary motive behind their creation. References to the latter can be found in sources from, to name only a few, Bozen, Meran, Basel, Constance and Lausanne.[3] In the hopes of preventing quarrels following her death Basilia from the parish of Marling near Meran, for example, arranged the situation as follows: her daughter Maetza and Maetza's husband were allowed

1 Ines Heiser, "Generationenkonflikte? Erbrecht und Elternfürsorge in der mittelhochdeutschen Literatur," in *Aufblühen und Verwelken. Mediävistische Forschungen zu Kindheit und Alter*, ed. Ines Heiser and Andreas Meyer (Leipzig: Eudora, 2009), pp. 145–58.

2 Stadtarchiv Meran (StAM), Notariatsimbreviaturen (NI) 5 (1369), fol. 4v.

3 Katharina Simon-Muscheid, "Diebstahl oder Erbrecht? Streit um letztwillige Verfügungen in den oberrheinischen Städten des 15. und 16. Jahrhunderts," in *Criminalità e giustizia in Germania e in Italia. Pratiche giudiziarie e linguaggi giuridici tra medioevo ed età moderna*, ed. Marco Bellabarba, Gerd Schwerhoff, and Andrea Zorzi (Bologna: Il Mulino, 2001), pp. 35–62, here p. 37; Paul Baur, *Testament und Bürgerschaft. Alltagsleben und Sachkultur im spätmittelalterlichen Konstanz* (Sigmaringen: Jan Thorbecke, 1989), p. 85.

 | DOI:10.1163/9789004456204_008

use of a specific vineyard for their lifetime (usufruct), however the main assets were bequeathed to Basilia's grandson, who promised to provide for her until the end of her life and also agreed to settle a pay-out with his sister.[4] This kind of planning testifies to the fact that the people of the late-medieval age were well aware of conflicts that might arise with regard to family and property.[5] Scholars speculate that demographic growth and increased mobility may have led to an increase in writing during the twelfth century. This may also have attributed to more sources exhibiting this concern for the future.[6]

This chapter examines the practice of inheritance and matrimonial property in the late medieval county of Tyrol, with a particular focus on conflicts within families, between different generations and the sexes. Before detailing legal practice, it is first necessary to delineate the marital property law and inheritance law of that region. Few historians have taken the trouble to consider premodern marriage property law in Tyrol, and thus archivist and legal historian Hans von Voltelini's (1862–1938) treatise "Geschichte des ehelichen Güterrechtes in Tirol" remains an important work.[7] Aware of the topic's complexity, Voltelini described regional variances in form and presented the conjuncture of legal traditions within the region. The article derives from his habilitation work on thirteenth century notaries in Bozen and Trento, and those records served as the primary sources for his work.[8] Voltelini's efforts to understand sixteenth century law code in conjunction with early medieval Germanic law, while methodological consistent with his own time, to some extent impeded his understanding of the late medieval marriage and property law. Given that older legal histories have highlighted the influence neighbouring legal traditions had on Tyrolean law, we can see that the social dimensions of this subject have long been neglected. Historic and ethnographic studies

4 StAM, NI 5 (1369), fol. 13v.

5 See Christian Hagen, Margareth Lanzinger, and Janine Maegraith, "Competing Interests in Death-related Stipulations in South Tirol, c. 1350–1600," in *Planning for Death: Wills and Death-related Property Arrangements in Europe, 1200–1600*, ed. Mia Korpiola and Anu Lahtinen (Leiden and Boston: Brill, 2018), pp. 88–118 and the other chapters in this volume.

6 Thomas Behrmann, "'Ad maiorem cautelam'. Sicherheitsdenken, Zukunftsbewußtsein und schriftliche Fixierung im Rechtsleben der italienischen Kommunen," *Quellen und Forschungen aus italienischen Archiven und Bibliotheken* 72 (1992), pp. 26–53.

7 Hans von Voltelini, "Zur Geschichte des ehelichen Güterrechtes in Tirol," in *Festgaben zu Ehren Max Büdinger's von seinen Freunden und Schülern* (Innsbruck: Wagner, 1898), pp. 331–64; on Voltelini see Thomas Olechowski, Tamara Ehs, and Kamila Staudigl-Ciechowicz, *Die Wiener Rechts- und Staatswissenschaftliche Fakultät 1918–1938* (Göttingen: V&R unipress, 2014), pp. 298–300.

8 Hans von Voltelini, ed., *Die Südtiroler Notariatsimbreviaturen des dreizehnten Jahrhunderts*, part 1 (Innsbruck: Wagner, 1899).

that have focused on the Tyrolean peasantry have paid little attention to property issues.[9]

Siglinde Clementi has revisited this topic with a special interest in noble marriage and inheritance.[10] The "Aushandeln von Ehe" comparative study took a broad look at marriage contracts in modern Austria, which included Tyrol.[11] This recent research shares a modern approach of social history that takes into consideration not only cultural and legal norms, but also gender specific perspectives and the consequences of these norms for familial life. The present chapter follows this approach in both content and method.[12]

We have as yet no comprehensive comparative survey of premodern marital property and inheritance law for German-speaking regions.[13] What studies we do have on early modern Germany also tend to consider older regional marital customs.[14] Joint ownership was predominant in most territories,

---

9 Otto Stolz, *Rechtsgeschichte des Bauernstandes und der Landwirtschaft in Tirol und Vorarlberg* (Bozen: Ferrari-Auer, 1949), pp. 64–74; Franz Kolb, "Vermögens- und Erbrecht in der Wipptaler Bauernfamilie," *Tiroler Heimat* 20 (1956), pp. 63–81.

10 Siglinde Clementi, "Deren von Wolkenstein. Familienstrategien, Heirat und Geschlechterbeziehungen bei den Wolkenstein-Trostburg (um 1500 bis 1650)," in *Die Wolkensteiner. Facetten des Tiroler Adels in Spätmittelalter und Neuzeit*, ed. Gustav Pfeifer and Kurt Andermann (Innsbruck: Wagner, 2009), pp. 111–48.

11 Margareth Lanzinger, Gunda Barth-Scalmani, Ellinor Forster, and Gertrude Langer-Ostrawsky, *Aushandeln von Ehe. Heiratsverträge der Neuzeit im europäischen Vergleich* (Cologne, Weimar, and Vienna: Böhlau, 2010, 2nd edition 2015); Margareth Lanzinger, "Marriage Contracts in Various Contexts: Marital Property Rights, Sociocultural Aspects and Gender-specific Implications. Late-Eighteenth-Century Evidence from two Tirolean Court Districts," *Annales de démographie historique* 121–1 (2011), pp. 69–97. See also Siglinde Clementi, "Zur Ökonomie der Ehre. Heiratsgüter in Tirol um 1800," *Geschichte und Region / Storia e regione* 19–1 (2010), pp. 109–22 (special iussue on Heiratsgüter / Doti).

12 The following resulted from the project "Legal Spaces and Gender Order as Social Processes in a Trans-regional Perspective. Negotiating and Stipulating Property in Urban and Rural Contexts of Southern Tyrol from the Fifteenth to the Early Nineteenth Century" (University of Innsbruck, Geschichte und Region / Storia e regione, Bozen/Bolzano), 2014–2016. See also Siglinde Clementi, Ellinor Forster, Christian Hagen, Margareth Lanzinger, and Janine Christina Maegraith, "Rechtsräume und Geschlechterordnungen als soziale Prozesse – transregional. Vereinbaren und Verfügen in städtischen und ländlichen Kontexten im südlichen Tirol vom 15. bis zum frühen 19. Jahrhundert – ein erster Projektbericht," *Geschichte und Region / Storia e regione* 22–2 (2013), pp. 165–72.

13 For an overview of the older literature, see Louis Pahlow, "Zwischen kirchlichem Dogma und wirtschaftlicher Vernunft. Ehe und eheliches Güterrecht in der mittelalterlichen Stadt," *Zeitschrift der Savigny-Stiftung für Rechtsgeschichte, Germanistische Abteilung* 128 (2011), pp. 377–90.

14 See Karin Gottschalk, *Eigentum, Geschlecht, Gerechtigkeit. Haushalten und Erben im frühneuzeitlichen Leipzig* (Frankfurt a. M. and New York: Campus, 2003); Gesa Ingendahl, *Witwen in der Frühen Neuzeit. Eine kulturhistorische Studie* (Frankfurt a. M. and New York: Campus,

and in other regions the separation of goods and community of acquisition (*Errungenschaftsgemeinschaft*) were common practice.[15] Nineteenth century jurists were primarily interested studying the premodern legal situation as a means of writing a modern law code, and thus their work touches little on the medieval situation. The higher nobility and their marriage patterns dating back as far as 1300 have been the subject of much research, however, few attempts have been made to tackle the dependencies of norm and practice as a central theme.[16]

In the following, legal practice will primarily be examined by means of social interaction and situational negotiation processes. The focal point of this chapter lies on the fourteenth and fifteenth centuries, as there are more preserved written records from this time. Only a few charters have been handed down to us from before the thirteenth century, and because they derive largely from rulers or church officials they rarely contain information relating to marriage property.[17] During the middle of the thirteenth century public notaries who offered their services in Trento also began working in the Adige Valley (Bozen, Meran) and the Vinschgau (Glurns).[18] Several Latin register books (*imbreviatur*) belonging to these scholars have been preserved, and they contain

---

2006); Peter Landau, "Bamberger Landrecht und eheliche Gütergemeinschaft," in *Landesordnungen und Gute Policey in Bayern, Salzburg und Österreich*, ed. Horst Gehringer, Hans-Joachim Hecker, and Reinhard Heydenreuter (Frankfurt a. M.: Klostermann, 2008), pp. 1–18; David Warren Sabean, *Property, Production, and Family in Neckarhausen, 1700–1870* (Cambridge: Cambridge University Press, 1990); Rolf-Dieter Hess, *Familien- und Erbrecht im Württembergischen Landrecht von 1555 unter besonderer Berücksichtigung des älteren württembergischen Rechts* (Stuttgart: Kohlhammer, 1968).

15 Richard Schröder, *Geschichte des ehelichen Güterrechts in Deutschland*, vol. 1–2 (Stettin: Saunier 1863–1871, New Print Aalen: Scientia-Verlag, 1967); Paul von Roth, "Das deutsche eheliche Güterrecht," *Zeitschrift für vergleichende Rechtswissenschaft* 1 (1878), pp. 39–94.

16 Karl-Heinz Spieß, *Familie und Verwandtschaft im deutschen Hochadel des Spätmittelalters, 13. bis Anfang des 16. Jahrhunderts* (Stuttgart: Franz Steiner, 1993); Gabriela Signori, *Von der Paradiesehe zur Gütergemeinschaft. Die Ehe in der mittelalterlichen Lebens- und Vorstellungswelt* (Frankfurt a. M. and New York: Campus, 2011).

17 See Franz Huter, ed., *Tiroler Urkundenbuch*, part 1, vol. 1–3 (Innsbruck: Wagner, 1937–1957); Martin Bitschnau and Hannes Obermair, eds., *Tiroler Urkundenbuch*, part 2, vol. 1–2 (Innsbruck: Wagner, 2009–2012).

18 Voltelini, *Die Südtiroler Notariatsimbreviaturen;* Hans von Voltelini and Franz Huter, eds., *Die Südtiroler Notariatsimbreviaturen des dreizehnten Jahrhunderts*, part 2 (Innsbruck: Wagner, 1951); Hannes Obermair, "The Use of Records in Medieval Towns: The Case of Bolzano, South Tyrol," in *Writing and the Administration of Medieval Towns. Medieval Urban Literacy 1*, ed. Marco Mostert and Anna Adamska (Turnhout: Brepols, 2014), pp. 49–68; David Fliri, "Das Meraner Notariat im Spätmittelalter," in *1317 – Eine Stadt und ihr Recht. Meran im Mittelalter*, ed. Gustav Pfeifer (Bozen: Athesia, 2018), pp. 213–28.

provisions on dowry and matrimony, testaments, waivers and testimonies. The present-day municipal archive of Meran maintains an inventory of sixty-seven register books that date from between 1328 and 1490.[19] While the local noble families primarily made use of charters with their own seals, the urban and rural population of southern Tyrol turned to notaries to record their marriages and inheritance property agreements. These records offer an abundance of information; however, they do not allow for an all-encompassing view of all social groups. Wealthy land-owning individuals tend to be better represented within these records than people with few or no possessions who had little need for the service of a public notary. Beginning in the fifteenth century Latin notaries' registers gradually began being replaced by German-language court books, which followed a similar form and used similar terminology.[20]

1 Customary and Territorial Law before and after 1500

Inheritance and marital property law principles in the county of Tyrol were put in place with the territorial law codes (*Landesordnungen*) of 1526, 1532 and 1573. These printed codifications were drafted by the government and representatives of the country, and embody the regulative power of the sixteenth century territorial state and its ruler.[21] Some of the regulations contained therein can be traced back to older laws, privileges and customs. Legal regulations from the relatively new criminal law of 1499, for example, also found their way in to the law codes. The principle of usucaption law (*Ersitzungsrecht*), elaborately described in the law of 1532, can be traced back as far as 1289.[22] Scattered diplomatic evidence confirms that there was some form of extensive territorial law that was valid for the entire county of Tyrol by as early as the end of the

19 For further scattered examples see Fliri, "Meraner Notariat," p. 215.

20 Christian Hagen, *Fürstliche Herrschaft und kommunale Teilhabe. Die Städte der Grafschaft Tirol im Spätmittelalter* (Innsbruck: Wagner, 2015), pp. 151–56; Franz Huter, ed., *Das älteste Tiroler Verfachbuch* (*Landgericht Meran 1468–1471*) (Innsbruck: Wagner, 1990), pp. 22–26.

21 Martin Paul Schennach, *Gesetz und Herrschaft: Die Entstehung des Gesetzgebungsstaates am Beispiel Tirols* (Cologne, Weimar, and Vienna: Böhlau, 2010), pp. 481–585; Josef Pauser and Martin P. Schennach, eds., *Die Tiroler Landesordnungen von 1526, 1532 und 1573. Historische Einführung und Edition* (Vienna, Cologne, and Weimar: Böhlau, 2018).

22 It describes how ownership of immobile property could be gained after rightful use of said property for more than ten years. Pauser and Schennach, *Tiroler Landesordnungen*, pp. 263–65 (II 51). See Hermann Wiesflecker, "Das Landrecht Meinhards II. von Tirol," in *Neue Beiträge zur geschichtlichen Landeskunde Tirols: Festschrift Franz Huter zum 70. Lebensjahr*, ed. Ernest Troger (Innsbruck and Munich: Wagner, 1969), pp. 455–65.

thirteenth century. It can be assumed that this *ius terre* (*Landrecht*), which was decided upon under the auspices of Count Meinhard II. (d. 1295) and his council, was based on extant customary law.[23] It seems befitting that Meinhard, who had fended off Bavarian claims to power, made efforts to present his county as a separate legal entity. As evidenced by well-known law books and custumals such as *Sachsenspiegel* and *Schwabenspiegel*, Meinhards actions coincide with a tendency to reflect on regional adapted law that can also be found at other regions at that time.

The formulaic mention of the law (*ius terre*) in Tyrolean sources from the fourteenth and fifteenth centuries indicates the continuing validity. As a rural award (*Weistum*) shows, the origin of the law was still remembered nearly two centuries later.[24] Due to a lack of written records, the exact content of the law unfortunately remains unknown, and it is therefore difficult to make an argument for legal continuity.

In late-medieval and early modern Tyrol, the concept of separation of goods is thought to have been predominant: family continuity and the idea of family lines were highly important within that property regime. As a rule, women received their marriage portion or *Heimsteuer* (*dos*) from their families. In return the grooms usually brought a gift that was intended to secure the bride. Sources sometimes refer to this as the *Widerlage* (*donatio propter nuptia*), but the terms *Morgengabe*, or morning gift (*donatio antelectum*), were most common. These properties were administered by the husband, as guardian, on the basis of gender guardianship – as it was legal tradition within the framework of matrimony.

The status of the husband as a guardian however did not mean that men had total command over the goods to the exclusion of their wives' consent. According to the statutes of Brixen (1379) with reference to territorial law, women had some degree of control over their marriage portion and morning gift.[25] The text of that territorial law remains unknown, so the precise

23 Hannes Obermair, Art. "Tiroler Landesrecht," in *Eines Fürsten Traum. Meinhard II. – Das Werden Tirols. Tiroler Landesausstellung 1995 im Schloss Tirol und im Stift Stams*, ed. Josef Riedmann (Dorf Tirol: Südtiroler Landesmuseum, 1995), pp. 130–32, here p. 130; Wiesflecker, "Landrecht".

24 Ignaz Vinzenz Zingerle, ed., *Tirolische Weistümer*, vol. 4/1 (Vienna: Braumüller, 1888), pp. 248–249: *"Da herzog Meinhart das lant zwang und* [...] *was herr über alles lant, da satzt er sein rät nider, ritter und knecht, die erfunden landsrecht, wie er das lant vestent."* "When Duke Meinhart conquered all land, he made his knights and servants devise territorial law, as he stabilized the land."

25 Josef Mutschlechner, *Alte Brixner Stadtrechte* (Innsbruck: Wagner, 1935), p. 40: *"Eß ist auch zewißßen, daß eyn igleich Frau mit irer Haimsteuer und mit irer Morgengab und Erbgut*

implications of this passage are unclear. The sources provide little information regarding the ways in which women exercised active control over their portions during marriage. Awarding the morning gift in their last wills might, for example, be regarded as the strongest evidence of a woman's right to have some authority over what happened with her property. The aforementioned regulation also appeared in charters, invoked to safeguard marriage portions and morning gifts with landed property, mandating that, in keeping with territorial law, each woman had command over her marriage portion, morning gift and property.[26] This phrasing, however, cannot hide the fact that married women had little control over their property consisting of their marriage portion, morning gift and inheritance shares. They could pledge only small amounts of money and had full control over only their jewellery – a control that extended to the right of sale.[27] Legally, these passages aimed to protect wives' property while it fell under their husbands' administration. For husbands, this primarily meant that they could neither sell nor mortgage the property used to safeguard these goods. As a result, a large number of registered land transactions initiated by married men note the formal consent of their wives. Be that as it may, it remains unclear whether a wife's property was safeguarded by the specific goods that were mentioned, or by all property brought into the union by the husband – a matter that would prove significant in the event of the husband's death. Little is known of the extent to which this formality might have served as leverage for women while keeping house as husband and wife.

The separation of goods emerges clearly in a case of death. Following a death, couples' assets fell in principle to their original side. Surviving wives were entitled to their marriage portion and morning gift. If the man survived the woman, he could use the morning gift, but the original marriage portion was passed to her heirs. The heirs were often their mutual children, but in the instance of a childless marriage this ultimately meant a refund to the respective original family line. This principle is recognised as normative with regard to territorial law. One of the earliest known documentations of this rule originates from the area of Brixen in 1307: As Elisabeth König was married, her brother awarded her with a marriage portion of 40 mark *Berner*

---

alles daß tun soll daß landes recht ist" – "It is to be known that every woman should do with her marriage portion and morning gift what is according to territorial law."

26 Archiv Kloster Neustift, Urkunden, 417 (17 April 1354): *"Darüber kann sie verfügen als ain igleich frawe mit irr haimstewer vnd mit irr morgent gabe vnd mit irem aygenleichen guote pilleichen tuon vnd lazzen sol nach landes recht."*

27 Mutschlechner, *Stadtrechte*, p. 40; for similar rules in Sterzing see Zingerle, *Tirolische Weistümer*, vol. 4/1, p. 425.

(Veronese pennies) and two farmyards as security.[28] In the event that she were to die without an heir, the source states, in accordance with territorial law the farmyards were to fall back to the rightful (König) family line (*an den rechten stam danne si her chomen sein nach landes recht*).[29] This reference to the family line, or stirps, is an expression that reoccurs within such contracts and remained in use up until the eighteenth century.[30] In the county of Tyrol non-noble daughters were not generally excluded from their parental inheritance by virtue of receiving their marriage portion. It was only in noble circles that daughters were generally forced to renounce inheritance claims in exchange for their marriage goods.[31] This custom was recorded among the nobility in the Tyrolean law code (*Tiroler Landesordnung*) of 1532.[32]

Overall children were the primary descendants entitled to inherit. According to the Tyrolean law code of 1532 children had, in principle, the right to inherit in equal parts. Fathers' moveable goods, such as clothes, jewellery, horses, weapons, seals and books, were intended for the sons, and daughters received mothers' movables, such as clothes and jewellery.[33] Movables were therefore handled to some degree separately from the main inheritance.[34] In order to preserve the family line and name, sons furthermore received the seemly advantage (*zimlicher Vortail*) in the allocation of other goods.[35] While

---

28 The primary currency of the medieval central alpine region was the Veronese penny, also called *Berner*, which referred to the old German name Bern for Verona. The counts of Tyrol had coined pennies based on the Veronese standard in Meran since the middle of the thirteenth century and since 1477 in Hall. Pound and mark were merely arithmetic units: a pound consisted of 240 pennies and a mark contained 10 pounds. All mentions of *Berner* will henceforth be normalised as Veronese penny. See Helmut Rizzolli and Federico Pigozzo, *Der Veroneser Währungsraum. Verona und Tirol* (Bozen: Athesia, 2015); Peter Spufford, *Handbook of Medieval Exchange* (London: Boydell and Brewer, 1986), pp. 93–95.

29 Archiv Kloster Neustift, Urkunde 50 (20 August 1307).

30 Margareth Lanzinger, "Von der Macht der Linie zur Gegenseitigkeit. Heiratskontrakte in den Südtiroler Gerichten Welsberg und Innichen 1750–1850," in Margareth Lanzinger, Gunda Barth-Scalmani, Ellinor Forster, and Gertrude Langer-Ostrawsky, *Aushandeln von Ehe. Heiratsverträge der Neuzeit im europäischen Vergleich* (Cologne, Weimar, and Vienna: Böhlau, 2010, 2nd edition 2015), pp. 205–367, here pp. 304 and 363.

31 Voltelini, "Geschichte," p. 349; Clementi, "Wolkenstein".

32 Pauser and Schennach, *Tiroler Landesordnungen*, p. 296 (III 34).

33 For the gendered ordering of objects see Karin Gottschalk, "Does Property have a Gender? Household Goods and Conceptions of Law and Justice in late Medieval and Early Modern Saxony," *The Medieval History Journal* 8 (2005), pp. 7–24; Gottschalk, *Eigentum*, pp. 39–47.

34 Karin Gottschalk, "Erbe und Recht. Die Übertragung von Eigentum in der Frühen Neuzeit," in *Erbe. Übertragungskonzepte zwischen Natur und Kultur*, ed. Stefan Willer, Sigrid Weigel, and Bernhard Jussen (Berlin: Suhrkamp, 2013), pp. 85–125, here p. 94.

35 Pauser and Schennach, *Tiroler Landesordnungen*, p. 287 (III 9).

based on the principle of equality, these injunctions on inheritance law were likewise informed by patrilineal dynastic thinking and intended to preserve the male line while maintaining the inheritance. The law prescribed neither partible nor impartible inheritance (*Anerbenrecht*) and, as had been the case in the late Middle Ages before the codification of Tyrolean law code, the law of succession was implemented differently in practice.[36]

2 Marriage and Securing the Marriage Portion

A notarial entry from 27 February 1414 contains a marriage contract between two families from the rural surroundings of Meran. Nikolaus and Sabina Gereuter from Partschins had agreed with Konrad Farmer from Mut that the former's daughter Gertrud should one day marry the latter's son Erhard. Sabina's sister Anne and the sister's husband Konrad Gamian likewise supported the union.[37] In the event that Erhard were to die before the marriage, another of Konrad Farmers' sons would succeed as the bridegroom. In the case that Konrad Farmer had no other son who resembled Erhard, he was expected to compensate Gertrud with ten mark (Veronese pennies). Interestingly, the property agreement for the marriage of Erhard and Gertrud also revolves around ten mark. At the end of the contract we find that the ten mark were a contribution from Gertrud's uncle Konrad Gamian. It seems that the sum was never paid in cash but represented Gertrud's marriage portion, and she had the right to claim this in the event that her husband died. Were she to be widowed, Gertrud would receive the ten mark as well as her widow's right.[38] Were she to die without children of her own, Konrad Farmer's family would have had to pay the sum to Gertrud's heirs.

This case contains another significant economic transfer: On 18 February 1414 Konrad Farmer sold a field and vineyard in Algund for 47 mark (Veronese pennies), likely in need of capital.[39] A week later he purchased the farmyard Preidlerhof in Haslach in the parish of Tyrol for 59 mark and 5 pounds

36 Rudolf Palme, "Die Entwicklung des Erbrechtes im ländlichen Bereich," in *Südtiroler Erbhöfe: Menschen und Geschichten*, ed. Paul Rösch (Bozen: Raetia, 1994), pp. 25–37.

37 StAM, NI 34 (1414), fol. 31v–32v.

38 Widow's right (*Wittiben Recht*) describes the widow's claims, including clothing, jewellery and trousseau, as well as a third of all movable goods. In addition to their endowment, widows could also demand a temporary livelihood tied to her social status, but the latter was subject to negotiation. See Hagen, Lanzinger, and Maegraith, "Competing Interests," p. 103; Pauser and Schennach, *Tiroler Landesordnungen*, pp. 300 (III 40) and 482 (III 40).

39 StAM, NI 34 (1414), fol. 24r–25v.

(Veronese pennies). The sellers were Konrad Gamian and his wife Anna Preidler, Gertrud's maternal aunt.[40] This farm is mentioned in the marriage contract, and once married, Gertrud and Erhard were in all likelihood intended to assume management of the Preidlerhof. The transfer of the farmyard accentuates the approval granted the marriage arrangement by Gertrude's aunt and uncle, who may have been without heirs. The last sentence of the contract underscores the couple's appreciation of their niece, stating that the uncle owed Gertrud ten mark (Veronese pennies) out of friendship or kinship rather than legal obligation (*causa amicicie et non causa iure*).[41]

This case illustrates a number of points. Firstly, it is rare that the sources allow a complete view of familial or individual financial circumstances – a factor that is important to keep in mind with regard to the Middle Ages. As a result, it is often only possible to observe the transfer of resources in a fragmented manner. Secondly, the case demonstrates the close integration of family and kinship relationships in connection with the transfer of wealth. Finally, we have before us an arranged marriage, which proves once again that this connectedness rendered marriage and inheritance matters that implicated the entire family. This was especially the case for social groups with assets, because marriage offered a substantial opportunity to consolidate or even raise a family's economic and social position. It is as a result of this that social control over marital affiliations (*conubium*) – in particular for the nobility, but likewise extending to wealthy citizens – is well documented.[42] The marriage contract described above shows that this also applied to the rural population. As Hermann von Weinsberg (1518–1597) a city councillor from Cologne put it: choose first, love follows (*eirst erweln, darnach lieben*).[43]

Thinking along family lines was the guiding principle behind the separation of marital property and led to numerous constellations of conflict. Most often

40 StAM, NI 34 (1414), fol. 29v–30r.

41 StAM, NI 34 (1414), fol. 32v. For the special relationship between aunts and nieces see Michaela Hohkamp, "Eine Tante für alle Fälle: Tanten-Nichten-Beziehungen und ihre Bedeutungen für die reichsfürstliche Gesellschaft der Frühen Neuzeit," in *Politiken der Verwandtschaft. Beziehungsnetze, Geschlecht und Recht*, ed. Margareth Lanzinger and Edith Saurer (Göttingen: V & R unipress, 2007), pp. 147–69.

42 Gerhard Fouquet, "Geschäft und Politik, Ehe und Verwandtschaft: Briefe an den Nürnberg-Lübecker Kaufmann Matthias Mulich vom Winter 1522/23," in *Die Stadt als Kommunikationsraum. Beiträge zur Stadtgeschichte vom Mittelalter bis ins 20. Jahrhundert. Festschrift für Karl Czok zum 75. Geburtstag*, ed. Helmut Bräuer and Elke Schlenkrich (Leipzig: Leipziger Universitätsverlag, 2001), pp. 311–46, here p. 329.

43 Konstantin Höhlbaum and Friedrich Lau, eds., *Das Buch Weinsberg*, vol. 5 (Leipzig and Cologne, 1926), p. 290.

this conflict took place between widows and the families of their deceased husbands, as for example in the case of childless widows. Widows with children and those who remarried also often found themselves at a variance with their children's guardians. Relationships between orphaned children and their stepparents were likewise burdened by financial issues. The sources handed down to us are thus to be understood as a safeguard against potential disputes and a tool for conflict prevention.

Considering that married women fell under the guardianship of their husbands, we see that women's families had a vital interest in documenting the exact sum of the marriage portion and morning gift. The documents that recorded this information played a central role in negotiating wealth should the husband die. The marriage portion was paid in cash or promised to be paid by the woman's family, commonly the father. In return, the husband documented the receipt thereof and, often in connection with the morning gift, promised to safeguard the sum by appointing his assets as collateral. This process occasionally appears in the sources as early as the thirteenth century. In 1237, for example, the blacksmith Lantemann of Bozen secured his wife Diemut's marriage portion and his morning gift and declared his house as security.[44] Sources from Bozen, Meran and the Vinschgau area evidence that the safeguarding of marital property had become the norm by the end of the fourteenth century at the very latest. The amounts of money to which women were entitled were guaranteed on the part of the husband by specific property named or all property. This practice of the guarantee is echoed in the law code of 1532, according to which wives are entitled to a lien on their husbands' property in order to secure their marital goods.[45] Thus, while a wife's property was secured on her husband's real estate her access to it was limited. But to protect her goods the husband in turn was prohibited to freely sell or trade the concerned property. In exceptional cases we find that women allowed the sale of the land in question by a waiver of appeal.[46]

The year 1396 represents a short but well-documented period in the Meran area from which we have more than 400 preserved notarial acts. About seventy-six of these entries concern inheritance and matrimonial matters, three of which are full marital contracts, and each of these addresses the future

44 Voltelini, *Notariatsimbreviaturen*, no. 592.

45 Pauser and Schennach, *Tiroler Landesordnungen*, p. 279 (III 1).

46 See Hannes Obermair, *Bozen Süd – Bolzano Nord. Schriftlichkeit und urkundliche Überlieferung der Stadt Bozen bis 1500*, vol. 1 (Bozen: Stadt Bozen, 2005), no. 125/126; Voltelini, "Geschichte," p. 355.

TABLE 7.1 Marital property according to notarial acts for Meran 1396[a]

Marriage portion (dos)	Morning gift (*donatio antelectum*)	Type of documentation
20 mark (Ver. pennies)		Receipt and guarantee by husband
50 mark (Ver. pennies)		Promise of payment by wife's family
25 mark (Ver. pennies)		Receipt and guarantee by husband
	16 mark (Ver. pennies)	Guarantee by husband
20 mark (Ver. pennies)		Receipt and guarantee by husband
6 mark (Ver. pennies) and 1 cow	4 mark (Ver. pennies)	Guarantee by husband (Ulten)
	Handover of a plot of land worth 30 mark (Ver. pennies)	Donation (*in dotem et dotis nomine ad uxorem suam dominam*) to the wife by the husband's parents
Plot of land		Handover to son-in-law (Lana)
12 mark (Ver. pennies)		Receipt and guarantee by husband (Riffian)
House		Handover to son-in-law
4 mark (Ver. pennies)	4 mark (Ver. pennies)	Receipt and guarantee by husband (Obermais)

[a] StAM, NI 12 (1396), fol. 9r–9v, 30v, 49r; NI 16 (1396), fol. 1v, 3v, 81v, 126v; NI 20 (1396), fol. 35r, 55r, 94r, 138r

marriage of children not yet of age.[47] A total of eleven acts served to secure marital property for marriages actually held in 1396. At that time many marriages were still arranged by verbal agreement, with for the most part only bigger property claims being put into writing.

The aforementioned marital goods primarily concern families with citizenship in Meran that were active in craft and trade; within these, it is possible to identify the occupation of only one person with any certainty: the innkeeper

47 StAM, NI 16 (1396), fol. 31r; NI 20 (1396), fol. 67r, 81 r.

Michael Fleisser.[48] With regard to records relating to the surrounding villages, such as Lana, Nals, Obermais, Riffian and Ulten, it remains unclear whether the men worked as craftsmen or farmers. It is not unreasonable to presume an agricultural background for the cases arising from villages in the vicinity of Meran that mention a cow or plot of land. In order to provide some context for the monetary measurements named, it is worth noting that at that time two whole pigs could be bought at the Meran market for a little less than one mark (Veronese pennies).[49] A vineyard could be purchased in the same area for four to six mark, and a house in the town of Meran could be purchased for fifty mark.[50] That considered, we can see that the maximum amount listed in the table would have been a considerable sum at that time. In this case we know very little besides the name of the bride, Klara, whose family presumably originated from Nals. Her father Ulrich, also called Arbais of Nals, promised the fifty mark to her groom, Otto Jaufner. He can be identified as important citizen of Meran who had ties to the town's council, and in 1401 Jaufner served as judge in Meran and the surrounding territory.[51]

Even this small sample shows that the nature and amount of marital property was subject to strong variance, and it was not just money that changed hands. Cash reserves were potentially more limited in rural areas. Pragmatic considerations also played a role: a citizen of Bozen, for example, assured his wife a spot (*canipassio*) in the local hospital as a morning gift, probably as a provision for her old age.[52] In general, it can be assumed that wealthier families are over-represented in the deeds, and the marriage portion for less wealthy social groups was likely limited to household effects and clothing.[53]

We find in rural areas in particular the emergence of contract constellations that were focused not so much on specific sums, but rather on the continuous operation of a farm by a single family. One marriage contract (*carta pactorum matrimonii*) of 1357 states that Heinzlin von der Niedereben from the parish of Partschins negotiated a marriage with the consent of his relatives or friends (*consencientibus et volentibus eius melioribus amicis suis*).[54] Each of those six men hailed from surrounding villages and were noted by name, but there is

48 StAM, NI 12 (1396), fol. 30v.
49 On coins and currency see footnote 28.
50 StAM, Urkundenreihe (UUR) 96 (28 August 1392).
51 Hagen, *Fürstliche Herrschaft*, pp. 99–103, here p. 100.
52 Obermair, *Bozen Süd*, vol. 1, no. 702.
53 Voltelini, "Geschichte," p. 349.
54 For the following StAM, NI 3 (1357), fol. 44v–45r.

no mention of their kinship relation to the future groom.[55] Heinzlin promised Diemline, the daughter of Konrad called Egger from the neighbouring parish of Algund, to accept and marry her as a wife as soon as she was of legal age. The contract stipulated that even before the marriage Konrad and Agnes, the parents of the bride-to-be, would move to the Niedereben-Hof along with the young couple. This farm (*curia*) was situated in Heinzlin's village, and its name suggests that it was his family's farm in his possession.[56] The elder couple were to have full authority over the farm while providing the future spouses with lodging and food as if they were both their children (*pueros*). Upon the realisation of the marriage, the new spouses would share authority over the farm with the Egger parents.

This case is somewhat remarkable, because the son-in-law married into the family but provided his farm as the primary economic foundation. As the contract makes no mention of a guardian, he appears to have been of age but willing to pass control of his farm over to his intended parents-in-law. It is possible that Heinzlin expected some economic benefit from this arrangement or was perhaps unable to cultivate the farm on his own. No additional context has been supplied, however, the contract itself included several terms of contingency. In the event that the intended marriage was not realised within eight years, Konrad Egger and his wife were to leave the Niedereben farm with the goods they had brought with them as well as some compensation for the amount of time that they had worked on the farm. Were the marriage to be annulled within the same time span, Konrad Egger and his wife had to pay Heinzlin and his heirs thirty pounds of Veronese pennies, with the proviso that Heinzlin had to compensate the parents for expenses associated with the repair or upkeep of the farm buildings. Should either party withdraw from the agreement, a penalty of ten mark (Veronese pennies) was due. In addition to the accommodations and provisions for the involved parties, stable management of the farm and economic survival seem to have been of central interest. In light of the long prospect, it appears crucial that each side had a written charter for this complex agreement.

---

55 The medieval terms *amicus* and *frunt* (friend) are ambiguous, but very often refer to (blood) relatives. See Simon Teuscher, *Bekannte – Klienten – Verwandte. Soziabilität und Politik in der Stadt Bern um 1500* (Cologne, Weimar, and Vienna: Böhlau, 1997), pp. 75–83; Kerstin Seidel, *Freunde und Verwandte. Soziale Beziehungen in einer spätmittelalterlichen Stadt* (Frankfurt a. M. and New York: Campus, 2009), pp. 213–26.

56 See also Josef Tarneller, *Die Hofnamen im Burggrafenamt und in den angrenzenden Gemeinden* (Vienna: Hölder, 1909–1911, New Print Meran: Antiquariat Unterberger, 1986), p. 95.

In another case from the middle of the fourteenth century we find that the marriage portion took the form of neither a fixed sum nor a plot of land, but rather the income from a small municipal office.[57] We learn from a compromise settlement that Greta married the summoner (messenger of the court) Konrad and as a result received two-thirds of the income from the office commissioned with handling cargo (*Aufgabeamt*) from her mother Diemut Kräflin.[58] The last third of the money was intended to remain with her mother. The exact *modus operandi* and the amount of the revenue however, apparently sparked a dispute between the mother and daughter that needed to be settled by arbitration in 1357. Greta and her husband were able to assert their claims by presenting the marriage contract that stipulated the aforementioned division of the income. The arbitrators decided that Greta's husband Konrad should run the office alone and repay the mother proportionally without trickery and fraud, while her mother had to accept the payoff without oath or proof.

Depending on family assets, marital property exchanged between regional nobility had the potential to add up to much higher sums. In the 1402 marriage between Ciprian Fuchs von Fuchsberg and Margaret, the daughter of Wilhelm von Belasi, we find that the bride was promised a marriage portion of 200 mark (Veronese pennies) and as a morning gift her husband was obligated to pay the same sum in annual 30-mark instalments.[59] As was custom, Margaret's sister Anna was given the same amount of money twelve years later upon her marriage to Heinrich von Payersberg.[60] Both daughters renounced their claims to paternal inheritance once they were endowed with the charters.

3 Widows and Remarried Women in Dispute with Their Husbands' Families

As mentioned, women's control over specific marital property such as the morning gift varied greatly during the Middle Ages.[61] In principle, women in late medieval Tyrol should have been able to freely determine what they wished

57 StAM, NI 3 (1357), fol. 71v.

58 There is unfortunately little known about this office; the name suggests that the *Aufgeber* loaded cargo for transit. The name may also correspond with Konrad's work as summoner at the court. It is unclear, however, how the mother and her new husband procured the rights to this income.

59 Südtiroler Landesarchiv Bozen/Bolzano (SLA), Archiv Gandegg, no. 49 (16 May 1402).

60 SLA, Archiv Oberpayersberg, no. 208 (13 May 1414).

61 Wilhelm Brauneder, Art. "Morgengabe," in *Handwörterbuch zur deutschen Rechtsgeschichte*, vol. 3 (Berlin: Erich Schmidt Verlag, 2016), col. 1628–34.

to do with their marriage portion and morning gift following their husbands' deaths. Widows frequently donated their marriage portion and morning gifts, with donations to religious institutions being particularly well documented. Bozen citizen Elisabeth Zwigelperger, for example, was married twice. In her last will she reassigned the morning gift from her second husband back to him, and in accordance with law and custom (*ius et usus huius terre et comitatus Tirolis*) was then able to transfer the morning gift from her first marriage to the Our Lady parish church.[62]

We repeatedly find that heirs were financially incapable of fulfilling widows' claims and demands to return goods such as the marriage portion. In the case of Verena, widow of Konrad Reinmann from Vöran, her six children were assigned a guardian who oversaw the upbringing of the underage children and also administered the children's entitlement to their father's estate. He emphasised that the children were already overburdened by overdue debts and interest. In August 1504 they found a compromise before a judge and jury. The widow and her heirs were to remain on the estate for life; she was urged to educate, feed and clothe the four children who were still underage, and to endow each of them with a decent garment.[63] The widow's claim for reimbursement of her property and payment of the morning gift worth 13 mark (Veronese pennies) had strengthened her bargaining position and secured her a basis for survival.

However, written proof did not always result in the rapid resolution of conflict. Barbara, daughter of the knight Hans von Seben, received a marriage portion (*Heimsteuer*) of 350 mark (Veronese pennies) for her marriage to Johann von Annenberg. Her husband, in return, promised a morning gift of 200 mark (Veronese pennies).[64] In the event that she outlived Johann von Annenberg, Barbara von Seben was entitled to lifetime interest on her morning gift (usufruct). These written assurances became highly important within the following years. In 1429, just a few years after their wedding, Johann von Annenberg was hanged during a dispute over the Bishop of Brixen Ulrich Putsch.[65] Barbara married Gerwig Gussen shortly thereafter, and appointed him as her

62 Hannes Obermair, *Bozen Süd – Bolzano Nord. Schriftlichkeit und urkundliche Überlieferung der Stadt Bozen bis 1500*, vol. 2, (Bozen: Stadt Bozen, 2008), no. 1075c.

63 StAM, UUR 522 (25 August 1504).

64 Tiroler Landesarchiv Innsbruck (TLA), Dornsberg Archiv (23 February 1424, 28 February 1425).

65 Victor Schaller, "Ulrich II. Putsch, Bischof von Brixen, und sein Tagebuch 1427–1437," *Zeitschrift des Ferdinandeums für Tirol und Vorarlberg* 36 (1892), pp. 227–322, 568–72, here pp. 263 and 294.

procurator in September 1430 in order to assert her claims to her marriage portion, morning gift and widow's rights against her children from her previous marriage. These negotiations must have proven difficult, for two years later she was still trying to claim the sum, which amounted to 350 mark, with the help of her husband and two brothers-in-law.[66] The payment was likely delayed by Johann's brother Sigmund von Annenberg, who represented the interests of the Annenberg family and acted on behalf of Barbara and Johann's underage sons. Whether or not Barbara ultimately asserted her claims remains unclear.

4 Last Wills and Their Implementation

A will was on one hand an instrument for conflict prevention in matters of inheritance. On the other hand, wills could be challenged and were not always followed. We have relatively little documentation of thirteenth century last wills, the writing of these documents seems only to have begun gaining popularity during the fourteenth and fifteenth centuries. Their form generally followed notarial regulations and Roman law.[67] Similar to marriage contracts, the phrasing of wills emphasises the separation of goods, as illustrated by childless marriages in which the goods ultimately returned to their families of origin. In a last will from 1369 Katherina bequeathed all of her goods to her husband Konrad Maienberger for the duration of his lifetime. Following his death, the will expressly stated that everything was to be returned to the "true stirps" (*retransire ad proximos heredes et ad verum stipitem ipsius testatricis*).[68] The document even details which goods should be returned to which family members. This clearly demonstrates that preparation for death involved not only provision for children and surviving spouses, but also consideration of the original bloodline.[69]

The formulation of last wills offered surviving spouses' options, greater flexibility, and bargaining power over heirs. Christina from Meran, wife of Hans Melauner, had her will drawn up on her sickbed in March 1471. She and Melauner had no children together, so she bequeathed portions of her fortune

66 TLA, Dornsberg Archiv (21 September 1432).

67 For changes to the freedom of testation see Peter Landau, "Die Testierfreiheit in der Geschichte des Deutschen Rechts im späten Mittelalter und in der frühen Neuzeit," *Zeitschrift der Savigny-Stiftung für Rechtsgeschichte, Germanistische Abteilung* 114 (1997), pp. 56–72.

68 StAM, NI 5 (1369), fol. 76r.

69 See Hagen, Lanzinger, and Maegraith, "Competing Interests".

to her stepdaughter and ecclesiastical institutions. In addition, she returned the morning gift of 100 mark to her husband and, in accordance with the law of the county of Tyrol (*nach landesrechten der grafschaft Tirol*), bequeathed all of her belongings to him.[70] Following her death, however, Christina's brother, a citizen of Vienna, made claims against her husband. Both sides eventually agreed in court that the widower and his heirs should be entitled to her estate with all rights, but should provide the brother with 54 mark of compensation.[71] Her brother's successful protest demonstrates the limitations of testamentary freedom. In another will from the same period, a woman provided her husband with two options in the case she died: to own either one-third of her entire estate – the other two-thirds would remain with her heirs – or to receive usufruct of her entire estate for the duration of his life.[72] In this case as in many others, the wording of the will explicitly references Tyrolean law. The law code of 1526 then codified this choice.[73]

Correspondence from the well-known poet Oswald von Wolkenstein evidences that deaths within a family, especially among the nobility, often spurred a host of relatives into action. When his cousin Veit von Wolkenstein died on 23 September 1442, Oswald was bedbound by illness. He nonetheless assumed an active part in the estate and guardianship negotiations. In detailed memoranda he explained how the assets should be inventoried and managed. It was unclear whether Veit had created a last will, so negotiations initially proved difficult.[74] Numerous letters to friends and family document Oswald requesting information and referring to the claims of various close relatives. In mid-October Oswald was informed by his brother-in-law Wolfgang von Freundsberg that there was a will. In the end, Oswald's ill health kept him from attending the Brixen-based family meeting, and he was represented by a relative.[75]

5 Conclusions

This final case again illustrates that for a time in history a death in the family remained important well beyond the nuclear family unit. The same is in

70 Huter, *Tiroler Verfachbuch*, no. 169.
71 Huter, *Tiroler Verfachbuch*, no. 194.
72 Huter, *Tiroler Verfachbuch*, no. 187.
73 Pauser and Schennach, *Tiroler Landesordnungen*, p. 168 (I 3, 2) and pp. 283–284 (III 3).
74 Anton Schwob, ed., *Die Lebenszeugnisse Oswalds von Wolkenstein: Edition und Kommentar*, vol. 4 (Vienna, Cologne, and Weimar: Böhlau, 2011), no. 377.
75 Schwob, *Lebenszeugnisse Oswalds*, vol. 4, no. 383.

principle true of premodern marriage. A wide circle of family members, friends, and peers participated in negotiations. The wedding itself was even more public, and the involvement of the community was considered fundamental. Oftentimes a loud and rowdy marriage procession made its way through the town to the church, where the wedding blessing took place. As Lyndal Roper has described with regard to sixteenth century Augsburg, the term "going to church and street" (*zu Kirche und Straße gehen*) was often synonymous with the marriage ceremony.[76] It is no coincidence that this phrase appears again and again within our sources, in particular in cases in which widows negotiated for their movables. The expression furthermore seems to have had a broader meaning in Tyrol and was used to refer to all manner of public appearances. Such public appearances could then help arguing for property claims, especially for clothing and jewellery. The marriage ritual "going to church and street" had a pragmatic basis that could decide over individual economic well-being.

Many of the interactions concerning marriage in late medieval Tyrol were never documented and remain ambiguous to this day. Most verbal marriage negotiations failed to result in a detailed contract, except for long term arrangements for underage children. Receipts and documents intended to safeguard specific goods were merely promises that can at best be infrequently verified.

As we have seen, the principle of separation of property implicated specific axes of conflict from the outset. The emphasis on a dynastic approach and the principle of gender guardianship generally tended to push women into the role of petitioner. Widows' need for protection, a principle that dated back to Roman law, was customarily implemented. The decided goal of the onus to secure marital goods was to keep widows from poverty.[77] In cases in which the decease of a husband was followed by lengthy negotiations with his family, however, it was widows who were likely in a worse financial position than those who remarried.

Nonetheless, not all bargaining and inheritance negotiations were characterised by unresolvable conflict. The written sources handed down to us did indeed serve as instruments of conflict prevention. As discussed in the opening paragraphs, many a letter was written with the express aim of suppressing discord.

During the Middle Ages, the primary means of settling a dispute was the convening of an arbitral tribunal, and parties submitted to the arbitrators that

76 Lyndal Roper, "'Going to Church and Street': Weddings in Reformation Augsburg," *Past and Present* 106 (1985), pp. 62–101.

77 See the chapter by Janine Maegraith in this volume.

they had chosen. Should those peers prove incapable of coming to an agreement, additional individuals were consulted, including lordly representatives. As we have seen, the referees too made an emphatic attempt to honour written safeguards and agreements.

References

Baur, Paul. *Testament und Bürgerschaft. Alltagsleben und Sachkultur im spätmittelalterlichen Konstanz*. Sigmaringen: Jan Thorbecke, 1989.

Behrmann, Thomas. "'Ad maiorem cautelam'. Sicherheitsdenken, Zukunftsbewußtsein und schriftliche Fixierung im Rechtsleben der italienischen Kommunen." *Quellen und Forschungen aus italienischen Archiven und Bibliotheken* 72 (1992): pp. 26–53.

Bitschnau, Martin, and Hannes Obermair, eds. *Tiroler Urkundenbuch*, part 2, vol. 1–2. Innsbruck: Wagner, 2009–2012.

Brauneder, Wilhelm. "Morgengabe." In *Handwörterbuch zur deutschen Rechtsgeschichte*, vol. 3, col. 1628–34. Berlin: Erich Schmidt Verlag, 2016.

Clementi, Siglinde. "Deren von Wolkenstein. Familienstrategien, Heirat und Geschlechterbeziehungen bei den Wolkenstein-Trostburg (um 1500 bis 1650)." In *Die Wolkensteiner. Facetten des Tiroler Adels in Spätmittelalter und Neuzeit*, edited by Gustav Pfeifer and Kurt Andermann, pp. 111–48. Innsbruck: Wagner, 2009.

Clementi, Siglinde. "Zur Ökonomie der Ehre. Heiratsgüter in Tirol um 1800." *Geschichte und Region / Storia e regione* 19–1 (2010): pp. 109–22.

Clementi, Siglinde, Ellinor Forster, Christian Hagen, Margareth Lanzinger, and Janine Christina Maegraith. "Rechtsräume und Geschlechterordnungen als soziale Prozesse – transregional. Vereinbaren und Verfügen in städtischen und ländlichen Kontexten im südlichen Tirol vom 15. bis zum frühen 19. Jahrhundert – ein erster Projektbericht." *Geschichte und Region / Storia e regione* 22–2 (2013): pp. 165–72.

Fliri, David. "Das Meraner Notariat im Spätmittelalter." In *1317 – Eine Stadt und ihr Recht. Meran im Mittelalter*, edited by Gustav Pfeifer, pp. 213–28. Bozen: Athesia, 2018.

Fouquet, Gerhard. "Geschäft und Politik, Ehe und Verwandtschaft: Briefe an den Nürnberg-Lübecker Kaufmann Matthias Mulich vom Winter 1522/23." In *Die Stadt als Kommunikationsraum. Beiträge zur Stadtgeschichte vom Mittelalter bis ins 20. Jahrhundert. Festschrift für Karl Czok zum 75. Geburtstag*, edited by Helmut Bräuer and Elke Schlenkrich, pp. 311–46. Leipzig: Leipziger Universitätsverlag, 2001.

Gottschalk, Karin. "Does Property have a Gender? Household Goods and Conceptions of Law and Justice in late Medieval and Early Modern Saxony." *The Medieval History Journal* 8 (2005): pp. 7–24.

Gottschalk, Karin. *Eigentum, Geschlecht, Gerechtigkeit. Haushalten und Erben im frühneuzeitlichen Leipzig*. Frankfurt a. M. and New York: Campus, 2003.

Gottschalk, Karin. "Erbe und Recht. Die Übertragung von Eigentum in der Frühen Neuzeit." In *Erbe. Übertragungskonzepte zwischen Natur und Kultur*, edited by Stefan Willer, Sigrid Weigel, and Bernhard Jussen, pp. 85–125. Berlin: Suhrkamp, 2013.

Hagen, Christian. *Fürstliche Herrschaft und kommunale Teilhabe. Die Städte der Grafschaft Tirol im Spätmittelalter*. Innsbruck: Wagner, 2015.

Hagen, Christian, Margareth Lanzinger, and Janine Maegraith. "Competing Interests in Death-related Stipulations in South Tirol, c. 1350–1600." In *Planning for Death: Wills and Death-related Property Arrangements in Europe, 1200–1600*, edited by Mia Korpiola and Anu Lahtinen, pp. 88–118. Leiden and Boston: Brill, 2018.

Heiser, Ines. "Generationenkonflikte? Erbrecht und Elternfürsorge in der mittelhochdeutschen Literatur." In *Aufblühen und Verwelken. Mediävistische Forschungen zu Kindheit und Alter*, edited by Ines Heiser and Andreas Meyer, pp. 145–58. Leipzig: Eudora, 2009.

Hess, Rolf-Dieter. *Familien- und Erbrecht im Württembergischen Landrecht von 1555 unter besonderer Berücksichtigung des älteren württembergischen Rechts*. Stuttgart: Kohlhammer, 1968.

Hohkamp, Michaela. "Eine Tante für alle Fälle: Tanten-Nichten-Beziehungen und ihre Bedeutungen für die reichsfürstliche Gesellschaft der Frühen Neuzeit." In *Politiken der Verwandtschaft. Beziehungsnetze, Geschlecht und Recht*, edited by Margareth Lanzinger and Edith Saurer, pp. 147–69. Göttingen: V & R unipress, 2007.

Höhlbaum, Konstantin, and Friedrich Lau, eds. *Das Buch Weinsberg*, vol. 5. Leipzig and Cologne, 1926.

Huter, Franz, ed. *Das älteste Tiroler Verfachbuch (Landgericht Meran 1468–1471)*. Innsbruck: Wagner, 1990.

Huter, Franz, ed. *Tiroler Urkundenbuch*, part 1, vol. 1–3. Innsbruck: Wagner, 1937–1957.

Ingendahl, Gesa. *Witwen in der Frühen Neuzeit. Eine kulturhistorische Studie*. Frankfurt a. M. and New York: Campus, 2006.

Kolb, Franz. "Vermögens- und Erbrecht in der Wipptaler Bauernfamilie." *Tiroler Heimat* 20 (1956): pp. 63–81.

Landau, Peter. "Bamberger Landrecht und eheliche Gütergemeinschaft." In *Landesordnungen und Gute Policey in Bayern, Salzburg und Österreich*, edited by Horst Gehringer, Hans-Joachim Hecker, and Reinhard Heydenreuter, pp. 1–18. Frankfurt a. M.: Klostermann, 2008.

Landau, Peter. "Die Testierfreiheit in der Geschichte des Deutschen Rechts im späten Mittelalter und in der frühen Neuzeit." *Zeitschrift der Savigny-Stiftung für Rechtsgeschichte, Germanistische Abteilung* 114 (1997): pp. 56–72.

Lanzinger, Margareth. "Marriage Contracts in Various Contexts: Marital Property Rights, Sociocultural Aspects and Gender-specific Implications. Late-Eighteenth-Century Evidence from two Tirolean Court Districts." *Annales de démographie historique* 121–1 (2011): pp. 69–97.

Lanzinger, Margareth. "Von der Macht der Linie zur Gegenseitigkeit. Heiratskontrakte in den Südtiroler Gerichten Welsberg und Innichen 1750–1850." In Margareth Lanzinger, Gunda Barth-Scalmani, Ellinor Forster, and Gertrude Langer-Ostrawsky. *Aushandeln von Ehe. Heiratsverträge der Neuzeit im europäischen Vergleich*, pp. 205–367. Cologne, Weimar, and Vienna: Böhlau, 2010, 2nd edition 2015.

Lanzinger, Margareth, Gunda Barth-Scalmani, Ellinor Forster, and Gertrude Langer-Ostrawsky. *Aushandeln von Ehe. Heiratsverträge der Neuzeit im europäischen Vergleich*. Cologne, Weimar, and Vienna: Böhlau, 2010, 2nd edition 2015.

Mutschlechner, Josef. *Alte Brixner Stadtrechte*. Innsbruck: Wagner, 1935.

Obermair, Hannes. *Bozen Süd – Bolzano Nord. Schriftlichkeit und urkundliche Überlieferung der Stadt Bozen bis 1500*, vol. 1. Bozen: Stadt Bozen, 2005.

Obermair. Hannes. *Bozen Süd – Bolzano Nord. Schriftlichkeit und urkundliche Überlieferung der Stadt Bozen bis 1500*, vol. 2. Bozen: Stadt Bozen, 2008.

Obermair, Hannes. "The Use of Records in Medieval Towns: The Case of Bolzano, South Tyrol." In *Writing and the Administration of Medieval Towns. Medieval Urban Literacy 1*, edited by Marco Mostert and Anna Adamska, pp. 49–68. Turnhout: Brepols, 2014.

Obermair, Hannes. "Tiroler Landesrecht." In *Eines Fürsten Traum. Meinhard II. – Das Werden Tirols. Tiroler Landesausstellung 1995 im Schloss Tirol und im Stift Stams*, edited by Josef Riedmann, pp. 130–32. Dorf Tirol: Südtiroler Landesmuseum, 1995.

Olechowski, Thomas, Tamara Ehs, and Kamila Staudigl-Ciechowicz. *Die Wiener Rechts- und Staatswissenschaftliche Fakultät 1918–1938*. Göttingen: V&R unipress, 2014.

Pahlow, Louis. "Zwischen kirchlichem Dogma und wirtschaftlicher Vernunft. Ehe und eheliches Güterrecht in der mittelalterlichen Stadt." *Zeitschrift der Savigny-Stiftung für Rechtsgeschichte, Germanistische Abteilung* 128 (2011): pp. 377–90.

Palme, Rudolf. "Die Entwicklung des Erbrechtes im ländlichen Bereich." In *Südtiroler Erbhöfe: Menschen und Geschichten*, edited by Paul Rösch, pp. 25–37. Bozen: Raetia, 1994.

Pauser, Josef, and Martin P. Schennach, eds. *Die Tiroler Landesordnungen von 1526, 1532 und 1573. Historische Einführung und Edition*. Vienna, Cologne, and Weimar: Böhlau, 2018.

Rizzolli, Helmut, and Federico Pigozzo. *Der Veroneser Währungsraum. Verona und Tirol*. Bozen: Athesia, 2015.

Roper, Lyndal. "'Going to Church and Street': Weddings in Reformation Augsburg." *Past and Present 106* (1985): pp. 62–101.

Roth, Paul von. "Das deutsche eheliche Güterrecht." *Zeitschrift für vergleichende Rechtswissenschaft* 1 (1878): pp. 39–94.

Sabean, David Warren. *Property, Production, and Family in Neckarhausen, 1700–1870*. Cambridge: Cambridge University Press, 1990.

Schaller, Victor. "Ulrich II. Putsch, Bischof von Brixen, und sein Tagebuch 1427–1437." *Zeitschrift des Ferdinandeums für Tirol und Vorarlberg* 36 (1892): pp. 227–322, 568–72.

Schennach, Martin Paul. *Gesetz und Herrschaft: Die Entstehung des Gesetzgebungsstaates am Beispiel Tirols*. Cologne, Weimar, and Vienna: Böhlau, 2010.

Schröder, Richard. *Geschichte des ehelichen Güterrechts in Deutschland*, vol. 1–2. Stettin: Saunier 1863–1871, New Print Aalen: Scientia-Verlag, 1967.

Schwob, Anton, ed. *Die Lebenszeugnisse Oswalds von Wolkenstein: Edition und Kommentar*, vol. 4. Vienna, Cologne, and Weimar: Böhlau, 2011.

Seidel, Kerstin. *Freunde und Verwandte. Soziale Beziehungen in einer spätmittelalterlichen Stadt*. Frankfurt a. M. and New York: Campus, 2009.

Signori, Gabriela. *Von der Paradiesehe zur Gütergemeinschaft. Die Ehe in der mittelalterlichen Lebens- und Vorstellungswelt*. Frankfurt a. M. and New York: Campus, 2011.

Simon-Muscheid, Katharina. "Diebstahl oder Erbrecht? Streit um letztwillige Verfügungen in den oberrheinischen Städten des 15. und 16. Jahrhunderts." In *Criminalità e giustizia in Germania e in Italia. Pratiche giudiziarie e linguaggi giuridici tra medioevo ed età moderna*, edited by Marco Bellabarba, Gerd Schwerhoff, and Andrea Zorzi, pp. 35–62. Bologna: Il Mulino, 2001.

Spieß, Karl-Heinz. *Familie und Verwandtschaft im deutschen Hochadel des Spätmittelalters, 13. bis Anfang des 16. Jahrhunderts*. Stuttgart: Franz Steiner, 1993.

Spufford, Peter. *Handbook of Medieval Exchange*. London: Boydell and Brewer, 1986.

Stolz, Otto. *Rechtsgeschichte des Bauernstandes und der Landwirtschaft in Tirol und Vorarlberg*. Bozen: Ferrari-Auer, 1949.

Tarneller, Josef. *Die Hofnamen im Burggrafenamt und in den angrenzenden Gemeinden*. Vienna: Hölder, 1909–1911, New Print Meran: Antiquariat Unterberger, 1986.

Teuscher, Simon. *Bekannte – Klienten – Verwandte. Soziabilität und Politik in der Stadt Bern um 1500*. Cologne, Weimar, and Vienna: Böhlau, 1997.

Voltelini, Hans von, ed. *Die Südtiroler Notariatsimbreviaturen des dreizehnten Jahrhunderts*, part 1. Innsbruck: Wagner, 1899.

Voltelini, Hans von. "Zur Geschichte des ehelichen Güterrechtes in Tirol." In *Festgaben zu Ehren Max Büdinger's von seinen Freunden und Schülern*, pp. 331–64. Innsbruck: Wagner, 1898.

Voltelini, Hans von, and Franz Huter, eds. *Die Südtiroler Notariatsimbreviaturen des dreizehnten Jahrhunderts*, part 2. Innsbruck: Wagner, 1951.

Wiesflecker, Herrmann. "Das Landrecht Meinhards II. von Tirol." In *Neue Beiträge zur geschichtlichen Landeskunde Tirols: Festschrift Franz Huter zum 70. Lebensjahr*, edited by Ernest Troger, pp. 455–65. Innsbruck and Munich: Wagner, 1969.

Zingerle, Ignaz Vinzenz, ed. *Tirolische Weistümer*, vol. 4/1. Vienna: Braumüller, 1888.

CHAPTER 8

Gender Imbalance in the Use, Ownership, and Transmission of Property in Early Modern Southern Tyrolean Urban and Rural Contexts

Janine Maegraith

Damit nun aber Sy die gemellte Wittib in Irem Wittiblichen Stannd nit waislos gehallten unnd aufs weit Velld getriben werde, sonnder ain Zeit lanng ain Unndterschlaiff habe.[1]

So that said widow would not be kept orphaned and sent into the open field, but have shelter for a time.

∴

As the above quote indicates, future provisions for widows were highly dependent on local property systems, on their own property situations, and on the settlements of their endowments at court.[2] In this case, the widow had no right to remain on her late husband's estate and so that she would not become homeless, the court settled her in temporary lodgings. This was a case study in southern Tyrol, but the multiplicity of different European legal property regimes used to determine specific access to property through inheritance and marriage reveal a highly fragmented picture.[3] According to various sources

1 Südtiroler Landesarchiv Bozen/Bolzano (SLA), Verfachbuch (VfB) Sonnenburg 1587, no folio numbers, 9 March 1587.

2 Research and analysis are based on results from the project "Legal Spaces and Gender Order as Social Processes in a Trans-regional Perspective. Negotiating and Stipulating Property in Urban and Rural Contexts of Southern Tyrol from the Fifteenth to the Early Nineteenth Century" (University of Innsbruck; Geschichte und Region / Storia e regione, Bozen/Bolzano), 2014–2016. Additional cases and the land purchase contracts are being extracted in the context of the project "The Role of Wealth in Defining and Constituting Kinship Spaces from the Sixteenth to the Eighteenth Century", financed by the Austrian Science Fund (FWF, project number P 29394).

3 See Karin Nehlsen-von Stryk, Art. "Witwe. A. Rechtsgeschichte, II. Germanisches und Deutsches Recht," in *Lexikon des Mittelalters*, vol. 9 (Munich: LexMA-Verlag, 1998), col.

 DOI:10.1163/9789004456204_009

there were about 200 different property regimes in the early modern German speaking territories, but a comparative study of these remains to be realised.[4] The comparative study on negotiating marriage in Lower Austria, Salzburg, and Tyrol, for example, illustrates not only substantial territorial differences, but also the fruitfulness of such an approach when put into a European context.[5] A look at Tyrol's surrounding areas offers a glimpse of the aforementioned diversity and fragmentation of property regimes: in Württemberg, for example, an area with partible inheritance and community of acquisition (*Errungenschaftsgemeinschaft*),[6] widowed spouses inherited half of their deceased spouse's acquired assets but, according to inventories, also retained usufruct of the property of the deceased spouse.[7] In areas with community of property systems such as Lower Austria or parts of Silesia, widowed spouses had a claim on half of the assets of the deceased, and enjoyed a stronger position than their children and better safeguarding of their provisions.[8] In

---

277–78, where she stresses that the diversity and fragmentation of the matrimonial property regime renders a general description of provisions for widows impossible. Similarly, many different regimes coexisted in France, see Barbara B. Diefendorf, "Women and Property in Ancient Regime France. Theory and Practice in Dauphiné and Paris," in *Early Modern Conceptions of Property*, ed. John Brewer and Susan Staves (London: Routledge, 1995), pp. 170–93, here p. 170. See also Beatrice Moring and Richard Wall, *Widows in European Economy and Society 1600–1920* (Woodbridge: Boydell Press, 2017), pp. 67–79.

4 See, for example, Claudius von Schwerin, *Deutsche Rechtsgeschichte* (Leipzig and Berlin: Teubner, 1912), p. 90.

5 Margareth Lanzinger, Gunda Barth-Scalmani, Ellinor Forster, and Gertrude Langer-Ostrawsky, *Aushandeln von Ehe. Heiratsverträge der Neuzeit im europäischen Vergleich* (Cologne, Weimar, and Vienna: Böhlau, 2010, 2nd edition 2015).

6 See Rolf-Dieter Hess, *Familien- und Erbrecht im württembergischen Landrecht von 1555 unter besonderer Berücksichtigung des älteren württembergischen Rechts* (Stuttgart: Kohlhammer, 1968), pp. 93–101.

7 See also Janine Maegraith, "Opportunity or Constraint? Partible Inheritance, Family Property and Household Structure in Southwest Germany – Evidence from Inventories," in *Finding "Ie" in Western Society*, ed. Motoyasu Takahashi (Ehime: Ehime University Economics Study Series, 2013), pp. 133–61.

8 See Margareth Lanzinger, "Ehegütermodelle und Balanceakte. Resümee," in Margareth Lanzinger, Gunda Barth-Scalmani, Ellinor Forster, and Gertrude Langer-Ostrawsky, *Aushandeln von Ehe. Heiratsverträge der Neuzeit im europäischen Vergleich* (Cologne, Weimar, and Vienna: Böhlau, 2010, 2nd edition 2015), pp. 459–67, here p. 461; Gertrude Langer-Ostrawsky, "Vom Verheiraten der Güter. Bäuerliche und kleinbäuerliche Heiratsverträge im Erzherzogtum Österreich unter der Enns," in ibid., pp. 27–119, here pp. 61–63. On Silesia see Ellinor Forster and Janine Maegraith, "Alte Gewohnheiten unter neuem Namen? Die Angleichung Schlesiens durch die österreichischen Eherechtsnormen im späten 18. und frühen 19. Jahrhundert," *Szkice archiwalno-historyczne* 12 (2015), pp. 13–53. Community of property regimes could also be found in Bavarian and Alemannic law, see Hans von Voltelini, "Zur Geschichte des ehelichen Güterrechts in Tirol. Eine

Italian areas with dowry systems, on the other hand, widows faced uncertainty about the return of their dowries, whether they would have to leave the money with the estate of their deceased husband or, in cases of dowry restitution, whether they would have to leave the estate and their children behind.[9] A look at widows' endowments in early modern German noble families shows that the dower was for the most part negotiated before the marriage and regulated through marriage contracts. Nevertheless, Karl-Heinz Spieß has shown that, as wives and then widows remained "strangers without property" in their husband's household, discrepancy, and thus uncertainty, remained between contractual settlement and actual practice.[10]

If "without property" means without landownership, then this would be an apt description of widows in Tyrol, where separate marital property and an emphasis on consanguinity were codified by the Tyrolean law code of the sixteenth century. This resulted in a similar extent of uncertainty for widowed spouses who had entitlement only on their own property and not on that of their spouse. Consequently, if a widow had no real estate of her own she was a "stranger" in her late husband's household, reliant on the money she had brought in as a marriage and/or inheritance portion and a beneficial settlement at court to keep her from being "sent into the open field". This brief survey illustrates how different property regimes as well as different inheritance

rechtshistorische Skizze," in *Festgaben zu Ehren Max Büdinger's von seinen Freunden und Schülern* (Innsbruck: Wagner, 1898), pp. 1–34, here pp. 26–27.

9 Isabelle Chabot in this volume and Isabelle Chabot, "Lineage Strategies and the Control of Widows in Renaissance Florence," in *Widowhood in Medieval and Early Modern Europe*, ed. Sandra Cavallo and Lyndan Warner (London and New York: Routledge, 2014), pp. 127–44, here pp. 134–35; on problems of reimbursement of the full dowry and how many widows opted for this in Venice see Anna Bellavitis, "Die Mitgift in Venedig zwischen Mittelalter und Früher Neuzeit," *L'Homme. Z.F.G.* 22–1 (2011), pp. 23–37, esp. pp. 29 and 32–36; see also Margareth Lanzinger, "Variationen des Themas: Mitgiftsysteme," in Margareth Lanzinger, Gunda Barth-Scalmani, Ellinor Forster, and Gertrude Langer-Ostrawsky, *Aushandeln von Ehe. Heiratsverträge der Neuzeit im europäischen Vergleich* (Cologne, Weimar, and Vienna: Böhlau, 2010, 2nd edition 2015), pp. 469–92, here 487–88.

10 *Eigentumslose Fremde*; see Karl-Heinz Spieß, "Witwenversorgung im Hochadel. Rechtlicher Rahmen und praktische Gestaltung im Spätmittelalter und zu Beginn der Frühen Neuzeit," in *Witwenschaft in der Frühen Neuzeit. Fürstliche und adelige Witwen zwischen Fremd- und Selbstbestimmung*, ed. Martina Schattkowsky (Leipzig: Leipziger Universitätsverlag, 2003), pp. 88–114, here p. 105, with reference to Marianne Weber, *Ehefrau und Mutter in der Rechtsentwicklung* (Tübingen: Mohr, 1907), p. 223: "*In den aristokratischen Kreisen stand die Frau vermögensrechtlich regelmäßig dennoch als eigentumslose Fremde ihrem Mann und seinen Verwandten gegenüber.*" (In aristocratic circles, the wife regularly faced her husband and his relatives in questions of property law as a stranger without property.)

systems had a substantial influence on the property situation of both men and women, especially during widowhood.

These diverse settings and imbalances between the parties involved brought along with them different issues of contention and processes of arbitration. In this chapter I will analyse which conflicts arose from the specific configuration in Tyrol, how these were attempted to be resolved, and the aspects that played important roles in the resolution of each. The results from the analysis of the court books suggest that whilst negotiation prevailed, litigation was comparatively rare. In order to demonstrate this, I will examine the gender specific distribution of property, and especially landownership, in sixteenth century southern Tyrol in view of the prevailing property and inheritance laws and the legal practice. Marital property arrangements and property agreements for widowhood in southern Tyrol were analysed in order to gain a better picture of women's access to property in their position as daughters, wives, and widows, and to establish legal practice, contracts, and settlements in regard to inheritance.

The so called *Verfachbücher*, or court books, of Sonnenburg in the Puster Valley and Brixen serve as the basis of this study. These court books contain documents on all property-related issues such as wills, inheritance proceedings, obligations, guarantees on marriage portions (*Heiratsgut*), widows' and widowers' endowment contracts, usufruct contracts, land purchase contracts, lease agreements, endowments, and property transfers, as well as conflict settlements.[11] To a lesser extent they also contain marriage contracts for this period. The endowment contracts for widowhood constitute an especially rich source for the investigation of the legal and economic situation of widows and widowers, and thus the use and distribution of family property. The two areas, the monastic rural territory of Sonnenburg/Castel Badia in the Puster Valley, and the city court of the independent prince-bishopric of Brixen/Bressanone, are located within the same region and were chosen for a comparison between town and countryside. The period of investigation is the sixteenth century, which was subject to three consecutive versions of the Tyrolean law code (*Tiroler Landesordnung*), implemented in 1526, 1532, and 1573.[12] A focus on this

11 *Heiratsgut* or marriage portion describes the money brought into a marriage by one spouse. Legally, it is not equivalent to a dowry which is why the expression "marriage portion" was chosen in this context.

12 Josef Pauser and Martin P. Schennach eds., *Die Tiroler Landesordnungen von 1526, 1532 und 1573. Historische Einführung und Edition* (Vienna, Cologne, and Weimar: Böhlau, 2018); Martin P. Schennach, *Gesetz und Herrschaft. Die Entstehung des Gesetzgebungsstaates am Beispiel Tirols* (Cologne, Weimar, and Vienna: Böhlau, 2010); see also the chapter by Christian Hagen in this volume.

period facilitates the study of the implementation and practice of law in different social strata and political entities. Within our project research we have observed that, in comparison for example with the eighteenth century, the sixteenth century evidenced a wider spectrum of negotiations, and the options provided by the newly written down legal system were broadly exploited.[13] At the same time, this study enables to look at the socio-economic impact that legal spaces and gender order had on household structures.

1 The Meaning of Property

Property can have different meanings according to the legal space in which it is located. In Tyrol, as well as in other areas, property is comprised of assets both movable and immovable. The Tyrolean law code, for example, mentions *freye Besitzung der Gueter*[14] – free ownership of assets – or *Hab und Gut* – chattels and assets – which implies both movable and immovable property. There were three ways in which real estate could be held: first, in ownership. Landownership had important implications, as it could facilitate access to means of production, common rights, and income, in both rural and urban contexts.[15] As it technically remained under the authority of the landlord, landownership in southern Tyrol was also linked to dues and obligations. Here, hereditary land tenure (*Erbleihe* and *Baurecht*), which granted the holders of such tenure far-reaching rights to dispose over their land, was dominant. However, changes such as land sales were subject to formal seigneurial consent – here by the Abbess in Sonnenburg and the Prince-Bishop in Brixen. This condition having been met, the *Baurecht* was free to be owned, cultivated, and inherited by the owner and his or her heirs.[16]

13 Margareth Lanzinger and Janine Maegraith, "Konkurrenz um Vermögen im südlichen Tirol des 16. Jahrhunderts," *L'Homme. Z.F.G.* 27–1 (2016), pp. 15–31, here p. 30; Christian Hagen, Margareth Lanzinger, and Janine Maegraith, "Verträge als Instrumente der Vermögensabsicherung im südlichen Tirol vom 14. bis zum 18. Jahrhundert," *Historische Anthropologie* 25, 2 (2017), pp. 188–212, here pp. 197–198.

14 Tiroler Landesordnung (TLO) 1573, III, 33. The Tiroler Landesordnung is edited in Pauser and Schennach, *Die Tiroler Landesordnungen.*

15 Margareth Lanzinger and Janine Maegraith, "Houses and the Range of Wealth in Early Modern Gender- and Intergenerational Relationships," *Jahrbuch für Europäische Geschichte / European History Yearbook* 18 (2017), pp. 14–34.

16 Rudolf Palme, "Die Entwicklung des Erbrechtes im ländlichen Bereich," in *Südtiroler Erbhöfe. Menschen und Geschichten*, ed. Paul Rösch (Bozen: Raetia, 1994), pp. 25–37, here p. 29.

This definition of property distinguishes it from the second way real estate could be held, which was a temporary right of use, or usufruct. Under usufruct the user of the property had right of administration over the property, but only the property gains remained in ownership of the user, the property itself did not. Usufruct rights could entail land and houses as well as monies and movables and, as the user was obliged to retain the property unchanged, were supervised by the heirs or guardians of underage or unmarried inheriting children. Following the death of the user, the property reverted to the original owner's next of kin.[17] Usufruct might not have equalled free ownership of assets, but it enabled users to profit from property income and made it possible for widows to remain in the house in a managing capacity, while in other situations they would have had to make do with a chamber and hardly any managing capacity.[18] A third way property could be held was as a fief. Fiefdoms could be hereditary as well. But as they hardly feature in this sample, they will not be included in this analysis.[19]

Most of the property that was negotiated in inheritance and endowment cases was lineage property. The owner of such property was bound by the responsibility to keep it intact for the blood relatives and future heirs, and therefore only a third of such assets were disposable as, for example, a testamentary bequest. Barbara Diefendorf describes this concept of property aptly by saying that the owner was more the "custodian" of such property.[20] On the other hand, half of all acquired assets were disposable.[21] This mattered: whereas acquired property was individual property of which half could be disposed of, lineage property – including marriage and inheritance portions – was protected and only a third of this was disposable.

2 Marital Property and Widows' Endowments

The following case illustrates the legal context and social implications of widows' endowment negotiations in Tyrol: in 1627, the carpenter Sebastian Ziser

17 TLO 1573, III, 6.

18 On France see, for example, Diefendorf, "Women and Property," pp. 178–82.

19 On fiefdoms in this area see Erika Kustatscher, *Die Städte des Hochstifts Brixen im Spätmittelalter. Verfassungs- und Sozialgeschichte von Brixen, Bruneck und Klausen im Spiegel der Personengeschichte (1200–1550)* (Innsbruck: Studienverlag, 2007), pp. 83 and 140–43.

20 Diefendorf, "Women and Property," p. 185.

21 TLO 1573, III, 3.

died in Pflaurenz, a village in the dominion of Sonnenburg.[22] He left behind a widow named Maria Ziser, but no children. At the behest of Sebastian Ziser's sisters and their husbands, a probate inventory was drawn up by the judge of the court of Sonnenburg following his death. The widow, who was present with her gender guardian, was legally obliged to assist with the inventory, and to disclose all of her husband's belongings; otherwise she would have lost all of her widow's entitlements.[23] The inventory listed half a dwelling with half a garden in Pflaurenz worth 122 Gulden and all of her deceased husband's movables, including carpentry tools and his liabilities. Each of the items was valued but no total was calculated at the end. As the marital property in southern Tyrol was separated, this was not seen as necessary, and consequently the widow's possessions were likewise not listed.

After the inventory was drawn up, the widow's endowment was negotiated at court and the amount of her marriage portion established, as well as her claims relating to the length of her marriage, the "wear and tear of her time and clothing",[24] and any other potential claims that she had on her husband's estate by virtue of the Tyrolean law code. She had to defend her claims against the blood relatives of her late husband – his sisters – who, as the principal heirs, tried to protect as much of the estate as possible from her claims. A standard expression that the judge had taken the parties' *Red und Gegenrede*, or statement and counter-statement, into account indicates, that disagreements between the two parties preceded this settlement. The judge ultimately acted as arbitrator, and in the resulting judicial settlement the widow was granted the following: firstly, she was affirmed ownership of the movables she had brought into her marriage, which were mostly stored in her locked trunk. These were comprised of her clothes, fabrics, and adornments – in so far as she had worn those items in church and in public (*vnnd die Sy zů Kirchen vn{d} Strassen getragen hat*),[25] including items she had received as gifts or bought during the course of her marriage. Secondly, she was allocated some household items such as kitchenware, bedding, bedclothes, and several ells of cloth – but no foodstuff or grain. Some of these items comprised roughly a third of the movables to which

22 SLA, A 742, Sonnenburg Inventare 1618–1631, 1 July 1627, "*Sebastian Zisers seeligen Inventari*" (including the widow's endowment contract), fol. 60v–66r.

23 TLO 1573, III, 38.

24 This phrase appears frequently in court records and refers to the length of her marriage. See, for example, SLA, VfB Sonnenburg 1588, fol. 241–255, 18 August 1588, "[*ihre*] *erlitne unnd Verschlissne Zeit unnd Tägs Begwäntung*".

25 TLO 1573, III, 40.

she was entitled by law from her husband's estate.[26] Maria Ziser was allowed to stay in the dwelling rent-free for three months, until Michaelmas. Thirdly, the heirs were obliged to give the widow six Gulden in return for her marriage portion. Although the widow claimed she had brought in a marriage portion of 31 Gulden, she had no entitlement to this sum because she had no legal proof of it. For her 21 years of housekeeping and her "wear and tear" the heirs were instructed to give her 14 Gulden. Altogether she was entitled to 20 Gulden – less than her claimed marriage portion. The first instalment of ten Gulden was scheduled for Michaelmas, when she had to move out. The rest was settled for May 1628. Upon receipt of the payments the widow had to renounce all further claims on her deceased husband's estate. However, should she be able to provide legal proof of her marriage portion, she would be entitled to the 31 Gulden. The heirs, in turn, were required to pay the court fees. The settlement was accepted and both parties pledged to observe it.

This case illustrates several aspects of use, ownership, and transmission of property in southern Tyrol. According to the law code, inheritance was restricted to the bloodline of the deceased: children were the intended primary heirs and were, in principle, entitled to inherit in equal shares. This allowed for the division of property between all children, including daughters, as well as impartible succession or undivided fraternal succession. Sons were expected to receive preference on behalf of the agnatic line, in order to preserve "stem and name".[27] In the absence of children the next of kin – in this case the sisters of the deceased – were entitled to inherit. Consequently, marital partners were in principle excluded from the inheritance of their deceased spouses as this would have meant assets crossing the bloodline.[28] Separation of property was the established marital property regime, and any claims a widowed spouse might have had on the estate of his or her late spouse were strictly regulated by the law code and hotly contested by the blood relatives of the deceased. After the death of one spouse or in case of separation of bed and board, the property was split up into the two different sets of assets. This ruled out any

---

26 TLO 1573, III, 40. Voltelini assumed that a third of the movables was put in place of the community of acquisition, see Voltelini, "Zur Geschichte des ehelichen Güterrechts," pp. 27–28.

27 TLO 1532, 1573, III, 9, "*ain zimlicher Vortail / zu erhaltung Stam{m}ens vnd Namens*".

28 See Christian Hagen, Margareth Lanzinger, and Janine Maegraith, "Competing Interests in Death-related Stipulations in South Tirol c. 1350–1600," in *Planning for Death: Wills, and Death-Related Property Arrangements in Europe, 1200–1600*, ed. Mia Korpiola and Anu Lahtinen (Leiden and Boston: Brill, 2017), pp. 88–118; Lanzinger and Maegraith, "Konkurrenz um Vermögen," pp. 15–31.

possible accrual through marriage, and thus had serious implications.[29] In the case of the property of Sebastian Ziser's wife, the legal documentation of her marriage portion that would have been necessary to reclaim the same from his heirs was missing. Such legal proof, mainly in the form of guarantees of marriage portions wherein the husband pledges his property as security for her marriage portion, appears frequently in the court books.[30] Without such legal proof, a widow had basically no claim to her money, and was reliant on the leniency of the heirs and the court. This illustrates the precarious position in which widows could find themselves, especially if she lacked any legal proof of her property or the marriage remained childless.[31]

This example also shows that property consisted of several different components, and that the widow was entitled to a complex set of claims as specified in the Tyrolean law code. She was entitled to her material possessions such as her trousseau with all her clothes, fabrics, and ornaments. During marriage, the material goods – located in her "locked trunk" – remained under her administration, whereas the marriage portion, the morning gift, and any other financial assets she might inherit from her blood relatives – including the gains on those assets – remained in her husband's administration.[32] In turn, the husband was not allowed to sell or diversify any of her assets without her approval, not least because he pledged her marriage portion on his property. In widowhood, the marriage portion, morning gift, and inherited assets in the form of money or

29 See Voltelini, "Zur Geschichte des ehelichen Güterrechts," p. 26.

30 See ibid., p. 25.

31 On the precarious position of widows in Europe see also Olwen Hufton, *The Prospect Before Her: A History of Women in Western Europe 1500–1800* (London: Harper Collins, 1995), p. 223.

32 For Brixen, the ordinance of 1379 states that wives could only administer their clothing and adornments. All of the wife's other assets came into the management of her husband, Josef Mutschlechner, *Alte Brixner Stadtrechte* (Innsbruck: Wagner, 1935), p. 40 (*Von den Frauen*). See also Voltelini, "Zur Geschichte des ehelichen Güterrechts," p. 24 (*Schlüsselgewalt*). TLO 1573, III, 1. The law stated that the wife had no claim on the gains but that they remained in the property of her husband. As a widow, she only had claims on her marriage portion, morning gift, and inherited assets. Margareth Lanzinger discussed this issue in view of the 1786 legal change in the introduction of the *Josephinisches Gesetzbuch*, see Margareth Lanzinger, "Von der Macht der Linie zur Gegenseitigkeit. Heiratskontrakte in den Südtiroler Gerichten Welsberg und Innichen 1750–1850," in Margareth Lanzinger, Gunda Barth-Scalmani, Ellinor Forster, and Gertrude Langer-Ostrawsky, *Aushandeln von Ehe. Heiratsverträge der Neuzeit im europäischen Vergleich* (Cologne, Weimar, and Vienna: Böhlau, 2010, 2nd edition 2015), pp. 205–367, here pp. 251 and 254. Kustatscher highlights how separation of marital property ensured independence for spouses. But in the light of restricted management rights this has to be questioned, see Kustatscher, *Die Städte des Hochstifts Brixen*, pp. 85–87.

real estate had to be returned to the widow. In the case described, however, Maria Ziser lacked any proof of her marriage portion and also no morning gift was mentioned, so that she was dependent on the good will of the court and the relatives of her husband. In addition, the widow was entitled to a third of the movables that comprised household goods such as bedding, bedclothes, kitchenware, and knives – but no cash or silverware. In principle, the widow had a claim to free lodging on the estate until at least the first instalment of the endowment, which in this case allowed her to stay for three months. The law provided for the arrangement of a "reasonable livelihood, according to her status", which in some cases included foodstuff, clothing, and free firewood – essential for cooking and heating – in the settlements; but Maria Ziser's settlement lacked any such agreement.[33] Other than this she had no claim on her late husband's estate more generally, and on the real estate in particular. The house and garden were now the property of the sisters of the deceased. The outcome of this settlement was not exactly in her favour. Her late husband's heirs had successfully defended their succession. But on the other hand, the court could alleviate the consequences of the principles of separation of marital property and in some other cases widows reached settlements where the outcome actually exceeded their legal claims. However, it was rare for widows to own the main estate, which meant that in this case they had to negotiate for favourable endowments.

Given that a major part of property in early modern Europe was transferred by inheritance and marriage, the fact that male heirs were given preference in Tyrol, and that a regime of separation of marital property prevailed suggests that few women were able to acquire additional property through marriage or gain access to landownership by any means other than purchase.[34] Landholdings were mostly owned by the husbands; this moreover indicates that widows found themselves in a precarious economic position more often than widowers. Similar precarious positions of widows have been identified in several parts of Europe. Olwen Hufton has stressed the predicament of widows in seventeenth- and eighteenth-century European towns, whereby widows made up about a third of the recipients of poor relief. Hufton moreover estimates that two or three in five farmers' widows, who themselves maintained a farm, were poor or depended on relatives.[35] The high proportion of widows in towns is especially significant: Sheilagh Ogilvie has calculated that in 1736 fifteen percent of heads of household in Wildberg in Württemberg were widows,

---

33 TLO 1573, III, 40, "*vnnd zimblich vnnderhaltung / nach gelegenhait jres Stanndts*".

34 Similar in Moring and Wall, *Widows*, p. 67.

35 Hufton, *The Prospect Before Her*, pp. 250 and 235.

while only 4.2 percent were widowers. This is very close to Hufton's calculation of widows making up about twelve percent of urban household heads with many more being lodgers.[36] Research also shows that there were more widows than widowers in early modern Germany. Widowed men were far more likely to remarry than widowed women, which probably accounts for the relatively high number of households headed by widows.[37] Similarly, a 1679 census in the court district of Sonnenburg reveals that about 20 percent of households were headed by women, of these 16.5 percent were probably widowed.[38] What did this mean for widows in southern Tyrol? And if access to landownership for women was restricted, what were the alternatives? What meaning, then, did other property components such as marriage portions, movables, and claims have, especially during settlement proceedings?

3 Inheritance Practice and Distribution of Landownership

With regard to inheritance, the sixteenth-century versions of the Tyrolean law code stipulated no particular regulations for succession to ownership other than that of children or, in their absence, blood relatives, and thus left some extent of leeway. Although the law code mitigated the principle of equal shares among children, and gave preference to the male line, it specified neither partible nor impartible inheritance. There were therefore several inheritance patterns practiced in Tyrol.[39] But gendered inheritance patterns were further enhanced in the Tyrolean law code: daughters were to receive their mother's movables, such as her trousseau and clothing, and sons were to receive their father's clothing, weapons, books, etc.[40] Other assets of the mother were to be equally divided amongst children or, in their absence, went to her blood

36 See Sheilagh C. Ogilvie, *A Bitter Living: Women, Markets, and Social Capital in Early Modern Germany* (Cambridge: Cambridge University Press, 2003), p. 177, see also chapter 5; Hufton, *The Prospect Before Her*, p. 245.

37 On early modern Germany see, for example, Dagmar Freist, "Religious Difference and the Experience of Widowhood in Seventeenth- and Eighteenth-Century Germany," in *Widowhood in Medieval and Early Modern Europe*, ed. Sandra Cavallo and Lyndan Warner (London and New York: Routledge, 2014), pp. 164–78, here p. 166.

38 Tiroler Landesarchiv Innsbruck (TLA), Stift Sonnenburg, Fasz. VI. Position 18 Karton 13: Volkszählung im Gericht Sonnenburg 1679.

39 See Paul Rösch, "Lebensläufe und Schicksale. Auswirkungen von zwei unterschiedlichen Erbsitten in Tirol," in *Südtiroler Erbhöfe. Menschen und Geschichten*, ed. Paul Rösch (Bolzano: Raetia, 1994), pp. 61–70; Palme, "Die Entwicklung des Erbrechtes," pp. 25–37.

40 TLO 1573, III, 9.

relatives. The preference of sons was even more marked among noble families, wherein daughters were expected to make a renunciation of their inheritance, as Siglinde Clementi has shown in her work.[41] Thus, although both men and women in practice had property rights, access, disposition, and rights of use of real estate were governed by gender specific concepts. In addition, the predominance of the bloodline had serious implications on marital property, which was clearly defined as separate in the law code. As we have seen, and in contrast to areas with community of property, the widowed spouse had no claim on provisions other than temporary lodgings until the first down payment.[42] The definition of the widow's claims does include a "reasonable livelihood", but befitting of her social status, and therefore the interpretation of the livelihood was up for negotiation with the heirs. According to the law code, the husband was obliged to guarantee his wife's marriage portion on his estate in order to secure its amount.[43] However, this guarantee was not always issued in written form. He could promise her a voluntary morning gift of a value up to as high as the third of the marriage portion; from 1532 onward he could also bequeath her by will lifelong usufruct or up to a third of his assets as property.[44] But again, such arrangements were also subject to negotiation with the heirs.

Consequently, the interests of the heirs and those of the widow often collided: although a widowed spouse had no inheritance claim on the property of the diseased spouse, the marriage portion, any inheritance portions she had received from her birth family, and the widow's claims all had to be separated out from the estate. Therefore, the heirs tried to limit her claims as much as possible to protect their inheritance and limit financial disadvantage resulting from a pay-out. In many cases the marriage portion and the morning gift rested as obligation on the estate, and a pay-out required additional solvency which could pose a major problem for the heirs, but it could also be an opportunity for the widow for potential usufruct. A clash of interests was thus predetermined and further complicated by the fact that there was scope for negotiation within the legal claims – for example regarding the "reasonable

41 See Siglinde Clementi in this volume and Siglinde Clementi, "Undivided Brothers – Renouncing Sisters. Family Strategies of Low Nobility in Sixteenth- and Seventeenth-Century Tyrol," in *Gender, Law and Economic Well-being in Europe from the Fifteenth to the Nineteenth Century*, ed. Anna Bellavitis and Beatrice Zucca Micheletto (London and New York: Routledge, 2019), pp. 149–64.

42 TLO 1532, 1573, III, 38. See Voltelini, "Zur Geschichte des ehelichen Güterrechts," p. 29, where he stresses that, in contrast to Bavarian and Austrian law, no *Leibzuchtrecht* remained in Tyrol.

43 TLO 1573, III, 1.

44 TLO 1532, 1573, III, 3.

livelihood" of the widow. The outcome of settlements therefore depended on a myriad of prerequisites: the existence of contractual stipulations, such as marriage contracts or wills; the marital and parental status of the widowed person, whether or not there were, for instance, underage or of age children, children of other marriages, or whether the marriage remained childless; and finally the solvency of the estate, which determined whether a pay-out to the widow would be possible or ruinous to the estate. Similar prerequisites have been identified in other areas, as shown for example by Jurgita Kunsmanaitė's work on sixteenth-century Lithuania.[45] But settlement proceedings were also influenced by the assertiveness of the persons involved: the role of the judge and his assessors (*Beisitzer*), the interests of the heirs, whether they wanted to retain or sell the estate; the interests of the widow, whether she intended to stay on the estate or remarry; and the intentions of guardians of underage children, who were responsible for keeping the children's inheritance intact. As a result, endowment proceedings become highly complex. Although it is possible to determine tendencies in regard to the frequency of certain stipulations, when analysing this data, one must always consider that a multitude of legal and personal aspects were involved in each of these proceedings.

The sample used for this study consists of 351 cases extracted from the court books of Sonnenburg from the period of 1549 to 1600, and 148 cases from the court books of the city court of Brixen for 1528, 1533–40, 1574, and 1600.[46] All of these cases are related to inheritance and marital property. The extraction of the cases and analysis of the court books is work in progress, and the sample does not represent an exhaustive selection. The numbers and analyses presented here are therefore tentative. The data consists of a variety of documents, in particular, endowment contracts of siblings and widows, wills and mutual wills, and guarantees of marriage portions (see Table 8.1).

The documents treat several different life stages, from inheritance of parents' estates, stipulation and guarantee of marital property at marriage, will making, *inter vivos* property transfers in return for lodging and sustenance in old age (retirement contracts), and widowhood settlements. As the higher proportion of wills, and correspondingly the lower proportion of sibling settlement contracts in Brixen indicate, the ratios of the documents reveal a

45 We have discussed these prerequisites in Hagen, Lanzinger, and Maegraith, "Competing Interests". Jurgita Kunsmanaitė established these for sixteenth-century Lithuania as well, see Jurgita Kunsmanaitė, *Provisions for Widowhood in the Legal Sources of Sixteenth-Century Lithuania* (Kiel: Solivagus, 2015), pp. 17–18.

46 Due to the very high number of court cases in Brixen, a sample was chosen and the cases for the years 1528, 1533–40, 1574, and 1600 extracted.

TABLE 8.1 Type and number of selected documents from Sonnenburg (1549–1600) and Brixen (1528, 1533–40, 1574, 1600)[a]

Type of document	Sonnenburg	Brixen
Sibling settlement contracts	79 (22%)	14 (9%)
Widow endowment contracts	67 (19%)	33 (22%)
Widower endowment contracts	13 (4%)	9 (6%)
Wills and mutual wills	45 (13%)	36 (24%)
Guarantees of marriage portions	30 (9%)	9 (6%)
Continuing probate proceedings	31 (9%)	12 (8%)
Marriage contracts	2 (1%)	10 (7%)
Other	85 (24%)	25 (17%)
Sum	**352 (100%)**	**148 (100%)**

a SLA, A 742 Verfachbuch (VfB) Sonnenburg 1540–1558, 1564–1573 (1559–1563 missing); VfB Sonnenburg 1573–1600; VfB Brixen Stadtgericht 1512–1556 (compilation); VfB Brixen Stadtgericht 1528–1540, 1574, 1598–1600 (1600). I would like to thank all the members of the archive in Bozen/Bolzano for their invaluable support

distinction between town and countryside. Analysis of these documents can also indicate specific inheritance practices. In 1578, for example, following the death of the widow of Christoph Ox, a former judge in Sonnenburg, the inheritance shares for the children of his second marriage were settled at the court in Sonnenburg.[47] The widow had held the estate in usufruct from 1569 until her death in 1571, after which the children were put under guardianship, and their settlement delayed. The son received 100 Gulden more than his sisters on the grounds that this would help secure the male family line as specified in the law code and that he would furthermore be of more use in the support of his sisters, because he was trained as a clerk. If the principal estate included land, the principal heir was, unless otherwise stated in a parents' will, chosen on a case-by-case basis. Sometimes it was the eldest son, sometimes the youngest, in some cases, especially in Sonnenburg, the eldest and youngest succeeded together, or all sons held the estate as undivided fraternal property until the brothers agreed on a division of the property. The other sisters and brothers

47 SLA, VfB Sonnenburg 1578, fol. 145–169, 31 May 1578. The children of his first marriage were settled on 18 June 1571; and on occasion of the marriage of one daughter the settlement of the other children was negotiated in 1578.

TABLE 8.2 Inheritance practice in Sonnenburg and Brixen[a]

Cases	Sonnenburg	Brixen
Sibling inheritance cases concerning main estate	54	9
Sibling inheritance cases with sons & daughters present	40	9
Daughters principal heirs with sons & daughters present	3	2
Sibling inheritance cases with only daughters present	5	0

[a] Sources see note for Table 8.1

were paid out with their inheritance shares or, alternatively, future instalments were arranged. Although daughters often received a smaller amount of money, they could garner a larger number of material goods as part of their future endowment. In a settlement from 1587, for example, the son received a set of clothes in addition to his share, but the daughters received a trunk, bedding, bedclothes, linen, and some clothing.[48] To identify the inheritance practice in regard to daughters, Table 8.2 shows all transcribed cases, where a settlement for the children of a deceased parent were negotiated, with special attention to cases in which both sons and daughters were present and daughters became principal heirs.

In 40 of the 79 cases of siblings' settlements in Sonnenburg, both brothers and sisters were present, and the main estate was negotiated. Of these 40 cases, there were only three cases, or 7.5 percent, in which the sister was declared principal heir.[49] But of the nine equivalent cases in Brixen, two sisters received the title of the main estate, equalling ca. 22 percent.[50] Although the sample for Brixen is comparatively small, we can nonetheless make some assumptions. In most cases – in Sonnenburg in 92.5 percent and in Brixen in 78 percent of the cases – one or several sons became principal heirs, whilst the sisters and other brothers were settled with their shares in movables, monies, or investments.

48 SLA, VfB Sonnenburg 1587, no folio numbers, 13 May 1587.

49 In 18 of the 79 cases in Sonnenburg the mother's estate was negotiated, in six cases only brothers were present, in three all siblings inherited in equal shares, and seven with alternative or unknown arrangements.

50 Of the nine siblings' settlements in Brixen two concerned the mother's estate.

Consequently, in a constellation where brothers and sisters were present, sisters seldom inherited land or buildings. Only when no brothers were present, the brothers could not take the succession, or the brothers who were principal heirs died without leaving children of their own, did daughters inherit real estate. According to the extracted cases, the preferential treatment of sons was, as stipulated by the law code, indeed put into practice. These proportions seem to be even lower than findings from other areas. Raffaela Sarti refers to estimates by Jack Goody and Antoinette Fauve-Chamoux for the countryside, according to which no male heirs were present in about 20 percent, and women inherited in 30.[51] In Sonnenburg, only in five cases, or about nine percent of 54 sibling inheritance proceedings in which the main estate was negotiated, no male heirs were present; considered alongside women as principal heirs, only ca. 15 percent of daughters inherited land.

Another way to approach gender specific distribution of property is to look at the marriage portions of wives and at land transmission during widowhood. Information on what and how much brides brought into their marriages, and if they received land as part of their widow's endowment, can be retrieved from marriage contracts, widow endowment settlements, wills, and guarantees on marriage portions (see Table 8.3). The information in Table 8.3 shows only 16 cases or ca. 13 percent, in which wives and widows in Sonnenburg brought land into their marriage, purchased it later, or received land as part of their settlement. In Brixen the proportion was slightly higher, with 18 cases, or ca. 18 percent.

In order to establish the general gender specific distribution of property in both places, information regarding wives, widows, sisters, and daughters who owned land has been retrieved from all the cases in both samples. From these, a total of 28 cases, or ca. eight percent, in which women were named as either owning or receiving real estate could be extracted for Sonnenburg. Of those, 18 cases entailed a whole or part of a *Baurecht* with farmland (*Hof*), and ten a building. The Brixen sample contains 20 cases, or 13.5 percent, in which women either owned or inherited real estate, or were adjudicated their late husband's landed property. Of those 20 cases, twelve owned buildings, and two buildings with land attached, four owned a farm and two a vineyard. There is a clear difference between town and countryside regarding the type of real estate ownership: although the proportion of women owning real estate was lower in Sonnenburg, the proportion of women owning farms and land was

51 Raffaella Sarti, *Europe at Home. Family and Material Culture, 1500–1800* (New Haven, CT: Yale University Press, 2002), p. 44.

TABLE 8.3 Landownership by wives and widows

Cases	Sonnenburg	Brixen
Marriage contracts and widow/widower endowment contracts, wills, guarantees of marriage portions	124	98
Women owning land	16	18
Women owning land, whole sample	28	20

higher in Sonnenburg than in urban Brixen, where women with real estate proportionally owned more buildings. The overall low number of women owning real estate seems to confirm the thesis that women occur less as landowners as a result of the specific property regime. In a study on property transfers from the eighteenth to the beginning of the twentieth centuries in the rural area of Innichberg, which is close to the market town of Innichen in the Puster Valley, Margareth Lanzinger has shown that in 205 property transfers concerning 27 farms, daughters comprised only 15 percent of those succeeding in title.[52] Although there might have been an improvement over time, the proportion remained very low.

The question remains, whether the prevailing property regime in Tyrol created imbalances solely in respect to gender, or whether this had wider implications. Since women did have property rights and, in some cases, held real estate, it would in principle have been possible to counterbalance this situation. In this sense it is illuminating to look at the cases in which the wife was the owner of the main estate and the husband married into this estate, bringing with him a monetary marriage portion. These husbands were called *einfahrende Gesellen* or fellows literally "arriving" in their wife's property, thus signifying them as not the principal property holder. The Sonnenburg sample contains ten and Brixen six identified cases in which the husband married into property and brought no real estate into the marriage. As we see many inheritance cases in which some sons were successors to the estate and others were paid off with their due share, this is not particularly unusual. These

52 See Margareth Lanzinger, "'aus khainer Gerechtigkeit …, sondern aus Gnaden'. Erbinnen – Handlungsoptionen und Geschwisterkonstellationen," *Frühneuzeit-Info* 15–1/2 (2004), pp. 20–28, here p. 21. Kustatscher found eight cases where real estate formed part of the bride's marriage portions, see Kustatscher, *Die Städte des Hochstifts Brixen*, p. 85.

cases show that those husbands were bound by the same principle as wives without landed property. In 1574, for example, the inheritance proceedings of Katharina Hinterkirchin's late husband Christian Vollunger were initiated, and his estate, which consisted of his marriage portion, morning gift, wages, the "wear and tear of his time and clothing", and his faithful housekeeping, was negotiated.[53] The fact that she had given him a morning gift indicates that she had been a widow at the time of their marriage.[54]

These cases point to property, rather than gender, being the central aspect for participation in the land market, and to the fact that both men and women could gain real estate if they had sufficient means. As we have seen, however, sons were favoured as successors. Consequently, fewer women brought real estate into their marriage as a marriage portion, and the system of separated marriage property reinforced this imbalance because wives – or husbands marrying into property – had no claim on their spouse's property, and thus no prospect on any gains.[55] In addition, husbands retained administration rights of their wife's property during marriage and often usufruct on it as widowers, especially when underage children were involved, creating a situation in which widowhood rarely brought any change to the widower's property situation.[56] All these factors established a higher proportion of landownership among men.

However, most women received a marriage portion in the form of money and material endowments from the parental estate. The wife's money was then invested into the husband's estate, and the material goods entered daily use in housekeeping, so that both components constituted a vital part of the household economy. The meaning of these should therefore not be underestimated.[57] The movables brought into a marriage were seldom attributed a

---

53 SLA, VfB Brixen Stadtgericht, fol. 40r–43r, 9 February 1574.

54 TLO 1573, III, 44.

55 The only exception was when a spouse bequeathed a third of his or her property to the other spouse. This was usually part of an option between lifelong usufruct or a third of the property in ownership. While this option was not found offered to a wife in the Sonnenburg sample, the sample for Brixen contains eight such stipulations.

56 See also Sandra Cavallo and Lyndan Warner, "Introduction" to *Widowhood in Medieval and Early Modern Europe* (London and New York: Routledge, 2014), pp. 3–23, here p. 12. By law they could hold the morning gift in usufruct, TLO 1573, III, 42.

57 Margareth Lanzinger and Janine Maegraith, "Vermögen als Medium der Herstellung von Verwandtschaftsräumen vom 16. bis zum 18. Jahrhundert – ein Projektbericht mit Objektperspektive," *Frühneuzeitinfo* 28 (2017), pp. 202–08. On material goods brought in by brides see also Karin Gottschalk, *Eigentum, Geschlecht, Gerechtigkeit. Haushalten und Erben im frühneuzeitlichen Leipzig* (Frankfurt a. M. and New York: Campus, 2003), where she had found that research of the trousseau is often neglected because of the focus on landownership (pp. 15–16); see also Renata Ago, *The Gusto for Things. A History of Objects in Seventeenth-Century Rome* (Chicago: University of Chicago Press, 2013).

TABLE 8.4 Distribution of values of marriage portions (in Gulden)

Place	N	Mean	Median	Minimum	Maximum	Quartile 1	Quartile 3
Brixen	51	334	140	12	2000	44	480
Sonnenburg	74	137	95	0	677	48	160

value, but it is possible in many cases to identify the monetary marriage portion (see Table 8.4).

As might be expected when looking at the wide range of marriage portion values, mean, and median differ significantly in Sonnenburg and Brixen. The Quartiles for Brixen describe a broad distribution of marriage portion values, and the minimum and maximum of both are far from the median of the sample. Marriage portions could range from very low, for instance zero in Sonnenburg, to very high, as high as 2,000 Gulden in Brixen. Marriage portions originated from parental assets, mostly those of the father, and reflect the different social and economic contexts of the brides. However, husbands could add to this a morning gift in the amount of up to a third of the value of the marriage portion.[58] This could be a considerable addition to her marriage portion. In the case of Maria Ziser, for example, this would have confirmed her marriage portion and made a substantial difference. The morning gift remained on the husband's estate until his death; thereafter the widow could claim the money. In cases for which we have listings for the value of both the marriage portion and morning gift it becomes clear that husbands in Brixen decided in most cases to give more than the recommended third as a morning gift – six cases even exceeded the third by up to 100 or more Gulden. In Sonnenburg, on the other hand, more than half of the husbands decided to give exactly, or less than, the third.[59] This striking difference between Brixen and Sonnenburg could indicate different legal practices as well as differences in cash availability or diverse real estate value and income rates. It is also important to consider that women had

58 See comments on the Tyrolean law code concerning the third book of the law code recommending that the morning gift should amount to a third of the marriage portion, Tiroler Landesmuseum Ferdinandeum, Dip. 904, Teil II, fol. 16r–27v, here fol. 21v.

59 There are 27 cases in Brixen in which both values are listed, most of the morning gifts exceed the suggested third. In Sonnenburg there are twelve such cases, half give less, three give exactly a third, and only three give more.

the right to bequeath their morning gift back as a gift to their husbands.[60] The two samples reveal that very few women did so, two in Sonnenburg and six in Brixen. But their decision is linked to the fact that the morning gift was the only asset that actually crossed the bloodline if the couple had no children: a widowed husband could keep the morning gift he gave his late wife in usufruct, but following his death it would go to either their children or, in case of childlessness, to her heirs.[61] In bequeathing morning gifts back to their husbands, wives assured that these assets would remain in their husband's family and not cross the bloodline. That Sonnenburg showed lower morning gifts would strengthen the thesis that rural areas safeguarded lineage property much more than urban areas. However, the fact that proportionally more women bequeathed their morning gift back in Brixen, where the morning gift was actually higher than in Sonnenburg, is significant and will be further investigated.

Apart from the marriage portion, brides brought material goods consisting primarily of their clothing, ornaments, household goods, bedding, fabrics, and sometimes material for textile production (spinning wheel, hemp, and wool) or livestock. The value of these material goods remained in most cases unspecified. It is only in some probate inventories that endowments can be found itemised and valued. In 1574, for example, a day labourer's wife in Brixen left movables worth 14 Gulden and an obligation with 22 Gulden, probably her marriage portion. In 1588 a merchant's wife in Brixen, in contrast, left over 156 Gulden worth of material goods, of which one of her trunks alone was worth 16 Gulden. Her marriage portion was 280 Gulden.[62] These two examples illustrate that, as mentioned above, the value and use of goods should not be underestimated, these constituted not only a vital part of the household economy, but along with her marriage portion and morning gift, also constituted part of the widow's security.

4 Widow's Endowments

So far the sample has revealed that the inheritance practice in southern Tyrol was prone to favour sons over daughters, that marriage portions generally came

60 The law code provided women with the right to bequeath their morning gift, which offers additional evidence that, although it was not paid out to her during marriage, the morning gift was indeed legally the wife's property. See TLO 1573, III, 7. See also Kustatscher, *Die Städte des Hochstifts Brixen*, pp. 85–86.

61 TLO 1573, III, 42.

62 SLA, VfB Brixen Stadtgericht, 1574.2, fol. 153v–156r, 9 June 1574; SLA, VfB Brixen Stadtgericht, 1588, fol. 253r–255v, 8 June 1588.

in the form of money and material goods, and that the proportion of land owning women was low in both localities. This property situation would likely have left widows in a very vulnerable situation. Since the law code did not provide for claims on a permanent residence, for example, and left the amount of a livelihood or provision up for negotiation, we can deduce that widows could indeed be left without any security or provision. As testified by the opening quote, however, endowment proceedings reveal a variety of stipulations and show that widows were not always left to their own devices.

Tables 8.5 and 8.6 show the various aspects that could have had influence on the outcome of an endowment settlement: land or landownership on the side of the widow, for example, or the presence of underage children, and whether or not the care of underage children was part of the contract. One should keep in mind that if there were children, underage or grown up, the widow had to negotiate with or against her own children (or her stepchildren) and their guardians. Also, if she was allowed to remain on the estate with her small children, this was usually on the condition that she left her money invested on that estate. In the case of her remarriage, she would be required to leave. It is often difficult to determine whether or not the widow was allowed to stay on the estate. In many cases that entitlement was not part of the settlement. In these cases, the widow was probably allowed to stay until her receipt of the first down payment. As there are no church records available for this time period the widows' ages remain unknown. Whether the presence of underage children or old age had any influence on negotiations remains therefore uncertain.

Apart from the material and monetary endowments, the specific familial or property situation might have led to certain outcomes of the settlements. Landownership, for example, could have led to a favourable outcome for the widow. Land was involved as either a marriage portion or other contribution in five of the cases in Brixen. Small children were present in two of those cases, and their care was part of the negotiation that led to the widow coming into ownership or use of the estate. In additional three cases no underage children were present. The widow received ownership in one case because she owned half of the estate and her late husband's will added weight to the negotiation. Landownership, therefore, mattered, and it is here where Brixen differs from Sonnenburg, which evidenced less landownership. The role of taking on the care of underage children is more distinct in instances where there was no female landownership. In eight out of ten cases in Brixen this condition secured the widow further lodgings, usufruct, or ownership of the estate. Other cases in which underage children were present but the widow was not granted responsibility for their care evidence a different outcome. Only in two cases she received permanent or temporary lodgings but in five such cases lodgings were left undecided or were not granted. In nine cases

TABLE 8.5 Widows' endowments: contractual negotiations in Brixen

	No land			Land involved		
	Presence of children			Presence of children		
	Care of small children	Small children, no care	No small children	Care of small children	Small children, no care	No small children
N = 33	10	7	11	2	0	3
		Lodgings			Lodgings	
Yes	8	1	4	2		2
Temporary	0	1	1	0		1
No / unclear	2	5	6	0		0
		Endowment			Endowment	
Usufruct	2	0	2	1		0
Choice, half or third	0	1	2	0		2
Endowment only	2	5	9	0		2
Lease	0	1	0	0		0
Ownership	6	0	0	1		1

out of eleven wherein there were no small children the widows received only an endowment payment and only in four permanent and in one temporary residence.

In 1548, for example, the endowment proceedings for the widow Magdalena Morlin in Brixen ended in a favourable settlement because she had underage children and was pregnant, and her late husband had bequeathed her lifelong usufruct of the estate. Consequently, her marriage portion of 300 Gulden and morning gift of 200 Gulden were to remain on the estate, paying five percent interest, and she as beneficiary was required to raise her children on the estate until they were of age. She was expected to administer the estate responsibly with the assistance and advice of the children's guardians, who could also pay her an advance should she prove herself apt at running the estate well.[63]

63 SLA, VfB Brixen Stadtgericht, 1538–1540, fol. 138r–142v, 5 May 1548.

TABLE 8.6 Widows' endowments: contractual negotiations in Sonnenburg

	No land			Land involved		
	Presence of children			Presence of children		
	Care of small children	Small children, no care	No small children	Care of small children	Small children, no care	No small children
N = 64	**12**	**20**	**30**	**1**	**0**	**1**
		Lodgings			**Lodgings**	
Yes	10	6	11	1		1
Temporary	1	11	7	0		0
No / unclear	1	3	12	0		0
		Endowment			**Endowment**	
Usufruct	1	1	2	1		0
Choice, half or third	0	0	0	0		0
Endowment only	5	19	27	0		1
Lease	2	0	0	0		0
Ownership	4	0	1	0		0

In this case, the widow was entrusted with looking after the children and was in possession of a will written by her husband that strengthened her case. In some instances, such decisions could also have been linked to the circumstance that her marriage portion exceeded the solvency of the estate.

Only two women brought land into their marriages in Sonnenburg of which one received the estate in usufruct. But the small number renders it almost impossible to draw any conclusions in this respect. However, providing for the care of small children did seem to add weight in negotiations; in ten out of twelve such cases the widow was granted unlimited lodgings. Mothers were urged to either remain in the lodgings looking after their children until they wished to leave, or to stay on a temporary basis as long as the children were very small. In one case the widow was granted usufruct, in two the lease of the land, and in another four ownership of the estate, as a pay-out would have likely ruined it financially. In most cases in which the widow was granted lifelong lodging, her money was left on the estate and no interest paid; she was only paid out if she decided to leave the estate and remarry. Most settlements included the condition that, in return, the widow was expected to further contribute with her labour. This illustrates the significance of her work which is otherwise rarely mentioned in the records. Old age was the reason for lodgings in three of the cases, which points to the possibility that age and ability to work may have been additional factors in the negotiations. In 19 cases, the widow retained temporary lodgings especially when no care was negotiated for children or the widow was childless, and in 15 cases the widow could stay on the estate until her death or departure if no small children were present or no care negotiated. Lodgings were not always explicitly part of the settlement and were in most cases granted until the widow's first pay out. In addition, her claim on lodgings often ended when she remarried. Significantly, in 18 instances where no small children were present the widow received lifelong or temporary lodgings, and no lodgings were mentioned or granted in twelve cases, which left future arrangements open for negotiations – this was also the case with Maria Ziser. It is noteworthy that whereas the presence of small children helped to gain a better outcome, still about a third of all widows were left without guaranteed shelter.

With so few cases where women owned land in Sonnenburg, it is difficult to establish how this may have influenced the outcome of settlements. However, mutual wills can provide insight into property arrangements between husband and wife and show that claims on land through investment could lead to improved future provisions for the wife. In a mutual will in Sonnenburg from 1596, for example, the married couple Georg Rauchegger and Maria Siggin arranged for the future use of their jointly purchased property. The land title remained with the husband, but in the case of his death she would retain the property in lifelong usufruct. Following her death, it would go to their children, or to the husband's blood relatives.[64] Although the wife did not have legal ownership of the property, the investment of her marriage portion led to an arrangement in her favour. That the Sonnenburg sample contains a significantly smaller proportion of mutual wills than Brixen might again point to differences between town and countryside, with towns showing a higher tendency toward the use of legal instruments as safeguarding.

In case a widower owned the main estate, widowhood did not fundamentally change his property situation, and thus endowment settlements were the subject of less urgency than they were for widows. Only in cases where

64 SLA, VfB Sonnenburg 1596, no folio numbers, 12 June 1596.

the deceased wife had been the owner of the main estate, the widower was treated similarly to a widow with no real estate; the exception here being that he had no claim to widow's rights, and was held responsible for paying the debts that had been accrued during marriage.[65] In Brixen there were two cases with *einfahrende Gesellen* as widowers, and three in Sonnenburg. These settlements were negotiated similarly to the widows' settlements, and the presence of underage children or financial problems had substantial influence in their outcome. In Brixen, for example, the widower was required to give his children their mother's goods and financial assets of 120 Gulden. But he was allowed to retain the rest of the estate on the grounds that he had cared for her in her long illness and had invested all of his money in her estate. In return, he was responsible for raising his underage children.[66]

All in all, the proportion of landowning widows in Brixen is slightly higher than in Sonnenburg. This could reflect the differing nature of landholdings in town and countryside, between crafts with predominantly house- and workshop ownership, and agriculture where ownership of a farm and arable land was important. In her sample, Kustatscher found a few women running workshops, such as bakeries since it was possible for widows to continue the trade of their late husband.[67] This could also indicate a tendency towards a more dynastic approach in the countryside that favoured sons over daughters.

The results so far suggest that widows were dependent on court settlements for the assignment of their lodgings and provisions. Having young children could, to some extent, lead to a more favourable settlement, but in many cases this was only for a limited time. Landownership or substantial investments by way of their marriage portions could support widows' negotiations in obtaining a better settlement and even in gaining lifelong usufruct of the estate. As usufruct supplied a mode by which women could both manage an estate and retain the gains from an estate, this was an important way in which women could partake in the local economy.[68] At the same time, usufruct could pose a daunting task if a widow faced numerous debts or was raising small children, but it could also be an opportunity. One example in Sonnenburg is Christina Neuhauserin in Sonnenburg, who received the right to lifelong usufruct from her deceased husband by will, and thereafter managed to accrue huge gains on the estate. Her will shows that she was able to dispose of over 2,000 Gulden

65 TLO 1573, III, 44.
66 SLA, VfB Brixen Stadtgericht 1600, no folio numbers, 14 January 1600.
67 See Kustatscher, *Die Städte des Hochstifts Brixen*, p. 88.
68 See the chapter by Beatrice Moring in this volume in view of access to land.

made up entirely of acquired assets, whereas the property in usufruct returned to her husband's kin following her death.[69]

5 Conclusions

Although women were in possession of land less often than men, they did have control over some assets that were comprised of different components: their material goods, livestock, and in widowhood money and investments. In some cases, marriage portions proved to be quite powerful, as a pay out to the widow might have either exceeded the solvency of the estate or the value of the estate altogether. In such cases, in order to avoid indebtedness and thus secure the estate for the children, the widow was granted lifelong usufruct or even received the estate as property – in both cases on the condition that she raised the children on the estate. The marriage portion that was invested in the estate thus became a powerful tool for negotiation. The morning gift could be a considerable addition to this circumstance. This analysis has shown that the role and significance of lifelong usufruct should not be underestimated. Although women did not gain full ownership of the estate, and the guardians of the children technically controlled her property management, women with usufruct were the administrators of the real estate in their care, and the profits remained their own. This granted them some extent of independence and participation in the local economy. Also, women were active on the credit market.[70] Their marriage portions and endowment payments could be invested and lent to family members or neighbours against an interest payment in either cash or in kind. Although in most cases women lacked landownership that could have offered them collateral, they could draw on the amount of their marriage portions, which were mortgaged on the assets of their husbands, and were thus secured. However, in most cases and especially when the marriage portions were low or average, widows saw their property during marriage only marginally increased – if at all, unless they received a morning gift after the marriage. Their work and contributions to their husbands' estates thus remained little remunerated. It is only in cases where the widows were allowed to continue to live on the estate, and that their labour is named as one of the conditions for this, that the necessity of

69 SLA, VfB Sonnenburg 1592, fol. 43–44, 28 March 1592.

70 Sheilagh Ogilvie, Markus Küpker, and Janine Maegraith, "Household Debt in Early Modern Germany: Evidence from Personal Inventories," *Journal of Economic History* 72–1 (2012), pp. 134–67.

their labour input is implied. This analysis has also shown that the situation of widowers who married into property was very similar to that of unpropertied widows. This implies that not only gender and kinship, but even especially property itself was a decisive factor.

The next step will therefore be to analyse the purchase deeds to determine how many women made use of their money to purchase real estate on the market as some cases in the sample suggest.[71] It also remains to be analysed, to which extent gender can be considered the main category responsible for creating such an imbalance in landownership, or if this imbalance was consolidated by an amalgam of specific practices of law, gender, wealth, and kinship. As we have seen the law left leeway in inheritance practices and lineage property by definition did not exclude women from inheritance. This was illustrated by the case of Maria Ziser, where her late husband's sisters inherited his house and garden. But if inheritance practices which favoured sons over daughters were maintained, this imbalance could not be corrected.

Access to landed property or investment in land was important and could secure a favourable settlement for the widow. This means that the imbalance of the distribution of landownership reinforces the thesis that widows were in a precarious economic situation – albeit not always one that led to poverty.[72] It was also in the interest of the court and the community to avoid leaving widows orphaned and "sent into the open field", as becomes evident in the role of the judge as arbitrator and the fact that most of the contracts were based on previous negotiation rather than litigation. Negotiating parties, furthermore, used the open definitions in the law code leading to a wide range of settlements between the parties involved.

References

Ago, Renata. *The Gusto for Things. A History of Objects in Seventeenth-Century Rome.* Chicago: University of Chicago Press, 2013.

Bellavitis, Anna. "Die Mitgift in Venedig zwischen Mittelalter und Früher Neuzeit." *L'Homme. Z.F.G.* 22–1 (2011): pp. 23–37.

71 Janine Maegraith, "Fenced in or out? Women and Property in Early Modern Southern Tyrol," in *Gender, Law and Material Culture. Immovable Property and Mobile Goods in Early Modern Europe*, ed. Annette Caroline Cremer (London and New York: Routledge, 2021), pp. 123–45.

72 Moring and Wall, *Widows*, pp. 20 and 251.

Cavallo, Sandra, and Lyndan Warner. "Introduction." In *Widowhood in Medieval and Early Modern Europe*, edited by Sandra Cavallo and Lyndan Warner, pp. 3–23. London and New York: Routledge, 2014.

Cavallo, Sandra, and Lyndan Warner, eds. *Widowhood in Medieval and Early Modern Europe*. London and New York: Routledge, 2014.

Chabot, Isabelle. "Lineage Strategies and the Control of Widows in Renaissance Florence." In *Widowhood in Medieval and Early Modern Europe*, edited by Sandra Cavallo and Lyndan Warner, pp. 127–44. London and New York: Routledge, 2014.

Clementi, Siglinde. "Undivided Brothers – Renouncing Sisters. Family Strategies of Low Nobility in Sixteenth- and Seventeenth-Century Tyrol." In *Gender, Law and Economic Well-being in Europe from the Fifteenth to the Nineteenth Century*, edited by Anna Bellavitis and Beatrice Zucca Micheletto, pp. 149–64. London and New York: Routledge, 2019.

Diefendorf, Barbara B. "Women and Property in Ancient Regime France. Theory and Practice in Dauphiné and Paris." In *Early Modern Conceptions of Property*, edited by John Brewer and Susan Staves, pp. 170–93. London: Routledge, 1995.

Forster, Ellinor, and Janine Maegraith. "Alte Gewohnheiten unter neuem Namen? Die Angleichung Schlesiens durch die österreichischen Eherechtsnormen im späten 18. und frühen 19. Jahrhundert." *Szkice archiwalno-historyczne* 12 (2015): pp. 13–53.

Freist, Dagmar. "Religious Difference and the Experience of Widowhood in Seventeenth- and Eighteenth-Century Germany." In *Widowhood in Medieval and Early Modern Europe*, edited by Sandra Cavallo and Lyndan Warner, pp. 164–78. London and New York: Routledge, 2014.

Gottschalk, Karin. *Eigentum, Geschlecht, Gerechtigkeit. Haushalten und Erben im frühneuzeitlichen Leipzig*. Frankfurt a. M. and New York: Campus, 2003.

Hagen, Christian, Margareth Lanzinger, and Janine Maegraith. "Competing Interests in Death-related Stipulations in South Tirol c. 1350–1600." In *Planning for Death: Wills, and Death-Related Property Arrangements in Europe, 1200–1600*, edited by Mia Korpiola and Anu Lahtinen, pp. 88–118. Leiden and Boston: Brill, 2017.

Hagen, Christian, Margareth Lanzinger, and Janine Maegraith. "Verträge als Instrumente der Vermögensabsicherung im südlichen Tirol vom 14. bis zum 18. Jahrhundert." *Historische Anthropologie* 25–2 (2017): pp. 188–212.

Hess, Rolf-Dieter. *Familien- und Erbrecht im württembergischen Landrecht von 1555 unter besonderer Berücksichtigung des älteren württembergischen Rechts*. Stuttgart: Kohlhammer, 1968.

Hufton, Olwen. *The Prospect Before Her: A History of Women in Western Europe 1500–1800*. London: Harper Collins, 1995.

Kunsmanaitė, Jurgita. *Provisions for Widowhood in the Legal Sources of Sixteenth-Century Lithuania*. Kiel: Solivagus, 2015.

Kustatscher, Erika. *Die Städte des Hochstifts Brixen im Spätmittelalter. Verfassungs- und Sozialgeschichte von Brixen, Bruneck und Klausen im Spiegel der Personengeschichte (1200–1550)*. Innsbruck: Studienverlag, 2007.

Langer-Ostrawsky, Gertrude. "Vom Verheiraten der Güter. Bäuerliche und kleinbäuerliche Heiratsverträge im Erzherzogtum Österreich unter der Enns." In Margareth Lanzinger, Gunda Barth-Scalmani, Ellinor Forster, and Gertrude Langer-Ostrawsky, *Aushandeln von Ehe. Heiratsverträge der Neuzeit im europäischen Vergleich*, pp. 27–119. Cologne, Weimar, and Vienna: Böhlau, 2010, 2nd edition 2015.

Lanzinger, Margareth. "'aus khainer Gerechtigkeit ..., sondern aus Gnaden'. Erbinnen – Handlungsoptionen und Geschwisterkonstellationen." *Frühneuzeit-Info* 15–1/2 (2004): pp. 20–28.

Lanzinger, Margareth. "Ehegütermodelle und Balanceakte. Resümee." In Margareth Lanzinger, Gunda Barth-Scalmani, Ellinor Forster, and Gertrude Langer-Ostrawsky. *Aushandeln von Ehe. Heiratsverträge der Neuzeit im europäischen Vergleich*, pp. 459–67. Cologne, Weimar, and Vienna: Böhlau, 2010, 2nd edition 2015.

Lanzinger, Margareth, "Variationen des Themas: Mitgiftsysteme." In Margareth Lanzinger, Gunda Barth-Scalmani, Ellinor Forster, and Gertrude Langer-Ostrawsky. *Aushandeln von Ehe. Heiratsverträge der Neuzeit im europäischen Vergleich,* pp. 469–92. Cologne, Weimar, and Vienna: Böhlau, 2010, 2nd edition 2015.

Lanzinger, Margareth. "Von der Macht der Linie zur Gegenseitigkeit. Heiratskontrakte in den Südtiroler Gerichten Welsberg und Innichen 1750–1850." In Margareth Lanzinger, Gunda Barth-Scalmani, Ellinor Forster, and Gertrude Langer-Ostrawsky. *Aushandeln von Ehe. Heiratsverträge der Neuzeit im europäischen Vergleich*, pp. 205–367. Cologne, Weimar, and Vienna: Böhlau, 2010, 2nd edition 2015.

Lanzinger, Margareth, Gunda Barth-Scalmani, Ellinor Forster, and Gertrude Langer-Ostrawsky, *Aushandeln von Ehe. Heiratsverträge der Neuzeit im europäischen Vergleich.* Cologne, Weimar, and Vienna: Böhlau, 2010, 2nd edition 2015.

Lanzinger, Margareth, and Janine Maegraith. "Houses and the Range of Wealth in Early Modern Gender- and Intergenerational Relationships." *Jahrbuch für Europäische Geschichte / European History Yearbook* 18 (2017): pp. 14–34.

Lanzinger, Margareth, and Janine Maegraith. "Konkurrenz um Vermögen im südlichen Tirol des 16. Jahrhunderts." *L'Homme. Z.F.G.* 27–1 (2016): pp. 15–31.

Lanzinger, Margareth, and Janine Maegraith. "Vermögen als Medium der Herstellung von Verwandtschaftsräumen vom 16. bis zum 18. Jahrhundert – ein Projektbericht mit Objektperspektive." *Frühneuzeitinfo* 28 (2017): pp. 202–08.

Maegraith, Janine. "Fenced in or out? Women and Property in Early Modern Southern Tyrol." In *Gender, Law and Material Culture. Immobile Property and Mobile Goods in Early Modern Europe*, edited by Annette Caroline Cremer, pp. 123–45. London and New York: Routledge, 2021.

Maegraith, Janine. "Opportunity or Constraint? Partible Inheritance, Family Property and Household Structure in Southwest Germany – Evidence from Inventories." In *Finding "Ie" in Western Society*, edited by Motoyasu Takahashi, pp. 133–61. Ehime: Ehime University Economics Study Series, 2013.

Moring, Beatrice, and Richard Wall. *Widows in European Economy and Society 1600–1920*. Woodbridge: Boydell Press, 2017.

Mutschlechner, Josef. *Alte Brixner Stadtrechte*. Innsbruck: Wagner, 1935.

Nehlsen-von Stryk, Karin. Art. "Witwe. A. Rechtsgeschichte, II. Germanisches und Deutsches Recht." In *Lexikon des Mittelalters*, vol. 9, col. 277–78. Munich: LexMA-Verlag, 1998.

Ogilvie, Sheilagh C. *A Bitter Living: Women, Markets, and Social Capital in Early Modern Germany*. Cambridge: Cambridge University Press, 2003.

Ogilvie, Sheilagh, Markus Küpker, and Janine Maegraith. "Household Debt in Early Modern Germany: Evidence from Personal Inventories." *Journal of Economic History* 72–1 (2012): pp. 134–67.

Palme, Rudolf. "Die Entwicklung des Erbrechtes im ländlichen Bereich." In *Südtiroler Erbhöfe. Menschen und Geschichten*, edited by Paul Rösch, pp. 25–37. Bozen: Raetia, 1994.

Pauser, Josef, and Martin P. Schennach, eds. *Die Tiroler Landesordnungen von 1526, 1532 und 1573. Historische Einführung und Edition*. Vienna, Cologne, and Weimar: Böhlau, 2018.

Rösch, Paul. "Lebensläufe und Schicksale. Auswirkungen von zwei unterschiedlichen Erbsitten in Tirol." In *Südtiroler Erbhöfe. Menschen und Geschichten*, edited by Paul Rösch, pp. 61–70. Bolzano: Raetia, 1994.

Sarti, Raffaella. *Europe at Home. Family and Material Culture, 1500–1800*. New Haven, CT: Yale University Press, 2002.

Schennach, Martin P. *Gesetz und Herrschaft. Die Entstehung des Gesetzgebungsstaates am Beispiel Tirols*. Cologne, Weimar, and Vienna: Böhlau, 2010.

Schwerin, Claudius von. *Deutsche Rechtsgeschichte*. Leipzig and Berlin: Teubner, 1912.

Spieß, Karl-Heinz. "Witwenversorgung im Hochadel. Rechtlicher Rahmen und praktische Gestaltung im Spätmittelalter und zu Beginn der Frühen Neuzeit." In *Witwenschaft in der Frühen Neuzeit. Fürstliche und adelige Witwen zwischen Fremd- und Selbstbestimmung*, edited by Martina Schattkowsky, pp. 88–114. Leipzig: Leipziger Universitätsverlag, 2003.

Voltelini, Hans von. "Zur Geschichte des ehelichen Güterrechts in Tirol. Eine rechtshistorische Skizze." In *Festgaben zu Ehren Max Büdinger's von seinen Freunden und Schülern*, pp. 1–34. Innsbruck: Wagner, 1898.

Weber, Marianne. *Ehefrau und Mutter in der Rechtsentwicklung*. Tübingen: Mohr, 1907.

PART 3

Social Spaces – Legal Cultures: Patricians and Nobles

CHAPTER 9

Family Justice and Public Justice in Dowry and Inheritance Conflicts between Florentine Families (Fourteenth to Fifteenth Centuries)

Isabelle Chabot

Patrimonial and inheritance conflicts pitting families against one another were a structural phenomenon in medieval Florence. These conflicts have left abundant documentary traces: court records preserved in the various archives of civil justice remain yet to be explored, but scholarly literature focusing on *consilia* – legal advice provided by experts upon request of the conflicting parties or the courts – has already illustrated how intense and complex conflicts on female property could become.[1] The rich private documentation preserved in the Florentine State Archives (notarial deeds, wills, family diaries, account books, tutorship books etc.) allows for further investigation into not only the reasons at the heart of these controversies but also the various ways in which conflicts were resolved – private, non-procedural, and judicial – and how these interacted during the course of litigation. This chapter aims to investigate this interplay between family justice and public justice in patrimonial disputes involving women. While primarily focusing on the restitution of dowries, I will also investigate cases in which daughters challenged the *exclusio propter dotem*, claiming more than the dowry that they had received from their paternal inheritance.

1 See, in particular, the pioneering studies by Lauro Martines, *Lawyers and Statecraft in Renaissance Florence* (Princeton: Princeton University Press, 1968); Julius Kirshner, *Marriage, Dowries and Citizenship in Late Medieval and Renaissance Italy* (Toronto: University of Toronto Press, 2011); Thomas Kuehn, *Law, Family and Women: Toward a Legal Anthropology of Renaissance Italy* (Chicago: Chicago University Press, 1991); Thomas Kuehn, *Heirs, Kin and Creditors in Renaissance Florence* (Cambridge: Cambridge University Press, 2008) and the recent Thomas Kuehn, *Family and Gender in Renaissance Italy, 1300–1600* (Cambridge: Cambridge University Press, 2017).

 | DOI:10.1163/9789004456204_010

1 Family Justice and Public Justice

When Florentine women and their families initiated a dispute over property, they had various options for conflict resolution at their disposal that often interacted with each other. The first stage of the litigation process generally involved informal bilateral negotiations, which would lead the parties to a "domestic" agreement (*dimesticamente*).[2] The two parties would meet to discuss the issue and a *ricordanza* would be written in the family diary, or else they would draw up a private *scritta* (writ) that reported the terms of the agreement or "pact", with which everyone was expected to comply within a certain amount of time. In addition to the involvement of prominent relatives and close acquaintances in finding a non-procedural solution, legal experts were often employed as representatives of the conflicting parties, providing counsel and mediation. Notaries were responsible for drawing up the acts and were moreover often called to act as arbiters with, or on behalf of, the relatives of the conflicting parties. A woman could also choose a notary as her *mundualdus*, a legal guardian who represented her in formal undertakings[3] or as a legal agent (*procuratore*) who appeared in court on her behalf. From a legal standpoint, patrimonial and inheritance disputes were extremely complex, and thus jurists were often called in by private individuals, the courts, or the officers of municipal magistracies (*uffici*) to provide their professional opinions.[4]

An inability to reach a bilateral agreement or the need for a more formal agreement required the intervention of a third party – arbitrators or judges – and hence recourse to arbitration or a judicial authority. Arbitration was a means of arriving at a solution through private negotiation,[5] while

2 This term is used by Donato Velluti: cf. note 58.

3 Thomas Kuehn, "Cum Consensu Mundualdi: Legal Guardianship of Women in Quattrocento Florence," in Thomas Kuehn, *Law, Family and Women. Toward an Anthropology of Renaissance Italy* (Chicago: University of Chicago Press, 1991), pp. 212–37, here p. 222.

4 Julius Kirshner, "Consilia as Authority in Late Medieval Italy: The Case of Florence," in *Legal Consulting in the Civil Law Tradition*, ed. Mario Ascheri, Ingrid Baumgärtner, and Julius Kirshner (Berkeley: University of California Press, 1999), pp. 107–40; Thomas Kuehn, "Lawyers and Housecraft in Renaissance Florence: the Politics of Private *Consilia*," in *The Politics of Law in Medieval and Renaissance Italy: Essays in Honour of Lauro Martines*, ed. Lawrin D. Armstrong and Julius Kirshner (Toronto: University of Toronto Press, 2011), pp. 124–40.

5 Luciano Martone, *Arbiter-arbitrator. Forme di giustizia privata nell'età di diritto comune* (Naples: Jovene, 1984); Thomas Kuehn, "Law and Arbitration in Renaissance Florence," in Thomas Kuehn, *Law, Family and Women: Toward a Legal Anthropology of Renaissance Italy* (Chicago: Chicago University Press, 1991), pp. 19–74; Massimo Vallerani, "Liti private e soluzioni legali. Note sul libro di Thomas Kuehn e sui sistemi di composizione dei conflitti nella società tardo medievale," *Quaderni storici* 89 (1995), pp. 546–57.

seeking a procedural resolution shifted the dispute into the sphere of public justice. As we shall see, however, the use of infrajudicial methods and recourse to judicial authority during the course of disputes were by no means mutually exclusive. But as Thomas Kuehn has observed, they always interacted: conflicting parties shifted from one arena to another with a certain flexibility, entering and exiting the courts before or after seeking mediation by arbitration.

With the reformed statutes of 1325, and perhaps earlier, the Florentine commune deliberately removed relatives – blood relatives and relatives by marriage – from the courts of justice, therewith obliging them to resolve family disputes by arbitration. If even one of the implicated parties resorted to a judge, the judge was obliged to reject both litigants and each party was required to appoint its own arbitrators within eight days, under penalty of 300 *lire*. The article *Quod consaguinei et consortes habentes questionem vel controversiam teneantur ipsam commictere in arbitros* in the statute of the Podestà of 1325,[6] listed all relatives – descendants (up to the third degree), ascendants (up to the third degree) and collaterals (up to the fourth degree), male and female – who were obliged to resolve their conflict through arbitration rather than in civil court. To apply to the court was prohibited for them by the statutes. This article also established rules and timeframes for arbitration and guaranteed a public, and therefore legal, framework. The *compromisum* was a preliminary agreement in which the main points of the dispute were formulated and parties involved agreed to observe the decision of one or more arbitrators of their choosing. Arbitrators were generally allowed up to two months to settle an issue (*laudum*), and in cases of disagreement it was the judge's responsibility to appoint a third arbitrator to resolve the conflict. The statutes furthermore guaranteed the execution of the arbitration settlement by charging unobservant parties with fines or time in the city jail.

The Florentine statutes, however, stipulated that "women could not be forced into arbitration on their dowry".[7] This restriction was significant, as it resulted by and large in the subtraction of dowry issues from family justice, relinquishing the resolution of these conflicts to public authority. According to the statutes, female patrimonial rights were best defended in a legal and

6 *Statuti della Repubblica fiorentina,* ed. Romualdo Caggese (Florence: Tip. Galileiana, 1921), new edition: Giuliano Pinto, Francesco Salvestrini, and Andrea Zorzi, eds., *Tomo II: Statuti del Podestà dell'anno 1325* (Florence: Olschki, 1999), pp. 152–54; Kuehn, "Law and Arbitration," pp. 27–28.

7 "*Nulla quoque mulier vigore dicti statuti compellatur compromictere litem questionem seu discordiam quam haberet pro dote sua vel occasione dotis*", *Statuti della Repubblica fiorentina,* p. 154.

public space such as the court, where the rules were established by law, rather than according to the logic or interests of male relatives and family acquaintances who were generally appointed arbitrators. Thomas Kuehn's analysis of a sample of 123 arbitrations (1422–1430) – the only such study so far – reveals that women were involved in only one case out of every four (41 out of 123), but "women's arbitration was more likely to include kin as the other party – 18 out of 31 (58 percent)".[8] This data suggests that resolution of controversial disputes was generally obtained by either resorting to informal non-procedural modalities, or by appealing directly to public justice.

Conflicts regarding dowries and succession involved numerous judges who instructed civil lawsuits.[9] Competence in these issues fell not only to the primary courts presided over by foreign judges (the *Podestà*, the *Capitano del Popolo* and, as of 1364[10] even the *Esecutore degli Ordinamenti di giustizia*),[11] but also to the *Mercanzia*, the merchant court which, in dealing with bankruptcies, could receive cases in which dowry payments were given precedence,[12] or even to guild courts.[13] Some of the new urban magistracies – including for example the *Ufficiali dei Pupilli*, established in 1368 to administer inheritances of minors whose intestate fathers had failed to designate a tutor,[14] the *Ufficiali della Torre*

8 Kuehn, "Law and Arbitration," pp. 40–41.

9 In Florence, Thomas Kuehn has counted about forty different judicial authorities "Some Ambiguities of Female Inheritance Ideology in the Renaissance," *Continuity and Change* 2–1 (1987), pp. 11–36, here p. 13, and in Kuehn, *Law, Family and Women*, pp. 238–57.

10 On 3 June 1364, the city councils approved a provision that granted the *Esecutore* the same authority in dowry trials that up until then had been reserved for the *Podestà*, Archivio di Stato di Firenze (ASF), *Provvisioni, Registri*, 51, fol. 147, 151.

11 Guidobaldo Guidi, *Il governo della città-repubblica di Firenze del primo Quattrocento*, 3 vols. (Florence: Olschki, 1981); Andrea Zorzi, "The Judicial System in Florence in the Fourteenth and Fifteenth Centuries," in *Crime, Society and the Law in Renaissance Italy*, ed. Trevor Dean and Kate J. P. Lowe (Cambridge: Cambridge University Press, 1994), pp. 40–58.

12 In 1423, for example, the *Mercanzia* mandated the return of a 1,200-florin dowry to Nanna, widow of Matteo Ridolfi. ASF, *Carte strozziane*, II serie, 11 fol. 3v, diary of Antonio di Lionardo Rustichi. Antonella Astorri, *La Mercanzia a Firenze nella prima metà del Trecento* (Florence: Olschki, 1998); Elena Maccioni and Sergio Tognetti, eds., *Tribunali di mercanti e giustizia mercantile* (Florence: Olschki, 2016).

13 In 1431, Maddalena presented a petition to the court of the wool worker's guild against a weaver to force him to pay her 50 lire as a dowry and to give her the clothing items that she had been promised upon her engagement as an apprentice: Franco Franceschi, *Oltre il "Tumulto". I lavoratori fiorentini dell'arte della lana fra Tre e Quattrocento* (Florence: Olschki, 1993), p. 177.

14 Caroline M. Fisher, "Guardianship, the Family and the Rise of Renaissance Florentine State, 1368–93," in *Famiglie e poteri in Italia tra Medioevo ed Età moderna*, ed. Anna Bellavitis and Isabelle Chabot (Rome: École française de Rome, 2009), pp. 265–82; ASF,

from 1364, and the *Ufficiali sopra i beni dei ribelli*, the latter two of which were responsible for the management of goods confiscated from the banished – were inevitably faced with the claims of wives or widows.[15] Scholars have yet to fully chart the judicial authorities that had jurisdiction over conflicts concerning dowries and succession, and countless petitions of wives, widows, and heirs regarding these issues that were addressed to the *Signoria* remain yet to be investigated, and it will be interesting to develop a fuller understanding of how women could use this extraordinary judicial complexity to their advantage.[16]

The most complex cases involve more than one jurisdiction. In 1415, a particularly intricate litigation was the execution of the highly indebted inheritance of Ugolini di Piero Michi, a Florentine silk merchant. The merchant's two orphans (who refused the inheritance) opposed their late father's many creditors who, however, did not have priority on three dowry credits of Ugolino's widowed mother (300 florins), first wife (1,500 florins), and second wife (1,050 florins). The twin's maternal grandfather and guardian battled for a whole year, juggling between appeals to the podesterial court, an arbitration, a *sindacato*, and appeals to the court of the *Mercanzia*, in order to at least secure the mother's inheritance (1,500 florins) for the children.[17] During litigation the two procedures of arbitration and lawsuit intersected, because disputes were generally extremely complicated, and women (and their legal representatives) often took recourse to one and then the other method. In order to unblock a stalemate and reach an agreement it was sometimes necessary to appeal to a court, or simply threaten to do so. Awareness that the case might be lost could induce either party to interrupt a trial. In October 1411, Bartolomea, widow of Bartolomeo di Falco, brought the heirs of her brother-in-law Paliano di Falco to court to secure a lifetime provision of food in compliance with her late husband's will. Six months later, on 2 April 1412, Paliano's testamentary executors gave in, and handed her eight florins as her first annuity. The three jurists who were in the meantime asked for their professional opinion (*consilium*), had assured that Bartolomea's claims were based on solid grounds. Thus, it was "in

---

Santa Maria Nuova, Carte Galli-Tassi, 850, account book of the inheritance of Niccolò di Sanminiati de' Ricci, by the *Ufficiali de' Pupilli*: for the reimbursement of the dowry to the widow (950 florins), cf. fol. 133v–134r, 135r.

15 Cf. notes 20 and 21.

16 On Bologna, see Massimo Vallerani, "La supplica al Signore e il potere della misericordia. Bologna 1337–1347", *Quaderni storici* 131 (2009), pp. 411–41; Massimo Vallerani, "La pauvreté et la citoyenneté dans les suppliques du XIVe siècle", *L'atelier du centre de recherche historique* 13 (2015), pp. 2–16 (dossier: *Supliques. lois et cas dans la normativité de l'époque moderne*, ed. Simona Cerutti and Massimo Vallerani).

17 ASF, *Manoscritti*, 82, account register of the testamentary execution, 1414–1420.

the best interest of Paliano's heirs," not to incur additional legal expenses by waiting for an unfavourable sentence.[18] In this case, the litigation was resolved by the advisors of the conflicting parties rather than a judge.

Frequent sources of conflict, dowry restoration and instances of dowered daughters challenging their exclusion from paternal succession are two specific issues upon which I would like to dwell. In the ensuing section I will observe negotiation strategies and the flexibility of resolution methods in the resolution of patrimonial conflicts involving women.

2 Recovery of Dowry Credit

Up until the beginning of the fifteenth century, a Florentine woman could formally claim her dowry only upon her husband's predecease. Yet there were at least two situations in which married women frequently separated their paternal inheritance from the fates of their husbands. First, if their husband's business went askew, thereby jeopardizing the family's well-being. Second, when a husband was banished for political or economic reasons and his assets were confiscated by the commune. From the mid-thirteenth century onward, eminent Italian jurists upheld wives' rights to claim their dowries even during marriage. Although this right wasn't incorporated into the statutes in Florence until 1415, the podesterial court had begun considering cases against insolvent husbands well before this amendment was introduced.[19] In the second half of the fourteenth century, the government demonstrated in fact a certain receptiveness to this trend, welcoming petitions from wives of exiles or bandits,[20] as

18 ASF, *Carte strozziane*, IV serie, 366, fol. 137v, 140r.

19 Julius Kirshner, "Wives' Claims Against Insolvent Husbands in Late Medieval Italy," in *Women of the Medieval World: Essays in Honor of John H. Mundy*, ed. Julius Kirshner and Suzane F. Wemple (Oxford: Blackwell, 1985), pp. 256–303, now in Julius Kirshner, *Marriage, Dowries and Citizenship in Late Medieval and Renaissance Italy* (Toronto: University of Toronto Press, 2011), pp. 131–60. See the sentence dated 14 June 1400 as a result of which Mea Busini was assigned a farm belonging to her husband in return for her dowry: ASF, *Carte strozziane*, IV serie, 564, fol. 2v; Isabelle Chabot, *La dette des familles. Femmes, lignage et patrimoine à Florence aux XIVe et XVe siècles* (Rome: École française de Rome, 2011), pp. 172–74.

20 The records of the *Ufficiali della Torre* spanning from 1375 to 1431 attest to the dowry restoration of ninety wives of bandits. The credits were paid using money from the sale of confiscated goods or with the assignment of the same goods (39 cases between 1431 and 1509), Randolph Starn, *Contrary Commonwealth: The Theme of Exile in Medieval and Renaissance Italy* (Berkeley-Los Angeles: University of California Press, 1982), p. 114. Between the end of the thirteenth and the early decades of the fourteenth centuries, the dowries of wives and widows of exiled men were not reimbursed. Instead, they were provided an annual

the livelihoods of the families left behind in the city were dependent on those dowries.[21]

The dowry was a credit guaranteed by pledges and sureties and its return to the widow was furthermore regulated by the *ius proprium*. The Florentine statutes of 1325 gave the family of the deceased six months to satisfy a widow's request, and as of 1415 the term was reduced to just two months.[22] Such a short span of time served well the interests of widows who were young enough to consider remarriage and urgently wanted to reclaim the dowry – if possible as it had been conveyed upon marriage: in cash.[23] Debtor families also preferred to restore dowries in cash, and would generally try to avoid reimbursing widows with immovables. Nonetheless, it was very difficult, not to say impossible, for heirs to assemble sizeable amounts of cash in so brief a time.

Statutory provisions were aimed at keeping dowry disputes out of the private realm of family justice by arbitration. Consequently, we can expect to find many references to widows in court records, since they benefitted from summary procedure that accelerated dowry reimbursement. While their presence still needs to be verified, private documentation such as merchant family diaries allow us to underscore two important aspects in the use of public justice within such litigation. Recourse to court was not always immediate: it was necessary in particularly complex cases of bankruptcy or to resolve more dire conflicts, but absent these, widows and their families first attempted to find an infrajudicial solution. For the most common forms of litigation, which generally resulted from payment delays or incomplete reimbursements as a result of

---

pension in wheat: Isabelle Chabot, "Il matrimonio di Dante," in *Dante attraverso i documenti*, vol. 1: *Famiglia e patrimonio (secolo XII–1300 circa)*, ed. Giuliano Milani and Antonio Montefusco, special issue of *Reti Medievali Rivista* 15–2 (2014), pp. 1–31, here pp. 24–29, http://rivista.retimedievali.it, accessed 10 April 2018.

21 In 1427 Bernardo Lamberteschi, father of Maddalena, wife of Quirico Tornaquinci, banished by the commune, declared to the *catasto* that the *Sei Ufficiali delle vendite* had assigned his daughter a tower and a farm valued at 1,200 florins (equivalent to her dowry) "so as she and her sons would be able to sustain themselves". ASF, *Catasto*, 47, fol. 297*r*.

22 *Statuti della Repubblica fiorentina*, vol. 2: *Statuti del Podestà dell'anno 1325*, pp. 98–100; *Statuta populi et communis Florentiae publica auctoritate collecta castigata et praeposita anno salutis Mccccxv*, Friburgi apud Michaelem Kluch (but Florence: Cambiagi), s.d. (but 1777–1781), 4 vols, liber 2, rub. 61, pp. 156–59. On dowry recovery in Venice see Stanley Chojnacki, "Getting Back the Dowry," in Stanley Chojnacki, *Women and Men in Renaissance Venice. Twelve Essays on Patrician Family* (Baltimore: John Hopkins University Press, 2000), pp. 95–111.

23 The analysis of 4,000 Florentine dowry contracts distributed in three samples between 1242 and 1436 showed that, in both the city and countryside, between 91 percent and 99 percent of dowries were conveyed in cash. Maristella Botticini and Aloysius Siow, "Why Dowries?," *American Economic Review* 93 (2003), pp. 1385–98.

a lack of cash, the court was often a temporary and provisional stage aimed at bringing insolvent debtors back to (private) negotiation in an effort to quickly settle the matter.

In informal private negotiations, widows could act autonomously, and did not need a *mundualdus* or legal agent. They usually granted their debtors a more comfortable margin of time than allowed by law. The parties agreed on a potential rate, however, widows could also request an annual interest on credit. In 1427 Francesco di Betto Busini had owed his stepmother Vaggia 600 florins from her dowry for two years. Francesco agreed to pay her 48 florins per year and to provide her with a "writ" attesting her debt, "as she wants".[24] Payment of annuities did not extinguish the debt, but it did postpone the return of the dotal fund. Failure to comply with these deadlines led creditors to seek public justice. For Costanza, whose husband Lotto di Duccio Mancini had died in 1486, the pension of 55 florins (a seven percent interest) per year, negotiated with her husband's nephews and heirs, was intended to be a temporary solution. But five years had passed, and, in March 1491, the woman filed a lawsuit at the podesterial court in order to force her debtors to restore her dowry, valued at 950 florins. It was, however, an arbitration settlement (*laudum*), pronounced in January 1492 rather than the court trial, that put an end to the dispute and established that the debt was to be paid in three instalments between November 1491 and January 1492.[25]

On 22 February 1388, messer Pazzino Strozzi, who was in charge of the affairs of his nephews, orphans of messer Palla di messer Francesco Strozzi, recorded in the inheritance account book that he delivered 770 florins in "cash" to his sister-in-law, Francesca Adimari. Another note stated that on the same day, Francesca's two notary prosecutors were instructed to go to the *Palagio* (of the *Podestà*) to interrupt the judicial proceedings. The account book does not explain the reasons or development of the controversy: Francesca Adimari had been a widow for ten years (Palla had died on 10 October 1377) and while remaining in the deceased's home with her five children she had, for some reason, requested her dowry. This met with initial resistance from her brother-in-law until, after threat of bringing the case to a judge for intervention, messer Pazzino hastened to find the money.[26]

Widows were prompted to turn to public justice by non-fulfilment, fraud, or unfairness on the part of the other party. In her tax report to the *catasto* of 1427, Ginevra, daughter of Baldassare Ubriachi, widow first of Alamanno di Giovanni

24 ASF, *Catasto* 35(II), fol. 1472*r*.

25 ASF, *Carte strozziane*, IV serie, 566, fol. 3r, 6v–7r.

26 ASF, *Carte strozziane*, III serie, 277, fol. cxxxvijr.

Mannini and then of Roberto di Luigi Canigiani, acknowledged that both of her late husbands' families were still in debt to her. The debt of the Mannini was the oldest: Ginevra was still waiting to receive 100 florins of her dowry and some testamentary legacies bequeathed by her first husband, but her brothers-in-law were "forcefully" keeping all the assets of the deceased. Ginevra finally came to "certain pacts" with one of them, Salvestro, who had acted surety on her dowry, and, between March and October 1425, he had signed "three writs". Be that as it may, he rendered the terms of the agreements void "through contrived ways", and Ginevra ended up dragging him to court. The dispute with the Canigiani, her second husband's heirs, from whom Ginevra had received only a portion of her dowry valued at 900 florins, resulted in a complicated court case, the outcome of which seemed very uncertain, and the results of the same are not a matter of record.[27]

In the face of bankruptcy, inheritance or dire financial straits, widows were expected to immediately resort to judicial authorities, because in cases where they were not the sole creditor of the deceased, law regulated that widows' dowries had precedence over all other creditors. Following the death of Niccolò Busini on 28 February 1491 his young children had to refuse a highly indebted inheritance.[28] As a result of the delicate situation their mother and guardian, Lisabetta Mancini, immediately requested that the podesterial court protect her dowry and, at the same time, save her children from a ruinous future. Within four months, in June 1491, the judgment awarded her the family house and a portion of her late husband's real estate.[29]

Cilia, whose notary husband died in 1419, was forced to leave the house with her two children as a result of disagreements with her stepsons. She immediately initiated a lawsuit to retrieve the 200 florins that constituted her dowry.[30] Eight years of litigation in court failed to overcome her stepsons' resistance, and to remedy the situation she addressed a petition to the *Palagio* (of the *Signoria* or the *Podestà*) in May 1427. As a result, Cilia was able to have one of her stepsons imprisoned for debt by summary procedure. After spending seventeen days in the city jail ser Antonio agreed to find an immediate "agreement" with his stepmother. In the notary's presence, he pledged, alongside his brothers, to return Cilia her dowry in July 1428. Cilia granted her debtors a year, but she requested seven percent interest on the 200 florins and, in the

27 ASF, *Catasto* 15, cc. 916r–v, 936r.

28 On repudiation of inheritance: Kuehn, *Heirs, Kin, and Creditors.*

29 ASF, *Carte strozziane*, IV serie, 567, c. 1v, 89r.

30 Tax report of Cilia, widow of ser Betto del maestro Giovanni: ASF, *Catasto*, 17, fol. 434r–435r.

meanwhile, also obtained tenancy on her stepsons' landed property.[31] A case that had dragged on for eight years was thus closed thanks to a combination of the coercive power of public authority (with the imprisonment of the recalcitrant debtor) and a private agreement that plausibly reiterated the judge's sentence (the dowry had to be restored) but allowed the parties to renegotiate the terms thereof. The agreement provided the debtors with enough time to find the money, and Cilia obtained additional guarantee with an immediate deposit on her stepsons' estate, in addition to securing compensation by way of interest that her stepsons had to pay for another year. Once again, we can see how the procedural decision and the use of summary procedure intersected with negotiations at an infrajudicial level that proved to be more effective in arriving at rapid dispute resolution.

Family diaries, even more than notarial deeds or judicial records, allow us to follow the entire development of a dispute and to grasp the flexibility of the negotiation processes during which various methods – private, infrajudicial and judicial – interacted. Based on two such detailed accounts I would like to chart the main stages in two disputes concerning Paolo Sassetti, an uncle and guardian,[32] and Giovanni Bandini, the father of two young widows.[33] First we should consider their timing: the first dispute began in September 1395 and ended in November 1396, more than a year later; the second dispute lasted two years, from January 1449 to January 1451, that is to say, disputes over the return of dowries generally lasted much longer than anticipated by law.

In 1384, Paolo Sassetti married off Lena, his young niece who was an orphan, to the merchant Lodovico Tolosini, to whom he handed a sizeable dowry of 700 florins bequeathed by the bride's father. Her husband Lodovico and his two brothers, Filippo and Geri Tolosini, acted surety. In October 1385 Lena received an additional 425 florins from her mother Simona's succession. The marriage lasted eleven years: in September 1395 news of Lodovico's death (in Catalonia on 2 July 1395) arrived in Florence; Lena was 28 years old. The second marriage in question, of Tancia Bandini to Gregorio Megli (dowry of 300 florins),

31 Tax report of ser Antonio di ser Betto del maestro Giovanni, ASF, *Catasto*, 34, fol.71*r*–74*v*. On conflicts between stepmothers and stepsons, see also Isabelle Chabot, "Matrigne. Le altre madri dei Fiorentini (secc. XIV–XV)," in *Tra archivio e storia. Scritti dedicati ad Alessandra Contini Bonaccossi* (Florence: Florence University Press, 2018), pp. 65–89.

32 ASF, *Carte strozziane*, II serie, 4, (1363–1400), fol. 69v–70r; 74v–75r, 111v–112r. For the English version of the text see Isabelle Chabot, "Marriage, Dowry and Remarriage in the Sassetti Household (1384–97)," introduced and translated from Italian by Isabelle Chabot, in *Medieval Italy. Texts in translation, ed.* Katherine L. Jansen, Joanna Drell, and Frances Andrews (Philadelphia: University of Pennsylvania Press, 2009), pp. 446–50.

33 ASF, *Conventi soppressi*, 102, 82, fol. 14v.

celebrated in January 1447, lasted only two years. By January 1449, aged twenty, she was already a widow. Lena Sassetti and Tancia Bandini were young and could still remarry: their natal families brought them back home the same day as their husbands' funerals and "according to the custom of Florence". Their return to their natal homes signalled that they would soon claim their dowries.

In the early months following the news of Ludovico's death, informal contacts with the Tolosini served to clarify the financial situation of the deceased and to establish the time line and means by which the dowry could be returned. Far from Florence, the merchant Lodovico who had died intestate on his trading route in Catalonia appears to have been in dire economic straits. The men of the Sassetti family – Paolo always used the first person plural as if to emphasise that he was representing his kin – were also international merchants. They were no doubt aware of the difficulties merchants were bound to encounter in getting hold of cash, and were perhaps inclined to allow their own debtors some time. Although the situation would have recommended it, they did not go to court immediately: the bilateral negotiations with the Tolosini lasted eight months, from September 1395 to April 1396, without reaching an agreement.

Apparently, the dispute between the Megli family and Tancia's father, the notary ser Giovanni Bandini, came to a more expedient end: an agreement was reached within the three months following Tancia's husband's death and formalised on 2 April 1449. It is interesting to note that while not formally an arbitration, the negotiation also involved two external parties: Giovanni Gianfigliazzi – the *mezzano* who, two years earlier, had arranged the marriage of Tancia – and a notary named ser Antonio Danti that was most likely chosen by the Megli family. Thanks to their "mediation", the parties "agreed" to a "return" to be paid in two instalments within five months: the two brothers of the deceased signed a "writ" prepared by ser Antonio Danti in which they agreed to reimburse 160 florins by the end of April, and 140 florins by the end of September 1449; ser Giovanni was expected to register the payments in his diary.

In both cases, the first stage consisted of a more or less successful negotiation that remained in the private sphere. The parties resorted to public justice later, when the Sassetti took note of the failure of bilateral negotiations, and Giovanni Bandini of the Megli's noncompliance with the agreement.

On 19 April 1396, after eight months of unsuccessful attempts, the Sassetti decided to file a lawsuit against Geri Tolosini, Lena's only surviving former brother-in-law, who had acted surety on her dowry. It was a difficult decision for the Sassetti, and one that they would rather have avoided because, as Paolo pointed out, both sides would have to bear the costs. But it turned out to be an effective move: six months passed, and Geri probably convinced himself that he would have more to lose from an unfavourable sentence. On 6 November 1396, he asked the Sassetti to forgo court action – "and we were happy", Paolo commented, suggesting that they entrust the arbitration to two family acquaintances: "And this was done because the said Geri did not want action being taken against the movable and immovable property of Lodovicho." From then on, everything went smoothly: in the *compromisum*, drawn up on 7 November 1396, Geri pledged to return the 700 florins and, no more than three days thereafter Lena's *procuratore* received the money. The arbitration settlement failed to mention Lena's maternal inheritance: probably Sassetti likely preferred giving that up in the interest of quickly settling the dispute. A few months later, Lena remarried.

In the second case, the Megli did not meet the deadlines set in April 1449: during the course of the year they had repaid a little more than half the dowry in small instalments. Thus, in May 1450, ser Giovanni decided to take them before the *Podestà* to recover the 140 florins still owed. When, a month later, the judge assigned ser Giovanni tenancy of all the assets that secured Tancia's dowry credit and ordered the expropriation of livestock and crops from the Megli farms, they rushed to request that court proceedings be interrupted. On 16 June, "not wanting to go to trial", they resumed private negotiations with ser Giovanni and concluded a new agreement that entailed the reimbursement of the three florins of court fees he had already paid, assignment of a farm to his daughter and, by September, the delivery of 36 *staia* of grain as interest on the dowry credit. For their part, the Megli reserved the right to repurchase the farm if they were able to provide Tancia with 140 florins in cash (which they did, six months later on 30 January 1451).[34]

In both these disputes we see that the Tolosini and the Megli lacked the cash to satisfy the widow's request, however, they were in possession of property in the form of land. They of course wanted to avoid the property being transferred to the widow at all costs and knew a judge would not hesitate to do so in an effort to close the dispute. In dowry restoration litigation recourse to a judicial authority was an effective weapon that creditors used to unblock a stymied situation: sooner or later the debtors would forgo trial, and this would lead to the initiation of private negotiations that often brought about an almost immediate resolution and payment in cash.

In 1418 Lapo Niccolini was faced with returning the dowry to Tancia Guadagni, widow of his nephew Giovanni Niccolini who had died in 1417. The likelihood of ending up in court was serious, Giovanni had left a pile of debts to his five children and their mother, the latter immediately returned to her natal family, leaving the children behind and permanently destitute. Yet Lapo

34 Chabot, *La dette des familles*, pp. 328–29.

managed to convince the Guadagni to seek resolution through arbitration by resorting to a trusted notary: "for the wellbeing and peace and rest of the parties", he said, but above all, "so as to avoid a trial".[35] In such a ruinous situation, the responsibility of the debt of 900 florins fell upon those who had acted as guarantors at the time of Giovanni Niccolini's marriage. In this case it had been Giovanni's brother Francesco, by that time deceased, and therefore the responsibility fell to Francesco's sole son and heir. But Lapo Niccolini feared that he would also become involved because, at the time, he had purchased a house for his nephew Giovanni. The arbitration was settled to the advantage of the Niccolini heirs, who only reimbursed 120 of the 900 florins due to the widow. Lapo's house, which a judge would have probably expropriated in order to secure Tancia's dowry, did not become embroiled in the negotiations.

In dowry restoration litigation we can therefore observe a constant dialectic between family justice and public justice that often prevented trials from coming to a final sentence. Widows and their families made strategic use of the court's appeal, while indebted families were too afraid of losing control over real estate and property to come up against a judge. The impression one gets is that both sides preferred to avoid the intrusion of public authority in their private affairs – and dowry issues were very private matters – and shared a similar interest in finding a compromise that would allow dowries to be recovered or repaid in cash.[36]

A conflict around the maternal inheritance that pitted Nanna, daughter of Tommaso di Iacopo de' Pecori, against her father's heirs for nine years, suggests another dialectical, perhaps contrasting relationship between podesterial public justice, which was administered by foreign judges, and a state magistracy, the *Ufficiali de' Pupilli* that remained in the hands of citizens with no legal expertise.[37] Let us chart the main points by following the story of Nanna's husband, Domenico Busini, as narrated below in his tax report to the *catasto* of 1427.

Tommaso de' Pecori was a widower when he died, sometime before 1418, and without direct male heirs. In his will he choose his only daughter Nanna, as not only his universal heir but also left her her mother's dowry, valued at

35 Christian Bec, *Il libro degli affari proprii di Lapo di Giovanni Niccolini de' Sirigatti*, édition critique et commentée (Paris: SEVPEN, 1969), pp. 142 and 135.

36 Obviously, husbands' heirs did not always succeed. A tax census such as the *catasto* of 1427 elucidates how female wealth transformed with widowhood: women became owners of houses and other property that had been a part of their late husbands' inheritance.

37 On family policy, which the Florentine state entrusted to new magistracies (*magistrature*) see Isabelle Chabot, "Le gouvernement des pères: l'État florentin et la famille (XIVe–XVe siècles)," in *Florence et la Toscane, XIVe–XIXe siècles. Les dynamiques d'un État italien*, ed. Jean Boutier, Sandro Landi, and Olivier Rouchon (Rennes: Presses Universitaires de Rennes, 2004), pp. 241–63.

1,100 florins, as a credit on his estate. Widowers usually retained usufruct of both the dotal and non-dotal assets of their late wives. Upon their fathers' deaths, sons would collect the maternal inheritance alongside the paternal one,[38] while daughters had to request that their fathers' heirs settle the dotal credit, and daughters often encountered the same resistance as widows in this deferred dowry restoration.[39] In fact, to obtain the 1,100 florins of her maternal inheritance from Tommaso de' Pecori's heirs (all collateral relatives), Nanna had to bring them to court: in 1418 the *Podestà* ruled that it was her legitimate right to receive the sum. At that time, the *Ufficiali de' Pupilli*, which administered Tommaso's inheritance on behalf of his underage heirs, promised to immediately deliver an initial instalment of 500 florins and 100 florins per year thereafter for the following six years. Nanna never received anything and, her husband claimed, the officers had "always mocked her". As the de' Pecori had failed to pay, Nanna turned to the guarantors who had acted surety to her mother's dowry in 1424 and requested that grain, wine, and other products that had been produced on their landed property be seized: "But the *Ufficiali de' Pupilli* wanted her to quitclaim, promising that she would obtain [her money]." Three more years passed, in vain. In July 1427, Nanna's husband, Domenico Busini, exasperated, announced that he would from then on take matters in his own hands: "I promise you that I shall soon be in the possession of the goods of the guarantors of the dowry and I'll take them and I will not have anything to do with the *Ufficiali de' Pupilli* and I will be proven right." This time the threat was taken seriously and, a month later, Nanna finally collected her first instalment, 498 florins.[40] For nine years, the execution of a sentence issued by the main court of justice (the court of the *Podestà*) had been stymied by state officers (the *Ufficiali de' Pupilli*) suspected by Nanna's husband of defending a "family justice" aimed at protecting the interests of heirs and guarantors against Nanna's legitimate rights to her mother's inheritance.

---

38 In Florence, Siena, Arezzo, Genoa etc. the statutes reserved maternal inheritance for sons only (in Florence this also applied to grandsons), thus excluding the daughters *propter masculos*: Chabot, *La dette des familles*, pp. 16–19 and 35; for the statutes of Milan see Thomas Kuehn, "Gender and Law in Milan," in A *Companion to Late Medieval and Early Modern Milan. The Distinctive Features of an Italian State*, ed. Andrea Gamberini (Leiden and Boston: Brill, 2015), pp. 406–31.

39 In 1488, Filippo Strozzi, for example, requested the advice of a few jurists and had to go to court to defend the inheritance rights of his second wife. In his personal register, he recorded the expenses "for the trial for her mother's inheritance that she expects", "to get the mother's dotal contract" and "to purchase many *consilia* in regard to her mother's inheritance that she expects". ASF, *Carte strozziane*, V serie, 41, fol. 79v.

40 ASF, *Catasto*, 34, fol. 501r; Chabot, *La dette des familles*, pp. 120–21.

3 Inheritance: Challenging the *Exclusio Propter Dotem*

The de' Pecori dispute introduces the issue of the (often denied) access of women to inheritance, and the options they had to challenge this exclusion. The medieval dowry system provided many inherent reasons for conflict. Included in communal statutory law (*ius proprium*) since the mid-twelfth century, the dowry system reintroduced gender inequalities in the portioning out of patrimonies that had been abolished by late Roman civil law. As Kuehn observes, "In particular, with regard to intestacy, in Florence and elsewhere, statutory rules were intended to supplement or preclude the exercise of the rules of the communes which resided largely in the Roman law text of the *Corpus iuris civilis* of Justinian".[41]

Unlike the shares of the father's inheritance that each son received, a daughter's dowry was proportional to neither the global size of the estate nor to the number of children. Municipal law did not equate the dowry with the *legitima portio*, and carefully avoided setting criteria in the definition of its value:[42] in Florence, for example, statutes merely specified that daughters had to be dowered *competenter*. Thus, they allowed fathers broad discretion on the one hand; on the other hand, they prevented daughters from claiming goods beyond their dowries, symbolically depriving them of their status as "legitimate heirs". In those very rare instances in which data on the global value of the paternal patrimony is available, and the relationship between daughters' dowry and sons' share of inheritance can be calculated, the gender imbalance in the transfer of wealth from one generation to the next is such as to induce us to consider dowries as a form of "compensation" owed daughters on account of their being essentially disinherited.[43] Moreover in Florence, and elsewhere,

---

41 Thomas Kuehn, "Intestate Inheritance as a Family Matter: Ius Commune, Statutes and Cases from Florence," in *How Nordic are the Nordic Medieval Laws? Ten years after, Proceedings of the Tenth Carlsberg Academy Conference on Medieval Legal History 2013*, ed. Per Andersen, Kirsi Salonen, Helle Sigh, and Helle Vogt (Copenhagen: DJØF Publishing, 2014), pp. 59–80, here p. 59.

42 Thomas Kuehn, "Dos non teneat locum legitime: Dowry as a Woman's Inheritance in Early Quattrocento Florence," in *Law and Marriage in Medieval ad Early Modern Times*, ed. Per Andersen, Kirsi Salonen, Helle Møller Sigh, and Helle Vogt (Copenhagen: DJØF Publishing, 2012), pp. 231–48. Justinianean law (sixth century) established that the *portio legitima* – the minimum amount mandatorily due children (sons and daughters) – was equivalent to one-third of the inheritance if there were four children or less, and half if there were more than four children (*Novellae constitutiones, Novella* 18).

43 Diane Owen Hughes, "From Brideprice to Dowry in Mediterranean Europe," *Journal of Family History* 3 (1978), pp. 263–96 [reprinted in *The Marriage Bargain. Women and Dowries in European History*, ed. Marion Kaplan (New York: Routledge, 1985), pp. 13–57].

daughters were excluded *propter dotem* from paternal inheritance as well as *propter masculos* from maternal inheritance: a double exclusion that additionally heightened discrimination between siblings.

There is early evidence of this remarkable disparity between female dowry and male share of inheritance. In a Genoese document dated 1223, for example, a certain Enrico de *Uxecio* sold immovable property valued at 3,000 lire to the commune. The same document mentions that Enrico had dowered his only daughter with 120 lire, i.e. 3.6 percent of the share of his patrimony specified in the document. It follows that Enrico's three sons would plausibly share an even larger fortune.[44] In order to provide an idea of the relationship between endowment and succession in late medieval Florence, Table 9.1 presents data concerning the gender distribution of inheritance in six families of merchants-bankers: the first five lived in the second half of the fourteenth century (Giovanni di Bartolomeo Morelli (d. 1363),[45] his brother Pagolo di Bartolomeo Morelli (d. 1374), Vanni of ser Lotto Castellani,[46] and one of his sons Michele,[47] and messer Niccolò degli Alberti),[48] while the last, Tommaso Spinelli, was active one century later.[49] The

44 Manlio Bellomo, *Ricerche sui rapporti patrimoniali tra coniugi. Contributo alla storia della famiglia medievale (XII–XIII secc.)* (Milan: Giuffré, 1961), pp. 180–81.

45 Giovanni had a single daughter, Mea, to whom he left a dowry of 700 florins. When he died in 1363, he bequeathed a fortune of 15,000 florins to his four sons, this according to a nephew's estimate in his diary: Giovanni di Pagolo Morelli, *Ricordi*, nuova edizione e introduzione storica, ed. Claudia Tripodi (Florence: Florence University Press, 2019) p. 189. When he died, in 1374, his brother Pagolo di Bartolomeo left two daughters and two sons. He bequeathed a fortune of 20,000 florins, he left a dowry of 1,500 florins to both the daughters (ibid., pp. 194, 207). See also Chabot, *La dette des familles*, p. 72.

46 In his diary, Michele registered 33,000 florins as the paternal share of the inheritance, which consisted of invested capital, commodities and credits. ASF, *Corporazioni religiose soppresse*, 90, 131, fol. ijv, while the real estate was worth almost 13,000 florins. Giovanni Ciappelli, "I Castellani di Firenze: dall'estremismo oligarchico all'assenza politica (secoli XIV–XV)," *Archivio storico italiano* 149–1 (1991), pp. 33–91, here pp. 44–47.

47 Will of Michele di Vanni Castellani (1370), ed. G. Brucker, *Firenze nel Rinascimento* (Florence: La Nuova Italia, 1981). p. 267; Ciappelli, "I Castellani di Firenze," p. 48 – the real estate, purchased between 1355 and 1383, was worth 47,000 fiorini. In his will (1389), Michele's brother, Stefano di Vanni Castellani, left his daughters the same amount of money (1,000 florins) in dowry as their cousins (Michele's daughters); his wife's dowry was worth 700 florins, ASF, *Notarile antecosimiano* 13948, fol. 11r–3v.

48 Isabelle Chabot, "Messer Niccolò degli Alberti, 'pater pauperum'. Lettura del testamento," in *L'ospedale dell'Orbatello. Carità e arte a Firenze,* ed. Cristina De Benedictis and Carla Milloschi (Florence: Polistampa, 2015), pp. 73–81, here p. 80.

49 Lorenzo Fabbri, "The Magnificent Arbitrator: Lorenzo de' Medici and the Patrician Families," in *Florence, in Studies on Florence and the Italian Renaissance in Honour of F. W. Kent*, ed. Peter Howard and Cecilia Hewlett (Turnhout: Brepols, 2016), pp. 95–113, here p. 103.

exceptionality of these few cases lies in the fact that, by crossing different sources, we know the value of the men's entire inheritance, data that in most cases remains inaccessible.

Although the table above should by no means to be taken as statistical evidence, these data nonetheless enable us to gauge gender inequality in inheritance at the same social level. In the second half of the fourteenth century, the budget which these Florentine mercantile elite families reserved for dowries did not exceed five percent of the gross wealth of each household (except Pagolo Morelli). A century later, Tommaso Spinelli's budget more than doubled, due to the absence of direct male descendants and dowry inflation, but the dowries assigned to his three daughters were worth just over a third of the *legitima* they could claim, in this case equivalent to one-third of their father's inheritance, or 20,000 florins. In 1363, the dowry of 700 florins for an only daughter like Mea Morelli could be worth about one fifth of the share of the inheritance received by any one of her four brothers. A decade later, in the Alberti household, however, in which there were five daughters, although dowered generously, their share could not be remotely compared to the portion received by any one of their brothers (2.9 percent).[50] The fact that, in the same decades, an upper-echelon merchant like messer Niccolò Alberti, whose

50 Two economists, Maristella Botticini and Aloysius Siow ("Why dowries?"), are convinced that there was substantial parity between female dowries and male inheritance in late medieval Florence. In order to "draw a comparison between the size of the dowries assigned to the daughters and the expected bequests to their *brothers*" (p. 1393, italics are mine), they cross-analysed the following data: the value of a daughter's dowry (indicated in the marriage contract) on the one hand, and on the other hand an "estimate of the bequest to each of the bride siblings" obtained by dividing the estimate of the family's property (*imponibile*) declared in the 1427 *catasto* per number of children listed in each household. In a sample of 296 households, "[w]e find that the existence of dowries, by itself, did not prevent daughters from receiving roughly equal, or higher, share of their parental wealth. Even if parents did not leave bequests to their daughters [...], these data suggest that *children* did not receive disproportionately large share of parental wealth" (p. 1394, italics are mine). However, the authors point out that they have "ignored gender composition of siblings" (Table 3), and have therefore divided the value of the paternal patrimony by the number of siblings, males and females. A rather odd methodological choice, which completely ignores the municipal law, unfortunately vitiates their data, and invalidates their conclusion: firstly, because by resorting to this method they fail to register the "bequests to the *brothers*" (p.1393) or the share of parental wealth reserved for the "sons": they consider the share received by *all* the children, including daughters; and secondly the authors therefore assume that upon a father's death, there would be an egalitarian division between brothers and sisters of the estate registered in the 1427 *catasto*. Equal division had been abolished three centuries earlier with the introduction of the *exclusio propter dotem*. With the data at their disposal, the authors could have considered the relationship between the dowry of a daughter (specified in the dotal contract) and

fortune was twenty times greater than that of Giovanni Morelli, gave each daughter a dowry of "only" 1,200 florins (not even double the worth of Mea Morelli's dowry of 700 florins) indicates that the value of the dowry was not proportional to paternal wealth. It is interesting to note that affluent fathers such as Niccolò Alberti and Michele Castellani not only conveyed a dowry to their daughters, but also provided them 800 florins as non-dotal assets. In any event, the 10,000 florins given to the five daughters as dowry and non-dotal goods accounted for just three percent of messer Niccolò Alberti's entire fortune. Lastly, analysis of last wills elucidates that Florentine fathers' dowry budgets were inflexible.[51] In addition, from 1480 onward, dowry inflation led to a reduction in female marriages, and more and more women were destined to take religious vows so as to maintain a net worth of dowries consistent with family status without impinging on the share of inheritance that was to be transferred to the sons.[52]

Wills also show that fathers rarely overrode the rule of the *exclusio propter dotem*. When they did correct some of the adverse effects of this norm, they left their daughters only paltry revenue in cash or kind, as well as the right to return to the family home in case of widowhood or need.[53] The new dowry and inheritance system, established by the municipal law from mid-twelfth century, which was designed to keep women away from the lion's share of the inheritance, nonetheless left some margin of inclusion as a result of the coexistence of and interplay between the *ius proprium* and the *ius commune*. Thanks to its silences and ambiguities, the *ius proprium* gave daughters a real chance at challenging inheritances, both intestate and by will, by invoking the rules of Roman civil law (*ius commune*). Again, as Kuehn observes, "this litigiousness is attributable to the confusing normative situation where statutory exclusions stood in contrast to the *ius commune*'s rules of equality in

the entire estate declared by their father in the 1427 *catasto*: a useful approach that they unfortunately failed to consider.

51 Chabot, *La dette des familles,* chapter 3.

52 Anthony Molho, *Marriage Alliances in Late Medieval Florence* (Cambridge, Mass. and London: Harvard University Press, 1994), chapter 7, figure on p. 305.

53 Chabot, *La dette des familles*, pp. 87–97, on a sample of 282 male wills (1350–1440). Botticini and Siow came to the same conclusions by observing the "bequest behavior in Florentine households with both sons and daughters" in two small samples of wills dating from two different periods (20 acts between 1260 and 1299 and 85 acts between 1420 and 1436): if three-quarters of thirteenth-century testators did not leave any legacy to daughters beyond the dowry, this attitude became even more evident in the early decades of the fifteenth century (79 percent), Botticcini and Siow, "Why Dowries?," p. 1390.

TABLE 9.1 Gender distribution of inheritance in six Florentine merchant families (fourteenth to fifteenth centuries)

Families	Inheritance (in florins)	Daughters	Dowry	Dowry budget (and *non dotal*)	Relationship dowry budget /inheritance	Sons	Share of inheritance of a son (subtracted dowries)	Relationship dowry/share of inheritance
Morelli (1363)	15 000	1	700	700	4,6 %	4	3575	19,6%
Morelli (1374)	20 000	2	1500	3000	15%	2	8500	17,6%
Castellani (1354)	46 000	3	700	2100	4,5 %	3	15 000	4,6%
Castellani (1370)	**47 000*	3	1000	3000	6,4%	5	-	-
			***+ 500*	*+ 1500*	*3,2%*			
Alberti (1376)	300 000	5	1200	6000	2,0%	4	70 000	***2,9%
			***+ 800*	*+ 4000*	1,3%			
Spinelli (1472)	60 000	3	2380	7140	11,9 %	-	-	-

* *only real estate*
** *non dotal goods*
*** *dowry + non dotal goods*

inheritance and when rules of law and jurists could obviously disagree, so that each side could pretend to some bit of justice".[54]

In Florence, the *exclusio propter dotem* was extensive in genealogical terms: the statutes of 1325 stipulated that a dowered daughter was excluded from her father's intestate inheritance by a plethora of male relatives: descendants (sons, grandsons, and other male descendants in direct line), and collaterals (brothers, nephews). By virtue of the 1415 redaction the male ascendants (father and grandfather) of the deceased also took precedence over dowered daughters. In the absence of direct male descendants (sons and grandsons), however, daughters regained some rights. The rules of succession granted them life usufruct on the paternal inheritance before male collaterals collected the patrimony. As of 1415, this right to usufruct was transformed into a simple right to an annuity (*alimenta*). But jurists went even further: according to Baldus de Ubaldis (citing a *consilium* by Bartolo), if there were no surviving direct male descendants, dowered daughters could demand the *legitima portio*, calculated in a third of the patrimony including the dowry which they had already received, but they did not have the right to *trebelianica*, that is, the fourth part of a *fideicommisaria* succession.[55]

Florentine women kept some of their inheritance rights even in the presence of a paternal will. It is true that the statutory norm on testamentary succession prevented dowered daughters from contesting their fathers' last wills, but *only* in the presence of sons and, as of 1415, even of direct male descendants: in this case, they had to "content themselves" with what they had received and the judges (the *Podestà* and the *Capitano del Popolo*) were to immediately reject their petitions.[56] But "in Florence and elsewhere [in other statutes], it was only

54 Thomas Kuehn, "Person and Gender in the Laws," in *Gender and Society in Renaissance Italy*, ed. Judith C. Brown and Robert C. Davis (London: Longman, 1998), pp. 87–106, here p. 97.

55 Julius Kirshner, "Baldus de Ubaldis on Disinheritance: Contexts, Controversies, Consilia," *Ius Commune: Zeitschrift für Europäische Rechtsgeschichte* 27 (2000), pp. 119–214, here p. 163. Thomas Kuehn concluded that the dowry was different from the legitim: "legitim could include more than a dowry, but dowry would always be part (if not all) of legitim", Kuehn, "Dos non teneat locum legittime," p. 242.

56 "Si vero testatus decesserit is de cuius hereditate et bonis ageretur, relicto filio masculo legiptimo et naturali [aut filiis vel ex eo vel eis descendentibus masculis] et descendente seu descendentibus masculis, et aliquid reliquid, quoquo relicti titulo, alicui mulieri que iure romano possit ei succedere, sit et esse debeat ipsa contenta [ipsa mulier] et eius heredes et descendentes, tali relicto, et plus nullo modo [aliquis vel aliqua eorum] petere possit. *Et teneatur dominus Potestas et Capitaneus et ad iustitiam constituti talibus mulieribus et eorum heredibus et descendentibus et cuilibet eorum ius non redere nec eorum petitiones audire, sed conventos incontinenti absolvere et sint absoluti ipso iure.* [Et si nihil reliquerit quoquo relicti titulo dictis mulieribus, que de jure romano succederent, tunc

in the absence of the close male heirs who excluded her from receiving more than her dowry that a woman could look for a supplement to her share that would be calculated in terms of *legitima*".[57] The *exclusio propter dotem* could be challenged when men who had no direct descendants left their belongings to collaterals, to distant relatives or even strangers, such as charitable or religious institutions, even in Florence. As we shall see, Florentine women did not "content themselves" with their dowries, and did not hesitate to claim the *legitima*, both by infrajudicial means and in resorting to public justice.

The first case to illustrate this brings us back to Florence in the mid-fourteenth century and concerns a conflict between Donato Velluti and his cousin, Tessa, on the intestate inheritance of Tessa's father, Gherardo Velluti. The plague had claimed the lives of the girl's father, mother, two brothers and sister in the summer of 1348, leaving Tessa the only surviving member of her family. According to the Florentine statutes, being the closest male in the collateral line, Donato was the legitimate heir of his paternal uncle, Gherardo; an inheritance which included a few items of furniture and furnishings in the deceased's Florence home, and a farm in Montalbino in Valdesa. Donato was aware, however, that his cousin also had some rights to the inheritance: he therefore expressed the intention of leaving her usufruct (as per statute) and invited Tessa and her husband to "domestically" (*dimesticamente*) discuss his proposal. "But they were dishonest and spiteful and they had other intentions, that is to obtain everything", complained Donato. Again, by statute, Tessa could not only claim her mother Maddalena's inheritance – her dowry was still included in the patrimony – but also claim the *legitima* on her father's inheritance, as the patrimony was transmitted to a collateral relative.

Together with her husband Filippo, Tessa embarked a long and bitter conflict with her cousin. The dispute unravelled in a succession of surprise moves (or "betrayals", according to Donato), attempts at intimidation, violent verbal quarrels, and various arbitrations which were promptly dismissed. The battle lasted more than five years – four pages of a special "notebook" written by Donato document its various stages – until the umpteenth arbitration assigned the Montalbino farm to Donato but obliged him to pay his cousin

---

dicte mulieres habeant, et habere debeant in bonis talis huiusmodi defunti illud, quod haberent, seu petere possent si ab intestato totaliter decesserint secundum formam presentis statuti tantum, et dicto iure sint contente, nihil ulterius petere possint, et propterea non rumpatur testamentum]", *Statuti della Repubblica fiorentina*, vol. 2, *Statuti del Podestà dell'anno 1325*, rub. 69 In italics the sentence which was omitted in the 1415 redaction; between [] the part added in 1415, *Statuta populi et communis Florentiae*, rub. 130, p. 225.

57 Kuehn, "Dos non teneat locum legittime," p. 246.

200 florins: in the end, Tessa received much more than Donato had initially offered.[58]

Another Tessa, daughter of Neruccio Gianni, was a relative of Donato Velluti by way of marriage to Sandro di Zanobi dello Scetto, whose mother was a Velluti. Neruccio was "a man of vast fortunes" who was able to give his daughter in marriage with a "good dowry" (sometime after 1340). He also had an only son, whom he named universal heir, but if the child were to die, Neruccio left his entire fortune to Orsanmichele, a prominent Florentine confraternity. Tessa, therefore, was not considered a possible "heir": she had to content herself with her "good dowry".

First Neruccio and then his young son died in the plague of 1348. Tessa's husband Sandro envisioned collecting some, if not all, of his father-in-law's fortune on behalf of his wife. Donato Velluti depicted Sandro as a "a prodigal spender", "the opposite" of Tessa who was a "wise woman", and insinuated that Sandro was driven by personal interests in claiming his wife's paternal inheritance.[59] Sandro proceeded in two different directions. The first, which would have been the most advantageous, consisted in challenging the will on account of a technicality by accusing Neruccio, who had been suspected of usury, of having failed to meet the obligations imposed by the bishop in case of *male ablata*. If the will were invalidated, Neruccio's legacy would have been transmitted in compliance with the Florentine rules of intestacy and, in the absence of all the male candidates listed by such law, Tessa would remain the sole heir to her father.

Neruccio's will was considered valid, but Tessa could invoke the *ius commune* and claim "half [of the inheritance], that is, a third part as the *legitima* and a fourth part as *trebelliania*". The resolution of the dispute between Tessa and the confraternity of Orsanmichele was entrusted to an arbitration which was favourable, at least in part, to the woman. The *laudum* only recognised her right to the *legitima portio* and assigned her a third of the paternal inheritance, or "the Montughi farm and some other objects and cash, which amounted to several thousand florins".[60] It was much more than a dowry. In the fourteenth century challenging the paternal last will, and in so doing challenging the *exclusio propter dotem* in the presence of collaterals allowed daughters to acquire a better share of inheritance as well as improve their status as "heir".

58 *La cronica domestica di messer Donato Velluti, scritta fra il 1367 e il 1370*, ed. Isidoro Del Lungo and Guglielmo Volpi (Florence: Sansoni, 1914), p. 109.

59 On the active role of husbands in the legal doings of their wives see Kuehn, "Cum Consensu Mundualdi," pp. 235–36.

60 *La cronica domestica di messer Donato Velluti*, pp. 52–53. On *trebelianica*, cf. note 55.

The two following cases, recently studied by Lorenzo Fabbri, took place in the 1470s during Medici rule, a period of change.

Tommaso Spinelli died in 1472 without male descendants. He left a fortune estimated by the court of the *Podestà* at 60,000 florins to his brother Nicodemo, in order to favour his nephew Gaspare and therewith make him his "foster son". The inheritance was transmitted to the collateral line, and Spinelli's daughters Giana, Bice, and Lisabetta had to be satisfied with the substantial sum of 2,380 florins they each received upon their weddings (Table 9.1). Their cousin Gaspare would collect the lion's share of the fortune. Yet, the three sisters, with their husbands, all scions of the Florentine elite, immediately challenged the father's will before the court of the *Podestà*, claiming a third of the paternal inheritance as *legitima*: 20,000 florins, almost triple their three dowries. The three sisters won the trial in July 1472, Nicodemo and Gaspare appealed to the court of the *Capitano del Popolo*, but four months later, in November 1472, they lost the case. Despite these two unfavourable judgments, their uncle did not give up: Giana, Bice, and Lisabetta Spinelli accepted (or could not refuse) his request to submit the dispute to the arbitration of Lorenzo de' Medici. On 15 February 1473, the Magnificent completely overturned the two judicial decisions, which he considered "unjust": he ruled in favour of Nicodemo and Gaspare, granting each of the three sisters a supplement of just 1,200 florins in addition to their dowries.[61] In validating the pre-eminence of *ius proprium* over *ius commune*, this *laudum* – a private and irrevocable decision – affirmed the superiority of family justice over public justice in conflicts concerning inheritance. A few years later, an arbitration settlement along these same lines, once again made by the Magnificent, pushed this logic much further, with remarkable legal and political consequences.

In 1476–1477, a similar conflict found Beatrice, daughter of Giovanni Borromei, a wealthy banker, in opposition to her cousin (the son of her father's brother), Carlo di messer Antonio, and her father's two grandnephews, Achille and Iacopo (at the time still in their teens), whom her father had chosen as heirs.[62] In May 1463, Beatrice Borromei had married Giovanni di Antonio dei

61 Fabbri, "The Magnificent Arbitrator," pp. 102–103. Lorenzo the Magnificent's intense activity as arbitrator was part of his policy of *patronage* and control of the elite.

62 I would like to thank Lorenzo Fabbri for having shared and discussed his forthcoming (now published) essay with me entitled: "Women's Rights According to Lorenzo de' Medici: The Borromei-Pazzi Dispute and the Lex de testamentis," in *The Art and Language of Power in Renaissance Florence: Essays for Alison Brown,* ed. Amy Bloch, Luca Boschetto, Carolyn James, and Camilla Russell (Toronto: Centre for Reformation and Renaissance Studies, 2019).

Pazzi. A year earlier, on 8 April 1462, when Giovanni Borromei concluded the marriage alliance with this powerful family, he made two important acts: first, he emancipated Beatrice from his *patria potestas*,[63] and second he promised a truly exceptional dowry worth 5,500 florins (3,000 florins from the *Monte delle doti*, another 1,500 florins in cash and a sumptuous trousseau worth 1,000 florins), but he also received the formal commitment of his future son-in-law and other relatives of the Pazzi family that, upon reaching the age of eighteen, Beatrice would make an oath in presence of a notary that she would not advance further claims on the paternal inheritance. As a matter of fact, in November 1464, Beatrice, at the time eighteen and legally emancipated, gave quittance to her father.

It should be remembered that a few years earlier, in 1455, the only son of Giovanni Borromei had died, a tragic loss that forced him to rethink his succession strategy: as was clarified at the time of her marriage, his only remaining descendant, Beatrice, had to be completely excluded, albeit with an exceptional dowry, and she was to "content herself" with what was given her. The intent of this champion of patrilineage was clear: in the absence of direct male descendants, he wanted to prevent his fortune from ending in the hands of his daughter (and through her, the Pazzi). He therefore preferred to entrust the continuation of the Borromei family to his collaterals, his nephews Carlo, Achille, and Iacopo, who shared his surname.

Following his son's death, Giovanni Borromei cancelled his 1451 testament and rewrote his last will several times before deciding, in 1472, to revoke all of these and die intestate. He thus obtained two results: first, he prevented his daughter from challenging his will; second, intestacy resulted in a situation whereby base line for succession established by the statutes necessarily had to be followed. This gave precedence to collaterals over his daughter. In the summer of 1474, Giovanni changed his strategy again, and left his belongings to his grandnephews through a *donatio mortis causa*, which could not be challenged. As he was dying in Padua on 26 October 1476, Giovanni modified the 1474 *donatio*. He left usufruct of his possessions to his widow, and an annuity of 55 florins to his daughter in addition to her dowry. His fortune passed to his grandnephews, who were obliged to leave Padua (where they had been born) and settle in the Borromei Palace in Florence.

---

63 "Emancipation allowed a daughter to give up her share or to make some arrangement with her father [...]. By the later years of fourteenth century, this use of female emancipation had become relatively common." Thomas Kuehn, *Emancipation in the Late Medieval Florence* (New Brunswick: Rutgers University Press, 1982), p. 118.

All these precautions aside, this did not prevent Beatrice, with the help of her husband, from renouncing the donation and immediately claiming the paternal inheritance. The case went on to have considerable public resonance. The Pazzi and the Borromei did not go to court, and relied instead on the arbitration of Lorenzo de' Medici, who evidently took the opportunity to avenge himself of an antagonistic family, ruling against Beatrice and in favour of her cousins. But this time, the Magnificent resolved the case by asking the councils of the Republic to approve a legislative measure that amended the 1415 statutes regarding rules of testamentary succession. The *lex de testamentis*, voted in between 18 and 20 March 1477, prevented daughters from challenging the paternal will even in the presence of collaterals.[64] Not only that: the new law likewise prohibited daughters from challenging the *donationes cause mortis* and, if this was not enough, it was retroactive. Clearly, the *lex de testamentis* had been tailored to damage Beatrice, and by damaging her, the Magnificent wanted in particular to wound her husband and his family. The law fuelled much resentment among the Pazzi and, according to Bernardo Machiavelli, was even one of the main reasons behind the notorious "conspiracy" that struck Lorenzo in April 1478 and cost the life of his brother Giulian.

Striking in both the Spinelli and Borromei disputes, is the contrast between public justice (administered by professional judges in compliance with statutory law which, in 1472, still acknowledged daughters' rights to challenge the *exclusio propter dotem*) and private justice by arbitration (administered by a "Lord" who was able to rewrite the *ius proprium*, making it less "unfair" to families). These episodes shed light on the political use of a private dispute such as the Pazzi-Borromei conflict, certainly, but so too the crucial amendment to the statutes of 1415 – the *lex de testamentis* of 1477 – removed any chance Florentine women had left to advance legitimate claim on a part of the paternal inheritance that was no doubt heftier than a dowry.

References

Astorri, Antonella. *La Mercanzia a Firenze nella prima metà del Trecento*. Florence: Olschki, 1998.

Bec, Christian. *Il libro degli affari proprii di Lapo di Giovanni Niccolini de' Sirigatti*, édition critique et commentée. Paris: SEVPEN, 1969.

64 The *lex de testamentis* is edited by Lorenzo Fabbri, "Women's Rights". See also Kuehn, *Heirs, Kin, and Creditors*, pp. 74–77.

Bellomo, Manlio. *Ricerche sui rapporti patrimoniali tra coniugi. Contributo alla storia della famiglia medievale (XII–XIII secc.)*. Milan: Giuffré, 1961.

Botticini, Maristella, and Aloysius Siow. "Why Dowries?." *American Economic Review* 93 (2003): pp. 1385–98.

Brucker, Gene. *Firenze nel Rinascimento.* Florence: La Nuova Italia, 1981.

Chabot, Isabelle. "Il matrimonio di Dante." In *Dante attraverso i documenti*, vol. 1: *Famiglia e patrimonio (secolo XII–1300 circa)*, edited by Giuliano Milani and Antonio Montefusco, special issue of *Reti Medievali Rivista* 15–2 (2014), pp. 1–31.

Chabot, Isabelle. *La dette des familles. Femmes, lignage et patrimoine à Florence aux XIVe et XVe siècles*. Rome: École française de Rome, 2011.

Chabot, Isabelle. "Le gouvernement des pères: l'État florentin et la famille (XIVe–XVe siècles)." In *Florence et la Toscane, XIVe–XIXe siècles. Les dynamiques d'un État italien*, edited by Jean Boutier, Sandro Landi, and Olivier Rouchon, pp. 241–63. Rennes: Presses Universitaires de Rennes, 2004.

Chabot, Isabelle. "Marriage, Dowry and Remarriage in the Sassetti Household (1384–97)."Introduced and translated from Italian by Isabelle Chabot. In *Medieval Italy. Texts in translation*, edited by Katherine L. Jansen, Joanna Drell, and Frances Andrews, pp. 446–50. Philadelphia: University of Pennsylvania Press, 2009.

Chabot, Isabelle. "Matrigne. Le altre madri dei Fiorentini (secc. XIV–XV)." In *Tra archivio e storia. Scritti dedicati ad Alessandra Contini Bonaccossi*, pp. 65–89. Florence: Florence University Press, 2018.

Chabot, Isabelle. "Messer Niccolò degli Alberti, 'pater pauperum'. Lettura del testamento." In *L'ospedale dell'Orbatello. Carità e arte a Firenze*, edited by Cristina De Benedictis and Carla Milloschi, pp. 73–81. Florence: Polistampa, 2015.

Chojnacki, Stanley. "Getting Back the Dowry." In Stanley Chojnacki, *Women and Men in Renaissance Venice. Twelve Essays on Patrician Family*, pp. 95–111. Baltimore: John Hopkins University Press, 2000.

Ciappelli, Giovanni. "I Castellani di Firenze: dall'estremismo oligarchico all'assenza politica (secoli XIV–XV)." *Archivio storico italiano* 149–1 (1991): pp. 33–91.

Cronica (La) domestica di messer Donato Velluti, scritta fra il 1367 e il 1370, edited by Isidoro Del Lungo and Guglielmo Volpi. Florence: Sansoni, 1914.

Fabbri, Lorenzo. "The Magnificent Arbitrator: Lorenzo de' Medici and the Patrician Families." In *Florence, in Studies on Florence and the Italian Renaissance in Honour of F. W. Kent*, edited by Peter Howard and Cecilia Hewlett, pp. 95–113. Turnhout: Brepols, 2016.

Fabbri, Lorenzo. "Women's Rights According to Lorenzo de' Medici: The Borromei-Pazzi Dispute and the Lex de testamentis." In *The Art and Language of Power in Renaissance Florence: Essays for Alison Brown*, edited by Amy Bloch, Luca Boschetto, Carolyn James, and Camilla Russell. Toronto: Centre for Reformation and Renaissance Studies, 2019.

Fisher, Caroline M. "Guardianship, the Family and the Rise of Renaissance Florentine State, 1368–93." In *Famiglie e poteri in Italia tra Medioevo ed Età moderna*, edited by Anna Bellavitis and Isabelle Chabot, pp. 265–82. Rome: École française de Rome, 2009.

Franceschi, Franco. *Oltre il "Tumulto". I lavoratori fiorentini dell'arte della lana fra Tre e Quattrocento*. Florence: Olschki, 1993.

Guidi, Guidobaldo. *Il governo della città-repubblica di Firenze del primo Quattrocento*, 3 vols. Florence: Olschki, 1981.

Hughes, Diane Owen. "From Brideprice to Dowry in Mediterranean Europe." *Journal of Family History* 3 (1978): pp. 263–96 [reprinted in *The Marriage Bargain. Women and Dowries in European History*, edited by Marion Kaplan, pp. 13–57. New York: Routledge, 1985].

Kirshner, Julius. "Baldus de Ubaldis on Disinheritance: Contexts, Controversies, Consilia." *Ius Commune: Zeitschrift für Europäische Rechtsgeschichte* 27 (2000): pp. 119–214.

Kirshner, Julius. "*Consilia* as Authority in Late Medieval Italy: The Case of Florence." In *Legal Consulting in the Civil Law Tradition*, edited by Mario Ascheri, Ingrid Baumgärtner, and Julius Kirshner, pp. 107–40. Berkeley: University of California Press, 1999.

Kirshner, Julius. *Marriage, Dowries and Citizenship in Late Medieval and Renaissance Italy*. Toronto: University of Toronto Press, 2011.

Kirshner, Julius. "Wives' Claims Against Insolvent Husbands in Late Medieval Italy." In *Women of the Medieval World: Essays in Honor of John H. Mundy*, edited by Julius Kirshner and Suzane F. Wemple, pp. 256–303. Oxford: Blackwell, 1985 [reprinted in Julius Kirshner, *Marriage, Dowries and Citizenship in Late Medieval and Renaissance Italy* (Toronto: University of Toronto Press, 2011), pp. 131–60].

Kuehn, Thomas. "Cum Consensu Mundualdi: Legal Guardianship of Women in Quattrocento Florence." In Thomas Kuehn, *Law, Family and Women. Toward an Anthropology of Renaissance Italy*, pp. 212–37. Chicago: University of Chicago Press, 1991.

Kuehn, Thomas. "Dos non teneat locum legitime: Dowry as a Woman's Inheritance in Early Quattrocento Florence." In *Law and Marriage in Medieval ad Early Modern Times*, edited by Per Andersen, Kirsi Salonen, Helle Møller Sigh, and Helle Vogt, pp. 231–48. Copenhagen: DJØF Publishing, 2012.

Kuehn, Thomas. *Emancipation in the Late Medieval Florence*. New Brunswick: Rutgers University Press, 1982.

Kuehn, Thomas. *Family and Gender in Renaissance Italy, 1300–1600*. Cambridge: Cambridge University Press, 2017.

Kuehn, Thomas. "Gender and Law in Milan." In *A Companion to Late Medieval and Early Modern Milan. The Distinctive Features of an Italian State*, edited by Andrea Gamberini, pp. 406–31. Leiden and Boston: Brill, 2015.

Kuehn, Thomas. *Heirs, Kin and Creditors in Renaissance Florence*. Cambridge: Cambridge University Press, 2008.

Kuehn, Thomas. "Intestate Inheritance as a Family Matter: Ius Commune, Statutes and Cases from Florence." In *How Nordic are the Nordic Medieval Laws? Ten years after, Proceedings of the Tenth Carlsberg Academy Conference on Medieval Legal History 2013*, edited by Per Andersen, Kirsi Salonen, Helle Sigh, and Helle Vogt, pp. 59–80. Copenhagen: DJØF Publishing, 2014.

Kuehn, Thomas. "Law and Arbitration in Renaissance Florence." In Thomas Kuehn, *Law, Family and Women: Toward a Legal Anthropology of Renaissance Italy*, pp. 19–74. Chicago: Chicago University Press, 1991.

Kuehn, Thomas. *Law, Family and Women: Toward a Legal Anthropology of Renaissance Italy*. Chicago: Chicago University Press, 1991.

Kuehn, Thomas. "Lawyers and Housecraft in Renaissance Florence: the Politics of Private *Consilia*." In *The Politics of Law in Medieval and Renaissance Italy: Essays in Honour of Lauro Martines*, edited by Lawrin D. Armstrong and Julius Kirshner, pp. 124–40. Toronto: University of Toronto Press, 2011.

Kuehn, Thomas. "Person and Gender in the Laws." In *Gender and Society in Renaissance Italy*, edited by Judith C. Brown and Robert C. Davis, pp. 87–106. London: Longman, 1998.

Kuehn, Thomas. "Some Ambiguities of Female Inheritance Ideology in the Renaissance." *Continuity and Change* 2–1 (1987): pp. 11–36.

Maccioni, Elena and Sergio Tognetti, eds. *Tribunali di mercanti e giustizia mercantile*. Florence: Olschki, 2016.

Martines, Lauro. *Lawyers and Statecraft in Renaissance Florence*. Princeton: Princeton University Press, 1968.

Martone, Luciano. *Arbiter-arbitrator. Forme di giustizia privata nell'età di diritto comune*. Naples: Jovene, 1984.

Molho, Anthony. *Marriage Alliances in Late Medieval Florence*. Cambridge, Mass. and London: Harvard University Press, 1994.

Morelli, Giovanni Di Pagolo. *Ricordi*, nuova edizione e introduzione storica, edited by Claudia Tripodi. Florence: Florence University Press, 2019.

Starn, Randolph. *Contrary Commonwealth: The Theme of Exile in Medieval and Renaissance Italy*. Berkeley and Los Angeles: University of California Press, 1982.

Statuti della Repubblica fiorentina, vol. 2: *Statuti del Podestà dell'anno 1325*, pp. 98–100.

Statuti della Repubblica fiorentina, edited by Romualdo Caggese. Florence: Tip. Galileiana, 1921, new edition: Giuliano Pinto, Francesco Salvestrini, and Andrea Zorzi eds., *Tomo II: Statuti del Podestà dell'anno 1325*. Florence: Olschki, 1999.

Statuta populi et communis Florentiae publica auctoritate collecta castigata et praeposita anno salutis Mccccxv, Friburgi apud Michaelem Kluch (but Florence: Cambiagi), s.d. (but 1777–1781), 4 vols., liber 2, rub. 61, pp. 156–59.

Vallerani, Massimo. "La pauvreté et la citoyenneté dans les suppliques du XIVe siècle." *L'atelier du centre de recherche historique* 13 (2015): pp. 2–16 (dossier: *Supliques. Lois et cas dans la normativité de l'époque moderne*, edited by Simona Cerutti and Massimo Vallerani).

Vallerani, Massimo. "La supplica al Signore e il potere della misericordia. Bologna 1337–1347." *Quaderni storici* 131 (2009): pp. 411–41.

Vallerani, Massimo. "Liti private e soluzioni legali. Note sul libro di Thomas Kuehn e sui sistemi di composizione dei conflitti nella società tardo medievale." *Quaderni storici* 89 (1995): pp. 546–57.

Zorzi, Andrea. "The Judicial System in Florence in the Fourteenth and Fifteenth Centuries." In *Crime, Society and the Law in Renaissance Italy*, edited by Trevor Dean and Kate J. P. Lowe, pp. 40–58. Cambridge: Cambridge University Press, 1994.

CHAPTER 10

Border Patrimonies: The Transmission and Claiming of Property in Women's Everyday Writings in Sixteenth to Eighteenth-Century Friuli

Laura Casella

The geographical backdrop of this chapter is Friuli, a border territory divided between the Republic of Venice and the County of Gorizia. Friuli was part of Habsburg Inner Austria, an area in which different political and juridical entities encountered one another. The western part of the region – predominantly feudal, with a few small cities – which had been under the dominion of the Patriarchs of Aquileia throughout the Middle Ages, was conquered by the Venetians in 1420 and subsequently made part of the Venetian mainland. In 1500, upon the death of the last Count of Gorizia, the eastern part came under the direct rule of the Habsburgs, *avvocato* and vassal of the Patriarch. The more stable definition of the border would be grounds for political bargaining between the two powers for the entire early modern period.

Until a few decades ago, historiography has mainly insisted on highlighting the differences between these two areas, and underlining their political aspects. An alternative reading emerges, however, if we analyse this border area from a social point of view. By focusing on the family strategies, the alliances or divisions of the aristocratic elite – an elite too often interpreted from a political and conflictual view of the border[1] – we arrive at a reconsideration of the history of this area. This allows us to overcome a binary view of the nobility's political positions that has served nationalistic historiographical constructs of the nineteenth and twentieth centuries, and treating the personal, social, and cultural lives of the figures involved as central and closely interconnected. The

1 For a critical examination of these positions see Laura Casella, "Storia di un territorio di confine. Il Friuli veneto e asburgico in età moderna," in *Gli ebrei nella storia del Friuli Venezia Giulia. Una vicenda di lunga durata. Atti del convegno internazionale di studi, Museo Nazionale dell'Ebraismo Italiano e della Shoah (Ferrara, 12–14 ottobre 2015)*, ed. Miriam Davide and Pietro Ioly Zorattini (Florence: Giuntina, 2016), pp. 23–37; Laura Casella, "Un laboratorio politico di confine. La Patria del Friuli prima dell'Italia (secc. XVIII–XIX)," in *Nazioni d'Italia. Identità politiche e appartenenze regionali fra Settecento e Ottocento*, ed. Angela De Benedictis, Irene Fosi, and Luca Mannori (Rome: Viella, 2012), pp. 151–78.

 | DOI:10.1163/9789004456204_011

border families evidently shared material and ideal horizons, lifestyles, and behaviours.[2] From a socio-economic point of view their interests were mainly linked to rental income and, although they owned *palazzi* and other residences in the major cities (Udine in Venetian Friuli and Gorizia in Habsburg Friuli), they shared a feudal character in their cultural outlook and a rootedness in the castles and country houses of the Friulian countryside.

My aim is to draw attention to the administration of assets by the nobility that lived astride this border, and to decisions concerning the transmission of property, including dowries. The fact that family and patrimonial interests in many cases straddled the border makes it particularly interesting to compare the positions and choices of men and women with regard to the different juridical regimes that characterised the Venetian and Habsburg areas, as well as the opportunities or constraints and potential conflicts that these implied. Indeed, these cases enable us to develop a more general social and gendered history of the border region.[3]

Many specific aspects must be explored before it is possible to delineate a general social profile of the Friulian nobility: educational and career paths for men, strategies for social mobility and matrimonial alliances, decisions regarding the transmission of property, the running of the household, the material aspects of life, and domestic consumption. Without losing sight of this more general perspective, the immediate purpose of this chapter is to foreground the spheres of agency of aristocratic women in order to trace a gendered reading of family roles and responsibilities in household administration. This interpretive viewpoint seems useful for measuring the real possibilities women had to dispose of their own and their family's property and for evaluating, through these practices, the respective rights of a husband and wife to the ownership and use of property.

My chosen subject matter – the agency of women of the feudal aristocracy in Friuli – may seem characterised by more than one form of marginality. First, by spatial marginality: this research concerns a territory on the periphery both of the Habsburg Empire and of the Republic of Venice, a borderland often

2 Laura Casella, "Noblesse de frontière. Espace politique et relations familiales dans le Frioul à l'époque moderne," *Mélanges de l'École française de Rome. Italie et Méditerranée* 125–1 (2013), pp. 1–14 (15 December 2017, doi 10.4000/mefrim.1134); see also the editors' introduction to the dossier *Famiglie al confine*, ed. Laura Casella, Anna Bellavitis, and Dorit Raines, in the same volume, https://mefrim.revues.org//1007, accessed 15 December 2017.

3 Laura Casella, "I beni della nobiltà nel Friuli moderno: un quadro d'insieme e alcuni casi di rivendicazioni maschili e femminili a cavallo del confine," *Geschichte und Region / Storia e Regione* 27–2 (2018), pp. 70–101, special issue *Vermögen und Verwandtschaft / Patrimonio e parentela*, ed. Siglinde Clementi and Janine Maegraith.

described as culturally and economically backward. Second, by social marginality, as I am concerned with families who, for the most part, belonged to the feudal nobility, often described as "residual" with respect both to processes of social and economic evolution centred upon the cities and with respect to political processes inherent in the building of the modern state. And, in addition, there is the marginality of gender: little attention has been given to women in the history of early modern Friuli.[4]

I would, however, suggest that we reconsider this emphasis on marginality.[5] The border constituted an opportunity for aristocratic families to weave social networks between the territories, to take up opportunities for career or economic enterprise within a very broad compass, and make political matrimonial unions that were socially and territorially diverse. Moreover, as far as aristocratic women were concerned, documentation enables us to trace the physiognomy of several figures that had the authority to make decisions, the strength to defend their positions, and the awareness to conciliate and negotiate. They showed themselves to be, in other words, amply qualified for the administration not only of their own goods and properties but also of the houses into which they entered in matrimony, running economic interests and managing properties that were, in some cases, situated on both sides of the border.

The choice of my sources is a fundamental point that I would like to address in order to emphasise that interpretive and methodological revision go hand in hand. Before describing the kind of sources I have used, and the criteria for their selection, going on to provide some case studies that enable us to analyse the decisions women made regarding the management and transmission of their property, I would like to briefly consider the presence of women's writings in family archives and their interpretive possibilities for several areas of research.

4 There is no overview, and only a few case studies, of these see Liliana Cargnelutti, *Per la nobile signora. Una causa matrimoniale friulana del secolo XVIII* (Udine: Casamassima, 1992); Roberta Corbellini, ed., *Interni di famiglia. Patrimoni e sentimenti di figlie, madri, mogli, vedove. Il Friuli tra Medioevo ed età moderna* (Udine: Arti grafiche friulane, 1992); Stefania Pascolini, *Dal Talamo al chiostro. Ruoli femminili ed ideologia nobiliare in un matrimonio friulano del Seicento* (Udine: Forum, 2000); Laura Casella, "Donne aristocratiche nel Friuli del Cinquecento tra strategie familiari e conflitti di fazione," in *Donne di potere nel Rinascimento*, ed. Letizia Arcangeli and Susanna Peyronel (Rome: Viella, 2008), pp. 89–128.

5 It is not possible here to reference the many studies that have appeared in recent decades on the subject of border. A work that remains of fundamental importance for the study of borders and their permeability is Peter Sahlins, *Boundaries. The Making of France and Spain in the Pyrenees* (Berkeley: University of California Press, 1989).

1 Women's Everyday Writing in Family Archives: Many Possible Readings

My recent research in family archives in Friuli provides a body of women's everyday writing that is both unexpected and difficult to categorise.[6] The volume of such sources, as well as their different types and functions, which I will describe below, suggests that the practice of everyday writing was quite common among women – even more so in Friuli than in Tuscany, with which a comparison can be established.[7]

Only very recently has systematic attention been paid to women's sources in this field of research in Friuli. In terms of quantity, the most significant women's writings are letters. A first survey, conducted a few years ago, of female correspondence between 1650 and 1800 showed how common this form of writing was.[8] Through these sources it is possible to begin to analyse various fields in which women were active and expressed themselves: from matters of family ties and taking care of children to the running of the household, from the administration of agrarian properties or commercial activities – shared to a greater or lesser extent with husbands, sons, and other male members of the family – to social relations, negotiations, and conflicts, interwoven with matrimonial ambitions, or with political relations, albeit of an informal nature. A pertinent example of the latter is the case of the noblewoman Barbara Malvezzi from Bologna, who through marriage entered the Colloredo family, a family of soldiers like her birth family. Her copious correspondence, consisting of over

6 I have consulted the following family archives at the Archivio di Stato di Udine (ASUD): Archivio Perusini (which holds the papers from a branch of the Colloredo family, and in particular those of Silvia Rabatta Colloredo, 1717–1801); Archivio Savorgnan; Archivio Della Torre (relating to Sofonisba Antonini, first decades of the seventeenth century); Archivio Toppo (for the papers of Eleonora Fabris, Bianca Prampero, and Olimpia di Varmo, mid-seventeenth century to the early eighteenth century); and at the Archivio di Stato di Gorizia (ASGO), Archivio Coronini Cronberg (which also contains the papers of the Degrazia family and of Venere Bosina, second half of the sixteenth century). More precise references will be provided in the relevant individual notes that follow.

7 On women's accounting and memoir writing in Tuscany see Serena Galasso, "Il mestiere di sposa: genere, organizzazione domestica e scrittura contabile a Firenze nel XVI secolo," in *Donne e lavoro: attività, ruoli, complementarietà (sec. XIV–XIX)*, ed. Paola Avallone and Gemma Colesanti (Cagliari: Istituto di storia dell'Europa mediterranea, 2019), pp. 121–51; Serena Galasso, "La memoria tra i conti: alcune riflessioni sulle scritture domestiche di donne a Firenze (XV–XVI secolo)," *Quaderni storici* 1 (2019), pp. 195–223.

8 Albina De Martin Pinter, "Lettere di donne. La scrittura epistolare femminile in Friuli tra 1650 e 1800. Un primo censimento, un'analisi di casi" (PhD diss., Università degli studi di Udine, 2012/2013).

700 letters, shows how she was able to use her skill in building new social networks and in taking advantage of those that her aristocratic origins and marriage had enabled her to weave in order to intervene in favour of her son-in-law Carlo della Torre. He was an illustrious member of the highest nobility of the County of Gorizia and, as its *Capitano*, the most important representative of its institutions. Imprisoned for many years in Graz (from 1671 until his death in 1689), Carlo found in his mother-in-law someone willing to concern herself both with coordinating the administration and interests of the family on both sides of the border, and with his personal legal affairs. From the castle of Dobra in the County of Gorizia where Barbara lived, she kept in close contact with Carlo's descendants living in Venetian Friuli and with all those who might act as effective mediators to free her son-in-law via her prolific correspondence.[9]

In addition to private letters, other important sources can be found in family archives: a complex range of handwritten books, diverse in both content and form, to the pages of which, for various reasons, their female authors added notes. This kind of documentation is even less recognised than women's correspondence, and thus remains to be studied. These writings often are "invisible" in the archives, as the latter were generally structured according to masculine and patrilinear logics. Modern cataloguing of archival material has often reproduced the same organizing logic as that of the documentation itself, and thus has perpetuated the difficulty that this represents for research. There is not necessarily an absence of women's sources, but a more systematic and minute approach it certainly requires to find them.

Account books, memoirs, and diaries allow us, through personal and self-representational documents, to approach family structures and networks that, as we have seen, could be transnational. They also provide for the reconstruction of women's roles in the management of a family and its assets: in such a range of matters as providing for the household, dealing with servants, agents and suppliers, the education of children, the maintenance and construction of social and familial networks. These documents allow us to trace both women's decision making regarding economic management and the transmission of property, as well as their role as mediators in situations of conflict.

Though their forms differ, these materials are all eloquent examples that help us understand where, when, and why women wrote in modern Friuli. The activity of writing and agency of aristocratic women are therefore two subjects

9 Albina De Martin Pinter, "Reti di donne sul confine friulano. Lettere femminili nell'archivio Della Torre (XVII secolo)," *Mélanges de l'École française de Rome. Italie et Méditerranée* 125–1 (2013), pp. 97–114 (doi: 10.4000/mefrim.1200) https://mefrim.revues.org//1007, accessed 30 September 2020.

that must be considered in relation to each other, interweaving research perspectives.

The documentation described serves, as mentioned above, to highlight the role of women in domestic administration and economic activities in pre-industrial agrarian contexts. It also enables us to understand domestic work and family economic roles in a wider, revised sense and evaluate not only *agency*, but also the *recording of agency* – that is, the production and conservation of papers as well as the formation of the archives of elite families. In doing so, the very construction of family memory is subjected to a gendered reading. This contributes to a reconsideration of the exclusively masculine and patrilinear structure of these collections of documents.

Historians concerned with women's written expression have only recently begun to turn their attention to everyday writing undertaken for practical purposes.[10] This perspective sets out with different questions from those that have been posed with regard to intellectual or literary women's writings. Studies of these written forms have sought the expression of female "genius" in various fields of culture and erudition, and have measured the presence of female figures in intellectual social networks.[11] Approaching sources such as those I will shortly describe in more detail, involves, on the other hand, revising several fields of historical research, and considering them together, in relation to one another. In this respect I propose to particularly focus on three topics.

The first is the link between writing on the one hand, and literacy and numeracy on the other. The women I have encountered in my research used writing for ordinary and practical purposes concerned with record-keeping, as opposed to intellectual ones. They wrote to make arrangements, to run things, to administer, to explain their decisions, and left a record of their behaviour – and thus often to avoid dispute and promote conciliation. The material quality of the writing, the handwriting and autograph character of these writings are in themselves very important indicators for understanding some features of the sociocultural identity of these women: their level of literacy, for example,

---

10 Isabelle Lacoue-Labarthe and Sylvie Mouysset, eds., *Écrire au quotidien*, special issue of *Clio. Histoire, Femmes et Sociétés* 35 (2012); see also, more generally, Daniel Fabre, ed., *Écritures ordinaires* (Paris: Éditions POL, 1993).

11 An overview of both fields of writing offers Tiziana Plebani, *Le scritture delle donne in Europa. Pratiche quotidiane e ambizioni letterarie (secoli XIII–XX)*, (Rome: Carocci, 2019). Women's education, writing skills, and women's agency in eighteenth century Friuli are discussed in Laura Casella, "Sapere e saper fare. Il 'Colloquio sopra gli studi delle donne', l'educazione e le scritture femminili nel Friuli del Settecento," in *Atti dell'Accademia udinese di scienze lettere e arti*, CX-2017 (2020), pp. 143–69.

of numeracy, as shown in their accounting, as well as their economic and juridical competence.

The second is the economic role and work of women in the pre-industrial rural economy. In fact, despite the marked growth in research in recent years into the subject of women's work, one has to agree with Scarlette Beauvalet's assertion that "*il existe relativement peu de travaux qui portent spécifiquement sur les femmes dans le milieu rural à l'époque moderne*",[12] above all as far as the aristocracy is concerned. Research interest in the economic weight of women's activities in non-urban areas is hard to come by, in particular with regard to all those "unpaid" occupations that had to do with the management – economic as well as affective-relational management – of the noble household.[13]

The third also relates to the rural setting, but more specifically concerns the position of feudal aristocratic women within it. Although recent Italian studies have attributed a "modern" character to feudality, the agency of women still needs to be investigated in feudal contexts[14] with regard to, for example, the education of children and decisions on their matrimonies, and to inheritance strategies. Juridical models and feudal law would suggest that women were powerless in disposing of and inheriting property. We still need to investigate, however, to what extent this was the case in practice. The juridical system of Friuli in particular is characterised by the co-existence of a common law of Roman origin and Germanic influences on the one hand and, on the other, Venetian and Habsburg legislation, a complex juridical system that involved

---

12 Scarlett Beauvalet, "Les femmes dans le monde rural à l'époque moderne, XVIe–XVIIIe siècles," in *Ruralité française et britannique XIIIe–XXe siècles. Approches comparées*, ed. Nadine Vivier (Rennes: Presses Universitaires de Rennes, 2005), pp. 89–102, here p. 89; see also the entire section of the volume dedicated to "Le travail des femmes dans les exploitations agricoles (XVe–XXe siècles)" and, in particular, Jane Whittle, "Le travail des femmes dans les ménages ruraux anglais, 1450–1650: trois approches alternatives," ibid., pp. 77–87.

13 See, however, Manuela Martini and Anna Bellavitis, eds., *Household Economies, Social Norms and Practices of Unpaid Market Work in Europe from the Sixteenth Century to the Present*, special issue of *The History of the Family*, 19–3 (2014); Anna Bellavitis, Manuela Martini, and Raffaella Sarti, eds., *Familles laborieuses. Rémunération, transmission et apprentissage dans les ateliers familiaux de la fin du Moyen Âge à l'époque contemporaine en Europe*, special issue of *Mélanges de l'École française de Rome*, 128–1 (2016). An important reassessment of women's work is provided by Cristina Borderías and Manuela Martini, eds., *Per una nuova storia del lavoro*, special issue of *Genesis* 15–2 (2016). On the work of women in urban contexts see Anna Bellavitis, *Women's Work and Rights in Early Modern Urban Europe* (London: Palgrave McMillan, 2018, orig. Ital. 2016).

14 Renata Ago, *La feudalità in età moderna* (Rome and Bari: Laterza, 1994); Aurelio Musi, *Il feudalesimo nell'Europa moderna* (Bologna: Il Mulino, 2007); Elisa Novi Chavarria and Vittoria Fiorelli, eds., *Baroni e vassalli. Storie moderne* (Milan: Franco Angeli, 2011).

many parties: feudal jurisdictions, cities, and territorial assemblies on both sides of the border. In reconstructing social practices, it is difficult to establish, above and beyond the statement of rules, the real spheres of decision making. The writings of women, in the form of memoirs or record-keeping, constitute a valuable testimony and help us to reconstruct their effective agency.

2 What Kind of Books? First Categorisations

In the initial phase of my research I set about preparing a survey of these writings, making a first attempt to classify them by type. A subsequent step will involve comparing these with family books and books kept by men. Important aspects to consider in regard to these books, which I mentioned here only briefly, are: the social rank and family status of their "authoresses" – be they a daughter, wife, mother, widow, etc. – the question of autography, the form and content of the documents, and whether they are singular documents or part of a collection. Starting with these characteristics we can begin to develop a better understanding of the degree of literacy and numeracy of these women, their competence in household management, and in accounting. We can also develop some ideas about the "canon" of these written sources and reflect on differences and similarities in analogous texts by men.

Several of the women to whom I have dedicated particular attention belong to the aristocracy: Eleonora Fabris, Bianca Prampero, Olimpia di Varmo (all of whom entered by marriage into the family of Savorgnan della Bandiera between the mid-seventeenth and the beginning of the eighteenth century); Lucrezia (first decades of the seventeenth century), Silvia Rabatta and Claudia Prampero (eighteenth century and first decades of nineteenth century) who all married into the Colloredo family; Sofonisba Antonini della Torre (first decades of the seventeenth century). The case of Venere Bosina can be added to these, exceptional both for her time (second half of the sixteenth century) and for the importance of the documentation relating to her. She belonged to the artisan and commercial milieu of western Friuli but had growing interests in land investments and family ties with a family belonging to the Habsburg nobility, the Degrazia, which is the reason she is included in this research.

Most of the writings considered were autographs, whether in part or as a whole. It is not possible here to go into the question of autography, an issue that is not crucial in measuring the agency of women. In fact, it was customary in noble families to entrust the keeping of registers and papers to a secretary and one finds several hand writings, especially in some account books, with that of the lady of the house often appearing only in reviewing the entries.

Autography is a determining feature, on the other hand, when we find thoughts, comments, wishes, and problems committed to the page.

The material aspect of these books also constitutes a criterion for analysis. Indeed, it is important to reflect on the variety of forms they take, consider their material characteristics, observe the objects that are in themselves eloquent both as far as the quality of paper and binding are concerned – indicative of the standard of living of their author – and in regard to their dimensions: small notebooks, easy to carry, in which to register money lent;[15] taller registers typical of account books for the recording of rent collection, personal or household expenses, and many other varieties of "books" with diverse shapes and functions.[16]

In some archives these books are linked to each other and to other household registers by internal references. The archive of Silvia Rabatta Colloredo's papers is a prime example of a structured system of interconnected writings; the systematic nature of the recording of household income and expenditures affords us a detailed picture of the family's consumption and the author's role in domestic life.[17]

In other cases, we cannot count on structured archives but find single, albeit very significant, written traces of a life, including the one of Sofonisba Antonini, to whom I will return. In other instances the relationship between practical record keeping and the writing of reflections and self-expression was more developed, such as in some memorial writing separate from and independent of accounts, although in account books comments and decisions are

15 For example, the *Libro de mi* in which Venere Bosina records money lent to various people during the second half of the sixteenth century (ASGO, Archivio Coronini Cronberg, b. 88) and the *Libro di memoria di soldi imprestadi,* 1788 in which Silvia Rabatta similarly notes such loans (ASUD, Archivio Perusini, b. 390, fasc. 5).

16 For some first reflections on this matter see Laura Casella, "Forme della memoria quotidiana. I libri femminili come oggetti materiali (Friuli, secc. XVI–XVIII)," in *Per Furio. Studi in onore di Furio Bianco*, ed. Alessio Fornasin and Claudio Povolo (Udine: Forum, 2014), pp. 133–42. On personal writings as "objects" in general see Michel Cassan, Jean-Pierre Bardet, and François-Joseph Ruggiu, eds., *Les écrits du for privé. Objects matériels, objects édités* (Limoges: Pulim, 2005).

17 Laura Casella and Albina De Martin Pinter, "Il cibo e la casa. Amministrazione domestica e consumi nelle scritture quotidiane di Silvia Rabatta Colloredo," *Genesis* 16–1 (2017), pp. 43–65. A fundamental reference for the reconstruction of domestic life through women's account books is Jane Whittle and Elizabeth Griffiths, *Consumption and Gender in the Early Seventeenth-Century Household. The World of Alice Le Strange* (Oxford: Oxford University Press, 2012). In addition to an organised archive of accounts, Silvia Rabatta Colloredo leaves a rich collection of over 400 letters. See De Martin Pinter, "Lettere di donne".

often written next to the entries. This is the case of Venere Bosina and her *Libro delle cose che son degne de eser notate et tenute a memoria* (*Book of things worth noting down and remembering*).[18] There are, then, women who wrote between the lines or on the blank pages of account books and those who, in addition, found time specifically for the writing of memoirs, which they entrusted to a book serving specifically for this purpose.

But it is worth introducing another level of interpretation for analysing this variety of everyday memorial writing by asking the following questions: how much writing of oneself is contained within writing of the family, thus becoming a part of it? To what extent do these words have a proto-autobiographical value as existential records, which obliges us to look for expressions of the self in places and forms that have not been considered until now? For women and men alike, the problem arises of placing "autobiographical" writing in relation to family writing.[19]

3 Writing of the Self and Family Memory

These writings have a dual nature: on the one hand, they are economic documents that stem from the concrete practice of administration; on the other, they can be considered as "writing of the self". Before dealing with the functional nature of these books, which enables us to take the measure of women's spheres and agency, I will first consider their narrative potential, that is the importance they may have as a kind of proto-autobiography – before autobiography existed as an established stylistic form.[20] These books do not represent a deliberate "autobiographical project". The written lives of women like Sofonisba or Venere, to whom I will return shortly, took shape in the recording of memoranda regarding the everyday and "material quality" of life, of biological stages and events that punctuate the flow of existence. The "self" and the "writing of the self" were often defined in relation to the family, to the roles that women had within it as daughters, sisters, wives, mothers, daughters-in-law,

---

18 Biblioteca Statale Isontina di Gorizia, ms. 40 [Rosina di Porcia], *Libro de le cose che son degne de eser notate et tenute a memoria dal 1541 in qua.*

19 Michel Cassan, *Écritures de familles, écritures de soi. France-Italie XVI–XIX siècles* (Limoges: Pulim, 2010).

20 On account books and their potential value as writings of the self cf. Adam Smyth, "Money, Accounting and Life-Writing, 1600–1700: Balancing a Life," in *A History of English Autobiography*, ed. Adam Smyth (Cambridge: Cambridge University Press, 2016), pp. 86–100; Rebecca E. Connor, *Women, Accounting and Narrative. Keeping Books in Eighteenth-Century England* (London and New York: Routledge, 2004).

mothers-in-law, aunts, nieces, granddaughters, or grandmothers but also in relation to economic interest, social relations, religion, the life of the community, and the political landscapes that these women managed to discern.

Some of these texts present notes similar to those of Italian family books, a type of book that derived from the account books of Tuscan merchants in the late medieval period which, in addition to accounts, registered both the most important events of the lives of family members and notes on current affairs and politics. These tended to be multi-generational texts in which the family was at once "author" (several members took part in keeping the book), "subject" and "recipient" (in the form of future generations).[21] They had a place alongside other registers in a complex system of family and personal writings that constituted the memorial patrimony of a house, sometimes its paper "monument", one of the ways in which the house narrated and represented itself.[22]

As with family books written by men, some of these women inserted notes in account books about transitions in their lives or in that of their family members: births, baptisms, names of godparents, their children's weddings. Bianca Prampero Savorgnan noted down important life changes regarding some of her family members in several account and expense books. On these pages, as well as in notes on expenses and income, the noblewoman recorded, for example, the birth of two grandchildren, the daughters of her son Girolamo, both born in June in 1673 and June 1674. She reported when they were baptised and the names of the godfathers and godmothers, Girolamo Antonini and Elena Mantica in the case of the first, Marzio di Sbrojavacca and Giacoma Valvason in the second.[23]

---

21 Angelo Cicchetti and Raul Mordenti, *I libri di famiglia in Italia*, vol. 1: *Filologia e Storiografia letteraria* (Rome: Edizioni di storia e letteratura, 1985); Raul Mordenti, *I libri di famiglia in Italia*, vol. 2: *Geografia e storia* (Rome: Edizioni di storia e letteratura, 2001); Giovanni Ciappelli, ed., *Memoria, famiglia, identità tra Italia ed Europa nell'età moderna* (Bologna: Il Mulino, 2009); Giovanni Ciappelli, *Memory, Family, and Self: Tuscan Family Books and other European Egodocuments (14th–18th Century)* (Leiden and Boston: Brill, 2014).

22 Only two examples, Tuscan and Friulian: that of the family book of the Ciurianni family studied by Isabelle Chabot, *Ricostruzione di una famiglia. I Ciurianni di Firenze tra XII e XV secolo, con l'edizione critica del "Libro proprio" di Lapo di Valore Ciurianni e successori (1326–1429)* (Florence: Le Lettere, 2012), and that of the Amaseo family, on which cf. Laura Casella, "Mémoire de la révolte et mémoires de famille. La 'crudel zobia grassa' (1511) dans les livres de famille du XVIe siècle: brève histoire des manuscrits et des éditions," in *La Mémoire des révoltes en Europe à l'époque moderne, ed.* Alexandra Merle, Stéphane Jettot, and Manuel Herrero Sánchez (Paris: Classiques Garnier, 2018), pp. 143–69.

23 "*Li 18 Giugno 1673. A ore niove nacque una fanziolina à Gerolamo mio Figliollo, et questo e il primo parto della signora Olimpia sua consorte, et il medesimo giorno fu batizata essendo giorno di Dominica. Furono compadri il signor conte Gerolamo Antonino et comadre la*

These kind of notes are important for many reasons. The presence of the godparents – the first two belonging to families of the newer urban nobility, the second to the older feudal nobility of the land – is indicative of the compass of the family's social network, shifting from new to old nobility, from urban to feudal. The note also shows, above all, that it was the woman, in this case a widow, who took on the task of keeping records concerning the social position of her family in account books, undertaking a duty usually fulfilled by the masters of the household, and thus contributed to the construction of a family history.

4 Venere's Diary and the Life of Sofonisba

One case worthy of attention as is the aforementioned *Book of things worth noting down and remembering from 1541 until now*, by Venere Bosina. It is a prime example of family and personal writing in which the writer bore witness to her economic activity and her familial and social relations, to her vision of life and of the motivations and times in which she wrote. The text represents a highly unusual case in terms of what it recorded and of the social profile of its author.

In this notebook of about sixty pages, the writer recorded facts about her private life, her economic activities, current affairs relating to the community in which she lived (a sizeable village in the west of Friuli, Porcia), and political events, covering exactly fifty years, from 1541 to 1591. Her writing shows what she chose to record at times of reflection. She wrote with the explicit intention of "not remaining idle" on the "holy days", as in non-working days, as she herself gave information on the title page, which indicates she usually had work to do. The phrase is indicative of her desire to write about her own life when she was not engaged in her usual activities. Her handwriting is functional, as opposed to that of a cultivated woman: letters with spaces between them, big letters, dialect terms that are italianised and echo the sounds of the words, ungrammatical phrases.

signora contessa Elena Mantica: il suo nome fu Bianca et sopra nome Antonia" and "Li 30 giugno 1674. A ore 22 la sudetta signora Olimpia mia nora partori una altra fanziolina in giorno di sabato e nel dimani fu batizata. Fu compadre il signor Marzio di Sbroiavacha et comadre la signora Contessa Giacoma Valvasona: il suo nome fu Eleonora et Isabeta." Cf. ASUD, Archivio Toppo, b. 48, *Libro di notte della Sig.a Bianca Savorgnana*, 9v. For studies on godparents see Guido Alfani and Vincent Gourdon, eds., *Spiritual Kinship in Europe, 1500–1800* (Basingstoke: Palgrave McMillan, 2012).

First, we can find events relating to family ties. The diary begins in 1566, but with the recording of a date from the past, an important stage in her life, 25 November 1541: "On St. Catherine's Day I was married to Gerolamo Bosina of Porcia and I lived with him until the year 1565. He died on St. James's Day which falls on 25 July."[24] The day of her wedding and that of the death of her husband were the two temporal poles of her marital life. Although Venere's Book opens with reference to her status as a widow, we know that even before her husband's death she was already used to running family affairs and being concerned with economic and patrimonial matters. This is confirmed by the fact that Venere kept other notebooks, all written in her hand: account books, registers of loans, including money lent to her husband when he was alive. The second entry in the notebook relates to the time when Venere began to write and refers again to her family and to her now active role in matrimonial strategies. Venere, who had no children from her marriage, noted that her nephew (from her husband's side) Bernardino was marrying her niece Marina, daughter of her sister Maria and Francesco De Grazia, a gentleman of Gorizia. This passage represents a double matrimonial tie and leads us to observe an interesting and unusual social alliance that was almost certainly sought for economic reasons. Both Bernardino, and, before him Venere's sister, were joined in wedlock to the De Grazias, a noble family from Gorizia with interests in the commerce of wheat, whose social standing would increase considerably over the course of the sixteenth and seventeenth centuries until it became part of the imperial nobility.

Using this text as my starting point, I have reconstructed Venere's biography. She was the daughter of Pietro, a *calegher*, the Venetian term for "shoemaker", from a small coastal community near Venice. She married Girolamo della Massara, a rich artisan of leather and later a wheat merchant. Girolamo was called Bosina (or Bossina) because of his commercial dealings with Bosnia.

The reconstruction of this complex family network to which Venere belonged merits further study for not only what it can tell us about the familial and economic relations that can straddle class barriers (those between artisan-merchants and nobility) and political borders (between the Republic of Venice and the imperial Habsburg territories). It also provides insight into religious matters and the diffusion of heterodox and reformed ideas. Venere's husband, Girolamo Bosina, was a prominent figure in those heterodox circles of western Friuli that embraced reformed ideas. Venere must also have participated

24 *"Il di de Santa Caterina fui maritata in messer Geronimo Bosina da Porcia et stete con lui fina l'ano del 1565. Lui morse poi il dì de Santo Iacomo che vien de luio a vinti et 5."* [Rosina di Porcia], *Libro*, 1r.

in this climate of renewed religiousness because her sister, Maria De Grazia, a more orthodox Catholic, repeatedly advised her to abandon "your anti-Christ of Babylon" and "remember your errors and turn to God in true penitence, begging him to forgive you".[25]

In Venere's book we also find ample space devoted to another aspect of her everyday life: her economic affairs. There are many notes regarding the weather that mentioned dangers to her agrarian interests, like, for example, in 1569 when extreme heat compromised the harvest causing famine and, consequently, a rise in prices. She wrote: "in the month of July bread was scarcely found, and their hunger was so great that people took it out of the oven before it was cooked – they couldn't wait."[26] Venere's powerful words and vivid imagery show her involvement.

Venere, then, gave careful consideration to a wide range of conditions affecting her own affairs. Among these, political affairs, whether at the local or broader level, have obvious weight. We must remember that her economic interests straddled an unstable political border, a border that was from time to time subject to wars between the Republic of Venice and the Habsburgs, as well as to Turkish incursions. Venere described "power" carefully, especially when it manifested itself in the bloodshed, ambushes, feuds, and vendettas that shook her community. She showed herself to be aware of group dynamics and how factions worked, whether she was writing about ordinary people or the noble family of Porcia, feudal lords of the area. But Venere's attention and commentary were not limited to local affairs, which she knew from personal experience. She also recorded military and diplomatic matters involving international politics: for example, the news that the Turks had taken Nicosia (Cyprus) in 1571, the year of the battle of Lepanto; the decision the following year not to mount a naval expedition because of the lack of Spanish help in organizing a fleet, and the peace that followed in 1573.

The fragments I have presented here are not many, but enough to bear witness to a narrative fabric in which family matters and political episodes alternate with considerations on agricultural and commercial profitability and meteorology as if it were all equally entitled to belong to Venere's day and give form to her life.[27]

25 ASGO, Archivio Coronini Cronberg, Atti e documenti, b. 200, filza 568, Lettera di Maria De Grazia alla sorella.

26 "[…] *quando fu il mese de luio non se trovava pan, che le persone il tirava fora del forno che non lo lasava coser per gran fame che non poseva aspetar che si cosese.*" [Rosina di Porcia], *Libro*, 12v–13r.

27 In recent years European historical research has dedicated increased attention to investigating the "materiality" of personal writings from various viewpoints (cf. note 16), the

The diary is in itself of exceptional value and a rich source that we can also compare with other papers and notebooks by Bosina. Of course, it is only possible to compare different text types when we are lucky enough to come across extensive archives. There are other cases of writings by women that are limited to a sole, small document, and these are nonetheless very significant. The life of a noblewoman from the early seventeenth century, Sofonisba Antonini della Torre provides a clear example. It is narrated in the first person. Punctuated by a recurring "*Nota come* […]" ("note how […]") she summarised the most important stages of her life: betrothal at the age of eleven, her wedding the following year, entry into her husband's house, the births of her children, the death of her mother at "the age of 63 years" of which "42 were spent in marital company with my lord father". But she also noted the spread of the plague, her husband's military engagements, the good match made for her daughter Lucina who in 1649 would marry a "gentleman worth half a million in gold". In the space of a few pages we find the sequence of a noblewoman's life pressed between that of the previous generation and the generation to follow.[28]

relationship between autobiography and family history (cf. note 21), and between the writing of the self and other forms of everyday writing (cf. note 20). Rich research interests have been developed that relate to several European countries: research in France, for example, has led to, among other publications, the following collective volumes: Jean-Pierre Bardet, Elisabeth Arnoul, and François-Joseph Ruggiu, eds., *Les écrits du for privé en Europe. Du Moyen Âge à l'époque contemporaine. Enquêtes, analyses, publications* (Bordeaux: Presses Universitaires de Bordeaux, 2010); Jean-Pierre Bardet and François-Joseph Ruggiu, eds., *Au plus prés du secret des cœurs? Nouvelles lectures historiques des écrits du for prive en Europe du XVIe au XVIIIe siècle* (Paris: Presses de l'Université Paris-Sorbonne, 2005); for research relating to Germany see Gabriele Jancke and Claudia Ulbrich, eds., *Vom Individuum zur Person. Neue Konzepte im Spannungsfeld von Autobiographietheorie und Selbstzeugnisforschung* (Göttingen: Wallstein, 2005) and Claudia Ulbrich, Kaspar von Greyerz, and Lorenz Heiligensetzer, eds., *Mapping the "I". Research on Self-narratives in Germany and Switzerland* (Leiden and Boston: Brill, 2015). A gendered reading of everyday personal writings appears in numerous studies: cf. for example Danièle Tosato-Rigo, ed., *Appel à témoins. Écrits personnels et pratiques socioculturelles* (*XVIe–XXe s.*), special issue of *Études de Lettre*, 1–2 (2016) and Oscar Jané and Patrice Poujade, eds., *Memòria personal. Construcció i projecció en primera persona e l'època moderna* (Madrid: Casa de Velazquez, 2015). The publications cited in note 10 and 11 and Emmanuelle Berthiaud, ed., *Paroles de femmes. Rôles et images de soi dans les écrits personnels, Europe, XVIe–XXe siècle* (Paris: Éditions Le Manuscrit, 2017) concentrate on women's writings in particular. As far as the present state of research is concerned, memorialistic accounts such as that of Venere Bosina remain rare, however, both in terms of the complex layers of the writing and the chronological period covered.

28 ASUD, Archivio Torriani, b.79, 1v–2r.

5 Practical Skills and Archival Papers

Cases such as those just described above are rare. Much more frequent are abundant accounting documents that can be gleaned for fragmentary evidence, which are nonetheless equally laden with significance. More than one of the documents relating to Bianca Prampero Savorgnan permits us to focus on her managerial ability. These registers – some of which she kept for her own purposes and some in her role as her son's tutor – contain precious information about members of the family, their roles and tasks, their respective positions, and the sphere of women's agency. In addition to account books, such as *Rotoletto dell'anno 1693* (*Roll for the year 1693*),[29] in which Bianca recorded the income from her properties, there are others in which she noted income owed to her son,[30] much like his wife Olimpia would in the years to follow.[31] It is evident how over the span of three generations – that of Bianca's mother-in-law Eleonora, Bianca herself, and her daughter-in-law Olimpia – the women of the family had a direct responsibility in the management of the income of their respective sons and husbands. In particular, *Libro di notte della Sig.a Bianca Savorgnana* (*Signora Bianca Savorgnana's book of notes*) clearly illustrates the various activities of the noblewoman.[32] This book is a register of land rents, particularly credit notes held by the Savorgnans, and capital interests for a little over a decade (from 1667 to 1680). Many of these notes concern properties situated in the countryside beyond Aquileia, not far from an unstable "multiple" border, recently redrawn: the Republic of Venice to one side, the territories of the County of Gorizia and the new County of Gradisca, which had been separated from the County of Gorizia and therewith become an administratively

29 ASUD, Archivio Toppo, b. 113, *Rotoletto dell'anno 1693. Rotoletto che si consegna di scodere alla M.ma Bianca Savorgnana cavatto dalle partite del rottolo del Intrada del Feudo di Savorgnano*. A similar "roll" of accounts goes under the title *Rotolo di me Bianca Savorgnan 1692*, see ibid., b. 112, like others such as *Rotolo della entrata 1667–1675 di Bianca rel. del q. Aquilio Savorgnan*, ibid., b. 111.

30 ASUD, Archivio Toppo, b. 113, *Rotolo di Bianca Savorgnan q. Aquilio faciente per suo figlio Girolamo, 1693*.

31 Ibid., b. 113, *Rottolo di Olimpia Savorgnan faciente per Girolamo Savorgnano marito 1694 usque 1707*. In these documents we note that it is Girolamo's mother and wife respectively who keep his accounts. Also the *Rottolo 1690 di Girolamo Savorgnan* in fact contains notes by both Bianca and Olimpia. See ibid. b. 112. Girolamo's will mentions "*molte mie indisposizioni*" ("my many ailments") and the "*lunga compagnia di molti anni sofferta appresso di me*" ("long companionship of many years endured by my side") providing a glimpse of an uncertain state of health, perhaps the reason it was not possible for him to take care of the family's business.

32 ASUD, Archivio Toppo, b. 48, *Libro di notte della Sig. a Bianca Savorgnana*.

separate territory in 1647, to the other. On 17 September 1670, Bianca noted how her land agent had acquired and then sold wheat.[33] It was one note amidst the other specific accounting records, written to explain an entry in which the agent recorded increased earnings as a result of the acquisition of wheat based on two different measures – that of Gradisca (in the territory of Inner Austria) and that of Aquileia (in the Venetian territory) – and selling it according to the more profitable Gradisca system.[34]

The note is significant for more than one reason: it evidences that this noblewoman was accomplished in and knowledgeable about matters of economic management in general, and that her knowledge extended to an awareness of different systems of measurement and wheat prices concerning the strip of the border pertaining to the family's land rents, divided between different administrative and political systems.[35] It is furthermore significant because it allows us to approach, albeit within the confines of a single case, the realities of the everyday economic practices that took place on and across the border, and the often direct, not merely supplementary role assumed by women in these practices.[36]

---

33 "*Memoria come costuma il fattore alle Basse tior il formento dei Coloni a Campo Longo, san Lenardo e Fiumicello a misura di Gradischa; il resto tutto a misura d'Aquileia, e sul venderlo lo dà tutto a misura di Gradischa sì che ogn'anno per questa causa nel render conto mi dà qual cossa d'achresimento come apar nei miei registri.*" ASUD, Archivio Toppo, b. 48, *Libro di notte della Sig.a Bianca Savorgnana*, 6v.

34 The Gradisca *staio* (bushel) was equal to 85.79576 litres, while that of Aquileia was equal to 89.5791 litres. These measurement conversions for solids and liquids are drawn from Aleksander Panjek, *Terra di confine. Agricoltura e traffici tra le Alpi e l'Adriatico: la contea di Gorizia nel Seicento* (Mariano del Friuli: Edizioni della Laguna, 2000), p. 15 (for Gradisca) and from Gaetano Perusini, "Consuetudini giuridico-agrarie della Provincia di Udine," in Gaetano Perusini, *Vita di popolo in Friuli* (Florence: Olschki, 1961), pp. 173–270, here p. 253 (as far as Aquileia is concerned).

35 Bianca carefully checks the quantities of grain sold and the prices charged, demonstrating dexterity in dealing with the different units of measurement in use and their conversion. She writes on 11 January 1669: "*Ho fato la prova quante misure delle nostre d'avena che vano per pesenale quali sono giusto 10, fano misure 60 per starro.*" cf. ASUD, Archivio Toppo, b. 48, *Libro di notte della Sig.a Bianca Savorgnana*, 7v. See Alessio Fornasin, *Il mercato dei grani di Udine. Indagine per una storia dei prezzi in Friuli (secoli XVI–XVIII)*, in www.storiadivenezia.net/sito/saggi/fornasin_mercato.pdf, accessed 30 September 2020, for a general picture of the prices of grain.

36 It is interesting to investigate by means of their relationships with agents and administrators what specific competence and how much scope for decision making these women had in the running of family businesses. A detailed example concerning the division of roles between the lady of the house and her agents is that relating to Silvia Rabatta Colloredo, for which see Casella and De Martin Pinter, "Il cibo e la casa".

The assumption of economic management also involves control over documents and their conservation. In Bianca's case, the attention that she dedicated to the completeness and order with which the papers were kept is also evident on numerous other occasions, for example in June 1672 when she observed that some acts establishing the rent terms of some fields were missing.[37] Perhaps the noblewoman was prompted to organise her domestic papers because of a dispute that had arisen or simply out of the need to inform herself and check the contractual conditions of two leaseholders. Having established that some papers were missing from the household archive, and in order to check the basis of rights and legal entitlements, she began a retrospective search that allowed her to reconstruct the personal chain of those contracts' guarantees, the dates from which the stipulations applied, and the conditions upon which the properties were leased.

6 Expressing One's Will and Avoiding Conflict

The certifying function of the written word, of documentation, applies not only to relations with servants, agents, and leaseholders. It also holds true with regard to family members and serves to explain one's decisions more fully: women authors often made more ample use of words than men, either to justify the entire conduct and running of the household, or because they needed to support their decisions more forcefully in regard to the transfer of property and were thus writing to avert contestation or to promote conciliation.

As an example, we may consider the particularly pressing need of the noblewoman Bianca Prampero Savorgnan to keep records of her activities regarding her daughter's dowry in the final decades of the seventeenth century. Among the many "rolls" regarding Bianca there is one recording the income from her various properties (listed in alphabetical order at the beginning, as was customary, and, in this case, also in an index at the end) in which she subsequently

37 *"Per diligenca c'abi usata non ho mai potuto ritrovar in Casa ne l'instromento del livello ch'abiamo col Merlo, ne tan poco quello del Columbina, onde io ho regavato nei Rotoli antichi che quel del Merlo ha per sue sigurta il signor Camilo et il signor Paolo Caimi, onde dalle medesime sigurtà ho fato dar lume dove sia l'instrumento di questo livello mi diedero la presente memoria. L'anno 1627 9 febraro fu stipulato questo instrumento tra il signor Antonio del Merlo, et il signor Aquilio Savorgnano per mano del signor Mattia Paulitti, notaro colegialle. Quello del signor Columbina ho regavato che lo possede detto signor Isepo come herede della roba del signor Martio Brombila onde in caso di non poter haver il pagamento, serve per memoria come tutti i suoi beni di Nimis sono hobligati a questo livello, et anco altri beni ch'io non so specificarli."*

made use of the final two pages to address the question of her daughter's dowry in more specific and detailed notes. The issue was regarding land in the countryside south of Udine that, in 1675, was given as a dowry to Maddalena, who had married into the noble Arcoloniani family. Bianca claimed she had bought this land, as indicated by the registration of the act documented in the same notebook. This declaration of property served to anticipate the possibility – or, rather, the probability – of a contestation by other members of the family who might have opposed her decision or laid claim to their rights. It was, at the same time and more generally, an opportunity to provide a justification for her management of the family property following the death of her husband. Bianca was aware of possible objections and forestalled them with these words: "Whoever sees this register, may perhaps be surprised that I have given as a dowry to my daughter properties and rent income and may be surprised that I have not set aside a dowry with the surplus from the income over the twelve years that I have administered the house following the death of my husband; but I affirm that I would have endowed [her] fully [with money] had it not been for the circumstances that I will go on to describe."[38]

The circumstances Bianca referred to were all attributed to the difficulties, or rather, the misfortunes, as she called them, that occurred when a poor widow was left to run a family. She listed in detail the problems regarding her family interests or related expenses that she inevitably had to face after Aquilio's death: lawsuits and trials – for the most part successful – in the courts of Udine and Venice costing little less than a thousand ducats; the acquisition of properties and land; the revision and improvement of the terms of contracts relating to management and rent; further thousands of ducats in building expenses on the properties spread across Friuli and in the city of Udine, and on improvements and decorations in many of her houses that were now, she stated, in perfect condition. The expenses for the maintenance of her son, for his education in Bologna, and for his marriage were added to these. A son who, once married, "wants to do everything as it suits him and leaves me to untangle all our problems."[39]

38 *"Forse stupirano chi vedra il presente Rotollo ch'io abi dati beni in Dote questa mia Figliolla, et anco Livelli,* [...] *dico stupirano che non abi fatta questa Dotte coi avanzi del entratta per il corso d'anni 12 che sin ora ho manegiata la Casa dopo la morte del q.n Sig.r mio Consorte: onde dico che certo l'averei preparata abbondantissimamente se non fusero statte le ocasioni, che qui sotto rapresento".* ASUD, Archivio Toppo, b. 111, *Rotolo della entrada, 1667–1675 di Bianca rel del q. Aquilio Savorgnan*, 108r.

39 *"vuol far tutto a suo modo et mi lascia a me tutti gli intrichi"*, ibid., 109r.

Her daughter's dowry, as well as *il suplimento di dote* (the supplement to the dowry), is clearly traceable from her administrative records, kept year by year, and was set aside from other surplus from her income. Bianca did not fail to mention that among her duties was also to care for her elderly mother-in-law. Her intergenerational attitude was very explicit, and she explained without any circumlocution or concessions to an often superficial pietas that the *gran spesa* (great expense) involved would, a *Dio piacendo* (God willing), one day be repaid by the wealth that her mother-in-law would leave to her grandson, Bianca's son.[40]

Some years later, in 1680, after Bianca had seen to it that her son Girolamo was handsomely provided for and married, she saw fit to complain about his behaviour and took pains to define more clearly her daughter Maddalena's rights concerning the property I referred to earlier. The land should have been redeemed, but Bianca complained of a lack of liquid assets. The failure to conclude the redemption procedure and concern about the possible seizure of the property by Venice prompted Bianca to transfer some documents relating to this land to her son-in-law, under guarantee of his decision regarding the transfer of the property and her daughter's right of use.[41] So in this case it was the son-in-law who had to protect the dowry of his wife and the wishes of his mother-in-law. The writings act as repositories of memory and wishes and constituted the origin of a claim, the material for bringing an action to court and having one's rights recognised against those of rival claims by other individuals or the state.

This example illustrates quite clearly the strong links between direct involvement in the administration of property and family income, dowry choices and transfer, and concern with avoiding both conflict and legal claims. Bianca made a written memorandum of every action and administrative passage in the attempt to protect her choices and ward off the danger of legal claims. These notes provide us with a detailed and 'authentic' version of how Bianca's household was run during her widowhood. They also open up interpretive possibilities concerning both the various fields of family interest – patrimonial, judicial, administrative – through which her part can be traced, and her attention to "preserving the memory" of and justifying her activities and decisions.

A century earlier, Venere Bosina had also entrusted information about the properties that she had acquired, and those she wanted her ownership and wishes regarding transfers to be recognised, to paper specifications. Much

---

40 *"et anco ma bisogniato sempre mantener la vechia con gran spesa perche cumula dinari che dopo la sua morte mio figliollo li godera piacendo al Sig[no]re"*, ibid., 108r.

41 Ibid.

as Venere regularly recorded her loans and income, she also kept detailed accounts of every acquisition or decision that may subsequently have served to promote her rights. Some writings function to identify acquisitions that had not derived from her dowry. On a paper bearing the title *Memoria de li miei mobili ch' ho comprado mi che non sono a conto de dota* (memorandum of my furniture that I purchased that is not from dowry) we find a detailed list of personal property and clothing belonging to her as well as the respective beneficiaries of these items. It has been noted that the passing on of material objects was one form of female transfer with which women expressed preferences and emphasised the importance of certain ties.[42] Venere took care to record that the aforementioned clothes were bought with money from her income.[43] Her numerous memoranda – lists of household linen, furniture, and soft furnishings with which she had adorned her house, but also sums of money to maintain Bernardino (her nephew and, as she was childless, one of her heirs) on numerous occasions, on a trip to Venice, to Gorizia, and to buy fields and *vestir* Marina[44] (clothe Marina, his wife) – all served to emphasise her personal economic contribution to the maintenance of her family and to assure that it was recognised.[45]

In Venere Bosina's papers, as in those of Bianca Savorgnan, decisions concerning transfer – how, what, and to whom – were not rare or isolated occasions for making relatively autonomous decisions regarding their wealth. On the contrary, the documentation shows that they were accustomed to making decisions as a result of their relatively wide scope for self-determination and decision-making in economic and family administration. Undoubtedly, the act of making one's will, of leaving a record of one's own wishes, is a particularly delicate constellation that can influence both the balance of relationships and expectations that are taken for granted by heirs. At first, and in consideration of the continuation of the name of the family, Venere left her possessions to

42 Sandra Cavallo, "Proprietà o possesso? Composizione e controllo dei beni delle donne a Torino (1650–1710)," in *Le ricchezze delle donne. Diritti patrimoniali e poteri familiari in Italia (XIII–XIX secc.)*, ed. Giulia Calvi and Isabelle Chabot (Turin: Rosenberg & Sellier, 1998), pp. 187–207, here p. 202.

43 ASGO, Archivio Coronini Cronberg, Atti e documenti, b. 220, *Memoria de li miei mobili*; *Memoria de alcune cose che ho messo in casa*, (s.d.), with Venere Bosina's notes regarding expenses and credits dating back to 1552.

44 ASGO, Archivio Coronini Cronberg, Atti e documenti, b. 220, *Memoria de li dinari che ho dati ha m Barnardin.*

45 "*Memoria de alcune cose che ho messo in casa che ha queli che le receve non ten conto e si lava la bocha che non ha auto nente del mio se non la mia dota, per tanto li voio far veder in qualche parte*", cf. ASGO, Archivio Coronini Cronberg, Atti e documenti, b. 220.

her nieces and nephews from her husband's side. When, over time, she recognised that the male line would not continue, she altered her arrangements in favour of the children of her sister of the noble family Degrazia, inhabitants of the County of Gorizia.[46] Other examples could be cited, but the point to note is that with regard to both large and small patrimonies, possessions crossed the border leaving and entering families living in Venetian or Imperial Friuli. This phenomenon is such that when a considerable number of possessions were moved, there were wider public repercussions. These examples provide only a glimpse into a subject – that of dowries and the passage of goods in families extending across a border – that deserves further study in regard to both its juridical and economic implications. The problem with dowries is confirmed by an annotation placed in a document recording the economic situation in the territory of Gorizia in May 1655. The provincial States of Gorizia were engaged in estimating the wealth of the territory in the context of negotiations with the sovereign, which would soon afterwards have established new taxes. With this note the local nobility strategically emphasised the pervasive impoverishment of the territory in previous decades. Self-interestedly it informed the sovereign that there was one particular channel of impoverishment pertaining to elite families caused by cross-border marriages. As a result, the note continued, the sum of 90,000 Rhenish florins had passed to the Venetian State through dowries in the space of just a few years.[47] We know neither how this figure was calculated nor if it was accurate, but it was certainly big enough to signal an economic problem, and above all a recurrent practice, though not without a range of collateral effects and possible controversies.

Dowries, matrimony, and patrimony constitute, on both public and domestic levels, cause for attention, concern, and conflict. This is a well-known historiographical concept, but the ways in which I am concerned with these themes assume nuances and implications made greater by the fact of the border. Silvia Rabatta's testimony is very clear in this regard. The desire of one of her children to marry caused her concern, not only because of the economic burden on a family already embarked upon the marriage of another son but also because of his wish to set up house 'beyond the border'. Silvia Rabatta was born in the County of Gorizia, in Dornberg, at the heart of the *signoria* of her house but had come to live in Venetian Friuli when she had entered into the Colloredo family, marrying Filippo and abundantly safeguarding its continuance with the birth of

46 "*avea fato questo pur pensando che li fosse qualche eredi de lori ma quando ho veduto che ne m*[*esser*] *barnardin ne m*[*esser*] *francesco non auto eredi, me par che così vol il dovere e cosi voio che sia che vada a li mie nevodi da Goricia*". Ibid.

47 See Casella, "Noblesse de frontière," p. 6.

seven sons (as well as two daughters). In one of her many letters she expressed in no uncertain terms her opposition to the marriage and urged her eldest son to convince his brother to abandon this idea.[48] At the time that she wrote these words, in which she openly criticised her son's intention to strengthen ties with a family from the county, Silvia had already gained personal experience in the problems that could arise in managing 'transnational' legal claims. She had in fact been involved in a dispute about inheritance against the claims of Antonia Coronini who, like Silvia, belonged to one of the most important families of the county.[49] The dispute had, over a long period, cost her considerable expense. In a letter to her son Cesare she reminded him of the costs and (hoped for) benefits of that legal case: "Now I find myself in a dispute with the Rabatta heirs, and pray to God that I live long enough to see the end of this costly dispute to ensure that you will be richer than you are now."[50]

7 Conclusions

Along these lines, I could cite other such cases of 'border disputes'. Suffice it to say for now, that the legal views expressed involved, in this as in other cases, the interpretation of a complex framework of regulations relating to the subject of succession, and refer on both sides to different juridical systems layered with judicial particularisms, local customs, and sovereign legislations.

Too few studies on Friuli have placed a woman centre stage or considered the economic and decisional role of women within the family or in relations between families. Similarly, there is a lack of in-depth studies of matrimonial and patrimonial alliances and of the social relations between families in the two territories that straddled the border. Such studies are necessary to gain

48 ASUD, Archivio Perusini, b. 387, Lettera di Silvia Rabatta Colloredo al figlio Carlo, s.d., s.l.

49 In 1648 Antonio Rabatta established a *fideicommissum* for the male line of the family. In the absence of male heirs, his possessions would go to the next woman in the line of succession. Upon the 12 September 1794 death of his grandson Michele Rabatta (the son of Silvia's brother Antonio), who was the last male heir, Silvia and Antonia Coronini, sister of the late Michele, came into conflict over the inheritance. Silvia claimed to be the legitimate heir in so far as she was the closest in the line of succession to the testator; Antonia claimed she was the heir because she was the closest in the line of succession to the most recent heir.

50 "*Ora mi ritrovo in lite con li eredi Rabatta, ed pregate Dio che viva infine e terminata questa lite che molto mi costa che al ora restarete più sig.ri di quello siate*", ASUD, Archivio Perusini, b. 387, Lettera di Silvia Rabatta Colloredo, s.d.

a general understanding of the spaces for women's agency in the handling of minor and major conflicts that arose within families and the wider social sphere. On the basis of the abundant evidence found in individual and family documentation, it seems possible to infer a widespread and proven competence in the economic administration of property and the management of legal contentions. It is also fair to assume that women of the Friulian aristocracy – though the case of Venere Bosina suggests to apply this consideration beyond the nobility – maintained considerable spheres of influence that have hitherto been neglected by historians.

Widowhood has long been associated with greater liberty, and rightly so. However, it is not the only condition that allowed the women I have studied thus far to manage various aspects of the household and its economy. In some cases, married women as well were also active in a broad range of family matters: the running of family agrarian properties, buying of provisions, dealing with administrators and agents, suppliers, and traders as shown in the case of Silvia Rabatta; the record keeping and ordering of domestic papers or the handing down through women of administrative skills as in that of Bianca Savorgnan and the other women of that family. Writings concerned with the ordinary running of the house enable us to trace the outer limit of this sphere of influence, and related to the authority of husbands and sons, and the roles of other household figures (agents etc.) involved in its economic management. This is a first step in tracing the role of women in the rural economy, particularly in Friulian society.

Women, moreover, made decisions concerning the transmission of their property and expressed their wishes in all the written forms available to them: wills, memoirs, notes inserted in family books. It is interesting to see how legally binding documents sit side by side with memorialist writings that were intended to offer guidance to heirs.

To leave behind one's expressed wishes where one cannot compel was a concern these women shared, and one intended to avert conflict. But when conflict was inevitable, the ability to defend their interests and those of their families in a legal setting was no less of a common feature, whether on a grand or small scale, in the public or private sphere, on either side of the border: from Barbara Malvezzi who worked to free her son-in-law, the *Capitano* of the county, as a matter of great political importance, to Silvia Rabatta who opposed her niece's claims to properties across the border, which she maintained belonged to her. Although all of the issues addressed here require further research, the women I have discussed were clearly active in both conflict and mediation, whether of a formal or informal variety.

References

Ago, Renata. *La feudalità in età moderna*. Rome and Bari: Laterza, 1994.

Alfani, Guido, and Vincent Gourdon, eds. *Spiritual Kinship in Europe, 1500–1800*. Basingstoke: Palgrave McMillan, 2012.

Bardet, Jean-Pierre, Elisabeth Arnoul, and François-Joseph Ruggiu, eds. *Les écrits du for privé en Europe. Du Moyen Âge à l'époque contemporaine. Enquêtes, analyses, publications*. Bordeaux: Presses Universitaires de Bordeaux, 2010.

Bardet, Jean-Pierre, and François-Joseph Ruggiu, eds. *Au plus prés du secret des cœurs? Nouvelles lectures historiques des écrits du for privé en Europe du XVIe au XVIIIe siècle*. Paris: Presses de l'Université Paris-Sorbonne, 2005.

Beauvalet, Scarlett. "Les femmes dans le monde rural à l'époque moderne, XVIe–XVIIIe siècles." In *Ruralité française et britannique XIIIe–XXe siècles. Approches comparées*, edited by Nadine Vivier, pp. 89–102. Rennes: Presses Universitaires de Rennes, 2005.

Bellavitis, Anna. *Women's Work and Rights in Early Modern Urban Europe*. London: Palgrave McMillan, 2018 (orig. Ital. 2016).

Bellavitis, Anna, Manuela Martini, and Raffaella Sarti, eds. *Familles laborieuses. Rémunération, transmission et apprentissage dans les ateliers familiaux de la fin du Moyen Âge à l'époque contemporaine en Europe*, special issue of *Mélanges de l'École française de Rome*, 128–1 (2016).

Berthiaud, Emmanuelle, ed. *Paroles de femmes. Rôles et images de soi dans les écrits personnels, Europe, XVIe–XXe siècle*. Paris: Éditions Le Manuscrit, 2017.

Borderías, Cristina, and Manuela Martini, eds. *Per una nuova storia del lavoro*, special issue of *Genesis* 15–2 (2016).

Cargnelutti, Liliana. *Per la nobile signora. Una causa matrimoniale friulana del secolo XVIII*. Udine: Casamassima, 1992.

Casella, Laura. "Donne aristocratiche nel Friuli del Cinquecento tra strategie familiari e conflitti di fazione." In *Donne di potere nel Rinascimento*, edited by Letizia Arcangeli and Susanna Peyronel, pp. 89–128. Rome: Viella, 2008.

Casella, Laura. "Forme della memoria quotidiana. I libri femminili come oggetti materiali (Friuli, secc. XVI–XVIII)." In *Per Furio. Studi in onore di Furio Bianco*, edited by Alessio Fornasin and Claudio Povolo, pp. 133–42. Udine: Forum, 2014.

Casella, Laura. "I beni della nobiltà nel Friuli moderno: un quadro d'insieme e alcuni casi di rivendicazioni maschili e femminili a cavallo del confine." *Geschichte und Region / Storia e Regione*, 27–2 (2018): pp. 70–101.

Casella, Laura. "Mémoire de la révolte et mémoires de famille. La 'crudel zobia grassa' (1511) dans les livres de famille du XVIe siècle: brève histoire des manuscrits et des éditions." In *La Mémoire des révoltes en Europe à l'époque moderne*, edited by Alexandra Merle, Stéphane Jettot, and Manuel Herrero Sánchez, pp. 143–69. Paris: Classiques Garnier, 2018.

Casella, Laura. "Noblesse de frontière. Espace politique et relations familiales dans le Frioul à l'époque moderne." *Mélanges de l'École française de Rome. Italie et Méditerranée* 125–1 (2013): pp. 1–14, https://mefrim.revues.org//1007.

Casella, Laura. "Sapere e saper fare. Il 'Colloquio sopra gli studj delle donne', l'educazione e le scritture femminili nel Friuli del Settecento." *Atti dell'Accademia udinese di scienze lettere e arti*, CX-2017 (2020): pp. 143–69.

Casella, Laura. "Storia di un territorio di confine. Il Friuli veneto e asburgico in età moderna." In *Gli ebrei nella storia del Friuli Venezia Giulia. Una vicenda di lunga durata. Atti del convegno internazionale di studi, Museo Nazionale dell'Ebraismo Italiano e della Shoah (Ferrara, 12–14 ottobre 2015)*, edited by Miriam Davide and Pietro Ioly Zorattini, pp. 23–37. Florence: Giuntina, 2016.

Casella, Laura. "Un laboratorio politico di confine. La Patria del Friuli prima dell'Italia (secc. XVIII–XIX)." In *Nazioni d'Italia. Identità politiche e appartenenze regionali fra Settecento e Ottocento*, edited by Angela De Benedictis, Irene Fosi, and Luca Mannori, pp. 151–78. Rome: Viella, 2012.

Casella, Laura, Anna Bellavitis, and Dorit Raines. "Introduzione" to *Famiglie al confine*, special issue of *Mélanges de l'École française de Rome. Italie et Méditerranée* 125–1 (2013), https://mefrim.revues.org//1007.

Casella, Laura, and Albina De Martin Pinter, "Il cibo e la casa. Amministrazione domestica e consumi nelle scritture quotidiane di Silvia Rabatta Colloredo." *Genesis* 16–1 (2017): pp. 43–65.

Cassan, Michel. *Écritures de familles, écritures de soi. France-Italie XVI–XIX siècles.* Limoges: Pulim, 2010.

Cassan, Michel, Jean-Pierre Bardet, and François-Joseph Ruggiu, eds. *Les écrits du for privé. Objects matériels, objects édités*. Limoges: Pulim, 2005.

Cavallo, Sandra. "Proprietà o possesso? Composizione e controllo dei beni delle donne a Torino (1650–1710)." In *Le ricchezze delle donne. Diritti patrimoniali e poteri familiari in Italia (XIII–XIX secc.)*, edited by Giulia Calvi and Isabelle Chabot, pp. 187–207. Turin: Rosenberg & Sellier, 1998.

Chabot, Isabelle. *Ricostruzione di una famiglia. I Ciurianni di Firenze tra XII e XV secolo, con l'edizione critica del "Libro proprio" di Lapo di Valore Ciurianni e successori (1326–1429)*. Florence: Le Lettere, 2012.

Ciappelli, Giovanni. *Memoria, famiglia, identità tra Italia ed Europa nell'età moderna.* Bologna: Il Mulino, 2009.

Ciappelli, Giovanni. *Memory, Family, and Self: Tuscan Family Books and other European Egodocuments (14th–18th Century)*. Leiden and Boston: Brill, 2014.

Cicchetti, Angelo, and Raul Mordenti. *I libri di famiglia in Italia*, vol. 1: *Filologia e Storiografia letteraria*. Rome: Edizioni di storia e letteratura, 1985.

Connor, Rebecca E. *Women, Accounting and Narrative. Keeping Books in Eighteenth-Century England.* London and New York: Routledge, 2004.

Corbellini, Roberta, ed. *Interni di famiglia. Patrimoni e sentimenti di figlie, madri, mogli, vedove. Il Friuli tra Medioevo ed età moderna*. Udine: Arti grafiche friulane, 1992.

De Martin Pinter, Albina. "Lettere di donne. La scrittura epistolare femminile in Friuli tra 1650 e 1800. Un primo censimento, un'analisi di casi". PhD diss., Università degli studi di Udine, 2012/2013.

De Martin Pinter, Albina. "Reti di donne sul confine friulano. Lettere femminili nell'archivio Della Torre (XVII secolo)." *Mélanges de l'École française de Rome. Italie et Méditerranée* 125–1 (2013): pp. 97–114, https://mefrim.revues.org//1007.

Fabre, Daniel, ed. *Écritures ordinaires*. Paris: Éditions POL, 1993.

Fornasin, Alessio. *Il mercato dei grani di Udine. Indagine per una storia dei prezzi in Friuli (secoli XVI–XVIII)*. Online available at www.storiadivenezia.net/sito/saggi/fornasin_mercato.pdf, accessed 30 September 2020.

Galasso, Serena. "Il mestiere di sposa: genere, organizzazione domestica e scrittura contabile a Firenze nel XVI secolo." In *Donne e lavoro: attività, ruoli, complementarietà (sec. XIV-XIX)*, edited by Paola Avallone and Gemma Colesanti, pp. 121–151. Cagliari: Istituto di storia dell'Europa mediterranea, 2019.

Galasso, Serena. "La memoria tra i conti: alcune riflessioni sulle scritture domestiche di donne a Firenze (XV-XVI secolo)." *Quaderni storici* 1 (2019): pp. 195–223.

Jancke, Gabriele, and Claudia Ulbrich, eds. *Vom Individuum zur Person. Neue Konzepte im Spannungsfeld von Autobiographietheorie und Selbstzeugnisforschung*. Göttingen: Wallstein, 2005.

Jané, Oscar, and Patrice Poujade, eds. *Memòria personal. Construcció i projecció en primera persona e l'època moderna*. Madrid: Casa de Velazquez, 2015.

Lacoue-Labarthe, Isabelle, and Sylvie Mouysset, eds. *Écrire au quotidien*, special issue of *Clio. Histoire, Femmes et Sociétés* 35 (2012).

Martini, Manuela, and Anna Bellavitis, eds. *Household Economies, Social Norms and Practices of Unpaid Market Work in Europe from the Sixteenth Century to the Present*, special issue of *The History of the Family*, 19–3 (2014).

Mordenti, Raul. *I libri di famiglia in Italia*, vol. 2: *Geografia e storia*. Rome: Edizioni di storia e letteratura, 2001.

Musi, Aurelio. *Il feudalesimo nell'Europa moderna*. Bologna: Il Mulino, 2007.

Novi Chavarria, Elisa, and Vittoria Fiorelli, eds. *Baroni e vassalli. Storie moderne*, Milan: Franco Angeli, 2011.

Panjek, Aleksander. *Terra di confine. Agricoltura e traffici tra le Alpi e l'Adriatico: la contea di Gorizia nel Seicento*. Mariano del Friuli: Edizioni della Laguna, 2000.

Pascolini, Stefania. *Dal Talamo al chiostro. Ruoli femminili ed ideologia nobiliare in un matrimonio friulano del Seicento*. Udine: Forum, 2000.

Perusini, Gaetano. "Consuetudini giuridico-agrarie della Provincia di Udine." In Gaetano Perusini, *Vita di popolo in Friuli*, pp. 173–270. Florence: Olschki, 1961.

Plebani, Tiziana. *Le scritture delle donne in Europa. Pratiche quotidiane e ambizioni letterarie (secoli XIII-XX)*. Rome: Carocci, 2019.

Sahlins, Peter. *Boundaries. The Making of France and Spain in the Pyrenees*. Berkeley: University of California Press, 1989.

Smyth, Adam. "Money, Accounting and Life-Writing, 1600–1700: Balancing a Life." In *A History of English Autobiography*, edited by Adam Smyth, pp. 86–100. Cambridge: Cambridge University Press, 2016.

Tosato-Rigo, Danièle, ed. *Appel à témoins. Écrits personnels et pratiques socioculturelles (XVIe–XXe s.)*, special issue of *Études de Lettre*, 1–2 (2016).

Ulbrich, Claudia, Kaspar von Greyerz, and Lorenz Heiligensetzer, eds. *Mapping the "I". Research on Self-narratives in Germany and Switzerland*. Leiden and Boston: Brill, 2015.

Whittle, Jane. "Le travail des femmes dans les ménages ruraux anglais, 1450–1650: trois approches alternatives." In *Ruralité française et britannique XIIIe–XXe siècles. Approches comparées*, edited by Nadine Vivier, pp. 77–87. Rennes: Presses Universitaires de Rennes, 2005.

Whittle, Jane, and Elizabeth Griffiths. *Consumption and Gender in the Early Seventeenth-Century Household. The World of Alice Le Strange*. Oxford: Oxford University Press, 2012.

CHAPTER 11

A Dispute over Guardianship: The Trentino-Tyrolean Noble Trapp Family between 1641 and 1656

Siglinde Clementi

When Osvaldo Trapp, member of the Tyrolean low nobility, died in 1641, he not only left behind his widow Maria Anna Trapp, née Thun, and his seven-year-old son Osvaldo Ercole Trapp, but also a large amount of debt and numerous ongoing, unresolved conflicts.[1] In addition, his death sparked new constellations of family conflict. The most bitter disputes were between Osvaldo Trapp's widow Maria Anna and his brother Ernesto, canon of the cathedral of Trent.

This chapter analyses an individual case based on an interfamilial conflict between a widow of low nobility and the brother of her deceased husband. In so doing, it outlines the issue of maternal guardianship and widowhood within the low nobility, and domestic conflicts and constellations of power in families of low nobility during the seventeenth century.[2] The principal hypothesis

1 This chapter has been judiciously translated into English by Janine Maegraith. The original Italian quotes were translated into German by the author, and then translated into English. In order to illustrate the source material, original Italian passages of particular significance are indicated in brackets. I am grateful to Margareth Lanzinger and Janine Maegraith for their comments and numerous suggestions.

2 There is now an extensive body of literature on noblewomen: Heide Wunder, ed., *Dynastie und Herrschaftssicherung in der Frühen Neuzeit. Geschlechter und Geschlecht* (Berlin: Duncker & Humblot, 2002); Heide Wunder, "Geschlechterverhältnisse und dynastische Herrschaft in der Frühen Neuzeit," in *Frauen und Bildnis 1600–1750. Barocke Repräsentationskultur an europäischen Fürstenhöfen*, ed. Gabriele Baumbach and Cordula Bischoff (Kassel: kassel university press, 2003), pp. 15–37; Anke Hufschmid, *Adlige Frauen im Weserraum zwischen 1570 und 1700. Status – Rollen – Lebenspraxis* (Münster: Aschendorff, 2001); Beatrix Bastl, *Tugend, Liebe, Ehre. Die adelige Frau in der Frühen Neuzeit* (Vienna, Cologne, and Weimar: Böhlau, 2000); Martha Schad, *Die Frauen des Hauses Fugger von der Lilie (15.–17. Jahrhundert). Augsburg – Ortenburg – Trient* (Tübingen: Mohr, 1989); Ebba Severidt, *Familie, Verwandtschaft und Karriere bei den Gonzaga. Struktur und Funktion von Familie und Verwandtschaft bei den Gonzaga und ihren deutschen Verwandten (1444–1519)* (Leinfelden-Echterdingen: DRW-Verlag, 2002); Michaela Hohkamp, "Eine Tante für alle Fälle: Tanten-Nichten Beziehungen und ihre politische Bedeutung für die reichsfürstliche Gesellschaft der Frühen Neuzeit (16. bis 18. Jahrhundert)," in *Politiken der Verwandtschaft. Beziehungsnetze, Geschlecht und Recht*, ed. Margareth Lanzinger and Edith Saurer (Göttingen: v&r-unipress, 2007), pp. 147–68; *Tanten*, special issue of WerkstattGeschichte, 46 (2007). On medieval Tyrol see: Ute Monika Schwob, " 'Herrinnen' in Tiroler Quellen. Zur rechtlichen und sozialen Stellung der

 | DOI:10.1163/9789004456204_012

of this chapter is that different personal interests and property constellations entertained a high potential for conflict, whereby emotions and material interests formed a specific relationship that fundamentally shaped the conflicts and their character, and determined their basis, courses, and outcomes.[3] Transitional stages that permanently change familial relations are sensitive moments in family life and were especially prone to the outbreak of conflict. Such stages include the formation of a new family unit through marriage and offspring, and the threat to interfamilial balance by way of the death of a family member, especially the head of the household – the latter was the case with the Trapp family. Such moments were accompanied by rites of passage that can be understood both as modalities to overcome emotions, and as conflict prevention strategies.[4] Conflict prevention was most difficult in instances

adeligen Frau im Mittelalter," in *Literatur und bildende Kunst zum Tiroler Mittelalter*, ed. Egon Kühebacher (Innsbruck: Institut für Germanistik, 1982), pp. 157–82; Julia Hörmann-Thurn und Taxis, ed., *Margarete "Maultasch". Zur Lebenswelt einer Landesfürstin und anderer Tiroler Frauen des Mittelalters* (Innsbruck: Wagner, 2007); Christina Antenhofer, *Briefe zwischen Süd und Nord. Die Hochzeit und Ehe von Paula de Gonzaga und Leonhard von Görz im Spiegel der fürstlichen Kommunikation (1473–1500)* (Innsbruck: Wagner, 2007); on the early modern period see Siglinde Clementi, "Deren von Wolkenstein. Familienstrategien, Heirat und Geschlechterbeziehungen bei den Wolkenstein-Trostburg (um 1500 bis 1650)," in *Die Wolkensteiner. Facetten des Tiroler Adels in Spätmittelalter und Neuzeit*, ed. Gustav Pfeifer and Kurt Andermann (Innsbruck: Wagner, 2009), pp. 111–47; Siglinde Clementi, "Zur Ökonomie der Ehre. Heiratsgüter in Tirol um 1800," *Geschichte und Region / Storia e regione* 19–1 (2010), pp. 109–22 (special issue on Heiratsgüter / Doti). On noble family strategies see esp. Heinz Reif, *Westfälischer Adel 1770–1860. Vom Herrenstand zur regionalen Elite* (Göttingen: Vandenhoeck & Ruprecht, 1979); Karl-Heinz Spieß, *Familie und Verwandtschaft im deutschen Hochadel des Spätmittelalters: 13. bis Anfang des 16. Jahrhunderts* (Stuttgart: Steiner, 1993); Sylvia Schraut, *Das Haus Schönborn. Eine Familienbiographie. Katholischer Reichsadel 1640–1840* (Paderborn: Schöningh, 2005); and Stanley Chojnacki, *Women and Men in Renaissance Venice. Twelve Essays on Patrician Society* (Baltimore and London: The Johns Hopkins University Press, 2000).

3 See esp. Hans Medick and David Sabean, "Emotionen und materielle Interessen in Familie und Verwandtschaft: Überlegungen zu neuen Wegen und Bereichen einer historischen und sozialanthropologischen Familienforschung," in *Emotionen und materielle Interessen. Sozialanthropologische und historische Beiträge zur Familienforschung*, ed. Hans Medick and David Sabean (Göttingen: Vandenhoeck & Ruprecht, 1984), pp. 27–54; on marriage, see also Christoph Duhamelle and Jürgen Schlumbohm, "Einleitung: Vom 'europäischen Heiratsmuster' zu Strategien der Eheschließung?," in *Eheschließungen im Europa des 18. und 19. Jahrhunderts. Muster und Strategien*, ed. Christoph Duhamelle and Jürgen Schlumbohm (Göttingen: Vandenhoeck & Ruprecht, 2003), pp. 11–33; and on nobility see Silke Lesemann, "Liebe und Strategie. Adelige Ehen im 18. Jahrhundert," *Historische Anthropologie* 8–2 (2000), pp. 189–207.

4 See in general Arnold van Gennep, *The Rites of Passage* (*Les rites de passage, 1909*) (Chicago: University of Chicago Press, 1960).

where substantial and competing economic interests clashed, and in the emergence of a tug-of-war between different familial entities. Widowhood was thus a time that was especially prone to conflict; with the death of the head of the household we see the emergence of two difficult, controversial, and occasionally existential central issues. Firstly, who should take up the role of head of the household? Within the noble context, this also meant assuming a role of power that essentially determined the history of the noble "house" and therefore the livelihood of the family group. Secondly, how would provisions for the widow be organised, and which family group would be responsible for this? Where should the widow reside, who would finance the widow's seat?[5]

Following the tried and tested micro-historical approach,[6] this chapter takes up an individual case, namely the issue of guardianship following the death of Osvaldo Trapp in 1641 up until the death of his widow Maria Anna in 1656. The case study is reconstructed and contextualised as extensively as possible on the basis of the existing documents. The main issues discussed will include marital guardianship and widowhood, gender relations, familial lines of conflict, and power constellations amongst families of the lower nobility during the seventeenth century. My main thesis points to the agency of women in the

5 On (noble) widows see Giulia Calvi, *Il contratto morale. Madri e figli nella Toscana moderna* (Rome and Bari: Laterza, 1994); Giulia Calvi, "Diritti e legami. Madri, figli, Stato in Toscana (XVI–XVIII secolo)," *Quaderni storici* 86–2 (1994), pp. 487–510 (this is a special issue on *Costruire la parentela. Donne e uomini nella definizione dei legami familiari*, ed. Renata Ago, Maura Palazzi, and Gianna Pomata); Giulia Calvi, "Widows, the State and the Guardianship of Children in Early Modern Tuscany," in *Widowhood in Medieval and Early Modern Europe*, ed. Sandra Cavallo and Lyndan Warner (Harlow and New York: Longman, 1999), pp. 209–19; Giulia Calvi, "Rights and Ties that Bind: Mothers, Children, and the State in Tuscany during the Early Modern Period," in *Kinship in Europe. Approaches to Long-term Development (1300–1900)*, ed. David Warren Sabean, Simon Teuscher, and Jon Mathieu (New York and Oxford: Berghahn, 2007), pp. 145–62; Pauline Puppel, *Die Regentin. Vormundschaftliche Herrschaft in Hessen 1500–1700* (Frankfurt a. M. and New York: Campus, 2004); Sandra Cavallo and Lyndan Warner, eds., *Widowhood in Medieval and Early Modern Europe* (Harlow and New York: Longman, 1999); Martina Schattkowsky, ed., *Witwenschaft in der Frühen Neuzeit. Fürstliche und adelige Witwen zwischen Fremd- und Selbstbestimmung* (Leipzig: Leipziger Universitätsverlag, 2003).

6 On the possibilities of microhistory as a link between detailed history and macro level studies see Jürgen Schlumbohm, ed., *Mikrogeschichte – Makrogeschichte, komplementär oder inkommensurabel?* (Göttingen: Wallenstein, 1998), esp. his introduction "Mikrogeschichte – Makrogeschichte. Zur Eröffnung einer Debatte," pp. 9–32. See also Carlo Ginzburg, "Microstoria: due o tre cose che so di lei," *Quaderni Storici* 86 (1994), pp. 510–39; Hans Medick, *Weben und Überleben in Laichingen 1650–1900. Lokalgeschichte als Allgemeine Geschichte* (Göttingen: Vandenhoeck & Ruprecht, 1996); and Margareth Lanzinger, *Das gesicherte Erbe. Heirat in lokalen und familialen Kontexten. Innichen 1700–1900* (Vienna, Cologne, and Weimar: Böhlau, 2003).

lower nobility, who as widows, guardians, and regents could come into positions of considerable power. They were able to do so in spite of relatively precarious life situations that positioned them between two families and within a familial property regime characterised by undivided fraternal property, separation of marital property, and renunciation of inheritance against payment of dowry. Strategically used gender images and a likewise strategically deployed ambivalence in the use of property rights played a central role in the controversy surrounding this position of power.

1 Story and Contexts: Family Assets and Dividing Lines

When Osvaldo Trapp, the territorial ruler of Caldonazzo, died 1641 at the age of seventy-three, the event shook the family like an earthquake: numerous points, such as the central issue of the allocation of property between the Trapp brothers Osvaldo, Ferdinando, and Ernesto, had remained unresolved. Osvaldo also left a will that was prone to engender conflict. Apart from his wife, Osvaldo also left behind his seven-year-old son Osvaldo Ercole Trapp. Osvaldo Ercole was the son of Osvaldo's fourth, and Maria Anna Thun's second, marriage and was born in 1634 at the *Magnifica Corte di* Caldonazzo.[7] After three childless unions, Osvaldo's fourth marriage can be viewed as an extreme attempt to continue his own Trapp-Caldonazzo line; his brother Ferdinando and wife Anna Maria d'Arco, on the other hand, had secured the continuity of the Trapp-Beseno line with an abundance of children: nine children stemmed from the marriage, amongst them Giorgio Sigismondo Trapp, who would later become the curator of Osvaldo Ercole. Osvaldo Ercole's mother Maria Anna Thun was 20 years old when she remarried, and already the widow of the count Giorgio Filippo Liechtenstein. She had left a son from her first marriage behind at the house of Liechtenstein when she remarried.[8]

---

7 Südtiroler Landesarchiv (SLA), Archiv Trapp Churburg (ACh), Ältere Registratur (ÄR) 4314: autobiographical notes.

8 On the history of the Trapp family during the sixteenth and seventeenth century see Siglinde Clementi, *Körper, Selbst und Melancholie. Die Selbstzeugnisse des Landadeligen Osvaldo Ercole Trapp* (Cologne, Weimar, and Vienna: Böhlau, 2017), pp. 67–134. More cursorily but covering a longer period Andreas Trentini, *La Magnifica Corte di Caldonazzo: Castello Trapp*, dt. Ausgabe (Rovereto: Longo, 1993), *La Magnifica Corte di Caldonazzo: Castello Trapp* (Caldonazzo: Comune di Caldonazzo, 1990); Michelangelo Lupo, *I Trapp. Storia di una famiglia nel vecchio Tirolo* (Trento: Provincia Autonoma di Trento, 1997). In addition to Clementi on Osvaldo Ercole Trapp in *Körper, Selbst und Melancholie* see also Luciano Brida, "Appunti di vita di un feudatario secentesco: Osvaldo Ercole Trapp (1634–1710)," *Studi Trentini di Scienze Storiche* 62–1 (1983), pp. 335–66.

The family Trapp belonged to the most eminent of noble families in Tyrol and was well-integrated within the political structure of the county of Tyrol and the bishoprics of Trent and Brixen. The family held three important dominions and fiefdoms: Churburg, Beseno, and Caldonazzo. The Churburg, with the municipality of Matsch, was a fief of the counts of Tyrol, and Beseno was a fief of the prince-bishop of Trent. Caldonazzo held an intermediate position: it was sold to the Trapp family as a possession of the Tyrolean counts, but then assigned as a fiefdom by the prince-bishop of Trent; the authorities at the court in Innsbruck nonetheless continued to claim their sovereign rights. Throughout the entire early modern period this was the source of imbalances and power struggles that directly affected the Trapp family.[9] The family was also of special significance to the Tyrolean sovereigns in another respect: with Beseno and Caldonazzo the family held two strategically important dominions situated at the southern border of the Reich that had needed to be defended against the Venetians repeatedly.[10] Although their dominions were situated in the southern areas of the Tyrolean territory and within the reach of the prince-bishop of Trent, the Trapps, like most Tyrolean noble families, oriented themselves towards the court in Innsbruck. Innsbruck was the seat of the court and

9 Tiroler Landesmuseum Ferdinandeum, Bibliothek 841, pp. 33–38; Bibliothek 2114; SLA, ACh, ÄR 1411: Copia des Kaufvertrages von Caldonätsch, 6. März 1461 (copy of the sale contract of Caldonätsch, 6 March 1461); SLA, ACh, Lehenbriefe Caldonazzo: Lehenbrief 1523. See also Archivio di Stato di Trento (ASTN), Archivio del Principato Vescovile di Trento (APV), Atti Trentini XVII, Pos. 5, Signorie Trapp: Beseno e Caldonazzo: Lehenbrief Beseno 1604; Lehenbrief Caldonazzo 1604; Lehenbrief Beseno 1532; Lehenbrief Caldonazzo 1664.

10 On the history of the sovereignty of early modern southern Tyrol see esp. Marco Bellabarba, "Il principato vescovile di Trento dagli inizi del XVI secolo alla guerra dei Trent'anni," in *Storia del Trentino*, vol. 4: *L'età moderna*, ed. Marco Bellabarba and Giuseppe Olmi (Bologna: Il Mulino, 2000), pp. 15–70; Claudio Donati, "Il principato vescovile di Trento dalla guerra dei Trent'anni alle riforme settecentesche," in ibid., pp. 71–124; Marco Bellabarba and Serena Luzzi, *Il territorio trentino nella storia europea*, vol. 3: *L'età moderna* (Trento: Fondazione Bruno Kessler press, 2011); Sergio Benvenuti, *Storia del Trentino*, vol. 1: *Periodizzazione e cronologia politico-istituzionale* (Trento: Ed. Panorama, 1994); Marcello Bonazza, *Il fisco in una statalità divisa. Impero principi e ceti in area trentino-tirolese nella prima età moderna* (Bologna: Il Mulino, 2001); Reinhard Stauber, *Der Zentralstaat an seinen Grenzen. Administrative Integration, Herrschaftswechsel und politische Kultur im südlichen Alpenraum 1750–1820* (Göttingen: Vandenhoeck & Ruprecht, 2001); Hans von Voltelini, *Das welsche Tirol* (Erläuterungen zum Historischen Atlas der österreichischen Alpenländer 1/3/2) (Vienna: Holzhausen, 1919); for a comparison see Otto Stolz, "Geschichte der Gerichte Deutschtirols," *Archiv für österreichische Geschichte* 102 (1913), pp. 86–334 and more generally, Otto Stolz, *Geschichte des Landes Tirol* (Innsbruck: Tyrolia, 1955); Hans von Voltelini, *Giurisdizione signorile su terre e persone nel Trentino medievale* (Trento: Gruppo Storico Argentario, Bibl. Cappucini, 1981).

of the government of Tyrol, and the *Landstände* (estates) also met there for the *Landtage* (state diets).[11] Several members of the Trapp family had served the Tyrolean sovereigns.[12] The two lines had been ennobled to the rank of barony in 1605, and to earldom in 1655 and 1691 respectively.

The Trapp Beseno-Caldonazzo brothers lived on undivided property, in other words, the whole of the brothers' property comprising the dominions of Beseno and Caldonazzo was legally jointly owned and managed.[13] Five brothers from two marriages had initially lived on the undivided property, but the oldest brother Karl had died in 1602, and Giovanni and Ernesto from the second marriage had become clergymen: Giovanni joined the Teutonic Order and died in 1625, and Ernesto, who will take up an important role in this case study, became canon of Trent. In return for an annual apanage or payment from the family property and assurance that they would not be made responsible for the destiny of the house, both clerical brothers waived their property rights in favour of their married brothers Osvaldo and Ferdinando. The latter stipulation referred primarily to the high debts and simmering conflicts within the other line of the family, the Trapp of Churburg in Vinschgau.[14]

In spite of their formal joint management of the property, Osvaldo had taken on a role of leadership in the house of Trapp Beseno-Caldonazzo. He was the eldest and had managed affairs up until his brother Ferdinando's marriage in 1609. Thereafter, the two brothers often appeared together, or even in a

---

11 Werner Köfler, *Land, Landschaft, Landtag. Geschichte der Tiroler Landtage von den Anfängen bis zur Aufhebung der landständischen Verfassung 1808* (Innsbruck: Wagner, 1985).

12 Art. "Trapp," in *Genealogisches Handbuch des Adels*, Adelslexikon, vol. XIV, pp. 501–503.

13 On the undivided property of the Trapp brothers and on the following see Clementi, *Körper, Selbst und Melancholie*, pp. 73–80; Siglinde Clementi, "Undivided Brothers – Renouncing Sisters. Family Strategies of Low Nobility in Sixteenth- and Seventeenth-century Tyrol," in *Gender, Law and Economic Well-being in Europe from the Fifteenth to the Nineteenth Century*, ed. Anna Bellavitis and Beatrice Zucca Micheletto (London and New York: Routledge, 2019), pp. 149–64.

14 In contrast to the sons of the Gonzaga family of high nobility, who joined the clergy during the fifteenth century, two Trapp brothers actually renounced their property rights. On the Gonzaga see Charlotte Zweynert, "Ausgleichende Verfügungen, verbindende Gegenstände, konkurrierende Interessen. Das Testament des zweitgeborenen Francesco Gonzaga aus dem Jahr 1483," in *Beziehungen, Vernetzungen, Konflikte. Perspektiven Historischer Verwandtschaftsforschung*, ed. Christine Fertig and Margareth Lanzinger (Cologne, Weimar, and Vienna: Böhlau, 2016), pp. 37–65; and on the Trapp brothers Clementi, *Körper, Selbst und Melancholie*, pp. 88–91 and SLA, ACh, ÄR 1411: *Cessione delle ragioni* (transfer of claims) 1625; SLA, ACh, RA (rote Ablage) 42/11 (olim 15 ÄR 1141): renunciation of inheritance claims; SLA, ACh, 15 ÄR 1173: renunciation by Giovanni Trapp, 7 January 1625.

group of four (and following Giovanni's death, three) for major transactions.[15] The house of Trapp was heavily indebted; the Caldonazzo fiefdom had been used again and again to counter a lack of money. Amongst other instances, the tithe of Caldonazzo had been transferred to the house of Welsperg in 1613, and in 1616 the whole jurisdiction of Caldonazzo was sold to Giovanni Battista Someda di Chiaromonte, a brother-in-law of the Trapp brothers, for 40,000 Gulden.[16] Within a few months of the transaction, however, Osvaldo Trapp regretted the decision to sell and de facto rescinded the sale citing noncompliance with the terms of contract on the part of the Someda family. This initiated a conflict that proved highly problematic long after his death.

A second major area of conflict concerned the entire Trapp family in Tyrol, including the Churburg line. This opens up an area of research that has thus far been the subject of very little study: *Auszeigungen* amongst noble brothers or cousins.[17] *Auszeigung* meant the allocation of usage rights amongst noble brothers or cousins with undivided property. The entire property was, in principle, divided into approximately equal parts and allocated to the brothers, while remaining a joint estate. Usage rights, rather than property rights, were assigned. This practice had real advantages in comparison with an actual division of the estate: the procedure was, technically speaking, neither a definite nor actual division. Thus other heir claimants, such as sisters or brothers who had joined the clergy (*abgeschichtet*), could be excluded from the division by way of an *Auszeigung* and were unable to claim their dues. The provisional character of an *Auszeigung* made stipulations based on allocation of usage rights extremely conflict-prone. Within the Trapp family one such *Auszeigung* was stipulated in 1558 amongst the cousins Jakob and Oswald, therewith creating the two lines of the Trapp family in Tyrol, Churburg and Beseno-Caldonazzo.[18] The 1558 settlement was intended to be valid for seven years, and as long as it remained unrevised. The settlement effectively remained legally valid for many decades and generations, and was the cause of repeated controversy between

15 Clementi, *Körper, Selbst und Melancholie*, p. 90.

16 Ibid., p. 91.

17 Ibid., pp. 70–79; Clementi, "Undivided brothers"; Tiroler Landesordnung (TLO) 1573, III, 35. The Tiroler Landesordnung is edited in Josef Pauser and Martin P. Schennach, eds., *Die Tiroler Landesordnungen von 1526, 1532 und 1573. Historische Einführung und Edition* (Vienna, Cologne, and Weimar: Böhlau, 2018).

18 Clementi, *Körper, Selbst und Melancholie*, pp. 75–79; SLA, ACh, ÄR 3358: *Auszeigung zwischen Jakob und Oswald Trapp, 11. Jänner 1558* (allocation of usage rights between Jakob and Oswald Trapp, 11 January 1558); SLA, ACh, RA Schachtel 8 37/02 75(84): *Abschrift der Auszeigung zwischen Jakob und Oswald Trapp vom 25. August 1610* (copy of the allocation of usage rights between Jakob and Oswald Trapp on 25 August 1610).

the two main Trapp family lines of the Churburg and Beseno-Caldonazzo in Tyrol. At the end of the seventeenth century Sigismondo, the curator of Osvaldo Ercole, even invoked and successfully demanded an amendment to the settlement on the grounds of losses of territory to the disadvantage of the Beseno-Caldonazzo line.

When Osvaldo Trapp died in 1641, his will effectuated a settlement that curtailed the power of his brother and favoured his widow. Osvaldo used his will to pursue his firm intention to establish a separate line: he appointed his son Osvaldo Ercole as sole heir, and his wife Maria Anna as guardian, curator, and regent (*tutrice, curatrice e gubernatrice*).[19] Astonishingly, she was fixed to retain this role even in the case of remarriage; but she chose not to remarry. Seen in the context of the early modern low nobility, Osvaldo Trapp's will is in many respects remarkable: he allowed his widow an unmitigated position of power and, in spite of the undivided property situation of the brothers, favoured her over the male claimants of the Trapp-Beseno line of his brother Ferdinando in every respect. Even if there had been no legitimate children present, the widow would have been appointed principal heir and, again, would retain the position in the instance of remarriage. In fact, Osvaldo tried to prevent any interference from male claimants by making their restraint a precondition for their promised bequest. It was clearly Osvaldo's main objective to create a separate Trapp-Caldonazzo line, and to protect it against the hereditary titles of his brothers and their descendants.

Osvaldo's will was validated by the guardianship court in Innsbruck that was, according to the Tyrolean law code (*Tiroler Landesordnung*), responsible for the nobility.[20] On 26 April 1641, Maria Anna was officially appointed guardian of her son. Prior to this and as required by the Tyrolean law code, a probate inventory had been drawn up.[21] Subsequently, Maria Anna officially assumed legal guardianship of her son and pledged not to expose him *indefeso*, or unprotected, to the many interests of others.[22] In accepting the guardianship Maria Anna took on multiple responsibilities: the well-being and education of Osvaldo Ercole; the administration of the house of Trapp-Caldonazzo and therewith the preservation and, if possible, increase of assets; and the regency

19 SLA, ACh, ÄR 10/3: will of Osvaldo Trapp, 23 December 1635; SLA, ACh ÄR 3779: copy of Osvaldo Trapp's will by his son Osvaldo Ercole Trapp. See also Clementi, *Körper, Selbst und Melancholie*, pp. 95–97.

20 TLO 1573, III, 48.

21 SLA, ACh, ÄR 1689: probate inventory Osvaldo Trapp, 6 April 1641.

22 SLA, ACh, ÄR V-1e: guardian deed of Maria Anna Trapp; SLA, ACh, ÄR 1411: comprehensive holdings on the guardianship of Maria Anna Trapp.

of the land court of Caldonazzo, which comprised the high and the low jurisdiction. Maria Anna herself summarised her fields of duties as follows:

> Nel governo tutelare conferitomi begnignam.te da V.A.S. per la dispositione testamentaria del q. Sig.r Barone Osbaldo mio consorte e sig.re devo osservar molte cose, ma principalm.te l'infrascritti capi
>
> 1. Devo prestar l'esata obedienza e riverenza à V.A.S.
> 2. Amministrar la giustizia indifferentemente, senza aggravio di alcuno
> 3. Governar bene il pupillo et procurar ch'impari et riesca virtuoso
> 4. Haver bona cura della sua roba contener buona economia
> 5. Tener neta la giurisditione da banditi, e mantener la quiete nei sudditi.[23]
>
> According to the guardianship and regency which I was awarded by His Majesty on the basis of the testamentary decision of baron Osvaldo, my husband and lord, I have to observe many things, but especially the following:
>
> 1. To show strict obedience and subservience to His Majesty
> 2. To exercise just Jurisdiction without burdening anybody
> 3. To educate the ward well and to see that he learns well and grows into a virtuous man
> 4. To administer and duly run his estate well
> 5. To keep the municipality free of criminals and to keep the subjects calm.

Ernesto Trapp, the brother of Osvaldo, did not agree with the transfer of guardianship to his sister-in-law. He pointed out that the agnates had not been sufficiently involved in this process, and repeatedly intervened by way of the government in Innsbruck.[24] The guardianship commission, on the other hand, referred to the Tyrolean law code, which allowed parents to appoint each other as guardians, and the fact that these intentions must, in principle, be respected.[25] According to that law code, and within the jurisdiction thereof, it

23 Tiroler Landesarchiv (TLA), Allgemeines Leopoldinum, Littera D, Nr. 66: letter from Maria Anna Trapp, 15 October 1641.

24 TLA, Allgemeines Leopoldinum, Littera D, Nr. 66: letters from Ernesto Trapp to the *Landesfürstin* Claudia de Medici, 15 February 1641 and 21 February 1641; SLA, ACh, ÄR 1261: papers on the bankruptcy proceedings 1616–1641.

25 TLO 1573, III, 48.

was not only fathers that decided on who should be the guardian of their children, but theoretically mothers as well. This was not the case in early modern Tuscany where, as Giulia Calvi has shown, fathers were solely responsible for deciding who would be the child's guardian.[26] How this legal norm was practised in Tyrol and, more precisely, whether both mothers and fathers determined the guardian or guardians of their children by will and whether this decision was respected by the guardianship court, is still in need of investigation. That notwithstanding, the intentions of the parents could not simply be ignored.[27]

The accusations lodged against Maria Anna by Ernesto Trapp at the court in Innsbruck were serious: according to him, Maria Anna squandered the little remaining wealth and posed a burden to the heavily indebted house; she was unable and unjust in exercising jurisdiction, the subjects needed a "padrone," a master. Moreover, and whereas the Trapp brothers had repeatedly rendered good service to the sovereign, in his eyes the widow was not suited to command the strategically important southern border of the Reich. He had not waived his share of the income of Caldonazzo only to leave it to his sister-in-law to harm the house. He would be prepared to take responsibility for the indebted house. His former renunciation should not be used against him but rather act to nullify his brother's will. The brothers' property remained undivided, and the thought of being dependent on the widow was intolerable. Maria Anna should redeem her dowry and withdraw to her birth family so that he could exercise his – in his view legitimate – sovereign rights without impediment (*ordinata a Casa sua a godersi la Sua dotte, et io possa senza molestia e pericolo procedere*).[28] In addition to Ernesto, Ferdinando, the married brother and holder of Beseno also intervened. Maria Anna clearly understood the intentions of her two brothers-in-law. In a letter to the government in Innsbruck she wrote that they tried to interfere with the jurisdiction of Caldonazzo by using the argument that the Trapp brothers' property was still undivided (*che non syino seguite fra il sig.r mio consorte e sig.ri frat.i le perfette divisioni*).[29] Against this she argued that she, as guardian and regent, had received the jurisdiction of Caldonazzo, and that her brother-in-law Ferdinando held that of Beseno. Now,

26 Calvi, *Il contratto morale*; Calvi, "Diritti e legami"; Calvi, "Widows, the State"; Calvi, "Rights and Ties".

27 TLO 1573, III, 48.

28 TLA, Allgemeines Leopoldinum, Littera D, Nr. 66: letters from Ernesto Trapp to the Landesfürstin, 15 February 1641 and 21 February 1641; SLA, ACh, ÄR 1261: papers on the bankruptcy proceedings 1616–1641.

29 SLA, ACh, ÄR 206: letter from Maria Anna Trapp to the Landesfürstin 1641.

on the pretext of helping her, he was attempting to incorporate Caldonazzo as well. Ernesto acted solely out of personal interest.

Maria Anna knew how to defend herself against the accusations that were brought forward against her in Innsbruck. As quoted above, she wrote a pre-emptive letter to the government, carefully listing her duties as a guardian, regent, and head of the household. She declared that she was aware of her duties, and that she performed them conscientiously. She appealed to Claudia de Medici who, as *Landesfürstin* (territorialsovereign),[30] played the roles of protector and supreme guardian. She presented Claudia de Medici a declaration from every mayor in the jurisdiction of Caldonazzo as well as the dean of Calceranica – the deanery to which Caldonazzo belonged to – who all certified her *buon governo*, good governance. In spite of heavy debts, she had not sold anything, and had curtailed household expenses. She exercised proper jurisdiction and took rigorous action against criminals.[31]

Maria Anna also faced severe incrimination from the princely Fiscal: Fiscal Giovanni Battista Hippolito, who the Upper Austrian Tyrolean government had appointed the court official in the "Welsch Confines," which were the southern-most territorial confines that belonged to the county of Tyrol, had accused her of turning to the prince bishop of Trent. This, in view of the political balance of power in southern Tyrol at that time, brought her under suspicion of treason.[32] The county of Tyrol and the prince-bishopric of Trent disputed their respective influence over Caldonazzo: Tyrol claimed jurisdiction while Trent insisted that it was their episcopal fief. By turning to Trent, Maria Anna could be regarded as having been disloyal to the county of Tyrol. The Fiscal's accusations are otherwise astoundingly similar to those of her brother-in-law Ernesto: according to Hippolito, who argued as a deputy of the county of Tyrol to defend its interests in the southern parts of the county, she led a profligate life, did not take good care of the jurisdiction, and was utterly unsuitable

30 As guardian and regent of her underage son Ferdinand Karl, Claudia de Medici was sovereign of Tyrol from 1632 to 1646. The older as well as the newer historiography ascribe to her a prudent and independent regency. See Sabine Weiss, *Claudia de' Medici. Eine italienische Prinzessin als Landesfürstin von Tirol (1604–1648)* (Innsbruck: Tyrolia, 2004).

31 TLA, Allgemeines Leopoldinum, Littera D, Nr. 66: letter from Maria Anna Trapp to the Landesfürstin, 15 October 1641.

32 TLA, Allgemeines Leopoldinum, Littera D, Nr. 66: letter, 5 April 1641. On the trial of power between the territorial prince of Tyrol and the prince bishop of Trent see Clementi, *Körper, Selbst und Melancholie*, pp. 81–86 and the bibliography in note 10. The *Fiskal* was a princely court official who was responsible for the collection of fines and for distraints. He had his seat at the princely law courts in Rovereto.

to command the strategically important borderland.[33] The accusations against Maria Anna dragged on for the entire year of 1641, but the widow was nevertheless able to assert her position. Neither the petitions of her brothers-in-law nor that of Hippolito were successful: the government in Innsbruck affirmed Maria Anna's position as guardian of Osvaldo Ercole Trapp, as head of the Trapp-Caldonazzo house, and as regent of the dominion of Caldonazzo.[34] In the ensuing years Maria Anna weathered a costly bankruptcy proceeding that considerably weakened the dominion of Caldonazzo: the main creditors pushed their demands through, the Welsperg regained the tithe of Caldonazzo, and the Someda obtained half of the dominion of Caldonazzo. The Trapp family book contains an entry describing how, following the bankruptcy of the house, Caldonazzo yielded a miserable sum (*somma misera*).[35]

Maria Anna conducted the guardianship and regency in the face of the constant animosity of brother-in-law Ernesto, who could not come to terms with her holding legal guardianship. In letters to her son she complained that Ernesto wanted to move her out (*sgomberare*), that he did not shy away from conspiring with Someda, and that he was even trying to win over Osvaldo Ercole.[36] Maria Anna's letters also bemoan that her son showed her too little sympathy (*poca carita filiale*), and that she faced unjustified accusations; it was not her fault that the house was fraught with problems, and she had done her utmost to restore it (*se la Casa è travagliata mia non è la colpa, havendo fatto il mio potere per riparare al possibile*).[37] During his mother's guardianship, Osvaldo Ercole clearly found himself in a conflict of loyalty between his mother and uncle Ernesto. He was only eighteen years old, and far away from home: he had been a page at the court of the archduke Ferdinand Karl in Innsbruck since 1652. In the end, Osvaldo Ercole decided in favour of the more powerful party and asked the court in Innsbruck to revoke his mother's guardianship and transfer

33 TLA, Allgemeines Leopoldinum, Littera D, Nr. 66: letter from Hippolito to the government, 17 October 1641.

34 TLA, Allgemeines Leopoldinum, Littera D, Nr. 66: letter from Wolkenstein/Pappen, 11 July 1641 and 15 March 1641.

35 Clementi, *Körper, Selbst und Melancholie*, pp. 102–09. SLA, ACh, ÄR 1261: papers on the bankruptcy proceedings 1616–1641; SLA, ACh, ÄR 1303: Concursio Trappio Biseni 1649; TLA, Kopialbuchserie, Prozessakten Nr. 2392: Prozessakten in Sachen Maria Anna Freyin von Trapp 1648 (litigation records on the case of Maria Anna Freyin von Trapp 1648); SLA, ACh, ÄR 1369: Urteil Cosmo de Cosmi im Trappschen Konkursverfahren (verdict Cosmo de Cosmi on the Trapp bankruptcy proceedings); SLA, ACh, *Libro degli Annali della Famiglia de Conti di Trapp*.

36 SLA, ACh, ÄR 1847: letter from Maria Anna to Osvaldo Ercole, 30 October 1653; SLA, ACh, ÄR 1570: letter from Maria Anna to Osvaldo Ercole, 1 June 1652.

37 Ibid.

it to his uncle Ernesto. In April 1652, he sent a petition concerning the matter in which he substantiated his request to the government in Innsbruck: owing to his mother's impotence (*impotenza*), little of his property remained (*ridotto il mio patrimonio quasi a nulla*).[38] Worse still was the protest of the remaining subjects, who did not feel sufficiently protected by Maria Anna as regent, and who would refuse to obey him; they indicated that they could not serve two lords – him and the Someda: "*quelli pochi sudditi che restano mi hanno con piu lettere avisato e ultimamente anche protesta, che non vedono in detta mia madre protetione alcuna ni sufficienza di diffesa vogliono di tutto negarmi l'obbedienza, allegando non poter nello stesso tempo servir di due padroni che son io et i sig. Somedi.*"[39]

According to this letter, it was not only Maria Anna's posited weakness that was the problem, but also the peculiar property situation following the bankruptcy proceedings, which had resulted in the dominion of Caldonazzo having two owners: Osvaldo Ercole as the heir of Osvaldo Trapp, and the Someda brothers as principal creditors. In his petition to the territorial prince, Osvaldo Ercole described himself as a poor abandoned ward (*povero abandonato pupilo*) who had no man to advocate for him (*non ho huomo, che per me dici la ragione*). He emphatically requested the appointment of his uncle Ernesto as his next agnate as his guardian, who was a man of recognised integrity (*homo giá di conosciuta integrità*),[40] Osvaldo Ercole also referred to the fact that, as an eighteen-year-old, he had the right to choose his own guardian.[41] This was nothing less than an instance of averting his outright ruin (*massime concorrendo le cause della mia totale rovina*).[42] This time, Innsbruck agreed and informed the relevant parties about the change of guardianship at the beginning of May 1652. The official letter mentions Maria Anna Trapp's alleged bad administration and economy (*ybler administration vnd haushaltung*).[43] A decisive factor may also have been a recurrent and severe illness of the widow; documents

38 SLA, ACh, ÄR 1382: petition by Osvaldo Ercole to the Landesfürst, regarding the *Kuratel* of his mother Maria Anna Trapp, undated.

39 Ibid.

40 Ibid.

41 The Tyrolean law code does not contain a reference to a free choice of a guardian (*Gerhab* and *Curator* in the TLO.) Perhaps Osvaldo refers to a common practice, and perhaps even women had, in practice, the right to choose their own gender guardian (*Geschlechtsvormund*) beginning at the age of eighteen.

42 SLA, ACh, ÄR 1382: petition by Osvaldo Ercoles to the Landesfürst, regarding the *Kuratel* of his mother Maria Anna Trapp, undated.

43 TLA, Kopialbuch, Parteibuch 1652: letter from Ernesto Trapp, 3 May 1652, letter from Ernesto Trapp, 5 June 1652, fol. 177r.

frequently mention a dangerous indisposition (*grave indispositione* or *geferliche leibsindisposition*), but provide no further specification or description.[44]

Consequently, Maria Anna found herself in a very difficult situation: in 1652, at the age of forty-nine, she was deprived of both the guardianship and regency. She was now entirely cut off from the revenues of the jurisdiction of Caldonazzo, which she had administered for over ten years since the death of her husband in 1641. As a result of the bankruptcy proceedings, she had not benefited from the generosity shown in her husband's will through a bequest of over 2,000 Gulden and her dowry remained with her birth family, in the hands of her brothers Thun. In letters to her son she complained bitterly about her situation in life: she had no money (*priva di soldi*) and, since Ernesto had forbidden everybody to give her anything, she was cut off from the subject's rent in kind. She didn't even have firewood to heat, which made her many phases of her illness nearly unbearable. In June 1653 she furthermore wrote that her dowry did not yield enough upon which to survive (*la mia dotta non mi rende stipendio*).[45] Maria Anna's dowry comprised 2,000 Gulden, but as a widow she could count on a capital of 6,175 Gulden which, with the effective interest rate of five percent, yielded 300 Gulden per year. To compare, Osvaldo Ercole was awarded an annual bequest from the family property of over 600 Gulden when he was put under tutelage in 1669.[46] The available capital for Maria Anna was composed of her dowry of 2,000 Gulden and additional inheritances from her father, brother, and mother. The fund remained, however, with her birth brothers and was never paid out. She received only annual accrued interest of five percent. During this time of relative need, Maria Anna turned again and again to her brothers, pleading for early payment of the annual interest.[47] The separation of marital property that was at that time prevalent in Tyrol resulted in a situation wherein non-governing widows had to live off the returns of their dowry, marriage portion, or ideally, and as was the case for Maria Anna, further bequests. If no other provisions, such as a marriage contract, had been

44 SLA, ACh, ÄR 1570: letter from Maria Anna to Osvaldo Ercole, 11 October 1653; TLA Kopialbuch, Parteibuch 1649: letter to Cosmo de Cosmi, 21 January 1649, fol. 25r–v; Archivio Provinciale di Trento (APTN), Archivo Thun di Castel Thun (ATh) 33.14 (1): letter from Maria Anna Trapp to Monsignor Sigmund Graf Thun, 3 October 1649.

45 SLA, ACh, ÄR 1971: letter from Maria Anna to Osvaldo Ercole, 28 June 1653.

46 APTN, ATh A 21.11 (4): Kostenaufstellung; A 33.10 (1): Rechnungsbuch, 22. April 1647; on Osvaldo Ercoles bequest SLA, ACh, Libro degli Annali della Famiglia de Conti di Trapp.

47 See for example: APTN, ATh A 33.14 (1): letter from Maria Anna Trapp to Christoforo Thun, 6. June 1652 or APTN, ATh A 33.14 (1): letter from Maria Anna Trapp to Christoforo Thun, 26 March 1656.

made this situation could result in relative and status-specific poverty during widowhood.[48]

Following the bankruptcy of the house and change of guardianship, Maria Anna and her brother-in-law Ernesto interpreted the situation of the family and of rule in entirely different ways. Maria Anna insisted on her rights: in spite of the loss of the legal guardianship, a part of the revenues of the dominion of Caldonazzo were due to her, surely because she saw herself as part of the house of Trapp-Caldonazzo, and specifically because Osvaldo had, in addition to her dowry, made her a bequest in his will. Ernesto, on the other hand, demanded that Maria Anna settled for the revenues of her dowry and hoped, as was clearly worded, that she would leave the estate in Caldonazzo. This, however, the widow did only sporadically and tentatively. As she herself clearly suspected when she wrote of disposal (*rimozione*) and removal (*sgomberare*), the much-lamented bad treatment she received was intended to make her leave. Accordingly, Maria Anna remained in Caldonazzo until she died in 1656.

2 Interpretations: Gender Images and Relations

This case study makes it possible to address open questions and debates surrounding early modern gender relations and familial power constellations

48 On early modern noble marital property regimes in Tyrol see Siglinde Clementi, "Hybrid Legal Culture among the Early Modern Tyrolean Nobility. Marriage Contracts and the Symbolic Value of Assets," in *Gender, Law and Material Culture. Immobile Property and Mobile Goods in Early Modern Europe*, ed. Annette Caroline Cremer (London and New York: Routledge, 2021), pp. 93–119; Siglinde Clementi, "Heiraten in Grenzräumen. Vermögensarrangements adeliger Ehefrauen und -männer im frühneuzeitlichen Tirol," *Geschichte und Region / Storia e regione* 28–2 (2018), pp. 44–69; Clementi, "Deren von Wolkenstein"; Clementi, "Zur Ökonomie der Ehre". The marriage contracts of the Wolkenstein family included provisions to prevent any financial difficulties by awarding the daughters a dower befitting their social status. On marital property arrangements in early modern Tyrol see also Margareth Lanzinger, "Von der Macht der Linie zur Gegenseitigkeit. Heiratskontrakte in den Südtiroler Gerichten Welsberg und Innichen 1750–1850", in Margareth Lanzinger, Gunda Barth-Scalmani, Ellinor Forster, and Gertrude Langer-Ostrawsky, *Aushandeln von Ehe. Heiratsverträge der Neuzeit im europäischen Vergleich* (Cologne, Weimar, and Vienna: Böhlau, 2010, 2nd edition 2015), pp. 205–367; Margareth Lanzinger and Janine Maegraith, "Konkurrenz um Vermögen im südlichen Tirol des 16. Jahrhunderts," *L'Homme. Z.F.G.* 27–1 (2016), pp. 15–31; Christian Hagen, Margareth Lanzinger, and Janine Maegraith, "Competing Interests in Death-Related Stipulation in South Tirol c. 1350–1600," in *Planning for Death. Wills and Death-Related Property Arrangements in Europe, 1200–1600*, ed. Mia Korpiola and Anu Lathinen (Leiden and Boston: Brill, 2017), pp. 88–118; and Janine Maegraith in this volume.

within the low nobility. The conflicts between widow Maria Anna and her brother-in-law Ernesto Trapp illustrate two fundamentally clashing positions that revolve around different interpretations of property situations. Based on her deceased husband Osvaldo's will, Maria Anna Trapp referred to her rights as guardian and regent, and believed that the administration of the individualised property was due to her, and basing his argument on the brothers' undivided property, Ernesto Trapp insisted on his rights as Osvaldo's brother. Following the logic of undivided property as he understood it, Ernesto Trapp denied Maria Anna's administrative expertise, and worked to prevent a situation wherein he would be dependent on her as regent of Caldonazzo. Maria Anna, according to the logic of individualised property, accused him of pursuing purely personal interests.

Both men and women employed deep-seated gender concepts as weapons within the conflict over guardianship. Gender roles were used as arguments against the female regency in situations where women were considered most vulnerable: rule and defence. Control and protection of the subjects and border defence were principal responsibilities for both male and female regents. Women could easily be denied the respective skills on the basis of their weaker constitution and reputation to this effect. In spite of legal concessions for widows or in instances of absent male heirs, (male) reservations against female regency and women as vassals have a long tradition. These objections repeatedly make use of the same arguments and notions regarding the gender roles of women: unfitness to bear arms, inconsistency (important for the legal obligation of providing advice as a vassal), lack of assertiveness, and constrained legal capacity above all in respect to the gender guardianship.[49] As shown by the decision of the guardianship court regarding the controversy between Ernesto and Maria Anna Trapp, such arguments were not always successful.

The accusation of mismanagement and squandering the estate were perhaps less relevant in terms of gender roles, this was aimed more at the fact that squanderers could, independent of gender, be put under guardianship.[50] In this case too, however, the accusation was unsuccessful. Osvaldo Ercole's petition evoked the image of the strong, honourable man in contrast

49 See Hedwig Röckelein, "De feudo femineo – über das Weiberlehen," in *Herrschaftspraxis und soziale Ordnung im Mittelalter und in der frühen Neuzeit. Ernst Schubert zum Gedenken*, ed. Peter Aufgebauer and Christine van den Heuvel (Hanover: Hahnsche Buchhandlung, 2006), pp. 267–84 and Elisabeth Koch, *Maior dignitas est in sexu virili. Das weibliche Geschlecht im Normensystem des 16. Jahrhunderts* (Frankfurt a. M.: Klostermann, 1991), pp. 167–78.

50 TLO 1573, III, 53.

to the non-assertive mother.[51] The government's considerations in disempowering Maria Anna and transferring guardianship to Ernesto Trapp are unfortunately not recorded, and thus cannot know the extent to which gender preconceptions affected the judicial decision-making process. The fact is that gender preconceptions were made use of and strategically deployed. This was done by women as well as men: Maria Anna described herself as a poor, undefended (*indefesa*) widow who deserved, and was in need of, special protection from the *Landesfürstin*. The image of, and discourse surrounding the poor widow in need of protection was prevalent during early modern times.[52] In this case, it served Maria Anna as an effective appeal to the sovereign who was herself a regent by virtue of widowhood. In her lawsuit against the fiscal court official Hippolito, Maria Anna presented a gender and status-specific argument: Hippolito treated her not as a lady, but in a disrespectful way one wouldn't even treat a peasant woman (*mi fa di quei torti che non si farebbero a una povera contadina no che a una Dama della mia nascita*).[53] She blamed Ernesto for self-interest, and therewith took the same line as the law, which defined self-interest as a reason for exclusion from a guardianship case. The Tyrolean law code provided that persons with claims on the property of the children in question could not be their guardians.[54] Giulia Calvi has shown that, in early modern Tuscany for example, the local guardianship court preferred mothers over male family members as guardians, as the former were not entitled to inherit and one might expect that they were more strongly interested in the welfare of the children than the agnates might have been.[55]

---

51 SLA, ACh, ÄR 1382: petition by Osvaldo Ercole to the Landesfürst, regarding the *Kuratel* of his mother Maria Anna Trapp, undated.

52 Gesa Ingendahl, "Elend und Wollust. Witwenschaft in kulturellen Bildern der Frühen Neuzeit," in *Witwenschaft in der Frühen Neuzeit. Fürstliche und adelige Witwen zwischen Fremd- und Selbstbestimmung*, ed. Martina Schattkowsky (Leipzig: Leipziger Universitätsverlag, 2003), pp. 265–79; Eve Rosenhaft, "'... mich als eine Extraordinarium'. Die Witwe als widerstrebendes Subjekt in der Frühgeschichte der Lebensversicherung," in *Stationen einer Hochschullaufbahn. Festschrift für Annette Kuhn zum 65. Geburtstag*, ed. Udo Arnold, Peter Mayers, and Uta C. Schmidt (Dortmund: edition ebersbach, 1999), pp. 292–309, here pp. 304–05; in general see Britta-Juliane Kruse, *Witwen. Kulturgeschichte eines Standes in Spätmittelalter und Früher Neuzeit* (Berlin and New York: de Gruyter, 2007).

53 TLA, Allgemeines Leopoldinum, Littera D, Nr. 66: letter from Maria Anna Trapp to the Landesfürstin, 17 October 1641.

54 TLO 1573, III, 48.

55 Calvi, *Il contratto morale*; Calvi, "Widows, the State"; Calvi, "Rights and Ties"; Calvi, "Diritti e legami". See on the practice of widows as "donna et madonna" in patrician families in late medieval Venice Chojnacki, *Women and Men*.

During his conflict "with" sister-in-law Maria Anna Trapp, Ernesto Trapp tried to take advantage of the precarious intermediate position of wives, and in particular widows, of the low nobility, who lived between two families and two houses – their family of origin and the family into which they had married. He demanded the disempowerment of Maria Anna as guardian and regent, and her withdrawal into her own house – by which he meant her birth family. He ultimately denied her affiliation to the house of Trapp-Caldonazzo, denigrated her familial affiliation by marriage to the gentry Trapp family, and demanded her retreat to her family of birth. This amounted to the relinquishment of her role as guardian, regent, and head of household. During married life, wives of the low nobility were, on the one hand, forced to live with the ambivalence of separation from affiliation with their birth family, and belonged to the new family only during matrimony. On the other hand, and in keeping with agnatic logic, which called for undivided property and rule amongst brothers, they could be rejected from the family into which they had married upon reaching widowhood. The role of women as interface between two families and houses was very demanding, and could result in their relegation to a relative, status-specific poverty.[56] Even if they were not supported by all institutions, brothers clearly held the stronger social position in the patrilineal context. The logic of brothers, who regarded themselves as one entity, one family, and one house, was backed by the constellation of wealth made up by the undivided property of brothers, the separation of marital property, and the dowry system. This brothers' logic differed from the logic of the guardianship court, which was first and foremost responsible for protecting the interests of the ward. The Tyrolean law code also provided for this by stipulating that, if at all possible, persons with self-interest in the ward's property were not allowed to become guardian of the same.[57] As mentioned, Giulia Calvi has also shown evidence of this practice in Tuscany.[58] In a marital

56 See Clementi, "Deren von Wolkenstein," pp. 146–47; Severidt, *Familie, Verwandtschaft*, pp. 41 and 69. With her focus on the role of sisters and aunts within the aristocratic kinship network, Michaela Hohkamp drew attention to the fact that this in-between status of noble women between two families and dynasties could sometimes entail a significant position of power, see Michaela Hohkamp, "Do Sisters Have Brothers? The Search for the 'rechte Schwester'. Brothers and Sisters in Aristocratic Society at the Turn of the Sixteenth Century," in *Sibling Relations and the Transformation of European Kinship 1300–1900*, ed. Christopher H. Johnson and David Warren Sabean (New York and Oxford: Berghahn, 2011), pp. 65–83; Hohkamp, "Eine Tante für alle Fälle".

57 TLO 1573, III, 48.

58 Calvi, *Il contratto morale*; Calvi, "Widows, the State"; Calvi, "Rights and Ties"; Calvi, "Diritti e legami".

property regime based on the separation of property and on dowry, mothers were regarded as being beyond all suspicion because they had no claim on the property of their late husband's family, and therefore had a higher chance of being awarded guardianship. First, however, we must ascertain whether these findings applied in Tyrol in practice and whether, as provided for in the Tyrolean law code, women themselves actually intended and determined guardians for their children in their wills.[59]

Not only were Maria Anna's relations to her brothers-in-law of the house Trapp-Caldonazzo strained during her widowhood, but so too were her relations to her birth brothers. These tensions arose from the intermediate position of widows of low nobility, wherein they were suspended between two houses and families. Indeed, Maria Anna was separated from her birth family Thun by marriage, but substantial property concerns still linked her to them, even as a widow. Her dowry of 2,000 Gulden and additional inheritances from her father, brother, and mother were never paid out. Instead, the respective fund of 6,175 Gulden remained with her brothers, and they paid out only the annual interest. In addition, the question of where the widow would live was pending at the time Maria Anna lost the guardianship and regency. The marriage contract between Maria Anna Thun and Osvaldo Trapp was unfortunately not recorded. We know from other low nobility marriage contracts of the same period that the dower often comprised not only money but a seat befitting the widow's rank.[60] It is highly likely that the marriage contract between Maria Anna Thun and Osvaldo Trapp provided no dower, and therefore no widow's seat. Maria Anna had to be content with the revenue of her fund and, much to the dismay of her brother-in-law Ernesto, remained on the Caldonazzo estate. The conflict between the widow Maria Anna Trapp and her brother-in-law Ernesto Trapp can also be interpreted as a struggle for the rights of disposition over the court in Caldonazzo – especially as, following the change of guardianship and regency, the main issue according to Ernesto's objective was that the widow should leave the court. Unimpeded exercise of power was linked to unrestricted disposal of the seat of power. This principle would later be used

59 These questions regarding guardianship and matters such as gender order among Tyrolean nobility, marriage and inheritance practices, property arrangements, and kinship and friendship constellations is subject of my ongoing research project *Vermögensarrangements, Geschlechterbeziehungen und Verwandtschaft in landadeligen Familien Tirols 1500–1700* (Property Arrangements, Gender Relations and Kinship in Families of the Lower Nobility in Tyrol 1500–1700).

60 Clementi, "Deren von Wolkenstein," pp. 140–41; see also Hufschmidt, *Adlige Frauen*, pp. 374–77.

at the expense of her son Osvaldo Ercole Trapp: after his legal incapacitation in 1669, he had to leave the court in Caldonazzo. After taking possession of the guardianship, Ernesto assumed that Maria Anna's birth family would be responsible for her accommodation as widow. Here again we see the collision of two different ideas of widowhood that, in their contrariness are perhaps characteristic of the transitional legal space of southern Tyrol, situated in between German and Italian legal cultures.[61] Ernesto's reasoning is reminiscent of practice in large parts of middle and northern Italy, where the widow went back to the house of her birth family – thus underlining the transitory character of marriage.[62] The Tyrolean law code provides for the *Entrichtung,* or provision, for the widow, but does not mention her residence or widow's seat. This legal vacuum was largely regulated within the nobility through marriage contracts. In the sixteenth and beginning of the seventeenth century, for example, the Wolkenstein marriage contracts consistently provided for a widow's seat.[63] This was likewise the case for widows of the low nobility in other German speaking territories.[64]

Maria Anna, however, did not feel obliged to leave the Caldonazzo estate, perhaps because she saw herself as in the right and part of the house of Trapp-Caldonazzo, or perhaps because she could not envisage any other solution befitting of her rank. In her circumstances, she would have had difficulty affording a widow's seat without the help of the family; she remained in Caldonazzo and saw herself compelled to plead with her brothers for money as a result of her financial difficulties. As the case of Maria Anna Trapp, née Thun, shows, an intermediate familial position – between two families and houses – could render a widow of the low nobility dependent on the good will of two groups of brothers.

61 Siglinde Clementi, Ellinor Forster, Christian Hagen, Margareth Lanzinger, and Janine Christina Maegraith, "Rechtsräume und Geschlechterordnungen als soziale Prozesse – transregional. Vereinbaren und Verfügen in städtischen und ländlichen Kontexten im südlichen Tirol vom 15. bis zum frühen 19. Jahrhundert – ein erster Projektbericht," *Geschichte und Region / Storia e regione* 22–2 (2013), pp. 165–72. On legal history in Tyrol see Martin P. Schennach, *Gesetz und Herrschaft. Die Entstehung des Gesetzgebungsstaates am Beispiel Tirols* (Cologne, Weimar, and Vienna: Böhlau, 2010).

62 Cecilia Cristellon, "Das Haus als Bühne: Vor- und nachreformatorische Heirats- und Ehepraxis," in *Das Haus in der Geschichte Europas. Ein Handbuch*, ed. Joachim Eibach and Inken Schmidt-Voges in collaboration with Simone Derix, Philip Hahn, Elizabeth Harding, and Margareth Lanzinger (Berlin and Boston: de Gruyter-Oldenbourg, 2015), pp. 303–18.

63 Clementi, "Deren von Wolkenstein," pp. 140–41.

64 Hufschmidt, *Adlige Frauen*, pp. 374–77.

3 Conclusions

The story of Maria Anna Trapp illustrates that women could attain a certain extent of power, even within a familial property regime that consistently disadvantaged them in material aspects as a result of undivided fraternal property, separation of marital property, and dowry with renunciation of inheritance. As a widow and as guardian and regent Maria Anna possessed the rule over the fiefdom of Caldonazzo, the jurisdiction of the land court (*Landgericht*), and the administration of the house of Trapp-Caldonazzo. Her husband Osvaldo, who elevated her into this position by testamentary bequest, had intended to create a counterbalance to his overly powerful brothers and to establish his own line of Trapp-Caldonazzo. The legal situation, which stipulated that guardians have no personal interest in the property of the ward, favoured the widow as guardian because of her lack of claims in this respect and economic weakness. This is likely the reason that the guardianship and regency controversy between Maria Anna and her brother-in-law Ernesto was decided in her favour. In the end, Maria Anna did not fail as a result of the legal situation or ostensible power relations, but as a result of the fact that her son Osvaldo Ercole decided in favour of his allegedly more socially influential uncle Ernesto, and the court followed suit. Maria Anna therefore failed due to the subtle and highly effective power relations within the family. Until that point Maria Anna had fought for her rights as guardian and regent. In spite of harsh hostilities, she tried to push her views through, and she initially succeeded. Different interpretations of property rights and various conceptions of gender had distinctive parts in this.

The essentially ambivalent management of property rights in the early modern period made different perspectives on property highly dependent on the personal interests involved. Ernesto tried to enforce his own agenda by stressing the logic of undivided property of brothers, while Maria Anna successfully referred to her rights to the individualised property of Osvaldo Trapp. Both interpretations of property rights had a legal basis. Crucial for the legal practice was how the interpretations accommodated the authorities and their specific interests. The guardianship court in Innsbruck was primarily interested in the well-being of the ward, and appointed Maria Anna as guardian because it was Osvaldo Trapp's last will and the Tyrolean law code provided for deference to parents' intentions. Widows and mothers were moreover regarded as free of personal interest, and therefore more suitable guardians than uncles, because mothers' marginality in inheritance law within a marital property regime based on separation of property and a dowry system meant that they had no claim on their deceased husband's inheritance.

Gender concepts played a key role in guardianship controversies, where women were censured for their weakness in political power. In the end, Maria Anna failed as guardian because of the conflict of loyalty in which her son Osvaldo Ercole was embattled and whereby he eventually opted for the socially stronger party, his uncle Ernesto. In order to effect a change of guardianship Osvaldo Ercole put forward an argument regarding the political and social weakness of Maria Anna, and the strong social position and reputation of Ernesto, the canon of Trent. The guardianship court obviously accepted his reasoning, withdrew the guardianship and regency from Maria Anna, and transferred these to Ernesto Trapp. As a result, the widow was pushed into a socially marginal position, between two families of low nobility, two groups of brothers controlling property in positions of power.

References

Antenhofer, Christina. *Briefe zwischen Süd und Nord. Die Hochzeit und Ehe von Paula de Gonzaga und Leonhard von Görz im Spiegel der fürstlichen Kommunikation (1473–1500)*. Innsbruck: Wagner, 2007.

Bastl, Beatrix. *Tugend, Liebe, Ehre. Die adelige Frau in der Frühen Neuzeit*. Vienna, Cologne, and Weimar: Böhlau, 2000.

Bellabarba, Marco. "Il principato vescovile di Trento dagli inizi del XVI secolo alla guerra dei Trent'anni." In *Storia del Trentino*, vol. 4: *L'età moderna*, edited by Marco Bellabarba and Giuseppe Olmi, pp. 15–70. Bologna: Il Mulino, 2000.

Bellabarba, Marco, and Serena Luzzi. *Il territorio trentino nella storia europea*, vol. 3: *L'età moderna*. Trento: Fondazione Bruno Kessler press, 2011.

Benvenuti, Sergio. *Storia del Trentino*, vol. 1: *Periodizzazione e cronologia politico-istituzionale*. Trento: Ed. Panorama, 1994.

Bonazza, Marcello. *Il fisco in una statalità divisa. Impero principi e ceti in area trentino-tirolese nella prima età moderna*. Bologna: Il Mulino, 2001.

Brida, Luciano. "Appunti di vita di un feudatario secentesco: Osvaldo Ercole Trapp (1634–1710)." *Studi Trentini di Scienze Storiche* 62–1 (1983): pp. 335–66.

Calvi, Giulia. "Diritti e legami. Madri, figli, Stato in Toscana (XVI–XVIII secolo)." *Quaderni storici* 86–2 (1994): pp. 487–510.

Calvi, Giulia. *Il contratto morale. Madri e figli nella Toscana moderna*. Rome and Bari: Laterza, 1994.

Calvi, Giulia. "Rights and Ties that Bind: Mothers, Children, and the State in Tuscany during the Early Modern Period." In *Kinship in Europe. Approaches to Long-term Development (1300–1900)*, edited by David Warren Sabean, Simon Teuscher, and Jon Mathieu, pp. 145–62. New York and Oxford: Berghahn, 2007.

Calvi, Giulia. "Widows, the State and the Guardianship of Children in Early Modern Tuscany." In *Widowhood in Medieval and Early Modern Europe*, edited by Sandra Cavallo and Lyndan Warner, pp. 209–19. Harlow and New York: Longman, 1999.

Cavallo, Sandra, and Lyndan Warner, eds. *Widowhood in Medieval and Early Modern Europe*. Harlow and New York: Longman, 1999.

Chojnacki, Stanley. *Women and Men in Renaissance Venice. Twelve Essays on Patrician Society*. Baltimore and London: The Johns Hopkins University Press, 2000.

Clementi, Siglinde. "Deren von Wolkenstein. Familienstrategien, Heirat und Geschlechterbeziehungen bei den Wolkenstein-Trostburg (um 1500 bis 1650)." In *Die Wolkensteiner. Facetten des Tiroler Adels in Spätmittelalter und Neuzeit*, edited by Gustav Pfeifer and Kurt Andermann, pp. 111–47. Innsbruck: Wagner, 2009.

Clementi, Siglinde. "Heiraten in Grenzräumen. Vermögensarrangements adeliger Ehefrauen und -männer im frühneuzeitlichen Tirol." *Geschichte und Region / Storia e regione* 28–2 (2018): pp. 44–69.

Clementi, Siglinde. "Hybrid Legal Culture among the Early Modern Tyrolean Nobility. Marriage Contracts and the Symbolic Value of Assets." In *Gender, Law and Material Culture. Immobile Property and Mobile Goods in Early Modern Europe*, edited by Annette Caroline Cremer, pp. 93–119. London and New York: Routledge, 2021.

Clementi, Siglinde. *Körper, Selbst und Melancholie. Die Selbstzeugnisse des Landadeligen Osvaldo Ercole Trapp*. Cologne, Weimar, and Vienna: Böhlau, 2017.

Clementi, Siglinde. "Undivided Brothers – Renouncing Sisters. Family Strategies of Low Nobility in Sixteenth- and Seventeenth-Century Tyrol." In *Gender, Law and Economic Well-being in Europe from the Fifteenth to the Nineteenth Century*, edited by Anna Bellavitis and Beatrice Zucca Micheletto, pp. 149–64. London and New York: Routledge, 2019.

Clementi, Siglinde. "Zur Ökonomie der Ehre. Heiratsgüter in Tirol um 1800." *Geschichte und Region / Storia e regione* 19–1 (2010): pp. 109–22.

Clementi, Siglinde, Ellinor Forster, Christian Hagen, Margareth Lanzinger, and Janine Christina Maegraith. "Rechtsräume und Geschlechterordnungen als soziale Prozesse – transregional. Vereinbaren und Verfügen in städtischen und ländlichen Kontexten im südlichen Tirol vom 15. bis zum frühen 19. Jahrhundert – ein erster Projektbericht." *Geschichte und Region / Storia e regione* 22–2 (2013): pp. 165–72.

Cristellon, Cecilia. "Das Haus als Bühne: Vor- und nachreformatorische Heirats- und Ehepraxis." In *Das Haus in der Geschichte Europas. Ein Handbuch*, edited by Joachim Eibach and Inken Schmidt-Voges in collaboration with Simone Derix, Philip Hahn, Elizabeth Harding, and Margareth Lanzinger, pp. 303–18. Berlin and Boston: de Gruyter-Oldenbourg, 2015.

Donati, Claudio. "Il principato vescovile di Trento dalla guerra dei Trent'anni alle riforme settecentesche." In *Storia del Trentino*, vol. 4: *L'età moderna*, edited by Marco Bellabarba and Giuseppe Olmi, pp. 71–124. Bologna: Il Mulino, 2000.

Duhamelle, Christoph, and Jürgen Schlumbohm. "Einleitung: Vom 'europäischen Heiratsmuster' zu Strategien der Eheschließung?" In *Eheschließungen im Europa des 18. und 19. Jahrhunderts. Muster und Strategien*, edited by Christoph Duhamelle and Jürgen Schlumbohm, pp. 11–33. Göttingen: Vandenhoeck & Ruprecht, 2003.

Ginzburg, Carlo. "Microstoria: due o tre cose che so di lei." *Quaderni Storici* 86 (1994): pp. 510–39.

Hagen, Christian, Margareth Lanzinger, and Janine Maegraith. "Competing Interests in Death-Related Stipulation in South Tirol c. 1350–1600." In *Planning for Death. Wills and Death-Related Property Arrangements in Europe, 1200–1600*, edited by Mia Korpiola and Anu Lathinen, pp. 88–118. Leiden and Boston: Brill, 2017.

Hohkamp, Michaela. "Do Sisters Have Brothers? The Search for the 'rechte Schwester'. Brothers and Sisters in Aristocratic Society at the Turn of the Sixteenth Century." In *Sibling Relations and the Transformation of European Kinship 1300–1900*, edited by Christopher H. Johnson and David Warren Sabean, pp. 65–83. New York and Oxford: Berghahn, 2011.

Hohkamp, Michaela. "Eine Tante für alle Fälle: Tanten-Nichten Beziehungen und ihre politische Bedeutung für die reichsfürstliche Gesellschaft der Frühen Neuzeit (16. bis 18. Jahrhundert)." In *Politiken der Verwandtschaft. Beziehungsnetze, Geschlecht und Recht*, edited by Margareth Lanzinger and Edith Saurer, pp. 147–68. Göttingen: v&r-unipress, 2007.

Hohkamp, Michaela, ed. *Tanten.* Special issue of *WerkstattGeschichte*, 46 (2007).

Hörmann-Thurn und Taxis, Julia, ed. *Margarete "Maultasch". Zur Lebenswelt einer Landesfürstin und anderer Tiroler Frauen des Mittelalters*. Innsbruck: Wagner, 2007.

Hufschmid, Anke. *Adlige Frauen im Weserraum zwischen 1570 und 1700. Status – Rollen – Lebenspraxis*. Münster: Aschendorff, 2001.

Ingendahl, Gesa. "Elend und Wollust. Witwenschaft in kulturellen Bildern der Frühen Neuzeit." In *Witwenschaft in der Frühen Neuzeit. Fürstliche und adelige Witwen zwischen Fremd- und Selbstbestimmung*, edited by Martina Schattkowsky, pp. 265–79. Leipzig: Leipziger Universitätsverlag, 2003.

Koch, Elisabeth. *Maior dignitas est in sexu virili. Das weibliche Geschlecht im Normensystem des 16. Jahrhunderts*. Frankfurt a. M.: Klostermann, 1991.

Köfler, Werner. *Land, Landschaft, Landtag. Geschichte der Tiroler Landtage von den Anfängen bis zur Aufhebung der landständischen Verfassung 1808*. Innsbruck: Wagner, 1985.

Kruse, Britta-Juliane. *Witwen. Kulturgeschichte eines Standes in Spätmittelalter und Früher Neuzeit*. Berlin and New York: de Gruyter, 2007.

La Magnifica Corte di Caldonazzo: Castello Trapp. Caldonazzo: Comune di Caldonazzo, 1990.

Lanzinger, Margareth. *Das gesicherte Erbe. Heirat in lokalen und familialen Kontexten. Innichen 1700–1900*. Vienna, Cologne, and Weimar: Böhlau, 2003.

Lanzinger, Margareth. "Von der Macht der Linie zu Gegenseitigkeit. Heiratskontrakte in den Südtiroler Gerichten Welsberg und Innichen 1750–1850." In Margareth Lanzinger, Gunda Barth-Scalmani, Ellinor Forster, and Gertrude Langer-Ostrawsky, *Aushandeln von Ehe. Heiratsverträge der Neuzeit im europäischen Vergleich*, pp. 205–367. Cologne, Weimar, and Vienna: Böhlau, 2010, 2nd edition 2015.

Lanzinger, Margareth, and Janine Maegraith. "Konkurrenz um Vermögen im südlichen Tirol des 16. Jahrhunderts." *L'Homme. Z.F.G.* 27–1 (2016): pp. 15–31.

Lesemann, Silke. "Liebe und Strategie. Adelige Ehen im 18. Jahrhundert." *Historische Anthropologie* 8–2 (2000): pp. 189–207.

Lupo, Michelangelo. *I Trapp. Storia di una famiglia nel vecchio Tirolo*. Trento: Provincia Autonoma di Trento, 1997.

Medick, Hans. *Weben und Überleben in Laichingen 1650–1900. Lokalgeschichte als Allgemeine Geschichte*. Göttingen: Vandenhoeck & Ruprecht, 1996.

Medick, Hans, and David Sabean. "Emotionen und materielle Interessen in Familie und Verwandtschaft: Überlegungen zu neuen Wegen und Bereichen einer historischen und sozialanthropologischen Familienforschung." In *Emotionen und materielle Interessen. Sozialanthropologische und historische Beiträge zur Familienforschung*, edited by Hans Medick and David Sabean, pp. 27–54. Göttingen: Vandenhoeck & Ruprecht, 1984.

Pauser, Josef, and Martin P. Schennach, eds. *Die Tiroler Landesordnungen von 1526, 1532 und 1573. Historische Einführung und Edition*. Vienna, Cologne, and Weimar: Böhlau, 2018.

Puppel, Pauline. *Die Regentin. Vormundschaftliche Herrschaft in Hessen 1500–1700*. Frankfurt a. M. and New York: Campus, 2004.

Reif, Heinz. *Westfälischer Adel 1770–1860. Vom Herrenstand zur regionalen Elite*. Göttingen: Vandenhoeck & Ruprecht, 1979.

Röckelein, Hedwig. "De feudo femineo – über das Weiberlehen." In *Herrschaftspraxis und soziale Ordnung im Mittelalter und in der frühen Neuzeit. Ernst Schubert zum Gedenken*, edited by Peter Aufgebauer and Christine van den Heuvel, pp. 267–84. Hanover: Hahnsche Buchhandlung, 2006.

Rosenhaft, Eve. "'... mich als eine Extraordinarium'. Die Witwe als widerstrebendes Subjekt in der Frühgeschichte der Lebensversicherung." In *Stationen einer Hochschullaufbahn. Festschrift für Annette Kuhn zum 65. Geburtstag*, edited by Udo Arnold, Peter Mayers, and Uta C. Schmidt, pp. 292–309. Dortmund: edition ebersbach, 1999.

Schad, Martha. *Die Frauen des Hauses Fugger von der Lilie (15.–17. Jahrhundert). Augsburg – Ortenburg – Trient*. Tübingen: Mohr, 1989.

Schattkowsky, Martina, ed. *Witwenschaft in der Frühen Neuzeit. Fürstliche und adelige Witwen zwischen Fremd- und Selbstbestimmung*. Leipzig: Leipziger Universitätsverlag, 2003.

Schennach, Martin P. *Gesetz und Herrschaft. Die Entstehung des Gesetzgebungsstaates am Beispiel Tirols*. Cologne, Weimar, and Vienna: Böhlau, 2010.

Schlumbohm, Jürgen, ed. *Mikrogeschichte – Makrogeschichte, komplementär oder inkommensurabel?* Göttingen: Wallenstein, 1998.

Schraut, Sylvia. *Das Haus Schönborn. Eine Familienbiographie. Katholischer Reichsadel 1640–1840*. Paderborn: Schöningh, 2005.

Schwob, Ute Monika. "'Herrinnen' in Tiroler Quellen. Zur rechtlichen und sozialen Stellung der adeligen Frau im Mittelalter." In *Literatur und bildende Kunst zum Tiroler Mittelalter*, edited by Egon Kühebacher, pp. 157–82. Innsbruck: Institut für Germanistik, 1982.

Severidt, Ebba. *Familie, Verwandtschaft und Karriere bei den Gonzaga. Struktur und Funktion von Familie und Verwandtschaft bei den Gonzaga und ihren deutschen Verwandten (1444–1519)*. Leinfelden-Echterdingen: DRW-Verlag, 2002.

Spieß, Karl-Heinz. *Familie und Verwandtschaft im deutschen Hochadel des Spätmittelalters: 13. bis Anfang des 16. Jahrhunderts*. Stuttgart: Steiner, 1993.

Stauber, Reinhard. *Der Zentralstaat an seinen Grenzen. Administrative Integration, Herrschaftswechsel und politische Kultur im südlichen Alpenraum 1750–1820*. Göttingen: Vandenhoeck & Ruprecht, 2001.

Stolz, Otto. "Geschichte der Gerichte Deutschtirols." *Archiv für österreichische Geschichte* 102 (1913): pp. 86–334.

Stolz, Otto. *Geschichte des Landes Tirol*. Innsbruck: Tyrolia, 1955.

Art. "Trapp." In *Genealogisches Handbuch des Adels*, Adelslexikon, vol. XIV. (Limburg: Starke, 2003), pp. 501–503.

Trentini, Andreas. *La Magnifica Corte di Caldonazzo: Castello Trapp*, dt. Ausgabe. Rovereto: Longo, 1993.

Van Gennep, Arnold. *The Rites of Passage* (*Les rites de passage, 1909*). Chicago: University of Chicago Press, 1960.

Voltelini von, Hans. *Das welsche Tirol* (Erläuterungen zum Historischen Atlas der österreichischen Alpenländer 1/3/2). Vienna: Holzhausen, 1919.

Voltelini von, Hans. *Giurisdizione signorile su terre e persone nel Trentino medievale*. Trento: Gruppo Storico Argentario, Bibl. Cappucini, 1981.

Weiss, Sabine. *Claudia de' Medici. Eine italienische Prinzessin als Landesfürstin von Tirol (1604–1648)*. Innsbruck: Tyrolia, 2004.

Wunder, Heide, ed. *Dynastie und Herrschaftssicherung in der Frühen Neuzeit. Geschlechter und Geschlecht*. Berlin: Duncker & Humblot, 2002.

Wunder, Heide. "Geschlechterverhältnisse und dynastische Herrschaft in der Frühen Neuzeit." In *Frauen und Bildnis 1600–1750. Barocke Repräsentationskultur an europäischen Fürstenhöfen*, edited by Gabriele Baumbach and Cordula Bischoff, pp. 15–37. Kassel: kassel university press, 2003.

Zweynert, Charlotte. "Ausgleichende Verfügungen, verbindende Gegenstände, konkurrierende Interessen. Das Testament des zweitgeborenen Francesco Gonzaga aus dem Jahr 1483." In *Beziehungen, Vernetzungen, Konflikte. Perspektiven Historischer Verwandtschaftsforschung*, edited by Christine Fertig and Margareth Lanzinger, pp. 37–65. Cologne, Weimar, and Vienna: Böhlau, 2016.

PART 4

Urban and Rural Spaces: Ascribing and Defending Property, Bequests, and Occupation

CHAPTER 12

Little to Leave: Labourers' Goods and the Probate Process in Early Modern England

Craig Muldrew

In studies investigating the material culture of households in early modern Europe, the probate inventory has proven to be one of the most fruitful of sources. In English historiography, especially, they have been subject to a great deal of mostly quantitative analysis. Many tens of thousands of inventories have been examined to measure the changing ownership of household goods such as pewter tableware, chairs, feather beds, cupboards and specific luxury goods such as pictures, mirrors and silver.[1] Inventories have also been used extensively to measure agrarian production and credit relationships. Probate inventories provide listings of rooms in the house and their contents as well as tools, production equipment both in the house and in outbuildings or the yard, as well as farm animals and growing or harvested crops. In addition, debts owed to the deceased were listed, and on rare occasions the debts they owed to others as well. Occasionally clothing was also itemised and valued, as was cash if more than a small amount was possessed.

However, the inventory was only one stage of the entire probate process, which also included an administration bond to appoint the executors, a will if one had been made, and a final account subtracting all liabilities from the estate including outstanding debts, funeral and nursing costs, and any expenses for looking after orphaned children. A will could bequeath both land and movable goods, however it is important to note that the law relating to real property was customary and governed by different rules than the transfer of movable goods, and so land was not inventoried. The inventory was meant to be a listing of *movable assets* only, and the account was the document where the final balancing of the estate took place. In contrast to other European probate documents no information on age or family members was required, only the names of the deceased, executors, assessors, and witnesses were recorded. In terms of survival, the document to have survived in the largest numbers in English

1 Janine Maegraith and Craig Muldrew, "Consumption and Material Life," in *Oxford Handbook of Early Modern European History*, ed. Hamish Scott (Oxford: Oxford University Press, 2015), pp. 369–97.

 | DOI:10.1163/9789004456204_013

record repositories is the will, of which many millions are extant. Somewhere between one to two million inventories have survived, and somewhere around 30–50,000 probate accounts.[2] Wills have been used by religious historians for signs of protestant phraseology, and also by Jane Whittle and Amy Erickson to investigate changes in female inheritance patterns and voluntary bequests.[3] Some probate accounts have also been analysed in comparison to inventories to look at relative indebtedness and credit, but as Ian Mortimer has shown probate accounts are more likely to have survived in cases where the deceased was more indebted.[4] However, wills have rarely been used in conjunction with either inventories or accounts in such economic investigations as listed above.

The main reason for this is that, sometime in their archival history, most of these related documents were separated from each other, and either stored separately or disposed of. Wills, because they were the only document which listed the bequest of land, were kept the most meticulously, and the survival of wills is fairly constant over time.[5] However, the number of surviving inventories and probate accounts rises to a peak in the later half of the seventeenth century before declining in the eighteenth century, and only a small number have remained from the end of the century. Evidence from canon law in 1604 indicate that the lack of survival for earlier dates was due to lack of record

2 Craig Muldrew, *The Economy of Obligation: The Culture of Credit and Social Relations in Early Modern England* (London: Palgrave, 1998), chapter 4, n. 58.

3 Jane Whittle, "Inheritance, Marriage, Widowhood and Remarriage: A Comparative Perspective on Women and Landholding in North-East Norfolk, 1440–1580," *Continuity and Change*, 13–1 (1998), pp. 33–72; Amy Louise Erickson, *Women and Property in Early Modern England* (London: Routledge, 1993), chapters 9–12.

4 Muldrew, *Economy of Obligation*, pp. 103–07; Ian Mortimer, "Why were Probate Accounts Made? Methodological Issues Surrounding the Historical use of Administrators' and Executors' Accounts," *Archives* 31 (2006), pp. 2–17. There are probably over 30,000 surviving probate accounts. These have been collected by Dr. Peter Spufford, and information from them has been entered into a computer database. They are described in Peter Spufford, ed., *Guide to the Probate Accounts of England and Wales*, 2 vols. (London: British Record Society, 1999); Amy Louise Erickson, "An Introduction to Probate Accounts," in *The Records of the Nation*, ed. G. H. Martin and Peter Spufford (Woodbridge: Boydell, 1990), pp. 273–86.

5 The actual transfer of the land and its nature (inheritance, *inter-vivos*, gift or sale) would be recorded in the court rolls of the manor in which it was located at the time of transfer. Customs of inheritance could differ from manor to manor, and wills were expected to respect them, but increasingly over time marriage settlements could override custom, however these were not common among poorer families. Disputes over inheritance were usually dealt with in the same ecclesiastical courts but are kept as separate records. More complex cases went to the central equity courts, of which Chancery was the most important. For more on this very complex issue see Lloyd Bonfield, *Devising, Dying and Dispute: Probate Litigation in Early Modern England* (Farnham: Ashgate, 2013); Erickson, *Women and Property*; Jane Whittle, *The Development of Agrarian Capitalism: Land and Labour in Norfolk 1440–1580* (Oxford: Clarendon, 2000), pp. 46–177.

keeping facilities, and from 1685 onwards an Act of Parliament restricted the need for probate accounts to be made.[6] But, since it seems unlikely that the church archives would have disposed of eighteenth century inventories while retaining those from the seventeenth century, the lack of eighteenth century inventories is more likely attributable to the fact that they were not exhibited or deposited as a record.[7] Perhaps to save space, the decision was left up to the executors, administrators, and family. But, this must remain conjecture until any evidence is discovered. Wills were a more necessary record, because under English law, land tenure was customary, as opposed to common law which governed movable property, financial contracts, and lease holdings. Inventories and accounts only dealt with the latter, most of which could be settled in the months or years after the death of the testator. But any division of real property was either governed by manorial custom, or by the provisions of a will, and thus the will could be a relevant document in establishing title to land.[8] Even where no land was involved, the division of the estate in a will usually contained instructions relating to the death of spouses and minors well into the future. Thus, wills are an essential tool in understanding the nature of the probate process in that they are the only document which indicate if the deceased was a landholder or not. They also contain very valuable information concerning the size of bequests to children and other kin, servants and neighbours.

In England it had long been the practice to dispose of moveable goods by will, but during the sixteenth century Parliament passed a number of statutes encouraging people to settle the transfer of landed property as well, rather than relying solely on the custom of the manor.[9] This was done by the church

---

6 Tom Arkell, "The Probate Process," in *When Death do us Part: Understanding and Interpreting the Probate Records of Early Modern England*, ed. Tom Arkell, Nesta Evans, and Nigel Goose (Hertfordshire: Leopard's Head Press, 2000), pp. 3–13, here p. 12.

7 Jeff and Nancy Cox, "Probate 1500–1800: A System in Transition," in *When Death do us Part: Understanding and Interpreting the Probate Records of Early Modern England*, ed. Tom Arkell, Nesta Evans, and Nigel Goose (Hertfordshire: Leopard's Head Press, 2000), pp. 14–37, here pp. 26–27.

8 A good example can be found in John Money, ed., *The Chronicles of John Cannon Excise Officer and Writing Master*, vol. 1–2 (Oxford: Published for the British Academy by Oxford University Press, 2010), p. 268. Because of the great length of the manuscript, this edition has had to summarise some of the material. This reference is to Cannon's original pagination. The manuscript is in the Somerset Record Office DD/SAS/1193/4: *John Cannon's Chronicles*.

9 Arkell, "The Probate Process," pp. 7–8. Free bench, or the widow's third, was often practiced, as was primogeniture, but will making allowed much more freedom than strictly enforced customary arrangements in providing capital for younger siblings. There is a literature which suggests that over the course of the seventeenth century daughters increasingly received less than they would under customary arrangements. This was done in order to bolster the survival of patriarchal family landholding by bequeathing more to the sons,

courts and involved, as noted, a will, administration bond, inventory and finally an account. In 1529 a statute was passed to regulate the fees and charges which could be taken by the courts for registering testamentary documents. The cost of copying the will was set at 6d. [pence], and another 6d. for the administration bond in the case of intestacy. If the property was above £5 in value then a charge of 3s. [shillings] was added, and 5s. for estates valued at £40 or more. The act also stated that the courts could not refuse to process any probate documents properly made for whatever value. However, given that court time spent on more valuable estates was profitable in a way that time spent on poor people's estates was not, court officials probably discouraged the latter.[10] Where probate accounts have survived, the costs of making and exhibiting the inventory are given so they can be calculated. The 143 probate accounts which have survived for labourers are almost all for exceptionally wealthy individuals worth typically £30–50, and for these individuals the cost of the process of inventorying was typically between 12s. and £1 6s.[11] For two labourers from Kent worth less, £13 13s. and £11 8s., the costs were £1 11s. 4d. and 10s. respectively. The cost of the administration in these cases also typically added another pound or more.[12] Since around 40 percent of surviving labourers inventories were worth less than £15, this represents a significant charge on such a small estate and would have been a disincentive to make a will and/or inventory unless necessary.[13]

Indeed, very few poorer people's wills, inventories and accounts have survived in comparison than those of their wealthier neighbours. The one

especially those in financial trouble. However, there is debate on this matter as much of the evidence comes from elite court sources. Erickson, *Women and Property*, pp. 24–25; Susan Staves, *Married Women's Separate Property in England, 1660–1833* (Cambridge, Mass.: Harvard University Press, 1990); Barbara Todd, "Freebench and Free Enterprise: Widows and their Property in Two Berkshire Villages," in *English Rural Society 1500–1800: Essays in Honour of Joan Thirsk*, ed. John Chartres and David Hey (Cambridge: Cambridge University Press, 1990), pp. 196–200.

10 Arkell, "The Probate Process," pp. 11–13.

11 For a discussion of these documents see Craig Muldrew, "From Credit to Savings? An Examination of Debt and Credit in Relation to Increasing Consumption in England, c.1650 to 1770," *Quaderni Storici* 137 (2011), pp. 391–413, here pp. 402–04.

12 Oxfordshire Record Office 56/3/18, 172/4/38, 299/1/48, 298/5/67, 296/2/51; Kent Archives PRC/20/3/3/4. The cost for inventorying much more valuable estates seems to have been about the same. See for instance the account of a Kentish clothier worth over £500 where it cost £1 12s. Ibid., Account of Alexander Wesser, 06/10/1631.

13 This figure is taken from the sample of 927 labourers' inventories I studied in Craig Muldrew, *Food, Energy and the Creation of Industriousness: Work and Material Culture in Agrarian England, 1550–1780* (Cambridge: Cambridge University Press, 2011), p. 186.

occupational title which refers, in the vast majority of cases, to poor people is "labourer". In the English context, while the definition is imprecise, it generally referred to a man who earned his living from wages paid for manual labour, and most of these were agricultural labourers. Such individuals will be what the term labourer refers to in this chapter.[14] In the diocese of Cheshire, for instance, between 1550 and 1800, 82 labourers' inventories have survived compared to 3,624 husbandmen's (smaller farmers) and 11,764 yeomen's (larger farmers), or 262 butchers' inventories.[15] However, the main reason for this is not because of the actions of any court officials, but due to the obvious fact that the smaller the estate, the easier it was to bequeath with little effort or potential conflict. This would make it less likely that an accurate legal will or inventory would need to be made and exhibited.

The recent work of Sebastian Keibek on probated individuals from the county of Cheshire and the area of Lancashire covered by the diocese of Chester demonstrates that there is a statistically measurable relationship between the probability of being inventoried and wealth. To do this he calculated the ratio of the practitioners of any one single occupation being probated in parishes where the registers of births contained the fathers' occupations which could be matched to surviving inventories from the same parish.[16] Using this data, together with the total value of each inventory, an iterative probability function of leaving an inventory based on wealth was worked out for populations at a country level. Using Cheshire as an example, in the period 1661–1670 (this was when the largest number of inventories have survived), 34 percent of adult male householders left an inventory. By 1751–60 this figure had dropped to only 19 percent.[17] There, in the early eighteenth century, almost every yeoman left an inventory, while only one out of every 3.1 butchers did so, and one out of every five tailors. But by far the occupation least likely to leave an inventory were labourers. Only about one out of every 14 did so (seven percent). This is because the probability of being inventoried did not begin to rise very much until the value of an inventory was about £25 (Keibek's Figures 4 and 5).[18] The probability function can also be used to reconstruct the curve along which

---

14 For a fuller discussion see Muldrew, *Food, Energy*, pp. 18–21.

15 Cheshire Record Office, "Wills Database Online," accessed 7 October 2020, https://www.cheshirearchives.org.uk/family-history/wills-and-probate-records.aspx.

16 Sebastian Keibek, "Correcting the Probate Record for Wealth Bias," Cambridge Working Papers in Economic and Social History No. 28, March 2017, pp. 1–25, here pp. 4–5. http://www.econsoc.hist.cam.ac.uk/docs/CWPESH_number_28_March_2017.pdf.

17 Keibek, "Correcting the Probate Record," p. 5.

18 Ibid., pp. 16 and 18–19.

the wealth of inventoried households would fall.[19] Keibek, together with Shaw Taylor, has also argued that the reason why it was wealthy agricultural occupations which had the highest propensity to be inventoried was the fact that the greatest percentage of their wealth consisted of livestock, crops and other farm equipment.[20]

Using this process Keibek was able to make new estimates of the median values of household wealth. Thus, the median value of inventories from Cheshire and Lancashire between 1700–1760 is reduced from £27 to £8.50.[21] The value of the household goods of farmers from Cheshire and Lancashire when corrected declines from a median of £12.44 to £5.56, while for labourers, this results in a reduction from £5.46 to £1.54, or 72 percent.[22] Labourers' possession of pewter also goes down from 44 percent to 17 percent.[23] Currently, though, this function can only be done for the period around ca. 1700 because of the survival of parish registers with occupational data, and to date the iterative probability calculation has only been done for the diocese of Cheshire.

Looking at actual surviving inventories, out of a sample of around 52 labourers' inventories which have survived for Cheshire after 1660, there are only three in which the household goods are worth less than £2, while about a half have household goods worth less than £5. In my 2011 study of agricultural labourers in England, *Food, Energy and the Creation of Industriousness* I analysed a set of 970 labourers' inventories drawn from Cheshire, Lincolnshire, Norfolk, Cambridgeshire, Kent and Hampshire. This was a first attempt to examine the material wealth of those with the occupational designation labourer. Some of these were unusually wealthy labourers worth over £100, but the majority were worth less than £20, and many were valued at less than £5.[24] At that time the standard method for determining relative poverty and wealth was to use record linkage to match individuals with the numerous tax registers produced during the late seventeenth century. The most useful of these from the point

19 Ibid., p. 21.

20 Sebastian Keibek and Leigh Shaw-Taylor "Early Modern Rural By-Employments: A Re-examination of the Probate Inventory Evidence," *Agricultural History Review* 61–2 (2013), pp. 244–81.

21 Sebastian Keibek, "From Inventories to Households: What Removing Inventories' Social Bias Reveals about Eighteenth-Century English Consumption" (unpublished paper presented at the European Social Science History Conference, Valencia, 2016), Slide 18.

22 Here household goods are defined as things like furniture, linen, decorative items, tableware and cooking implements, while clothing is excluded because it was valued together with money. Keibek, "Inventories to Households," Slide 25.

23 Ibid., Slide 28.

24 Muldrew, *Food, Energy*, pp. 169–73.

of view of social history were the hearth taxes which were intended to tax all but the most poor in society, and the collection procedure involved making a list of those who were exempt from the tax mostly for reasons of poverty. The hearth tax was established in the 1660s by Charles II as a new way of raising money, and was designed to be a progressive tax charging people more who had a higher standard of living as measured by the number of hearths in their households. The increase in rooms and fireplaces in houses was a significant development in the seventeenth century, and the tax was designed to use this increase in standards of living as a measurement of wealth.[25] This linkage could be done for 144 labourers' inventories and of these 26 were exempted and the median value was £15.62.[26] Based on this limited sample, I concluded that it would be reasonable to assume if exempt households were similar to poorest labourers', then the latter were not significantly worse off in terms of the things they possessed than the inventoried sample. However, Keibek's work decisively shows that this is not true, and that it must have been the case that assessors simply neglected to list many households as exempt where there could be no question that they might be liable for any payment.[27]

This scepticism about the representativeness of hearth tax exemptions is further reinforced in Alexandra Shepard's *Accounting for Oneself: Worth, Status and the Social Order in Early Modern England*. Her sample of occupational wealth is taken from the need for deposing witnesses in trials which came before the English church courts, to state what they were worth in goods and taking into account all debts. This was done to establish the credit of the witnesses, as the poor were considered to be more financially susceptible to

25 There is currently a project by the British Records Society to publish the lists of the 1668 tax for every county which describe the nature of the tax. See for instance, Duncan Harrington, Sarah Pearson, and Susan Rose, eds., *Kent Hearth Tax Assessment, Lady Day 1664*. Hearth Tax Series, vol. II (London: British Record Society in association with the Kent Archaeological Society, 2000), pp. xiii–cxii. The best general introduction is Kevin Schurer and Tom Arkell, eds., *Surveying the People: The Interpretation and Use of Document Sources for the Study of Population in the Later Seventeenth Century* (Oxford: Leopard's Head Press, 1992), part I.

26 Muldrew, *Food, Energy*, pp. 188–92.

27 National Archives, Cambridgeshire Hearth tax Exemptions 1672–3 E179, 84, 440. Nesta Evans and Susan Rose, *Cambridgeshire Hearth Tax Returns, Michaelmas 1664* (London: British Record Society in association with The Cambridgeshire Records Society, 2000), pp. xxvi, xxxviii–xlii; Harrington, Pearson, Rose, eds., *Kent Hearth Tax*, pp. li–liii; Craig Muldrew, "Credit, Market Relations, and Debt Litigation in Late Seventeenth Century England, with Particular Reference to King's Lynn" (PhD diss., University of Cambridge, 1990), pp. 77–79.

bribery.[28] These included 273 statements by labourers compared to 1,104 for yeomen and 2,127 for husbandmen, for instance.[29] In the period 1625–49 these values ranged from a mean of £29.04 and a median of £10 for husbandmen and a mean of £143.06 and median of £100 for yeomen, compared to only an mean of £4.75 and median of £2 for labourers.[30]

Given this, what I wish to do here is to return to my sample of labourers' inventories together with a new smaller sample of wills from Cambridgeshire to explore the nature of surviving labourers' inventories which are not obviously exceptional in terms of either large agricultural assets, credit, or the number of household goods, to try to understand why they might have been probated. In the original sample of labourers' inventories I collected, the median value of all the inventories was £18.49, and where there was enough information to measure the value of household goods, the median was £6.07.[31] To get a sense of the range of wealth of these labourers' inventories, Graph 12.1 below simply plots both the total and the household value of these from the whole period on two independent curves from the lowest to highest value.[32] What can be seen here is that the total value of the inventories, including assets such as farm animals and credit in the form of debts owed to the deceased, rises more steeply than the value for their household goods at all levels of wealth. It also demonstrates that, in the case of the exceptionally wealthy labourers, the value of household goods does not rise nearly as steeply as the value of their other assets.

Graph 12.2 presents the curve of the household goods, only in more detail. The curve rises slightly more quickly at the bottom, indicating that inventories of less than £2 are fewer (83), but the most important information this figure provides is that the curve starts to rise significantly more steeply at a value of about £10, or inventory 550, which means that 28 percent of inventories had household goods more valuable than this, and that these can be taken as atypical. Of the 550 inventories worth £10 or less, 56 percent were worth £5 or less and 44 percent between £5 and £10. Thus, it was the case in this sample that someone was almost as likely to be inventoried if they were worth £10 as one pound or less. Hypothetically if we were to reduce the median of the total value of the labourers' inventories (£18.49) by the same percentage

28 Alexandra Shepard, *Accounting for Oneself: Worth, Status, and the Social Order in Early Modern England* (Oxford: Oxford University Press, 2015), pp. 10–27.

29 Ibid., p. 14.

30 Ibid., pp. 69–70.

31 Muldrew, *Food, Energy*, pp. 172–73.

32 Independent here means that the inventory represented at each point on the horizontal axis is not the same on each curve.

(72 percent) as Keibek's iterative probability function produced for Cheshire and Lancashire, this results in a figure of £5.2, and a value of £1.7 for household goods. However, if we calculate the actual median value of household goods in all inventories below the value of £5.2 the amount is considerably more: £2.62. It must be stressed that this is only *hypothetical* without a proper comparison with parish register data.

Graph 12.3 shows the *actual* relationship between the value of household goods in all inventories of less than £26, which is where the curve on Graph 12.1 began to get steeper. What we can see here is that the value of household goods fluctuates enormously in comparison to the total value of the inventory. Using a 50-inventory moving average, there is an overall linear relationship, but the value of household goods rises much less and remains under £10. If we measure the correlation between the value of total assets and the value of household goods in each inventory itself for the whole sample, the result is fairly weak (.44). This means that labourers with more capital goods and credit did not always use that wealth to purchase more household goods. The correlation between the possession of farm animals (.24) or cash (.06) and household goods is even weaker.

Thus, as labourers became poorer in total assets, the value of their household goods declined less steeply. This is due to the fact that most possessed

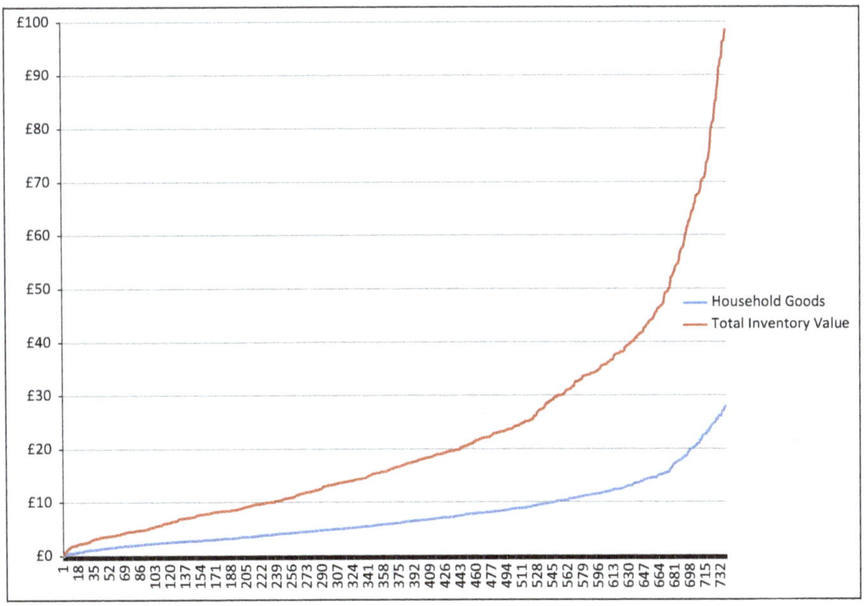

GRAPH 12.1 Value of household goods compared to total inventory values[a]

[a] This omits twenty outlying inventories worth over £100 for clarity of presentation

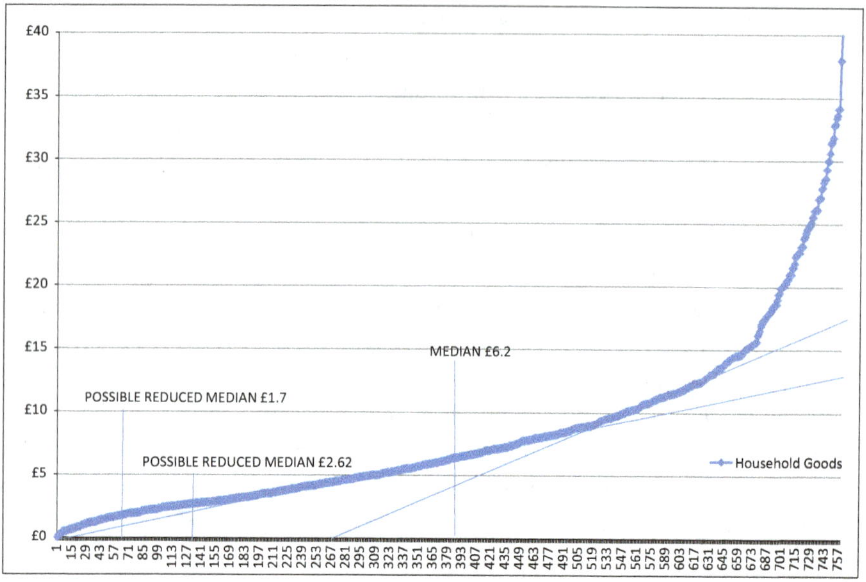

GRAPH 12.2 Value of household goods in labourers' inventories on a curve[a]

[a] Muldrew, *Food, Energy*, pp. 169–72. 760 inventories are used here out of a sample of 970, where each category could be clearly measured. Inventories where values are missing, or items of different categories are valued together could not be added up. Inflation has not been taken into consideration here

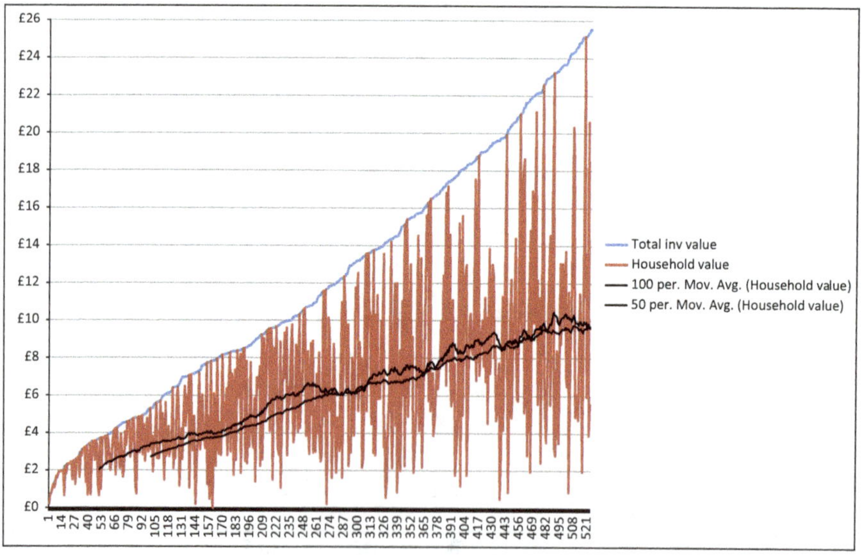

GRAPH 12.3 Value of inventories and their household goods worth £30 or less

basics such as beds and bedding, a table and chairs as well as some basic eating and cooking utensils, and the difference between goods valued between ca. £3–7 was not that great. Looking at Graph 12.3 it can be clearly seen that many inventories with a total value of £20–25 had household goods worth no more than inventories valued at £6 or less. What this suggests is that for most labourers who were inventoried, there was a wide range of factors which affected their ability or need to buy household goods. If their earnings were lower, or if they owed debts for clothing, rent or food, remains unknown to us.

1 Labourers' Wills

We can now turn to a small sample of wills drawn in the diocesan courts of Ely which could be matched to some of the labourers' inventories in the larger sample. This will hopefully provide some indication as to why the small percentage of labourers living in that area who decided they needed to make a will, and their executors, who felt an inventory was needed, made one. The north of Cambridgeshire was dominated by the fenland economy, in contrast to the south of the county which was suited to profitable market oriented arable corn-livestock farming. In terms of area, northern Cambridgeshire was about twice the size, encompassing the areas to the north of the city of Cambridge. Although some fen drainage was being undertaken in the late seventeenth century, the majority of the economy was based on livestock grazing and fishing for eels and catching wildfowl. But most importantly, for labourers, the unenclosed land there meant that there was probably more opportunity for them to retain smallholdings in the edge of fens. As Margaret Spufford has shown for some of these poor will makers in the fens, it was still important to bequeath even a house or small number of capital goods such as cows.[33] The following two examples provide a sense of the nature of such holdings both customary and by lease:

James Sibley, 1690

> To my daughter Sarah Benton … that part of a freehold messuage in St. Marys parish Ely which I now enjoy, the other part belonging to the heirs of John Gotobed deceased together with the proportion of lets lately decreed as in right to the same part thereof in padmal near the let of John

33 Margaret Spufford, *Contrasting Communities. English Villagers in the Sixteenth and Seventeenth Centuries* (Cambridge: Cambridge University Press, 1974), pp. 142–44.

> Cranwell deceased: the other part thereof lying in boyall fen near wickham bridge: and my will is that she shall enjoy the same part of house and lets ... during her natural life. ... after her decease ... my will is that the let in Padmal be tied as an Ingagement for some legacies hereafter: ... to Nicholas Benton my grandson, a piece of turf ground in west fen called Hammonds ground containing two acres which I enjoy for a time ... also a boat. ... I give and bequeath unto Hannah Shipthorpe my grandchild daughter of Edward Shipthorpe ... the sum of five pounds as a legacy.[34]

Thomas Nicks, 1672

> To my daughter Prudence Nicks, four acres of arable land and ley in the fields and bounds of Oakington for the term of three years beginning this twenty first of March. After that time is expired I give my son ... the said land only, the three rood lay I give unto my daughter and her heirs for ever but the three acres and one rood to him and his heirs for ever provided always and upon this condition that my said son William Nicks shall pay my daughter four pounds to be paid unto her three years after my death. Also for want of payment hereof I give and bequeath unto my daughter Prudence Nicks the land next against the brook in Ofmer field.[35]

In Sibley's case it is probable that his wife and possibly another daughter who had been married to Gotobed, had died by this time, as they are not mentioned in the will, which was probably made to ensure that his land would become the property of his one living daughter and her son.[36] Nicks' wife must also have died, but his children still seem to have been young, and he desired to give his only son, who was presumably not yet of age, the largest part of his land. He also made a third child Ann his executor, and although he did not leave her any land, he left her all of his movables subsequently valued at £30 6s. which included four milk cows. In both these cases we can see that there were complexities which can explain the making of the will.

In Cambridge roughly 1,712 labourers left wills mostly from 1660–1750, compared to 360 inventories which have survived from the same period. For the sample used in *Food, Energy and Industriousness*, 263 of these inventories were transcribed, and of these I was able to match 116 wills with the individual deceased labourers. This means that a majority of the transcribed inventories

34 Cambridgeshire Archives Service (hereafter CAS), Will of James Sibley or Ely, 1690.
35 CAS, Will of Thomas Nicks of Oakington, 1672.
36 On female inheritance patterns, see Erickson, *Women and Property*, pp. 61–78.

from Cambridgeshire have survived without a matching will. Of those with a will, only 20 percent were worth less than £5 compared to 37 percent of inventories with no will. This implies that those who left a will were more wealthy, but then begs the question what was the reason for inventories to be made if someone died intestate? Edward Hill who died intestate in 1728 left only two beds and some unnamed goods worth 13s. in two rooms. John Hitch who died a year earlier left much more including a bed with curtains, a chest, five tables, twelve chairs, a pewter case and dressing board and cooking and fireplace equipment, but this was still only worth £2 12s.[37] There is nothing to indicate these individuals possessed any land, and the cost of the appraisal would hardly seem worth it, but for some reason lost to us, they were exhibited. Twenty out of 62 intestate inventories (32 percent) with household goods worth £6 or less had no crops or animals, credits or money worth over £1.5 which might have justified making an inventory. In contrast, only seven out of 75 intestate inventories (nine percent) with household goods valued at more than £6 had no crops or animals, credits, or money worth over £1.5.

In Table 12.1 the nature of bequests in the Cambridgeshire wills are presented together with the values of the inventories they could be matched with. Here the average total value of the inventories in this matched sample at £22 14s. is similar the average value of £24 12s. of all 263.[38]

We can see that this sample of labourers includes a majority who bequeathed some land, and 22 percent who bequeathed animals. Unsurprisingly the value of farm capital possessed by those who left animals as bequests was 70 percent higher than for those who did not. But, very surprisingly, those with land had a less valuable portion of their property accounted for by crops, animals, and farm equipment. This is probably because in numerous wills, when land is described it is said to be fen land which might well be some form of marsh or peat and not more valuable grazing land, although it is impossible to say for certain without any valuation. These labourers' household goods were also worth less on average (£18) than those who had no property, implying that possession of such land was not a means to increase material wealth. Also, we can see that labourers who bequeathed no land, and those who bequeathed neither land nor animals actually had more valuable household possessions and more debts owed to them, implying that whatever work they did gave them the ability to purchase more household goods. Although this sample is limited, this fact seems to agree with what Arthur Young complained of in the

37 CAS, YW [1728], Inventory of Edward Hill, 1728.

38 Muldrew, *Food, Energy*, p. 172.

TABLE 12.1 Cambridgeshire will and inventory matched sample 1660–1750: average amounts (median values)

	Number	Value of inventory (£)	Value of household goods	Value of animals and outdoor goods	Value of debts owed
All wills matched with inventories	116 (100%)	22.7 (16.3)	8.4 (8)	9.4 (5.89)	4.5
Wills bequeathing landed property	67 (58%)	18	8.2	6.3	3
Wills bequeathing animals	25 (22%)	30.6	9.3	17.5	3.8
Wills not bequeathing landed property	49 (42%)	29.1	12.8	10.2	6.1
Wills bequeathing neither animals nor property	34 (29%)	28.1	10.7	10.5	7
Inventories without wills	137	25.5 (15.75)	7.3 (6)	11.6 (6.4)	5.6

1770s, that after ca. 1650, a small piece of land provided a secure rather than a prosperous standard of living which labourers who had possession thereof were happy to maintain as long as they could, even when they had an opportunity to increase their prosperity through more "industrious" but insecure wage labour.[39] Finally, those inventories which have survived where no will was made have less valuable household goods, but more valuable capital goods, but certainly do not indicate any financial reason why a will was not made.

39 Muldrew, *Food, Energy*, pp. 1–2.

There were some unusual cases where one can see an obvious reason for the making of the will, such as Stephen Watson, who ordered his house sold to pay a debt of £4 16s. he had borrowed on its security, or Edward Tisdall who willed that his freehold of three acres should be rented out to fellow Quakers, or William Lacey who bequeathed £5 each to a wool comber and butter weigher to help build a Meeting House in Wisbech.[40] Other labourers bequeathed the remaining terms of leases they had (William Harrison, William Mason).[41] One other labourer gave his ground and barn to his son, but instructed him to pay his sister's child £5 and to give her free passage through his house (John Green).[42] A variety of other reasons included in the wills indicate possible reasons for their creation. Henry Marshall willed his house and garden and the residue of goods to his wife for her life, after which these were to be bequeathed to Cornelius Austin, a joiner, and Richard Thompson. He also, amongst other legacies, gave the daughter of his brother £4, which was to be paid by Austin and Thompson one year after his wife's decease, provided that she was not forced to sell the house for necessary want.[43] Richard Graine willed that all of the household goods his wife brought into the marriage should go to her, and that she should also have what she wanted of the goods he possessed before marriage, during her life, and that they should go to his eldest son thereafter. He also willed that his wife and eldest son should act as co-heirs of his saffron ground, and gave his eldest son, Richard, five guineas, another son William four guineas, and his granddaughter one guinea.[44] Other wills were more complicated, such as that of Lawrence Hammond who willed that if his wife was to remarry he gave to his two sons £3 each, and if she did not, his goods were to be divided amongst four people after her decease.[45]

We can often gain valuable information by comparing the bequests in wills to the goods listed in the inventories, which were usually taken a few days after the will was drawn up. The inventory of Thomas Cole printed below contains £6 worth of livestock, but his household possessions were modest, and he possessed no land. This did not stop him, however, from making a will in which he bequeathed almost every item he had to various people including a servant who had probably taken the role of a housemate since his wife had already

40 CAS, Will of Edward Tisdall or Teasdale of Wisbeach, 1708; Will of William Lacey of Ely, 1690.

41 CAS, Will of William Harrison of Ely, 1706; Will of William Mason of Stow-cum-Quy, 1707.

42 CAS, Will of John Green of Gamlingay, 1676.

43 CAS, Will of Henry Marshall of Over, 1662.

44 CAS, Will of Richard Grain or Graine or Green of Great Shelford, 1731.

45 CAS, Will of Lawrence Hammond of Barton, 1680.

died. Both the will and inventory are reproduced here so that this relationship can be seen. Also, as his wife had died and there was no main beneficiary named for the residue of his estate, all the bequests here can be located in the inventory.

Bequests in the Will of Thomas Cole, 22/09/1671[46]

- To son William: my best bedstead with a flock bed, one pair of sheets, one blanket, one pillow, one pillowbear, a press cupboard, one white tailed cow, one bolster.
- To son John: 30s. one weather hogget [sheep], one pair of sheets, pillowbare.
- To daughter Rosemond Witt: one black cow, one pair of sheets, one pillowbare, the great box, the backtub, one cimdell.
- To granddaughter Witt: one great brass kettle, the best ewe and lamb.
- To granddaughter Susanna Cole: one hogget.
- To his servant Elizabeth Morlin: one boarded bed with a flockbed, one blanket, one little kettle, one skillet, one pail.
- To John Ratford: my linsey wosly doublet.

Inventory of Thomas Cole senior, Maddingly, 25/9/1671[47]

Purse and apparel £1
1 hofeell [?] 3s. 4d.
hay 6s. 8d.
2 cows £4
6 sheep £1 5s.
1 hog 10s.

Chamber
1 half-headed bed, 1 flock bed, bolster, pillows, blanket 16s.

Hall
2 chests, 1 little table, 1 drinking vessel, 1 tub, 1 meal stand 12s.

Kitchen
1 press cupboard 5s.

46 CAS, Will of Thomas Cole of Madingly, 1671.

47 CAS, VC29:167, inventory of Thomas Cole, 1671.

4 brass kettles 10s.
4 pair-sheets, 4 pillowbears 13s. 4d.
lumber 6d.

Sum £10 13s. 4d.

One unmarried labourer, John Tinworth, who died in 1662 worth £14 10s. was only inventoried for what he left in his will; a cow worth £2 10s., which he left to his sister, and "what money he hath," which his inventory identified as £12 together with his apparel, which he left equally to Sarah Larkin and Ellen Smith, although his mother was to have the interest on Ellen Smith's part as long as she lived. Most likely, being unmarried, he was living in someone else's house.[48] Thomas Christmas, who died a widower in 1686, possessed a valuable amount of livestock worth £29 14s., and household goods worth £8 9s. (but which included £1 13s. 4d. worth of pewter and brass). After dividing many of these goods between his children and grandchildren, he evidently felt his livestock made him wealthy enough to give 8s. 4d. to the poor of Chatteris.[49] In another case, when we compare a will with a lot of detailed bequests of individual goods to the inventory there is a large discrepancy. In his will made March 12, 1651 William Hudson left to Margaret his wife,

> four pair of hemptare sheets, six pillowbeares, six table napkins, two hand towels, eleven pewter platters, five pottingers, four little saucers, one warming pan, two wicker chairs, one buffet stool, one feather bed, one bolster, two pillows, one coverlet, one cupboard, one hutch, one bed settle, one long table in the custody of John Bromis of Ely, two forms, one carved coffer in the parlour and one box, one bedstead in the parlour.

He also left 5s. to his son to be paid by his executor six months after his death if it be demanded. The rest of his goods he gave to his other son John, who was also made executor.[50] Here there are numerous items such as the hand towels, napkins, saucers, warming pan, pewter platters together with the cupboard and hutch in which these items were perhaps stored which were not listed in the inventory made up six days later:

48 CAS, Will of John Tinworth of Comberton, 1662; VC29:187.
49 CAS, Will of Thomas Christmas of Meapal, 1686; VC33:163.
50 CAS, Will of William Hudson of Ely, 1651.

William Hudson, Cambridgeshire/18/3/1651[51]

Purse and apparel £1 8s.
1 furnished feather bed £2 10s.

Little room
1 boarded bed, 1 pair-cobirons 6s. 8d.
2 hutches, 1 box, 4 pewter dishes 13s. 6d.

Parlour
1 bedstead, 1 little table, 3 stools, 1 chair, 1 old flock bed 17s.

Buttery
2 brass pots, 1 kettle and things 1s. 11d.

Hall
1 table, 2 forms, 3 chairs, 2 forks. 1 cheese press, 1 pair bellows 12s.
2 cows £4
Sum £11 18s. 2d.

Presumably, these goods were already taken by the wife at some point in the six days before the inventory was made up. It would certainly be instructive to compare more wills and inventories where large numbers of bequests are itemised to their respective inventory to see how common this practice was. If it was common, it would mean that inventories of married men who died before their wives actually underestimate the possession of goods. Since the majority of inventoried individuals fall into this category this could be significant.

A number of wills also show that debts owed to labourers in their inventories were being used to earn interest, demonstrating the importance of savings.[52] John Brooks, who died in 1689, left £13 and various clothes, as well as bonds and bills due to him which were worth £18.[53] Five wills mentioned bonds, four money put to use, and four used the word interest.[54] A very interesting example is that of Richard Fox of Orwell, who in his will dated 15 January 1697 left: £12 with interest on bond due from Peter Brumbly of Barrington, Cambridge to his

51 CAS, Inventory of William Hudson of Ely, 1651.

52 Muldrew, "From Credit to Savings?," pp. 400–06; Ann Kussmaul, *Servants in Husbandry in Early Modern England* (Cambridge: Cambridge University Press, 1981), pp. 81–83.

53 CAS, Will of John Brooks of Rampton, 1689.

54 For examples see CAS, Will of Stephen Watson of Teversham, 1685; John Brooks above.

son Richard. He also bequeathed to his daughter Elizabeth, "the full sume of fifty pounds of lawfull money of England to be paid to her when she shall attaine to the age of one and twenty years by my Trusty and welbeloved friend William Fairechloe of Orwell … shopkeeper whom I ordaine is to bee trustee for taking Care of the said fifty pounds, the same to secure and put out to Interest."[55]

Here the inventory lists debts owing to him of £62, exactly the sum that was mentioned in the will. The will also gives his wife three rooms on the west side of his copyhold cottage where he dwelled until his death, with a little barn in the yard and 3.5 acres of land, and the inventory lists hay, barley and a cow and pig. The cottage was then in the occupation of his son-in-law Richard Harrup, who was granted first regress and egress to the said dwelling through the other part of the cottage. Four rooms with two beds were listed in the inventory, including a kitchen, but with no fireplace equipment, implying this was probably shared with the son-in-law's family. The fact that he was sharing a house with his daughter and her husband and possibly more children shows how poorer families could co-habit and share things like cooking goods.[56] The will of John Fann, a labourer from Ely, who died in 1691 possessing a small feather bed with a bolster pillow and seven sheets, two old tables, three old chairs and a frying pan, indicates he was living with a landlady when he became sick and made the will to bequeath 40s. to her. Curiously the inventory also lists £99 of good and bad debts owed to Fenn, which are unmentioned in the will, and had no effect on his very poor material standard of living.[57] How he came to be owed such a massive amount of money is impossible to know form these documents. Possibilities include a disputed legacy, or accumulated seaman's wages, but the debt perhaps indicates that the landlady had the will made to secure her small wages out of this legacy.

Fourteen labourers' wills (twelve percent) made specific bequests of individual household goods. The most common items to be specified were beds. It was not only Shakespeare who felt it was important to pass on his bed, and indeed in the inventories a bed, especially a feather bed, with its appurtenances was almost inevitably the most valuable item in a house. In the inventory of John Gaunt listed below, fully 60 percent of the value of the inventory was in the form of beds and their appurtenances. In this case the will simply bequeathed 5s. to his sister, 2s. 6d. to his son, 10s. to the daughter of Henry Thomas and the rest to his wife.[58]

55 CAS, Richard Fox of Orwell, 1697.

56 CAS, VC35:324, inventory of Richard Fox.

57 CAS, Will of John Fann of Ely, 1691.

58 For a discussion of the legal position of widows of intestate husbands see Erickson, *Women and Property*, pp. 174–86.

John Gaunt, Wisbech, Cambridgeshire/3/6/1700[59]

Purse and apparel £1 6s. 4d.

Low Room
1 feather bed, pillows, bolsters, blankets, 1 coverlet, 1 bedstead as it stands, furniture £4 10s.
5 sheets, 6 napkins, 4 pillowbears £1 5s.
1 nest of drawers 16s.
1 old cupboard 5s.
1 joined stool, table 2s. 6d.
6 chairs 3s. 6d.
1 pair-fire grates, irons, 1 warming pan £1 7s. 6d.
2 pewter dishes, 1 pewter pottinger, 1 pewter salt, earthenware 5s.
1 brass kettle, 1 brass pot kettle 15s.

Chamber
2 feather beds, pillows, bolsters, blankets, bedstead £4
2 old chests, 1 trunk, 1 lantern, 1 basket, 2 pairs brass scales, 2 sieves 6s. 9d.

Back Room
1 wash keeler, 3 beer vessels 2s. 6d.
lumber 2s. 6d.

Sum £15 7s. 6d.

Many other things were listed in wills as well, including cupboards, pewter dishes, tables chests, "a pot in the kitchen" and a lock and key. But bequests which detailed individual items were in the minority in almost every will. Whether a will listed land, animals or goods, the main type of bequest was in the form of a monetary sum. As the work of Donald Spaeth has noted, goods itemised in inventories were most often intended to go to auction rather than as bequests, which is why they were listed in batches with a price given for the entire group rather than individually.[60] George House, who died in 1717 worth £10.23 ordered in his will that his goods were to be sold by his brothers to put his son out as apprentice, and from the remainder 3/5 and 2/5 were to go to

59 CAS, VC35:484, inventory of John Gaunt, 1700.

60 Donald Spaeth, "Valuing Household Goods in Early Modern England," (paper presented at the North American Conference on British Studies, Montreal, 2012).

his two daughters respectively and 1s. each to his nephews and his brother-in-law. Again in this case it would be worth considering the extent to which a wife would have wished to remove goods willed to her before the remainder was auctioned off.[61] Most of the wills with neither livestock or land gave the majority of the goods to a surviving wife or some other primary recipient if the deceased was unmarried or widowed.

What is perhaps most striking about many of the wills is how often labourers went to the trouble of bequeathing very small amounts to various individuals. One shilling was a very common sum to give to children, relatives or friends. Ambrose Bent who died possessing a bullock, a bed, a table a few chairs and little else, worth only £3 10s. wrote his will to give a shilling each to his brother and sister, and the rest to his wife.[62] Thomas Wadnam of Barton gave his son-in-law his year-old calf, a shilling to his cousin of Trinity College, another 1s. to his second cousin and the remainder to his intended wife Ann Cook.[63] Presumably the will was needed because he was not yet married, but this does not make the bequests less significant. Thomas Maulden of Stapleford, who died in 1670 with £12 5s. worth of inventoried assets, left 1s. each to two brothers and one sister married to a labourer. The rest of his estate he left to Jane Joyce, a widow from the Isle of Ely.[64] There are even twelve wills where such bequests were the only ones listed, apart from the majority of the estate being given to a wife or child. In such cases perhaps the making of a will was an important part of recording valuable social relations, which were obviously no less important simply because someone was poor.[65] Jeffrey Marsh, who died in 1693 left his house and barn to his wife and 20s. each to three siblings, however when his inventory was taken it only listed the bare necessities to sleep and eat:

> 1 furnished bed, 10s.[66]
> 1 iron pan, 1 hutch, 1 chair 4s.
> 1 press cupboard, 1 kneading trough 4s.
> 1 table, 1 form, 2 chairs 3s. 6d.
> 1 kettle, 1 skillet, 1 brass pot 4s.

61 CAS, Will of George House of Wittlesey, 1717.
62 CAS, Will of Ambrose Brett of Cottenham, 1666; VC29:306.
63 CAS, Will of Thomas Wadman of Barton, 1691; VC34:220.
64 CAS, Will of Thomas Maulden of Stapleford, 1670.
65 Ilana K. Ben-Amos, *The Culture of Giving: Informal Support and Gift-Exchange in Early Modern England* (Cambridge: Cambridge University Press, 2008).
66 The lack of clothing is unusual and presumably it had already been taken by someone.

1 barrel, 2 tubs, 1 ale-stoole 6s.
1 pair tongs, 1 fire pan, 1 little pair hob irons 1s. 6d.
3 pewter dishes 3s. 6d.
Sum £1 16s. 6d.

2 Labourers' Inventories and Change over Time

Returning to my larger inventory sample already discussed (see above pp. 316–19 and Graph 12.1), it can be recalled that the correlation between the total value of everything in the inventory and the value of the household goods was somewhat low (.44). However, if we look at the 278 labourers' inventories which survive from *before 1650*, the correlation between total value of everything in the inventory and the value of the household goods is much stronger (.59). This suggests that the value of household goods was more strongly related to the chances of an inventory being taken before 1650, which then declined afterwards. Looking only at inventories from after this date, the correlation between total value of the inventory and the value of the household goods drops to only .39 and that between agricultural wealth and household wealth to an extremely weak .18. This is not surprising given that the percentage of the population inventoried went up after 1650 (see above), but it makes it more difficult to trace change over time. One possible way of dealing with this is to look at only those inventories which have fewer valuable agricultural goods, given that much of the value which triggered the probate process for all occupations was contained in capital farm goods such as animals.[67]

Using this observation, we can reduce the labourers' inventory sample by eliminating all those who possessed crops and animals and other farm goods worth more than £1.5, which covers most instances where more than one cow or a few sheep were possessed. We also need to exclude all those with unusually high assets of money of over £25, and debts due to them of over £35, as well unusually wealthier labourers as outliers.[68] This results in a greatly

67 Keibek and Shaw-Taylor, "Early Modern Rural By-Employments," pp. 244–81.

68 £35 worth of debts is obviously a lot, and it might be argued that this would make such labourers unusually wealthy, but I have chosen these figures to enlarge the sample. Since labourers could use bonds, and have wages in arrears as a form of saving, it might represent a form of security, but was not necessarily used on consumption. When all debts of over £10 are removed from the sample, the average value of the inventory excluding the debts remain about the same, and the value of the household goods are only about 10s. less on average. Also, only two out of fourteen people with debts over £30 lived outside of Hampshire and Kent, so these individuals might well have accumulated arrears

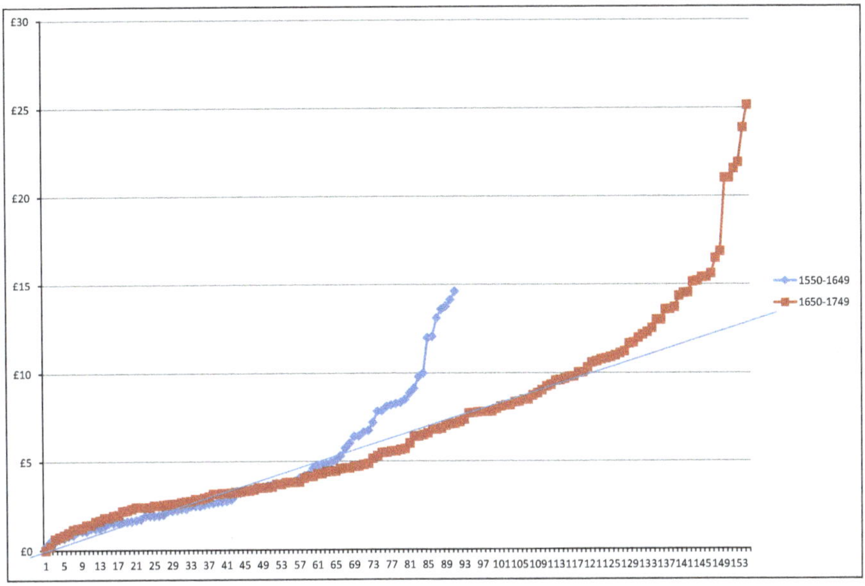

GRAPH 12.4 Value of household goods in labourers' inventories on curves for the periods 1550–1649 and 1650–1750

reduced sample of 245 inventories, but one still large enough to make meaningful observations for each time period. In Graph 12.4 this reduced sample has been put on two curves, one for before 1650, and one after, to determine where each curve starts to rise more steeply because of wealthier outliers. For the earlier period this is about £6.5, and for that latter period about £12.5. If inventories above these amounts are removed, this results in a sample of 205 inventories which are broken down into components of the inventories in Table 12.2.

Once this is done, the total value of the inventories is, of course, much smaller than the larger sample, but so too is the value of household goods. Looking at the median figures in column six, the value of household goods is between 32 percent and 54 percent lower than those in column seven. Using the same reduction on just inventories from Cheshire between 1660 and 1750, to compare to Keibek's sample, leaves us with a sample of 26 inventories form the original sample of 51.[69] This results in a reduction of median inventory

while working at sea previously in their life. Non-agricultural labourers working in the Hampshire dockyards which were included in the original sample for comparison have, however, been removed. Muldrew, *Food, Energy*, pp. 200–07.

69 Ibid., p. 172.

TABLE 12.2 Values in the Muldrew reduced inventory sample of debts, outdoor goods, and household goods over time with outliers removed (in £)

Time period[a]	Total inventory value	Outdoor goods	Debts owed to	Money	Household goods	Household goods in the total Muldrew sample[b]
1550–99 mean (27)	6.65 (8.3)[c]	0.26	3.46 (4.32)	0.09	2.84 (3.55)	5.61 (7)
1550–99 median	4.66 (5.83)	0.00	0.00	0.00	2.69 (3.36)	4 (5)
1600–49 mean (43)	11.28	0.27	7.9	0.25	2.86	8.58
1600–49 median	5.14	0.00	0.95	0.00	2.49	5.39
1650–1700 mean (81)	13	0.23	6.39	1.24	5.15	10.03
1650–1700 median	8.42	0	0.00	0.00	4.3	7.69
1700–1749 mean (55)	14.35	0.21	6.34	1.57	6.23	13.12
1700–1749 median	8.67	0.00	0.00	0.00	6.57	9.57

a The numbers in parenthesis in this column are the numbers of inventories used
b Muldrew, *Food, Energy*, p. 183
c The figures in parenthesis in this line have been adjusted upwards by 25 percent to account for the inflation of prices. See Muldrew, *Food, Energy*, p. xvi for further explanation of which prices have been used
d The numbers in parenthesis are cases used

value of £23 and median household goods value of £5.95 to a median inventory value of £11.6 (50 percent) and a median household value of £3.75 (37 percent). For the total reduced sample, the reduction of the median value of household goods is almost exactly the same; £3.7 (39 percent), but the median value of the total inventory is less, only £7.1 (62 percent). This is less of a reduction than Keibek's method, which was 72 percent. But it provides a reasonable enough sample to measure change over time.

In column six, we can see that there is still an increase in the value of household goods after the English civil war (1642–49), and a continued increase into the eighteenth century, just as there is in the larger sample (column seven). In the reduced sample, though, the percentage rise is 73 percent for the median value between 1600–49 and 1650–1699, and a 53 percent jump in the median value moving to the period 1700–1749, or an overall rise of 163 percent. This compares to a 43-percent and 17-percent rise in the median over the same two periods, and a total rise of 77 percent for the unadjusted sample. Obviously, the amounts are less than the larger sample as these are poorer individuals, but the overall rise from the early seventeenth century is much greater. In part, we can also see that this was because the median value of household goods actually *fell* by 39 percent between 1600–1649, when inflation is taken into account. The rise in both the amount of cash found, and the debts owed in the reduced sample mirrors the larger sample of inventories, but again is obviously less because of the removal of the wealthier labourers. There is evidence, from the very few probate accounts that survive from some wealthier labourers, to suggest that the value of labourers' liabilities against their estates went down in the eighteenth century. If this was true for poorer labourers as well it would raise the actual value of labourers' estates, but that has not been taken into consideration here.[70]

This sample would seem to confirm that there was a significant *percentage* increase in the value of labouring families' material goods after the civil war, *but* this value was only in the range of £2–4 here. It would probably have been less for most labouring households if we were able to use Keibek's method of correction, but this does indicate that some extra income was available to spend. In comparison, the median, uncorrected, value of yeomen's consumption goods in just the county of Kent rose by £25.5 to £53.54.[71] Even that of husbandmen rose by £8.8 between the periods 1600–49 and 1700–1749.[72] Also, the *fall* in median household value when inflation is taken into consideration in the period 1600–1650, reinforces the great difficulty of this period, when population growth was outstripping the opportunities for agricultural labour, leading to a large increase in migrants seeking work in towns and cities, especially London. In addition, possibly as many as 400,000 mostly young men travelled abroad as indentured servants to the new world before 1660.

70 Muldrew, "From Credit to Savings?," pp. 402–07.

71 If these figures were reduced by a similar amount to farmers in Cheshire and Lancashire from 1700–1760 (55 percent), they would be £11.5 and £24 respectively.

72 Mark Overton, Jane Whittle, Darron Dean, and Andrew Hann, *Production and Consumption in English Households, 1600–1750* (Abingdon: Routledge, 2004), p. 188.

Also, we need to put inventory evidence in the age context of a society where around 50 percent of the population was below the age of 26, and about 17 to 18 percent between the ages of 15 to 24, and the average age of first marriage for men was about 26. Although no ages are given in probate documents, the one parish study which has been done shows about 70 percent of inventories were made for married individuals with children who were between the ages of 27 and 59.[73] Given the need to save enough to pay for the cost of small children before they could work for themselves, it was generally the poor who had to wait longer to get married, and in the period between 1600–1660, many did not get married at all.[74] Thus, for the approximately 30 percent of the population who were between circa 15 and 35 years of age, their standard of living was based on dependence as servants, or they were trying to find steady work as day labourers. And young, recently married couples, would have been poorer as they incurred the expenses of raising a family.[75] This can be seen in the inventories with very few, if any, household goods worth less than £2, which might well have been made for those unlucky enough to die in their twenties or early thirties.

3 Labourers' Inventories Compared to Worth Statements

There is one other source which we can use for comparison to further contextualise the wealth of labourers who left inventories, and to obtain more information on younger people. These are the witness statements from the church courts analysed by Shepard in *Accounting for Oneself*, which provide evidence of wealth from a much broader more inclusive and random social sample. These statements result from the need for witness deponents to declare what they were worth in goods, taking into account all debts, in trials which came before the English church courts. Occupational designators were listed in 8,782 out of 13,686 statements collected from between 1550–1649.[76] These included 273 statements by labourers, 1,104 for yeomen and 2,127 for husbandmen, for instance. Such self-evaluations were supposed to include the same range of

73 Overton, Whittle, Dean, and Hann, *Production and Consumption*, p. 27.

74 Edward A. Wrigley and Roger S. Schofield, *The Population History of England* (Cambridge: Cambridge University Press, 1989), pp. 261–65.

75 Edward A. Wrigley, Rosalind S. Davies, Jim E. Oeppen, and Roger S. Schofield, *English Population History from Family Reconstitution 1580–1837* (Cambridge: Cambridge University Press, 1997), p. 615.

76 Shepard, *Accounting*, p. 14.

movable goods as inventories, but with the crucial difference that here *any negative balance of debts owed by the witness over debts owed to them was to be subtracted*. Using the period 1625–49 as an example, these values ranged from a mean of £29.4 and a medium of £10 for husbandmen and a mean of £143.06 and median of £100 for yeomen, compared to a £4.75 mean and £2 median for labourers.[77] These figures, however, cannot be simply equated with inventory values because the latter omit any liabilities in the form of unpaid debts and so inflate the net value of the surviving goods.[78]

Shepard examined this by first comparing worth statements to some samples of inventories from similar places and time periods. Here she found that in general inventoried wealth was a little over twice the value of comparable worth statements.[79] In her Table 3.3 she also made a similar appraisal of a sample of probate accounts from Kent compared to worth statements from the Canterbury church courts, and probate accounts from Wiltshire and worth statements from the Salisbury church courts.[80] When compared to the charge in these probate accounts (which is the final net worth with debts and funeral and other costs on the estate *subtracted*), the value of the worth of witnesses in the diocese of Salisbury was roughly the same as the charge for gentry and yeomen in Wiltshire, but about 50 to 100 percent lower for husbandmen witnesses, and even lower in Kent. Given Keibek's estimation that almost all gentry and yeomen would have been probated, a rough match for these groups should be expected, but husbandmen, being poorer, would be much less likely to be inventoried, and even less likely to have had an account made for their estate, so it is not surprising that the mean and median worth statements were less.[81]

The proportion of witnesses who gave their occupation as "labourer" was roughly as unrepresentative of their proportion in the total population of the country as for probate inventory survival. There are 273 labourers in the witness sample compared to 2,145 husbandmen and 1,104 yeomen.[82] The highest

77 Ibid., pp. 69–70.

78 Spufford, "The Limitations," pp. 139–74.

79 Shepard, *Accounting*, p. 93 table 3.2. This table shows that there was quite a bit of variation between areas. Shepard also compared a sample of labourers with Everitt's sample but as Leigh Shaw-Taylor has shown many of these were not actually listed as labourers but were poor husbandmen selected by Everitt as proxies for labourers. These inventory values were still 18–40 percent higher than worth statements. Muldrew, *Food, Energy*, pp. 165–67, n. 9.

80 Shepard, *Accounting*, pp. 92–95.

81 Keibek, "Correcting the Probate Record," p. 16.

82 Shepard, *Accounting*, p. 69.

incidence of appearance was in the diocese of Cambridge and Ely where 6.3 percent of witnesses who provided an occupation stated they were labourers.[83] This was because poverty was suggestive of dependence and a vulnerability to influence – the very rationale behind the asking about worth in the first place. Because of this, if possible, plaintiffs and defendants would turn to witnesses who were less vulnerable to being doubted. Selection could also be influenced by the nature of the disputes, many of which were over probate, which would have involved fewer labourers as witnesses as well. However, proximity to the events concerning the case in question was undoubtedly the most important criterion of being a witness.

Also, in many cases another question was posed about "maintenance" or income separately to that of total worth, and in the answers to these questions we find much more evidence of people describing their maintenance as being "by their own labour". Twenty four percent of men and 22.5 percent of women claimed they lived by their labour (out of a total subset of 2,177 of which 1,459 were men and 718 were women).[84] In comparison, only a small percentage (2.7) of witnesses asked this question provided an occupational answer of "labourer". This means that 352 men and 161 women styled themselves as living by their labour. The median worth of individuals who stated that they were living by their labour was £0.5 before 1600 and £1.25 between 1600–1624 and £1 from 1625–49.[85] However, the men who claimed this were a disproportionally young group. 45.9 percent of them who claimed they were worth 40s. or less, or little or nothing, and/or poor were below the age of 25.[86] This was in contrast to women who identified themselves this way throughout their life course. Possibly this was an important reason why the median worth of those witnesses, living by their labour, who gave monetary evaluations of their goods was lower than those with the occupation labourer. In Shepard's Table 2.10 the median wealth of the six labourers under the age of 25 who provided an occupational title was £0.38 before 1660 and £.5 between 1600 and 1649. In this same table, of the 10.3 percent (1,410) of men who did not value their wealth, responding that they were worth little or nothing or poor, only seven to eight percent were over 35 years of age.[87] An occupational title, as one might expect, was something which was usually associated with marriage and establishment.

83 Ibid., p. 21.

84 Ibid., pp. 151–52. Page 160 lists the occupation of witnesses and how they answered the questions. There were only 30 matches for labourers.

85 Ibid., p. 177.

86 Ibid., p. 132.

87 Ibid., p. 78.

Also it should be noted that those witnesses who described themselves as poor, and who *also* gave cash values, 66 percent provided round figures of 20s. before *c*.1600 and 40s. until 1660, and then either £5 or £10 after this date (numbers are not given).[88] Since 20.9 percent of labourers who gave an occupational title responded they were worth little or nothing or poor (compared to 71.9 percent who gave a positive monetary value), this means that about 13.7 percent of total labourers gave round figures. Such round figures probably reflect an uncertainty about their level of indebtedness rather than an accurate valuation of goods, but the unchanging value of £2 as the median on Shepard's Table 2.7 suggests that this practice was quite common, and this also needs to be kept in mind when comparing worth values to inventory values.

In Table 12.3 below I have entered the values of total inventoried wealth from the reduced labourers' inventory sample in Table 12.2 above for the same four time periods in the first two rows. Immediately below this I have entered the worth amounts from Shepard's analysis which are only available for the first two periods. Here we can see that the inventory values are still significantly higher than the worth statements. However, we still need to deal with the problem of debts. It is important to consider in such comparisons, that the value of inventories alone, before any liabilities are subtracted from an estate will be higher than a worth statement given the prevalence of credit in this society.[89] However, it is difficult to know just how much, given the bias of probate accounts toward more indebted individuals. In a rare sample of inventories in which both inward and outwards debts were listed, from Darlington between 1600–1625, in 115 inventories worth less than £100 the value of the debts owed by the deceased was on average £14.4 which was £5 higher than those owed to the deceased. The average total value of these inventories was £62.8 which means that their net worth was 23 percent lower than simply a listing of their goods and debts owed to them would have indicated. Presumably, if they would have made worth statements, they would have been about 23 percent lower than their inventoried value.[90]

To do this, in the final two rows, I have eliminated the value of debts owed to the deceased on the assumption that their liabilities would have been 25 percent higher. As a result, the mean figures are almost the same. The median figures are more difficult to interpret since 57 percent of the deceased labourers

88 The large jump after 1660 is quite striking, although it might have something to do with the increasing predominance of London in the sample after 1660. Shepard, *Accounting*, p. 64, Table 2.5; pp. 94–95, pp. 124–25, pp. 128–29.

89 Muldrew, *Economy of Obligation*, chapters 1–4.

90 Ibid., p. 118.

had no debts owing to them on death, which makes the mean equal zero in all but the period 1600–1649. If, instead, the average debts are subtracted from the mean total value then the result is actually lower than the worth figures. This is somewhat artificial but many labourers with large debts owing to them had very few household goods. For instance, 60 percent of the poorest labourers in my sample in terms of household goods (less than £1.75 in value) had outstanding debts owed to them. The correlation between debts owed and household value is, furthermore, almost negative (.18).

The final two columns of Table 12.3 also give the values of inventories after 1650 for comparison, as Shepard's worth sample stops in 1649 owing to a reduction in the use of church courts after this date. As noted above, the period from 1575–1650 was a period when the cost of food was continually rising, causing many labourers to be constantly indebted for basic necessities, which is a main reason for their lack of credit, and suspicion that they would be forced to take bribes to keep their access to purchases alive. Indeed, there is much evidence that a lot of debts of the poor had to be forgiven as a form of charity.[91] In contrast, the period after 1650 was one in which population growth was stagnant and opportunities for work increased as more farmland was cultivated and industry and trade expanded.[92]

This rough correlation suggests that the reduced labourers' inventory sample presented in Table 12.2 represents a range of experience for the *working adult* labouring population. At any one time, some percentage of labourers would have found themselves bereft of many goods living with some relative, or on the road sleeping rough in a barn at some point in their life cycle. As mentioned at the beginning, probate evidence is a snapshot which excludes such individuals. It has been estimated that rarely did those on relief form more than five to six percent of parish populations at any one time.[93] But the number of those on the road before 1650 was certainly higher, as indicated by the many witnesses who appeared before the church courts claiming little maintenance or that they were worth nothing. But these individuals were most likely to be young and unmarried or very old, when the possession of goods was limited for most individuals in society. Some middle-aged labourers may have had to sell goods to pay their debts as well, but whether their creditors would force them to sell everything is hard to say. Overall, the fact that Keibek's method

91 Ibid., pp. 304–09.

92 Muldrew, *Food, Energy*, pp. 260–319.

93 Steve Hindle, *On the Parish? The Micro-Politics of Poor Relief in Rural England c.1550–1750* (Oxford: Clarendon, 2004), pp. 271–73.

TABLE 12.3 Comparison of the total Muldrew inventory sample with Shepard's worth estimates (in £)

	1550–99	1600–49	1650–99	1700–49
Reduced Muldrew inventory sample (mean)	6.65	11.28	13.0	14.35
Reduced Muldrew inventory sample (median)	4.66	5.14	8.42	8.67
Shepard worth evaluations (mean)[d]	2.85 (104)	4.54 (169)		
Shepard worth evaluations (median)	2.0	2.0		
Reduced Muldrew inventory sample; debts owed to (mean)	3.46	7.9	6.39	6.34
Reduced Muldrew inventory sample without debts owing (mean)	3.19	3.38	6.61	8.01
Reduced Muldrew sample without debts owing (median)	1.47	0	2.03	2.33

of correcting for wealth bias produced a lower median than that achieved in Table 12.2 suggests the number with few possessions was considerable.

One thing we can tell from this study is that there were reasons not directly related to wealth for making a will. For some labourers making a will was perhaps a way of expressing their "worth" in Shepard's terms. For others it was evidently worth making a will to avoid potential familial conflict over the estate. Although the values might not have been great in absolute terms, they might have been so in relative terms to the recipients of the bequests. The most important finding of this admittedly small sample of will/inventory comparisons is that the possession of some heredity small holding or more than one or two animals worth less than £1 10s., was not directly correlated to household consumption goods. The finding that some inventories might have been taken after certain goods had been taken by the surviving spouse also needs to be investigated further. Certainly, it would now be instructive to look at a broader sample of wills from some other county. Also, it would be very interesting to perform a similar reductive exercise to select the inventories of rural spinsters and widows with few animals and limited debts and cash to compare their wealth and bequests to those of labourers. For even those with little to leave, the distribution of assets between the surviving spouse, children and other remained important. A poor family was still a family.

References

Arkell, Tom. "The Probate Process." In *When Death do us Part: Understanding and Interpreting the Probate Records of Early Modern England*, edited by Tom Arkell, Nesta Evans, and Nigel Goose, pp. 3–13. Hertfordshire: Leopard's Head Press, 2000.

Ben-Amos, Ilana K. *The Culture of Giving: Informal Support and Gift-Exchange in Early Modern England*. Cambridge: Cambridge University Press, 2008.

Bonfield, Lloyd. *Devising, Dying and Dispute: Probate Litigation in Early Modern England*. Farnham: Ashgate, 2013.

Cox, Jeff and Nancy. "Probate 1500–1800: A System in Transition." In *When Death do us Part: Understanding and Interpreting the Probate Records of Early Modern England*, edited by Tom Arkell, Nesta Evans, and Nigel Goose, pp. 14–37. Hertfordshire: Leopard's Head Press, 2000.

Erickson, Amy Louise. "An Introduction to Probate Accounts." In *The Records of the Nation*, edited by G.H. Martin and Peter Spufford, pp. 273–86. Woodbridge: Boydell, 1990.

Erickson, Amy Louise. *Women and Property in Early Modern England*. London: Routledge, 1993.

Harrington, Duncan, Sarah Pearson, and Susan Rose, eds. *Kent Hearth Tax Assessment, Lady Day 1664*. Hearth Tax Series, vol. II. London: British Record Society in association with the Kent Archaeological Society, 2000.

Hindle, Steve. *On the Parish? The Micro-Politics of Poor Relief in Rural England c.1550–1750*. Oxford: Clarendon, 2004.

Keibek, Sebastian. "Correcting the Probate Record for Wealth Bias." Cambridge Working Papers in Economic and Social History No. 28, March 2017: pp. 1–25.

Keibek, Sebastian. "From Inventories to Households: What Removing Inventories' Social Bias Reveals about Eighteenth-Century English Consumption." Unpublished paper presented at the European Social Science History Conference, Valencia, 2016.

Keibek, Sebastian, and Leigh Shaw-Taylor. "Early Modern Rural By-Employments: A Re-examination of the Probate Inventory Evidence." *Agricultural History Review* 61–2 (2013): pp. 244–81.

Kussmaul, Ann. *Servants in Husbandry in Early Modern England*. Cambridge: Cambridge University Press, 1981.

Maegraith, Janine, and Craig Muldrew. "Consumption and Material Life." In *Oxford Handbook of Early Modern European History*, edited by Hamish Scott, pp. 369–97. Oxford: Oxford University Press, 2015.

Money, John, ed. *The Chronicles of John Cannon Excise Officer and Writing Master*, vol. 1–2. Oxford: Published for the British Academy by Oxford University Press, 2010.

Mortimer, Ian. "Why were Probate Accounts Made? Methodological Issues Surrounding the Historical use of Administrators' and Executors' Accounts." *Archives*, 31 (2006): pp. 2–17.

Muldrew, Craig. "Credit, Market Relations, and Debt Litigation in Late Seventeenth Century England, with Particular Reference to King's Lynn." PhD diss., University of Cambridge, 1990.

Muldrew, Craig. *Food, Energy and the Creation of Industriousness: Work and Material Culture in Agrarian England, 1550–1780*. Cambridge: Cambridge University Press, 2011.

Muldrew, Craig. "From Credit to Savings? An Examination of Debt and Credit in Relation to Increasing Consumption in England, c. 1650 to 1770." In *Quaderni Storici* 137 (2011): pp. 391–413.

Muldrew, Craig. *The Economy of Obligation: The Culture of Credit and Social Relations in Early Modern England*. London: Palgrave, 1998.

Overton, Mark, Jane Whittle, Darron Dean, and Andrew Hann. *Production and Consumption in English Households, 1600–1750*. Abingdon: Routledge, 2004.

Schurer, Kevin, and Tom Arkell, eds. *Surveying the People: The Interpretation and Use of Document Sources for the Study of Population in the Later Seventeenth Century*. Oxford: Leopard's Head Press, 1992.

Shepard, Alexandra. *Accounting for Oneself: Worth, Status, and the Social Order in Early Modern England*. Oxford: Oxford University Press, 2015.

Spaeth, Donald. "Valuing Household Goods in Early Modern England." Paper presented at the North American Conference on British Studies, Montreal, 2012.

Spufford, Margaret. *Contrasting Communities. English Villagers in the Sixteenth and Seventeenth Centuries*. Cambridge: Cambridge University Press, 1974.

Spufford, Peter, ed. *Guide to the Probate Accounts of England and Wales*, 2 vols. London: British Record Society, 1999.

Staves, Susan. *Married Women's Separate Property in England, 1660–1833*. Cambridge, Mass.: Harvard University Press, 1990.

Todd, Barbara. "Freebench and Free Enterprise: Widows and their Property in Two Berkshire Villages." In *English Rural Society 1500–1800: Essays in Honour of Joan Thirsk*, edited by John Chartres and David Hey, pp. 196–200. Cambridge: Cambridge University Press, 1990.

Whittle, Jane. "Inheritance, Marriage, Widowhood and Remarriage: A Comparative Perspective on Women and Landholding in North-East Norfolk, 1440–1580." *Continuity and Change*, 13–1 (1998): pp. 33–72.

Whittle, Jane. *The Development of Agrarian Capitalism: Land and Labour in Norfolk 1440–1580*. Oxford: Clarendon, 2000.

Wrigley, Edward A., Rosalind S. Davies, Jim E. Oeppen, and Roger S. Schofield. *English Population History from Family Reconstitution 1580–1837*. Cambridge: Cambridge University Press, 1997.

Wrigley, Edward A., and Roger S. Schofield. *The Population History of England.* Cambridge: Cambridge University Press, 1989.

CHAPTER 13

Property, Power, Gender: Conflicts and Agency of a "Merchantess" in the Archduchy of Austria below the Enns in the Eighteenth Century

Andrea Griesebner

It was nearly a quarter of a century ago that Heide Wunder first drew our attention to the important functions of women in workshops and trade during the early modern period, formulating the thesis of the married couple as a "working couple".[1] If the bride and groom agreed on a community of marital property (*Ehegütergemeinschaft*) – as was the rule well into the nineteenth century in the Archduchy of Austria below the Enns, a core territory of the Habsburg Monarchy[2] – the couple also formed an "assets couple". The following pattern can be seen in marriage contracts evaluated by Gertrude Langer-Ostrawsky: First, the bride and groom "married" their respective wealth together. The wealth the bride brought to the union was often referred to as dowry (*Heiratsgut*), while the wealth of the groom was referred to as counter-dowry (*Widerlage*). There are also marriage contracts in which the bride counter-dowried (*widerlegte*) the groom's dowry.[3] Second, bride and groom agreed that the assets and property accumulated over the course of their marriage "should be and remain joint property". The couple had joint power of administration over both the "married" property and assets earned together over the course of the marriage. As the marriage

1 Heide Wunder, *He Is the Sun, She Is the Moon. Women in Early Modern Germany* (Cambridge, MA: Harvard University Press, 1998) (German version Munich: Beck, 1992). See also Olwen Hufton, *The Prospect Before Her. A History of Women in Western Europe* (London: Fontana, 1995).

2 On the marital regime of "community of marital property" see Gertrude Langer-Ostrawsky, "Vom Verheiraten der Güter. Bäuerliche und kleinbäuerliche Heiratsverträge im Erzherzogtum Österreich unter der Enns," in Margareth Lanzinger, Gunda Barth-Scalmani, Ellinor Forster, and Gertrude Langer-Ostrawsky, *Aushandeln von Ehe. Heiratsverträge der Neuzeit im europäischen Vergleich* (Cologne, Weimar, and Vienna: Böhlau, 2010, 2nd edition 2015), pp. 26–119.

3 See for example the 1698 marriage contract between Georg Winkhler and Kunigunde Fuxis. The widow contra-dowried (*widerlegt*) her husband's dowry (*Heyrath gueth*) with her "marital love and faithfulness" as well as her "complete assets". Quoted from Langer-Ostrawsky, "Vom Verheiraten der Güter", p. 80.

 | DOI:10.1163/9789004456204_014

contracts also evidence, the bride and groom could reserve the right of disposition for specific portions of their property and/or choose to add these to the community of marital property on the condition that the spouse proved his or her "good conduct".[4] Third, the marriage contract made provisions for the inheritance.

Following the death of a spouse, the surviving spouse and children succeeded as heirs instead of the family of the deceased (*Herkunftsfamilie*), as was the case in the separation of matrimonial property regime.[5] Depending on the number of children, the surviving spouse received between half to two-thirds of the joint property. The remaining portion went to the children as paternal or maternal inheritance. Marriage contracts also regulated the concrete distribution between the widow or widower and possible children resulting from the marriage. Should the marriage have remained childless, bride and groom also determined the amount the surviving spouse was expected to pay the relatives of the deceased. Such agreements vary from nothing to one-third of the matrimonial property.

Then as now, marriage was not the same for everybody. As Gertrude Langer-Ostrawsky has argued, we should not expect to find "normal" biographies among early modern period individuals or married couples. Although marriage was deemed to be "forever", growing old together was in no way usual. Spouses died as a result of accidents, sickness, epidemics, and in childbirth.[6] In regard to the balance of power within a marriage, it made a significant difference if the marriage was the first for bride and groom, or if one or both spouses had been previously married, and if the bride and groom had similar or divergent positions within the social hierarchy. Widows were sought-after partners on the marriage market. Apart from movable property, they often brought houses, land, and businesses or trade rights into their new marriages, and "married" these to their new husbands. In such constellations, it was not

4 See for example the 1647 marriage contract between Hanns Khorner and Margareth Hörzogin. The widow reserved her complete ("*ganz und gar*") right of disposition for certain pieces of land, and she kept her field in Lehenfeld "until her husband-to-be has proved his good conduct" ("*auf Ihres zukhunfftigen Ehewierths woll verhalten*"). Quoted from Langer-Ostrawsky, "Vom Verheiraten der Güter", p. 98.

5 On the marital regime of "separation of marital property" see Margareth Lanzinger, "Von der Macht der Linie zur Gegenseitigkeit. Heiratskontrakte in den Südtiroler Gerichten Welsberg und Innichen 1750–1850," in Margareth Lanzinger, Gunda Barth-Scalmani, Ellinor Forster, and Gertrude Langer-Ostrawsky, *Aushandeln von Ehe. Heiratsverträge der Neuzeit im europäischen Vergleich* (Cologne, Weimar, and Vienna: Böhlau, 2010, 2nd edition 2015), pp. 205–367.

6 Cf. Langer-Ostrawsky, "Vom Verheiraten der Güter," p. 67.

the women, but rather the men who "married-in" and, as Claudia Ulbrich put it so nicely, "had to adjust and learn to fit in".[7] The conflict potential rendered inherent in these marital constellations as a result of the prevailing gender order postulating men's superiority intensified when previously widowed brides brought children or stepchildren from earlier marriages into the new marriage. "Married-in" husbands not only had to deal with being married to a wife who was socially and economically much better positioned, but also with stepchildren who could accept or reject him as an "authority". With marriage laws assigning at least half of joint property to the surviving spouse, "married-in" spouses with few or no assets posed a financial threat to the children. In turn, the payment of paternal or maternal inheritance to the (step)children, due at the latest at the time of their wedding, could also lead to conflict for the new couple.

Although in the community of marital property system "married" assets as well as assets and property acquired during marriage were de jure joint property (*gemeinsames gut*), in instances of economic crisis, it mattered whether the assets threatened by bankruptcy had been brought in by the wife or the husband, as can be seen in some well documented marriage proceedings. Together with a team of collaborators, I am analysing early modern marriage proceedings carried out at the ecclesiastical court of the Lower Officialat of the Diocese of Passau and the ecclesiastical court of the Diocese of Vienna, courts to which most of the people of the Archduchy were subjected to.[8] It is remarkable that wives initiated 1,276, or 73 percent of the examined matrimonial proceedings between 1558 and 1783 and this percentage hardly changed in the various time segments examined. Women not only sued their husbands more often; they were also more likely to request a separation or divorce. With 39 percent, the husbands' most frequent legal interest was cohabitation, while only eight percent of the women sued for marital cohabitation with their separated husbands. 66 percent of the women but only 32 percent of the men approached the ecclesiastical courts to demand the right to live apart from the spouse.

---

7 Cf. Claudia Ulbrich, *Shulamit and Margarete. Power, Gender, and Religion in a Rural Society in Eighteenth-Century Europe* (Boston and Leiden: Brill, 2004), p. 109 (German version Cologne, Weimar, and Vienna: Böhlau, 1999).

8 The research was supported by the Austrian Science Fund (FWF) between 2011 and 2018 (P 23394 and P 28063) and by the Anniversary Fund of the Oesterreichische Nationalbank between 2018 and 2020 (17913). For the research projects, the funding and the collaborators see "Web portal. Marriages at Court 3.0," ed. Andrea Griesebner, accessed August 2020, https://www.univie.ac.at/ehenvorgericht/?lang=en.

We can, with some caution, put forth the thesis that women often took the initiative, either by initiating separation without authorisation, or by submitting separation or divorce litigation to the consistory if they believed that the assets or trades they brought into the marriage were threatened by their husbands' management. In cases where husbands demanded the consistorial court to order wives to return to the common household, it can reciprocally be assumed that litigations for "order of cohabitation" had often been introduced by "married-in" husbands.

In the sources on marriage litigation these conflict constellations are adumbrated, but, due to a lack of detailed descriptions of the origin and composition of matrimonial property and inheritance rights of children or stepchildren, cannot be analysed and therefore cannot be measured numerically. The ecclesiastical courts were not interested in a couple's economic conflicts, but rather in whether or not there was a reason acceptable under canon law for a limited separation or a permanent divorce from bed and board. Nonetheless, marriage proceedings before the consistories are a good starting point for microstudies. The inclusion of additional sources – from council minutes to marriage contracts and wills – renders visible structural conflict potential that otherwise remains hidden.

At the centre of this chapter is a microstudy concerning the Catholic "merchantess" (*Handelsmännin*) Eva Maria Neudorferin, widowed Mayerhoferin, whose second husband, Franz Neudorfer, sued her at the Viennese Ecclesiastical Court (hereafter referred to as the Vienna Consistory) for "unauthorised divorce" in 1771. I am interested in the narration of the conflicts Eva Maria brought forward as justification and, above all, the contexts of the conflicts.

Using a praxeological approach, the aim here is to investigate the relation between property, power, and gender. The basic tenet of this approach goes back to Pierre Bourdieu who, put simply, stated that individual actors develop their patterns of perception, thought, and action (habitus), and the social practices on which these are based, in response to the conditions they encounter and in relation to their own position within a social space.[9] The first section will explore the arguments Eva Maria brought forward as justification for her separation. Using a type of flashback in the second section, I will draw attention to Eva Maria's first marriage to Joseph Mayerhofer. As a result of this union, Eva Maria brought considerable property and a trade licence into her

9 Pierre Bourdieu, *The Logic of Practice* (Cambridge: Polity Press, 1990) (French version Paris: Les Éditions de Minuit, 1980).

marriage to Franz Neudorfer, as well as inheritance obligations to six stepchildren and four children of her own. The third section attempts to contextualise the reasons given by Eva Maria for her "unauthorised divorce" and argues that the economic and social failure of the couple was due to the conflict potential inherent in their marriage constellation. Another marriage litigation, in which Franz Neudorfer once again demanded the cohabitation of his wife, is at the centre of the brief fourth section. I will close with an examination of the provisions taken by Eva Maria to transfer her resources to her daughter Josepha and Josepha's spouse. From among the 870 couples that resolved their marital conflicts before the Viennese Consistory in several timespans between 1656 and 1783, I chose the Neudorfers because of the potential their case provided for drawing on auxiliary sources to interpret their disputes, actions, and options.[10] The comparatively rich eighteenth-century civil and criminal justice material available in the archive of the market town of Perchtoldsdorf allowed me to use the last name, as suggested by Carlo Ginzburg and Carlo Ponti in 1979, as a sort of "Ariadne's thread".[11] In addition to the bound council minutes held in the archives there, local census (*Seelenbeschreibungen*) from the mid-eighteenth century, bequest papers, wills, and marriage contracts are also available. Furthermore, I could make use of a study of the market town's houses that reconstructs ownership of the houses from the Middle Ages onwards on the basis of entries in the land title registers (*Grundbücher*) of the various lordships (*Grundherrschaften*).[12] Finally, baptismal, marriage, and death registries of the parish churches have also been utilised as additional resources. Research and access to these sources has been materially facilitated by the genealogical database GenTeam and by matricula, the online portal for church registries.[13]

10 Concerning the time spans studied, see the explanations given in the menu item "data collection" at the web portal "Marriages at Court 3.0", https://www.univie.ac.at/ehenvorgericht/?page_id=10514&lang=en.

11 Carlo Ginzburg and Carlo Poni, "The Name and the Game: Unequal Exchange and the Historiographic Marketplace," in *Microhistory and the Lost Peoples of Europe*, ed. Edward Muir and Guido Ruggiero (Baltimore: Johns Hopkins University Press, 1991), pp. 1–10 (Italian version 1979).

12 Gregor Gatscher-Riedl and Johannes Seidl, *Von Menschen und Häusern in Perchtoldsdorf. Zur Besitzgeschichte des Hausbestandes einer niederösterreichischen Kleinstadt* (Perchtoldsdorf: Marktgemeinde, 2013), pp. 148–49.

13 See "GenTeam," http://www.genteam.eu/; "Matricula," ICARUS – International Centre for Archival Research, accessed 17 September 2020, http://icar-us.eu/cooperation/online-portals/matricula/.

1 Franz Neudorfer Sues Eva Maria for Cohabitation, 1771

On 12 July 1771, the Viennese Consistory heard the cohabitation complaint deposited by Franz Neudorfer. This Catholic court, located on Wollzeile (now part of Vienna's first district), had power to adjudicate not only in religious (*spirituals*) and church matters (*ecclesiastica*), but was also the court of jurisdiction for matrimonial matters (*matrimonales*). While the latter was a prerogative shared by secular courts (*causae mixti fori*), judgements annulling marriages or allowing spouses to live apart remained the exclusive right of the church up until the introduction of Joseph II's Marriage Patent that came into effect on 1 November 1783. Ecclesiastical judges could grant spouses permission to live independently from one another for either a limited period of time ("separation from bed and board") or permanently ("divorce from bed and board"). The decision of whether to address the consequences of annulment, separation or divorce from bed and board before the church or a secular court was at the discretion of the spouses. Because the couple's place of residence was in the parish of Perchtoldsdorf, a village located south of Vienna and within the Viennese diocese, the Viennese Consistory was responsible for the Neudorfer couple's marriage proceedings.

According to the protocol of the court hearing on 12 July 1771, Franz Neudorfer requested the judge to order his wife, "who had separated herself highhandedly from his bed and board," to resume conjugal life.[14] Eva Maria Neudorferin, accompanied by her lawyer Dr. Strahl, gave well founded reasons for leaving her husband. She argued, first, that her husband had "maliciously caused bankruptcy", had lost a great sum in "lotteries", and had forced her under "threat of death" to "vouch" for two debt obligations, i.e. forced her to act as his guarantor. Second, she mentioned violence against her person and her son, whom Franz Neudorfer had "beaten bloody".[15] And third, Eva Maria stated that "together with her daughter, his stepdaughter, she had to leave because he had used the girl for his lust, to which the girl is prepared to attest".[16]

14 Entry from 12 July 1771, Diözesanarchiv Wien (DAW) (Viennese Diocese Archive), Wiener Protokolle (WP) (Viennese minutes) 154, 562.

15 Michaela Hohkamp has drawn attention to the mention of blood as a verbal marker for violence: "Grausamkeit blutet – Gerechtigkeit zwackt: Überlegungen zu Grenzziehungen zwischen legitimer und nicht-legitimer Gewalt," in *Streitkultur(en). Studien zu Gewalt, Konflikt und Kommunikation in der ländlichen Gesellschaft* (16. bis 19. Jahrhundert), ed. Magnus Eriksson and Barbara Krug-Richter (Cologne, Weimar, and Vienna: Böhlau, 2003), pp. 59–79.

16 Entry from 12 July 1771, DAW, WP 154, 562.

Franz Neudorfer could not respond to the accusations, because he was in the Perchtoldsdorf jail for domestic violence at the time of the hearing. Continuing with the sentence, the minutes likewise make no note of a reply from Franz Neudorfer's lawyer. The judges rejected Franz Neudorfer's cohabitation request and granted Eva Maria permission to live "alone and honourably and quietly". The husband was ordered to refrain from "all violence in the house of his wife". This court ruling is remarkable in multiple respects: First, because the judges granted Eva Maria a "tolerance", the term at that time for the right to live apart from a spouse. Among the marriage litigations examined for the research projects mentioned, there are only a few isolated cases in which a wife succeeds in having her husband's "cohabitation demand" rejected. Such requests were generally only successful in instances when the wife could prove the husband's adultery, or he confessed to adultery. Second, although the judges of the consistory did not explicitly grant a divorce from bed and board, they put no time limit on the "tolerance". Third, they not only forbade Franz Neudorfer from exercising physical violence in general but forbade him from doing so "in the wife's house" in particular. With this amendment, they confirmed Eva Maria's right to stay in the house and ordered Franz Neudorfer to move out.

The sources on the marriage litigation mention neither how long Eva Maria and Franz Neudorfer were married nor their ages. The marriage registries of the Perchtoldsdorf parish church list their wedding date as 3 August 1766. As usual, we find the groom's biographical data listed first: "Franz Neudorfer, single, merchant's servant from the Vienna parish of St. Stephen, son of the deceased sacristan of Winsdorf in Bavaria and Eva, his wife." The information given about the bride is even briefer: "the respectable Eva Maria Mayerhoferin, widow of Joseph Mayerhofer, former member of the inner town council."[17] We can establish from the entry that the Neudorfer couple had been married for five years at the time of the marriage litigation. We also learn that the groom married into the household, and that the bride and groom had very different social statuses. Eva Maria and her deceased first husband belonged to the political elite of the market town, whereas Franz Neudorfer worked as a commercial servant for a

17 Parish of Perchtoldsdorf, Trauungsbuch (Marriage register) 1756–1771, 126, entry from 3 August 1766, quoted from the digital reproduction at Matricula online. The entries can very easily be found in the registers, and thus I do not cite the books and the pages concerning entries from the Perchtoldsdorf parish. This information will be provided for entries from other parishes. I owe a great deal of thanks to Susanne Hehenberger for helping me locate the names in the parish registers, to Finbarr McLoughlin, Markus Reisenleitner, and Jennifer Blaak for assistance with translation, to the editors for their useful comments, and to Brooke Penaloza Patzak for thorough proofreading.

Viennese merchant. Using the Perchtoldsdorf death registers, which state that Eva Maria died on 3 September 1789 at the age of 66, we can calculate that she was about 43 years old when she married Franz Neudorfer. Franz Neudorfer, who was baptised on 9 April 1733 in Windorf,[18] was 33 at the time of their wedding, thus ten years her junior. My search for their marriage contract has thus far brought no results, however, information from Eva Maria's first marriage has made it possible to reconstruct her fortune at the time of her marriage to Franz Neudorfer.

2 Eva Maria and Joseph Mayerhofer: an Unequal Pair, 1745–1766

Canon law prescribed that weddings take place in the bride's parish church. As the Perchtoldsdorf parish registers have no record of the wedding between Eva Maria and her first husband Joseph Mayerhofer, it can be assumed that she was not from Perchtoldsdorf but had come there upon her marriage. I have not yet been able to find out where she and Joseph Mayerhofer were married, nor her birth name. According to the sources, we can presume that they married in the mid-1740s. It was the fourth marriage for Joseph Mayerhofer, baptised on 16 January 1694, and presumably the first for Eva Maria, who was twenty years old at the time. Joseph Mayerhofer was about thirty years older than Eva Maria. Along with his property, he brought six children into their marriage. While the marriage contract between the two presumably no longer exists, we can assume that they had also been an economically unequal pair. Nevertheless, as his will testifies, he and Eva Maria had, as was the case in each of his previous marriages, agreed on a community of marital property.

Joseph Mayerhofer himself had married up the ladder of society. He contracted his first marriage with Rosina Stögerin in June 1720. Rosina's mother had died in 1717, and her father died two months before the wedding in April 1720. Rosina and her four siblings had inherited the parental home at Hochstrasse 55. While the marriage register referred to Joseph Mayerhofer as a vintner (*Hauer*), the christening entry for their first son on 17 March 1724 notes him as a merchant, meaning that his social status had improved by this time. In December 1724, the couple bought Rosina's family home from her siblings for 450 Gulden.[19] Rosina died on 28 November 1730. The entry in the land

18 Parish of Windorf, Taufbuch (Baptism register) 1733–1777, 4.

19 Gatscher-Riedl and Seidl, *Von Menschen und Häusern*, p. 149. He likely had to mortgage the house to guarantee the inheritance of the children.

title register notes that Rosina bequeathed him the house on Hochstrasse.[20] According to the model of community of marital property in force in the archduchy, Joseph Mayerhofer presumably inherited half of their joint property; the other half went as maternal inheritance to the children, to be managed by their father until their marriages. Joseph Mayerhofer brought three children from his first marriage into his marriage with Eva Maria: Joseph (b. 17 March 1724), Franz Augustin (b. 27 August 1725) and Eva Theresia (b. 20 December 1726).

Joseph Mayerhofer married his second wife, Juliana Schürauerin, the unmarried daughter of the Perchtoldsdorf cooper master couple, Gotthard Schürauer and Catharina Schürauerin, on 21 January 1731, only seven weeks after the death of Rosina. Juliana's father was a member of the inner town council, as were the two witnesses at their wedding. With this second marriage Joseph Mayerhofer married into the political elite of Perchtoldsdorf. At the time of the baptism of their daughter Maria Anna on 28 February 1733, Joseph Mayerhofer was already a member of the outer town council.[21] As the entry in the land title register shows, Juliana was registered as co-owner on 19 August 1732.[22] Juliana died on 4 January 1741. In her will, signed on 1 January 1741,[23] she bequeathed her four children 240 Gulden each and listed Joseph Mayerhofer as sole heir. Their house, with an estimated value of 500 Gulden, became his in full again. From this second marriage Joseph Mayerhofer brought another four children into his union with Eva Maria: Maria Anna (b. 28 February 1733), Maria Barbara (b. 10. December 1735), Andreas (b. 30 November 1737) and Juliana (b. 26 November 1739).

On 15 May 1741, four and a half months after Juliana's death, Joseph Mayerhofer, then 45 years old, married 27-year-old Theresia Braitheneckerin, the unmarried daughter of the linen merchant couple Tobias and Barbara Braithenecker. The entries in the land title register and, more precisely, the transcriptions of these entries in the book by Gregor Gatscher-Riedl and Johannes Seidl note that Joseph Mayerhofer inherited the house following the death of his wife Juliana on 3 December 1742, but not that Theresia was registered as a joint owner.[24] Theresia died less than three years after their wedding

20 Ibid., p. 149.

21 The town judge, who also held the position of a judge of the local criminal court, and the members of the outer town council were elected every two years, the members of the inner town council were selected by the members of the outer town council.

22 Gatscher-Riedl und Seidl, *Von Menschen und Häusern*, p. 149.

23 Will of Juliana Mayrhoferin, Marktarchiv Perchtoldsdorf (AMP) (archive of Perchtoldsdorf), carton 56.

24 It has not yet been possible to compare with the original to ascertain if the author forgot to include the entry in the transcription, or if it was in fact not mentioned in the land title register. See Gatscher-Riedl und Seidl, *Von Menschen und Häusern*, p. 149.

on 17 March 1744. None of the children from their marriage survived. In accordance with the law of the time, Joseph Mayerhofer inherited either all, or at least two-thirds of their joint property.

The presumed date of the mid-1740s for the wedding of Eva Maria and Joseph Mayerhofer is based, on the one hand, on his evidenced habit of remarriage and, on the other, on the fact that Eva Maria had four stillbirths before giving birth to their son Leopold, baptised on 5 November 1750. A dispute between the couple and the locally appointed midwife in March 1758 not only confirms the miscarriages, but furthermore demonstrates very clearly how dangerous giving birth was at that time. Each of Joseph Mayerhofer's previous three wives had died during, or as a result of, childbirth.[25]

On 3 March 1751, Eva Maria and Joseph Mayerhofer, the latter by then a member of the town's inner council, sold their house on Hochstrasse to Andreas and Anna Binder for 550 Gulden and moved to Perchtoldsdorf Marktplatz 2 (Market Square). What they paid for the new house is unknown. From the address and the estimated worth of 1,000 Gulden mentioned in Joseph Mayerhofer's will, we can assume that their trade establishment was flourishing.[26] Eva Maria's second (surviving) child, Franziskus, was baptised on 23 December 1752. According to the local household list of 1754,[27] which notes Leopold (3), Franz (1.5) and two female servants,[28] the only stepchildren still living with the couple at Market Square 2 in March 1754 were Maria Anna (21)

25 On 8 March 1758 Anna Maria Kellin, appointed midwife of the market, made the complaint that at the time of birth, Eva Maria Mayerhoferin called not her, but the former midwife Anna Maria Joiser. Kellin demanded compensation for lost wages from the married couple and requested a certification that they would not avoid using her as their midwife in the future. Joseph Mayerhof explained why the couple chose to act against regulations in turning to their former midwife in stating that he "had already woefully lost three wives and the children in childbirth". In addition to this, the first four children with which Eva Maria had been pregnant "had, to their great grief, been born dead." It was not until Anna Maria Joiserin "had been called upon as the midwife for his wife" that, thanks to her experience, "four births were carried out successfully." Entry from 8 March 1758, AMP, RP 32, 190. Regarding this conflict see also Gertrude Ostrawsky, *Geschichte des Marktes Perchtoldsdorf 1683–1983*, vol. 2 (Perchtoldsdorf: Marktgemeinde, 1983), pp. 78–80.

26 Along with most houses in the western part of the market square, house no. 2 belonged to the manorial estate of the Perchtoldsdorf church. According to Gatscher-Riedl and Seidl, the transmission of the land title registers of houses owned by the church is "complicated" and therefore not included in their history of the houses.

27 Seelenbeschreibung of 1754, AMP, carton 152, which lists all 266 houses in the town, along with their "housefathers" (247 houses), "housemothers" (19 houses), and all "persons living therein". The household list erroneously lists their one-year-old son Franz as a one-year-old daughter named Anna.

28 Elisabeth Pämeterin (19) and Magdalena Schaupin (41).

and Juliana (15).[29] Both soon left home: on 24 January 1757, Anna Maria married the Perchtoldsdorf binder master Franz Gensberger, and on 24 September 1758, Juliana married master baker Anton Thoma from Maria Enzersdorf, a village thirty kilometres away. It is worth noting that all three sons from Mayerhofer's previous marriages completed apprenticeships and married "outside", whereas the three daughters from the previous marriages likely worked in the family business, and two remained in town following their marriages.

The town council minutes show that Eva Maria and Joseph Mayerhofer jointly ran their commercial business. To quote an early source: on 3 January 1752, the town council ratified Joseph and Eva Mayerhofer's acquisition of rope products from rope-maker Johann Georg Würger.[30] The sources examined do not reveal if at that time the couple had a licence to deal only in linen and rope products, or if they also had one to sell groceries.[31] After their two sons, the couple had two daughters: Josepha, baptised on 8 November 1755, and Theresia, baptised on 5 March 1758.

2.1 *Eva Maria, Sole Heiress and Widow, 1766*

The will Joseph Mayerhofer signed on 8 January 1766,[32] shortly before his death, follows the marital property regime prevalent in the region at that time. Eva Maria inherited half of the couple's property. The other half went to Franz Mayerhofer's ten children, whose claims to their paternal inheritance played an important role in the conflict between Eva Maria and her second husband.

After the invocation and making arrangements for his funeral, Joseph Mayerhofer gave a list of the joint assets and property: the house at Market Square 2 (1,000 Gulden); movable assets, wine press, and animals (450 Gulden); various plots of land (2,874 Gulden); 600 buckets of wine[33] and empty wine barrels (2,914 Gulden); the stock, including linen and rope products (1,597

29 Andreas (16) was an apprentice to a glazier, Eva Theresia (27) had been married to stove-maker Georg Hameter of Perchtoldsdorf since November 1750; Franz Augustin (29) was a saddler journeyman and was married in Leitschau (most likely the town located in what is now North Slovakia); Joseph (30) worked as barber and surgeon in nearby Mödling, where he married the daughter of the master cooper couple Ludwig and Maria Magdalena Jungitsch in August 1752, see Parish of Mödling St. Othmar, Trauungsbuch 1751–1784, 16.

30 Entry from 22 December 1756, AMP, Ratsprotokolle (RP) (council minutes) 1756–1758.

31 Concerning the different trade licenses see Sigrid Kretschmer, *Wiener Handwerksfrauen. Wirtschafts- und Lebensformen im 18. Jahrhundert* (Vienna: Milena, 2000), pp. 202–24. For local merchants in Würtemberg see Sheilagh Ogilvie, Markus Küpker, and Janine Maegraith, "Krämer und ihre Waren im ländlichen Württemberg zwischen 1600 und 1740," *Zeitschrift für Agrargeschichte und Agrarsoziologie* 59–1 (2011), pp. 54–76.

32 Will of Joseph Mayrhofer, AMP, carton 59.

33 A bucket is an old measure of capacity amounting to 56.59 litres.

Gulden); and owed payments (1,466 Gulden). As in many wills of the early modern period, there is no mention of cash, which was probably distributed in advance.

From these total assets of 9,522 Gulden Joseph Mayerhofer deducted first bills to pay (649 Gulden), then the cost of his burial (100 Gulden) and the fee for drafting his will (six Gulden). He then detailed his additional debts: the maternal inheritance portion owed to two of his adult daughters (50 Gulden each), donations undertaken by his deceased wife Juliana (110 Gulden); memorial services for his former wives and his parents (three Gulden 18 Kreuzer), his own requiem masses (26 Gulden), legacies for several churches and fraternities (13 Gulden), and debt relief for individuals recorded as "poor customers" in the trading book (twelve Gulden). The last item on the list of debts was the dowry (400 Gulden) for his and Eva Maria's four underage children, which he considered fair, as it was the same amount he had given his other children. After subtracting his debts of 1,326 Gulden, Mayerhofer left, as he called it, "real wealth" of 8,226 Gulden.

In making detailed provisions, Mayerhofer tried, as he wrote at the end of his will, to distribute his wealth "among his bereaved spouse and many children" in a way that they might all be "satisfied" and accept it, and that no disagreement might ensue. Eva Maria received not only half of the "real wealth", but he also named her as his sole heir. She should receive "not only one half of my wealth without any exceptions, but also be the undisputed and sole heir of my mobile and immobile, attested and non-attested wealth without restriction." Mayerhofer distributed the second half of the joint property among his ten children. In place of his oldest son Joseph, who had died in 1763,[34] he recognised his son's children as heirs. In adherence with the practice of his time and place, he left an inheritance to each of the children from his four marriages – regardless of sex, age, or marital status – of 379 Gulden each. In addition, the married daughters Theresia, Maria Anna, and Juliana each received a vineyard and 2,700 litres of wine; his four sons received his clothes. He favoured his two eldest sons in as much as they were to additionally receive, in order to "remember him", his silver shoes and silver buckles. There were no extra portions for his two youngest daughters or the grandchildren. Aside from his wife and children, Joseph Mayerhofer made note only of the servant Elisabeth Pämeterin. For her thirteen years of service she received 32 Gulden.

He also determined when his children would receive their inheritance: Eva Maria was to give one half (without interest) to the married children one year

34 Parish of Mödling St. Othmar, Sterbebuch (Death register), 1755–1784, 66.

after the probate proceedings and the second half, (including interest) one year later. The underage children were to receive their portions upon marriage. Although Joseph Mayerhofer left a very detailed will, he made no mention of the commercial licences. This seems to imply that the licences were not tied to the house, and could not therefore be bequeathed or sold, but expired with the death of the licence-holder.

The will was opened and published on 29 January 1766 in the presence of Eva Maria, the adult daughters, Magdalena Vöcklin (perhaps in the name of the grandchildren) and the witnesses to the will: Franz Josef Au, the local judge, and Johann Au, a member of the town's outer council. The council postponed further proceedings until 26 February 1766 in order to hear the opinions of the absent sons, who had been sent a copy of the will by mail. Those present were requested "to use the time in between to consider their objections, if any."

Magdalena Vöcklin was absent from the 26 February 1766 probate proceedings. An additional person now present was Andreas, the youngest of the adult sons, a married master glazier in the town Friesach, 250 kilometres away. All four children present declared that "they were completely satisfied with their father's last will and did not intend to have it changed".[35] Andreas, however, requested that the local judge ensure not only that all the children received their inheritance "in full" but also "at the time" determined by their father. Franz Augustin sent a written acceptance of the will's terms, but the probate proceeding was again postponed because the guardians of the children of the deceased son Joseph neither appeared nor wrote.

On 12 March 1766, Eva Maria was appointed executor of her husband's will under the following conditions:[36] first, she promised to pay the debts as set down in the will, to carry out the legacies listed by her husband, and to take care of the memorial services (966 Gulden in total). Second, she committed herself to pay out the inheritance to the five married stepchildren within two years (total of 1,895 Gulden plus interest) and to the step-grandchildren and the underage children at marriage. Third, she agreed to secure the paternal inheritance and dowries for the four minor children with a mortgage on the house at Market Square 2 and some vineyards (1,916 Gulden). The councillor appointed the witnesses to the will, Franz Au and Johann Georg Au, as guardians to the underage children.

35 Entry from 26 February 1766, AMP, RP B–1–35, 250v–251r.

36 Annotation in the will of Joseph Mayerhofer.

3 Eva Maria and Franz Neudorfer: An Unequal Pair, 1766–1782

With the acceptance of the inheritance, several plots of land (meadows, vegetable gardens, and vineyards), the house at Market Square 2, and a large stock of goods were transferred into Eva Maria's sole ownership. In regard to the commercial licence(s), it is possible that she and her deceased husband had been joint holders and that the government of Lower Austria transferred the husband's half of the licence(s) to her. A later entry in the town council minutes confirms that Eva Maria had received a licence to sell groceries "ad personam" from the Lower Austrian government, and she may in the same manner have received a licence to continue selling linen and rope products.

Like her first husband, Eva Maria chose to remarry after a short period of time. As mentioned above, she married the commercial servant Franz Neudorfer, ten years her junior, on 25 July 1766. The rapid replacement of spouses was – as Sigrid Kretschmer has shown in her study of eighteenth-century Viennese businesswomen – quite common in commercial circles of the middle classes. "In the eighteenth century the cooperation of both spouses was understood to be of vital importance for running a business."[37]

Even though I have not been able to locate the marriage contract of Eva Maria and Franz Neudorfer so far, it can be concluded from other sources that they too agreed on a community of marital property. In marrying Eva Maria, Franz Neudorfer not only became co-owner of the house at Market Square 2 and several plots of land, but also rose from a commercial servant to a bourgeois (*bürgerlicher*) merchant. The sources do not note if, or with what, he may have counter-dowried Eva Maria's property.

Having "married in", Franz Neudorfer was in a structurally difficult position from the outset. Moreover, he failed to make himself popular in the town from the very beginning. After causing an accident in which the carriage of inner council member Franz Strohl was damaged, and Strohl's labourer and the parish priest were injured, the injured parties had to sue him several times for damage compensation. It was not until 20 November 1766, after being threatened with imprisonment, that Franz Neudorfer finally paid 14 Gulden and 15 Kreuzer for damages caused.[38] Franz Neudorfer seems to have tried to create an economic basis for himself in addition to co-managing the couple's business. In March 1767, he informed the council that Count Collalto had awarded him "the right to collect the lottery in the market town."[39] In the same month

37 Kretschmer, *Wiener Handwerksfrauen*, p. 205.

38 Entry from 20 November 1766, AMP, RP B–1–35, 305r.

39 Entry from 27 March 1767, AMP, RP B–1–35, 345r.

he was given a licence to deal in nails. As we lack studies on the everyday business of local shops, and because of presumably abbreviated record taking, it is difficult to make sense of the entry that follows in the council minutes.[40] On 20 April 1768, the council decided on his demand "to buy from his wife" the licence to sell groceries, which had been granted to "Eva Maria in person" by the Lower Austrian government.[41] After he had increased his initial offer of 150 to 200 Gulden, payable to the town's chamber office, the town council approved the transfer of the licence from wife to husband. The offer was, in fact, for half of two licences, since we see that in 1771, Eva Maria and Franz Neudorfer were joint holders of one licence to sell rope and linen products (200 Gulden), and another to sell groceries (200 Gulden).

Three years after the inheritance was handed over to Eva Maria, council minutes evidence the first signs that she and her second husband had failed to fulfil all of the financial obligations she had taken on in accepting her inheritance. On 19 April 1769, the city council informed Franz Neudorfer that his stepson Andreas Mayerhofer had applied for payment of his paternal inheritance and for mortgage securities for the inheritance portion of the children of his deceased half-brother Joseph. Only three days later, the council called upon Eva Maria, and a month later upon Franz, to "provide security" for the as yet outstanding portions of 120 Gulden, provided for in her previous husband's will, by means of a mortgage on their plots of land.[42] The beginning of these economic problems were accompanied by conflicts between Franz Neudorfer and his stepson Franz that, as the former argued at the hearing before the city council on 5 June 1770, infected the marital relationship. Franz Neudorfer brought forward that "he could no longer control" his stepson, who "frequently went out to dance and gamble" and "reacted defiantly" to his admonishments.[43] Because the conflict had already become "a cause for dispute with his wife", he requested the council "to order his stepson to move out of the house." Franz, seventeen and a half years old at the time, replied "that if he had no work to do he could go where he pleased, and he had been living in the house longer than his stepfather." This last remark again highlights the difficult structural position of a "married-in" spouse.[44] An entry in the city minutes

40 This chapter was completed in autumn 2017. Literature that has appeared in the meantime could therefore not be included.

41 Entry from 20 April 1768, AMP, RP B–1–36, 10r.

42 Entry from 19. April 1769, AMP, RP B–1–36, 96v, from 22 April 1769, AMP, RP B–1–36, 98v and from 22 May 1769, APM, RP B–1–36, 104r.

43 Entry from 5 June 1770, AMP, RP B–1–36, 203v.

44 See also Margareth Lanzinger, "Emotional Bonds and the Everyday Logic of Living Arrangements: Stepfamilies in Dispensation Records of Late Eighteenth-Century

from the end of November 1770 documents that Franz Neudorfer and his stepson also confronted one another with physical violence. Franz Neudorfer told the council that after he reprimanded Franz Mayerhofer for his "dissolute life" and "gambling", his stepson "began to grapple with him, tossed him against a wall and dragged him through the dung". Franz Mayerhofer excused himself by claiming "that he had to defend himself, and that he was not responsible for his father falling over." The council sentenced Franz Mayerhofer to two 24-hour stays in jail, adding that the "father" had asked for a lenient sentence.[45]

The couple was apparently running out of land that could be burdened with an additional mortgage. In August 1770, summoned by the city council to either pay the outstanding sum of 200 Gulden "for the groceries licence" or to mortgage the promissory note, Franz Neudorfer paid 30 Gulden and offered, instead of a mortgage, his wife as guarantor for his debts.[46] The council accepted Eva Maria as a debt guarantor only under the condition that she "certiorised" the debts therewith renouncing her "female freedoms" (*weibliche Freiheiten*).[47] As she later argued before the Viennese Consistory in July 1771, she had stood as guarantor not voluntarily, but under threat of death.[48]

Austria," in *Stepfamilies in Europe, 1400–1800*, ed. Lyndan Warner (London: Routledge, 2017), pp. 168–186.

45 Entry from 28 November 1770, AMP, RP B–1–36, 243v.

46 Entry from 17 August 1770, AMP, RP B–1–36, 216r.

47 The Latin term "certioration" then, as now, refers to the instruction of legal relationships.

48 As Ursula Floßmann stated as early as her article from 1992, the first traces of codification of "female legal benefits" (*weibliche Rechtswohltaten*) in the territory of modern-day Austria go back to the 1616 Civil Law Code of the Archduchy of Austria above the Enns (*Landtafel ob der Enns*). Referred to as "female good deed" (*weibliche guetthat*), the code formulated restriction of female intercessor rights, from which, however, farmers' wives and businesswomen were explicitly excluded. Ursula Floßmann, "Die weiblichen Rechtsfreiheiten in der Landtafel ob der Enns," in *Vestigia iuris Romani. Festschrift für Gunter Wesener*, ed. Georg Klingenberg, J. Michael Rainer, and Herwig Stiegler (Graz: Leykam, 1992), pp. 131–45, here p. 136. For Saxony see Hendrikje Carius, "Strategien vor Gericht? Die 'velleianischen Freyheiten' im sächsischen Recht (1648–1806)," in *Less Favoured – More Favoured in Law and Legal Practice: Gender, Power and Authority, 12th–19th Centuries*, ed. Grethe Jacobsen, Inger Dübeck, and Helle Vogt (Copenhagen: The Royal Library, 2005), accessed 17 September 2020, http://www5.kb.dk/export/sites/kb_dk/da/nb/publikationer/fundogforskning-online/pdf/A07_Carius.pdf. For a European overview see Ernst Holthöfer, "Die Geschlechtsvormundschaft. Ein Überblick von der Antike bis ins 19. Jahrhundert," in *Frauen in der Geschichte des Rechts. Von der Frühen Neuzeit bis zur Gegenwart*, ed. Ute Gerhard (Munich: C.H. Beck, 1997), pp. 390–459 and Karin Gottschalk, ed., *Gender Difference in European Legal Cultures. Historical Perspectives* (Stuttgart: Steiner, 2013). On legal development in the territory of modern-day Austria see Ursula Floßmann, Herbert Kalb, and Karin Neuwirth, *Österreichische Privatrechtsgeschichte* (Vienna: Verlag Österreich, 2014, 7th edition).

Council minutes delineate the process of her "certioration". On 17 August 1770, the promissory note to the chamber office was "read to her slowly and clearly" in the presence of her legal advisor Franz Wider, member of the inner council.[49] According "to the instructions"[50] Eva Maria was reminded of the "female freedoms", consisting of the "*senatus consultum velleianum* and the *authentica si qua mulier*", and then "renounced her female freedoms voluntarily and explicitly". The fact that the city council requested her renunciation of the "female freedoms" even though they did not apply to her as a businesswoman, indicated that the city council was concerned about potential bankruptcy of the couple's business. With regard to the community of marital property regime the renunciation is important, because the wife's dowry and husband's counter-dowry belonged to the second category of creditors and held a privileged position within that category. Dowries and counter-dowries had priority over all other claims secured by a mortgage. Other debts, such as outstanding wages or claims not secured by a mortgage, belonged to the third category.[51] Claims resulting from bankruptcy proceedings belonged, as they continue to today, to the first category.

3.1 *Bankruptcy Proceedings of Franz Neudorfer, 1771*

The mortgage sum that the couple offered to secure the inheritance of the (step-)grandchildren with did not suffice for their guardians. On 14 January 1771, the council of nearby Mödling mailed the debt obligation signed by Eva Maria and Franz Neudorfer to the council of Perchtoldsdorf, claiming that the existing mortgage did not cover "the outstanding debt of 379 Gulden". In the name of the children, the Mödling council demanded "cash or a guarantee from the Perchtoldsdorf's council".[52] The latter did not provide a guarantee for the couple, ordering them instead to mortgage yet another vineyard "in order to provide further security for the grandchildren."

Ten days later, the couple was asked to appear at the city council once again, this time at the request of Franz Kerber, who had applied in his mother's name to have the Neudorfer's "assets frozen".[53] His mother, as he argued at the 24 January 1771 hearing, had lent the couple 350 Gulden and received neither

49 Entry from 27 August 1770, AMP, RP B–1–36, 220r.

50 Certiorirung deren Weiber auf dem Lande vom 15. Oktober 1710, printed in *Codex Austriacus*, vol. 3 (Leipzig: Eisfeld, 1748), pp. 616–618.

51 Güter-Abschätzungs-Norma für das Erzherzogthum Oesterreich unter der Enns vom 29. Juni 1765, printed in *Codex Austriacus*, vol. 4 (Vienna: Trattner, 1777), pp. 718–34.

52 Entry from 16 January 1771, AMP, RP B–1–37, 10r.

53 Entry from 24 January 1771, AMP, RP B–1–37, 10v–11v.

repayment nor adequate security. Whereas Franz Neudorfer simply replied that "he could not repay anything at the moment", Eva Maria was prepared to give back the 200 Gulden that she had borrowed from her before her marriage to Neudorfer. The remaining debt, "which her husband had borrowed without her knowledge, was not her concern and should be repaid by Mr. Neudorfer". As requested in Eva Maria's claim, the town council decided that Franz Neudorfer would be responsible for repaying the outstanding 150 Gulden and granted Franz Kerber's mother the right to obtain enforced repayment. Barely a fortnight later the couple was called to make another appearance before the council. This time the councillors confronted the couple with "their many debts", and asked Eva Maria "if she would like to contribute to the debt repayment."[54] Eva Maria requested two weeks for reflection, and only three days later requested the initiation of a bankruptcy suit against her husband.[55]

The convocation of Franz Neudorfer's creditors was published in the Viennese Diarium of 20 March 1771. Everybody who believed themselves to have claims against him was to report this in person or through authorised persons at the town hall of Perchtoldsdorf on 30 April 1771.[56] The city council entrusted the bankruptcy proceedings to the town's legal expert, Dr. Bernhard Brauner. Strikingly, the city council assigned a trustee not to Franz Neudorfer, but rather to Eva Maria, "to collect all funds and clear the accounts".[57] As trustee the council appointed Franz Au, guardian and godparent to Eva Maria's underage children. He was to make sure that nothing was sold from the shop in his absence, and thus the council directed him to "take home the key to the store when leaving."[58]

Eva Maria most likely forbade her husband from entering the shop and banished him from "bed and board" from February 1771 onward. On 22 March 1771, the town council threatened him with arrest should he once more break open the door of the house or take items from it.[59] On 31 May, Eva Maria again complained that her husband "had broken into the cellar and unhooked the door."[60] Franz Neudorfer did not deny that he had forcibly gained entry to the cellar, justifying his action by arguing that "he had nothing to drink" and was therefore compelled to break in. A month later Eva Maria reported that Franz

54 Entry from 6 February 1771, AMP, RP B–1–37, 14r.
55 Entry from 9 February 1771, AMP, RP B–1–37, 16r.
56 Wienerisches Diarium (Viennese Diarium), 20 March 1771, 17–18.
57 Entry from 23 March 1771, AMP, RP B–1–37, 25rv.
58 Entry from 23 March 1771, AMP, RP B–1–37, 25v.
59 Entry from 23 March 1771, AMP, RP B–1–37, 25v.
60 Entry from 31 May 1771, AMP, RP B–1–37, 34v.

Neudorfer, "despite the warning, had become violent again", for which he was arrested and put in jail, where he remained during the hearing at the Viennese Consistory.

Franz Neudorfer used the 12 July 1771 verdict of the Viennese Consistory, which allowed Eva Maria to live separately from him, to demand alimony from his wife. On 4 September 1771, Eva Maria asked the town council to support her by warning Franz Neudorfer "to refrain from all illegal claims and violent actions under threat of further arrest."[61] Two weeks later, she justified her refusal to pay maintenance by making a clever reference to the prevailing gender order: "the woman should not support the man, but the man the woman".[62] Franz Neudorfer countered that "he had been pushed out of the business and she, Neudorferin, is running it alone". Not least because "it is not yet ruled that he is no longer co-owner", he would be entitled to maintenance payments from the store's revenues. His maintenance claim was not immediately rejected by the town council, but rather delegated to the town's legal expert, Dr. Bernhard Brauner. Whether or not Brauner awarded the husband any type of alimony has not come down to us.

The time of Neudorfer's bankruptcy proceedings provides our first evidence of conflict between Franz Neudorfer and his older stepson Leopold. Following Neudorfer's complaint that his older stepson was "treating him badly" and slandering him as a "bad man", the council warned the couple and stepson "to keep the peace as long as the bankruptcy case was still under way."[63]

While council minutes provide traces of the physical violence Eva Maria mentioned at the consistory, no evidence of the sexual violence committed against one of her daughters is given, which she had previously described before the consistory as the primary reason why she and her daughter had to "hit the road". As Eva Maria and her children continued to live in the house at Market Square 2, the wording used here is to be understood in the metaphorical sense. It is conceivable that Eva Maria used the accusation of sexual violence simply as an additional argument to contest Franz Neudorfer's claim for cohabitation. It is also possible that, in the hopes of protecting her daughter, she declined reporting the sexual violence to the authorities. The latter explanation seems plausible in consideration of a criminal proceeding that took place around the same time.[64] Market judge (*Marktrichter*) Johann Anton Cavalini had arrested

---

61 Entry from 4 September 1771, AMP, RP B–1–37, 45v–46r.

62 Entry from 18 September 1771, AMP, RP B–1–37, 48v–49r.

63 Entry from 3 October 1771, AMP, RP B–1–37, 50r.

64 See Andrea Griesebner, *Konkurrierende Wahrheiten. Malefizprozesse vor dem Landgericht Perchtoldsdorf im 18. Jahrhundert* (Vienna, Cologne, and Weimar: Böhlau, 2000), pp. 248–52 and Andrea Griesebner, "Physische und sexuelle Gewalt – ein Malefizverbrechen?

22-year-old Franz Riedler and his nine-year-old sister Katharina on suspicion of incest on 29 November 1770. Both were interrogated in detail about their sexual activity and sentenced in February 1771. Seeing that a nine-year-old girl had been arrested, jailed, and subsequently convicted "because of the vice of incest carried out with her brother", Eva Maria Neudorferin may have calculated the potential consequences of a report to the city council for one of her daughters – Josepha was thirteen in the spring of 1771, Theresia fifteen and-a-half. The sexual violence would not, in all probability, have resulted in a charge of *stuprum violenti* or rape, but rather in one of incest, which, according to the criminal law in place, included all sexual acts between persons who were considered such close relatives by blood or by marriage that they were not allowed to marry one another.[65]

3.2 *Bankruptcy of Eva Maria, 1772*

On 4 December 1771, Eva Maria herself filed for bankruptcy, arguing that her "fortune had been so impaired by the malicious transactions of her husband that she was no longer able to pay her many debts".[66] Her application to summon "her creditors per edicta ad valvas" was approved, which explains why it was not announced in the Viennese Diarium. While city council minutes note of Franz Neudorfer's bankruptcy proceedings only that Dr. Bernhard Brauner took note of the debts applied for on 30 April 1771, the minutes recorded Eva Maria's creditors' claims in detail.[67] At the 27 January 1772 meeting of her creditors, eleven individuals claimed a total of 3,842 Gulden. The highest single amount was claimed by Viennese master tailor Johann Michael Purgstaller. He produced a promissory note from Franz Neudorfer for 1,600 Gulden, for which Eva Maria had acted as a guarantor on 7 January 1771. This, along with the above-mentioned guarantee from August 1770, was presumably the second certioration referred to by Eva Maria at the Viennese Consistory. As this certioration is not recorded in the minutes of the Perchtoldsdorf council, she likely had this done at the Viennese city council. While the grounds for Franz Neudorfer owing that much money to the master tailor are not documented,

Strafrecht und Gerichtspraxis im Erzherzogtum Österreich unter der Enns im 18. Jahrhundert," in *Streitkulturen. Gewalt, Konflikt und Kommunikation in der ländlichen Gesellschaft (16.–19. Jahrhundert)*, ed. Magnus Eriksson and Barbara Krug-Richter (Cologne, Weimar, and Vienna: Böhlau, 2003), pp. 81–124.

65 Constitutio Criminalis Theresiana, Art. 75, § 1.

66 Entry from 4 December 1771, AMP, RP B–1–37, 60v.

67 Entry from 30 April 1771, AMP, RP B–1–37, 31r, and entry from 27. January 1772, AMP, RP B–1–37, 69r.

it is clear that Viennese merchant Andreas Hubmer requested half of the total of 945 Gulden, the couple owed him "for goods received." Ignaz Leopold Strohl also asked for "half" of 54 Gulden 49 Kreuzer "for goods obtained." Carl Kumßmiller, in contrast, a linen merchant from Lembach, remained unsure if his demand should be lodged against the bankruptcy of Eva Maria or that of Franz Neudorfer, and thus requested 1,058 Gulden and six and a half Kreuzer "from the couple". The remaining debts of nearly 700 Gulden pertained to smaller amounts, for example a bill from town surgeon Adam Ruef for medicine (four Gulden 37 Kreuzer), and one from Johann Anton Cavalini, the town's market judge and chimney sweep (one Gulden 30 Kreuzer).

As in the bankruptcy proceeding of Franz Neudorfer, Dr. Brauner acted as liquidator, and was provided with a list of debts claimed, mortgages on the house and lands, and a list of money owed to the chamber office. The search for the files pertaining to each bankruptcy within the Perchtoldsdorf archives has thus far proven unsuccessful, but I did discover an undated document entitled "inventory and assessment"[68] enumerating the extant (*ad concursum gediehne*) property of Eva Maria Neudorferin, referred to as "burgher merchantess from here". The following are listed as assets and property of Eva Maria: half of the house on Market Square 2, valued at 1,350 Gulden (625 Gulden); half of two vineyards (175 Gulden); half of seven vegetable gardens (60 Gulden, 30 Kreuzer); and one half each of the "licence to sell linen and rope products" (100 Gulden) and the "grocery licence" (100 Gulden). Additionally, she was the sole owner of a vineyard of 1,400 square metres for which no estimated value was mentioned. According to four cash books from the store, the "debts due" amounted to nearly 290 Gulden, all of which is listed as belonging to her individual assets rather than joint property. It is worth noting that the joint property listed consisted without exception of property brought into the marriage by Eva Maria.

3.3 *Announcement of Imminent Foreclosure, 1772*

Dr. Brauner decided not only to merge the two bankruptcies, but furthermore reported to the city council on 28 March 1772 that "all assets of the couple" would be sold by means of compulsory auction.[69] The foreclosure sale was announced in the Viennese Diarium on 25 April 1772.[70] The announcement stipulated that all of the property of Franz Neudorfer, referred to as "burgher merchant", and that of his wife Eva Maria would be sold to the highest bidders

68 Undated paper, probably February 1772, AMP, carton 83.

69 Entry from 28 March 1772, AMP, RP B–1–37, 79r.

70 Viennese Diarium, 25 April 1772, 19.

on 18 May 1722 at "the Neudorfer house". Explicitly mentioned are: the house at Market Square, the linen and the grocery licence, the stock, various vineyards, meadows, and vegetable gardens, 188 barrels of wine from the years 1766, 1770, and 1771, over 600 empty barrels, a horse with harness and cart, the house furnishings, and male and female clothing.

Eva Maria turned to the next legal instance, the government of Lower Austria, in an attempt to ward off the foreclosure sale. As evidenced in the council minutes, this body ordered a "halt to the proceedings" until their decision had been made, and summoned Eva Maria to a hearing on 19 May 1772.[71] The councillors granted her permission to attempt an out of court settlement, which she then managed to accomplish. On 31 March 1773, Eva Maria requested the town council to ratify the settlements "between her and her creditors", and "between Franz Neudorfer and his creditors". The council approved both settlements under the condition that she paid the inheritance debts due to her step-grandchildren and the chamber office with interest.[72] Eva Maria not only succeeded in averting bankruptcy and a compulsory auction, but also managed to be accepted as the sole owner of the rest of the joint marital property.

On 8 November 1773, Dr. Brauner informed the council that "the bankruptcy proceeding of Eva Maria and Franz Neudorfer was suspended", the ban on jurisdiction (*Jurisdiktionssperre*) lifted, and that the entire property was "to be given back to Eva Maria Neudorferin."[73] The fact that the minutes show only Eva Maria as active in the proceedings is remarkable. It was she who initiated all steps to avoid the compulsory auction, she who negotiated the out of court settlement with her and her husband's creditors, and she who finally received the remaining matrimonial property. There is no information on the role her husband played in any of this. That they still lived separated from one another remained irrelevant until three years later.

3.4 *Franz Neudorfer Sues Eva Maria for Cohabitation, 1776*

In mid-May 1776, the Perchtoldsdorf parish priest denounced four couples, the Neudorfer couple among them, to the Viennese consistory for separating themselves from bed and board without authorization.[74] At the hearing before the consistory, Franz Neudorfer, referred to as "former merchant", was acting as plaintiff, Eva Maria as defendant. As in the hearing four years earlier, Eva Maria did not deny that she lived apart from her husband. She justified the separation

71 Entry from 13 May 1772, AMP, RP B–1–37, 86rv.

72 Entry from 31 March 1773, AMP, RP B–1–37, 137r.

73 Entry from 21 November 1773, AMP, RP B–1–37, 175.

74 Entry from 22 May 1776, AMP, RP B–1–38, 26r.

by stating that "her husband had wasted many thousand Gulden" and would continue to incur debts; she would live "in great poverty". She had already separated from him five years earlier as a result of his "dissolute behaviour".

Franz Neudorfer replied only "that she had contributed to the downfall of their fortunes." The Viennese consistory deferred the hearing to 3 June 1776 in order to obtain "additional information about the grounds for dispute" from the town council.[75] On 3 June, Eva Maria appeared with her lawyer, Dr. Lichtenauer. She requested an extension of the "tolerance" granted her in July 1771, and presented medical proof that her husband had beaten and threatened to kill her.[76] Franz Neudorfer, in contrast, requested cohabitation, declaring that he would seek "paid employment" and would pay maintenance to his wife. The church minutes also record that the Perchtoldsdorf town council had characterised Neudorfer "as a bad housekeeper", and further reported "that his stepchildren had also squandered large amounts of money." The consistory refused "an additional tolerance" and sentenced Eva Maria to live with her husband: "that both should live in peace and harmony as Christian couples should, and should not, under threat of arrest, separate without authorization, should refrain from all instances of bad behaviour, especially Neudorfer, such as gambling and bad housekeeping."

It is highly unlikely that Eva Maria obeyed the order to allow Franz Neudorfer to move back into her house at Market Square. Council minutes note only that three months later, on 18 September, he asked the town council to order his stepsons Leopold and Franz Mayerhofer "to leave the house."[77] After this point Franz Neudorfer disappeared from the Perchtoldsdorf town council minutes. Eva Maria, in contrast, went on to be mentioned in the minutes on various occasions. On 7 June 1777, for example, she was granted permission to sell the wine that had previously been sealed as a result of her debts to the chamber office. She had to use the proceeds to pay out the inheritance of her step-granddaughter, who was about to marry and had requested her portion.[78] That Franz Mayerhofer was still living with his mother one year later, and that their relations too were not free of conflict is revealed by the criminal proceedings against him. When market judge Johann Anton Cavalini ordered him to spend the night in jail on 7 October 1777, Mayerhofer wounded Cavalini severely, albeit not mortally, with a knife. As Eva Maria testified on 18 October 1777, she had pleaded with Cavalini some hours before the incident to reprimand her

75 Entry from 24 May 1776, DAW, WP 157, 230–231.

76 Entry from 3 June 1776, DAW, WP 157, 237–238.

77 Entry from 18 September 1776, AMP, RP B–1–38, 52r.

78 Entry from 7 June 1777, AMP, RP B–1–38, 116v.

25-year-old son so that "he would behave better in the future and obey her". Her son, she said, "does not show her respect", "behaves badly" and "had pushed her once or twice".[79] The records of the criminal proceedings provide evidence that at that time Eva Maria was running the grocery with her younger son and her daughters. After Franz was arrested, Eva Maria requested the release of her older son Leopold from military service because she "needed him in the business". In November 1779, the district administration office (*Kreisamt*) permitted his release on the condition that the town council replace him with another man.[80]

Johann Anton Cavalini, who once again assumed the office of market judge in February 1780, decided that he would rather have Leopold in the army than in the market town. On 9 May 1780, Cavalini informed the city council that the bailiff had told him that Leopold, who was on leave in Perchtoldsdorf, carried his rifle openly within the market town.[81] Albeit a rather strange deduction on his part, Cavalini determined Leopold Mayerhofer to be dangerous because he himself had been dangerously wounded by Leopold's brother Franz Mayerhofer. Cavalini moreover argued that Leopold could not help his mother, "a merchantess, in any way", on the contrary, he "contributes to the fragmentation of what little wealth she has". Upon Cavalini's request the city council decided to prevail upon Mister von Auerhammer, senior of Leopold's regiment, to "order Leopold Mayerhofer to return" to his post. After this entry Leopold Mayerhofer likewise disappears from the town records. As his death is not recorded in the death registers, one can presume that he did not return to Perchtoldsdorf.

4 Eva Maria Transfers Her Assets, 1782

From spring 1780 onwards, Eva Maria Neudorferin ran her commercial enterprise with her daughters Theresia and Josepha. Her older son Leopold was in the army and younger son Franz in jail, where he died on 29 October 1780. On the occasion of the upcoming marriage of Josepha, Eva Maria regulated the passing on of her property in her daughter's marriage contract. The marriage contract proves that despite the bankruptcy at the beginning of the 1770s Eva Maria continued to own the house at Market Square 2, two trading licences, and plots of land. As she is described in the marriage contract as "currently

79 Summary statement of Eva Maria Neudorferin on 18 October 1779, AMP, carton 96/3. For the criminal proceeding see Griesebner, *Konkurrierende Wahrheiten*, pp. 195–204.

80 Entry from 17 November 1779, AMP, RP B–1–38, 291rv.

81 Entry from 9 May 1780, AMP, RP B–1–38, 323v.

married Neudorferin", we can assume that Franz Neudorfer was still alive as of 15 May 1782.

In the presence of Eva Maria and witnesses,[82] the "unwed" Josef Berghofer and the "virgin" Josepha Mayerhoferin agreed in their marriage contract of 15 May 1782 upon a community of marital property:[83] First, bride and groom promised each other "all marital love and faithfulness". Second, Josepha Mayerhoferin contributed (*verheiratete*), as "true dowry", her paternal inheritance portion of 479 Gulden, secured with a mortgage "on the house of her mother", to her groom. Third, Joseph Berghofer counter-dowried (*widerlegte*) the dowry with 500 Gulden. Fourth, the groom promised to purchase both of Eva Maria's licences for 400 Gulden. Fifth, Eva Maria promised to sell the groom the house on Market Square 2 for the estimated price of 1,200 Gulden. Sixth, Eva Maria agreed to sell the groom her plots of land "one after the other" at the current market price. She promised to give the bride and groom "free bed and board" in her house until the transfer was completed in full. Seventh, the groom guaranteed his mother-in-law "one room, one chamber, and a kitchen on the first floor, as well as board" free of charge following the transfer of the property. In the event that the mother and son-in-law should not get along, the groom assured Eva Maria 100 Gulden per annum in financial support. Up to this point the marriage contract would have us believe that the resources transferred following the marriage would go to the son-in-law, however, point eight stipulated that everything "both spouses would, thanks to the mercy of God, acquire during the marriage or would obtain in any lawful way, should be and remain joint property." In addition to this, point eight also dictated that both spouses "are free to have registered their co-ownership of the house, the licences, and further plots of land they may acquire or receive." As usual, the final clause dealt with the eventuality of a childless marriage or one of the spouses dying. It was agreed that the relatives of the deceased should not receive more than one third of the joint property. From the perspective of the spouses, this meant that the surviving spouse, regardless of sex, was entitled to one half of the joint property plus two-thirds of the amount that would have been distributed to potential children. Five days after signing the marriage contract, 26-year-old Josepha Mayerhoferin and Joseph Berghofer were married in the bride's parish church. The entry in the Perchtoldsdorf marriage register

---

82 Georg Au, member of the council inner circle, and Vincenz Kennerknecht, clerk of the town council, served as witnesses.

83 Marriage contract between Josepha Mayerhoferin and Josef Berghofer from 15 May 1782, AMP, carton 58.

tells us only that Joseph Berghofer was a "commercial servant in Vienna", listing neither the names of his parents nor where he was born.

A little more than a year after the marriage of her daughter, Eva Maria sold her trading licences to her son-in-law for 400 Gulden. However, as the council minutes make clear, he needed the permission of the Lower Austrian government in order to take over the licences. The councillors ordered the district administration office (*Kreisamt*) to find out if the commercial licences were tied to the house (*radiciret*) and to ask for the opinion of all parties concerned. The district court requested a report from the town council and extracts from the land title register dating back to 1740.[84] In addition to Eva Maria and her son-in-law, businessman Jakob Regenhardt appeared at the town council hearing on 15 October 1783. Regenhardt and his wife Barbara had been running the second grocery in Perchtoldsdorf since 1774.[85] Eva Maria explained that she could not produce extracts from the land title register because "her licenses were not tied to the house". Josef Berghofer proved with testimonials dated 17 October 1779 that he had learned the mercantile trade and had thereafter worked for Viennese merchant Joseph Angerer. Jacob Regenhardt stated that he had no objections to the transfer of the licences, because "he did not care if Eva Maria or her son-in-law carried on the trade."[86] On 19 March 1784, council minutes note that the Lower Austrian government granted Joseph Berghofer permission to take over the trade from his mother-in-law, and that the trade licences were not to be sold in the future for more than 400 Gulden.[87] It can be assumed that Josef Berghofer had been working alongside Eva Maria and Josepha before formal permission was granted. On 17 September 1783, he deposited 197 Gulden and 2 Kreuzer in the name of his mother-in-law at the chamber office. This money was intended for Eva Maria's step-grandson Ludwig Mayerhofer who, like his deceased father, had become an "examined surgeon" in nearby Mödling. In addition to a third of the 379 Gulden he had inherited, Ludwig Mayerhofer charged the 70 Gulden and 42 Kreuzer in interest that he was likewise due as per Eva Maria's agreement on 31 March 1773.[88] On 3 September 1789, Eva Maria died of "a stroke" in the house at Market Square 2. The death register additionally notes that, "she had been given the last sacraments by the local priest." I do

---

84 Entry from 19 September 1783, AMP, RP B–1–39, 74r.

85 Regenhart and his wife bought the store from Jakob Stumer, who went bankrupt in 1774. For further information on the Jakob and Barbara Regenhart couple see Gatscher-Riedl and Seidl, *Von Menschen und Häusern*, pp. 200–03.

86 Entry from 15 October 1783, AMP, RP B–1–39, 88r.

87 Entry from 10 March 1784, AMP, RP B–1–39, 128v.

88 Entry from 10 September 1783, AMP, RP B–1–39, 72r.

not know if she had sold the house and plots of land to her daughter Josepha and her son-in-law beforehand.

Her estate was settled one and a half years later, on 10 February 1791.[89] The delay between her death and the probate proceedings may have been a result of the fact that the residences of her husband Franz Neudorfer and her son Leopold were unknown. It is not clear from the records whether they had died or could simply not be found. Eva Maria named her daughter Josepha and son-in-law Joseph as sole heirs, both declared that they accepted the inheritance, property, and debts. Her second daughter Theresia, 33 years old and still unmarried, agreed to accept her sister and brother-in-law as "her debtors".

5 Conclusions

The aim of this chapter has been to contextualise the conflicts between Eva Maria Neudorferin and Franz Neudorfer. To this end, various sources of local and regional provenance have been taken into consideration. This microstudy makes clear that in the archduchy of Austria below the Enns houses, land, businesses, and trade licenses were not inherited along a patrilineal line but rather passed on to the surviving spouse and children independent of gender. Based on community of martial property, the surviving spouse received between half and two-thirds of the joint property. Trade and craft enterprises that served the local market were structurally designed as "working and economic units" and required both spouses to run profitably. Widows and widowers were sought-after marriage partners and often chose to remarry quickly.

As a result, "married-in" men were no exception in the archduchy. Nevertheless, they seem to have had more problems than "married-in" women in adjusting and learning to fit in. One explanation can be found in the contradiction between the prevailing "gender-neutral" matrimonial property regime on the one hand, and the socio-cultural and legal concepts of gender that postulated the superiority of men and conceded to husbands the right to corporally punish their wife (*potestas*), on the other.[90] In settings such as that shown in this microstudy, wherein the "married-in" man was furthermore in a socially and economically inferior position, conflict was structurally inherent. Difficult relationships between "married-in" husbands and stepchildren also affected couples' relationships, contributing to or respectively intensifying

89 Entry from 10 February 1791, AMP, RP B–1–42, 346r.

90 See Hohkamp, "Grausamkeit blutet – Gerechtigkeit zwackt," pp. 59–79.

conflict. This praxeological approach has also illustrated that as a result of the community of marital property, married couples were not only "working couples", as Heide Wunder has pointed out, but also "economic couples". If the husband failed to meet expectations, the question of the origin of the joint property became relevant in practice. In comparison to "married-in" women, women like Eva Maria had been in a much better position. In addition to the economic capital these women brought into their marriages, they also brought knowledge about their trade or business, and possessed social capital which they could and, as shown above, did use in instances of conflict with the "married-in" husband.

Despite intensive research into additional sources, many questions remain unanswered. First, there is the question of why Eva Maria decided to marry Franz Neudorfer, and why she contributed all of her property and assets with the exception of one single vineyard to the joint marital property. It is possible that Franz Neudorfer would not have agreed to a marriage contract in which Eva Maria reserved her right of disposition for more than a vineyard, or to one in which specific parts of her property remained hers until her husband-to-be had proven his good conduct. Another lingering question is why two bankruptcy proceedings were initiated, and how Eva Maria actually succeeded in regaining the sole ownership of the house, property, and trade, while Franz Neudorfer not only lost his part of the joint property, but also his legal status as a bourgeois (*bürgerlicher*) merchant. There are some studies available on local trade shops, but research addressing actual everyday life and the constraints and scope of agency remains a desideratum. This microstudy illustrates the strong position married women had in the archduchy, a positioning that the Josephine Civil Code, and more importantly the Austrian Civil Code (ABGB), attempted to restrict in 1786 and 1811 respectively. The ABGB declared the husband as the "head of the family" (§ 91), the separation of property to be the legal marital property regime, with the significant addition that when "in doubt" it was presumed "that the acquisition [during the marriage] is from the man" (§ 1237) and that the wife, in the legal assumption and as long as the wife did not explicitly disagree, "had entrusted the husband as her legal representative in the administration of her property" (§ 1238).[91]

91 Austrian Civil Code (*Allgemeines bürgerliches Gesetzbuch*), vol. 2, Marriage Law, http://alex.onb.ac.at/cgi-content/alex?aid=jgs&datum=1012&page=472&size=45; see also Ellinor Forster, "Handlungsspielräume von Frauen und Männern im österreichischen Eherecht. Geschlechterverhältnisse im 19. Jahrhundert zwischen Rechtsnorm und Rechtspraxis" (PhD diss., University of Innsbruck, 2008).

The divorce proceedings from the late eighteenth and the first half of the nineteenth century[92] confirm Gertrude Langer-Ostrawsky's findings that couples in the Archduchy of Austria continued to adhere to the practice of marriage contracts well into the second half of the nineteenth century, bypassing the legal provisions by agreeing on a community of marital property.

References

Bourdieu, Pierre. *The Logic of Practice.* Cambridge: Polity Press, 1990 [1980].

Carius, Hendrikje. "Strategien vor Gericht? Die 'velleianischen Freyheiten' im sächsischen Recht (1648–1806)." In *Less Favoured – More Favoured in Law and Legal Practice: Gender, Power and Authority, 12th–19th Centuries*, edited by Grethe Jacobsen, Inger Dübeck, and Helle Vogt. Copenhagen: The Royal Library, 2005. http://www5.kb.dk/export/sites/kb_dk/da/nb/publikationer/fundogforskning-online/pdf/A07_Carius.pdf

Floßmann, Ursula. "Die weiblichen Rechtsfreiheiten in der Landtafel ob der Enns." In *Vestigia iuris Romani. Festschrift für Gunter Wesener*, edited by Georg Klingenberg, J. Michael Rainer, and Herwig Stiegler, pp. 131–45. Graz: Leykam, 1992.

Floßmann, Ursula, Herbert Kalb, and Karin Neuwirth. *Österreichische Privatrechtsgeschichte.* Vienna: Verlag Österreich, 2014, 7th edition.

Forster, Ellinor. "Handlungsspielräume von Frauen und Männern im österreichischen Eherecht. Geschlechterverhältnisse im 19. Jahrhundert zwischen Rechtsnorm und Rechtspraxis". PhD diss., University of Innsbruck, 2008.

Gatscher-Riedl, Gregor, and Johannes Seidl. *Von Menschen und Häusern in Perchtoldsdorf. Zur Besitzgeschichte des Hausbestandes einer niederösterreichischen Kleinstadt.* Perchtoldsdorf: Marktgemeinde, 2013.

Ginzburg, Carlo, and Carlo Poni. "The Name and the Game: Unequal Exchange and the Historiographic Marketplace." In *Microhistory and the Lost Peoples of Europe*, edited by Edward Muir and Guido Ruggiero, pp. 1–10. Baltimore: Johns Hopkins University Press, 1991 [1979].

Gottschalk, Karin, ed. *Gender Difference in European Legal Cultures. Historical Perspectives.* Stuttgart: Steiner, 2013.

Griesebner, Andrea. *Konkurrierende Wahrheiten. Malefizprozesse vor dem Landgericht Perchtoldsdorf im 18. Jahrhundert.* Vienna, Cologne, and Weimar: Böhlau, 2000.

Griesebner, Andrea. "Physische und sexuelle Gewalt – ein Malefizverbrechen? Strafrecht und Gerichtspraxis im Erzherzogtum Österreich unter der Enns im 18.

92 See *Web portal. Marriages at Court 3.0*, ed. Griesebner, accessed August 2020, https://www.univie.ac.at/ehenvorgericht/?page_id=3201.

Jahrhundert." In *Streitkulturen. Gewalt, Konflikt und Kommunikation in der ländlichen Gesellschaft (16.–19. Jahrhundert)*, edited by Magnus Eriksson and Barbara Krug-Richter, pp. 81–124. Cologne, Weimar, and Vienna: Böhlau, 2003.

Hohkamp, Michaela. "Grausamkeit blutet – Gerechtigkeit zwackt: Überlegungen zu Grenzziehungen zwischen legitimer und nicht-legitimer Gewalt." In *Streitkultur(en). Studien zu Gewalt, Konflikt und Kommunikation in der ländlichen Gesellschaft (16. bis 19. Jahrhundert)*, edited by Magnus Eriksson and Barbara Krug-Richter, pp. 59–79. Cologne, Weimar, and Vienna: Böhlau, 2003.

Holthöfer, Ernst. "Die Geschlechtsvormundschaft. Ein Überblick von der Antike bis ins 19. Jahrhundert." In *Frauen in der Geschichte des Rechts. Von der Frühen Neuzeit bis zur Gegenwart*, edited by Ute Gerhard, pp. 390–459. Munich: C.H. Beck, 1997.

Hufton, Olwen. *The Prospect Before Her. A History of Women in Western Europe*. London: Fontana, 1995.

Kretschmer, Sigrid. *Wiener Handwerksfrauen. Wirtschafts- und Lebensformen im 18. Jahrhundert*. Vienna: Milena, 2000.

Langer-Ostrawsky, Gertrude. "Vom Verheiraten der Güter. Bäuerliche und kleinbäuerliche Heiratsverträge im Erzherzogtum Österreich unter der Enns." In Margareth Lanzinger, Gunda Barth-Scalmani, Ellinor Forster, and Gertrude Langer-Ostrawsky. *Aushandeln von Ehe. Heiratsverträge der Neuzeit im europäischen Vergleich*, pp. 26–119. Cologne, Weimar, and Vienna: Böhlau, 2010, 2nd edition 2015.

Lanzinger, Margareth. "Emotional Bonds and the Everyday Logic of Living Arrangements: Stepfamilies in Dispensation Records of Late Eighteenth-Century Austria." In *Stepfamilies in Europe, 1400–1800*, edited by Lyndan Warner, pp. 168–186. London: Routledge, 2017.

Lanzinger, Margareth. "Von der Macht der Linie zur Gegenseitigkeit. Heiratskontrakte in den Südtiroler Gerichten Welsberg und Innichen 1750–1850." In Margareth Lanzinger, Gunda Barth-Scalmani, Ellinor Forster, and Gertrude Langer-Ostrawsky. *Aushandeln von Ehe. Heiratsverträge der Neuzeit im europäischen Vergleich*, pp. 205–367. Cologne, Weimar, and Vienna: Böhlau, 2010, 2nd edition 2015.

Ogilvie, Sheilagh, Markus Küpker, and Janine Maegraith. "Krämer und ihre Waren im ländlichen Württemberg zwischen 1600 und 1740." *Zeitschrift für Agrargeschichte und Agrarsoziologie* 59–1 (2011): pp. 54–76.

Ostrawsky, Gertrude. *Geschichte des Marktes Perchtoldsdorf 1683–1983*, vol. 2. Perchtoldsdorf: Marktgemeinde, 1983.

Ulbrich, Claudia. *Shulamit and Margarete. Power, Gender, and Religion in a Rural Society in Eighteenth-Century Europe*. Boston and Leiden: Brill, 2004 [1999].

Wunder, Heide. *He Is the Sun, She Is the Moon. Women in Early Modern Germany*. Cambridge, MA: Harvard University Press, 1998 [1992].

CHAPTER 14

After Divorce: Disputes about Property and the Division of Wealth in the Context of Divorce from Bed and Board (Vienna, 1783–1850)

Georg Tschannett

In previous studies concerning divorce and separation scholarly research has focused on sources of conflict and spousal narrations of married life and its shortcomings.[1] Other studies have examined the significance of property in the context of divorce and separation, but have primarily concentrated on the legal circumstances and grounds for separation.[2] The chapter at hand will focus on how property was divided and alimony arranged in cases of divorce from bed and board. I will, in other words, analyse how married couples divided their "worldly goods" (as it is phrased in archival sources) in cases of conflict, and what influences played a role in this division. In concentrating research on the consequences of divorce, I tackle a new perspective that has been considered much needed for some time, and it will be necessary to focus attention beyond the content of divorce case-files to look into, among others, issues of who brought what amount of wealth into marriage, and to what extent this

1 Cf. Caroline Arni, *Entzweiungen. Die Krise der Ehe um 1900* (Cologne, Weimar, and Vienna: Böhlau, 2004); Suzanne Desan, *The Family on Trial in Revolutionary France* (Berkeley: University of California Press, 2004); Ellinor Forster, "Legitime Wut. Zum Ausdruck männlicher Gefühle in Ehescheidungsprozessen des ländlichen Tirol und Vorarlberg im 19. Jahrhundert," in *Die Präsenz der Gefühle. Männlichkeit und Emotion in der Moderne*, ed. Nina Borutta and Nina Verheyen (Bielefeld: Transcript, 2010), pp. 105–28; Sylvia Möhle, *Ehekonflikte und sozialer Wandel. Göttingen 1740–1840* (Frankfurt a. M. and New York: Campus, 1997); Birgit Stalder, *"Der Ehehimmel begann sich schon früh zu trüben." Geschlechterbeziehungen und Machtverhältnisse in Scheidungsprozessen zwischen 1876 und 1911. Ein interkonfessioneller Vergleich* (Berlin: Franz & Timme, 2008); Lawrence Stone, *Broken Lives. Separation and Divorce in England, 1660–1857* (Oxford: Oxford University Press, 1993). This chapter was written in the context of the projects *Matrimony before the Court. Arenas of Conflict and Courses of Action from the 16th to the 19th Century* (P 23394) and *Marriage Litigations from the 16th to the 19th Century. Regional and Social Differentiation* (P 28063), which were funded by the Austrian Science Fund.

2 Cf. Rainer Beck, "Frauen in Krise. Eheleben und Ehescheidung in der ländlichen Gesellschaft Bayerns während des Ancien Régime," in *Dynamik der Tradition*, ed. Richard van Dülmen (Frankfurt a. M.: Fischer, 1992), pp. 137–212; Alexandra Lutz, *Ehepaare vor Gericht. Konflikte und Lebenswelten in der Frühen Neuzeit* (Frankfurt a. M. and New York: Campus, 2006).

 | DOI:10.1163/9789004456204_015

was considered part of a couple's fortune.[3] It is also worthwhile to track the aftermath of marriage, i.e. to ask how divorce effected the living conditions of husbands and wives. What were the causes of dispute during the course of divorce?

In order to prevent misunderstanding, I will begin with some thoughts concerning the terminology used in this chapter. I have decided to use terms that were introduced into Austrian marriage law at the beginning of the nineteenth century. The meaning of these terms is the exact opposite of those in the canon law. Thus, this chapter uses the term "separation" (*Trennung*) for separations that allowed for the possibility of remarriage, and the term "divorce" or "divorce from bed and board" (*Scheidung von Tisch und Bett*) for separations that did not allow for the possibility of entering into a new marriage as long the partner remained alive.

The primary sources for my study are nearly 700 divorce case-files[4] from the magistrate of the City of Vienna (*Magistrat der Stadt Wien*). These of course reflect the views, expectations, and practices of predominantly middle-class, urban couples. To various degrees of extent and quality, this material documents marriages celebrated in the period from the 1760s to 1840s. In particular, the files emanate from the civil justice senate (*Ziviljustizsenat*, later *Magistratisches Zivilgericht*), which was the dedicated authority for cases of divorce from bed and board between November 1783 and the end of June 1850. Within the framework of the project "Matrimony before the Court. Arenas of Conflict and Courses of Action from the 16th to the 19th Century", I chose cases for analysis that span twenty-five-and a half years, which I then divided into four periods.

The first period (1783–1793, containing 113 cases) encompasses the early era of secular matrimonial courts. Prior to the reforms of Joseph II, ecclesiastical courts decided in matrimonial affairs, but his Marriage Act of 1783 placed jurisdiction over marital affairs in most of the Austrian hereditary lands in the remit of secular courts. Although the 1783 act held matrimony to be "a civil agreement", it retained the dogma of the indissolubility of Catholic marriage,

3 Among others, Siegrid Westphal also criticises the incomplete debate on the consequences of separation and divorce: Siegrid Westphal, Inken Schmidt-Voges, and Anette Baumann, *Venus und Vulcanus. Ehen und ihre Konflikte in der Frühen Neuzeit* (Munich: Oldenbourg, 2011), p. 178. Sylvia Möhle raised the question in the 1990s of what a divorce meant for men and women and which opportunities it opened up or did not open up: Möhle, *Ehekonflikte*, pp. 189–91.

4 Cf. Georg Tschannett, "Zerrissene Ehen. Scheidungen von Tisch und Bett in Wien (1783–1850)" (PhD diss., University of Vienna, 2015).

and marriage as a sacrament. In contrast to non-Catholic Christian or Jewish couples, who were allowed to dissolve their unions, Catholic spouses no longer wishing to live together had to make do with a divorce from bed and board. Whereas a separation allowed the innocent party the possibility of remarriage, couples granted divorce from bed and board were not permitted to remarry as long as their partner remained alive. Then and as now, Catholic doctrine saw marriage as indissoluble, even when husband and wife agreed that their marriage was at an end or when a civil court issued a divorce decree. As a result, in cases of divorce from bed and board, a spouse that remarried while the former husband or wife was living could be charged with bigamy. The Civil Code of 1786 and the Austrian Civil Code of 1811 (ABGB) made no modifications in this regard.

The second period (1807–1816, containing 314 cases) includes the five years before and after the implementation of the ABGB. As noted above, the ABGB, promulgated in 1811 and in force a year later, confirmed that Catholic marriages were indissoluble and permitted Catholics only divorce from bed and board. The ABGB, which in contrast to the Marriage Act of 1783 and Civil Code of 1786 permitted not only undisputed but also disputed divorce, included a list of grounds for legal divorce. In addition, it formulated a series of clauses in cases of dispute that regulated the division of wealth, provision for children, alimony for the divorced wife, and cancelation of the marriage agreement.

The third (1830–1832, containing 138 cases) and fourth periods (1848–1850, containing 124 cases) are both relatively short spans, and revealing for our purposes because they register a rise in the number of judicial divorce cases. As a consequence of the Revolutions of 1848 and resultant reorganisation of the judicial system, the municipal civil courts handed over divorce cases to courts sitting at district (*Bezirk*), county (*Kreis*) and provincial (*Land*) levels. The concordat signed by Rome and Vienna in 1855 during the restoration process that followed the defeated revolutions led to a revival of church law in matrimonial affairs. It stipulated that marital matters were once more to be the remit of the Catholic Church. Civil courts could only be engaged in settling the consequences of divorce, and even this could, provided both spouses agreed, be dealt with by church courts. The church courts acted in regulating marital disputes up until the 1870s.[5]

The majority of the matrimonial cases under review concerned Roman Catholics by confession, hardly surprising in light of the fact that 95 percent

5 Herbert Kalb provides an overview of the later development of marital jurisdiction in Austria. Herbert Kalb, "Das Eherecht in der Republik Österreich 1918–1978," *Beiträge zur Rechtsgeschichte Österreichs* 2–1 (2012), pp. 27–43.

of Vienna's population shared this faith.[6] In regard to the social aspect of the sample, the proportion of couples from families of skilled tradesmen is likely over-represented. If we subtract from the sample the quarter of the couples whose social origin is not clear from the records, almost two-thirds of the remainder belonged to the categories of small businesses (*Gewerbe*) or skilled workmen (*Handwerker*). One fifth of the couples seeking legal divorce represented middle-class civil servants. The remaining couples represented owners of large businesses or the educated bourgeoisie. Only a handful of couples were domestic servants, unskilled labourers or factory workers. More than one third of all couples under review were living apart before they sued for divorce. If we look at the gender aspects of the archival material, it seems remarkable that – as other studies confirm – over three-quarters of the proceedings were initiated by women.[7]

In addition to the court files I also consulted other documentation – marriage agreements, wills, and probate proceedings. It was a challenge to ascertain the years in which spouses died – a necessary task – because Vienna's municipal archive (*Wiener Stadt-und Landesarchiv*) files these documents according to year of death.[8]

1 Divorce Agreements

A divorce agreement is the primary document illustrating the manner in which couples divided their wealth and property in cases of divorce from bed and board. These are usually entitled "settlement" (*Vergleich*), "contract" (*Vertrag*), "marriage divorce contract" (*Ehescheidungskontrakt*), "marriage separation agreement" (*Ehetrennungsvertrag*), "separation certificate" (*Separations-Urkunde*), or "declaration" (*Erklärung*). All, in any event, document the agreement between the couple or their lawyers in respect to divorce

6 Cf. Anton Leo Hickmann, *Historisch-statistische Tafeln aus den wichtigsten Gebieten der geistigen und materiellen Entwicklung der k.k. Reichshaupt- und Residenzstadt Wien im neunzehnten Jahrhundert* (Vienna: Hölder, 1903), fig. 28 and 29.

7 Sylvia Möhle also concludes that women sued for divorce more often than men. Möhle, *Ehekonflikte*, p. 91.

8 ANNO, a virtual reading room provided by the Austrian National Library, was a vital resource for this research: Österreichische Nationalbibliothek, "ANNO – AustriaN Newspapers Online", accessed 21 July 2020, http://anno.onb.ac.at. The website includes a search function that allows for the searching of the names of spouses within obituaries published in the *Wiener Zeitung* and other newspapers. I then consulted the index of the archive to access the files accordingly.

and its consequences. These settlements can be considered products of Joseph II's marriage regulation of 1783, because this – in contrast to church jurisdiction – permitted divorce by mutual consent.[9] The clauses of the 1783 marriage regulation went a step further in fact, banning non-consensual divorces, which had been allowed in canon law for centuries past. While in accordance with most legal opinions of the time and with general contract law, this veto, a far-reaching option, was found to be to exclude too many couples in dispute and was dropped after only three years. It thus remained possible to apply for divorce by mutual consent and non-consensual divorces were once again permitted.[10]

A further novelty of the Josephine marriage reform was that secular courts, in contrast to church courts that differentiated between temporary or indefinite divorce from bed and board, usually decreed divorce without a time-limit. Resolving property matters therefore became to some extent more urgent, not least because the settlement was more temporally indefinite than in cases in which divorce was granted for only a few months or years.[11]

Divorce agreements were usually prefaced by a short introduction setting down the personal data of the involved parties. The next passage frequently stated that the husband and wife had "reached the following agreement" in respect to divorce. In some cases, there is an addendum that the agreement was entered into "voluntarily and unanimously".

Divorce settlements varied greatly in content, and we see various aspects appear on a case by case basis in the actual settlements. The amounts and frequency of alimony payments varied, as did the distribution of common property. There were few barriers to drafting the contents of divorce contracts. In the court files examined, I found only one instance in which a settlement was rejected by the court. This was the 1849 divorce proceedings between twenty-year old Johanna Dotzler, née Costenoble, and Rudolf August Dotzler, a civil servant seventeen years older, which the court rejected because there was no provision for maintenance for the underage wife. The judge remained unmoved by the young woman's plea (and that of her guardian) that she would apply

9 Canon law knew only two possibilities to permit divorce by mutual consent: If the spouses mutually agreed to enter an order or if the husband decided to become a priest and the wife agreed to this decision.

10 Cf. court decree from 13 October 1786, *Joseph des Zweyten Römischen Kaisers Gesetze und Verfassungen im Justiz=Fache, Jahrgang 1785 bis 1786, Zweyte Fortsetzung* (Vienna, 1817), No. 585, pp. 69–70, Österreichische Nationalbibliothek, "ALEX Historische Rechts- und Gesetzestexte Online", Justizgesetzsammlung (JGS), accessed 15 October 2020, http://alex.onb.ac.at/cgi-content/alex?aid=jgs&datum=1003&size=45&page=75.

11 Cf. the chapter of Andrea Griesebner in this book.

for maintenance neither now nor after reaching majority. That Rudolf August Dotzler was in financial straits and had to maintain a 74-year-old father, or that the underage wife possessed an annual income of 800 Gulden from properties, did not affect the rejection of the plea. A civil court decreed the divorce only in January of 1850 following the appeal of Rudolf August Dotzler.[12] In his plea, Dotzler repeated the arguments heard previously: it cannot be the intention of the court, he argued, "not to permit the divorce which was already a fact" and to tolerate "a relationship contrary to legal principles". He added that it was neither in his interest nor that of his wife to enter into a discussion about the reasons for the divorce, as this would reopen wounds that had hardly healed.

The Dotzler case provides us with insight into possible limits of tactical latitude in divorce settlements as well as the motives of a couple seeking undisputed divorce from bed and board. Not wishing to disclose details of their private lives, the majority of parties who entered a plea with the *Magistrat* abstained from judicial enquiry into causes of the dissolution of the marriage. Rather than confront the danger of re-awakening old emotions and conflict in a drawn out and costly trial (permitting or refusing divorce), couples usually took advantage of a consensual divorce from bed and board. But consensual divorce was not always the first choice. Numerous couples (increasing in proportion in the first half of the nineteenth century) reached a divorce settlement only during divorce proceedings. Between 1783 and 1850 eighty percent of divorce cases were settled by mutual consent. That does not mean, however, that mutual agreement was always advantageous for both parties, sometimes women relinquished rights and claims in advance in order to secure a final divorce.[13]

2 Non-consensual Divorces

Whereas an agreed settlement was the precondition for a divorce by mutual consent, cases where consent was absent were subject to the additional question of whether legal arguments concerning the consequences of the divorce would be addressed in a normal plea or separate trial. A court decree of

---

12 Rudolf August Dotzler's appeal, 27 December 1849, *Wiener Stadt- und Landesarchiv* (WStLA) 1.2.3.2.A6 Sch. 52, 59/1849.

13 As Monika Gimpel-Hinteregger points out, this risk continues: Monika Gimpel-Hinteregger, "Reformnotwendigkeiten im österreichischen Ehe- und Scheidungsrecht," in *Recht, Geschlecht und Gerechtigkeit. Frauenforschung in der Rechtswissenschaft*, ed. Ursula Floßmann (Linz: Trauner, 1997), pp. 193–216.

1788 stipulated that in such situations, judges had the right in a divorce trial to pass judgement on the distribution of the couple's property.[14] This ruling was revised in a later decree of November 1791.[15] Disputes about "the division of property and wealth", as the new text phrased it, were to be decided by a trial held separately from divorce proceedings. The Austrian Civil Code of 1811 retained this ruling, and declared that judges should strive to reach consensual settlements in cases of dispute (division of property, maintenance for children, alimony for the divorced woman, or annulment of the marriage agreement).[16] If this failed, the judge would hear the couple in a proper court proceeding and decide on a "reasonable sum for maintenance" for the woman and her children. This "provisional alimony", as it is formulated in relevant court files, was seen as a temporary solution, and offered the wife and her children support until a final maintenance sum was established.

The reasons for which divorced spouses initiated suits, and the claims they could thereby assert, were closely linked to the question of guilt. In disputed divorce cases, only the party declared innocent was entitled to "demand suitable maintenance".[17] Spouses that were declared in-part or wholly to blame for the end of the marriage had no right to alimony. In cases where blame was not apportioned, neither party could claim maintenance. The regulation that a woman seen as having contributed to the dissolution of marriage had no right to alimony from her husband was modified in a court decree of 1841. Although it was once more established that, as a rule, "a woman legally divorced from her husband on the basis of shared culpability" was not entitled to alimony. Cases in which the wife made maintenance claims remained at judge's discretion to "decide by taking all circumstances into account and factors in her favour".[18] According to Ellinor Forster, the principle of maintenance entitlement dependent on the question of guilt is to be found in the *Codex Theresianus* of 1766.[19] The Marriage Law of 1783 and Josephine law codex of

14 Cf. court decree from 9 May 1788, *Joseph des Zweyten Römischen Kaisers Gesetze und Verfassungen im Justiz=Fache, In dem achten Jahre seiner Regierung* (Vienna 1817), No. 824, p. 53, ALEX Historische Rechts- und Gesetzestexte Online, JGS.

15 Cf. court decree from 10 November 1791, *Leopold des Zweyten Römischen Kaisers Gesetze und Verfassungen im Justiz=Fache, In dem zweyten und letzten Jahre seiner Regierung* (Vienna 1817), No. 219, pp. 76–77, ALEX Historische Rechts- und Gesetzestexte Online, JGS.

16 Cf. Austrian Civil Code of 1811 (ABGB), §§ 108 and 117.

17 ABGB, § 1264.

18 Court decree from 4 May 1841, *Gesetze und Verordnungen im Justiz=Fache vom Jahre 1841, für die deutschen Staaten der österreichischen Monarchie*, No. 531, pp. 575–576, ALEX, Historische Rechts- und Gesetzestexte Online, JGS.

19 Cf. Forster, "Handlungsspielräume", p. 384; Codex Theresianus, 1. Theil, Caput II, § 4, 79.

1786, however, contained no such clause. Both legal texts allowed only for a consensual divorce.

The question of blame or guilt played an essential role in trials concerning the annulment of marriage contracts. "The continuation or annulment of marriage pacts" (Austrian Civil Code 1811) could be demanded by the party that was declared innocent, or by both parties, if both or none were declared guilty for the end of the marriage.[20] A husband or wife responsible for the end of the union had no such right. Annulling a marriage contract could have far-reaching consequences. According to legal expert Thomas Dolliner,[21] property a wife had brought into the marriage must be returned to her following such an annulment: "that bestowing on the other for whatever period the administration of or any benefits accruing from such wealth will be rendered null and void; that the agreed sharing of worldly goods will cease from the date of the pact annulment, and that the common property of the couple will be divided as upon the death of either spouse."

As there is only very scattered evidence of additional legal suits concerning the abolition of marriage agreements or the division of property, I place no emphasis on non-consensual divorces in the following pages, opting instead to focus on solutions to the division of property and alimony in divorce settlements. Before doing so, however, it is necessary to first examine the laws concerning marital property.

3 The Law of Marital Property and Marital Property Models

With regard to the legal aspects of marital property, we must distinguish between two models, i.e. differentiate between the division of property, and that which was commonly held.[22] In between lies a myriad of gradation and

20 ABGB, § 1264.

21 Thomas Dolliner, *Handbuch des österreichischen Eherechtes. Ausführliche Erläuterung des zweiten Hauptstückes des bürgl. Gesetzbuches von §. 93–110*, vol. 3 (Vienna: Braumüller, 1848, 2nd edition), p. 188. The first edition appeared in 1835, in this chapter I quote the second edition from 1848. Dolliner's texts were published as early as 1829 in the *Zeitschrift für österreichische Rechtsgelehrsamkeit*.

22 Cf. Ursula Floßmann, Herbert Kalb, and Karin Neuwirth, *Österreichische Privatrechtsgeschichte* (Vienna: Verlag Österreich, 2014, 7th edition), pp. 115–25; Margareth Lanzinger, Gunda Barth-Scalmani, Ellinor Forster, and Gertrude Langer-Ostrawsky, *Aushandeln von Ehe. Heiratsverträge der Neuzeit im europäischen Vergleich* (Vienna, Cologne, and Weimar: Böhlau, 2010, 2nd editon 2015).

mixed forms that could be chosen as legally binding by the couple. As Gertrude Langer-Ostrawsky and Margareth Lanzinger have established, the "separation of marital wealth tends to link the spouses to the respective partners' families of origin".[23] Shared property, in contrast, points to the significance ascribed to the marriage itself.[24] A variation of shared property is wealth accrued through common effort, which remained separate from that extant at the time of marriage and wholly comprised additional accruements made as the shared fortune of the couple.

The Austrian Civil Code was responsible for determining the state of the couple's worldly goods in all divisions of wealth. This meant that "husband and wife retain[ed] the right to their own property existing at the point of marriage or added to later by means of inheritance or work".[25] In practice, however, it was "customary and considered a legal standard that the wife entrusted the disposal of her property to her spouse", in order for him to "manage it in order to earn profit and use the same".[26] On closer examination, as Ursula Floßmann argues, a number of legal uncertainties exacerbated the "clear and comprehensive division of the property between man and wife", and thus the division of wealth on the basis of the legal codex turned out to be an "unclear" or "supposed" mutual management of the couple's property.[27] On the one hand the law stated that, "as long as she had not refused consent," the wife had handed control over her fortune to her husband; and on the other stated that, in cases of doubt, additional accruements were deemed his.[28] Wealth held in common, which had to be defined in a marriage agreement, could refer to the entire property of the couple (general wealth held in common) or to specific items (partial wealth held in common). The assent of the other party was essential to the administration of wealth held in common. Similar to the division of wealth, it was usual in such cases that the husband administered and earned profit from the property.

---

23 Gertrude Langer-Ostrawsky and Margareth Lanzinger, "Begünstigt – Benachteiligt? Frauen und Männer im Ehegüterrecht. Ein Vergleich auf der Grundlage von Heiratskontrakten aus zwei Herrschaften der Habsburgermonarchie im 18. Jahrhundert," in *Less Favoured – More Favoured: Proceedings from a Conference on Gender in European Legal History, 12th–19th Centuries,* ed. Grethe Jakobsen, Inger Dübeck, and Helle Vogt (Copenhagen: The Royal Library, 2005), pp. 1–41, here p. 1.

24 Langer-Ostrawsky and Lanzinger, "Begünstigt – Benachteiligt?", p. 1.

25 Forster, "Handlungsspielräume," p. 86.

26 Ibid., p. 396.

27 Floßmann, Kalb, and Neuwirth, *Privatrechtsgeschichte*, p. 116.

28 Cf. ABGB, §§ 1237–1238.

In practice, the marital conflicts I examined exhibited parallels to the early modern period observations described by Gertrude Langer-Ostrawsky in respect to the Duchy of Lower Austria, a region dominated by agrarian holdings and small businesses.[29] As in the agricultural regions she investigated, it was likewise common during the end of the eighteenth and first half of the nineteenth centuries for wider sectors of Vienna's urban population to regulate commonly held property by legal means. Although the "law intended otherwise", people adhered to "the socially and economically proven tradition of contracts".[30] Widow Anna Müllner, née Mayer, and Karl Dormann, for instance, agreed in their marriage agreement of June 1792 that "whatever the bridal pair during the marriage, either singly or jointly earns, inherits, or receives by other legal means should be their common property and remain so".[31] In a marriage pact between Johann Paul and Rosalia Kieninger signed forty years later, the text read that "whatever the bridal couple now possesses, or with God's blessing earns or inherits later, shall be and remain wealth held in common and to each an equal portion".[32]

As Gertrude Langer-Ostrawsky succinctly put it, "wealth held in common was equally a precondition for, and a result of, the strong position of the wife".[33] In cases where worldly goods were held in common, the property rights of both were entered into the land registry. As regards the debts and commitments that burdened wealth held in common, women carried the same responsibility as men, and were legally liable to the same extent. Changes to the state of common property could be made only with the consent of the other partner, and on the basis of agreement. A disadvantage was that the property wives brought into marriage was not protected. The model of commonly held property favoured widows and widowers, because the bereaved party usually received half of what had theretofore been held in common.

29 Cf. Gertrude Langer-Ostrawsky, "Vom Verheiraten der Güter. Bäuerliche und kleinbäuerliche Heiratsverträge im Erzherzogtum Österreich unter der Enns," in Margareth Lanzinger, Gunda Barth-Scalmani, Ellinor Forster, and Gertrude Langer-Ostrawsky, *Aushandeln von Ehe. Heiratsverträge der Neuzeit im europäischen Vergleich* (Vienna, Cologne, and Weimar: Böhlau, 2010, 2nd editon 2015), pp. 26–119, here p. 37.

30 Ibid.

31 Marriage contract between Anna Müllner and Karl Dormann, 2 June 1792, WStLA 1.2.3.2.A10 2/1810.

32 Marriage contract between Johann Paul and Rosalia Kieninger, 28 May 1831, WStLA 1.2.3.2.A6 Sch. 25, 2/1832.

33 Langer-Ostrawsky, "Vom Verheiraten der Güter," p. 40.

4 Divorce and the Division of Wealth

When a divorce from bed and board was granted, the commonly held wealth was distributed in the same way as in cases of the death of a spouse. In these cases, too, married women were in a favourable position, as shown in the example of the divorce between Leonhard Schierling and Eva Maria Schierlingin. The childless couple had been married for sixteen years and co-owned a factory that produced ladies' fans and their own house in the Alsergrund suburb outside the city walls. The business was likely located at their place of residence. The fan factory was property accrued during the course of the marriage; financing for the erection of the house in which they lived was, in contrast, primarily provided by monies inherited by the husband. It is clear that Leonhard Schierling and Eva Maria Schierlingin had built up a prosperous enterprise, and that they held their wealth in common. Husband and wife owned the house and the firm in equal portion.

In their divorce settlement of November 1790, the couple stated that the original marriage agreement should be annulled, and that they would live in separate apartments in their house.[34] At the same time, they stated that the property entitlements of the wife should entail half of the house in its present form and, should the house be extended, an equal share of its added value – she had gained joint property of the house when it was being built. The couple also decided that the husband should be the mortgage holder for the outstanding building debt of 2,200 Gulden; he, in return, would receive the tools and machinery, the income from outstanding credits, and the manufactured stocks. He would furthermore continue to act as administrator of their place of residence. In the divorce settlement, however, he bound himself to provide his wife with an annual account of his financial affairs. The alimony for his wife was to be derived from half of the rental income of the house, of which, as mentioned above, she was joint owner. In addition, Leonhard Schierling promised to give her as many work commissions as she will be able to complete in order to improve her income. As mentioned later in the settlement, all such work would only be paid when the product was well done, and when she agreed to refuse commissions from elsewhere. She was also barred from setting up her own distribution system, from selling fans, and from otherwise competing with her husband's business. The settlement delineated the price to be paid for her work in great detail.

34 Divorce settlement between Leonhard Schierling and Eva Maria Schierlingin, 28 November 1790, WStLA 1.2.3.2.A6 Sch. 1, 21/1790.

A similar divorce agreement was proposed by Elisabeth Sachs, née Schmid, and 46-year-old Johann Sachs in November 1812. The couple had been man and wife for twenty years. Elisabeth and Johann Sachs, who had agreed to share their worldly goods in common, earned their living as silk-manufacturers and possessed a house at Hundsturm, a city suburb predominated by small workshops. In contrast to the Schierlings, the Sachs couple was not childless. Elisabeth Sachs had brought fifteen children into the world, five of who had survived, and at the time of divorce was pregnant once more. As in the Schierling case, it was likewise the wife that initiated proceedings. She sued her husband for divorce, half of the rental income and one Gulden per day alimony. She also demanded funds for the upcoming birth and upkeep of the child. She stated that she could hardly refrain from claiming alimony seeing that, "her diligence and work" had contributed to the "present wealth of their marriage".[35]

During the divorce case at the end of November 1812 both spouses renounced their original marriage pact, agreeing that the house should, as had hitherto been the case, be owned in equal parts by both, and that Johann Sachs should remain administrator of the property. Elisabeth Sachs promised to leave the house, as a result of which she would receive the sum of 62 Gulden and 30 Kreuzer from her husband each quarter-year. What remained after expenditure as income from the house would be split between the spouses every three months. In regard to earning her future living, Elisabeth Sachs was to pursue the trade. She was to work on looms, and what she produced would be sold under her husband's name. In addition to household items such as a stove, bed, several pieces of furniture, and a portion of the kitchen fittings, she would also receive that which was necessary to continue working as a silk manufacturer: tools, machinery, and raw materials already at hand. In detail, this meant that she was to receive ten looms, with accessories, and several hundred yards of fabric. Monies owed to the business for goods sold or sums loaned would belong to each spouse in equal portions. When an outstanding debt could not be recovered, husband and wife were to suffer the loss equally.

During the reign of Maria Theresia, Vienna's silk industry had enjoyed special privileges. As Annemarie Steidl has shown, a ban was placed on the import of silk goods, and native silk manufacturers were granted loans, subsidies for apprentices, and prize money for good performance.[36] Not least because of these support measures, the silk industry in Vienna around 1800 held a

35 Elisabeth Sachs's divorce petition, 27 October 1812, WStLA 1.2.3.2.A6, Sch.7, 39/1812.

36 Cf. Annemarie Steidl, *Auf nach Wien! Die Mobilität des mitteleuropäischen Handwerks im 18. und 19. Jahrhundert am Beispiel der Haupt- und Residenzstadt Wien* (Vienna: Verlag für Geschichte und Politik, 2003), pp. 104–36.

dominant position. In 1801 there were 8,000 silk weaving looms in the city. The industry was organised around a triangle of workshops, centralised production in factories, and outwork. In the nineteenth century Viennese authorities granted manufacturing licences to couples. Widows were entitled to continue their business without asking permission from the guild. "She had the right", writes Steidl, "to train apprentices, to employ journeymen and by paying half the annual fee she became a member of the association of master weavers".[37]

In the Sachs case the pair agreed that the three older children (Jakob, 19; Theresia, 17; and Florian, 9) would reside in their father's care. Provided she found a new place to live, the mother would be responsible for the two younger children (Rosa, 7 and Ferdinand, 4). This was, however, a temporary six-month guardianship during which she had to demonstrate that her children were well looked after and wished to stay in her care.[38] She also had to pay for their upkeep and education, and the child she was expecting would likewise be under her care. Both spouses agreed to mutual visiting rights, promising one another "to send the children to the other from time to time". In the last clause of her divorce settlement, Elisabeth Sachs refrained from claiming maintenance for herself and the children in her household as (in her own words) "the property has been justly divided and the upkeep of the children sufficiently provided for".

Elisabeth Sachs died eleven years and two months after her divorce. In her will, written shortly before her death in January 1824, it was noted that she had sold her "silk manufacture" to her adult children Jakob and Theresia.[39] The house at Hundsturm was still in joint possession of the divorced husband and wife. In her will she granted her half of the house to her children Jakob, Theresia, Florian and Ferdinand – Rosa and the child she was carrying when divorced had died in the meantime. Another instruction was that the share of the house she bestowed upon her children was not to be sold or mortgaged until her son Ferdinand reached majority. The results of the probate proceedings demonstrate that the will of Elisabeth Sachs was carried out to the letter.[40]

Following her death, Johann Sachs married again, and his wife Barbara Machmajok bore him a daughter who was named Katharina. He died at the beginning of January 1849 at the age of 83. In his will he left his wife 1,600 Gulden and his daughter Katharina, still a minor, the sum of 700 Gulden.[41]

---

37 Ibid., p. 119.

38 Divorce settlement between Elisabeth Sachs and Johann Sachs, 30 November 1812, WStLA 1.2.3.2.A6, Sch.7, 39/1812.

39 Elisabeth Sachs's last will and testament, 8 January 1824, WStLA 1.2.3.2.A10 72/1824.

40 Elisabeth Sachs's probate proceedings, WStLA 1.2.3.2.A2 4004/1824.

41 Johann Sachs's last will and testament, 17 June 1835, WStLA 1.2.3.2.A10 41/1849.

The complete remnants of his movable and immovable property were to be divided in equal measure between his three sons from his first marriage (his daughter Theresia had died of "consumption" [tuberculosis] in 1830 at the age of 37) and the daughter from his second union. Probate papers reveal that his estate consisted of clothing, linen, and six-eighths of the house title at Hundsturm. We may assume that he had received one-eighth of the title from his deceased daughter Theresia, and had bought a further one-eighth from his son Ferdinand, the only child who had left the home at Hundsturm.[42] In his will he additionally noted that none of the fittings or material for his business belonged to him, as they had been purchased with the money of his second wife.

A third couple, Maria Anna Zauner, née Raablin, and Leopold Zauner, also divided their movables in the course of their divorce. They were married for twelve years and ran a market garden in the suburb Erdberg, where they possessed a house and several plots of land which they cultivated. Leopold Zauner had been previously married and had brought his gardening business into the marriage. According to the marriage agreement of July 1793, possession of one half of the land was to be transferred to Maria Anna Raablin once the first wife's will had been executed.[43] Maria Anna Zauner, a farmer's daughter, was in her early twenties when she married; she brought a dowry of 90 Gulden in cash and an endowment valued at 100 Gulden into the marriage. The couple decided to hold everything in common that they would "earn, inherit or purchase with God's blessing". They purchased the house in Erdberg in November 1800.[44] Maria Anna Zauner bore several children, two of whom survived.

At the end of July 1807, husband and wife entered a plea at court for an undisputed divorce from bed and board.[45] Three days earlier the couple had agreed in writing to share their worldly goods and the care and maintenance for both children.[46] In that document, Maria Anna Zauner promised to leave the house, which she jointly owned, within fourteen days. As compensation, Leopold Zauner committed himself to pay her 40 Gulden a year. In regard to household items and clothing, the wife was allowed to take two beds, several pieces of furniture, pictures, and the clothing she and her daughter possessed.

42 Johann Sachs's probate proceedings, WStLA 1.2.3.2.A2 52/1849.

43 Marriage contract between Leopold Zauner and Maria Anna Raablin, 12 July 1793, WStLA 1.2.3.2.A2, 2150/1825.

44 Maria Anna Zauner's probate proceedings, WStLA 1.2.3.2.A2 2150/1825.

45 Divorce petition from the Zauner couple, 24 July 1807, WStLA 1.2.3.2.A6, Sch.6, 16/1807.

46 Divorce settlement between Leopold Zauner and Maria Anna Zauner, 21 July 1807, WStLA 1.2.3.2.A6, Sch.6, 16/1807.

The rest of the movable property earned by common effort was valued at 300 Gulden, Leopold Zauner was to pay his wife half of this sum in two instalments.

In respect to the immovable common property, the couple agreed to continue joint ownership of the house. In the same passage of the divorce settlement, they stated that they wished to annul the original marriage agreement, meaning that neither Leopold nor Maria Anna Zauner would have claim on future acquisitions of the other party. In order to prevent dissent and conflict in connection with the use of the common property, the couple stipulated that Leopold Zauner could make use of the house, a "kitchen garden" and two "house gardens"; his wife was to have the use of one "kitchen garden". Because Leopold Zauner could not hand the "kitchen patch" over to his wife until early February 1808, he committed himself to pay her a daily compensation of half a Gulden between the time of her removal and the handover of the cultivation patch, and an additional Gulden for the period from the handover until the end of April 1808. Part of the divorce agreement contained a passage that Maria Anna Zauner was obliged to withdraw two complaints she had lodged against her husband in spring 1807. Therein she had demanded, on the one hand, half of a cultivated patch or its value (750 Gulden) and, on the other, that her husband make a statement under oath regarding their common property. They agreed, in connection with the children, that the male minor would stay with the father, and the female minor with the mother. Leopold Zauner was obligated to pay 60 Gulden yearly maintenance for the little girl.

Maria Anna Zauner died intestate in January 1825 at the age of 53. During the course of researching the extent of her estate it became clear that eight years before her death she and her ex-husband had purchased a gardening plot valued at 350 Gulden.[47] This transaction begs the question of whether the couple reunited following their divorce from bed and board, or worked together while continuing to live separately. Of the two children, only their daughter Elisabeth had survived. She had married, lived in the house in Erdberg, and now received the entire proceeds of her mother's estate, including Maria Anna Zauner's clothing, half of the house, and half of the numerous market-gardens.

These three reconstructed cases evidence common characteristics and reveal a pattern in the division of property following divorce: all three couples were home and business owners, had no or little debt, and were married for periods ranging from twelve to twenty years. At the time of their divorces they were probably aged 35–45 (Leopold Zauner, who had been married twice, may have been older). At the time of marriage, all three couples had agreed to share

47 Maria Anna Zauner's probate proceedings, WStLA 1.2.3.2.A2 2150/1825.

their worldly goods, including joint ownership of their houses and businesses, and to divide profits equally.

In the course of divorce each set of spouses remained joint owners of their respective houses. In most cases, the wives were obliged to move out of the apartment or house, and as a result received compensation from their husbands. We also find court files cases in which couples divorced from bed and board continued to live under the same roof, or in which the husband was obliged to leave the common domicile. This was particularly true of instances in which there was joint ownership of worldly goods and the wife, as an inheriting daughter or widow, became the sole owner of the house. Forty-two-year-old remarried widow Cäcilie Pollak and Korbinian Pollak, two years her senior, shared a market garden like the Zauner couple, and signed a contract in February 1850 that the husband had to leave the household within three days or face eviction. For her part, Cäcilie Pollak promised in writing to contribute eight Gulden monthly to her husband's rent for a quarter of a year.

Divorced wives earned their livings through their own labour and from rental revenue gleaned from their shares of property previously held in common. Eva Maria Schierlingin was accorded work in her ex-husband's fan workshop, Maria Anna Zauner received a "kitchen allotment", and Elisabeth Sachs ten weaving looms. In return, all three women renounced their rights to spousal maintenance. According to sex and age, children were alternately placed in the care of their fathers or mothers. Maria Anna Zauner received maintenance for her daughter. Elisabeth Sachs, in contrast, had to find ways and means to look after and educate her children on her own. The Zauner's joint purchase of land evidences that there was at times contact between husbands and wives following divorces from bed and board. Eva Maria Schierlingin and Leonhard Schierling continued to live and work under the same roof even after their divorce.

The March 1850 divorce agreement between thirty-year-old Franz König and his wife Anna, six years his junior, proves that the division of property model continued to be practiced into the middle of the nineteenth century.[48] The couple had been married for six years, ran a textile production workshop in the Leopoldstadt, a district of Vienna, and had three children. It is not clear what happened to their business but following their divorce the house remained in joint ownership. In any case, Anna König renounced her right to alimony, suggesting that she had her own income from either work or rental revenue. The

48 Divorce settlement between Franz König and Anna König, 12 March 1850, WStLA 1.2.3.2.A6, Sch.52, 12/1850.

three children were placed in care of the father and could be taken by a reliable person to visit their mother every Thursday, returning home the same day.

5 Arrangements for Maintenance

Regular maintenance payments were the counterpart to the division of property and wealth. In such cases one party, usually the man, maintained the business. In return, the divorced wife was granted a regular amount of maintenance, with evidence that in a few cases this was paid off in a lump sum. In a divorce settlement in 1793, for example, the middle-class gold and silver craftsman Karl Hauptmann committed himself to the payment of a yearly maintenance of 200 Gulden to his wife and their child. The wording in this document differs from that of other divorce agreements: therein it was explicitly stated in writing that the couple wished a divorce not only from bed and board, but also from "living together" (*Beisamenwohnen*) and joint work (*gemeinschäftlichen Wirthschaft*).[49]

Should the husband not fulfil his maintenance obligations the wife was granted the right to engage bailiff to enforce the maintenance and recover the money due to her. Women only met with success in such instances when their husbands possessed property or goods worth impounding, and there are few cases in which women demanded that the court seize a portion of their husband's wages or salary.

Some wives stipulated in divorce settlements that, should their husband fail to adhere to obligations set down therein or to pay maintenance, administration of the enterprise would fall to them. Coffee house owner Barbara Neumannin and glass-cutter Anton Neumann altered their divorce contract scarcely two months after it was granted in October 1787. In their first settlement, the couple agreed that the husband was to "carry out the coffee-house business of his wife and that he receives the necessary equipment."[50] Their three children were to be taken care of along gendered lines: the son to the father, both daughters to the mother. Anton Neumann was obliged by signature to pay his wife and two daughters a daily maintenance amount of 30 Kreuzer. The spouses also agreed that if Anton Neumann were either in part or wholly unable to pay the maintenance the wife would take over the coffee

49 Divorce settlement between Karl Hauptmann and Theresia Hauptmann, 11 October 1793, WStLA 1.2.3.2.A6, Sch.2, 34/1793.

50 Divorce settlement between Barbara Neumannin and Anton Neumann, 26 October 1787, WStLA 1.2.3.2.A6, Sch.1, 17/1787.

house. Anton Neumann fell into arrears with his maintenance payments and the couple therefore had to draft and sign a second divorce settlement. This stipulated that "the wife from this day henceforth run the coffee house and had all the necessary equipment put at her disposal".[51] The husband promised in writing to leave their common abode, of which the wife was now to become administrator. The debts owned by the business would fall to the responsibility of the wife. If Barbara Neumannin were to die before her husband, the coffee house and care of the children would revert to her husband. If their jointly owned house were to be sold during the couple's life time, both would share the proceeds after payment of outstanding debts.

Another couple changed their divorce settlement of November 1813 three years later. The Lehmers, who had been married for five years, ran a bakery and had one child. In their first agreement, they stipulated that the son should be in the care of his father until his eighth birthday, after which his mother would be responsible for his care.[52] As long as she was divorced from him and caring for their child, Johann Lehmer was obliged to grant his wife a yearly maintenance amounting to 700 Gulden. The couple furthermore stipulated that the husband must return the wife's dowry as well as the counter marriage portion accrued in the amount of 511 Gulden and 44 Kreuzer. An annulment of the portion of the marriage contract pertaining to gain from wealth held in common followed. The settlement was altered in March 1816. The reason, disputed by neither party, was that Johann Lehmer saw himself as incapable of paying further maintenance. He handed the child over to his wife, as well as the bakery, which she was to manage under his name.

In instances in which it was the divorced wife rather than husband that continued to carry out the business or skilled trade we generally see that she was a widow who had brought the business into a second union with a journeyman or master craftsman familiar with the business in question. Upon the death of her first husband Anna Bauer, née Stocker, for example, inherited a silk manufacture. In 1811, at the age of twenty-seven, she took ribbon maker Felix Broschat as her second spouse. During the marriage arrangements, she handed her trading licence over to her second husband. We thus find a November 1811 announcement in the *Wiener Zeitung* that "the Lower Austrian Provincial Government had transferred the provincial trade licence of Anna Bauer for the manufacture of silk ribbons to her present husband Felix Broschat with all the

51 Divorce settlement between Barbara Neumannin and Anton Neumann, 19 December 1787, WStLA 1.2.3.2.A6, Sch.1, 17/1787.

52 Divorce settlement between Johann Lehmer and Theresia Lehmer, 16 November 1813, WStLA 1.2.3.2.A6, Sch.7, 21/1813.

advantages and privileges attached thereto".[53] The Bauer-Broschat marriage was short-lived – after just sixteen months of wedded life the couple applied for a divorce and lodged a settlement to that end.[54] It was their mutual intention that the husband hand over the manufacture and all its contents to the wife, and Anna Broschat, for her part, pursued no maintenance claims. It is also clear from this divorce settlement that Felix Broschat was in debt, and his wife agreed to give him 5,000 Gulden to pay off his creditors – it may be that Anna Broschat was in part responsible for the debts.

Perhaps it was the end of her second marriage that prompted Anna Broschat to organise her affairs. In her will, drafted a few days before signing the divorce settlement, she left 500 Gulden to her stepfather and the same amount to her brother, along with three ribbon looms.[55] She also bestowed 200 Gulden and a ribbon loom each on two foremen in her employment. Two spinning women were to receive 50 Gulden each from her estate. At the time, she was pregnant with a child from the second marriage, who was to inherit its statutory portion of 3,000 Gulden. The sole heirs were her two minor sons from her first marriage. Following her death, the boys were to enter an educational establishment, and 1,000 Gulden per annum was set aside for their schooling and upkeep.

In August 1819, Anna Broschat died at the age of 35. She left behind three children: Matthias (16) and Ignaz (10) from the first marriage, and daughter Rosina (9) from the second. She was predeceased by Felix Broschat. Following her death, her entire property was sold at auction: jewellery, clothes, the factory equipment, silk stock, several houses, and partial ownership of houses. Although the probate proceedings estimated an estate of over 70,000 Gulden, it transpired that, following various deductions for auctioneers' fees, journeymen's wages, apprentices' allowances, the cook's pay, and all debts and unpaid invoices, all that remained was a slight debt. The will of December 1811 could therefore bestow nothing on her beneficiaries.

It was common practice, especially among civil servants, white-collar workers, and medical doctors, for a divorced husband to pay regular maintenance to his former wife. In divorce settlements entered into by such individuals one never finds reference to the division of housing property. Civil servants were seldom house-owners and, aside from clothing and bedlinen, possessed nothing other than their salaries. They lived in sets of rooms (*Quartiere*) for

53 *Wiener Zeitung*, 9 November 1811, p. 4094, ANNO AustriaN Newspapers Online.

54 Divorce settlement between Felix Broschat and Anna Broschat, 2 January 1813, WStLA 1.2.3.2.A6, Sch.7, 1/1813.

55 Anna Broschat's last will and testament, 21 December 1812, WStLA 1.2.3.2.A10 395/1819.

which they received rent (*Quartiergeld*). The dependence of wives in this milieu on alimony was greater than in cases where the couple was engaged in skilled workmanship or business. This hypothesis is supported by statistical material: almost every second wife in a total 191 divorced couples in the small business-skilled tradesman sector relinquished her maintenance rights, whereas only a sixth of wives in the 89 cases of civil servants did so.

Following divorce most wives of the civil servant middle-class received alimony from their husbands. An example typical of many others is that of the Staudinger couple. Josepha Staudinger and her husband Leopold, a senior civil servant with the municipal authority, divorced for the second time in May 1810 after reuniting for three years following their first legal divorce from bed and board in 1807. They both agreed in the settlement that the 40-year-old Leopold Staudinger should care for the five children and provide his wife an annual alimony of 800 Gulden. The "clothing allowance" (*Kleidungsbeitrag*) of 200 Gulden would expire once the divorce came into effect. Leopold Staudinger also agreed to allow his wife Josepha to remove several pieces of furniture, a bed, clothes, and linen from the apartment. A clause permitting the children to visit their mother twice weekly and go to the theatre or take walks in her company was also part of the agreement. In addition, Josepha was permitted daily visits to any of the children who had fallen ill.

An example of a wife of the civil servant middle-class who was capable of making a living on her own in the wake of divorce was Elisabeth Janda. In order to provide the court with evidence of her financial independence, she presented a certificate from her landlord stating that "during the four months in our house [she] had earned more than 130 Gulden in outwork (mainly by dressing lace and embroidery)". As a result of her "extraordinary diligence", the certificate further alleged, "she could easily earn 400 Gulden annually".[56]

6 Résumé

The case studies presented here in some detail illustrate what Peter Becker refers to in his study of St. Lambrecht (Styria) as "conflicts that have become chronic".[57] The couples had engaged in rows and disputes for months, or even years, and the divorce settlements were often not the first legal instrument that

56 Certificate, 2 January 1807, WStLA 1.2.3.2.A6 Sch. 6, 1/1807.

57 Peter Becker, *Leben und Lieben in einem kalten Land. Sexualität im Spannungsfeld von Ökonomie und Demographie. Das Beispiel St. Lambrecht 1600–1850* (Frankfurt a. M. and New York: Campus, 1990), p. 168.

documented their desire to end that strife. Couples regularly reached extra-judicial agreements before turning to the courts for divorce, particularly in an attempt to establish rules for further cohabitation. These rules not only served to preserve domestic peace, but might also outline conditions to keep people apart, thus obviating strife arising from working or living together.

Eva Maria Schierlingin and Leonhard Schierling, for example, signed such an agreement before their divorce was granted. It is probable – a written complaint by her points in this direction – that Leonhard was the initiator, and that his wife signed it "in order to keep the peace".[58] The pre-divorce pact of the Schierling couple contained the clause that each party was to reside in separate apartments in the house they owned jointly. This was the case leading up to the divorce hearing and, as court case files in Vienna demonstrate, is not a solitary example.

The marriage proceedings investigated in these pages indicate that couples often agreed that a divorce was necessary, but that consent often ended when it came to the consequences of the divorce. As studies on the history of marriage, gender relationships, and inter-family relations have shown, property ownership, property rights, and alimony claims had, and have, considerable potential for creating additional conflict.[59] Of late, Margareth Lanzinger, Ellinor Forster, Janine Maegraith, Siglinde Clementi and Christian Hagen have drawn attention to disputes about property in cases of bereaved spouses on the one hand, and the consequences of divorce on the other, cross paths. Lanzinger and others examine "if and in what way the interplay of marriage, family and relatives" inherently or structurally promotes conflict. For these scholars, the particular form of how property was commonly held in marriage and inherited in its aftermath fuelled marital dispute.[60] The law on marriage and inheritance, so their argument runs, are those sections of civil law that "define in a normative process rights, claims, duties and the precedence given to certain persons, which in legal case law establishes a pattern, either local or regional or milieu-based, of appropriateness which not all those affected by it can subscribe to."[61]

Looking closely at the legal norms that regulate the end of marriage and how spouses acted in such scenarios indicates that actors were influenced by

58 Eva Maria Schierlingin's divorce petition, 14 October 1790, WStLA 1.2.3.2.A6, Sch. 1, 21/1790.

59 Cf. Ellinor Forster and Margareth Lanzinger, "Stationen einer Ehe. Forschungsüberblick," *L'Homme. Z.F.G.* 14–1 (2003), pp. 141–55; Westphal, Schmidt-Voges, and Baumann, *Venus und Vulcanus*.

60 Margareth Lanzinger, Ellinor Forster, Janine Maegraith, Siglinde Clementi, and Christian Hagen, "Konfliktpotential und Streitgegenstände im Kontext ehelicher Vermögensregime," *Frühneuzeit-Info* 26 (2015), pp. 104–15, here p. 104.

61 Lanzinger, Forster, Maegraith, Clementi, and Hagen, "Konfliktpotenzial," p. 104.

many factors in addition to the writ of law. Gender, age, the point in a single private biography at which divorce proceedings were instituted, the social positions of each spouse, and who possessed what were additional factors that influenced the content and final form of divorce settlements. The model of shared worldly goods, dominant in this study, was to the advantage of women who ran businesses with their husbands. At even better advantage were daughters who had inherited businesses, or widows who brought such enterprises into their second marriage, both categories were in a strong position for settling a divorce by virtue of possession of half the couple's property or wealth. By virtue of possession of housing property and/or a business these women were in a comfortable position to secure their livelihood, as long as debts were few and the house was no more than slightly mortgaged. Whereas in cases of small businesses couples, property and work were the foundation for further prosperity following divorce, the question of alimony was a decisive factor in formulating divorce settlements for couples from the middle-classes and civil service backgrounds. Divorced couples with businesses were more likely than other divorcees to stay in contact, because their work patterns (often shared) and (common) place of residence made differing degrees of close contact a logical option after they had ended their marital union.

References

Arni, Caroline. *Entzweiungen. Die Krise der Ehe um 1900*. Cologne, Weimar, and Vienna: Böhlau, 2004.

Beck, Rainer. "Frauen in Krise. Eheleben und Ehescheidung in der ländlichen Gesellschaft Bayerns während des Ancien Régime." In *Dynamik der Tradition*, edited by Richard van Dülmen, pp. 137–212. Frankfurt a. M.: Fischer, 1992.

Becker, Peter. *Leben und Lieben in einem kalten Land. Sexualität im Spannungsfeld von Ökonomie und Demographie. Das Beispiel St. Lambrecht 1600–1850*. Frankfurt a. M. and New York: Campus, 1990.

Desan, Suzanne. *The Family on Trial in Revolutionary France*. Berkeley: University of California Press, 2004.

Dolliner, Thomas. *Handbuch des österreichischen Eherechtes. Ausführliche Erläuterung des zweiten Hauptstückes des bürgl. Gesetzbuches von §. 93–110*, vol. 3. Vienna: Braumüller, 1848, 2nd edition.

Floßmann, Ursula, Herbert Kalb, and Karin Neuwirth. *Österreichische Privatrechtsgeschichte*. Vienna: Verlag Österreich, 2014, 7th edition.

Forster, Ellinor. "Legitime Wut. Zum Ausdruck männlicher Gefühle in Ehescheidungsprozessen des ländlichen Tirol und Vorarlberg im 19. Jahrhundert." In *Die*

Präsenz der Gefühle. Männlichkeit und Emotion in der Moderne, edited by Nina Borutta and Nina Verheyen, pp. 105–28. Bielefeld: Transcript, 2010.

Forster, Ellinor, and Margareth Lanzinger. "Stationen einer Ehe. Forschungsüberblick." *L'Homme. Z.F.G.* 14–1 (2003): pp 141–55.

Gimpel-Hinteregger, Monika. "Reformnotwendigkeiten im österreichischen Ehe- und Scheidungsrecht." In *Recht, Geschlecht und Gerechtigkeit. Frauenforschung in der Rechtswissenschaft*, edited by Ursula Floßmann, pp. 193–216. Linz: Trauner, 1997.

Hickmann, Anton Leo. *Historisch-statistische Tafeln aus den wichtigsten Gebieten der geistigen und materiellen Entwicklung der k.k. Reichshaupt- und Residenzstadt Wien im neunzehnten Jahrhundert*. Vienna: Hölder, 1903.

Kalb, Herbert. "Das Eherecht in der Republik Österreich 1918–1978." *Beiträge zur Rechtsgeschichte Österreichs* 2–1 (2012): pp. 27–43.

Langer-Ostrawsky, Gertrude. "Vom Verheiraten der Güter. Bäuerliche und kleinbäuerliche Heiratsverträge im Erzherzogtum Österreich unter der Enns." In Margareth Lanzinger, Gunda Barth-Scalmani, Ellinor Forster, and Gertrude Langer-Ostrawsky, *Aushandeln von Ehe. Heiratsverträge der Neuzeit im europäischen Vergleich*, pp. 26–119. Cologne, Weimar, and Vienna: Böhlau, 2010, 2nd edition 2015.

Langer-Ostrawsky, Gertrude, and Margareth Lanzinger. "Begünstigt – Benachteiligt? Frauen und Männer im Ehegüterrecht. Ein Vergleich auf der Grundlage von Heiratskontrakten aus zwei Herrschaften der Habsburgermonarchie im 18. Jahrhundert." In *Less Favoured – More Favoured: Proceedings from a Conference on Gender in European Legal History, 12th–19th Centuries*, edited by Grethe Jakobsen, Inger Dübeck, and Helle Vogt, pp. 1–41. Copenhagen: The Royal Library, 2005.

Lanzinger, Margareth, Gunda Barth-Scalmani, Ellinor Forster, and Gertrude Langer-Ostrawsky. *Aushandeln von Ehe. Heiratsverträge der Neuzeit im europäischen Vergleich*. Vienna, Cologne, and Weimar: Böhlau, 2010, 2nd edition 2015.

Lanzinger, Margareth, Ellinor Forster, Janine Maegraith, Siglinde Clementi, and Christian Hagen. "Konfliktpotential und Streitgegenstände im Kontext ehelicher Vermögensregime." *Frühneuzeit-Info* 26 (2015): pp. 104–15.

Lutz, Alexandra. *Ehepaare vor Gericht. Konflikte und Lebenswelten in der Frühen Neuzeit*. Frankfurt a. M. and New York: Campus, 2006.

Möhle, Sylvia. *Ehekonflikte und sozialer Wandel. Göttingen 1740–1840*. Frankfurt a. M. and New York: Campus, 1997.

Stalder, Birgit. *"Der Ehehimmel begann sich schon früh zu trüben." Geschlechterbeziehungen und Machtverhältnisse in Scheidungsprozessen zwischen 1876 und 1911. Ein interkonfessioneller Vergleich*. Berlin: Franz & Timme, 2008.

Steidl, Annemarie. *Auf nach Wien! Die Mobilität des mitteleuropäischen Handwerks im 18. und 19. Jahrhundert am Beispiel der Haupt- und Residenzstadt Wien*. Vienna: Verlag für Geschichte und Politik, 2003.

Stone, Lawrence. *Broken Lives. Separation and Divorce in England, 1660–1857*. Oxford: Oxford University Press, 1993.

Tschannett, Georg. "Zerrissene Ehen. Scheidungen von Tisch und Bett in Wien (1783–1850)." PhD diss., University of Vienna, 2015.

Westphal, Siegrid, Inken Schmidt-Voges, and Anette Baumann. *Venus und Vulcanus. Ehen und ihre Konflikte in der Frühen Neuzeit*. Munich: Oldenbourg, 2011.

Epilogue

CHAPTER 15

Wealth in Its Diverse Meanings and Contexts – Concluding Comment

Margareth Lanzinger

The past few centuries have left us with abundant archival documentation of men's and women's efforts to clarify wealth-related questions, particularly associated with significant biographical junctures that had ramifications that extended beyond marriage or one's own lifespan.[1] Conflicts over the bequeathal and inheritance of money and goods and disputes concerning claims to and transfers of wealth in general were ubiquitous: between husband and wife, between parents, widowed or separated parents and their children or stepchildren, between guardians and the next of kin of the deceased or among siblings, with brothers- or sons-in-law etc. At the same time, peace in households, marriages, and families has historically been accorded a high priority. Ensuring or re-establishing such peace was an integrative component of *buon governo* – good government – as practiced by institutions such as courts and via proceedings geared more toward achieving consensus than toward hearing lawsuits and handing down judgments.[2] The significance of mediation and arbitration, and of the institutions – informal and formal – to which these tasks were entrusted, can therefore be considered significant. The choice of the words "stipulating, litigating, mediating" for the subtitle of this volume speaks to these consequential areas, which were distinct but interconnected in myriad ways.

The aim of this conclusion is to round out the volume, tying the chapters together by way of a transversal perspective that highlights and brings into conversation some of the themes raised by the contributing authors. These are

1 This chapter was translated by Christopher Roth. Basic literature on this overall thematic complex is listed in the introduction. This concluding comment thus cites only a few references that pertain to specific thematic areas. See most recently Mia Korpiola and Anu Lahtinen, eds., *Planning for Death. Wills, Inheritance and Property Strategies in Medieval and Reformation Europe* (Leiden and Boston: Brill, 2018); Lloyd Bonfield, *Devising, Dying and Dispute. Probate Litigation in Early Modern England* (Farnham: Ashgate, 2012).

2 Cf. Inken Schmidt-Voges, *Mikropolitiken des Friedens. Semantiken und Praktiken des Hausfriedens im 18. Jahrhundert* (Berlin: de Gruyter, 2015).

 | DOI:10.1163/9789004456204_016

aspects that also point beyond the scope of this volume and are equally relevant to the more general discussion of wealth between the late Middle Ages and the nineteenth century. The focus of the concluding comment is on access to wealth, on documenting wealth, on awarding and denying it, on contested wealth, and on the power of wealth. The horizon and overall framework are defined by the research projects comprising the context from which this volume has arisen.[3]

1 Wealth from a Variety of Perspectives

The chapters of this volume examine the acquisition and transfer of wealth as well as the disposition thereof, and the settlement of claims, conflicts, and arbitration from various perspectives. At the centre of interest here are premarital, marital, and post-marital wealth as well as the wealth of families and kin. Rural and urban spaces are also represented – occasionally in direct comparison –, as are various social milieus: agricultural labourers and farmers, craftspeople, merchants, tradesfolk, the urban petite bourgeoisie, and nobles. It is essential to draw social and gender-specific distinctions, not only with regard to the widespread estate- and gender-specific differences in early modern law and legal practice, but also in terms of the possibilities and limits of agency, and access to wealth and to positions in households, in families, and among kin.

1.1 *Legal Cultures*

The chapter investigate starkly contrasting regional legal orders and legal cultures: the extremely heterogeneous German-speaking region differs from the Northern Countries and just as clearly from the Italian territories, which were strongly characterised by dowries (*dote*) and were themselves heterogeneous. The aim of late eighteenth- and early nineteenth-century codifications such as the Josephine Code which took effect in Austria in 1787 and the French *Code*

---

3 The background for the conference and present volume was the research project "Legal Spaces and Gender Order as Social Processes in a Trans-regional Perspective. Negotiating and Stipulating in Urban and Rural Contexts of South Tirol from the Fifteenth to the Early Nineteenth Century" (2014–2016), funded by the Südtiroler Wissenschaftsfonds. This research is being continued using a more refined approach in the form of the "The Role of Wealth in Defining and Constituting Kinship Spaces from the Sixteenth to the Nineteenth Century" project (P 29394). The project is funded by the FWF Austrian Science Fund (2016–2020) and based at the University of Vienna, see http://kinshipspaces.univie.ac.at/en/.

civil of 1804 was to achieve greater legal uniformity. The latter had effects that extended far beyond the borders of France, providing the basic legal framework for French-occupied and -influenced territories – including large areas of what would later on become Italy.[4]

During the nineteenth century, customary practice was frequently challenged by processes of standardisation that took place both within territorial states in Europe's various regions and transnationally. And in some cases, the new laws themselves provided an opportunity to continue adhering to existing customs. It was thus that the 1811 Austrian Civil Code (*Allgemeines Bürgerliches Gesetzbuch*) established separation of goods as the legal norm in marriage, but still left it possible to opt for community of marital goods on a contractual basis. In France, on the other hand, the 1804 Code civil radically broke with the privileging of individual children as heirs and declared wills worded to this effect to be invalid. Even so, new strategies for circumvention came into play.[5] In other times and places, wills made it possible to soften legally mandated unequal treatment of for example daughters and sons by leaving them things to which they had no legal claim or by according a widow – to the disadvantage of her brothers-in-law – guardianship and administrative rights,[6] as we have seen in the case of Osvaldo Trapp analysed in the chapter by Siglinde Clementi. Alongside the German, Italian, French, and Northern regions, among which – despite all differences – there were some similarities resulting from their partial foundation in Roman law, there was also the English context, with its common law and system of coverture. This adhered to yet another logic, in that the property of women passed into the ownership of their husbands upon marriage.[7]

---

4 Peter A. J. van den Berg, *The Politics of European Codification. A History of the Unification of Law in France, Prussia, the Austrian Monarchy and the Netherlands* (Groningen: Europa Law Publishing, 2007); Filippo Ranieri, "L'influence du Code civil sur les codifications du 19e siècle: essor et déclin d'un modèle européen," in *Le bicentenaire du Code civil – 200 Jahre Code civil. Saarbrücker Kolloquium zum 50-jährigen Bestehen des CJFA am 26.11.2004*, ed. Claude Witz (Baden-Baden: Nomos, 2006), pp. 55–67.

5 On this, see also the case of Turin under French rule: Beatrice Zucca Micheletto, "L'introduzione del codice civile napoleonico a Torino: il regime patrimoniale dei coniugi tra norma e pratica," *Geschichte und Region / Storia e regione* 20–2 (2011), pp. 92–105.

6 Cf. Giulia Calvi, "Rights and Ties that Bind. Mothers, Children, and the State in Tuscany during the Early Modern Period," in *Kinship in Europe. Approaches to Long-Term Development (1300–1900)*, ed. David Warren Sabean, Simon Teuscher, and Jon Mathieu (New York and Oxford: Berghahn, 2007), pp. 145–62.

7 Cf. Amy Louise Erickson, *Women and Property in Early Modern England* (London and New York: Routledge, 1995); Amy Louise Erickson, "Coverture and Capitalism," *History Workshop Journal* 59–1 (2005), pp. 1–16, https://doi.org/10.1093/hwj/dbi001, accessed 18 January 2019.

Differing legal logics and means of classifying wealth have resulted in different types of archival sources that may have the same name, or that may otherwise seem comparable at first glance, but can actually contain different categories of wealth: a "dowry contract", for example, contains primarily the sum of money and the trousseau brought into the marriage as well as the arrangements associated therewith,[8] while a "marriage contract" may extend beyond those items to include comprehensive provisions for the eventuality of widowhood and with regard to inheritance. And in English probate inventories, for example, real estate property is absent – though from the sixteenth century on one sees more and more statutes that encouraged its inclusion in wills. Furthermore, in places where coverture was in practice, probate inventories failed to indicate which portions of the estate had been contributed by the wife.

Conversely, in the case of differing terms the question arises whether they express variations and provide access to crucial differences. While intergenerational contracts from the German-speaking world include the term *Übergabe* – "handover" or "transfer" –, the English term "retirement contract" also entailed the withdrawal of the older generation. There is, however, an important distinction to be made between these two concepts. The transferral itself embodied the same type of transaction, but the domestic power relations at play in any given case were weighted quite differently depending on which generation was in possession of authority, leading the household in an economic sense, and which was considered subordinate. In Beatrice Moring's chapter the term "retirement contract" is used in situations where the older generation withdrew. And as she emphasises, we must identify whether it was headship and/or ownership that was being transferred and the point in time when a retirement contract was concluded: alongside the property transfer, or only when age or illness rendered it necessary. Likewise associated with transfer and retirement are questions regarding the separate and common areas of the two generations, as to the older generation's share in household economic activity in relation to their being provided for by younger household members as well as the quality and quantity of that provision, and as to the period- and milieu-specific standard of living invoked by the formulation "appropriate maintenance".[9] Christian Hagen discusses a case from the late Middle Ages

8 Cf. Margareth Lanzinger, "Marriage Contracts in Various Contexts: Marital Property Rights, Sociocultural Aspects and Gender-specific Implications. Late-Eighteenth-Century Evidence from two Tirolean Court Districts," *Annales de démographie historique* 121–1 (2011), pp. 69–97.

9 Cf. Beatrice Moring and Richard Wall, *Widows in European Economy and Society, 1600–1920* (Woodbridge: Boydell Press, 2017); Christine Fertig, "Stem Families in Rural Northwestern

where shared authority by young and old was agreed upon in 1357 for the farm Niederedenhof in Partschins – a model that one seldom encounters in the early modern period.

The question as to what was considered separate and shared has also shown itself to be quite productive in conjunction with separations of bed and board. Georg Tschannett demonstrates in his chapter how the division of wealth in the wake of a separation did not necessarily entail the complete divergence of a separated couple's lives: shared house ownership or working relationships sometimes continued. One can draw certain parallels between the determination of alimony to be paid to separated women and the assignment of provisions for widows at the end of a marriage. And in both situations – separation and widowhood – it was often women who had to leave the marital household.

It was not customary everywhere, after all, for a widow to be sustained in the house of her deceased husband – Janine Maegraith has shown as much using the example of sixteenth and seventeenth century southern Tyrol which resulted from the system of separate marital property. This system, as in the Italian dowry system, rendered the existence of legally and contractually ensured widows' entitlements and regulated procedures following husbands' deaths particularly important and effectively necessary. The extent and nature of what could be and was negotiated and conceded varied considerably – both within the same region, such as Sonnenburg and Brixen, and compared in terms of time and space. While separation of goods puts the claims of widows or widowers firmly in the focus of Janine Maegraith's chapter, Beatrice Moring's chapter addresses the subsequent sustenance of bequeathing couples. This kind of focus simultaneously makes clear that there are fundamental differences depending on whether the contractual agreements were made for couples, widows, or widowers as well as depending on whether these persons were still in sufficient condition to economically sustain themselves or old and fragile enough to need provision. As Craig Muldrew emphasises, the category of age is an important point to consider when interpreting both transfer agreements and wills. In situations and milieus where we can assume a relatively low life expectancy, the age and the phase of life within which a will was written can provide an explanation for the type and extent of existing wealth. Wills and other archival documents, however, usually do not contain information on age, and this is thus an aspect that entails additional research.

Germany? Family Systems, Intergenerational Relations and Family Contracts," *The History of the Family* 23–2 (2018), pp. 196–217.

1.2 *Interrelated Perspectives*

We need a tightly entangled multi-layered perspective in order to gain insight into the social practice of law. Interrelated perspectives first and foremost include the legal framework of the investigated area and or milieu – which may, depending on the analytical emphasis, comprise contemporary commentary on legal interpretations. Second come legal instruments such as contracts and wills. Depending on the interests being served, these could facilitate and reinforce, allow for compromise on, or weaken wealth arrangements of a given type. Without fail these legal instruments also indicate the potential for conflict, they anticipate discord and react to conflict or mention the wish to avoid disputes as the explicit reason for drawing up a will or a contract, as seen in Christian Hagen's chapter on late-mediaeval southern Tyrol. The third level that is relevant in this respect is that of agreements and dispositions. And fourth, the efficacy and implications of each of these elements only becomes visible and comprehensible if established, negotiated, and utilised law can be interrelated with specific cases and with the social and legal position of affected men and women. The social and legal position of the parties competing for wealth was largely determined by who was competing with whom, by the situation in which that competition was taking place, by the question which parties may have gained support, and by the distribution of power within the actual configuration. Power could be based on gender, on immovable or financial wealth, and/or on legal assurances and claims.

Power can, in this sense, be regarded as an interdependent category. This is particularly evident in the position of men in "house systems", societies where house ownership played an enormous socioeconomic role, such as was the case in the French Pyrenees and southern Tyrol. Marie-Pierre Arrizabalaga writes that the social status of men who married inheriting daughters was considered "unnatural" because they were viewed as "servants" in their wives' houses. The *Tiroler Landesordnung* refers to such with the illustrative term *einfahrende Gesellen*, or "fellows marrying in". In the Lower Austrian community of Perchtoldsdorf, the prevailing community of marital goods model rendered the right of women to hold real estate and trade licenses much more favourable compared to areas with separation of marital goods or with dowries. But this could still result in gender imbalance – that of the unequal couple. As Andrea Griesebner has shown in her chapter about the case of Eva Maria Neudorferin, the potential for inequality to lead to conflict should not be underestimated. This type of gender imbalance likewise proved to be a contributing factor in conflicts, bankruptcies, and marital separation.

Women's power in systems with dowries and separation of goods, on the other hand – and more generally in contexts oriented on patrilineal continuity – was based on precisely the right that put them at a disadvantage in comparison with men. Their wealth was protected, and this – extended to instances in which their husbands were deeply indebted or had declared bankruptcy. A woman's wealth was secured by a mortgage on her husband's real estate wealth – a practice that had become typical in Tyrol as early as the fourteenth century – and had to be returned if she was widowed. In the case of Florence, for instance, we see that conflicts over dowries – typically relating to their return, particularly if the husband was insolvent – were handled in public court proceedings, whereas other conflicts within families and among other kin were addressed outside of court.

The fifth level is embodied by how conflict permits historians to recognise the seams and breaking points present in the various legal and social fabrics. These junctures might be inherent in existing laws, have originated in divergent interpretations and uses of law, or be based on competing logics and interests – the social relationships – involved. The sixth and final level that addresses conflict leads back to the legal institutions in cases when compromises were agreed out of court but documented there, reconciliations or resolutions were achieved, or lawsuits were filed. In this context interaction and negotiation have turned out to be central analytical concepts in social history and in the history of legal practice.

1.3 *A Cross-Period Approach*

This trans-epochal examination of ownership and wealth, conflict, and conflict resolution has proven particularly inspiring. This volume's chapters run from the late Middle Ages into the nineteenth century, revealing continuities while at the same time allowing for manifestations and implications of change to be all the more clearly perceived. Continuity of law as well as legal practices within and alongside codified laws could persist over a considerable period – and did in Italian territories, Vienna, and in Tyrol. At the same time, legal frameworks might undergo changes at the classic turning points between eras. Regina Schäfer and Simona Feci show this to be the case for the transition from the Middle Ages to the early modern period in the Southern German and Italian-speaking regions respectively, and Marie Pierre Arrizabalaga for the period around 1800 in the French Pyrenees. In this latter chapter we learn that succession to ownership needed to be completely reorganised following the introduction of the 1789 laws and 1804 Code Civil. As Beatrice Moring has ascertained in her investigation of the Northern Countries, on the other hand, significant changes there tended to take place independent of the commonly acknowledged divisions between historical periods. There we see that Norwegian law witnessed the advent of restrictions on women's rights to make economic decisions and transact in their husbands' absence towards the close of the seventeenth century. Subsequent changes continued until the end of the nineteenth century.

Fundamental processes of change did not necessarily coincide with the typical thresholds between historical periods – and some European chronologies differed greatly, particularly with regard to considerations of wealth and gender. Within this context, a catastrophe such as the late fourteenth century plague in Trento had the potential to expand individuals' opportunities and, as Silvia Mattivi shows, this was the case for women in particular. Legal changes could be introduced but did not automatically improve the situations of those who had previously been disadvantaged by laws relating to wealth. The groups of individuals thus disadvantaged include daughters vis-à-vis sons, younger people vis-à-vis older people or vice-versa, stepchildren and extramarital children vis-à-vis 'natural' children and children born in marriage, and women vis-à-vis men. Linear modernisation narratives do not apply where access to and distribution of wealth are concerned, no matter whether a married couple, a family, or kin are in question – and this is especially true when viewed from the perspective of gender relations.

1.4 *A Wide Range of Documents*

This volume also opens up a perspectival panorama, its case studies link specific lines of inquiry with comparative approaches while at the same time linking qualitative and quantitative methods. The basis for doing so is provided by the variety of sources upon which the authors have drawn. In addition to municipal statues, regional legal codes, and other forms of written and codified law the authors also evaluate court protocols – for both negotiation and legal conflicts –, various types of contracts, notarial registers, wills and mutual wills, inventories and records of probate proceedings, guardianship and bankruptcy documents, and documents concerning marital separations. As seen in the chapters by Laura Casella, Isabelle Chabot, and Siglinde Clementi, the spectrum also ranges beyond strictly court-related and legal sources, contributors have also analysed letters, family chronicles and diaries, notes and recollections that women wrote down in notebooks or account books. The parallel 'bookkeeping' on financial, personal, and familial matters found in the material studied by Laura Casella in some ways reflects the involvement of Friulan noblewomen in each of these areas. At the other end of the range of perspectives we see the dependence of aristocratic widows – amongst others – on the willingness of brothers and in-laws to honour contractually assured claims, in this volume represented by the figure of Maria Anna Trapp, née Thun. The coexistence of divergent views on where such women 'belonged' in widowhood was an artefact of the different legal cultures within the Tyrolean-Tridentine transitional region. Isabelle Chabot shows the dependence of women and families on dowries in the Florentine context with a special focus on cases involving husbands who had gone into exile as a result of bankruptcy or insolvency.

2 The Composition of Wealth

Wealth is the central thematic field of this volume, broadly defined to encompass both movable and immovable wealth: houses and landholdings, money and items of daily use, representation, and remembrance, as well as objects that functioned as stores of value. Wealth also encompassed legal and contractual entitlements, as those provided one access to and use of resources. Such entitlements might include a widow's claims to sustenance and maintenance, a separated wife's claim to alimony, or usufruct rights for parents who had handed down their property to the next generation, but also access to commons. Trade licenses and guild memberships are also considered forms of wealth – encountered, for example, in marriage contracts stating that the husband brought no money to the marriage, no house, and no property, but was qualified to practice a trade. The chapters of this volume demonstrate just how broad the possibilities for analysing wealth are, both in terms of their legal, economic, social, and cultural efficacy, and their interdependence and interrelation. It is in this sense, for example, that Janine Maegraith illustrates the differing of wealth categories at play in the claims of a widow, while Craig Muldrew does the same in his analysis of wills. Both of them elucidate the interplay between different types of wealth.

In each individual chapter wealth is brought into conversation with issues relating to spaces of negotiation, competition and conflict, and modes and agents of mediation. Wealth is thus linked with institutions such as marriage and kinship, with neighbourhood and community, with avenues of professional training, with ventures and professions, with migration and – quite centrally – with economic contexts within which livelihood was secured and power and prestige were consolidated. Many of the authors' chapters are situated in contexts where the closest social relationships – between spouses, between generations, among siblings, between relatives and kin – were regulated by formalised agreements, contracts, settlements, and compromises. These were instruments that, should conflict arise, were ideally intended to repair those relationships, or to at least lead to an outcome that was acceptable for both sides – an ideal that pertained across the entire range of social milieus.

In addition to jurists, court scribes, and other legal professionals, there were other mediators who could have assumed an institutionalised status and constituted a specific legal space, – especially neighbours or local court district commissioners who were referred to as "advocates" in the sense of representatives or councillors but had no formal legal training. In the late-medieval Ingelheim context discussed by Regina Schäfer elected *Fürsprecher*, or intercessors, mediated between parties at court. It was not uncommon for notaries in Renaissance Florence to assume a mediator function; procurators – comparable to the south German *Momper* – represented women at court, as did classically the gender guardians discussed by Isabelle Chabot. It is important here to emphasise that court and infrajudicial authorities interacted, and that women drew upon the advantages of both bodies, for which reason their legal actions were by no means always pursued to the point of regular court proceedings and rulings. The chapters by Janine Maegraith and Regina Schäfer ascertain that mediation and arbitration were preferred over court conflict, a fact that underlines the significance of mediators. Attempts at reconciliation were moreover an integral component of proceedings such as early modern Catholic marital separation suits, in which the competent priest was instructed to make three attempts at achieving reconciliation between the two parties.

3 Documented Wealth

Written documentation of wealth – and thus of rights and claims – played a particularly important role in safeguarding claims and eliminating potential sources of conflict, and practices in this regard were far from uniform. In some territories, legal and administrative frameworks obliged women and men to document their wealth in writing – either always or when in excess of a given amount –, and documentation could take the form of contracts, confirmations, receipts, wills, or inventories. In other territories, authorities merely issued recommendations aimed at motivating people to document their wealth. Notaries could also be involved, either in conformation with social norms or as a result of familial or personal need for a certain degree of assurance. The question here is what types of wealth were listed where and how – and what was considered the minimum value worth documenting? This leads to questions regarding the range of social strata represented in extant source material and what gaps remain. Research covering a broad range of social groups is more difficult to carry out in cases where the obligation to complete an inventory was tied to a certain minimum net worth – as was the case in England, where the lower limit was £5. This may have been related to a desire on the part of the authorities to save on court costs. Craig Muldrew estimates that the share of agricultural labourers for whom inventories were compiled amounted to around seven percent. This estimate has methodical implications in the context of British social history, in which the evaluation of inventories is so central. In such cases, it is all the more important to take the entire estate settlement procedure into account and to also make use of additional complementary materials such as wills, tax registers, witness statements from the church courts. Doing so can, however, give rise to new problems if no consideration is given to the logic behind the production of a source; an example here would be if one computed the share of the poorer British populace not contained in the inventories based on the lists of those people who were exempt from the hearth tax without noting or taking into account the fact that these lists did not include those whose exemption was uncontested – i.e., the poor.[10] Thus, as Craig Muldrew shows in his chapter, the careful analysis of wills can not only contribute to our ability to discern between socio-economic distinctions among early modern agricultural labourers, but also provides input for the wealth bias debate.[11] Indeed, the unequal representation of the social spectrum in source material is a fundamental problem.

This volume demonstrates the significance of written, institutionally catalogued, and preserved documents across historical periods. Producing a written version of an agreement and filing it with a notary or a court provided women and men with an elevated sense of assurance. Aristocratic families set up their own family archives, and these were places for memories just as much as they were stores of evidence. Oral agreements always entailed a certain inherent risk, even when they retained their importance and legal validity over the centuries. Witnesses and relatives could, after all, forget things over the years or pass away prematurely. In Janine Maegraith's study on the seventeenth-century South Tyrolean court district of Sonnenburg, the marriage portion that Maria Ziser from Pflaurenz brought into her marriage had not been documented in writing. Ziser's prospects of recuperating it once she was widowed were therefore poorer than they otherwise would have been. Laura Casella and Isabelle Chabot have likewise emphasised how important it was for patrician women

10 Cf. Craig Muldrew, *Food, Energy and the Creation of Industriousness: Work and Material Culture in Agrarian England, 1550–1780* (Cambridge: Cambridge University Press, 2011).

11 Cf. Sebastian Keibek, "Correcting the Probate Inventory Record for Wealth Bias," Cambridge Working Papers in Economic and Social History No. 28, accessed 5 October 2018, https://econpapers.repec.org/paper/cmhwpaper/28.htm.

in Friuli and Florence to possess written record of their wealth, therewith ensuring their rights and defending them against possible contestation. In this sense it is not only written agreements and dispositions that should be viewed as historically significant cultural means of using the law, but so too personal 'bookkeeping' that recorded open claims and receivables. In her study, Laura Casella was able to utilise documentation produced alongside 'official' notarial and court records. The documents she looked at concern wealth in the form of dowries, purchased land, inheritance, transfers separate from the dowry, and sums of money that had been lent.

Conflict avoidance was the primary aim of dispositions and agreements. There were various types of documents intended to arrange wealth-related matters in such a way that conflict would not arise in the first place. This interest in conflict avoidance represents an enormously important aspect of how extant law was used in instances where disagreement did arise, often even as a consequence of those wealth-related arrangements. As Craig Muldrew shows in his chapter, even those who owned comparatively little disposed of what they did have in their wills. That moves one all the more prompting to inquire into situative contexts and possible explanations.

One needs appropriate source material in order to relate the acts of stipulating, litigating, and mediating to one another. The contemporary institutional and administrative contexts have impacted the surviving body of documentation and the forms in which it survives – in terms of types and numbers of documents as well as in terms of their content, and degree of detail. Places and modes of archiving such bodies of documentation also depend on former institutional and administrative contexts – in the form of notarial archives, family archives, or protocol books and records of the courts, for example – each with its own respective logic of production and use. Networks of documents allow for the identification and reconstruction of interrelated transactions. That capacity can be affected – eased or made more difficult – by the specific characteristics of the respective bodies of documentation. The complexity of such relationships reveals itself in cases such as when the initiation of a marriage project entailed not only the broad involvement of relatives but also a large transfer of goods – as shown by Christian Hagen in the case of the Preidlerhof, which was sold to a niece. What exactly comes into view in such cases? Isabelle Chabot has pointed out the significance of both infrajudicial and court-based conflict resolution undertaken by friends and relatives in late-medieval Florence of which we find evidence in family records and families' books – *libri di famiglia*. Depending on the judicial area, conflict appears in court sources when either infrajudicial conflict resolution efforts had failed or when a court was called upon for arbitration.

4 Wealth Awarded and Denied

The significance of various types of wealth also depended on what men and women were allowed to dispose of and bequeath to others, what they were able to pass on. This varied considerably across Europe. In the Northern countries during the early modern period, Beatrice Moring has shown us that only movable goods – not land – could be disposed of in wills. In such cases, one can presume that movable wealth enjoyed a different, perhaps greater, importance. A more general factor underlying freedom of testation would therefore seem to be the extent of ownership rights to, possibilities of, and limitations on, an individual's ability to acquire immovable property. What rights and restrictions did ownership of immovable property imply? Across Europe there were different legal frameworks in this respect too, first, depending upon the chronology of the introduction of more comprehensive ownership rights and in terms of ownership variants that were more or less extensive. Second, a distinction must be drawn whether and under what conditions immovable property could be divided. A third question refers to the implications of joint ownership – such as among brothers – and, finally, it needs to be clarified whether women were able to own immovable property.

Some legal spaces featured extensive freedom of testation from spouse to spouse. This could produce conditions that were, as Regina Schäfer has shown based on the litigation record books known as *Haderbücher* from Ingelheim – all the more conflict-prone from the children's perspective. There, spouses had complete freedom of testation: they could use inheritance contracts to render the prevailing concept of separate goods null and void, and instead establish community of property. This situation is in contrast to legal spaces such as German-speaking Tyrol, in which there were graduated testamentary restrictions: inherited wealth was subject to greater testamentary restriction than acquired wealth, and children took absolute priority. There were also regions, French Pyrenees during the early modern period, in which the firstborn child – regardless of gender – succeeded to the ownership of houses and land via inheritance: in that instance, however, it was not possible for such property to be divided. This is the context in which Marie Pierre Arrizabalaga's study begins. And in the Northern Countries, on the other hand, only self-acquired land could be divided.

Regions where sons were preferred for succession differed from those where daughters were relegated to a subordinate position but not categorically excluded from succession to ownership – i.e., where daughters were not forced to yield to a nephew or cousin in the interest of guaranteeing continuation of the male line. In societies or social milieus that were structured in a strictly agnatic, patrilineal manner, however, daughters could not represent their families or lineages. This was frequently the case in aristocratic families and could also have implications within the Italian dowry system. It was then that cousins – preferably sons of the father's brother – were tapped for succession, a circumstance that entailed daughters renouncing their inheritances.

In the German-speaking area, however it was not intended – with the exception of aristocratic circles – that daughters who had received a dowry were considered as being fully compensated for their paternal inheritance claims. Women instead retained entitlement to their parental inheritance, or the compensation of their inheritance shares less the amount of the marriage portion that they had already received. In the case of the Italian dowry system the logic was different: there, daughters who had been provided with a dowry were excluded from further inheritance from their fathers, brothers, and sometimes mothers as well. In addition, the succession of daughters to ownership was no option. At least, this is the state of the art given by extant research into this subject. However, Simona Feci re-opened the debate with critical questions in her chapter to this volume. A crucial point here with regard to inequality between the sexes was that dowry values were significantly lower than those of sons' inheritance shares and what is more, sisters might be promised differing sums depending on the 'marriage strategy' in play.

This would suggest that there were highly diverse graduations of access to certain types of wealth via inheritance. These differences were shaped by gender and birth rank, either in accordance with the norm or in actual practice. There were also occasions, however, in which situational opportunities extended beyond those of the prevailing norm. Silvia Mattivi, for example, has found that daughters in Trento in the second half of the fourteenth century were bequeathed wealth beyond that which they had received via their dowries – a circumstance that stands in contrast to the situation that Isabelle Chabot described in Florence. Women generally appear to have been extensively present in diverse capacities relating to the administration and ownership of wealth during the period following the plague in Trento. Accordingly, Simona Feci calls for a more nuanced view of the normative discourse itself in her chapter on late-medieval and early modern Italy, suggesting that discussion of daughters' exclusion from succession to ownership is a still open and historiographically under-researched question.

This demand also shows that, compared with the focuses of the prevailing research perspectives regarding gender and wealth in the German-speaking area, the Italian discussion revolves around almost the exact opposite theme. While for decades dowries have stood at the centre of Italian gender history and micro-historical research in particular, there has been a marked tendency to overlook the issue of daughters' succession to ownership.[12] The German-speaking area, on the other hand, has been characterised by a focus on succession to ownership. The dominance of a social- and gender-historical perspective resulted in analyses of forms and strategies of inheritance, while the issue of marriage portions as equivalents to the dowry and the importance of marital property regimes long remained comparatively neglected.[13]

In the German-speaking context, it was typically only aristocratic daughters who – frequently under pressure or duress – signed declarations in which they renounced the inheritances that they would have received from their fathers and brothers. Nonetheless, such a renouncement had to be active and explicit, and was defined as a legal act in its own right. Women were not, therefore, automatically excluded from further claims to inheritance in the manner in which they were in the Italian dowry system. The renouncement of inheritance was not common in non-aristocratic social milieus. It is in this respect that the territory of present-day South Tyrol turns out to have been an interesting transitional space: the *Tiroler Landesordnung* only stipulated renouncement of inheritance for noble daughters,[14] but in a few individual courts in southern Tyrol – those of Neumarkt and Kaltern – we find sixteenth- and seventeenth-century renunciation declarations by daughters from the agrarian, trade, and merchant milieus. Borrowings from both sides came together here: the dowry or marriage portion was a de facto replacement for inheritance and inheritance renunciations had to be explicitly declared.

Silvia Mattivi's chapter on Trento is also situated in this transitional space. The *morgengab* (morning gift) listed in the notarial registries there would seem to indicate a proximity to German legal culture and, once again, still other modes of transfer: while the classic dowry system was primarily characterised by the transfer of the dowry from the bride's family to that of the groom, the morning gift represented a transfer from the groom's side to the bride. In this, one can see a certain reciprocity that was even more clearly evident in marriage portion systems with counter-dowries. The morning gift had the character of a gift over which wives were free to dispose, while the counter-dowry

12 Criticism of the focus on dowries has already been expressed by Ida Fazio, "Le ricchezze delle donne: verso una ri-problematizzazione," *Quaderni Storici* 101 (1999), pp. 539–50.

13 Margareth Lanzinger, Gunda Barth-Scalmani, Ellinor Forster, and Gertrude Langer-Ostrawsky, *Aushandeln von Ehe. Heiratsverträge der Neuzeit im europäischen Vergleich* (Cologne, Weimar, Vienna: Böhlau, 2010, 2nd edition 2015).

14 Tiroler Landesordnung 1532, 1573, III, 34; cf. Margareth Lanzinger and Janine Maegraith, "Konkurrenz um Vermögen im südlichen Tirol des 16. Jahrhunderts," *L'Homme. Z.F.G.* 27–1 (2016), pp. 15–31, here pp. 19–20.

typically consisted of rights of usufruct for the duration of widowhood, but the capital remained the property of the husband's family.

In the aristocratic and patrician context transitional spaces – such as the area between Venetian and Habsburg territory discussed in Laura Casella's research – were both legally and politically significant. In contrast to "border region", the term "transitional space" refers to permeability and exchange – in the sense of a 'realm of possibility' to take advantage of the legal opportunities, as seen for example in marriages, dowries, and goods. At the same time, transitional spaces also extended the potential for legal and political conflict that – as seen in the case of the Tridentine noble family Trapp – often revolved around power and economic interests.

5 Contested Wealth

Conflicts were ubiquitous, and some cannot be considered independent from the individuals by whom they were instigated and carried out. Such conflicts were nourished by personal characteristics, passions, and modes of behaviour. Such attributes are, however, accessible only in very well-documented cases, particularly in which ego documents or extensive court records have been preserved, such as those discussed by Regina Schäfer in her chapter that references this dimension of conflict. No less relevant were conflicts that were structured or fuelled by the interaction of specific factors – legal frameworks, everyday logics, gender hierarchies and inequalities, significance of landed property, patrilineal or bilateral orientation etc. – as they caused or contributed to the potential fragility of men's and women's positions in a social and economic sense. In the case of Tyrol, the combined consequences of separate marital property and the favouring of sons for succession – i.e., the interplay of a legal framework and a social practice – are identified as structuring factors in the sense sketched out above. One also needs to consider the extent to which the likelihood of conflict related to the amount of wealth in question. The power of disposition over owned real estate proved to be a very effective tool utilised by both men and women that, in some cases, reduced the significance of gender as a category of differentiation. Therefore, as Andrea Griesebner writes, the respective relationships between property, power, and gender must be considered on a case-by-case basis.

Viewed from this perspective, conflict extends beyond the personal to encompass contradictory ideas about claims and priorities, and about appropriateness and fairness. The chapters in this volume provide evidence of numerous configurations transversed by lines and axes of conflict that exhibit structuring components. Conflict could arise between spouses and lead to separation, and many such conflicts pertained to aspects outside of the couple and their married life: unequal property ownership – particularly when wives had brought immovable property and/or a trade license into the marriage – and stepfamily or blended family situations were both factors that have been demonstrated as increasing the potential for conflict. Lines of conflict over inheritance or inheritance shares could arise between parents and children, within groups of siblings, between brothers and sisters, or between older and younger generations. In this sphere of competition there were several types of situations that were especially delicate and thus likewise conflict-prone, such as the childlessness of a couple, widow or widower, the remarriage of widows, the legal, social, and economic position of widows as guardians, and step-constellations.

It was thus that, as Siglinde Clementi has reconstructed and discussed in her chapter, some widows had to either defend their rights in opposition to their children's guardians or – in instances where they themselves had assumed guardianship – suffer the hostility of brothers-in-law concerned with their own family interests. In the context of separate marital property, rights of usufruct ensured widows a comparably favourable position in which they could continue to make use of their husbands' wealth and were protected from being driven out of their homes. In such situations widows did, however, have to assume payment of all taxes as well as other obligations associated with the property in question. In the case of usufruct rights, there were a series of logics at play according to which wealth was bound to and ensured by kin. Usufruct did not endanger the succession of the deceased husband's relatives, but it did delay succession for an indeterminate period – which once again presented a potential for conflict.

Each of these situations raise questions as to the weighting of marriage and kinship and the balance of power between them. There were numerous graduations between the kin-centred separation of goods and the marriage-centred community of goods. In Ingelheim, studied by Regina Schäfer, both sides were given consideration in cases of childlessness and community of goods: two thirds of the couple's joint wealth went to the husband's relatives – this portion being referred to as the *Schwertteil* or "share of the sword" –, while one third went to the wife's relatives – the *Rockteil* or "share of the skirt". In early modern Finland, the wife – if widowed – had a claim on one third of the couple's joint property. One can also read the so-called *Einkindschaft* – literally "one childness", implying the intended legal equalising or "wholeness" of each child – as a tool intended to effect a certain balance between marital and kin interests, giving children from different marriages equal status and equal inheritance rights within their step-families. The legal context of Tyrol, on the other hand, was dominated by the claim of each spouse's line of descent, with priority given in many areas and increasingly over time to children from first marriages. The case of sixteenth-century Sonnenburg revealed, however, that in some court districts ultimogeniture was a strong customary entitlement which led to several instances where the eldest and the youngest son became joint successors to the estate.

Occurrences such as marriage, remarriage and death, and conditions such as old age, illness, and dependence on others for sustenance were among the particularly sensitive moments in individuals' lives. Marriages forged or strengthened alliances between families. They also entailed transfers of wealth and required the reorganization thereof. It is from this perspective in particular that efforts to combat so-called clandestine marriages (marriages that eluded familial and social control) must be considered. It is no coincidence that, as Silvia Mattivi has ascertained, there was more often a notary – rather than a priest – present in an official function at marriage ceremonies during the period prior to the Council of Trent (1545–1563). It was thus that attendant business-related matters – the "earthly", as some marriage contracts refer to it – were resolved during the course of the ceremony. The same goes for death, another turning point with which transfers and the reorganisation of wealth were inseparably linked.

Time and again, the focus of the chapters in this volume is asking whose claims took priority, how conflicts of interest were balanced or resolved, and whose consent was considered necessary for a settlement or decision. Inhabiting another context but likewise a bone of contention were debts and loans – particularly when they involved blood relatives and in-laws. The case reconstructed by Isabelle Chabot illustrates that if, as in the Italian dowry system, a dowry had to be repaid to the widow following her husband's death, that transaction could find itself in competition with the claims of other creditors. This means that debts and loans involved additional social relationships and axes of conflict that could lead beyond marriage, family, and kin to also involve guilds, brotherhoods, and neighbours.

A central issue of the whole volume is the question of the persons in their specific family, household, kin, and gender positions. Between these positions ran axes of competition depending on diverse situative contexts, and in many cases depending on separation of goods or community of goods in marriages. Within the context of our project, this fact confirms our hypothesis that it is crucial to think about inheritance practice and marital property regime practices in combination with one another. After all, marital property law and marital property practice were significant factors that governed the relationships between generations and the sexes. A pivotal point here is the ways in which marriage and kinship were positioned with relation to one another, and the relative importance accorded to marriage as a union and to the continuity of lineages. Adoptions of sons-in-law, for instance, took place not only in aristocratic families but also on Finnish farms. In Beatrice Moring's interpretation, the latter was primarily intended to ensure that parents-in-law were cared for as best as possible in their old age rather than to keeping a family name alive.

6 Wealth as a Power

In most of the societies featured in this volume's chapters, the overwhelming amount of real estate was owned by men – with exceptions being the French Pyrenees and to some extent Vienna and its surrounding region. The greater difficulty to near-exclusion women faced in terms of access to real estate ownership resulted in considerable inequality between the sexes. It also had serious repercussions for the position of inheriting daughters and of men who married into the properties of their wives or – as sons-in-law – married into their parents'-in-law households and businesses. Reference has already been made to the ambivalence to which such situations gave rise. The powerful position of a man as *pater familias* – based on various rights and reinforced in some German territories by their status as marital gender guardian (*Ehevogt*) – clashed with their otherwise less advantageous positions. This constellation bore within it considerable tension. How was this tension addressed? Precautionary measures were taken in many instances, often in the form of extensive and detailed marriage contracts, with an eye to avoiding conflict and ensuring the interests of the bride's family.

As the chapters by Andrea Griesebner and Georg Tschannett indicate, community of goods could provide women with a better negotiating position should a marriage end in separation whereas separation of goods proved advantageous if husbands were indebted: in the latter, wives' wealth need not be used to guarantee or to pay off such debts. Separation of goods did, however, put widows in a precarious position if they had brought only a modest amount of wealth into the marriage and were later turned out of their homes as widows, or if they had to argue about the return of their dowries in the dowry system. Even in such cases the widows' wealth enjoyed special protection against their deceased husbands' relatives and creditors. This means that none of the differing marital property regimes, including the Italian dowry system, can be described as having been fundamentally or clearly more or less advantageous for women, and that the advantages and disadvantages were to a certain extent situation-dependent. The disadvantaging of women does seem clearer in the common law system, but in all of these contexts, it was women's de facto latitude for action and negotiation that was decisive.

The legal quality of wealth and legal claims to wealth themselves affected social relationships, characterising and structuring them and, in turn, also being structured by them. A closer association between research on this topic and research on material culture could prove productive for both: the former could provide material culture studies with a new perspective on the legal quality of objects and things, while research on inheritance and marital property regimes could more broadly integrate new impulses from research into the power embodied by or associated with objects and things.

Spaces of negotiation are quite central when thinking about wealth. Using a research perspective that integrates spaces of negotiation broadens our view to include how both women and men from poorer milieus had the potential, despite restrictive legal situations, to exercise agency, negotiate, and make claims with respect to the disposal and management of a wide range of wealth. This volume's contributors associated spaces of negotiation with specific temporal and spatial situations: Isabelle Chabot and Silvia Mattivi show how spheres of action were altered and augmented as a result of the plague. Laura Casella investigated the extent to which the transitional situation inherent to border regions expanded women's latitudes for action and hence negotiation. "Space of negotiation" also implies the existence of various means of manoeuvring around the laws and practices in place. In this sense it is also worth noting that other chapters indicate that latitude for negotiation did not always work to the benefit of women. Microhistory has perceived the gaps, ambivalences, and contradictions in the realm of law as having been quite advantageous, these opened up spaces of negotiation, circumvented harsh conditions, and could be instrumentalised in a positive sense. This only applied, however, when those who were in a weaker position were capable of prevailing or obtain justice. As Siglinde Clementi and Regina Schäfer have shown, the coalescence of ambiguous and/or competing legal contexts, regulations, and institutions sometimes resulted in the opposite: this could also lead to the initiation of conflict or provide "opposing parties" with effective tools. Thus, the ability to negotiate was, like so many things, a double-edged sword.

This volume sheds light on marriage, family, and kinship as spaces of power and rule, and provides a great deal of insight into the power of law and of courts and non-court institutions that commented on the law and pronounced and implemented legal rulings as well as with a diverse range of legal instruments. Above all, however, the volume renders visible the power embodied by written documentation of wealth and by agreed-upon rights and claims, by written dispositions regarding property and wealth, by negotiation and battles over wealth's division along with the division itself, and last but not least by arbitration and mediation.

References

Bonfield, Lloyd. *Devising, Dying and Dispute. Probate Litigation in Early Modern England*. Farnham: Ashgate, 2012.

Calvi, Giulia. "Rights and Ties that Bind. Mothers, Children, and the State in Tuscany during the Early Modern Period." In *Kinship in Europe. Approaches to Long-Term Development (1300–1900)*, edited by David Warren Sabean, Simon Teuscher, and Jon Mathieu, pp. 145–62. New York and Oxford: Berghahn, 2007.

Erickson, Amy Louise. "Coverture and Capitalism." *History Workshop Journal* 59–1 (2005): pp. 1–16, https://doi.org/10.1093/hwj/dbi001.

Erickson, Amy Louise. *Women and Property in Early Modern England*. London and New York: Routledge, 1995.

Fazio, Ida. "Le ricchezze delle donne: verso una riproblematizzazione." *Quaderni storici* 101 (1999): pp. 539–50.

Fertig, Christine. "Stem Families in Rural Northwestern Germany? Family Systems, Intergenerational Relations and Family Contracts." *The History of the Family* 23–2 (2018): pp. 196–217.

Keibek, Sebastian. "Correcting the Probate Record for Wealth Bias." Cambridge Working Papers in Economic and Social History No. 28, March 2017.

Korpiola, Mia, and Anu Lahtinen, eds. *Planning for Death: Wills, Inheritance and Property Strategies in Medieval and Reformation Europe*. Leiden and Boston: Brill, 2018.

Lanzinger, Margareth. "Marriage Contracts in Various Contexts: Marital Property Rights, Sociocultural Aspects and Gender-specific Implications. Late-Eighteenth-Century Evidence from two Tirolean Court Districts." *Annales de démographie historique* 121–1 (2011): pp. 69–97.

Lanzinger, Margareth, Gunda Barth-Scalmani, Ellinor Forster, and Gertrude Langer-Ostrawsky. *Aushandeln von Ehe. Heiratsverträge der Neuzeit im europäischen Vergleich*. Cologne, Weimar, and Vienna: Böhlau, 2010, 2nd edition 2015.

Lanzinger, Margareth, and Janine Maegraith. "Konkurrenz um Vermögen im südlichen Tirol des 16. Jahrhunderts." *L'Homme*. Z.F.G. 27–1 (2016): pp. 15–31.

Moring, Beatrice, and Richard Wall. *Widows in European Economy and Society, 1600–1920*. Woodbridge: Boydell Press, 2017.

Muldrew, Craig. *Food, Energy and the Industrious Revolution: Work and Material Culture in Agrarian England, 1550–1780*. Cambridge: Cambridge University Press, 2011.

Ranieri, Filippo. "L'influence du Code civil sur les codifications du 19e siècle: essor et déclin d'un modèle européen." In *Le bicentenaire du Code civil – 200 Jahre Code civil. Saarbrücker Kolloquium zum 50-jährigen Bestehen des CJFA am 26.11.2004*, edited by Claude Witz, pp. 55–67. Baden-Baden: Nomos, 2006.

Schmidt-Voges, Inken. *Mikropolitiken des Friedens. Semantiken und Praktiken des Hausfriedens im 18. Jahrhundert*. Berlin: de Gruyter, 2015.

van den Berg, Peter A. J. *The Politics of European Codification. A History of the Unification of Law in France, Prussia, the Austrian Monarchy and the Netherlands*. Groningen: Europa Law Publishing, 2007.

Zucca Micheletto, Beatrice. "L'introduzione del codice civile napoleonico a Torino: il regime patrimoniale dei coniugi tra norma e pratica." *Geschichte und Region / Storia e regione* 20–2 (2011): pp. 92–105.

Index

www.ingramcontent.com/pod-product-compliance
Lightning Source LLC
LaVergne TN
LVHW010638300926
849161LV00005B/977
* 9 7 8 9 0 0 4 4 5 4 1 8 7 *